Social Indicators Research Series

Volume 71

This series aims to provide a public forum for single treatises and collections of papers on social indicators research that are too long to be published in our journal *Social Indicators Research.* Like the journal, the book series deals with statistical assessments of the quality of life from a broad perspective. It welcomes the research on a wide variety of substantive areas, including health, crime, housing, education, family life, leisure activities, transportation, mobility, economics, work, religion and environmental issues. These areas of research will focus on the impact of key issues such as health on the overall quality of life and vice versa. An international review board, consisting of Ruut Veenhoven, Joachim Vogel, Ed Diener, Torbjorn Moum, Mirjam A.G. Sprangers and Wolfgang Glatzer, will ensure the high quality of the series as a whole.

More information about this series at http://www.springer.com/series/6548

Olayinka Akanle • Jìmí Olálékan Adésìnà
Editors

The Development of Africa

Issues, Diagnoses and Prognoses

Springer

Editors
Olayinka Akanle
Department of Sociology
University of Ibadan
Ibadan, Nigeria

Jìmí Olálékan Adésìnà
SARChI Chair in Social Policy
University of South Africa (UNISA)
Tshwane, South Africa

ISSN 1387-6570 ISSN 2215-0099 (electronic)
Social Indicators Research Series
ISBN 978-3-319-66241-1 ISBN 978-3-319-66242-8 (eBook)
DOI 10.1007/978-3-319-66242-8

Library of Congress Control Number: 2017955373

Printed on acid-free paper

This Springer imprint is published by Springer Nature
The registered company is Springer International Publishing AG
The registered company address is: Gewerbestrasse 11, 6330 Cham, Switzerland

This book is dedicated to everyone laboring positively to understand, contribute to, and achieve Africa's development.

Preface

For generations of Africans (policymakers, intellectuals, and ordinary people), the development of the continent has always been an urgent task and a challenge that needs to be met. While there might have been divergent opinions on the most appropriate ways to ensure this objective, the focus, nonetheless, is broadly shared. That this collection of essays by two generations of African scholars would return to the issue is to be understood within the context of this long-term concern. The context, local and global, remains in flux and elusive, but as Mwalimu Nyerere observed, we must run while others walk.

As Samir Amin once noted, "'Economic development' was an important item in the nationalist programs and since every known path of economic development has involved industrialization and also partly because in no other sector was colonial blockage so transparent, the struggle for independence closely linked nationalism with the 'right to industrialize'." It was a matter on which the nationalists asserted themselves. While it is common to argue that development was an imperial agenda by Western powers, it is important to remind ourselves that the impulse for "catch-up" is grounded in the emancipatory aspirations and that the dominance of the West is underpinned by its developmental advantage. Victims of colonialism and persisting imperial order know that their technological disadvantage is a major factor in their subjugation and humiliation. The impulse that was eloquently expressed at the 1956 Bandung Conference would find expressions in the demand for "the right to development."

While Africa's efforts at industrialization have been out of sync with the international trend, the first generation of post-independence nationalists in Africa were animated by it. Between 1960 and 1975, Africa's industry grew at an annual rate of 7.5%, albeit from a low base. This growth rate masks significant variation on the continent. Over this initial period, five countries accounted for 53% of Africa's industrial output. In 27 other countries, the share of industry was less than 1%. Performance over the 15-year period was also unsteady, with much of the growth happening in the first decade of independence. In Nigeria's case, the growth rate in manufacturing value added increased from an average of 7.6% between 1963 and 1973 to 12% between 1973 and 1981. For all its weaknesses, in the first decade of independence, wage employment growth surpassed the population growth rate. Nor was development to be understood only in terms of industrialization; ultimately it was about reducing poverty and, in Arthur Lewis's terms, extending the "range of human choices." The understanding of "catch-up" in its wider sense of addressing human needs in the former colonies was aptly captured in the phrase "better life for all" that was common among early nationalists.

The balance of payment crises that emerged from the mid-1970s (first among oil importers) and fiscal squeeze at the end of the decade coincided with the rise of the New Right in the West. Africans, at all levels, were themselves aware of the development stumbling that the continent faced. Much of the response was driven by the demand for a more radical nationalist commitment to development. At the policymaking level, the consensus response was framed in the Lagos Plan of Action (1980) that sought to place development within a regional framework, transform the inherited colonial economic structures, and internalize the growth engine of the African economies. This effort was overtaken by the regime of structural adjustment and the neoliberal ascendance. Rather than the promised "accelerated development," what the wholesome deployment of market forces (liberalization, privatization) and state retrenchment produced was two lost decades, deindustrialization (of the limited industrial efforts of the first two decades of independence), explosion in the absolute number of people living in poverty, growing inequality, and widespread social dislocation. As soon as the growth rate in Africa ticked up, those who disavowed responsibility for the socio-economic collapse of the adjustment years claimed patrimony for it. While there has been some recovery from the depth of the economic crisis, Africa's economies remain dependent on external demand for Africa's resources, and the state of industrialization is fundamentally not much different from the mid-1970s. Manufacturing share of GDP is lower in 2011 than in 1974. Production of capital good remains rare.

After more than two decades of disavowing the value of intentional planning, we are back to the issue of the urgency of rapid economic development, with its attendant objective of expanding human choices. At national levels, "planning" is back on the agenda. At the continental level, we seem to have returned to mapping out long-term strategic framework with the African Union's *Agenda 2063*. What is required, beyond recovery, is long-term structural transformation of Africa's economies and society, one that deepens democracy, enhances equality, and expands human choice. Development, and development planning in particular, requires a measure of sovereignty and autonomy and focused commitment to the agenda; it requires the intentionality that market is not capable of delivering; it requires state capacity not only to plan and regulate but to constantly learn; it requires public leadership in mobilizing the social compact necessary for navigating the long road ahead and ensuring that the proceeds of development are shared equitably in society. Knowledge is central to the catch-up and latecomers can avoid the groping in the dark that marked the efforts of pioneers. This requires significantly high investment in higher education and skill. It vests Africa's institutions of higher education with a crucial role in meeting the challenge of Africa's development—in innovation and production of critical skills necessary for transforming Africa's economy and society.

The current volume reflects the persistence of the concern with development among Africans and I commend it to the reader.

London School of Economics
London, UK

Thandika Mkandawire

Acknowledgments

We, the editors, together with the publisher would like to extend our sincere gratitude to all those who contributed to this book. Without their contributions, commitment, understanding, and willingness to contribute, it would have been impossible to publish this very useful and important book. Thank you for your knowledge and dedication. It takes great effort and sacrifice to contribute to a book of this status, yet all contributors took time out of their often heavy and busy schedules to deliver their chapters, working under pressure as they did so. In all cases, the contributors were in addition required to revise and rework their chapters for resubmission after peer and editorial reviews—still under tight deadlines within their other busy schedules. We appreciate you all! We, the editors, are also especially grateful to Team Springer for their commitment, expertise, and professionalism in handling the publication of this book. They have been very helpful throughout the process, always following up with us and providing support. Hence, we would like to acknowledge everyone who has contributed in one way or another to the publication of this book. In many instances, some of these contributions were behind the scenes yet the publication would not have been possible without them. Thank you all very much.

Ibadan, Nigeria — Olayinka Akanle
Tshwane, South Africa — Jìmí Olálékan Adésìnà

Contents

Chapter 1
Introduction: The Development of Africa: Issues, Diagnoses and Prognoses

Olayinka Akanle and Jìmí Olálékan Adésìnà

Background

Africa's development is one of the most critical and important issues on the global agenda. This point has been attested to by the global adoption of the Millennium Development Goals (MDGs), and the immediate adoption of the Sustainable Development Goals (SDGs) on the expiry of the MDGs, to drive development in Africa and other developing countries, while simultaneously not isolating the developed countries. This is because the underdevelopment of Africa is a problem that does not affect Africa alone, but directly or indirectly affects the world at large. Today, Africa remains largely mired in underdevelopment rather than showing the needed signs of development. Generally, independence struggles in most African countries were contingent on the belief that decolonization and independence would lead to the requisite development on the continent. However, more than half a century after the demise of colonialism, development is still elusive on the continent despite repeated efforts.

In other words, over half a century after most African nations became independent, large parts of the continent remain underdeveloped despite the fact that Africa was originally projected to grow faster than Asia. Asia today has in the main has shown more promise (and signs) of growth and development than Africa, especially against the backdrop of the ascendancy of the Asian Tigers and the Asian transition economies such as India and China. These Asian countries have in particular been able to lift many of their populations out of poverty in contrast to Africa, where

O. Akanle (✉)
Department of Sociology, University of Ibadan, Ibadan, Nigeria
e-mail: yakanle@yahoo.com; yk.akanle@ui.edu.ng

J.O. Adésìnà
SARChI Chair in Social Policy, University of South Africa (UNISA), Tshwane, South Africa
e-mail: adesij@unisa.ac.za; adesij@gmail.com

O. Akanle, J.O. Adésìnà (eds.), *The Development of Africa*, Social Indicators Research Series 71, DOI 10.1007/978-3-319-66242-8_1

many remain in poverty. While Asia has shown resilience and focused development attempts and wealth creation, many parts of Africa, especially Sub-Saharan Africa, appear stuck at the level of negative development indicators.

What Africans and the world at large have come to realize is that Africa cannot and should not continue on the path of fixated underdevelopment. Unfortunately, the road to development is also not clear-cut or easy. While the issue of African development has become a universal demand and the need for positive change has become more urgent and profound, trajectories of development have also become more complex and more dynamic as the stakes of development have been raised and are constantly changing owing to the interface of local and global currents, undercurrents and political economy. While the manifestations of development are easy to identify, the processes and pathways are not. Hence, while the debates about African development exist and continue (OECD 2015; Africa Institute of South Africa [AISA] 2002; Muriith 1997; Moss 1997), the objects, natures and times of the debates are changing rapidly, as African development realities continue to emerge and evolve and thus necessitate continuous examination and interrogation.

For about the last 30 years most African nations have demonstrated underdevelopment potentiality rather than development capability, as can be seen in objective development indicators like the Corruption Index, poverty prevalence, unemployment rate, gender equality and literacy rate. According to the World Bank, even the economic growth rate witnessed in some parts of Africa has not translated to an improved standard of living for the people. Indeed, 48.5% of Sub-Saharan Africans continue to struggle with poverty while even more struggle with absolute poverty. Job creation has not kept pace with the booming population, which has reached the 1 billion mark – or 15% of the world's total population – and is projected to increase to 20% by 2030, in light of falling labor productivity figures and the fact that the manufacturing sector has remained largely stagnant since the 1970s. In addition, many African economies trail the rest of the world in competitiveness.

Unless specific, current, established and fresh comparative development problems confronting the continent are well examined, properly researched, well documented, and sufficiently understood, there cannot be positive development achievement in Africa. It is against this background that this book engages the development challenges confronting Africa with a view to presenting fresh and current examination, narratives, interpretations and pathways to the continent's established, current and evolving development problems. This book will interrogate and answer critical, current and pragmatic problems confronting Africa in definitive ways and provide workable pathways for resolving development problems that will have a positive impact on scholarship, policy and practice. The book adds depth to and broadens the knowledge base on development in Africa. Students, academics, scholars, practitioners, thinkers, policymakers, development partners and all those interested in issues affecting Africa's development should find this book very interesting, relevant and useful.

This book seeks to contribute to research and policy by expanding scholarly and practice knowledge on Africa's development trajectories. It is an academic, pragmatic and practical policy *toolkit* for Africa's development problems, providing new depth, and fresh theoretical, methodological and conceptual frameworks for understanding and resolving Africa's development quagmires within broader global sustainable development strategies. Generally, the book is relevant to people seeking a comprehensive, relevant, workable understanding of Africa's development issues. Certainly, Africa's development issues are complex, complicated, evolving, and dynamic. Thus, this book adds new on-the-ground, multilevel and multidimensional perspectives to the relevant issues hampering Africa's development. This book is practical and pragmatic yet methodical and scholarly; it is also highly comparative in ways that will account for problems, issues and solutions to Africa's development trajectories both multinational and transnational. It is current and contemporary and engages cutting-edge issues in great detail in ways that are very useful for teaching, research, policy, practice and general knowledge on development in Africa.

Structure and Orientation of the Book

Together with this introductory chapter, this book comprises 22 chapters. This chapter, frames the orientation and contextualizes the issues in the book, Chap. 2 conceptualizes and intellectually frames the development realities of Africa, while Chap. 3 accounts historically and theoretically for the occurrences that have come to shape and define development issues confronting Africa. Chapter 4 continues the focus and argument of Chap. 3 given the importance of the issues of interest to the two chapters. Chapter 4 further theorizes on Africa's development problems.

Chapter 5, 'Poverty in Africa', confronts, both theoretically and practically, one of the most definitive development issues of Africa. Poverty is one of the most significant issues confronting Africa today. In fact, poverty is key signifier of Africa's underdevelopment and is an overarching problem facing the continent. This chapter therefore examines the subject of poverty on the continent both empirically and theoretically. Chapter 6 discusses education in Africa. Education is at the very heart of human and material development for Africa, especially in view of the development experiences of China, India and Malaysia, among others. Therefore if Africa is to develop, education will have to play a central and important role. Against this backdrop, this chapter examines the state of education in Africa, adopting empirical data and descriptive/analytical approaches. The chapter is detailed, pragmatic and contemporary while also being future-oriented. The chapter is also analytical and problem-solving in a scholarly and a practical manner.

Chapter 7 covers agriculture, industrialization and the economy. Common narratives and interpretations of Africa's development and underdevelopment hinge on the role played by agriculture and industrialization in the economy. This is important as many accounts of development are centered on the state of the economy and, generally, most African nations are still agrarian and rural. What then is the interface between agriculture, industrialization and the economy in Africa? Can agriculture sustainably drive development in Africa? Can agriculture lead the industrial paths of Africa? What is the state of agriculture and industrialization in Africa? What is the missing link in the economy and can agriculture and industrialization reconnect the severed chain of Africa's development? What is the state of Africa's economy and what role can agriculture and industrialization play in it? What are the policy issues and what are the solutions? Are there country-specific issues that can drive home the points and the contours of Africa's development? At the end of the development tunnel is there any hope for the alignment of agriculture, industrialization and the economy in Africa? If yes, what is to be done? If not, what is to be done? Through a relevant up-to-date case study, this chapter engages the background issues.

'Politics, Democracy and Governance' in Africa is the title of Chap. 8. This chapter is very important because governance issues are central to Africa's development and underdevelopment. Nations' governance systems, processes and structures will ultimately determine how resources are aggregated, shared and distributed. They will also determine how resources are mobilized for development outcomes. Central to governance, however, are politics and democracy. Thus, this chapter uses a case study to examine the relationships among politics, democracy and governance in Africa as they affect the development realities on the continent. This chapter is conceptual, theoretical and empirical, dealing with the relevant data and cases in comparative terms. Chapter 9, 'Violence and Terrorism' boldly confronts unique issues confronting Africa. These two issues remain intractable in Africa today (see Akanle and Omobowale 2015). Unfortunately, most African countries appear to lack understanding of these problems and also have poor capacity for solving them. There is virtually no sub-region of Africa that is totally exempted from violence and terrorism. From North Africa to Southern Africa, West Africa to Central Africa, the Horn of Africa to East Africa, violence and terrorism exist and they certainly have various impacts on development and underdevelopment. This chapter is conceptual, theoretical and academic, yet practical and relevant to policy. Germane data are used as is a case study to drive home the relationships between the twin issues.

Chapter 10, 'Africa and the Media', also examines a very relevant issue at the center of Africa's development – the interface of Africa and the media. The role of the media in affecting and effecting change and development has been widely acknowledged and appreciated. This is particularly so in Africa against the background of the Arab Spring and the emergence of transparent elections driven by new media. The media[1] has, however, become a double-edged sword in Africa, playing both a positive and a negative role. In other words, while the media was instrumental in driving the change during the Arab Spring, it is also the engine of negative representations of Africa, the propagation Africa's negative image and the dissemination of propaganda, which has affected investments and development on the continent. Yet, the media is also sometimes positively implicated in directing development values to the continent. It is therefore very important to engage the manifestations, developments and ramifications of the media in Africa in search of sustainable development.

In Chap. 11, issues relating to childhood, youthhood and social inclusion in Africa are discussed. A major development issue in Africa is that of social inclusion.

[1] *CNN effects* on the continent, state TV [media], private media, social/new media and so on.

While most African countries are underdeveloped, it is the children and the youth in particular that suffer the consequences of underdevelopment of Africa. Children and youths are often excluded outright from the development processes of Africa and suffer more as a result of the underdevelopment outcomes of the continent. This is why, according to Alcinda Honwana, there is a prolonged period of waithood and youthhood in African countries as many youths are trapped, finding it difficult to transit to adulthood due to their large-scale disproportional experience of Africa's underdevelopment. The case is similar and sometimes worse for children, who suffer negative socio-cultural, economic and physical constructions on the continent; even the laws have failed to successfully address negative constructions and experiences of children in Africa (see Akanle 2012). Since childhood and youthhood are development flipsides, it is important to examine their development, socioeconomic and intergenerational interfaces in African countries. The background issues are discussed in this chapter through the life experiences of different individuals and groups across Africa.

'Health and Diseases in Africa' is the title of Chap. 12. Africa is one of the countries of the world with significant health and disease burdens. This is may be traced to the living environments, health belief systems and health infrastructure on the continent. These health and disease burdens have development implications especially seen against the backdrop of the axiom *health is wealth.* This chapter therefore examines the health and disease trajectories of Africa and demonstrates and documents their development implications. The chapter is strong, conceptual, empirical, engaging, polemic, theoretical and methodical with relevant data and perspectives for scholarship, policy and practice across the countries of Africa. Chapter 13 is entitled 'Corruption and Africa'. Corruption, like poverty, is among the most pervasive and dangerous problems confronting Africa today. In terms of causality, no other problem retards development in Africa like corruption (see Akanle and Adesina 2015). This chapter therefore critically examines corruption as a development issue in Africa through a comparative analysis of African countries. The chapter is empirical, theoretical, conceptual and comparative with specific case studies and transnational examples. Issues discussed include: What is corruption? How prevalent is corruption in Africa? Is corruption a way of life in Africa? How has corruption manifested in Africa over time and what is the trend? What data are available to demonstrate corruption in Africa? Are there differences among nations and sub-regions of Africa relative to the processes and nature of corruption? How has corruption affected development in African countries? Are there solutions to corruption in Africa? Specific examples are also discussed.

'Africa and the Climate Change Dilemma' is the title of Chap. 14. Climate change is a major issue confronting the world today and no continent or community is immune to it. In fact, climate change is one of the few issues on which it was very difficult to get global consensus until very recently. Implementing the consensus however remains a challenge. Despite contributing little to climate change in the world, Africans are among the most affected and yet capacity to understand and ameliorate its effects on the continent remains weak. It is against this background that this chapter investigates the trajectories and consequences of climate change on the continent. The chapter is comparative (continentally and intercontinentally), empirical, polemic, analytical, conceptual and theoretical.

Chapter 15 is called 'Gender in Africa'. Africa is a heavily patriarchal continent and this has huge implications for gender equality/equity and development (Akanle 2011). Traditional norms and values exist in Africa that always makes the gender question relevant in Africa's development engagements. It has been variously maintained that it is impossible for Africa to understand its development problems and develop without answering the gender question. This chapter therefore engages the gender question in Africa's development. Indicative questions include: What is gender? How does gender manifest in Africa and how has it affected the development of nations on the continent? How is gender affecting Africa's development? What are the conceptual, theoretical, and empirical and policy issues around gender and development in Africa? Are African countries different or the same in terms of gender and development? How can Africa manage its gender and development issues so that inclusive sustainable development may be possible in the short and the long run?

Chapter 16 engages the issue of 'Non-state Actors as the Strategic Realm in Africa's Development'. Non-state actors have been variously recognized as important engines of growth and development across the world. This is because they have an objective and critical existence that makes it possible for them to engage/disengage with the state in driving the development of nations and continents. Thus, this chapter examines the contributions of non-state actors to development on the continent, Africa. Their contributions are examined over time across African nations in terms of both positive and negative contributions. Issues relating to the abuses that have marked their contributions are also examined. Some of the questions asked in this chapter are: What is/who are non-state actors? What are their typologies? What development philosophies guide their existence and operations? What is their political economy? To what extent have they/have they not contributed to the development of countries in Africa? What are their challenges? What are their successes? Have there been abuses? Are they very important to Africa's development? How can they better drive development in Africa? Where are the cases of best practices in Africa and other developing and developed countries and what can be learnt from the best practices?

'Globalization and Africa's Development' (Chap. 17) discusses one of the most sensitive and controversial subjects in the social sciences and development studies—globalization. This is partly because of its multifaceted manifestations, as well as its global political economic and generalized impacts on developing countries. Thus, this chapter engages the many elements of globalization in policy, scholarship and practice manners. It traces the development of globalization, the place of developing countries, the role of developed nations and the overall implications of globalization for Africa in development terms. Indicative questions posed in this chapter include: What is globalization? What are the historical and developmental specificities of globalization? What are the drivers of globalization? What are the forces and elements of globalization? What are the theoretical contours of globalization? How has globalization influenced Africa's development to date? What roles has Africa played in globalization? To what extent has Africa benefited/not benefited from globalization? How can Africa positively appropriate globalization for sustainable development?

Chapter 18 gives a broad overview of regional and sub-regional organizations and Africa's development. It has been generally recognized that regional and sub-regional organizations are very important in driving growth and development. This is particularly so judging from the experiences of the European Union (EU). Africa is certainly a continent of regional and sub-regional blocs. However, the extent to which Africa's regional and sub-regional blocs have contributed to development on the continent remains a big question. This chapter therefore critically, theoretically and pragmatically engages the interlinkages of regional and sub-regional blocs and Africa's development, leveraging on continental and national issues through a case study of trade agreements.

'International Organizations and Africa' are the subject of Chap. 19. The chapter examines the implications of global/international organizations for Africa's development. The debates around the contributions of international organizations to the development of Africa are objectively engaged in this chapter. Chapter 20 examines 'African Development Initiatives'. This chapter interrogates the development philosophies and operational frameworks of development initiatives of Africa as the continent struggles to aggregate policies to drive common development on the continent. It links the continental development initiatives with global ones to prevent lopsided and vacuous analysis.

Chapter 21 engages the subject of 'Africa and International Migration' through a case study set in Cameroun. Africa is a continent of migrants. A significant proportion of international migrants in Europe, the United States of America (USA), Latin America, the Caribbean and Asia are Africans. While Africans immigrate to other continents, the continent is also a major recipient of migrants whether as a transit point or as a destination. Hence, due to large-scale migrations from Africa, the continent is among the highest recipients of remittances from abroad to the extent that remittances from migrants of African origin dwarfs foreign direct investments (FDIs) into Africa. Hence, a number of African countries may actually not be able to survive without remittances from their nationals abroad. Apart from remittances as development gains of international migration, Africa also benefits from extra-financial gains just as it suffers some losses from international migration. This chapter examines the relationship between international migration and the development of Africa from a historical perspective.

Chapter 22 is headed 'Aid and the Development of Africa'. Aid is among the most controversial development strategies in the world today (see Easterly 2006). Yet, Africa seems to be trapped in the aid web as many African countries remain, to varying degrees, somewhat dependent on aid from developed countries (Easterly 2006). Major issues around aid and development are whether they are necessary drivers of growth and development (by providing important materials and supports) or disablers of growth and development as they build a dependence syndrome and foster corruption. This chapter engages the trajectories of aid as development strategies and frameworks for Africa. Indicative questions this chapter will answer include: What is aid?

What are the philosophical, policy, empirical and practice issues around aid? How has aid driven or not driven development in Africa? How sustainable is aid in driving Africa's development? What are the established and emerging issues and debates around aid, especially in Africa? How can aid be made conformable and in tune to drive the development of Africa? Is aid necessary at all for Africa's development? And so on. This chapter, like the others, is detailed, polemic, objectively balanced, engaging, comparative, empirical, policy and practice-oriented and scholarly.

References

Africa Institute of South Africa (AISA). (2002). *Africa's development thinking since independence: A reader*. Pretoria: AISA. ISBN: 9780798301763.

Akanle, O. (2011). The sociology of gender equality and development in democratizing Nigeria. *The Nigerian Journal of Sociology and Anthropology, 9*, 22–36.

Akanle, O. (2012). Childhood construction, child rights and development in Nigeria: Trajectories from the Yoruba of south-western Nigeria. *African Journal for the Psychological Studies of Social Issues, 15*(2), 359–379.

Akanle, O., & Adesina, J. O. (2015). Corruption and the Nigerian development quagmire: Popular narratives and current interrogations. *Journal of Developing Societies, 31*(4), 421–446.

Akanle, O., & Omobowale, A. O. (2015). Trans-border banditry and integration in the ECOWAS region. In A. O. Olutayo & I. A. Adeniran (Eds.), *Regional economic communities: Exploring the process of socio-economic integration in Africa* (pp. 101–110). Dakar: CODESRIA.

Easterly, W. (2006). *The white man's burden: Why the West's efforts to aid the rest have done so much harm and so little good*. Oxford: Oxford University Press.

Moss, Todd J. (1997). *African development: Making sense of the issues and actors*. Boulder: Lynne Rienner. ISBN: 13:978-1588267-696.

Muriith, Samuel M. (1997). *African development dilemma: The big debate*. Lanham: University Press of America. ISBN: 0-7618-0546-X.

OECD. (2015). *African economic outlook 2015: Regional development and spatial inclusion*. Paris, AfDB, UNDP. ISBN: 9789264232822.

Olayinka Akanle, PhD, is a Lecturer in the Department of Sociology, University of Ibadan, Nigeria. He has received many scholarly awards like been a Postdoctoral Fellow at the South African Research Chair Initiative (SARChI) in Social Policy, College of Graduate Studies, University of South Africa (UNISA), South Africa; World Social Science Fellow (WSSF) of The International Social Science Council (ISSC), Paris, France, Laureate of Council for the Development of Social Science Research in Africa (CODESRIA) and University of Ibadan Postgraduate School Prize for scholarly publication awardee. He has published many articles internationally and he has co-edited many books. He is the author of ***Kinship Networks and International Migration in Nigeria*** (2013). His research interests include: Sociology of Development and Development Studies, Social Theory, Social Policy, Sociology of Religion, Migration and Diaspora Studies, Child, Youth, Gender and the Family in Post-Colonial Africa. E-mails: yakanle@yahoo.com, yk.akanle@ui.edu.ng.

Jìmí Olálékan Adésìnà is Professor and the DST/NRF SARChI Chair in Social Policy at the College of Graduate Studies, University of South Africa. Previously Professor of Sociology at Rhodes University and Professor and Head of Department at the University of the Western Cape, he serves on the Boards of the UN Research Institute for Social Development (Geneva). His research interests include Social Policy, Social Theory, and the Political Economy of Africa's Development. E-mails: adesij@unisa.ac.za, adesij@gmail.com.

Chapter 2
Conceptualizing and Framing Realities of Africa's Development

Abel Akintoye Akintunde and Ayokunle Olumuyiwa Omobowale

Introduction

The objective realities of Africa's development have remained vague to scholarship because epistemological lenses and levels of analysis continue to represent development as a skewed and ethnocentric and, hence, as a partial rather than an inclusive reality (Harrison 2005; Kolawole 2014; Konadu 2014). Most vivid and prominent in the literature is the representation of Africa's development in terms of the realities of other societies rather than those of Africa itself (Kolawole 2014). Development is hence represented and portrayed not as a subjective and interpretive experience of individual societies but rather as an experience of Africa imaged by non-African contexts when in fact development remains contextual and existential in nature. A projection of hierarchy and the stratification of Africa beneath other societies on the global socioeconomic ladder is the inevitable result of such an understanding of Africa's development in discourse. Such representations negate the tenets of philosophical phenomenology and interpretivism and their customary appeal for penetration into the subjective world of meaning of the actor(s) or research subject(s) as a basis for articulating their reality (Coser 1977, Thompson and Tunstall 1976), and in this case Africa's development reality.

Another consequence of such a representation is that development is construed as polarity between societies of the world. Hence, development is construed as a systemic, quantitative and comparative reality on the other hand, and as a subjective and qualitative experience on the other (Seers 1996). Leanings towards the former at the expense of the latter, however, makes it difficult to articulate anything close to

A.A. Akintunde (✉)
Bowen University, Iwo, Nigeria
e-mail: abelonhigh@gmail.com; abelonhigh@yahoo.com

A.O. Omobowale
University of Ibadan, Ibadan, Nigeria
e-mail: ao.omobowale@gmail.com

O. Akanle, J.O. Adésìnà (eds.), *The Development of Africa*, Social Indicators Research Series 71, DOI 10.1007/978-3-319-66242-8_2

Africa's realities of development in an empirical, existential sense. It is also in this sense that sustainable development as a people's subjective experience, particularly of Africans, becomes a mirage.

In this chapter we contextualize the realities of Africa's development as clearly epistemological. Nobles (2006) describes epistemology as a science involving the study of the nature of reality; how truth is defined; the relationship between the knower, knowing, and the known; what can be known; and what should/could be done with the known. Epistemology is a means of approaching knowledge and coming to know what is real from a culturally informed perspective (McDougal 2014). Hence, the articulation of Africa's realities of development requires an engagement with modes of knowledge production on Africa and attendant approaches underpinning this process. This thinking of development as an epistemological reality compels the necessary examination of some vital issues surrounding the realities of Africa's development. Fundamental to all is the concern for the evolution of knowledge production on the larger social reality of Africans but which ironically evolves from non-indigenous African perspectives developed particularly from non-African contexts and experiences (Higgs 2010). This makes it acceptable to argue further that epistemic relativism and intellectual myopia on what objectively constitutes Africa's social realities critically entangles any possible articulation and comprehension of Africa's realities of development (Bakari 1997; Waghid 2014). It is against this backdrop that this chapter examines the conceptual understandings and framings of development as an African reality precisely within the epistemic currents and popular understandings underpinning development as reality in prevailing debates. In essence, this study conceptualizes development initially as an epistemic construction which either enhances or blights the clear articulation of Africa's development realities and, secondly, as a subjective experience of Africa as a society in itself.

This chapter addresses the foregoing concerns in three major discussions under the headings: 'Defining the concept of development', 'Theoretic conceptualizations of development', and 'The epistemic sustainability of Africa's development'. The first section details the definition of the dynamics mediating conceptualizations of development and what these dynamics portend for any understandings of development as a concept applicable to Africa and any other human society. The second section addresses theoretic debates on development and underdevelopment. With development as an uneasy and difficult subject for theoretic pedagogy (Barnett 2005), the subsection provides an ideal framework for discussing, comprehending and critiquing the epistemology of development itself by showing that development is both a structural and an interpretive reality. The third section discusses Africa's development vis-à-vis epistemic sustainability and otherwise. It establishes how the hypothesis and theoretic understandings of development shape what evolves as the epistemology develops, showing how development informs and impedes a comprehensive representation and understanding of Africa's development realities.

The Concept of Development

A custom in definitions of development is its polar conceptualization as both a quantitative and qualitative reality. If development will truly ensue, it must comprise both quantitative and qualitative changes in the structure, composition and performance of the forces of production in any society (Rodney 1972; Harrison and Berger 2006). As a subjective and qualitative cultural process, development involves the innovation of tools, skills and the mobilization of required resources for development purposes. Supportively, Seers (1969) defines development as a transformative and qualitative experience that must be necessarily understood and engaged in view of three questions which for him must inform an adequate definition of development. These are: "What has been happening to poverty? What has been happening to unemployment? What has been happening to inequality" (Seers 1969, 3)?

The fact that development means different things for different people and that different societies and scholars have differently defined it makes the term conceptually ambiguous (Nieuwenhuijze 1982). Seers' definition for instance purports that development is a qualitative improvement and transformation in the empirical experience of a community, group or society of actors and these must inform their classification as developed. His three prerequisites for development are indicative of Rodney's (1972) and Harrison and Berger's (2006) assertion that development is a qualitative reality. The emphasis on 'poverty', 'unemployment' and 'inequality' depicts development as an existential and experiential concern that is both subjective and relative to a people. This outlook is clearly in contrast to the view of development as an absolute, unilinear or inevitable experience of all human societies. Shionoya and Nishizawa (2008) argue in fact that development is an interpretive reality that can only be fathomed from the perspective of philosophical hermeneutics through the methodological tool known as 'verstehen'. They also present development as a subjective experience of a society in terms of contexts and situations of meaning assignment by actors and members of such groups. For it is only when we know what has been happening to poverty in a society, to unemployment among its members and to inequality between these members that we can adequately and credibly speak of that society's development or otherwise.

Highlighting the subjectivity of development, Rodney (1972) argues that development in human society is a many-sided process. Development is first of all individual; it implies increased skill and capacity, greater freedom, creativity, self-discipline, responsibility and material wellbeing. These categories as he notes are virtually moral and are difficult to evaluate, and they depend in fact on the subjective experience, exposure, codes and standards that inform the outlook of the epistemologist.

At the structural level, the question of development lies at the heart of the political, economic and moral crises of the contemporary global society. Development is also central to the relations of power diplomacy and war in the contemporary world. As a qualitative reality development is decisively connected to the material wellbeing of humanity and the ways some people make a living and the ways some people hunger. It presents a fundamental dimension of social inequality and struggles for social justice (Archetti et al. 1987). Tony Barnett (2005) in fact presents three approaches for understanding the concept of development which inaugurate a general theoretical understanding of the epistemology of development. In the three approaches, development is proposed as both an internal attribute as well as an outcome of interaction between societies. He speaks of development from within, development as interaction and development as interpenetration.

- **Development from within:** Development can come from within, as in the case of China, where universal adherence to Confucianism as a religion instructs and motivates the indigenous development of ideals, thus fostering development leading to a potential change in society's form (Sanderson 1999). Accordingly, development can result only from processes within a given society.
- **Development as interaction**: Here the development of anything results from the interaction between an agent and his environment. Here the society changes as a result of the combination of the equalities and potentials within the object and the opportunities and resources available in that environment.
- **Development as interpenetration:** This view holds that we cannot really draw a sharp distinction between an object and its environment. For example, an animal is made of materials from outside itself; its actions in feeding and housing itself alter its environment. When applied to society, this view raises the question of where the boundaries of any society are located. How can we distinguish sociologically between, for example, Egyptian society—which is predominantly Muslim—and its 'environment' which also contains many other Muslim countries, the ideas, concerns and people of which may affect what goes on in Egypt.

These classifications provide an imperative for engaging development in epistemology as a theoretic concern in this section. Barnett's first construction of development is suggestive of development as an evolutionary process, the second is of development as an outcome of interaction between societies, and the third is of development as an outcome of a complex and interwoven interconnectivity of societies. We now turn to examine some theoretic epistemologies on development and its corollary underdevelopment.

Some Theoretic Conceptualizations of Development

The question of what constitutes development, and especially of the distinction between development and its flipside underdevelopment, has informed various debates, discourses and thought patterns (Archetti et al. 1987). With the general categorization in the literature of Africa, particularly Sub-Saharan Africa, as a developing region (Amin 1976; Rodney 1972), it becomes imperative to understand development within theory in order to articulate its implications for understanding and comprehending Africa's reality. This section therefore explores development as a theoretical subject that enhances understanding on Africa as a region within the global order. We therefore examine development and underdevelopment as two major concepts by which societies, including Africa, are engaged in modern debates. The two concepts are also customarily presented as a basis for classifying societies apart from one another. It is also on this basis that classifications are assigned to societies and by which distinction is made between them. While the economically prosperous nations of the Global North are often portrayed as the privileged side of such debates, the economically dependent nations of the Global South, and particularly Sub-Saharan Africa, are often painted as the disadvantaged category (Kolawole 2014).

In classifying societies, emphases in these debates often situate Africa and other developing countries apart from countries of the West in terms of their polar internal social and economic realities. This form of differential representation echoes one of Barnett's (2005) postulations that sees development as an internal experience that takes place 'from within' a society. Modernization theory, which emerged as a specialized version of an even broader theoretical strategy, the functionalist evolutionary approach (Marshall 1998; Sanderson 1999), is a prominent case in point. There is no one modernization theory, instead the term is shorthand for a variety of perspectives that were applied by non-Marxists to the Third World in the 1950s and 1960s (Harrison 2005). Modernization entails a total transformation of traditional or pre-modern society into types of technology and associated social organization common with the advanced, and economically prosperous and politically stable, societies of the Western world (Moore 1964). Among many definitions, modernization refers to what is 'up to date' in a specific location at any given time. It is usually the result of a process of 'Westernization', involving economic, political, social and cultural changes which contrast with a previous 'traditional' stability. Indeed, any reference to modernity somewhat implies some kind of contrast with a pre-existing order, and in such circumstances conflict may occur (Harrison 2005).

Modernization theories assume that development results from the internal presence of something—development ingredients—while underdevelopment in a society results from the direct opposite—certain internal deficiencies. They see underdevelopment as an original state and a condition of a society that has always existed at some point. These internal deficiencies responsible for underdevelopment include insufficient capital formation in which underdeveloped societies fail to successfully generate the capital required for experiencing a 'take off'—a point for inaugurating rapid economic growth (Sanderson 1999). Another deficiency is the use of outmoded techniques and practice for doing business. The failure of a society to adopt rational business practices impedes its chances for development and keeps its productivity and profit low. Ultimately, modernization theorists argue that underdeveloped societies generally lack the kind of consciousness and worldview on the world that promotes their development (Moore 1964; Sanderson 1999). By and large, modernization theory often tends to equate modernization and 'development', making them seems quite interchangeable (Harrison 2005; Shionoya and Nishizawa 2008). The position of modernization theory is generally that underdevelopment predates the emergence of modern capitalism and capitalist societies; that in fact the problem of underdevelopment became resolved with the arrival of capitalism, and that development and underdevelopment acquire meaning only when applied to nations incorporated into the capitalist world economy (Sanderson 1999).

For its rather generalizing position on development, the modernization approach is criticized for being too optimistic. In ascribing underdevelopment to those societies which fail to imitate the five stages of economic progress in the West, the theory is criticized for being too over-simplistic (Marshall 1998). In fact, Rostow's modernization approach, "in all its variations, ignores the historical and structural reality of the under-developed countries" (Harrison 2005). But modernization theory's assertion that imitation of the West is a sine qua non for development in any society is queried by Barnett (2005), who argues that it may be possible to perceive or postulate a developmental sequence in history, but it is another thing to say that sequence must happen that way or that it ought to cut across other societies. To say the latter is to make a value judgment. And in fact, exactly that kind of judgment has been made, and is made, about the development of political arrangements in many parts of the world (Barnett 2005, 13). Yet this trend is common with the evolutionary theorists of development in Western Europe and North America, who explain societies of the world according to Western ideals and histories. In fact, the epistemology of development reflects an essential ethnocentrism that weighs heavily on contemporary social sciences (Rodney 1972; Archetti et al. 1987).

Marxists known as dependency theorists also offer an alternative explanation of development which extensively criticizes tenets of modernization theory. Their assumptions are founded on the economic determinism of especially the historical materialism of Karl Marx, which posits that every society is characterized by a history of contestations known as dialectics—the thesis and anti-thesis. They see the historicity of societies as the imperative for understanding their development. They believe that the dialectics of societies rooted in their specific histories help to understand their development in terms of changes (synthesis) in material life occasioned by two major forces in history (thesis and antithesis). At the international level, they argue that in development and underdevelopment occasioned by the dialectics (bourgeoisie and proletariat), capitalism manifests as an unequal mode of interaction and as a mode of production exploited by the minority rich countries of the Global North to the detriment and disadvantage of the poor nations of the Global South.

Others, like Samir Amin (1976), construe development and underdevelopment more loosely as open rather than fixed experiences of any society in general, not necessarily any one society in particular. The concept of center and periphery is central to Amin's thoughts on development and underdevelopment and he begins his analysis with the international division of labor and the consequent unequal exchange between center and periphery. As he notes, technologically advanced heavy industry is concentrated in the center while the periphery is confined to light industry, the production of raw materials for the center, and an undeveloped agriculture. But again Amin argues that it is wrong to identify the underdeveloped countries with exporters of basic commodities. This is because many of the advanced capitalist countries also export basic commodities. From his Marxian outlook, Amin consequently defines underdevelopment as the blocking of the transition to capitalism of the peripheral social formations by the advanced capitalist social formations. In essence, underdevelopment is not simply non-development, but is a unique type of socioeconomic structure brought about by the integration of least developed countries (LDCs) into the world capitalist system (Marshall 1998).

Unlike the view of modernization that underdevelopment is an original state of a traditional society, dependency theorists identify underdevelopment as something created within a pre-capitalist society that relates economically and politically with capitalist societies. From the dependency thesis, underdevelopment results from the dependency of one society on another (Harrison 2005). Using concepts like metropolis–satellite and core–periphery to describe the world's rich bourgeoisie and the world's poor proletariats respectively, dependency theorists argue that underdevelopment is the flipside of development or, put differently, underdevelopment and development are two sides of a coin brought together by economic dependency of one society on another (Cardoso and Faletto 1979; Ritzer 2008). Dependency scholars also critique the writings of underdevelopment by showing that accumulation at the center (the advanced capitalist countries of the West) prevents development in regions like Africa and Indochina. This happens particularly within what they call the peripheral social formations—a description for underdeveloped countries (Amin 1976).

As Rodney (1972) argues, Africa as a developing country in Africa is often represented by the West as the proletariat society of the capitalist world from which countries of the core/metropolis expropriate surplus from which they extract raw materials. Yet the world's capitalist system is craftily designed to favor the West and to exploit Africa's wage labor as a part of the Global South. But as argued earlier, Africa's regime of underdevelopment in the satellite and periphery is not a fixed and inescapable fate. Rather this regime of exploitation, as argued earlier, is contingent on Africa's own level of class consciousness and, in this case, her epistemological class consciousness. It is in this consciousness that she potentially acquires the label of developed or underdeveloped, though this time as a self-imposed reality not as hegemony or direct exploitation from another. And since development and underdevelopment are jointly construed in this study as epistemological realities of Africa, then it follows automatically too that whatever in development discourse represents modern hegemony and the proletarianization of Africa is effectually contingent on the epistemic posture and disposition of the African scholars and scholarship towards the representation of their fate within the development epistemology.

For criticizing modernization theory and for taking a more hostile attitude to Westernization, dependency theorists are also classified in some quarters as underdevelopment theorists. Nevertheless, in concentrating on the mainly detrimental links of Third World with the world system, Marxists are criticized for paying relatively little attention to the domestic structures of Third World societies (Harrison 2005). Using the concept of class consciousness, Marxian thought also reveals that underdevelopment can however translate into underdevelopment if the proletariat (poor working class societies) do not move from a slavery mentality (of a class in itself) to a freedom mentality (class for itself) (Ritzer 2008).

The comparative analysis offered by the foregoing theories as an explanation for development and underdevelopment and their tendency to see development and underdevelopment as systemic processes within and between societies only succeeds in accounting for the structural nature and dimensions of development. Beyond their ethnocentric tendencies and oversimplification and overgeneralization of the development realities of societies, these structural explanations scarcely account for the qualitative (Harrison and Berger 2006) and the intrinsically interpretive nature and dimensions of development within societies they propose as developed and underdeveloped. In fact, as Shionoya and Nishizawa (2008) argue, economic sciences such as modernization are inherently and generally limited in providing an inclusive accounting of development as a historical experience of a people or society, because in equating evolution with development they limit and narrow down the qualitative realities of development. To this end, Archetti et al. (1987) note that the concepts of developing and underdeveloping or emerging societies are suffused with teleology which privileges parts of Europe and the USA as developed over developing nations in Africa. In portraying the world as a unilinear rise from barbarity to modernity as a substitute for the analysis of actuality—real and everyday experiences of people—modernization theory is weak. The evolutionary focus of modernization theory ignores the fact that in reality, the fundamental questions of the 'developing societies' are not of difference only but of relationships past and present with countries of advanced capitalism and industrialization. Indeed these very puzzles remain central to the sociology of development itself.

It is crucial to note at this point that although the foregoing theoretical efforts to understand development realities across societies (especially from the structural and macro-perspectives as already seen) are commendable, theories of development are bound by the selfsame limitations that bind social theory formulation, which is that their formulation is contextually informed and therefore also contextually relevant (Pratt 1978). Development theories too, because they are socio-culturally informed and specific, are thus inherently limited in explaining and comprehending African realities which naturally fall outside the province of the mostly Western cultures motivating their postulation. Tony Barnett (2005, 12–13) captures this reality aptly when he established the link between limits of social theorizing on development theorizing, arguing that:

> A 'theory' is never 'true'—rather it should be seen as being a very special form of language which sketches out the words we can use to discuss a particular problem and the ways in which we can test our language description against our experience. In the same way that it would be faintly absurd to ask whether the English, Russian or Swahili languages are 'true', so it is not relevant to ask whether the specialized 'theory language' we use in sociology or any other area of study is 'true'. Rather, we should be asking whether it is adequate for the job it is being asked to do. The English language is not very good at describing the life-world of, say, the!Kung* people of Southern Africa, because it was not invented to do that job. Similarly, the theoretical language of functionalist sociology has difficulty in describing and making sense of a society undergoing rapid change. In these senses, both English and functionalism are inadequate for those purposes. This problem becomes rather more complex (and interesting) in social science because social theory, being a produced thing—the result of people working/thinking together—reflects the experience and particular view of those who produce that theory. It often tends to support the beliefs which the theory producing group or groups hold about the way society is or ought to be working.

Implicitly, an inclusive understanding of Africa's development realities requires an interpretive turn in epistemologies on development in general and on Africa's development in particular. Owing to the impediments besetting comprehension of Africa's development realities within the macro-perspectives espoused earlier, Barnett's (2005) argument instructs an urgent turn towards a theoretical conceptualization of Africa's reality that acknowledges Africa's internal, compositional and historical attributes and situations. To therefore understand the realities of African development, epistemology must commence from the level of the subjective, micro-level interactions of African societies rather than setting out from the large-scale processes and systemic accounting of development and underdevelopment in societies (Shionoya and Nishizawa 2008). Theoretical representations would necessarily devote their commitment to subjective and interpretive understandings of development from the actors themselves, what Max Weber in the German sense aptly describes as *verstehen*, which depicts an understanding that is subjective and that pays tribute not to the researcher's position but to the research subject's meaning and interpretation of social reality (Coser 1977). Adherence to the tenets of verstehen would inspire interpretive understanding and interpretation of Africa's development that supports African studies based on what Peter Berger defines as the as 'calculus of meaning', that is, social construction development according to the subjective meanings attached to reality by Africans themselves.

Hence, Rodney (1972) explains that every people have shown a capacity for independently increasing their ability to live a more satisfactory life through exploiting the resources of nature. Because every continent independently participated in every epoch of the extension of man's control over his environment, and because in effect every continent can point to a period of economic development, it means that even in economic considerations, development is a subjective and not a corporate experience of societies of the world relative to themselves as modernization theory argues. For Rodney (1972), Africa being an original home of man, was obviously a major participant in the processes in which human groups displayed an ever increasing capacity to extract a living from the natural environment.

Sustainability and the Epistemology on Africa's Development

To achieve sustainably in the conceptualization of Africa's development realities, this subsection argues for inclusiveness in the epistemic articulation of African realities of development as an imperative for development. Although the drive towards sustainable development is topical in literature, we contextually conceptualize sustainability of development loosely as sustainable epistemology. Seeing development as an epistemological reality, achieving a sustainable epistemology of African realities enables the easy attainment of sustainable development in reality. Central to this conceptualization of development is the mode and patterns governing the representation of Africa in development scholarship and discourse. Epistemology is important because in discourse it not only shapes how a group is represented but also what becomes the fate of such a group as directed by policies prompted and driven by such discursive representation. Three important concerns connected with the prevailing representation of Africa's realities of development, especially those relative to the imaging of African in African studies and scholarship, are discussed. Representation is discussed vis-à-vis epistemic imperialism as the underdevelopment of Africa, the need for an articulated epistemology and the need for Africanizing the epistemology on Africa's development.

Epistemic Imperialism as the Underdevelopment of Africa

The central argument here is that a new form of imperialism, namely, epistemic imperialism constitutes a major impediment to the sustainable conceptualization of Africa's development realities. In his work, *How Europe Underdeveloped Africa* (1972), Rodney (1972) posited underdevelopment of Africa by the West. This study moves further to posit an epistemological underdevelopment of Africa through the medium already described as epistemic imperialism. Epistemic imperialism is indeed orchestrated through the Eurocentric epistemological enterprise. In the literature alluding to the epistemological underdevelopment of Africa through knowledge production and modes of knowledge production, misrepresentation, underrepresentation and denigrating representation are forms in which Africa witnesses underdevelopment. The mangled explanation of Africa, especially through the use of methodologies informing epistemic explanations that originate from outside Africa, and particularly from the West, remain the principal tools for perpetrating underdevelopment (Airoboman and Asekhauno 2012). As Kwasi Konadu (2014) argues, Eurocentric epistemology of Africa has its origins in the inception and development of African studies in the academy. Given the academic character of African studies in the USA and its geographical and cultural construction outside of Africa, it is evident that the 'founding' of the field lies ostensibly in anthropology and through agents of the European colonial enterprise. For him, the surest way of relocating Africa back into African studies is to relocate African studies back to Africa. But, even if African Studies cannot be relocated back to Africa geographically, the relocation could be done epistemologically and paradigmatically. He calls for an indigenous anchoring and ownership of the study of African(s) by Africans. Decrying epistemological imperialism, he notes that if the study of Africa has been and continues to be driven by paradigms and theories established by non-African scholars, then African studies are an invention of academia, which ultimately serves its own interests and those of non-Africans.

Kolawole (2014) for instance identifies orality, visuality and gestuality as cultural forms that express the African reality. There is therefore a need to contextualize issues from historical, political, sociological and cultural dimensions that add value to the specificity and validity of African data and concepts. Context mediates values and addresses the call for the authentication of African studies. Konadu (2014) aptly captures the colonialism and imperialism driving the discursive representation of Africa in African studies when he argues:

> Conceptual evidence for African studies being an invention by and created to serve the interests of non-Africans can be found in the parameters of African studies. African studies focused on the geographical entity of Africa rather than the movement and development of its people, thus suggesting that Africans who were forcibly brought to the United States and elsewhere stopped being Africans. The claim is a cultural and political stance which rejects the reality of African cultural-historical continuity, and conforms to a worldview and theoretical construct that also holds the principal unit of analysis to be the 'tribe. In this regard, it becomes clear not only that the "institutions of European society [have provided] … the categories of western (or European) social science," but also the unstated thrust in African Studies that non-European culture(s) either conform or exist in opposition to this authoritative model of social organization and knowledge production. The implication is that "African cultures are held as the primary obstacles to [their own] development."

In essence, the explanation for Africa using non-African lenses indicates nothing less than modernization carried forward. In discursively patterning Africa's structural, systemic and interpretive realities and outlook towards Eurocentric ends and agenda in terms of evolutionary theories and processes of development in the West, development scholarship and African studies clearly undermine the realities that are fundamental for understanding Africa's development. These explanations succeed only in sustaining the pristine Darwinian penchant for other worlds to imitate the foreign development stages of other worlds to be classified at all as developed. Such representations ensure epistemic modernization in which the explanation of Africa develops from naïve and external approaches.

Such approaches are weak because they are uncritically optimistic, ethnocentric in approach and they amount to oversimplifications (Marshall 1998). Leaning towards Marx, criticizes the modernization orientation of theory in understanding and explaining other human groups like Africa, arguing that historical and social formations of societies are heterogeneous rather than homogeneous. All histories and their differing conditions of existence must therefore be studied afresh. To understand development and change in any society, and in this case Africa, one must understand the peculiar and whole process of history of nature and the history of men, that is how the latter exploit the former. We therefore argue that approaches involved in representing Africa through non-African and particularly through Western lenses must be remodeled to image African realities from the contextual situations of Africans themselves. In fact, understanding how African culture influences the behavior of Africans and African societies, and what forces shape cultural change in Africa, accelerates the pace of progress, which informs a development that is sustainable (Harrison and Berger 2006). To achieve sustainable epistemological development in constructing the development realities of Africa then, what is pertinent are a discursive decolonization of the epistemological modernization mission and the epistemic imperialism of African realities.

Recognizing the underrepresentation and/or ethnocentric representation of Africa's development, this chapter posits that the implication for Africa of approaching the realities of Africa and those of Africa's development is a contemporary and an alternative form of underdevelopment. Indeed tenets of evolutionism may adequately apply to the realities of development in the West but they scarcely begin to sufficiently explain development in Africa because Africa's reality, like social reality itself, is subjectively and socially constructed and is not a given. In fact as Harrison and Berger (2006) observe, the realities of Africa's development are essentially interpretive in nature and require more cultural approaches that recognize and acknowledge the nexus between a people's culture and their development. Africa's realities of development are therefore defined by modes of production, especially their culture production, which is inherently peculiar and unique to each society in history. Epistemology on Africa's development must therefore focus on the actor and the system, on culture, values, and political and economic change, on diffusion and innovation, and on the importance of domestic structures, as well as links with external institutions and the world system. The role of epistemologists and social scientists themselves, as active diffusers of perceptions of development, whoever they are, must also be factored into consideration (Harrison 2005).

The portrayal of Africa's development as a 'dependent development' is another inadequacy underpinning the representation of Africa's development realities in development discourse. Indeed, the development realities of Africa as a host to developing countries may necessarily follow the path described by Cardoso and Faletto (1979) as 'associated dependent development', but to argue that Africa's development is all about dependency is a far too inadequate claim. Such representation of Africa indicates another form of epistemological colonialism entangling what constitutes development from a truly African lens. The trend is nowhere more rife than in the development policy discourses which emphasize that Africa's development history is intertwined with foreign aid. The realities of Africa's historical innovativeness, ingenuity and potential for self-sustenance are thus overlooked, making the region appear bereft of her development as a region. Hence, Africa is painted as a community of alms-receiving nations at the mercy of international donor groups controlled by the West (Akinola 2012).

We argue that the stigma associated with reliance on foreign aid is no different from that associated with the uncritical consumption of Western development epistemology on Africa. African elites have an obligation to shift paradigms from the consumption and recycling of Western development theses to the production of an indigenous African development thesis. As with the dependency tendency of African nations on foreign aid from the West, there is also a need in discourse for Africa to liberate herself from underrepresentation as a strictly underdeveloped region by directing domestic scholarship on development from the skewed western representation of her development realities towards decolonization. This position squares up with the argument of Amin (1976) that Africa must break out of the vicious cycle of dependence on and peripheralization from the West, which implies that each of her constituent underdeveloped societies must select their own appropriate planning techniques.

The Need for an Articulated Epistemology

Of course apart from acknowledging the nexus between Africa's culture and its development, an articulated epistemology is imperative for the evolution of a sustainable epistemology on Africa's realities of development. Serie McDougal III

(McDougal 2014) defines African epistemology as an approach to knowledge that includes the African: a conception of the meaning of knowledge; the means used to gain knowledge; the criteria for assessing the validity of knowledge; and the role that knowledge plays in human existence. Airoboman and Asekhauno (2012) argue that there is indeed an African mode of knowing, peculiar to Africans, that is context-dependent, social bound, and superior to other epistemologies. In fact what is presented as the dicta of African epistemology by its proponents (whether Africans or non-Africans) is colorized with a Western epistemological character. While Africa's realities may be peculiar, most proponents of African peculiar epistemology make the discipline of African epistemology too simplistic, commonplace and bereft of epistemological nitty-gritty. Yet epistemology, even as the universal theory of knowledge, is culturally ingrained and culturally provoked.

Kolawole (2014) observes that it is crucial to decenter knowledge on Africa in time and space, moving from exclusionist to positively inclusive ways of knowing such that the continuum of values sustained by Africa's indigenous history is not undermined. Concepts, theories and approaches sustaining epistemology must be repositioned because Africans like other societies of the world are constantly negotiating their position in the new world order. What is also necessary is a shift from the popular but much critiqued African studies noted for its uninclusiveness and ethnocentrism to the more inclusive Africana studies which is notable for its inclusive and objective representation of African realities (Konadu 2014). Part of the merits of Africana studies is its deconstructive outlook towards the Western representation of the world based on dualism as the epistemological social order and its social construction of the African social order as non-binary and rooted in communalism. In the latter, Africans for instance build and construct social reality based on the belief that 'I am, because we are; and since we are therefore I am'. Eurocentric epistemology in African studies hinges on dualism; Africana studies are predicated on "a sociocentric view of African communalism" that is compositionally non-binary in nature. The African as an individual is therefore a constitutive member of the collective (Waghid 2014).

Konadu (2014) therefore advocates for an African-centered approach that conceptualizes and situates Africans within their cosmological, symbolic and pragmatic universe. Such an unambiguous approach not only affirms African agency and serves Africa's best interests, but also authenticates the notion of an African cultural-historical continuum that predates African studies and would continue even if the academic field ceased to exist. Devoted to 'commitment, connectedness, and consciousnesses' and built on records and interpretations of Africans, Africana studies explores African culture as a whole. It accesses a temporal spiritual continuum of life within the composite of the ideational, spiritual and material realities of Africa. Africa should be viewed as a geographic, cultural, conceptual, socio-political and spiritual entity. With Africana studies it becomes easy to expose epistemology to the physical (land and people), ideational (philosophy and thought) and spiritual (temporal manifestation) aspects of Africa and its indigenous peoples living within the bounds of symbiotic relationships.

All knowledge results from an occasion of encounter in place. But the place remains a rightly shaped perspective that allows the researcher to put African ideals and values at the center of inquiry (Higgs 2010). And since African epistemology has always been informed by the beliefs, then the conceptualization of Africa's development epistemologically must not stray from this origin which draws roots from accumulated wisdom that has been passed on to the youth in the form of proverbs, revered traditions, myths and folktales; languages of multiple ethnic communities; traditional customs; and accepted authorities, whether people, institutions or texts, in matters of knowledge and belief. African epistemology has always been informed by the beliefs and concepts (Waghid 2014).

As Bakari (1997) notes, research on ancient African civilization suggests that Africans perceived the world differently from the worldview underpinning the explanation of Africans by their European oppressors who harness epistemology to enact oppression. While Western epistemology limits itself to the scientific method of abstraction and divides reality into the subjective and objective in consonance with Western ontology, African epistemology in consonance with African ontology conceives the world as a basic unitary system therefore seeing reality as interwoven and connected (Jimoh and Thomas 2015). Core to African epistemology for instance is that it is characterized by a strong interpersonal relationship with others as well as harmony, peace with nature, communalism, and spirituality. In fact, Afrocentric epistemology is rooted in spirituality, communalism, cooperation, ethics and morality. Afrocentric epistemology also recognizes science as a primary way of knowing. It equally places great emphasis on ethics and morality, spirituality, symbolic imagery, science, self-awareness and tradition. The universe, nature, humans and the spirit are all considered one through the use of symbolic imagery. The use of symbols provides the means for conveying a precise rationale. These symbols are the objectification of the subjective subliminal nature of Africans.

Conceptualizing Development by Africanizing the Epistemology of Africa's Development

Development is in fact part of a people's and to a society's culture rather than systemic. Hence, one cannot understand a long list of economic and political changes in a society without taking account of their relation to culture. In fact, different groups within a society have different values, which are relevant to the groups' role in economic development. Accordingly, development is necessarily contextual in nature and its definition cannot therefore be driven by any society or group in particular (Nyamnjoh 2004; Harrison and Berger 2006). Yet, narratives on development frequently suffer from what may be called the 'Westphalian fallacy'; that is, the notion that cultural boundaries coincide with political ones, so that entire societies can be analyzed and compared in terms of their values systems. In actual fact, though, the values operative within any society deemed 'national' are rarely monolithic. There are, typically, numerous regional, ethnic and religious variations, entire subcultures with divergent values, and even culture wars within and between societies. This pluralism, of course, is even more evident if one thinks in terms of 'civilizations.' And this peculiarity makes it difficult to speak of a society's development in comparison with other societies (Harrison and Berger 2006).

As Brown (2004) argues, a crucial tenet of traditional African culture is that there is more to reality and to the realm of experience than that which is readily accessible through empirical inquiry, and that we can acquire an understanding of natural phenomena only by appealing to experiences whose characterizations are not empirically confirmable but are nonetheless somewhat assertable. To therefore have a distinctive or unique African epistemology on development, it must be borne in mind that each race is endowed with a distinctive nature and embodies in its civilization a particular spirit. And that varied mindsets exist across human societies. Similarly, how each culture interprets experiences can be explained by uncovering those assumptions and concepts which underlie its experience and worldview. Hence, it would be presumptuous and inadequate to assess African development thought on the criteria developed within the context of Western cultures (Udefi 2014).

Another problem besetting the representation of development is the fact that domestic education, local efforts as well as modes of knowing in Africa have mostly been a journey fueled by an exogenously induced and internalized sense of inadequacy in Africans. Insofar as the study of Africa continues to be driven by the Eurocentric African studies and by paradigms and theories designed by non-African scholars, then African studies will continue to be understood chiefly in terms of Western ideals such as dualism which scarcely represents the sociocentric and communal outlook sustaining realities of development in Africa. African studies as an invention of academia also continues to serve its own interests and those of non-Africans (Konadu 2014). With this outlook comes the tendency to devalue or annihilate African creativity, agency and value systems. Such cultural estrangement has served to reinforce in Africans self-devaluation and self-hatred and a profound sense of inferiority that in turn compels Africans to 'lighten their darkness' both physically and metaphysically for Western gratification (Nyamnjoh 2004).

Consequently, we argue that an Africanist consciousness must also drive knowledge production on Africa if the African epistemology is to clearly articulate Africa's development. Such Africanist consciousness and representation of Africa must eschew aversion for local content. In fact it must necessarily draw from an inclusive, particularist unbiased and non-ethnocentric perspective which can be conveniently applied by anyone who seeks to engage the African reality (Udefi 2014). This is because the importance and development of Africa transcends the production and dissemination of knowledge about Africa by Africans. Hence, the African academy has to cross borders and build transnational multicultural bridges to expand the horizon of African epistemology or knowledge production and dissemination in order to have an articulate epistemology (Kolawole 2014). Africa's historicity is also core to evolving an Africanist epistemology because the historicity of societies is essential for understanding their development especially their economic historicity. In fact, as Shionoya and Nishizawa (2008) argue, the concern for the historicity of development is one of the premises of a universal social science.

Since development as echoed in the foregoing is contextual and subjective, a virile tool for achieving an Africanist social thought for development is to more frequently engage Africa using the lens of Africana studies as hinted earlier. As Serie McDougal III (McDougal 2014) notes, common approaches in Africana studies subject race and ethnicity to a reductive analysis to identify the most common qualities they possess. Africana studies also often seek to explain a wide range of dimensions of the lives of people of African descent. Among their several other characteristics is the recognition of the necessity of cultural specificity, the prioritization of Africana needs and interests, heterogeneous collectivism, collective emancipation and empowerment, agency and self-consciousness, historical location and cultural situating. The issues embedded in Africana studies are generally ingrained in what may be described as an indigenizing mission aimed at evolving an African thesis strictly in terms of the African context and nothing else.

The effectual role of African intellectuals in shaping cultural activities including those tied to development is also crucial to having an Africanist African epistemology of development. In other words, African intellectuals still play a critical part in shaping their culture via epistemology. So far, studies of traditional and contemporary African cultures are, for the most part, conducted by non-Africans, and both the reasons for undertaking such studies and the information on which they are based are foreign. The field covered by these cultures is consequently somewhat narrowed. In their narratives, realities of Africa development are simply derogated and reduced to a collection of animist religious practices, initiation symbols, functional objects of worship, and syncretic rites, superstitions and ceremonies (UNESCO 1974). Also noteworthy is that the engagement of Africa from an African lens as earlier noted is not the exclusive task of the African but that of an Africanist who would represent Africa in accordance with its characteristic internal qualities, culture and definition of development and not by external experiences and cultures foreign to Africa.

The solution is therefore for Africans and non-Africans alike to be involved insofar as paying tribute to the Africanity of development. Emerging African scholars who have accused European ethnologists of falsification and of rejecting their descriptions of African societies and cultures, recommend that Africans themselves should henceforth undertake research in the humanities and seek explanations of facts relating to traditional Africa. The consequence of non-involvement of Africans in the epistemology of African development is 'dual alienation'. That is, an alienation that ensues concurrently with the prevailing epistemic alienation birthed but one which is this time encouraged by inaction and non-involvement in the epistemic representation of Africa and her realities, including those relating to development. As Konadu (2014) argues, the African as an epistemologist must be like the sun, which contributes greatly to human life, but does not proselytize; in all humility, it shines brilliantly each day and simply does what a sun does. The sun (as we know it) does not attempt to be the moon or another star, because that is not its nature. An African proverb summarizes my point best: 'A piece of wood may stay in water for ten years, but it will never become a crocodile.' The obligation for building such an

Africanist and Afrocentric epistemology lies chiefly with the African but also with African institutions and with European scholars of African studies whose European views do not fully accommodate the historical development of Africans (Bakari 1997).

To complement the efforts of Africana studies, this chapter calls for an outlook known as *Afritude* as a necessary epistemology for understanding and representing Africa's development realities from an African lens. To resolve the challenge of alienating Africa's realities of development from African studies, *Afritude* is proposed as an approach but also an attitude for comprehending and representing Africa within the enterprise of knowledge production. As an approach *Afritude* is an interpretive lens and method that engages first with the qualitative dimensions of Africa's realities from Africans themselves before engaging with the quantitative dimensions. The attitudinal component of *Afritude* is an obligation to the epistemologist who must not necessarily be an African but must adopt the African worldview to represent the realities of Africa. His or her scholarly starting point must be Africans themselves and their subjective interpretations and symbols of social reality particularly that pertaining to development. As its mission, *Afritude* must heed the three major concerns raised so far, namely: the need to represent qualitatively the realities of Africa's development, to decolonize the epistemology of Africa's development and to evolve an articulate epistemology that evolves as a full tribute to the undiluted African worldview. The qualitative representation of Africa's realities is no more emphasized than in the views of Seers, Alalana, Barnett, as well as Harrison and Berger, who establish development as a subjective and qualitative experience of a people not just a perceptual hypothesis or conjecture about them. To this end, *Afritude* as a theory must be grounded in Africa's and the African experience to produce any knowledge on Africa. Secondly, *Afritude* must aim constantly at decolonizing extant and potential understandings of the realities of Africa's development. *Afritude* must also heed fully the tenets presented in this study for achieving an articulate epistemology. As a matter of importance, Afritude must also endeavor to see Africa as a sociocentric entity that stands opposed to the Western ideal of individualism that Western modernity begets.

Conclusion

This study commenced by construing development as an epistemological reality that is effectual and contingent on other realities, particularly processes underpinning epistemology on the realities of Africa's development. So far we have established that the concept of development is a coin with two inextricable sides, namely, the qualitative and quantitative dimensions. And these two sides must inform the understanding of development in Africa as a society and at any level of analysis. While development can be understood both as internal and external experience resulting from individual make-up and interaction between societies, the examination of Africa in terms of its development realities, and its subjective social historic and cultural capacities, as with any society, is more central to a clear comprehension of this region's development than by comparing Africa with other societies.

Evolutionary accounting and representations are significant for understanding the West but they certainly limit the understanding of Africa's realities of development. Hence, because such ethnocentric Western lenses have informed popular understandings of Africa's development, we established that the realities of Africa's development may not be missing in the enterprise of knowledge production but their representation from non-African lenses certainly blights the true image of Africa's development and affects epistemic imperialism which, in turn, triggers underdevelopment. This is because discussions and theorizing on Africa from the perspective of European social thought, whether by Western or even African development epistemologists, impedes sustainable development. Reliance on Africana studies and not just African studies for an inclusive, interpretive and existential orientation and representation of Africa's realities is identified as crucial for attaining the development of Africa within epistemology.

The holistic adoption of *Afritude* in its multipurpose essence as an approach, as an attitude, as a lens and as a mission is imperative for an epistemic arrival at a comprehension of Africa's realities of development. As earlier noted, *Afritude* as an approach and an attitude must be first of all adopt an interpretive lens that articulates very clearly both qualitative and quantitative dimensions of Africa's realities. The defining character of Afritude as an attitude instructs that Africa's development scholars and epistemologists may not be African but must adopt the Afrocentric lens to articulate Africa's development realities. The aim of Afritude as attitude is a tripartite devotion which entails that representation must be qualitative, that the study of Africa must aim chiefly at decolonizing epistemology and that what must result from the study of Africa is nothing but a sociocentric reality that stands culturally opposed to the reality of the West which is marked significantly by individualism.

References

Airoboman, F. A. & Asekhauno, A. A. (2012). Is there an 'African' epistemology? *JORIND*, *10*(3). ISSN 1596-8308. http://www.transcampus.org./journals; http://www.ajol.info/journals/jorind.

Akinola, A. O. (2012). Foreign aids in Africa: From realities to contradictions. *Global Advanced Research Journal of Social Science June, 1*(1), 012–017.

Amin, S. (1976). *Accumulation on a world scale: A critique of the theory of underdevelopment*. Review by Disney, N: MERIP Reports, October 51: 21–24.

Archetti, E. P., Cammack, P., & Robert, B. (1987). *Sociology of developing societies: Latin America*. Houndmills: Macmillan Education.

Bakari, S. (1997). *Epistemology from an Afrocentric perspective: Enhancing black students' consciousness through an Afrocentric way of knowing*. Greeley: University of Northern Colorado.

Barnett, T. (2005). *Sociology and development*. London: Hutchinson.

Brown, L. M. (2004). Understanding and ontology in traditional African thought. In L. M. Brown (Ed.), *African philosophy: New and traditional perspectives* (pp. 158–178). Oxford: Oxford University Press.

Cardoso, F. H., & Faletto, E. (1979). *Dependency and development in Latin America*. Berkeley: University of California Press.
Coser, L. (1977). *Masters of sociological thoughts*. New York: Harcourt Brace Jovanovich.
Higgs, P. 2010. Towards an indigenous African epistemology of community in education research. Procedia social and behavioral sciences 2: 2414–2421. Elsevier. Netherlands.
Jimoh, A., & Thomas, J. (2015). An epistemological approach to epistemic certitude and scepticism. *Research on Humanities and Social Sciences, 5*(11), 54–61.
Kolawole, M. E. (2014). *Perspectives on African studies: A multidisciplinary approach*. Ibadan: Ibadan University.
Konadu, K. (2014). *Transatlantic Africa: 1440–1888*. New York: Oxford University.
Harrison, D. (2005). *The sociology of modernization and development*. London/New York: Routledge.
Harrison, E. W., & Berger, P. L. (2006). *Case studies developing cultures*. London: Routledge.
Marshall, G. (1998). *Oxford dictionary of sociology*. New York: Oxford Press Inc.
McDougal, S., III. (2014). Africana studies' epistemic identity: An analysis of theory and epistemology in the discipline. *Journal of African American Studies, 18*, 236–250.
Moore, W. E. (1964). *Social change*. Englewood Cliffs: Prentice Hall.
Nobles, W. W. (2006). *Seeking the Sakhu*. Chicago: Third World Press.
Nieuwenhuijze, C. A. O. (1982). *Development begins at home: Problems and prospects of the sociology of development*. New York: Pergamon.
Nyamnjoh, F. B. (2004). A relevant education for African development: Some epistemological considerations. *Africa Development, 1*, 161–184. Council for the Development of Social Science Research in Africa.
Pratt, V. (1978). *The philosophy of the social sciences*. London: Methuen.
Ritzer, G. (2008). *Sociological theory* (7th ed.). New York: McGraw-Hill.
Rodney, W. (1972). *How Europe underdeveloped Africa*. United Kingdom: Bogle-L'Overture Publications.
Sanderson, S. K. (1999). *Macrosociology: An introduction to human societies*. New York: Longman.
Seers, D. (1969). The meaning of development. *International Development Review, 11*(4), 3–4.
Seers, D. (1996). The meaning of underdevelopment. *International Development Review, ii*(4), 2–6.
Shionoya, Y., & Nishizawa, T. (2008). *Marshall and Schumpeter on evolution: Economic sociology of capitalist development*. Northampton: Edward Elgar.
Thompson, K., & Tunstall, J. (1976). *Sociological perspectives*. New York: Penguin Books.
Udefi, A. (2014). The rationale for an African epistemology: A critical examination of the Igbo views on knowledge, belief, and justification. *Canadian Social Science, 10*(3), 108–117.
UNESCO. (1974, December 2–7). *Cultural development. Young people and African cultural values*. Obligation of the African Agency. Documents of the Regional Meeting of Abomey, Dahomey.
Waghid, Y. (2014). *African philosophy of education reconsidered on being human*. London/New York: Routledge.

Abel Akintoye Akintunde holds a Ph.D in Sociology of Development. His research revolves around Interpretive Sociological Theorizing of Indigenous African realities including but not limited to local social contexts of waste, waste materiality, waste value biographies, waste urbanity as well as the waste space and time. His Ph.D research unraveled the Social Relations underpinning local social Constructions of Imported Used Electronics and Electronic Wastes (E-wastes) within the second-hand market space of Lagos, Nigeria. His methodological devotion is to qualitative research approaches and their prospects for articulating nuances of taken-for-granted everyday African realities, particularly from the perspective of actors involved.

Ayokunle Olumuyiwa Omobowale holds a PhD in sociology from the University of Ibadan. His work focuses on development and society. He has won the University of Ibadan Postgraduate School award for scholarly publication (2007); the IFRA (French Institute for Research in Africa) research fellowship (2009); and the American Council of Learned Societies-African Humanities Program (ACLS-AHP) postdoctoral fellowship (2010). Before joining the University of Ibadan in 2008, Dr Omobowale taught sociology at the University of Lagos, Nigeria, in 2007–2008, and served as Assistant Editor of the International Encyclopedia of Revolution and Protest (2009). He is the author of The Tokunbo Phenomenon and the Second-hand Economy in Nigeria.

Chapter 3
Africa and the Development Narratives: Occurrences, History and Theories

Augustine Okechukwu Agugua

Introduction

A good starting point for discussing theories of African development might involve the invocation of a portion of the United Nations Economic Commission for Africa's (ECA) observation concerning the continent. According to that perspective, increasingly complex neoliberal globalization, changes in intercultural relations at the global level, climate change, poverty, rapid urbanization, the ICT revolution, the emergence of knowledge societies, the evolution of gender and intergenerational relations, the evolution of spirituality and of the status and the role of religion in modern societies, the emergence of a multi-polar world and the phenomenon of emerging powers in the South are some of the realities of our world today that are widely and extensively discussed by both academics and policymakers.

The question one must then ask is: How do all these affect Africa? And how prepared is the continent to face these development challenges as well as those that will arise in the future? In recent times, it has become rather difficult to keep pace with advances in science and technology, including areas of biotechnology and nanotechnology, genetic engineering and so on. The rapidity of the pace of change and development in virtually all spheres of social life at the local, national, continental and global levels makes it difficult to identify the challenges that Africa will be facing in the coming century beyond a few decades. Science itself is changing as a result of changes occurring in nature and in society. The ability of science to anticipate, read and interpret the processes of change has increased over the years. The ability of humanity to follow the developments taking place in nature, and to capture the major trends taking place within society, is likely to increase as science itself develops.

A.O. Agugua (✉)
Department of Sociology, University of Lagos, Lagos, Nigeria
e-mail: agugust@yahoo.com; aagugua@unilag.edu.ng

O. Akanle, J.O. Adésìnà (eds.), *The Development of Africa*, Social Indicators Research Series 71, DOI 10.1007/978-3-319-66242-8_3

Indeed, Africa has entered the twenty-first century with huge unresolved issues, such as poverty, rapid urbanization, the nationality question, regional integration, gender inequality, food insecurity, violent conflicts, political fragmentation, and the fact of occupying a subaltern position in the global community and in global governance. The weight of the past is a major handicap for Africa. The effects of the slave trade, colonization and neocolonialism that Africa has experienced are still being felt, as they have individually and together resulted in the suppression of freedoms, the violation of the human rights and dignity of the peoples of the continent, as well as the looting of human, natural and intellectual resources which have led to what the pan-African historian Walter Rodney called the "underdevelopment" of Africa, (Rodney 1972). Among the major challenges of the continent at the dawn of the twenty-first century are also the low level of education of many Africans, the lack of modern techniques of production and transport, a fragmented political space and the extrovert structure of the economies. The institutions of higher education and cultures of the elites are strongly marked, not necessarily by a philosophy and development strategies guided by the interests of African peoples, but by influences coming from the Global North, influences that are more alienating than liberating.

The foregoing captures the issue of sustainable development challenges in Africa, properly located within the rubric of global development dynamics or trends, a discussion of which follows immediately. It is also on that platform that discussions on theorizing Africa's development problems would be situated.

Global Development Dynamics

In many ways, development has been seen to have advanced more rapidly over the 15-year Millennium Development Goal (MDG) era than at any other time in human history. Since the launch of the MDGs, economic growth has been rapid, aided by strong commodity prices and generally improved macroeconomic policies. The MDGs helped frame the broader goals of development and build a coalition of partners to work toward common goals. One of the most remarkable achievements during the MDG era was the significant decline in the share of the extremely poor in the global population. The first MDG target, cutting the extreme poverty rate to half its 1990 level by 2015, was met 5 years ahead of schedule. As the number of the poor declined, the average shortfall in income below the poverty line improved as well from 13.2% in 1990 to 3.7% by 2012 (World Bank/IMF 2016). The 2012 estimate represents continued progress in poverty reduction as the revised headcount in 2011 was 987 million people (14.2% of the global population). A comparison of 2011 and 2012 reveals a modest decline in the number of poor in Sub-Saharan Africa, potentially heralding an era of poverty reduction not just in the share of the poor but also in their absolute number. The Global Monitoring Report 2015/2016 unveils poverty data based on a new $1.90 international poverty line, using 2011 purchasing power parity (PPP). To be comparable, the global poverty estimates are based on a common poverty line across all countries. As with the previous line of $1.25 a day, in 2005 prices, the new line is calculated by averaging the national poverty lines of the 15 poorest developing countries. Different methods were followed to estimate these lines. Beginning with the $1.25 line, the poverty line was calculated by taking the average of the 15 poorest countries (Chad, Ethiopia, The Gambia, Ghana, Guinea-Bissau, Malawi, Mali, Mozambique, Nepal, Niger, Rwanda, Sierra Leone, Tajikistan, Tanzania, and Uganda). Sadly, 13 of these countries are in Africa (World Bank/IMF 2016).

The implication is that the earlier expressed optimism on poverty reduction notwithstanding, major challenges to development still persist. The first key challenge is the depth of poverty, especially in Sub-Saharan Africa. The decline in poverty rates has been impressive, yet poverty still remains unacceptably high with around 900 million extremely poor people in 2012 and a projected 700 million people in 2015. Poverty is also becoming increasingly concentrated in Sub-Saharan Africa. Over the last decade, the vast majority (about 95%) of global poverty has been concentrated in three regions: East Asia and the Pacific, South Asia, and Sub-Saharan Africa. Over time, the composition of global poverty across these three regions has shifted dramatically. East Asia and the Pacific registered a spectacular decline. South Asia saw an initial increase and a later decline, with rates remaining high. Sub-Saharan Africa saw a steady increase in its share and is now home to 43% of the global poor. The growing global share of Sub-Saharan Africa reflects slower poverty reduction there amid rapid population growth: in 2012 the region's poverty rate stood at 42.6% (World Bank/IMF 2016).

With extreme poverty on the decline globally, a second key challenge is the unevenness in shared prosperity for the bottom 40% (B40). The B40 may include many possible populations. Among developing regions, the income of the richest person among the B40 makes that person either extremely or moderately poor, particularly in Sub-Saharan Africa and parts of East Asia. A third key challenge relates to the persistent disparities in the non-income dimensions of development. Compared with the MDG goal on income poverty, non-income goals saw more mixed success. Progress fell particularly short for targets related to health (maternal and infant mortality), nutrition (undernourishment and hunger), and sanitation (Kenny and Dykstra 2013). Close to one-fifth of all children below five remain undernourished and some 860 million people continue to live in slums. Access to primary school education and literacy rates have improved, yet the quality of education remains a concern.

In addition, little progress has been made in improving the long-term environmental sustainability of development. Although some countries have successfully 'delinked' trends in environmental degradation from growth, most have not. The cost of environmental degradation externalities associated with outdoor and indoor air pollution, water pollution, deforestation, carbon emission and other environmental hazards rose 50% during 1990–2010 (World Bank/IMF 2016). In 2010, between 11 and 21% of all deaths in developing countries were the result of pollution and other environmental risk factors. To sustainably end extreme poverty and promote shared prosperity, more attention is needed to the non-income dimensions of development. First, to end poverty in all of its forms everywhere, it must be recognized that poverty is multidimensional. Income poverty is typically accompanied by inadequate access to education, health, housing, employment and personal security, areas where improvements would increase the chances for escaping poverty. Second, the B40 consistently underperform in non-income dimensions. Children from B40 households are more likely to die before the age of five than children in the top 60% (T60) households and are also more likely to be underweight. Access to improved water sources (piped water) and technology (the Internet) is uneven, too. Despite rising enrollment rates in poorer countries, access to primary education remains inequitably low. Third, greater efforts are needed to monitor the sustainability of development progress in its economic, environmental and social aspects. Environmental sustainability concerns, particularly regarding natural resources, environmental health, and ecosystem sustainability, need to enter more fully into economic decision-making.

The foregoing concerns will naturally lead one to observe that in world development challenges, the outcome of the MDGs shows some traits of an unfinished agenda. Given this sense of unfinished agenda and the coterminous uncertain outlook, new schemes and additional efforts are therefore needed to promote broad-based growth, investment in people and insurance against risks. These three priorities require a strategy that promotes competitive economies and stable business environments, thus ensuring broad-based growth and income-earning opportunities to benefit the poor and the B40. Investment in human development is needed to tackle non-income deprivations and inequalities of opportunity so that these same groups can gain the capacity to benefit from and contribute to economic growth and prosperity (Fryer and Levitt 2004). And robust insurance mechanisms are required so that people, although not necessarily jobs, firms or industries, are protected against evolving risks for individuals, nations and the world, all in the spirit of nurturing a competitive economy and fostering an inclusive society as it informs sustainable development.

Among economies that have sustained growth for extended periods, five characteristics are noted to be key: effective leadership and governance; macroeconomic stability so that markets work; a market orientation to guide structural change; an outward orientation to achieve scale and impose discipline; and a future orientation to boost savings and meet investment needs (Commission on Growth and Development 2008). It is in this sense that we take a look at the evolving global trends that are now shaping the focus of development that informed the evolution of the Sustainable Development Agenda.

Emerging Trends in Development and the Sustainable Development Agenda

According to the World Bank/IMF (2016), several "megatrends" are playing a critical role in framing what will be feasible through to 2030. These include the unprecedented increase in global connectedness, including the cross-border movements of trade, services, capital and people; the shift of the global economic center of gravity toward the Global East; the pace of technological change and adoption; the move toward urbanization; the evolution of demographic trends; the general failure of countries to secure long-term environmental sustainability; and the impact of human activity on climate change. Trade, finance, communications and migration are all expanding rapidly, bringing the world closer together and increasing economic integration.

These megatrends may help or hinder efforts to reach the development goals. On the positive side, the shift in the global economic center of gravity to developing countries creates opportunities. The deepening of global trade and investment connections could help reverse slipping potential growth in some countries, and technological change is also proving to be a driver of productivity growth. On the other hand, increased connectedness permits the rapid spreading of economic crises in one country to the rest of the world. Urbanization is associated with economic growth, but it can also give rise to urban slums and environmental damage. Lower fertility rates reflect improved health and labor market opportunities for women, yet falling shares of the working-age population can produce headwinds to growth and put the fiscal sustainability of many public services at risk.

Cognizant of these trends, the Sustainable Development Goals (SDGs) are noted as representing a greater level of ambition and a more holistic vision of sustainable development. By shifting the focus to quality, the SDGs seek to address the unfinished agenda and scale up the impact of the MDGs. The SDGs recognize that collective action is needed to address global challenges such as the need for more resilient international financial systems, the sharing of trans-boundary resources and, most urgently, slowing and coping with climate change. Meeting the SDG investment needs requires a shift from 'billions' in official development assistance to 'trillions' in investments to unlock, leverage and catalyze domestic public resources and private capital flows. The SDGs need to be pursued in a changing world, with new opportunities and challenges brought by evolving global megatrends that shape development prospects. The SDGs recognize the interconnections between development objectives. There are important interactions between development goals and they cannot be effectively pursued separately from each other. For example, progress on health goals depends on investments in infrastructure that provides access to safe water and improved sanitation. Similarly, limiting carbon monoxide (CO_2) emissions to slow global warming requires the modernization of energy supplies. Hence, the SDGs explicitly articulate goals that are "integrated and indivisible and balance the three dimensions of sustainable development: the economic, social, and environmental" (Dobbs et al. 2015; Singh 2012).

In sync with the megatrends reshaping the world, the SDGs represent a new, more comprehensive approach for scaled-up impact. These megatrends, which include rising global connectedness, the importance of the dynamic economies in the Global East, the increasing pace of technological change and adoption, accelerating urbanization, changing global demographic trends, and the growing impact of human activity on environmental degradation and climate change, have all emerged over the past two decades and are having profound effects on the evolution of development outcomes. Whereas the MDGs of the Millennium Declaration were conceived as a framework committing nations to reduce extreme poverty through enhanced assistance to developing countries, the SDGs represent a global compact that is applicable to all countries, so that all may benefit more from global interconnections while safeguarding the environment and the global commons (World Bank/IMF 2016). The implication of the foregoing narrative makes it imperative to treat issues of development side by side with themes of sustainable development.

Africa's Development and Sustainable Development Challenges

Our presentations so far have shown development as a complex, global and multidimensional process, going beyond mere economic growth to include all dimensions of life and all the energies of a community, where all members must take part in the effort of economic and social transformation and its welfare. In tune with the foregoing views, Todaro and Smith (2003, 792) define development as "the process of improving the quality of human lives". In their analysis, they highlighted three important aspects of development:

1. Raising people's living level. This has to do with raising their income and consumption level of food, medical services, education etc.; through relevant economic growth processes.
2. Creating conditions conducive to the growth of people's self-esteem through the establishment of social and economic systems and institutions that promote human dignity and respect.
3. Increasing people's freedom by enlarging the range of their choice variable, such as by increasing varieties of consumer goods and services.

As noted earlier in this chapter, the overriding sustainable development challenge in Africa is poverty eradication. Thus the African Ministerial Statement to the World Summit on Sustainable Development (WSSD) identified poverty eradication as an indispensable requirement for sustainable development. As shown earlier in this work, Africa is the only region in the world where poverty has increased both in absolute and relative terms. Apart from being the poorest region in the world, Africa remains the least developed, the most technologically backward, the most indebted, the most food-insecure and the most marginalized. Furthermore, malnutrition, disease, environmental degradation, natural resource depletion, poor and inadequate infrastructure, unemployment and weak institutional capacities continue to pose serious development challenges for Africa. This state of affairs is exacerbated by recurring natural disasters and the AIDS pandemic, which is reversing decades of economic gains and imposing costs on Africa at least twice those in any other developing region, thus undermining sustainable economic growth (World Bank/IMF 2016).

It is striking that Africa is the only continent that was not able to meet most of the Millennium Development Goals (MDGs) by 2015. Sustainable development thrives best in an environment of good governance, peace and security, but armed conflict remains a major obstacle to development in several parts of the continent. The maintenance of an environment of peace and security is therefore one of Africa's foremost development imperatives. Apart from its costs in human and material terms, conflicts impede production, damage infrastructure, prevent the reliable delivery of social services and disrupt societies. Africa is the most subdivided continent, with small and fragmented economies that undermine the continent's position in the global development arena. In spite of the long-standing commitments and the emphasis placed by African leaders on the process of regional integration, this has been slow and therefore remains a major challenge for Africa.

From the work on cultural values and the human growth project (Harrison 2000), the relationship was also established more graphically in demographic details as follows: Of the roughly 7 billion people who inhabit the world today, fewer than 1 billion are found in the advanced democracies. More than 4 billion live in what the World Bank classifies as "low income" or "lower middle income" countries. The quality of life in those countries is seen to be dismaying, particularly after half a century of development assistance. HDI insight (World Bank 2009; Agugua 2015) gives a more daunting illumination by indicating that half or more of the adult population of 23 countries, mostly in Africa, are illiterate. Half or more of women are illiterate in 35 countries; prominent among them are Algeria, Egypt, Guatemala, India, Laos, Morocco, Nigeria and Saudi Arabia. Life expectancy is below 60 years in 45 countries, most of them in Africa. And in this vein, life expectancy is less than 50 years in 18 countries, all in Africa, and in West Africa's Sierra Leone life expectancy was found to be just 37 years. Children under five die at rates in excess of 100 per 1000 in at least 35 countries, most of them in Africa.

The population growth rate in the poorest countries is 2.1% annually, three times the rate in the high-income countries. The population growth rate in some Islamic countries is astonishingly high; from a high variant of 5% in Oman to a 'low' variant of 3.4% in Saudi Arabia. The most inequitable income distribution patterns among countries supplying such data to the World Bank are found in the poorer countries, particularly in Latin America and Africa. Democratic institutions are commonly weak or non-existent in Africa, the Islamic countries of the Middle East and the rest of Asia. The implication is that the world at the end of the twentieth century is far poorer, far more unjust, and far more authoritarian than most people had earlier anticipated. Thus the optimism of the people who waged war against poverty at the turn of the mid-twentieth century had been replaced by fatigue and pessimism.

Can one really adduce inadequacy and lack of the requisite traits to survive in a highly changing and complex world to be the issue at stake? Rather than this synchronic attitude that borders on ahistoricity, some authors advocate for a historical and causal path analogy. In this sense, one common perspective on the continent's current dismal state is linked to its colonial history of extraction and exploitation. Thus, Bairoch (1993) posits that no doubt a large number of structural features of the process of economic underdevelopment which its historical roots go back to European colonization. Bertocchi and Canova (2002) aver that African colonization exerted a direct impact on the postcolonial patterns of growth and human and physical capital accumulation. Grier (1999) also established that among former colonies, there is a link between a country's colonial experience and subsequent postcolonial growth. On his own, Englebert (2000) ambitiously claimed to have solved the mystery of Africa's underdevelopment by attributing Africa's poor performance to its weak, arbitrarily imposed postcolonial institutions. In the same vein, Acemoglu, Johnson and Robinson (Acemoglu et al. 2001, 2002) assert that in the former colonies, where the colonizer's focus was on extraction, as in Africa, weak institutions of private property were established and these poor institutions persist to date. At this point, a little interrogation of Africa's past and colonial experience might be useful.

Colonialism and Its Implications for Africa's Development

Colonialism is the practice of invading other lands and territories for the purpose of settlement and/or resource exploitation. Colonialism is neither new nor limited to any specific historical period (i.e. the 'colonial period' of the 15th to 19th centuries). Ancient civilizations were the first to begin colonizing other lands and people. The invaders then imposed their own forms of governance, laws, religion and education. Over time, these populations became assimilated into the culture and society of their conquerors. Fieldhouse (1966) gives an illustration of various forms of colonialism, but for the sake of this chapter, and as it concerns Africa, we shall restrict ourselves to two versions: the settler type and the commercial type. The settler type involves the displacement of the indigenous or native population by the colonist's own population. This is contrasted with the commercial type of colonialism in which the indigenous population is retained as a source of cheap labor and a future market (as noted in Ali Mazrui's theme of 'labor reserve'). As to be expected, settler colonization, with its dispossession of indigenous populations, is marked by conflict between the colonist and the colonized (Chinweizu 1975).

Although there were different motives for colonial adventures, as they also vary in form, a classical motive for colonialism as it affects Africa was essentially captured in the views of Cecil Rhodes. Cecil Rhodes, a British colonial official for which Rhodesia (now Zimbabwe) was named, articulated the motives and goals of European colonialism in the nineteenth century: "We must find new lands from which we can easily obtain raw materials and at the same time exploit the cheap slave labor that is available from the natives of the colonies. The colonies would also provide a dumping ground for the surplus goods produced in our factories" (Chinweizu 1975, 33).

It is often erroneously held that economic development occurs in a succession of capitalist stages and that today's underdeveloped countries are still in a stage, sometimes depicted as an original stage of history, through which the now developed countries passed long ago. Yet even a modest acquaintance with history shows that underdevelopment is not original or traditional and that neither the past nor the present of the underdeveloped countries resembles in any important respect the past of the now developed countries. Thus it is widely believed that the contemporary underdevelopment of a country can be understood as the product or reflection solely of its own economic, political, social and cultural characteristics or structure. Yet historical research demonstrates that contemporary underdevelopment is in large part the historical product of past and continuing economic and other relations between the satellite underdeveloped and the now developed metropolitan countries, as noted earlier in the views of Bairoch (1993), and others (Bertocchi and Canova 2002; Grier 1999; Englebert 2000; Acemoglu et al. 2001, 2002).

In this vein, Claude Ake endeavored to show how the nature of the capitalist mode of production and its internal contradictions, especially as it manifested in nineteenth century Europe, tended to hamper the accumulation of capital. In his view, as these contradictions developed, Western European capitalists tried to counteract their effects on accumulation; first, by making internal adjustments, but eventually, and inevitably, by transporting capitalism to new lands. And it is to be noted here that the whetted appetite of the colonists on the heels of capitalist instincts seem to be insatiable. Thus the more wealth they acquire, the hungrier they become for more. It is in this sense that Schurmann (1974) tried to link colonialism to capitalism with a related but different theme of imperialism (empire building). In his view, colonialism is expansion based on the actual needs and interests of the state, whereas imperialism is animated by expansion for expansion's sake in which every conquest is a way station to the next. In this sense, Schurmann (1974) compares imperialism to capitalism where money is the means to more money for its own sake and in endless acquisition. Since the theme of colonialism is closely tied to the concept of imperialism, it will be useful at this point to lace our understanding of colonialism with the related theme of imperialism.

Imperialism

Succinctly put, imperialism is the economic control and exploitation of foreign lands arising from the necessity for counteracting the impediments to the accumulation of capital engendered by the internal contradictions of the domestic capitalist economy. In a more encompassing sense, Brown (1974, 22) defined it as "the outward drive of certain peoples to build empires – both formal colonies and privileged positions in markets, protected sources of materials and extended opportunities for profitable employment of labour." The concept has thus been associated with an unequal economic relationship between states, not simply the inequality of large and small, rich and poor trading partners, but the inequality of the political and economic dependence of the latter on the former.

The beauty of the foregoing definition derives from the illumination it gives to the sequence of Africa's state of economic and socio-political progress when we address the theme of development and underdevelopment as it obtains in Africa today.

In assessing the extent and nature of capitalist penetration, and eventually the European colonization of African nations, Nnoli (1981, 97) wrote on the social conditions of Africa owing to the impact of colonialism. In his view, the most significant consequences of colonialism on social and economic progress in Africa lay in the impact on the production system; it replaced the subsistence economies of the pre-colonial societies with a capitalist one motivated and dominated by foreign private capitals and responding to their aims, serving the interests and needs of the external capitalists rather than the local population. By so doing, it caused a sharp and dramatic break with the past history of the African people and drastically altered the dynamics and direction of their future. It charted a new historical course for the people.

The point is further made that even though the traditional pre-colonial pattern of subsistence production continued, it was now subordinated to the productive ventures that were of interest to the colonialists who now dominated the economy and engaged most of the attention, efforts and resources of the new leadership. The focus was now anchored on the world market: export crop production, mining of minerals for export and the importation of manufactured goods from Europe predominated. Summarily, it is observed that in its desire to promote the new colonial activities, the colonial government acted to disrupt, disorganize and destroy the pre-capitalist system of production, subordinating it to the needs of the colonial economic zone.

Indeed, under the foregoing circumstances, the cost of external transaction increased. Dependence on external conditions and vulnerability to political pressures, as well as the manipulation of major local decisions by a coalition of external forces or the carving out of different territorial, functional and institutional spheres of influence by competing external forces characterized national life. Also it became difficult to weed out inefficient and inappropriate external resources. The dependence of national activities on external centers frustrated any attempt to transform the pattern of national and international economic life in a way consonant with the full and effective mobilization of internal resources. It imposed a straight-jacket pattern on the type and quantity of the factors of production and distribution of goods and services. In addition, by increasing external influence in the country, it imposed exorbitant costs on national independence. Such a situation served the interest of the colonialists. As competitors in the capitalist world market, they had no objective interest in increasing the bargaining power of the colony relative to that of their own country. This severely limited the power and influence of the colonies in international transactions.

The impact of the foregoing scenario on the state and psyche of the colonized lingered well into and after independence in what has been referred to as a neocolonial setting. In this sense, Acemoglu and Robinson (2012) were to aver that while the term ‘postcolonial neocolonial world’ might sound convoluted, it best captures the complex situation of the truncated African liberation project that gave birth to a problematic and fragile African nation-building process. It encapsulates an African state of ‘becoming’ that never materialized. The envisaged new African postcolonial world and a new African humanity that were expected to be borne by the decolonization struggle were soon captured and engulfed by strong neocolonial imperatives that shaped the African liberatory process into emancipatory reformism. Therefore, at the center of the 'postcolonial neo-colonized world' are the delicate issues of African liberation and freedom as well as African development and knowledge production that were never fully realized beyond some emancipatory pretensions. The main weakness of the emancipatory projects is that they do not question the core logic of Western modernity that globalized Euro-American views of the world and that constructed a racialized, hierarchical, hegemonic, patriarchal and capitalist global social system. At this point a look at the concept of neocolonialism will be useful.

Neocolonialism

An insight into the issue of colonialism and its implications for colonized African independent nations can be illustrated with the aftermath of their independence experience. Indeed a landmark in the history of the development and growth of most African nations was seen to have been recorded in the attainment of political independence. At least, the foreign control of the national apparatus of the African states was ended, and with it, the indignity, degradation and national humiliation that accompanied that control. The focus of national self-assertiveness and emancipations achieved an important victory and prognostications were made of emergent and ebullient great nations. At this point, however, the ovation tapers off and another series of tell-tale mixed feelings set in; sad to note, as has been observed in several quarters, the success of the African nations in those events of independence was seen to have been confined to the political realm.

The sore note here was that the battle for economic emancipation dignity and progress was yet to be waged. Thus, in spite of political independence, the pattern of production and economic activity forcibly instituted by colonialism survived largely unscathed. Rather, it grew stronger and more formidable. The nationalist movements made no significant effort to question the colonial export–import economy. Therefore, they neglected the consequences of that colonial economy for the marginalization of the vast majority of the African populace, distortion of the consumption pattern, neglect of local needs and resources, restriction of the capitalist mode of production from disintegrating the pre-capitalist modes and increasing production in accordance with its own internal dynamics, predominance of tertiary activities over the more productive primary and secondary sectors, the repatriation of capital/profits to foreign countries and, therefore, the loss of the benefits accruing from investments made with them. Other consequences included the high propensity to import and consequently the loss of benefits that would accrue from the use of the relevant income to purchase goods and services within the continent, and the confinement of African nations to the realm of imitative rather than innovative technology except in rare cases involving South Africa, as noted by Nnoli (1981).

The inherited pattern of production has not only persisted, it has been reinforced and strengthened by the expansion of its activities; greater orientation to the external environment, and growing divergence between local resource use and consumption on the one hand and consumption and local needs on the other. With increased activities in the field of manufacturing, importation and the construction industry, occasioned by the growth in oil wealth, the continent is more than ever before integrated into the world capitalist system in a manner which destroys self-reliance, increases external dependence and leads to the external control of local economic life. This scenario is seen as the basis for the onset of underdevelopment in societies like Nigeria as well as Africa in general (Nnoli 1981, 128).

In the views of Nnoli (1981), the aforementioned intensification has been possible largely because of the class character of the leadership of the nationalist movement. The economic motivations of the principal actors in the struggle for independence did not seek to make a clean break with the colonial production process. Members of this class merely sought promotion within the hierarchical system of distributing the benefits of that process, particularly between them and the foreign bourgeoisie who controlled production. They had no objective interest in abandoning an economic system which guaranteed their economic privileges, social prestige and political power. In order to improve their benefits from it, they were of course willing to make those reforms which do not threaten their privileged positions.

Indeed, the view is held that one of the most significant developments of the neocolonial period is the growth in the size and power of those local classes with vested interests in the reproduction of the inherited colonial production process. Over the years, increased urbanization, greater opportunities for education, proliferation of public projects, and increased economic opportunities at the supervisory level of the economy have produced an increased and increasing number of people who have joined the ranks of the privileged class. And these privileged classes have increased their powers through the use of public funds to build private financial empires. Thus the nagging view here is that the present African ruling class having acquired a vested interest in the neocolonial economy, has, therefore, become its political and socio-cultural guardians. They cannot therefore be expected to support, much less promote, a new economy in which their power and prestige would be severely damaged. Salvation must, therefore, lie with those classes which have antagonistic interests to those on which the neocolonial economy was founded; those who have not acquired vested interests in it and who have objective interests in a new system of production. This situation essentially requires the altering of power structures politically and bridging the gap of inequality economically.

The foregoing when anchored on the testy issue of development and underdevelopment x-rays why the cluster of modernization theories which arose in the 1960s were heavily criticized by scholars like Andre Gunder Frank, who posited that the underdevelopment of societies like African nations was caused by the dependency which former colonies endured under the aegis of their colonial rulers. Capitalist development in Third World countries (with the capitalist West being labeled the first world and the socialist bloc the second) is heavily dependent on the centers of core financial capital in the West. Immanuel Wallerstein further developed his viewpoint in his world systems theory which takes a comparative historical approach to show how capitalism first developed in a small number of core countries, with other countries forming semi-periphery or periphery states. The foregoing brings to the fore the essence of germane decolonization when development theories of Africa are discussed.

Colonialism and Decolonization

It is instructive to note here that during the twentieth century, 130 countries gained political independence from their colonial masters. This process of gaining political independence is known as decolonization. Decolonization is a process of undoing colonialism such that the colonized country achieves independence from the so-called mother country. Decolonization can be a peaceful process by which the parties negotiate the terms of independence; it can be a violent disengagement that involves civil disobedience, insurrection or armed struggle (war of independence). Effective decolonization entails the former of these. Colonization and decolonization are social processes even more than they are political processes. Governance over a people changes only after the people themselves have sufficiently changed. The meta-narrative of nationalist triumph takes two forms. First, which may be called the narrative of social mobilization by those who disparage it, the narrative of bourgeois nationalism goes like this: resistance to colonial rule, often local, which had been evident since the conquest was channeled into a unified anticolonial movement in the years after World War II by Western-educated intellectuals.

Mobilizing people through a wide range of organizations from ethnic associations to trade unions and bringing them into modern political parties, these leaders forged a movement that attacked head on the fundamentally racist construction of the colonial state and claimed its territory, its symbols and its institutions to bring material progress and a sense of national identity to the people of each African colony. The second meta-narrative is the revolutionary one, most powerfully articulated by Frantz Fanon: the anti-colonialism of Western-educated intellectuals and indeed of wage workers, aspiring only to become a labor aristocracy was false, and the revolutionary dynamic lay in a peasantry and lumpen proletariat willing to face up to the absolute denial of identity that colonialism necessarily entailed and to use violence to overthrow the colonial regimes. Fanon had little sympathy with the rhetoric of racial unity or the invocation of symbols of the African past which "bourgeois nationalists found easy to embrace as they set themselves up as brokers between African 'tradition' and post-colonial 'modernity'". His imagined future came out of the struggle itself: "The last shall be first and the first last." Decolonization is the putting into practice of this (Fanon 1966).

Economic (Mandan)/Marxist Theory of Development

Marxian theory rests on the fundamental assumption that changes in the economic 'infrastructures' of society are the prime movers of development. For Marx, society consists of two structures – 'infra-structure' and 'super-structure'. 'Infra-structure' consists of the 'forces of production' and 'relations of production'. The 'super-structure' consists of those features of the social system, such as legal, ideological, political and religious institutions, which serve to maintain the 'infra-structure', and which are molded by it. To be clearer, according to Marx, productive forces constitute 'means of production' (natural resources, land, labor, raw material, machines, tools and other instruments of production) and 'mode of production' (techniques of production, mental and moral habits of human beings). Both and their level of development determine the social relations of production, that is, production relations.

These production relations (class relations) constitute the economic structure of society—the totality of production relations. Thus, the socioeconomic structure of society is basically determined by the state of productive forces. For Marx, the contradiction between the constantly changing and developing 'productive forces' and the stable 'production relations' as the determinants of all social development or social change, is the order of nature and society (Turner 1999; Smelser 1976).

This is inherent in the matter through the contradiction of forces. Marx wrote: "Matter is objective reality, existing outside and independent of the mind. The activity of the mind does not arise independent of all the material. Everything mental or spiritual is the product of the material process." The world, by its very nature, is material (Turner 1999). Everything which exists comes into being on the basis of material course, and arises and develops in accordance with the laws of motion of matter. Things come into being, exist and cease to exist, not each independent of all other things but each in its relationship with others. Things cannot be understood each separately and by itself but only in their relations and interconnections. Marx believed that change occurs through the contradiction of forces and is present throughout history in some or other form. Accordingly, change, development and progress take place by way of contradiction and conflict and the resulting change leads to a higher unity (Smelser 1976). In particular, Marx viewed the class struggle and the transition from one social system to another as a dialectical process in which the ruling class viewed as 'thesis' evoked its 'negation' ('antithesis') in the challenger class and thus to a 'synthesis' through revolutionary transformation, resulting in a higher organization of elements from the old order. Marx believed that the class struggle was the driving force of change, progress and development. For him it was the "motor of history". He states that "the history of all hitherto existing society is the history of class struggles" (Communist Manifesto 1848 in Smelser 1976).

Modernization Theory

Modernization theory was developed in the 1950s–1960s to explain the change from traditional, pre-industrial society to industrialized modern society which was first experienced in the West, hence the tag on the West as the 'First World'. An efflux of the philosophy informing the conceptualization of the First World led to the observation that the non-existent or slow change in undeveloped countries, the Third World, can be explained by a difference in values in those countries which have developed. In this sense, Talcott Parsons argued that whereas in traditional societies there is a system of ascription whereby individuals obtain their roles by 'who' they are, in modern industrial societies achievement is valued, that is, individuals have to compete for positions on the basis of merit (Turner 1999). In the view of Parsons, pre-industrial societies will become modernized as they adopt and internalize the values held in developed countries. In this sense, the process of modernization is seen as being universal and a sine qua non for development (Gosling and Taylor 2005).

Modernization Theory and Its Relevance to Germane Development in Africa

According to modernization theory, modern societies are more productive, children are better educated and the needy receive more welfare. In a political sense, Coleman stresses three main features of modern societies: (i) differentiation of political structure; (ii) secularization of political culture with the ethos of equality, which (iii) enhances the capacity of a society's political system (Ohmae 1995). Modernization is a phased process, for example Rostow's theory of economic development for a particular society has five phases. In summary, these five stages are: traditional society, precondition for takeoff, the take-off process, the drive to maturity, and high mass consumption society. Modernization is a homogenizing process; in this sense, we can say that modernization produces tendencies toward convergence among societies, for example, Levy (1967 in Agugua 2003) maintains that "as time goes on, they and we will increasingly resemble one another because the patterns of modernization are such that the more highly modernized societies become, the more they resemble one another." Modernization is an Europeanization or Americanization process; in the modernization literature, there is an attitude of complacency toward Western Europe and the United States (Scholte 2002; Rostow 1960). These nations are viewed as having unmatched economic prosperity and democratic stability. In addition, modernization is an irreversible process, once started modernization cannot be stopped. In other words, once Third World countries come into contact with the West, they will not be able to resist the impetus toward modernization.

The application of modernization in Africa, therefore, provides strong indication of a new scramble for Africa which departs from the old imperialism (colonialism) only in form. The new imperialism does not seek political control of economies. Its main interest is to devise ways to assume direct control of a territory's natural resources and thereby accomplish the objectives achieved by colonialism. Many newly independent African governments served as "policemen" for the new "imperialists"; and the few African countries that dared to resist them were considered as subverting the process of modernization by stifling foreign investment and encroaching on expatriate right. It is in this sense that in certain quarters, globalization has been described as euphemism for neo-imperialism. At this point, a succinct overview of globalization theory and its implications for theorizing Africa's development becomes necessary.

Theory of Globalization

Globalization can be defined as the process of increased harmonization of national economies with the rest of the world to create a global coherent economy. The theory of globalization emerges from the global mechanisms of greater integration with particular emphasis on the sphere of economic transactions. In this sense, this perspective is similar to the world-systems approach. However, one of the most important characteristics of the globalization position is its focus and emphasis on cultural aspects and their communication worldwide. Rather than financial and political ties, globalization scholars argue that the main modern elements for development interpretation are the cultural links among nations. In this cultural communication one of the most important factors is the increasing flexibility of technology to connect people around the world (Gosling and Taylor 2005).

The main assumptions which can be extracted from the theory of globalization can be summarized in three principal points. First, cultural factors are the determinant aspects in every society. Second, it is not important, under current world conditions, to use the nation state as the unit of analysis, since global communications and international ties are making this category less useful. Third, with more standardization in technological advances, more and more social sectors will be able to connect themselves with other groups around the world. This situation will involve the dominant and non-dominant groups from each nation. The theory of globalization coincides with several elements from the theory of modernization. One aspect is that both theories consider that the main direction of development should be that which was undertaken by the United States and Europe. These schools maintain that the main patterns of communication and the tools to achieve better standards of living originated in those more developed areas. Regrettably, globalization may be seen as a force of exploitation, oppression and injustice. The rage that drives terrorists to commit obscene crimes can be said to be a response to globalization. Terrorism thrives on poverty, and international capitalism thrives on poverty too. The work of multinational companies like Coca Cola, Walmart and Shell in underdeveloped societies is seen as a new form of colonialism. The preaching of laissez faire as a modus operandi shortchanges undeveloped areas since it entrenches their underdevelopment. Globalization has also fueled the rise of transnational corporations and their power has vaulted to the point where they can now rival many nation states since majority of them are richer than some nations. For instance, based in Finland, Nokia represents nearly two-thirds of the stock market value, and provides a large share of the nation's tax revenue. With this much power, managers of the company have unprecedented influence in the politics of Finland (Gosling and Taylor 2005).

Dependency Theory

At this point, a look at the theme of dependency will complement the effort so far in explaining underdevelopment in Africa. Dependency theory as an approach in the explication of change and development in Africa came as a result of the criticism of modernization theories. The central argument is that the explanation given for some countries not having developed because of their traditional values and institutions is wrong. The theorist greatly associated with dependency theory is Andre Gunder Frank, who in 1967 argued that it is the perpetuation of an exploitative relationship between the developed and developing countries that keeps the developing societies such as Africa and Latin America dependent on the developed nations. In his own view, Frank used the phrase 'the development of underdevelopment' to explain how the exploitation of the capitalist system in the industrialized nations has not only prevented countries from developing but has actually reduced the overall level of development in the world (Gosling and Taylor 2005).

By the mid-1960s, dependency theory, which represents the first major shift from modernization in development conception and theory, was well formulated. In opposing the Ricardian-inspired claims that international specialization conferred benefits on Third World countries for exporting primary products to the European and American markets and receiving industrial goods in return, scholars within the United Nations Economic Commission for Latin America (ECLA), particularly Raul Prebisch, held that this international division of labor was at the root of the developmental problems of the Third World. This is because it bequeathed to the Third World the position of subordinate incorporation in the global economy polarized into a core and a periphery, where the core is the developed world and the periphery the Third World. Among the main authors of dependency theory we have Andre Gunder Frank, Raul Prebisch, Theotonio Dos Santos, Enrique Cardoso and Samir Amin (Scholte 2002; Elias 1987).

Dependency scholars are of the view that development and underdevelopment are two sides of the same coin The development of developed societies is as a result of the underdevelopment of underdeveloped societies and vice versa. They are of the view that in the beginning all societies were developing independently, but the development of others was hijacked by a culture which claimed to be superior, thereby aborting the development of cultures seen as inferior. Dependency scholars recommended selective diffusionism, a system for boycotting all that is unnecessary in their culture. It has been found, as in Andre Gunder Frank's case study of Latin America, that underdeveloped countries experience more growth when their ties to the monopolies are weak, contrary to the popular notion that societies are degenerate when their ties to capitalist centers are weak.

The Theory of World System

The form of negative influence imposed by the integration of developing societies into the developed nations, as adumbrated by the dependency theorists, was to metamorphose into an unholy alliance of what Immanuel Wallerstein described as world systems theory. This theory shows how the world, through the aforementioned global integration, has been partitioned into three compartments of unequal relationships, namely:

- Core: developed nations or the First World.
- Semi-periphery: developing nations or the Second World such as the Asian Tigers.
- Periphery: underdeveloped nations or the Third World such as Sub-Saharan African and Latin American nations (Olurode 2006).

A world system is a social system; one that has boundaries, structures, member groups, rules of legitimation and coherence. The world systems theory developed by the Colombian sociologist Immanuel Wallerstein is an approach to world history and social change that suggests that there is a world economic system in which some countries benefit while others are exploited. The core countries dominate and exploit the peripheral countries for labor and raw materials. Core countries own most of the world's capital and technologies and have great control over world trade and economic agreements. They are also cultural centers which attract artists and intellectuals. The peripheral countries are dependent on the core countries for survival. They focus on low-skill, labor-intensive production and extraction of raw materials; they have weak states. The semi-peripheral countries share the characteristics of both. They have less diversified economies and stringer state. This theory emphasizes the global structure of inequality. According to Ritzer (2008, 303–308), Wallerstein embarked on historical research and came up with the idea that there are two kinds of international systems: (i) *the world empire*, a system based on political and military domination, of which ancient Rome was an example; and (ii) *the modern capitalist world economy*, which relies on economic domination. The kernel of Wallerstein's world system theory is that once certain nations got rich, they reordered the international system to ensure that others remained poor. Thus the international economic system came to be seen as a deterministic framework within which countries would be either dominant or dominated and, then, remain as such.

In many models of economic analysis, the geopolitical North and South correspond to the mostly capitalist regions of Western Europe and North America (the *North*) and the poorer regions of Sub-Saharan Africa and South America (the *South*). However, this distinction does not deny the fact that quite a few emerging economies like Brazil, China and South Korea have displaced some economies of the traditional 'north'. Thus 'North' and 'South' are to be understood in this chapter as designations for the rich and the poor. Unfortunately, this theory having explained this exploitative relationship between these areas does not have a recommendation for underdeveloped societies. However, its deep insight regarding the workings of the world economic order and how it relates to African development challenges makes it necessary for us to discuss its viewpoints more deeply.

The World Capitalist System

The modern capitalist world system with which we are concerned probably came into being not long after the Industrial Revolution had seen the rise of the Western hemisphere as an economic power. But exactly how do the economic powers keep others underdeveloped? Wallerstein uses the concept of *core* and *peripheral* states. According to Ritzer (2008, 303), "the core economic area dominates the capitalist world-economy and exploits the rest of the system." The peripheral areas provide raw materials to the core and are heavily exploited by it. However, there is a residual semi-peripheral zone "that encompasses a set of regions somewhere between the exploiting and the exploited." It is within this region that may be located what are now being known as emerging economies as noted above. During the Western colonizing adventure in Africa, that was clearly the case. As Walter Rodney has brilliantly demonstrated in his seminal *How Europe underdeveloped Africa*, the colonizing powers simply structured the economies of the colonized peoples to serve the interests of the colonizing nations. And for all the economic benefits that accrued to the Europeans, the Africans got very little. For instance, Rodney notes that during the 500 years of Portuguese colonization of Mozambique, they did not even manage to train one doctor! (Rodney 1972). That of course, may have been an exception, but it certainly shows how exploitative colonialism was.

In the current world system, the dominant economic powers have set up the international trade system to ensure unfair trade practices which further impoverish the poorer nations of the South. The international aid institutions such as the International Monetary Fund (IMF) and the World Bank were set up ostensibly to assist the process of economic growth and reconstruction in the developing world. However, the policy of trade liberalization placed as a precondition for accessing the financial assistance provided by these organizations often implies that the aid recipients end up worse off, and thus remain dependent on the aid of these organizations. The upshot is now the call for fair trade as opposed to free trade. Some examples illustrate this.

According to Gregory Elich of the Jasenovic Research Institute: "In the US, Western Europe, and Japan, billions of dollars are provided to rice growers each year, allowing them to set an export price of rice well below the cost of production. Local growers in Sub-Saharan Africa cannot compete on equal terms, especially as they must manage without subsidies due to IMF/World Bank strictures." He adds that: "Under WTO agreements, Ghana is permitted to raise the tariff on poultry to as high as 99%. But when the nation actually attempted to raise its tariff from 20% to 40%, the IMF threatened to halt future loan disbursements and the tariff increase was never put into effect" (Elich 2010, 154).

With reference to the effect of liberalization on African countries, Elich (2010) explains: "In Cameroun, a threefold increase in poultry imports over a five-year period reduced local production and led to the loss of over 100,000 rural jobs every year. It took only five years to drive 92% of poultry farmers out of business. In Mozambique, vegetable oil imports now account for 81% of the total market, while most oil crushing operations have closed." He states further that economic restructuring in Cote d'Ivoire has led to the closure of the privatized rice mills and the elimination of fertilizer subsidies for the rice growers. "In their place there was only the removal of restrictions on imports." There is also the possibility that the lopsided structure of the capitalist may be sustained by certain enabling policies by the dominant powers. Acemoglu and Robinson (2012) identify technology and education as two important engines for economic growth. These engines, the authors note, are the products of what they describe as inclusive economics. They explain that inclusive economics create inclusive markets, which not only give people the freedom to pursue the vocations in life that best suit their talents but also a level playing field that gives them the opportunity to do so. Acemoglu and Robinson (2012) assert that this accounts for the economic prosperity of South Korea as opposed to the poverty of North Korea.

The skewed nature of the international capitalist system is also manifest in the discriminatory commodity-pricing system which ensures that the prices of most of the raw materials extracted in the developing countries are determined by international bodies controlled by the powerful nations. Of course, it can be argued that the organization of petroleum exporting countries (OPEC) is made up of mainly oil-producing developing nations. Still, we cannot underrate the fact that its power is severely limited by some crucial factors: (i) some developed nations and non-OPEC countries have very large deposits of oil which means they can significantly influence the oil market; then, the disposition of non-OPEC majors can lead to much speculation and hence price fluctuation (see also *The Nation* 2009); (ii) the extraction of crude oil from the poorer countries is largely undertaken by multinational companies since oil exploration requires very sophisticated technology which is not yet at the disposal of the developing nations; and (iii) the growing emphasis on the development of renewable sources of oil and clean energy can only mean declining export revenues for crude oil exporting nations.

Not to be forgotten too is the manifest division of trade in the international system such that while the countries of the South concentrate on primary products (i.e. raw materials), the countries of the North do more of the manufacturing and finished products (see also Ritzer 2008, 305 on Wallerstein). This widens the poverty gap in that the production of finished products often has greater value added and, consequently, more revenue and employment opportunities. For example, although Nigeria has oil refineries at Port Harcourt, Kaduna and Warri, the country exports much of her crude oil and imports almost 70% of refined petroleum products for domestic use. This means great advantage for the exporting countries because of the many by-products of the petroleum reefing process and, of course, loss for Nigeria in terms of employment generation and small business opportunities.

A particularly painful example is the case of coffee, a major export commodity of some African countries. Arguing for action on the part of US President Barack Obama to redress the gross injustices of the international coffee trade, an article in the pan-African magazine *New African* (2009, 11–17) quotes a Ugandan economist and coffee grower. The quote was actually lifted from a British newspaper *The Observer*. It is quoted in part here:

> African manufacturing and processing seldom adds much value to the raw product … Of the 35 billion pounds the global coffee market represents [only] 3.8 billion pounds accounts for the raw coffee beans traded annually … The industrialized countries' tariff and non-tariff barriers escalate with each stage of processing for most primary commodities. The vertical integration of transnational corporations means producers are usually unaware of their product's true value …
>
> One needs, approximately five grams of roasted and ground beans to make a cup of coffee that sells for 2 pounds, so one kilogram can make 200 cups worth 400 pounds. Green coffee beans are bought for an average price of 70p per kilogram. In other words, less than 0.2% of the value of processed coffee is retained by the growers.

Another manifestation of the world system is what can be described as the new Chinese imperialism. Extant evidence shows that China may be using her partnership with Africa to take advantage of the vulnerability of African economies and weak government regulation mechanisms to further impoverish the continent. A report on the shoemaking industry shows that although the shoemaking line of Ariaria market in Aba, South Eastern Nigeria, employs over 50,000, including apprentices, their masters and suppliers, lack of federal government patronage and inadequate infrastructure prevents it from performing much better than it is currently doing (*The Guardian* 2013, 44–5) The report adds that in the past, Aba sold leather bags, belts and shoes to traders from Cameroun, Ghana and Equatorial Guinea, but now on account of cheap and inferior products from China, the industry is dying. Then, in a case of intellectual property theft, one of the traders reported:

> [The] Chinese came in here and took samples of our shoes and brought them back in another way and in great quantity. Chinese designs are picked from us and put together with a special kind of gum. We locally manufacture our gums and most times, it makes our work last less than what it should.

As the traders have claimed, with electricity, raw materials and modern machines, Ariaria can become a world class manufacturing area. Another point of interest, though, is the question of intellectual property rights. Although the claim by this Ariaria trader might be debated, intellectual property rights have long been an issue in the lopsided world trade system: while industrial countries hold 97% of all patents worldwide, most of the knowledge that forms the basis of their technological breakthroughs was obtained from the locals who receive no compensation for their own contribution. This has been the case for years in the pharmaceutical industry (see Giddens et al. 2005, 643). The foregoing analysis illustrates how the capitalist world system places some nations at an ever-increasing advantage and others at an ever-increasing disadvantage, thus aggravating the poverty of the nations of the South. To be sure, certain instances may not necessarily derive from the distorted world system. For example, the non-functioning of Nigeria's refineries or Nigeria's generally poor infrastructure is less a matter of a lopsided world oil market than the patent incompetence and corruption that characterizes Nigeria's public service.

This analysis only illustrates the angle of the world system in the poverty of the nations of the south.

Conclusion: The Interplay of the World System and Development

Development is a multidimensional concept which embraces the multifarious economic and social objectives concerned with the distribution of income, the provision of basic needs, and the real and psychological well-being of people. Hence, in theorizing about Africa's development within the world economic order, what emerged from the discussion is that the world system is manifestly skewed against the poorer regions of the world. Thus it cannot be overemphasized that even with all the progress that has been made to make the international system more open with a view to spreading its opportunities, the poorer nations of the world may still struggle to catch up. This is because their poor infrastructure will limit the extent to which they can benefit from the opportunities of the age of information technology. For instance, telecommuting as noted means that considerably more work can be accomplished with fewer people and less space.

Also, on account of the progressive integration of new technology, an economy can develop rapidly once it begins to operate more efficiently. And then there are the multiplier effects. More efficient energy sources means less consumption of fossil fuels; this leads to less atmospheric pollution and, quite conceivably, healthier citizens and less health spending. The extra money can then be channeled to more developmental projects, with greater human development in view. Conversely, those who remain with inefficient technologies are somewhat condemned to run greater economic overheads so to speak. In short, technology—or more correctly, its application—can widen the gap between the rich and the poor.

The upshot is that once a nation gets on the train of development, it has attained a certain leverage that can enhance further development. The role of the political authorities in this regard is critical as well. Acemoglu and Robinson (2012) cite the example of two tribes—the Lele and the Bushong. These two tribes had almost everything in common, save for the fact that the Bushong became more prosperous than the Lele. The authors traced the difference in their economic prosperity to the purposeful political leadership of the Bushong which harnessed all available opportunities and reorganized the Bushong society such that they could achieve the level of prosperity they did (Acemoglu and Robinson 2012). It would then appear that the immediate solution to the poverty of the poor nations is to address their mode of social and political organization and their practices. This is something entirely within their power to handle despite whatever experiences such societies must have endured owing to colonialism, imperialism and the machinations of neocolonialists. And the issue is that African nations must stand up to the challenges as no level of theorizing can bail them out.

References

Acemoglu, D., & Robinson, J. (2012). *Why nations fail: The origins of power, prosperity and poverty*. London: Profile Books.

Acemoglu, D., Johnson, S., & Robinson, J. A. (2001). The colonial origins of comparative development: An empirical investigation. *American Economic Review, 91*, 1369–1401.

Acemoglu, D., Johnson, S., & Robinson, J. A. (2002). Reversal of fortune: Geography and institutions in the making of the modern world income distribution. *Quarterly Journal of Economics, 117*, 1231–1294.

Agugua, A. (2003). Social change in Nigeria since independence. In A. Osuntokun, D. Aworawo, & F. Masajuwa (Eds.), *History and cultures of Nigeria up to AD 2000*. Somolu: Frankad.

Agugua, A. O. (2015). The place of culture in economic growth and development in West Africa. In S. I. Koffi, J. O. Igue, & S. O. Akande (Eds.), *Growth and development in West Africa*. Berlin: Auflage.

Bairoch, P. (1993). *Economics and world history: Myths and paradoxes*. Chicago: University of Chicago Press.

Bertocchi, G., & Canova, F. (2002). Did colonization matter for growth? An empirical exploration into the historical causes of Africa's underdevelopment. *European Economic Review, 46*, 1851–1871.

Brown, B. (1974). *The economics of imperialism*. London: Harmondsworth.

Chinweizu. (1975). *The West and the rest of us: White predators, black slavers and the African elite*. New York: Random House.

Commission on Growth and Development. (2008). *The growth report: Strategies for sustained growth and inclusive development*. Washington, DC: World Bank.

Dobbs, R., Manyika, J., & Woetzel, J. (2015). *No ordinary disruption: The four global forces breaking all the trends*. New York: McKinsey and Co., Public Affairs.

Elias, N. (1987, September 29–October 2). *Technik and Zivilisation*. Paper presented at 23rd bi-annual meeting of the German Sociological Association (Soziologentag). Hamburg, West Germany,

Elich, G. (2010). What free trade is doing to Africa. *New African*, June: 72–74.

Englebert, P. (2000). Solving the mystery of the Africa dummy. *World Development, 28*, 1821–1830.

Fanon, Frantz. 1966. *The wretched of the earth*. (Constance Farmington, Trans.). New York: Grove.

Fieldhouse, D. K. (1966). *The colonial empires from the eighteenth century*. New York: Weidenfeld and Nicolson.

Fryer, R. G., & Levitt, S. D. (2004). Understanding the black–white test score gap in the first two years in school. *Review of Economics and Statistics, 86*(2), 447–464.

Giddens, A., Appelbaum, M., & Richard, A. (2005). *Introduction to sociology* (5th ed.). New York: Norton.

Gosling, R., & Taylor, S. (2005). *Principles of sociology*. London: London School of Economics and Political Science (LSE).

Grier, R. M. (1999). Colonial legacies and economic growth. *Public Choice, 98*, 317–335.

Harrison, L. E. (2000). Promoting progressive cultural change. In L. E. Harrison & S. P. Huntington (Eds.), *Culture matters: How values shape human progress*. New York: Basic Books.

Kenny, C., & Dykstra, S. (2013). *The global partnership for development: A review of MDG 8 and proposals for the post-2015 development agenda*. Policy Paper 026. Washington, DC: Centre for Global Development.

New African. (2009, August/September). *Obama, do something before you go*.

Nnoli, O. (1981). *Path to Nigerian development*. Dakar: CODESRIA.

Ohmae, K. (Ed.). (1995). *The evolving global economy: Making sense of the new world order*. Boston: Harvard University Press.

Olurode, L. (2006). Modernization and the dependency approaches. In S. A. Adebagbo, T. U. Obinyam, & L. Olurode (Eds.), *Family and social change: Essays in sociology and social welfare administration*. Lagos: Rebonik.

Ritzer, G. (2008). *Sociological theory* (7th ed.). New York: McGraw Hill.

Rodney, W. (1972). *How Europe underdeveloped Africa*. Washington, DC: Howard University Press.

Rostow, W. W. (1960). *The stages of economic growth: A non-communist manifesto*. Cambridge: Cambridge University Press.

Scholte, J. A. (2002). *Globalization: A critical introduction*. London: Macmillan.

Schurmann, F. (1974). *The logic of world power: An inquiry into the origins, currents and contradictions of world politics*. New York: Pantheon.

Singh, S. (2012). *New mega trends*. London: Palgrave Macmillan.

Smelser, N. J. (1976). *Comparative methods in the social changes*. Englewood Cliffs: Prentice Hall.

The Guardian. (2013, June 2). *Aba shoemakers threatened by unhealthy imports, poor infrastructure*.

The Nation. (2009, November 9). *OPEC identifies challenges in global oil business*, p. 28.

Todaro, M. P., & Smith, S. C. (2003). *Economic development* (8th ed.). Boston: Addison Wesley.

Turner, B. (1999). *Classical sociology*. London: Sage.

World Bank. (2009). *World development indicators 2009*. Washington, DC: Policy Research Department, World Bank.

World Bank/IMF. (2016). *Global monitoring report, 2015/2016: Development goals in an era of demographic change*. Washington, DC: The World Bank and the International Monetary Fund.

Dr. Augustine Okechukwu Agugua lectures in the Department of Sociology, University of Lagos, Akoka, Lagos, Nigeria. He has co-authored books in diverse fields of human endeavor and also contributed chapters in many highly rated books and journals both within and outside Nigeria. Dr. Agugua has equally been a benefactor of several fellowship programmes from reputed institutions of higher learning and is a member of the ECOWAS Regional Research Project. Dr. Agugua's major areas of research interest include Political Sociology; Social Policy; Inter-Group Relations, Criminology, and Sociology of Development. e-mails: agugst@yahoo.com, aagugua@unilag.edu.ng.

Chapter 4
Theorizing Africa's Development Problem

Natéwindé Sawadogo and Evéline M.F.W. Sawadogo Compaoré

Introduction

At the end of the nineteenth century, Africans were made to believe that the only civilization worth promoting was that of the Europeans, then colonizers (Ki-Zerbo 1978). When Africans started to appropriate science and technology after the Second World War, following their access to independence, they were drawn back to their own cultures as foundation for any meaningful development (Asad 1973; De Sardan 1995). As they began to consider this and were endeavoring to self-promote their development, again they were brought back to a new European myth, that of the market, supposed to flood the poor with wealth on condition that states observe minimum intervention in the working of the economy (Zagré 1994; Harvey 2005); the few remaining scientific resources of the 1960s and 1970s were finally crushed by the Structural Adjustment Programs (SAP), because it was strongly supported that the market forces would organize technological transfer to African countries wherever the best technologies originated (Oloruntoba 2015). Then, at the beginning of the second millennium, Africans who have long been educated to turn away from science and technology were suddenly called upon to strongly consider science and technology, because they are the key drivers of development! (World Bank 1999; UNESCO 2005; Kraemeer and Wamae 2010). This is the work of theory, and there is a need for balance if Africa's development is to be directed in a positive way.

N. Sawadogo (✉)
University of Ouaga II, Ouaga, Burkina Faso
e-mail: natwinde.sewadogo@yahoo.fr

E.M.F.W. Sawadogo Compaoré
Environmental and Agricultural Research Institute (INERA), National Research for Scientific and Technological Research Centre (CNRST), Ouaga, Burkina Faso
e-mail: zondel@hotmail.com

O. Akanle, J.O. Adésìnà (eds.), *The Development of Africa*, Social Indicators Research Series 71, DOI 10.1007/978-3-319-66242-8_4

In fact, about a century ago, Veblen (1921, 19) observed as follows:

> It has been usual, and indeed it still is not unusual, to speak of three coordinate 'factors of production': land, labor, and capital. The reason for this threefold scheme of factors in production is that there have been three recognized classes of income: rent, wages, and profits; and it has been assumed that whatever yields an income is a productive factor. This scheme has come down from the eighteenth century. Seen in the light of later events this threefold plan of coordinate factors in production is notable for what it omits. It assigns no productive effect to the industrial arts … The unexampled advance of technology during the past one hundred and fifty years has now begun to call attention to its omission from the threefold plan of productive factors handed down from that earlier time.

It took almost a century to come up to this truth in Africa, at least in its institutionalized form. In fact, as pointed out above, it was also the belief of anticolonialists and pan-Africanists such as Alioun Diop (Nyerere 1967). Early African leaders struggled for cultural and scientific emancipation, and worked to build higher learning and scientific institutions during the first decade of independence. It is these efforts that have been squeezed by the drastic economic reforms of the 1990s, supported by the World Bank, which, surprisingly, were developing at the same time a 'knowledge bank' as a new asset for international development banking (Kramarz and Momani 2013).

With the paradigmatic shift in development thinking from the end of the 1990s, which acknowledged the relevance of our fathers' vision, Africa had to again fall deeper into dependent relationships. It could be said that regretfully we had to wait until recently to see international awareness about such a contribution. A qualitative approach is used, through a documentary review, to map development theories so far applied in Africa, as a background to highlight the new knowledge-centered development paradigm. Using the same approach and methods, Africa's current and future development states are discussed in light of this paradigm. Materials from the PhD research by one of the authors are also used (Compaoré 2013, 2014, 2015). Our contention is that it is rather surprising that the debunking of the supposed autonomy of 'capital', as it was for the 'market' in the theory and practice of development, has not served for the recent debate about science and technology for development. The transfer of scientific knowledge is seldom discussed in debates on development without regard being given to the forms of political control (both domestically and internationally) that science and technology bring with them. However, as Dickson put it "the more an individual becomes dependent on a commodity owned and controlled by others, the more vulnerable he or she becomes to the ends that others seek to achieve through that ownership. Science is no exception" (1988, 4). When it is about developing countries, there is in the debate in academia, as among policy-makers, a kind of return to nineteenth century scientism and technological progressivism, despite the rich and large existing store of knowledge in the empirical social science studies of science and technology, as well as the critically large and rich accumulated literature in social sciences on development. In other words, to paraphrase Dickson, with respect to developing countries, "the increasing central *economic* importance of science gives it a *political* significance that is often lost in debates that focus on how it is applied to socially desirable or undesirable ends" (1988, 5).

There is a need to challenge this trend in development thinking and practice, so as to reinsert science and technology into the broader political economy of development, if it is to contribute to public welfare in Africa. The discourse on development in Africa is currently plagued with words such as 'science', 'technology', and 'innovation'. However, it is not sure that African policymakers have the right appreciation of these words. New ideas are implemented through old methods. We recommend that a large academic and policy debate be promoted in order to break the conceptual threshold that blocks the shift in policymaking toward a knowledge-centered approach to development, in which higher education and research will be pivotal.

The concept of development has a long history and has given rise to considerable controversy (Rostow 1960; UNDP 1991; Escobar 1991, 1992; Rist 1997; Tandon 2015; Mensah et al. 2016; Anyanwu et al. 2016; Kalai and Helali 2016). Gilbert Rist (1997), a specialist in development theory, offers the most comprehensive discussion about the concept, and as such provides the main source for the following conceptual discussion. According to Rist's historiography, the concept can be understood in three ways. First, development, in its intransitive sense, can refer to a natural phenomenon of growth. This definition is reflected in processes such as growth from small to big, young to old, immaturity to maturity, child to adult; that is, humans, animals and trees grow physically and naturally. Referring to the evolution of Western thought, Rist (1997) underlined that this natural development is thought to happen in three ways: (i) God's intervention, (ii) spontaneity, or (iii) just a natural phenomenon. This earlier conception of development has influenced the history of the concept. Considering Western society as the highest stage of development, this definition came to scale the history of all societies as passing from savage to barbarism before reaching the stage of civilization. Rist shows how such a conception underpins Western imperialism, and is played out through colonization. In this respect, development is seen to be synonymous with another term—civilization.

Second, in its transitive sense, development is considered as a process with the objective of modifying a reality in order to improve it. Development conceived as process emerged in the 1940s. This is strongly connected with European colonization and the fight for decolonization. Indeed, colonization is the beginning of the emergence of the difference between two different worlds: one is civilized and the other non-civilized. Such a distinction between the two worlds led to repeated invasions by the 'civilized world', which conquered the 'non-civilized'; this period of colonization was "a transitional period, then in which brutal power relations existed alongside paternalist feelings of responsibility towards 'natives' who needed to be civilized" (Rist 1997, 47). It was within this context that the concept of development as process enters policy circles. According to Rist, US President Truman first employed the concept in 1947. Since then and afterward, the concept has been widely used and promoted throughout academia and policy circles. Truman regarded development as a process, a way to help underdeveloped countries in their fight against poverty. This definition implies a purposive intervention, as is reflected in the following from the South Commission's report that defines development as

> … a process which enables human beings to realise their potential, build their self-confidence, and lead lives of dignity and fulfilment. It is a process which frees people from the fear of want and exploitation. It is a movement away from political, economic, or social oppression. Through development, political independence acquires its true significance. And it is a process of growth, a movement essentially springing from within the society that is developing (Rist 1997, 8–9).

What is stressed here is both the purposive intervention and the endogenous character of any development which aims to be sustainable.

Then, development consists of changing a reality by implementing activities. It is expected that these activities will result in a given desired state. Such a desired state is the third meaning of the concept of development. Consideration of the issue of development in development studies has generally concerned the second meaning. At policy level it is this understanding of development that underlies all technical cooperation for development (Gaillard 1999). Nonetheless studies of development as intervention often ask questions about the impacts of such intervention. This aspect concerns the third meaning of development, which refers to a change from position A to position B (B being better than A) (Aron 2006). For example, developed countries contrast with underdeveloped ones, as each refers to a particular point in a rank. Aron claims that the objectives for all countries are the same; they all aim for higher economic growth. It is from this perspective that the differences between rich and poor countries become more observable. This way of seeing development reduces it to increases (or not) in productivity; development in reality consists in producing goods in increased quantities and also different products with enhanced processes. For example, tools changed from manual to machines and increasingly complex machines in order to increase productivity. Underdevelopment was therefore characterized by a low level of gross domestic product (GDP). Low individual income is another consequence of underdevelopment.

Today, definitions of development are not limited to a simple reference to increases in GDP. Instead, the basic objective of human development is to enlarge the range of people's choices to make development more democratic and fully participatory. These choices are believed to include access to income and employment opportunity, education, health and a clean and safe environment (Rist 1997). Such a definition of development, which includes the second definition of the concept, goes back to the 1980s. This should enable individuals to enjoy human, economic and political freedoms in a sustainable way. Thus, there was an awareness of the interrelationship between modernization and the culture of people. Development became "a process of profound structural transformation—it cannot be simply imported" (Rist 1997, 202). In other words:

> Development is a process which enables human beings to realize their potential, build self-confidence, and lead lives of dignity and fulfilment. It is a process which frees people from the fear of want and exploitation. It is a movement away from political, economic and social expression. Through development, political independence acquires its true significance. And it is a process of growth, a movement essentially springing from within the society that is developing … the base for the nation's development must be its own resources, both human and material, fully used to meet its own needs … Development has therefore to be an effort of, by, and for the people. True development has to be people-centred (Rist 1997, 202).

From this standpoint, development becomes more than just an increase of income and wealth. It focuses more on individuals' wellbeing and freedom. This calls for a more critical assessment of the potential of theoretical proposals to improve the welfare of African societies.

The chapter is organized as follows: We first address methodological issues, which comprises a brief description of the background to the research problem, the literature review along with the theoretical framework and the research design. The description of the research methods closes the methodological discussion. Second, we map development theories so far applied in Africa, which end with an analysis of the new knowledge-centered development paradigm and its challenges for African countries. Finally, we make some suggestions in order for African countries to face these challenges.

Literature Review

Theorizing Africa's development requires a double attitude. First, it implies a break with possible existing forms of theorizing. Second, a proposal of an alternative theorizing is expected. In both cases there is a need for an epistemological justification to support the appreciation of the existing literature as well as the new proposal. These are questions of sociology of science. Yet, social sciences in Africa have generally been so far helpless in this regard. The evidence suggests that the interest has remained at the level of theoretical commentaries rather than thorough empirical research. The social sciences have approached the problem in terms of the development of an autonomous African science, with more focus on the social sciences. Indeed, there is a long-standing engagement of African scholarship with African social sciences for the promotion of an alternative discourse about African societies (e.g. Fyfe 1976; Zeleza 2006). However, recent evidence suggests that persisting structural and institutional factors still make the development of an indigenous social science a major challenge, particularly for West African social scientists (Sall and Ouedraogo 2009).

Structurally, in this region, the increase in programs and enrollment in social sciences is a recent trend. Indeed, before the end of the 1960s universities could only be found in very few countries: Ghana, Nigeria and Sierra Leone. In French West Africa, the earliest universities were created at the beginning of the 1960s (1959 for Dakar, 1963 for Abidjan, 1970 for Benin and 1974 for Ouagadougou). The significant increase in the number of higher education institutions occurred in the 1990s and 2000s, within a strained economic context which started from the 1980s. Institutionally, the 'epistemic rupture' that Adesina (2006) proposes in order to bring an indigenous social science about, that would contribute to global scientific debate, is constrained to remain a mere idea for a certain period because the mechanisms of institutional reproduction set by colonialism continue to operate through the training of academics staff and various cooperation schemes. As Sall and Ouedraogo (2009, 7) have underlined with regard to Sociology,

> … [a]lthough autonomous research and higher education institutions have now been established in most independent African countries, the foundations for strong academic cultures and theoretical propositions are yet to be established in many of them. The economic adjustments of the eighties and nineties came too quickly to restrict the development of the institutions and frustrate the hopes for progress of the science of sociology.

On the whole, West African social scientists, like those of the rest of Africa, seem to be experiencing a marginalizing condition in a global world, despite their paradoxical significant role in the reproduction of that global knowledge. Nevertheless, some optimistic views have been emerging in recent years which propose that a re-engineering of the publishing policy of African journals would improve the visibility of science in Africa by making it available in the global knowledge domain (Nwagwu 2006).

In the absence of these emerging channels for dissemination, West African scholars have long relied on 'chances' for publishing in international print journals, with more pressure to do so in recent years by 'university administrations and managements' (Omobowale 2010, 3). This quest for international publishing has become common behavior among African scholars (e.g. Nwagwu 2006; Nwagwu and Egbon 2011). These studies have two main weaknesses. First, they are meta-analyses and prospective reflections. Second, they emphasize the dimension of circulation of knowledge rather than the content of that knowledge. As a result the African individuality of what is circulated and accessed is left in the background. This literature takes further the traditional debate about the colonial roots of knowledge produced about African societies and its consequences for African development. This literature emerged first among African intellectual and political elites (e.g. N'Krumah 1974; Nyerere 1967).

It later became dominated by philosophical controversies complemented by historical contributions (e.g. Diop 2006; Fyfe 1976; Jewsiewicki and Mudimbe 1993; Ki-Zerbo 1973; Zeleza 2006). Social science of sciences in Africa remains a continuation of this social philosophy, without engaging in fieldwork research (Ajayi 1973; Sall and Ouedraogo 2009). Very few scholars have taken this empirical direction (Omobowale 2010). Nevertheless, at least this literature provides a theoretical attempt of understanding science. This aspect is particularly present within the small but rich empirical research from largely European scholars. This research developed a grounded literature from strong engagement with the classics in science studies in order to understand scientific and technological institutions in developing countries such as those of Africa (Arvanitis et al. 2000; Gaillard and Arvanitis 2013; Gault 2010; Mouton 2008).

This chapter adopts a constructivist approach. The relevance of this approach is that it enables one to follow and understand the process of negotiation between competing orders of knowledge production and their organizational consequences. In this connection, theorizing Africa's development problem entails investigating the relationships between discourse and power. It is these political processes in knowledge production that shape the socio-cognitive structure of development science, through which Diop foresaw current scientific and technological subordination denounced by African scholars, and with which Hountondji (1992) is particularly concerned. A qualitative approach is used, through a documentary review, to map development theories so far applied in Africa, as a background to highlight the new knowledge-centered development paradigm. Using the same approach and methods, Africa's current and future development challenges are discussed in light of this paradigm. When needed, illustrations are made from the case of Burkina Faso.

Institutionalist Theory of Development

The first attempt of development practices by African governments conformed to the institutionalist theory of development. This model dominated development policy between the 1950s and 1970s (Rapley 1997). When the concept of 'development' entered international relations at the end of the 1940s, it was on the basis that the application of a Western conception of market-based economics would produce the desired result—increased economic activity. It posited that high labor mobility from traditional to non-traditional activities is the driver of growth (Cimoli et al. 2009; Rist 1997). As a director of policy, the role of the state is to establish collaboration between the public and private sectors to overcome information and coordination failures; to develop institutions to support investment in self-discovery and the diffusion of new activities in markets (World Bank 1993, 1999; OECD 1997; Cimoli et al. 2009). Many African countries' development policies from the 1960s to the1980s were shaped by this institutionalist model and all aimed to improve people's living conditions. An example of the application of this model can be found in Burkina Faso's development policies[1] during this period.

They all believed, as clearly stated in the 1963–1967 development plan, that to bring about development, the policies should "make sure people in Upper Volta move to a higher technical and cultural stage" (in Gerardin 1964, 111), and "put in place development structures, schools etc., proper administrative and political measures to modify behavior, to make a certain number of public administrations work together or to facilitate an expansion" (in Gerardin 1964, 111). In line with modernization theory which is embedded in the institutionalist model, they expected that technical, cultural, and administrative modernization would be achieved through the importation of ready-made technology and trained staff from abroad, notably from developed countries (Gaillard 1999). This is supported by the data which shows that, during this period, higher education and research had not been mentioned in any of the policies. The technological transfer did not contradict the assumptions of the linear model of innovation which dominated this period (Manley 2003).

From the institutionalist perspective, indicators of development are the degree of diversification of the economy, and the degree of urban activities in the economic structure. However, by the end of the 1970s, the modernization paradigm did not result in the general prosperity promised. Instead, developing countries, and African countries in particular, continued to become increasingly poor, and within them only a small social category, representing the international capitalist branches and political elites, benefited from any wealth creation. The changes from traditional development strategies to more modern tactics did not happen. By the end of the 1970s, the policy measures taken by the Burkina Faso government, like those of

[1] 'Plan Triennal 1960–61–62'; 'Premier Plan Quinquennal de Développement 1963–1967'; 'Plan Cadre 1968–1970'; 'Plan Intérimaire 1971'; 'Deuxième Plan Quinquennal du Développement Economique et Social 1972–1976'; 'Troisième Plan Quinquennal du Développement Economique et Social, Avant Projet 1977–1981'.

many African countries, based on this model had not resulted in the improvement of the living conditions of the majority of the population, as reflected in the key development indicators (World Bank 1978).

Dependency Theory of Development

Between 1980 and 1990, many African countries sought to improve this situation by developing new policies[2] under the competing model of development based on dependency theory. Dependency theory interprets 'development' and 'underdevelopment' as socially embedded and interrelated processes. It supports the idea that the economies of the countries of the South are better understood within the international economic system. For example, according to this theory, colonization destroyed the social and economic features of countries under domination and blocked their natural evolution. Models based on dependency theory consider that market competition led to the formation of monopolies and 'free' trade arrangements enabled monopolies to continue their expansion through the internationalization of domestic markets. Proponents of dependency theory-based models "concluded from their own observation that the international system, far from guaranteeing the South's prosperity, brought the effects of domination to bear upon it and locked it in dependence" (Rist 1997, 109). In terms of policy these models advised that countries of the South should opt out of the system by developing their industry, including appealing for foreign capital, form regional groups and encourage state intervention to control inequalities through land reforms and the redistribution of investment. In most cases this would require radical social change (e.g. revolution) (World Bank 1993).

Several plans were designed within this framework. In Burkina Faso, for example, the revolutionary regime in place set out to achieve independence and economic autonomy. The efficiency of mass labor relies on a clear framework of a planned economy. It applied to all national and regional sectors. The aim was to deal with the urgent and pressing needs of the population which are food, water, housing, education, health, culture and sport. In relative terms, this strategy is considered by many analysts to have resulted in significant improvement in the living conditions of the majority of the population. However, like many left-oriented regimes between the 1970s and the 1980s, in Burkina Faso this revolutionary experience was stopped at the end of 1980s through political change. Everywhere in Africa, as in large parts of the rest of the world, the economy slowed down as it suffered from the international economic crisis in the context of newly liberalizing political regimes. It is in this context that a new development paradigm based on economic orthodoxy made a comeback, and dominated development discourse.

[2] 'Quatrième Plan Quinquennal de Développement 1982–1986'; 'Plan de Base ou Programme Populaire de Développement 1984–1985'; 'Rapport Sectoriel du Plan Quinquennal de Développement Populaire 1986–1990'.

The Market: The Neoclassical Theory of Development

The institutionalist model was later displaced by the market model. The market model dominated development discourse between the 1980s and 2000s. According to this model, markets have the potential to generate their own internal coordination (World Bank 1999). For this reason deliberate coordination of individual efforts is irrelevant and counterproductive, because competition provides opportunities for workers and producers and leads to high quality service. The Structural Adjustment Program (SAP) policy recommendations included the promotion of private investment in physical and human capital and new knowledge. Competition—market entry and exit, free-trade, export and foreign development investment—would enable knowledge spillover (Rist 1997). The argument was that developing countries do not need to invest in advanced science and high technology, because free trade would enable their transfer from developed countries. Politically, the displacement of the problem of development from international negotiation, as required by the New International Order, to a humanitarian framework allows intervention by Western countries using political pressure to change political regimes that do not respect 'human rights'.

Essentially, this conceptual shift owes much to the influence of a competing development paradigm commonly called 'dependency theory' and civil society action. This has resulted in the redefinition of the development concept as 'human development' which goes beyond the initial neoliberal understanding of development as growth. In the beginning of the 1990s, the concept of development had become almost uncontested as it managed through the past decades of debate to integrate a wider view, so that in addition to being universal, 'development' was becoming more and more trans-cultural. This is observable in the scope of indicators of measurement, which now included productivity growth rate, human rights (early 1980s), environmental protection (late 1980s), development as self-reliance, and human development (in 1990s). In the same way, for example, Burkina Faso development policies[3] at that time were shaped by the market. Indeed, in this country, in 1991, the authorities decided in line with the financial crisis to make structural reforms with the help of international financial bankers and, from the beginning of the 1990s, the SAP dominated Burkina Faso's development strategies. Many public sectors have been privatized and, until the end of the 1990s, development strategy was led by the SAP. However, by the end of the1990s, the achievements of the 1980s were lost.

Knowledge-Centered Development

The market model appeared to be undergoing a serious crisis. Indeed, Joseph Stiglitz and his collaborators observed in their book, *The Crisis of the Growth Paradigm,* as follows: "We began this book with the inevitable reference to the 'Washington

[3] 'Rapport Sectoriel du Plan Quinquennal de Développement Populaire 1986–1990'; 'Programme d'Ajustement Structurel 1990–2000'.

Consensus' and the damage done by the almost religious implementation of such an extremist version of economic orthodoxy. The times of the 'Consensus' are over, buried by the weight of its economic failures, in addition to its massive social disruptions" (Cimoli et al. 2009, 557). An opportunity had opened up for a new model of development, this time based on innovation. Towards the end of the 1990s, innovation came to be increasingly considered as an alternative means for development within the framework of knowledge-centered development. Many meetings were held in the African continent from 1998 onwards to debate the extent to which scientific and technological advances could aid development in underdeveloped countries.

Research and development as mechanisms to improve policy and promote technological innovation became part of the development agendas in Africa, as reflected in the titles of the 1998 World Bank report on *Knowledge for Development;* and the 1999 UNESCO conference in the African continent in 1999 on the *Role of Science in the Twenty-first Century, the New Commitment.* Moreover, in 1999, Knowledge Management Africa (KMA) organized a conference in South Africa on Knowledge to Address Africa's Development Challenges. The New Partnership for Africa's Development (NEPAD) was established in 2001 with the aim of creating new conditions for development in Africa. The African Ministerial Council on Science and Technology (AMCOST) held its first meeting in Johannesburg, South Africa in November 2003. The meeting emphasized that, as a matter of priority, all countries should have comprehensive national Science and Technology Innovation (STI) policies with emphasis on the development of effective National Systems of Innovation. In September 2005, a ministerial conference was held in Dakar and another in 2007, and the OECD made some guidelines available for African countries.

The sentiment was expressed as follows:

> We, the Heads of States and Government of the African Union, recalling our millennium commitments to achieve sustainable development for our Continent, realizing that the achievement of these goals depends on our countries' abilities to harness science and technology for development and also an increased and sustained investment in science, technology and innovation … commit ourselves to promote and support research and innovation activities and the requisite human and institutional capacities (UNESCO 2007, 5–6).

This sentiment was expressed in the Addis Ababa Declaration on Science, Technology and Scientific Research for Development at the African Union Summit in January 2007. Later, in January 2009, the OECD and the UNESCO organized a joint workshop which was held on Innovation for Development: Converting Knowledge to Value. In April 2009, a meeting of experts, Innovation out of Poverty, was held by the OECD Development Co-Operation Directorate. And in 2010, the OECD laid down a framework "for putting innovation on the development agenda" through its publication *Innovation and the Development Agenda.*

Because of its failure, the enthusiasm for 'market fanaticism' has given way to a new consensus that Stiglitz and his collaborators have called the "knowledge-centred development agenda" (Cimoli et al. 2009, 557). The World Bank in its first report at the beginning of the third millennium acknowledged that: "Poor countries—and poor people—differ from rich ones not only because they have less capital but because they have less knowledge" (World Bank 1999, 2). 'Knowledge' has taken the place of 'capital' as a production factor. The knowledge-centered development approach conceives of

> … development as a process that links micro-learning dynamics, economy-wide accumulation of technological capabilities, and industrial development. Different knowledge and different national 'political economies', of course yield different patterns of industrialization. However, it happens that all the countries which are nowadays developed undertook relatively high degrees of intervention to support their accumulation of technological capabilities and the transformation of their organizations of production especially in the early period of industrialization (Cimoli et al. 2009, 543).

Slowly taking off from the start of the current millennium, its establishment as a dominant discourse on development was prompted by the economic crisis of 2008. Cimoli and his collaborators reaffirmed that the role of knowledge in the economy is as old as economics: Smith (1937), List (1885), and Schumpeter (1934) had all addressed this basic problem.

Similarly, the 'development age' was opened up with the feeling of duty to "embark on a bold new program for making the benefits of our scientific advances and industrial progress available for the improvement and growth of underdeveloped areas" (Rist 1997, 71). The institutionalist development model which was promoted particularly by Rostow (1960) made technological progress the key to the diversification, specialization and modernization of the economic sectors. The dependency theory of development embraced by a large number of countries in the South were attempting to de-link from international systems in order to benefit more from the science and technology that they expected would result from a package of endogenous policy strategies. The UNESCO information policy in the early 1990s provided a framework for these initiatives. The period between the late 1970s and the late 1980s saw the development of the first science and technology policies and the erection of higher education institutions in many countries in the South and in Africa in particular (World Bank 1990). However, in the institutionalist development model developed earlier,

> … the role of learning (how to discover, how to identify opportunities and constraints, etc.) and the product space literature highlight the role of capabilities in defining the direction of diversification. They fail to address the process of learning and the link between structural transformation and accumulation of capabilities. Learning itself and the evolution of capabilities remain in a black box" (Nübler 2011, 7).

In other words, "[t]he thrust of institutional economics in the catching up debate is on the productivity-enhancing role of structural transformation" (Nübler 2011, 7). Catching up is defined as a process of diversification into higher productivity and value-added activities, and of enhancing the complexity of economic structures and the sophistication of the production and export structure (Nübler 2011).

In 1990, African states developed their own strategic plans, with the support of the UNESCO fully-fledged program, which terminated in 1994. The strategic position of the World Bank gave it the power to shape the initiative to fit the market paradigm, resulting in it prescribing for the states a program of internal reorganization aiming to boost African countries' economic development (Nübler 2011). Towards the end of the 1990s, innovation came to be increasingly considered as an alternative means for development within the framework of knowledge-centered development. Many meetings were held in the African continent from 1998 onwards to debate the extent to which scientific and technological advances could aid development in underdeveloped countries. Research and development as mechanisms to improve policy and promote technological innovation became part of the development agendas in Africa, as reflected in the titles of the World Bank report (1998) on *Knowledge for Development;* and the 1999 UNESCO conference on the Role of Science in the Twenty First Century: The New Commitment.

The first meeting of the African Ministerial Council on Science and Technology (AMCOST) held in November 2005 emphasized that, as a matter of priority, all countries should have comprehensive national Science and Technology Innovation (STI) policies with emphasis on the development of effective National Systems of Innovation. In Addis Ababa in 2007, the OECD made available some guidelines for African countries. The sentiment was expressed as follows:

> We, the Heads of States and Government of the African Union, recalling our millennium commitments to achieve sustainable development for our Continent … realizing that the achievement of these goals depends on our countries' abilities to harness science and technology for development and also an increased and sustained investment in science, technology and innovation, … commit ourselves to promote and support research and innovation activities and the requisite human and institutional capacities (UNESCO 2007, 5–6).

Later, in January 2009, the OECD and the UNESCO organized a joint workshop which was held on Innovation for Development: Converting Knowledge to Value. In April 2009, a meeting of experts on Innovation out of Poverty was held by the OECD Development Co-Operation Directorate. And in 2010, the OECD laid down a framework "for putting innovation on the development agenda" through its publication *Innovation and the Development Agenda.* African countries are now offered this agenda, which necessarily raises new challenges for them.

Options and Challenges for Africa: Concluding Reflections

There are no new options; there have only been varieties of options. The evolution of development theory brings the analysis back to the earliest positions defended by Africa's political and intellectual elites. As anticipated by these elites, the latest development theories agree that knowledge is key to development, not only as a means for the production of new goods but also as a good in itself. More importantly, they maintain that contrary to what some Western development theorists such as Rostow thought, it is not enough to transfer technology from abroad because, to be successful, technology transfer requires a strong domestic research and training system. The development of the sociology of science since the early 1970s has documented the socially constructed character of knowledge in terms of knowledge generation as its structure in a given society. Now that the international order has come to a consensus regarding the central role of science in development processes what are the challenges facing Africa?

The answer can be found in a series of international comparative science reports published over the last 6 years particularly by UNESCO and the African Union, which have regularly stressed that Africa is lagging behind in terms of science and technology. The UNESCO's 2015 report is clear on the matter. "The answers to global challenges … are increasingly dependent on technological innovation and the sound scientific advice brokered to decision-makers" (Aebischer 2015,4); then it warns that, "[i]n the long run, no region or nation can remain a simple 'user' of new knowledge but must also become a 'creator' of new knowledge" (Aebischer 2015,4). In the face of this, Africa has the most alarming record (UNESCO 2015). For example, as the report points out, in 2013, with a population of 14.3 million, Africa's share of global GDP was 5.1% of which only around 3% belongs to all of Sub-Saharan Africa, while the Americas reached 27.1% with its population of 13.7 million during the same period.

The gap between Africa and the other continents is reflected in its share of world expenditure on R&D. While all Africa is spending $19.9 billion, representing only 1.3% of world shares, North America alone spent $427 billion, corresponding to 28.9% of world share, just below Southeast Asia (36.9%), and above the European Union (19.1%). As for world shares of researchers, all Africa counted 2.4%, while the shares peaked at 18.5% for North America alone, 22.2% for the European Union and 36.9% for Southeast Asia. This is a continuation of the vicious circle of dependence, which has a very political significance in addition to its cultural and economic importance (Dickson 1988). The history of development in Africa displays a history of dependence and a lack of anticipation. Now that the consensus around what Africa's elites have long supported as central to development is institutionalized, there is an urgent need for African countries to make higher education their top priority not only to promote knowledge creation, but more importantly to create conditions for an appropriate organization of that knowledge to create wealth for social welfare.

Overall, from the 1980s up to the end of the early 2000s, many African governments justified their budget cuts to higher education by the pressures they were subjected from international financial institutions, such as the World Bank. There is no question that this order was backed up politically by international political forces, at the expense of early development vision and efforts by some African leaders. We have demonstrated through a thorough review of the literature and a strong synthesis of the pattern of theorizing regarding Africa development problem, that from the end of the first decade of the new millennium, the controversies around the role of science, thus of higher education, in development were over. These controversies have given way to a new consensus, that of science as a driver of development. African governments have no more reason to neglect their higher education, because promoting this will result in the needed improvements in all aspects of development. Current African governments' agenda about higher education may be now an indicator for understanding ex post the determinants of the crisis in African higher education during the 1980s and 1990s.

References

Adesina, O. O. (2006). Sociology, endogeneity and the challenge of transformation. *African Sociological Review, 10*(2), 133–150.

Aebischer, P. (2015). Universities: Increasingly global players. In United Nation Educational, Scientific Cultural Organization (Ed.), *Towards 2030: UNESCO science report* (pp. 3–5). Paris: UNESCO.

Ajayi, F. A. J. (1973). Towards an African academic community. In M. T. Yesufu (Ed.), *Creating the African university: Emerging issues in the 1970's* (pp. 11–19). Ibadan: Oxford University Press.

Anyanwu, J. C., Andrew, E., Erhijakpor, O., & Obi, E. (2016). Empirical analysis of the key drivers of income inequality in West Africa. *African Development Review, 28*(1), 18–38.

Aron, R. (2006). Theorie du Development et Ideologies de Notre Temps (1962). In R. Aron (Ed.), *Les Societes Modernes* (pp. 293–319). Paris: Press Universitaire.

Arvanitis, R., Waast, R., & Gaillard, J. (2000). Science in Africa: A bibliometric panorama using PASCAL database. *Scientometrics, 47*, 457–473.

Asad, T. (Ed.). (1973). *Anthropology and the colonial encounter*. New York: Humanity Books.

Cimoli, M., Dosi, G., & Stiglitz, J. E. (2009). *Industrial policy and development: The political economy of capabilities accumulation*. Oxford: Oxford University Press.

Compaoré, E. M. F. W. (2013). *Science, technology and development: A case study of agricultural biotechnology in Burkina Faso*. Unpublished PhD thesis, University of Nottingham.

Compaoré, E. M. F. W. (2014). *Science, technology and development: A case study of agricultural biotechnology in Burkina Faso*. Unpublished PhD Thesis, University of Nottingham.

Compaoré, E. M. F. W. (2015). *The role of the National Innovation Systems Framework in facilitating socio-economic development in Burkina Faso: Model and practice*. PhD thesis University of Nottingham.

De Sardan, J. P. O. (1995). *Anthropologie et developpement: Essai en socio-anthropologie du changement social*. Paris: APAD-Karthala.

Dickson, D. (1988). *The new politics of science*. Chicago: University of Chicago Press.

Diop, A. C. (2006). *Articles*. Dakar: Editions Silex.

Escobar, A. (1991). Anthropology and the development encounter: The making and marketing of development anthropology. *American Ethnologist, 18*(4), 658–682.

Escobar, A. (1992). Imagining a post-development era? Critical thought, development and social movements. *Social Text, 31*(32), 20–56.

Fyfe, C. (1976). *African studies since 1945*. London: Longman.

Gaillard, J. (1999). *La coopération scientifique et technique avec les pays du Sud: Peut-on partager la science?* Paris: Karthala Editions.

Gaillard, J., & Arvanitis, R. (2013). Science and technology collaboration between Europe and Latin America: Towards a more equal partnership? In J. Gaillard & R. Arvanitis (Eds.), *Research collaboration between Europe and Latin America: Mapping and understanding partnership* (pp. 1–22). Paris: Archives Contemporaines Editions.

Gault, F. (2010). *Innovation strategies for a global economy*. Cheltenham: Elgar.

Gerardin, B. (1964). Le Development de la Haute Volta avec un avant porpos de G. de Bernis. In Perroux F. (Ed.), *Cahiers de l'Institut de Science Economique Appliquee* 142(19).

Harvey, D. (2005). *A brief history of neoliberalism*. Oxford: Oxford University Press.

Hountondji, J. P. (1992). Recapturing. In V. Y. Mudimbe (Ed.), *The surreptitious speech: Présence Africaine and the politics of otherness 1947–1987* (pp. 238–248). Chicago: University of Chicago Press.

Jewsiewicki, B., & Mudimbe, V. Y. (Eds.). (1993). *History making in Africa: History and theory 32*. Middletown: Wesleyan University.

Kalai, M., & Helali, K. (2016). Technical change and total factor productivity growth in the Tunisian manufacturing industry: A Malmquist index approach. *African Development Review, 28*(3), 344–356.

Ki-Zerbo, J. (1973). Africanization of higher education curriculum. In M. T. Yesufu (Ed.), *Creating the African university: Emerging issues in the 1970s* (pp. 21–34). Ibadan: Oxford University Press.

Ki-Zerbo, J. (1978). *Histoire générale de l'Afrique*. Paris: Hatier.

Kraemeer, E., & Wamae, W. (Eds.). (2010). *Innovation and the development agenda*. Ottawa: OECD/IDRC.

Kramarz, T., & Momani, B. (2013). The World Bank as knowledge bank: Analyzing the limits of a legitimate global knowledge actor. *Review of Policy Research, 30*(4), 409–431.

List, F. (1885). *The national system of political economy* (Trans. from the original German (1841) by Sampson Lloyd). London: Longman, Green and Co.

Manley, K. (2003). Frameworks for understanding interactive innovation processes. *The International Journal of Entrepreneurship and Innovation, 4*(1), 25–36.

Mensah, J. T., Adu, G., Amoah, A., Abrokwa, K., & Adu, J. (2016). What drives structural transformation in Sub-Saharan Africa? *African Development Review, 28*(2), 157–169.

Mouton, J. (2008). Africa's science decline: The challenge of building scientific institutions. *Harvard International Review, 30*(3), 46–51.

N'Krumah, K. (1974). *Consciencism: Philosophy and ideology for decolonisation*. London: Panaf Books.

Nübler, I. (2011). *The thrust of institutional economics in the catching up debate*. Chicago: Chicago University Press.

Nwagwu, W. (2006). Peer-review and the electronic journal: Opportunities for the participation of developing countries' scientists in mainstream science. *Africa Media Review, 14*(1&2), 73–93.

Nwagwu, W., & Egbon, O. (2011). Bibliometric analysis of Nigeria's social science and arts and humanities publications in Thomson scientific databases. *The Electronic Library, 29*(4), 438–456.

Nyerere, K. J. (1967). The university in a developing society. *Revue Culturelle du Monde Noir* p. 61.

Oloruntoba, S. (2015). Politics of financialization and inequality: Transforming global relations for inclusive development. *Africa Development, XL*(3), 121–137.

Omobowale, O. A. (2010, November 3–6). *Academic dependence and scholarly publishing among social scientists in selected universities in Nigeria*. Paper presented at the II Workshop on Academic Dependence: The Challenge of Constructing Autonomous Social Sciences in the South, Mendoza.

Organization for Economic Cooperation and Development (OECD). (1997). *National innovation systems*. Paris: OECD.

Rapley, J. (1997). *Understanding development: Theory and practice in the third world*. Boulder: Psychology Press.

Rist, G. (1997). *The history of development: From western origins to global faith*. London: Zed Books.

Rostow, W. W. (1960). The process of economic growth. *The Economic History Review, 12*(1), 1–16.

Sall, I., & Ouedraogo, J.-B. (2009). Sociology in West Africa: Challenge and obstacles to academic autonomy. In S. Patel (Ed.), *ISA handbook of diverse sociological traditions* (pp. 225–234). London: Sage Publications.

Schumpeter, J. A. (1934). *The theory of economic development: An inquiry into profits, capital, credit, interest, and the business cycle* (Vol. 55). Cambridge, MA: Harvard University Press.

Smith, A. (1937). *The wealth of nations (1776)*. New York: Modern Library.

Tandon, Y. (2015). Development is resistance. *Africa Development, XL*(3), 139–159.

United Nations Development Program (UNDP). (1991). The human development index: A new development indicator? *Intereconomics, 26*(5), 236–243.

United Nations Educational, Scientific and Cultural Organization (UNESCO). (2005). *UNESCO science report 2005*. Paris: UNESCO.

United Nations Educational, Scientific and Cultural Organization (UNESCO). (2007). *A human rights-based approach to education for all: A framework for the realization of children's right to education and rights within education*. Paris: UNESCO.

United Nations Educational, Scientific and Cultural Organization (UNESCO). (2015). *UNESCO science report: Towards 2030*. Paris: UNESCO.

Veblen, T. (1921). *The engineers and the price system*. New York: Huebsch.

World Bank. (1978). *World development report*. Washington, DC: World Bank.

World Bank. (1990). *Structural adjustment and poverty: A conceptual, empirical and policy framework*. Washington, DC: World Bank.

World Bank. (1993). *The East Asian miracle: Economic growth and public policy*. New York: Oxford University Press.

World Bank. (1998/99). *Knowledge for development*. Washington, DC: World Bank.

World Bank. (1999). Capitals and capabilities: A framework for analyzing peasant viability, rural livelihoods and poverty. *World Development, 27*(12), 2021–2044.

Zagré, P. (1994). *Les politiques économiques du Burkina Faso: Un tradition d'ajustement structurel*. Paris: Karthala.

Zeleza, T. (Ed.). (2006). *The study of Africa Vol.1: Disciplinary and interdisciplinary encounters*. Dakar: CODESRIA.

Natéwindé Sawadogo is Assistant professor of Sociology at the University of Ouaga II, Burkina Faso. He holds a PhD in Science and Technology Studies from the Institute for Science, Technology and Society of the School of Sociology and Social Policy, at the University of Nottingham, in the United Kingdom. His work focuses on the interrelationships between science, technology, innovation and society. His area of interest includes, research and innovation systems, higher education, professions, health, law and politics. He is the Coordinator of the University of Ouaga II's interdisciplinary programme on Science, Technology, Innovation and Public Policy. E-mail: natewinde.sawadogo@yahoo.fr.

Dr Evéline M.F.W. Sawadogo Compaoré is Assistant Researcher of sociology at the Environmental and Agricultural Research Institute (INERA) of the National Research for Scientific and Technological Research Centre (CNRST), in Burkina Faso. She holds a PhD in Science & Technology Studies, from the Institute for Science and Society of the School of Sociology and Social Policy, at the University of Nottingham, in the United Kingdom. Her PhD investigated the transition of innovation policy in Burkina Faso. Her research area includes competence building system for innovation, Innovation, agricultural Innovation and development. e-mail: compeve@yahoo.fr.

Chapter 5
Poverty in Africa

Kolawole Emmanuel Omomowo

Introduction

It is imperative to engage with the discourse of poverty in Africa, beyond the MDGs and SDGs, by looking at the African Union (AU) *Agenda 2063, the Africa we want*, as the yearnings and aspirations of the African people. Moving from the MDG to the SDG objectives of halving by 2015 and eradicating by 2030 extreme poverty respectively remains a fundamental challenge to global development, and Africa development in particular. The celebrated achievement of MDG goal 1 of halving world poverty by 2015 is not a reflection of the achievement of Africa in poverty reduction. Rather it is the achievement of East Asia and the Pacific (especially China where over 500 million people moved out of extreme poverty between 1990 and 2010) and South Asia where the populations living in extreme poverty were reduced from 60.6% to 7.2% and 50.6% to 18.8% respectively between 1990 and 2012 using the $1.90 a day international poverty line at 2011 PPP (World Bank 2016; African Union 2015; United Nations 2013).

Africans living in extreme poverty only reduced from 56.8% to 42.7% of the population between 1990 and 2012. However, in head counts, the number of Africans living in extreme poverty increased from 288 to 389 million people between 1990 and 2012, an increase of 35.1%. The reduction in percentage is a function of the higher population growth rate. There are 897 million extremely poor people in the world, 389 million (43.4%) of them are Africans (World Bank 2016). The extreme poverty experienced by over 40% of the African population is a serious set-back for its development agenda, no matter how it is conceptualized. Therefore, poverty is central to the discourse of African development. The central attention given to poverty in the MDGs and SDGs is reinforced in the African Union Agenda

K.E. Omomowo (✉)
Archie Mafeje Research Institute, College of Graduate Studies, University of South Africa, Pretoria, South Africa
e-mail: Kolaskysy11@gmail.com

O. Akanle, J.O. Adésìnà (eds.), *The Development of Africa*, Social Indicators Research Series 71, DOI 10.1007/978-3-319-66242-8_5

2063, which spells out African aspirations for the next 50 years. The first aspiration, a prosperous Africa, driven by broad-based growth and sustainable development, hinges on poverty eradication and shared prosperity informed by socioeconomic transformation (African Union 2015). It is with this self-proclaimed aspiration in mind that I engage with poverty as a development challenge in this chapter.

The discourse of poverty must differentiate between concepts and the definition and measurement of poverty (Lister 2004). However, the conception, definition and measurement of poverty are contested; they often mirror the prevailing socioeconomic ideologies in a society, with the dominant view emanating from international institutions such as the World Bank and the United Nations. Barrett et al. (2008, 4–8) note that different conceptions of poverty in Africa have placed emphasis on issues such as ownership of assets, positive technological change, domestic and international market liberalization, favorable and unfavorable physical and political geographical areas. While they favor an asset-based approach to poverty in Africa, they emphasize that poverty could result from intricate social, political and historical relations.

Concepts of poverty are broad approaches to poverty that inform how it is defined and measured. It is about what it means to be poor from different perspectives and for different categories of people in a society and the world. It involves the discourses of poverty (Lister 2004). The definition of poverty speaks to the criteria for distinguishing 'the poor' from 'the non-poor'. It highlights the characteristics of poverty. The operationalization of the definition of poverty is its measurement of headcount or depth (Lister 2004; Noble et al. 2004). Noble et al. (2004) identified absolute, relative, commodities and capabilities and social exclusion as the broad conceptual approaches to poverty. Jones (2006) emphasizes understanding and explaining poverty beyond describing, defining and measuring it. The competing understanding and explanation of poverty informs responsive social action.

Poverty is located within the broader discourse of the political economy in order to connect it to consumption, social reproduction and social policy. The continuous appropriation of productive, individual and collective consumptions through the institutions of the economy, family and the state respectively is important for the persistence of a society. The consideration of poverty as a level of well-being speaks to the structure of the political economy and the appropriation of the productive, individual and collective consumptions in a society (Dickinson and Russell 1986). The level of well-being achieved defines the 'quality of social reproduction' of individuals or households. Sen (2009, 1999) sees well-being as achievement; it differs from 'advantage', which is an opportunity.

While income and expenditure remain very useful in poverty discourse vis-à-vis the standard of living, it will be argued in this chapter that the consideration of seemingly remote social institutions that might promote or reduce it is important in moving beyond description, to understanding and explanation. The kind of life that people wish and are able to live is important, which is a function of the conversion of income and assets into functioning (Sen 2009, 1999). To emphasize the difference between income or assets and the achieved functioning, Sen (1997) makes a distinction between income inequality and economic inequality.

The inability of individuals and households to adequately satisfy their individual consumption needs and the lack of collective consumption could account for the condition of poverty. It speaks to different modes of entitlement (Sen 1999, 2009) to appropriate a particular (socially defined) level of well-being or 'quality of social reproduction'. This approach to the consideration of poverty broadens its scope to include households living in the condition that has been described as "precarious prosperity" (Hübingers 1996, cited in Budowski et al. 2010). These are households that lack secured prosperity, and can easily slip into poverty due to various reasons. This category of people is often neglected in poverty discourse because they are above local or international poverty lines. Interestingly, the MDGs progress report of 2015 suggests that Africa's meagre achievement in reducing poverty is fragile and prone to a roll-back from shock (UNDP 2015).

Starting from what we know about the various conceptions, definitions and measurements of poverty, the discussion will be taken further to the not so clear precarious prosperous households in the South African context. The implications of the activities of micro-credit institutions, and patronage by those living in 'precarious prosperity' will be emphasized. Secondary data on socioeconomic indicators will be used to capture poverty trends in Africa. The international poverty line was used in this regard because it can be applied to most national contexts with Purchasing Power Parity (PPP) adjustment. This was complemented with primary data from a small-scale study in South Africa on the specific institutional practices of micro-credit institutions and their implications for the well-being of credit-consuming households. This was used to support the argument of the need to study the implications of social institutions that might create or reduce poverty within a society. It is the view here that the study of such institutions could be complementary to the descriptive power of income and expenditure approach to poverty to its explanation (Jones 2006).

Poverty as a Level of Well-Being

Poverty is taken to be a level of well-being here because it enables its connection to social reproduction and social policy. It means formal and non-formal collective consumption (the concern of social policy) can be interrogated in poverty discourse. Also poverty can be viewed as a particular 'quality of social reproduction' defined by different conceptual criteria as the different conceptions portend. Conceptually, if poverty is the opposing end of a continuum with prosperity, distinct points between the two ends are different levels of well-being or 'quality of social reproduction'. The various conceptions of poverty therefore speak to a particular characteristic level of well-being defined as poverty. This puts people's well-being at the center of political economy. The structure of individual, productive and collective consumptions is therefore informed by this (Fig. 5.1).

Sen (1997, 2008) emphasizes the concept of "well-being achievement" to differentiate "income inequality" from "economic inequality" in his capability

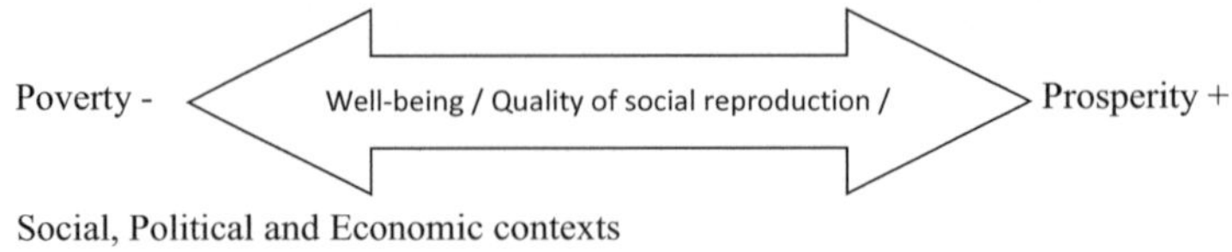

Fig. 5.1 Poverty as a level of well-being

conception of poverty (Sen 1999). This idea shows the limits of income and expenditure approach to poverty. There are environmental, social and individual variables that impact on the conversion of income to "well-being achievement" or functioning. Differences in individual advantages might result in the conversion of the same amount of income to different levels of "well-being achievement". The freedom to choose the functioning people value is fundamental to "well-being achievement" (Sen 2008). Poverty can hence be conceived as an undesirable level of "well-being achievement", in which the determining criteria have been variously conceptualized. Hence, we talk of the contested conception of poverty.

There are different approaches to the understanding of poverty that cannot be divorced from the history and culture of societies at a point in time. Contextual experience is important in the analysis of poverty. Hence the different explanations of poverty could have derived from differences in context and time (Stewart et al. 2007; Lister 2004, 3). Over the years, in what could be argued as heralded from Booth's and Rowntree's foundational research on poverty (Townsend 2009; Gordon 2002) in the United Kingdom, the notion of poverty has traversed different conceptual explanations, as it continues to define over 800 million people across the world. From its initial conception as a lack of means for subsistence to the deficiency of basic needs, the conception of poverty has include notions of relative and absolute deprivations, capabilities deprivation, culture of poverty, structural poverty and social inequality.

These various conceptions of poverty speak to material, relational and symbolic approaches to poverty in various combinations (Lister 2004; Baulch 1996). Jones (2006, 14–15), drawing the on Pierre Bourdieu's concepts of 'orthodoxy' and 'doxa', emphasizes power relations in the conception of poverty that becomes dominant. 'Orthodoxy' is the normalization of a particular position as truth and unchallenged about a contested phenomenon, and 'doxa' refers to the unidentified particular view that is latent and therefore uncontested. Baulch (1996, 2) uses "a pyramid of poverty concepts" to group the different conception of poverty into those that emphasize private consumption, common property resources and state-driven collective provision. Broad approaches emphasize physical capital assets, human capital, dignity and freedom. "Material and non-material wheel of poverty" is how Lister (2004) brings the different conceptions of poverty together. She emphasizes the interdependence between material and relational/symbolic (non-material) aspects in the conception of poverty. The material core or hub and the relational rim of the wheel of poverty are social structurally conditioned.

The conception of poverty remains contested. Noble et al. (2004, 3–4) classified the conceptions of poverty into absolute poverty, relative poverty, capabilities and commodities, and social exclusion. Their classification cannot be treated as exhaustive, and the delineation between concepts and definition is not always clear. *Absolute poverty* is described as an objective conception of poverty because it conceives poverty without a reference group. This conception of poverty is not limited by context or time (Noble et al. 2004). Sen (1981, 17) maintained that there is an "irreducible core of 'absolute deprivation'" in his conception of poverty as "absolute deprivation". This conception of poverty is emphasized through *subsistence* and *basic needs* approaches to poverty, and income is used as a proxy for the definition of poverty. The poverty threshold is determined by minimum income presumed necessary for subsistence (in term of human body nutritional requirement to physically function). Basic needs approach takes into consideration the provision of social services (health, education, shelter etc.) in addition to subsistence to define poverty (Gordon 2002; Townsend 1987, 1993). The subsistence and basic needs conception of poverty are limited by the assumption that people live on food alone and differences in the experiences of poverty by difference groups of people could undermine the effect of social services respectively (White et al. 2001).

The poverty line is synonymous and the dominant definition of poverty informed by subsistence and basic needs conceptions of poverty (Noble et al. 2007, 2004). Absolute poverty defined as the poverty line sets a threshold that divides the poor from the non-poor. The poverty line is "the monetary cost to a given person, at a given place and time, of a reference level of welfare" (Ravallion 1998, 3). Poverty lines could be problematic with regard to who and how the line is set. Also, how do we deal with people living just above the poverty line (the precarious prosperous) and transitory poverty (Blakemore and Griggs 2007; Kumar 2002)? The international poverty line is set by the World Bank, using the average poverty lines in the 15 poorest countries of the world at per capita GDP. It is applied to different countries by adjusting for purchasing power parity (PPP) in order to equalize the value of the poverty line across countries. The current international poverty lines are set at \$1.90 and \$3.10 a day for extreme poverty and poverty respectively at 2011 PPP (World Bank 2016).

The idea of relative poverty can be viewed as a response to the limitations of the absolute conception of poverty. It highlights the relational aspect and the implication of inequality in poverty discourse. *Relative poverty* was pioneered by Peter Townsend; it is the notion of poverty that considers poverty in relation to a reference group living standard that is socially acceptable for people to participate in the normal activities of their society. The minimum resources required to facilitating the reference living standard and social participation become the measure of poverty. Relativity can be in respect of other person(s)/group(s) or time period (Noble et al. 2004; Townsend 1979, 19). The relative deprivation conception of poverty transcends subsistence and basic needs approaches to poverty of income to include the provision of public goods, social and historical elements. It could expose the difference between poverty and inequality and speaks to human dignity and the unequal distribution of social infrastructures (Townsend 1987, 1993). Townsend's "deprivation index" (Townsend 1979, 250) and socially perceived necessities, as well as income and expenditure surveys, are used to measure relative deprivation

(Noble et al. 2004). Its limitation is that it might trade low income and inequality for poverty (Blakemore and Griggs 2007; Noble et al. 2004).

More recently, the conception of poverty as capability deprivation (Sen 1999, 2009) is an audacious shift away from the previous conceptions of poverty. *Capabilities poverty* emphasizes the deficiency of human capabilities and commodities at the heart of poverty. Noble et al. (2004) are of the view that while capabilities might be absolute, the required commodities to satisfy them are subject to individual, environmental and social conditions. Differences in advantages affect the conversion of monetary and non-monetary commodities to functioning (Sen 1999). It is achieved well-being (functioning), with available commodities that are important in the conception of poverty. The freedom to choose the functioning one value depending on individual, social and environmental advantages is a person's capabilities (Sen 2009, 1999). Poverty is defined in this view as "the denial of choices and opportunities for a tolerable life" (UNDP 1997 in Gordon 2002). This view prompted the UNDP to see poverty as a human development problem (Gordon 2002). A person is poor if his/her basic capabilities is below minimum acceptable level, and the life they live is not worthy of human dignity (Nussbaum 2011, 2003; Sen 1992 in Lister 2004, 16). This conception of poverty informs the UNDP Human Development Index (HDI) and the Human Poverty Index (HPI) to measure human development nationally and among deprived group respectively.

The s*ocial exclusion* conception of poverty takes into consideration the capability to participate in the ordinary activities of the society to which people belong (Millar 2007; Abrams and Christian 2007; Noble et al. 2004). The inability to fully participate could be constitutive of or instrumental to deprivation from a social relational perspective (Sen 2000). It is measured with the Bristol Social Exclusion Matrix (B-SEM) to reflect its multidimensionality of participation, resources and quality of life (Levitas et al. 2007).

Poverty—Further Conceptual Distinctions

The above four categorizations are not exhaustive; there are other characterizations of poverty, such as chronic poverty, transitory poverty, economically active and dependent poor and catastrophic poverty (Martins 2007; Hulme and Shephered 2003; White et al. 2001). While these situations might characterize poverty among different groups and contexts, they describe the characteristics of poverty rather than offering a causal explanation for poverty. However, what is worth mentioning here is the culture versus structure in poverty discourse. The idea that poverty results from the behavioral ineptitude of the poor against the position that poverty results from socio-structural imbalance and macroeconomic problems such as high rate of unemployment. This divide often plays out in the categorization of non-deserving and deserving poor respectively (Miller 1996), which is rooted English poor law of the 1600s. This idea is used to justify the targeting of social security benefits in the narrow sense and social policy broadly. It is my view that the choices that different countries make in this situation are a mixture of economic ideology, politics and scientific information.

The question of teleology arises in the conception of a culture of poverty. The ordering becomes difficult in terms of precedence and consequence. Does a culture of poverty cause poverty or it is poverty that causes a culture of poverty? The culture of poverty idea resonates with the notion of the 'underclass' and poverty (Murray 1996; Jencks 1992; Wilson 1987), often used to argue against the social provision of welfare even when there is no empirical justification (Jencks 1996). It is a value judgment language, which tends to blame the poor, pitch them against the rest of society and influence policy accordingly (Lister 1996). Rather than blaming the poor, the structure of poverty speaks to social structures that are constraining, historical and relational (Jones 2006). The question that this culture versus structure divides poses, in the final analysis, is whether a society should treat poverty as an individual or a social problem. The position taken by a society is often reflected in the structure of its political economy; how productive, individual and collective consumptions are satisfied.

White et al. (2001) noted that there are different causes and manifestation of poverty in Africa, although there are national and intra-national variations between different social groups. The different conceptions of poverty might therefore speak to different national and intra-national situations in Africa, I will argue. For example, Jones (2006) makes a compelling case for historical antecedents and the structure of global power relations as important for the consideration of the causes of poverty in Africa. He argues that we must take our engagement with poverty beyond description to causal explanations. Also, we might look at the causes from the perspective of different dimensions of poverty, such as geography (lack of natural endowment could cause poverty), gender, race and catastrophe such as famine, diseases and conflict. White et al. (2001) contend that dimensions of poverty are influenced by social positioning, time, physical location and distance from economic activities. Mbaku (2014) is of the view that the lack of rule of law and democratic institutions to create a conducive environment for creating wealth in postcolonial Africa is accountable for persistent poverty.

Poverty in Africa

The different conceptions of poverty might highlight different things in how we conceive and treat poverty (White et al. 2001). It is the position here that different empirical situations among different social groups and countries could provide important pointers to adapting or re-conceptualizing poverty in Africa. Conception is crucial because it informs the definition and measurement of and the policy response to poverty (White et al. 2001). The prevalence of poverty in Africa can be viewed from the culture and structure perspectives, an African problem caused by African ways of life—in the "local present" (Jones 2006, 7) or a global socioeconomic structural relations problem respectively—"the presence of the past and outside in the constitution of the local present (Bhaskar 1994 in Jones 2006, 7). Inadequate economic growth, a dearth of democratic and good governance, culture, conflict and diseases are viewed as some of the causes of poverty in Africa (Mbaku 2014; Gordon 2002). These causes emphasize the 'local present' without reference to the history and structure of global relations.

Adapting or Reconceptualizing Poverty in Africa

The prevalence and the characteristics of poverty in Africa warrant a closer look at how the different conceptions, definitions and measurements of poverty speak to African contexts. Such a look might call for the adaption of existing conceptions to the African situations or the reconceptualization of poverty from Africa's perspective. This process will involve paying attention to African contextual realities and the thinking that best captures the nature of poverty in Africa. Ikejiaku (2008, 2009a) tends to capture the unique nature of poverty in Africa with his conception of "poverty qua poverty"—a seemingly expanded absolute conception of poverty. For him, the consideration of absolute poverty precedes relative poverty. Therefore, relative poverty becomes relevant only when the problem of absolute poverty has been dealt with. Africa is still faced with the challenge of absolute poverty, unlike the developed world. Hence, she must prioritize absolute poverty compared to relative poverty.

The infusion of African realities into absolute poverty is what Ikejiaku describes with the notion of "poverty qua poverty"—the lack of basic needs with "hunger, thirst, poor health and living without decent shelter … not being able to read … chronic sickness … not finding any opportunities for you or your children; it is about being pushed around by those who are more powerful" (Ikejiaku 2009a, 6). Poverty in Africa therefore involves numerous situations that require understanding in order to explain them. This also reflects the mutually reinforcing multidimensionality (White et al. 2001) of poverty—different conditions may be described as poverty in the African context. Ikejiaku (2009b) is of the view that poverty qua poverty might be accountable for conflicts and instability in Africa. He contends that corruption in politics could hinder good governance, the provision of social goods and security, which might exacerbate poverty. This raises the question of causes and consequence in poverty discourse.

In a similar vein, the structure versus culture poverty debate is more nuanced than it seems. The conception of 'poverty breeds poverty' (Mafeje 2001, 20; Ikejiaku 2009a, 9) could cause the replacement of structure with 'culture of poverty'. Emphasizing the nature of the African context, Ikejiaku (2009a, 9) argues that economic stagnation is inevitable where a significant proportion of the population is living in poverty. Hence, dwelling on individual features of the poor is less rewarding than broad contextual engagement with the prevalence of poverty in Africa. Beyond the absolute poverty (measured with poverty line), we must consider 'poverty qua poverty'. The pervasiveness of poverty in Africa, Mafeje (2001) argues, merits its treatment as a problem of development, which needs fundamental reforms, and not ephemeral poverty alleviation policies. The treatment of poverty in Africa should therefore be informed by her development agenda.

Poverty in Africa—The Status Quo

Poverty persists in Africa (World Bank 2016; World Economic Forum 2015; Mbaku 2014), although social groups and national experiences vary because the causes also vary. The different causes of poverty are interacting, and there is a possibility of trading cause for effect (White et al. 2001). The consistent average economic growth rate of 5% for a decade has not reached a significant proportion of the population (World Economic Forum 2015; African Development Bank 2014). Growth has not led to a significant reduction in extreme poverty due to a lack of proper distribution and redistribution mechanisms. Therefore, market and the state must interact for effective engagement with poverty in Africa (White et al. 2001). In Africa, income inequality remains high, there is low productivity in all sectors of the economy, and sustainable inclusive growth and the creation of quality employment remain elusive. The best path to Africa development is not clear (African Development Bank 2014; World Economic Forum 2015).

The African Development Bank (ADB) (2014) categorizes the 54 African countries into low income ($785 or less), lower middle income ($786–$3115) and upper middle income ($3116–$9636) countries according to their 2013 gross national income (GNI) per capita. While GNI per capita shows the size of the economy in relation to the population, its relation to poverty is reflected in the Gini coefficient. The World Bank data on poverty quoted above excludes North Africa (Algeria, Egypt, Djibouti, Libya, Morocco and Tunisia) from Sub-Saharan Africa. The ADB data is more useful because it includes North Africa and uses local poverty lines of the respective African countries as well as the international poverty lines to determine the poverty rate. In addition, it speaks directly to national definition and policy response to poverty. The socioeconomic data presented in Table 5.1 captures the socioeconomic landscape of Africa.

There seems to be no clearly defined pattern to the data presented here. What is clear is that the level of poverty is high when national and international poverty lines are applied in most African countries. The few exceptions are Tunisia, Morocco and Mauritius. The Algerian data is rather old at 1995. The HDI seems to have a positive correlation with the GNI per capita. The countries in the upper middle income range record higher HDI values. However, the effect of the GNI per capita seems to be undermined by higher levels of inequality in some of the upper middle income countries. Botswana, Namibia, Seychelles and South Africa record a Gini coefficient of over 60% respectively. This is directly reflected in the level of poverty in most of the countries. Apart from Comoros with a Gini coefficient of 64.3%, no country in the low income and lower middle income categories recorded up to 60%.

Table 5.1 GNI per capita, HDI, inequality and poverty in Africa

Country	GNI per capita (US$) 2013	HDI value (scale 0–1) 2013	Gini coefficient		% of population in poverty (national poverty lines)		% of population in poverty (international poverty lines)		
			Year	Index	Survey year	%	Year	Below $1.25/day	Below $2/day
Low income countries ($785 or less)									
Burkina Faso	670	0.388	2009	39.8	2009	46.7	2009	44.5	72.4
Burundi	260	0.389	2006	33.3	2006	66.9	2006	81.3	93.5
Central African Rep	320	0.341	2008	56.3	2008	62.0	2008	62.8	80.1
Congo	430	0.564	2011	40.2	2011	46.5	2011	32.8	57.3
Eritrea	490	0.381	–	–	1993	69.0	–	–	–
Ethiopia	470	0.435	2011	33.6	2011	29.6	2011	36.8	72.2
Gambia	500	0.441	2003	47.3	2010	48.4	2003	33.6	55.9
Guinea	460	0.392	2012	33.7	2012	55.2	2012	40.9	72.7
Guinea Bissau	590	0.396	2002	35.5	2010	69.3	2002	48.9	78.0
Liberia	410	0.412	2007	38.2	2007	63.8	2007	83.8	94.9
Madagascar	440	0.498	2010	40.6	2010	75.3	2010	87.7	95.1
Malawi	270	0.414	2010	46.2	2010	50.7	2010	72.2	88.1
Mali	670	0.407	2010	33.0	2010	43.6	2010	50.6	78.8
Mozambique	610	0.393	2009	45.7	2009	54.7	2009	60.7	82.5
Niger	400	0.337	2011	31.2	2007	59.5	2011	40.8	76.1
Rwanda	630	0.506	2011	50.8	2011	44.9	2011	63.0	82.3
Sierra Leone	660	0.374	2011	35.4	2011	52.9	2011	56.6	82.5
Somalia	–	–	–	–	–	–	–	–	–
Tanzania	630	0.488	2012	37.8	2012	28.2	2012	43.5	73.0
Togo	530	0.473	2011	46.0	2011	58.7	2011	52.5	72.8
Uganda	550	0.484	2013	44.6	2009	24.5	2013	37.8	62.9
Lower middle income countries ($786–$3115)									
Benin	790	0.476	2012	43.5	2011	36.2	2012	51.6	74.3
Cameroon	1290	0.504	2007	40.7	2007	39.9	2007	27.6	53.2
Chad	1020	0.372	2011	43.3	2011	46.7	2011	36.5	60.5
Comoros	840	0.488	2004	64.3	2004	44.8	2004	46.1	65.0
Congo (DRC)	2590	0.338	2006	44.4	2005	71.3	2006	87.7	95.2
Côte d'Ivoire	1450	0.452	2008	43.2	2008	42.7	2008	35.0	59.1
Djibouti	–	0.467	2002	40.0	–	–	2002	18.8	41.2
Ghana	1770	0.573	2006	42.8	2012	24.2	2006	28.6	51.8
Kenya	1160	0.535	2005	47.7	2005	45.9	2005	43.4	67.2
Lesotho	1500	0.486	2010	54.2	2010	57.1	2010	56.2	73.4
Mauritania	1060	0.487	2008	40.5	2008	42.0	2008	23.4	47.7
Morocco	3020	0.617	2007	40.9	2007	8.9	2007	2.6	14.2

(continued)

Table 5.1 (continued)

Country	GNI per capita (US$) 2013	HDI value (scale 0–1) 2013	Gini coefficient		% of population in poverty (national poverty lines)		% of population in poverty (international poverty lines)		
			Year	Index	Survey year	%	Year	Below $1.25/day	Below $2/day
Nigeria	2710	0.504	2010	43.0	2010	46.0	2010	62.0	82.2
São Tomé & Principe	1470	0.558	2010	33.9	2009	61.7	2010	43.5	73.1
Senegal	1050	0.485	2011	40.3	2011	46.7	2011	34.1	60.3
South Sudan	960	–	–	–	2009	50.6	–	–	–
Sudan	1550	0.473	2009	35.3	2009	46.5	2009	19.8	44.1
Swaziland	2990	0.530	2010	51.5	2009	63.0	2010	39.3	59.1
Zambia	1810	0.561	2010	57.5	2010	60.5	2010	74.3	86.6
Zimbabwe	860	0.492	1995	50.1	2011	72.3	–	–	–
Upper middle income countries ($3116–$9636)									
Algeria	5330	0.717	1995	35.3	–	–	1995	6.4	22.8
Angola	5170	0.526	2009	42.7	2008	36.6	2009	43.4	67.4
Botswana	7770	0.683	2009	60.5	2009	19.3	2009	13.4	27.8
Cabo Verde	3620	0.636	2008	43.8	2007	26.6	2008	13.7	34.7
Egypt	3140	0.682	2008	30.8	2011	25.2	2008	1.7	15.4
Equatorial Guinea	14,320	0.556	–	–	2006	76.8	–	–	–
Gabon	10,650	0.674	2005	42.2	2005	32.7	2005	6.1	20.9
Libya	–	0.784	–	–	–	–	–	–	–
Mauritius	9290	0.771	2012	35.9	–	–	2012	0.4	1.9
Namibia	5870	0.624	2010	61.3	2009	28.7	2010	23.5	43.2
Seychelles	13,210	0.756	2007	65.8	2006	37.8	2007	0.3	1.8
South Africa	7190	0.658	2011	65.0	2011	45.5	2011	9.4	26.2
Tunisia	4200	0.721	2010	35.8	2010	15.5	2010	0.7	4.3

Source: African Development Bank (2014)

The high level of inequality in most African countries is an indication that the low level of economic success on the continent is not evenly distributed among its population. What is also worrying is the significant proportion of the populations that are sucked into poverty by moving from the international poverty line of $1.25/day to $2.00/day. This is a seeming indication that those above the poverty line have a tenuous prosperity. With poverty comes other challenges such as inadequate access to health services and a high mortality rate. Africa spent approximately 6% of it GDP on health in 2012, with a ratio of 47 doctors and 133 nurses to 100,000 people from 2004 to 2012. The crude death rate was 10.2/1000 in 2014 and a whopping 84/1000 for the under 5 mortality rate in 2012 (African Development Bank 2015).

Africa is not faring well in other development indicators such as education. Adult literacy rate remains low. Between 2001 and 2005, approximately 41% of persons 15 years and over could not read and write in Africa. This figure only slightly reduced to 37% in 2011–2015 (African Development Bank 2015). There is a significant reduction in the levels of the gross enrollment ratio between primary and secondary schools. From 2001 to 2015, the difference between gross enrollments from primary to secondary schools remained consistently high at over 50% attrition. For example, the enrollment ratios for 2011–2015 were 100% and 48% for primary and secondary schools respectively. The size and the structure of the national accounts do not portend a context prepared for significant growth. Africa's GDP remained small at approximately 2.3 trillion in 2015 at current market prices, with real GDP growth rate of 3.5% and $1932 per capita GDP in the same year. The structure of production continues to favor the agriculture and services sectors, with low industrial and manufacturing production. Between 2007 and 2014, industrial output dropped from 38.7% to 30.9%, and manufacturing output only slightly increased from 10.1% to 11.2%. In the same periods agricultural output remained constant at 16% while services output increased from 45.1% to 52.8% (African Development Bank 2015).

Therefore, Africa is not showing any serious signs of getting out of the poverty quagmire expediently. While the figures on poverty presented here might highlight low GNI per capita, a high level of inequality and low HDI, they offer more description than explanation of poverty in Africa. We cannot reduce variable association to causal explanation, and cause and effect relationships are not always unambiguous. With this in mind, I will highlight some of the reasons or causes that have been associated with the prevalence and persistence of poverty in Africa. I used associated consciously as a caution to avoid the problem of teleology.

Factors Associated with Poverty in Africa: Causes and/or Effects of Poverty

The identification of the causes and effects of any social phenomenon in an open system, such as a society, is often enigmatic because of the inability to control for all variables. It is not always clear which variable can be treated as cause or effect. Therefore we must tread cautiously rather than making emphatic claims. It is with this thinking that I engage with the causes and effects (factors associated with poverty) of poverty in Africa here. Bigman (2011) is of the view that a broad study of Africa's present and potential development must take into consideration her economic growth, urbanization and political development. The socioeconomic and demographic consequences of these factors underlie his contention for the persistence of poverty (poverty trap) in Africa.

Collier (2007 in Bigman 2011) opined that resource curse, bad governance, landlocked countries and conflicts are accountable for persistent poverty in Africa. For

Table 5.2 Causes of poverty in Africa

Causes of poverty	Political	Social and demographic	Economic	Situational
1	Governance	Household structure	Low productivity/growth	Remoteness of location
2	Social exclusion	Poverty creating social structure	Market instability and failures	Susceptible to shocks (disasters and diseases)
3	Political conflict	Low human capital and social services	Low productive assets	Environmental degradation
4		Gender biases	Income and wealth inequalities	
5		Disability and weak safety nets	Capital intensity—low job creation	
6			'Globalization' adjustment	

Source: White et al. (2001)

him, Africa's resources were plundered during the colonial and postcolonial periods by colonizers and corrupt politicians respectively. Bad governance, which undermines the development of efficient institutions, continues to define the political landscapes of significant numbers of African countries. He argues that land-locked countries are geographically disadvantaged by lack of access to the coast to facilitate their access to international market. Finally, conflict continues to adversely affect African economies. Bigman (2011) emphasizes a nuanced engagement with these factors, as their cause-and-effect relationship with poverty is not without ambiguity and the fact that there might be other intervening factors (variables). However, he notes that corruption, inequality, ineffective institutions and conflicts continues to stifle the improvement of the social well-being of African populations.

White et al. (2001) argue that there are diverse causes of poverty in Africa, which can be grouped into political, social and economic factors. These factors can be broadly divided into national (macro and micro) and international. In their specific analysis, White et al. categorized the causes of poverty into economic, situational, social-demographic and political. The identified elements in these categories were further classified as interactive, primary and proximate causes of poverty. Interactive factors are ambiguous with regard to cause/effect relationship to poverty. Primary causes are underlying, enduring causes of poverty, and they are fundamental to proximate causes. For instance, they suggest in their analysis that while economic growth is important, it is a proximate cause of poverty that depends on political and social primary factors. Table 5.2 shows the broad categories and their elements of causes of poverty in Africa.

It is imperative to note that these various factors and their elements play out in different dynamics and combinations in different African countries. White et al.

(2001) concluded broadly that markets and states are failing the poor in Africa. Barrett et al. (2006) note that vast literature emphasizes poor geographical location (unfavorable nature) and the corrupt colonial and modern state as contributing to persistent poverty trap in Africa.

Three key relational phenomena that should be taken into consideration in the "modern tragedy and a social crisis of enormous proportions" (Jones 2006, 4) of African poverty are the Structural Adjustment Program (SAP), external debt and international aid. This is not a claim that these are the primary causes of poverty in Africa, rather out of curiosity why they failed as a policy and practical approach to poverty eradication. Also, they highlight a particular understanding of poverty and how it should be dealt with. Their failure is perhaps a wake-up call for the consideration of alternative positions on the understanding and treatment of poverty.

The World Bank's policy idea of the SAP prescribes free market-driven production, distribution and consumption, with a significant cut-down in social spending. Its adoption and implementation failed in the African contexts because its conception does not capture the African situation appropriately (Ali 2003; Mafeje 2001). The SAP promise of economic growth and poverty alleviation were not achieved, rather the withdrawal of social provision was devastating for poor Africans (Mafeje 2001). The inadequate information base about poverty in Africa was at the center of the failure of the SAP (Ali 2003). The result of this failed policy is the targeting of social assistance for poverty alleviation, with its limitations, in the developing country context with the majority of the population living in poverty. Ali (2003) argues that a universal social policy is more appropriate in the African context due to high rates of poverty. It could be argued that this mismatch in policy and context is partly responsible for persistent poverty in Africa.

African countries credit and debt relations with international agencies, the International Monetary Fund (IMF) and the World Bank, as well as other developed countries agencies, can be viewed in the same light as the SAP. These are structural relations that failed to eradicate poverty in Africa. The result of borrowing by African countries has not resulted in the development of capital infrastructure and economic growth as a neoliberal postulation of development argues. Rather, most of the countries ended up with huge debt burdens that depleted their national fiscus, with little resources left for human and infrastructural development projects. Debt servicing in essence takes a large share of their GDP (Hope 2008; Mwega 2003). Debt is often connected to the SAP as a condition for African countries to access credit from international agencies. Therefore, their political economy was shaped by this condition without proper attention to the characteristics of their population.

This situation is not helped by the level of corruption among politicians and public and private sectors officials. This is often highlighted for the failure of the SAP and the inappropriate appropriation of debt funds. But we have cases where growth rate is lower than the high interest rate on debt (Hope 2008; Soludo 2003; Mkandawire and Soludo 2003). Ikejiaku (2008) is of the view that the African debt crisis is a case of dependency and collusion between African leaders, international agencies and the West. Servicing of debt is an avenue to extract substantial financial resources from Africa, which can be indirectly linked to poverty and underdevelopment. Closely associated to the SAP and external debt is international aid. It is also associated with conditionality of economic liberalization. Opening Africa to international financial systems and trade with advanced countries predisposed it to poverty and indebtedness (Ikejiaku 2008).

The paradox of aid dependence is that the amounts are often too small to make any significant socioeconomic or infrastructural development impact. Yet countries are compelled to take conditions, such as where to make purchases, which see a significant part of the fund staying in the donor country. This is what Ikejiaku (2008) calls the dependent and exploitative imperialist relationship. There is a connection between debt, aid and conditionality that undermines African development by causing aid dependence and outflow through debt servicing (Kanbur 2000). The thinking here is that in addition to defining and counting the poor, the structural relations of the SAP, foreign aid and the debt crisis have implications for poverty and African development. There is a need to consider alternative complements to economic liberalism in order to engage with poverty in Africa, if liberalism and targeted social provisions have failed to eradicate poverty in Africa. The consideration of structural issues might be an important complementary perspective, especially as they relate to different countries' contexts. Counting the poor only tells us part of the story (descriptive) about poverty, the concluding part might reside in the structural issues that can create or eradicate poverty.

Institutional Practices and Poverty in Africa: A Case Study in South Africa

Africa remains "the core of the world's poverty problem" (Bigman 2011, 3). The notion of 'poverty qua poverty' shows that poverty is beyond the lack of basic needs in Africa. Hope (2008, 2) describes African poverty as "characterized by lack of purchasing power, rural predominance, exposure to environmental risk, population displacement, insufficient access to social and economic services, rapid urbanization, and few opportunities for formal income generation". This shows that the nature of poverty on the African continent is unique, and should be treated accordingly. Disabled people, children, landless people and the working poor constitute a significant proportion of the poor in Africa. The poverty condition is aggravated by conflict, communicable diseases and inadequate formal employment (White et al. 2001).

To take this discussion further, I am of the view that embedded causes of poverty are more problematic to uncover, and are often not dealt with. These are institutions that may seem remote from poverty but could undermine or enhance social well-being. Institutions that could deplete the amount of household real income might gradually drive them into poverty, in the absence of collective consumption. The consumption of micro-credit in South Africa demonstrates this argument. Attempts to fill the gap in consumption needs and income with micro-credit, in the absence of collective consumption, could have either negative or positive consequences for the quality of social reproduction of the households concerned. It can push households living within the poverty range into poverty. In a small-scale study on poverty, micro-credit institutions and social reproduction in South Africa (Omomowo 2015), it was revealed that precariously prosperous households that consume micro-credit to meet individual consumption gaps, in the absence of collective consumption, are likely to gradually slip into poverty.

The argument here extracts from a qualitative research study on the effects of the consumption of micro-credit on the well-being of concerned households, using a case study of Pretoria and Cape Town in South Africa. Theoretical and purposive sampling methods were used to select participants for the study. Snowball sampling referral power facilitates the continuous selection of participants until saturation point. One-on-one semi-structured in-depth interviews were used for data collection (Yin 2009; Kumar 2005; Burgess 1984; Glaser and Strauss 1967). Fifty-four in-depth interviews, comprising four categories, were conducted. Thirty-six life histories, 13 micro-credit, four cultural and one legal interview were conducted. The life history interviews probed the implications of the consumption of micro-credit for the social reproduction of households. The interviews with micro-credit institution workers were used to corroborate the life histories interviews, while the cultural interviews probed cultural practices. The interview with a lawyer was to obtain legal views on credit relationships.

The textual data was manually analyzed using grounded theory and critical realism's 'constant comparative method' and 'analytical model' respectively. Thought processes of abduction, induction and retroduction were used to facilitate understanding, interpretation and explanation for conceptual abstraction (Danermark et al. 2002; Charmaz 2006; Dey 1999). Working with the conception of 'precarious prosperity', a poverty range was constructed, using the experience of the 2014 Ugandan report on poverty status. Setting the secured prosperity threshold at double the poverty line, 43% of the population was categorized as 'non-poor insecure' in Uganda. This approach was applied to the South African local poverty lines. South Africa uses three poverty lines—food, lower-bound and upper-bound poverty lines. These were rebased in the Income and Expenditure Survey of 2011 to R335, R501 and R779 respectively (Stats 2015; Ministry of Finance, Planning, and Economic Development 2014). In view of this, the 'poverty range' was taken to be from the lower-bound poverty line of R501 to the double upper-bound poverty line of R1558).

Out of a total of 36, 24 interviewees revealed the income and structure (number of adults and children) of their households, which were used to calculate their income per capita. Table 5.3 shows that 16 households' per capital incomes are within R501–R1558 poverty range, one household earn below it and seven households earn above it. The boundaries of the poverty range cannot be treated as rigid as there are indications of financial support of family not living in the same household, without clarity on frequency of support and amount. The voice of the people living within poverty range was emphasized.

Poverty discourse tends to overlook this category of people. Though they are categorized as non-poor, their prosperity is fragile and unsecured. The Uganda case

Table 5.3 Household per capita income taking children as half adult

S/N	[a]Name (interviewee code)	No of persons	No of adults	No of children	No of persons taking children as ½ adult	Household income (rand)			Household per capita income (rand)
						Salary/wage	CSG/DG/Pen/gift	Total	
1	Lerato (SR30)	10	6	4	8	4500	1000	5500	687[b]
2	Refilwe (SR31)	11	5 [2]	1 [3]	5 ½	6000	660	6600	1200[b]
3	Fibi (SR12)		5	4	7	3500	1400	4900	700[b]
4	Teballo (SR9)	10	5	5	7 ½	2600	1750	4350	580[b]
5	Mr. Ahmed (SR19)	6	4	2	5	1114	500	1614	323[b]
6	Tebogho (SR14)	3	1	2	2	5500	–	5500	2750
7	Mr. Hendricks (SR16)	3	2	1	2 ½	–	2580	2580	1032[b]
8	Lebo (SR29)	2	2	–	2	1500	–	1500	750[b]
9	Motapelo (SR28)	3	1	2	2	3000	–	3000	1500[b]
10	Impilo (SR27)	4	2	2	3	4900	–	4900	1633
11	Olwethu (SR33)	7	5	2	6	7500	500	8000	1333[b]
12	Peter (SR10)	7	6 [1]	–	6	5200	–	5200	867[b]
13	Ruth (SR7)	5	3	2	4	6000	–	6000	1500[b]
14	Tumi (SR6)	4	4	–	4	2500	2200	4700	1175[b]
15	Pamela (SR5)	6	4	2	5	2600	1100	3700	740[b]
16	Angela (SR4)	4	2	2	3	3000	500	3500	1166[b]
17	John (SR3)	6	2	4	4	2900	1000	3900	975[b]

(continued)

Table 5.3 (continued)

S/N	[a]Name (interviewee code)	No of persons	No of adults	No of children	No of persons taking children as ½ adult	Household income (rand)			Household per capita income (rand)
						Salary/wage	CSG/DG/Pen/gift	Total	
18	Unathi (SR2)	8	4	4	6	3540	1100	4640	773[b]
19	Simphiwe (SR13)	4	3	1	3 ½	2536	250	2786	796[b]
20	Mitchelle (SR15)	4	4	–	4	12,300	–	12,300	3075
21	Rose (SR23)	4	2	2	3	10,700	–	10,700	3567
22	May (SR21)	3	2	1	2 ½	5500	1100	6600	2640
23	Ingrid (SR18)	5	3	2	4	8300	1100	9400	2350
24	Phumi (SR17)	3	3	–	3	9000	1100	10,100	3367

CSG Child support grant, *DS* – Disability grant, *Pen* Old age pension
[a]All names are pseudonyms
[b]Household per capita income within 'poverty range'

shows that they have started paying attention to this category of people because they constitute a substantial part of their population. My sense here is that an anti-poverty or poverty eradication program that does not cast its net wide enough to include people living within the poverty range might not be very successful. It becomes imperative that embedded institutional practices, seemingly remote, that might undermine the quality of social reproduction of the precarious non-poor be studied. This will unveil the contextually peculiar causes of poverty to inform appropriate policy responses. It is with this thinking that the activities of micro-credit institutions and the consumption of micro-credit by the precarious non-poor were studied in two South African cities. Cash loans (micro-credit institution that lend against salary/wage income), retail goods credit (hire-purchase of durable goods and clothes) and 'mashonisa' (informal moneylenders) micro-credit institutions were considered in this study.

The study revealed that the purpose and dimension at which credit is consumed is important for its implications for a credit consuming household. There is a distinction between the productive consumption of micro-credit and micro-credit to smoothen individual consumption. While the productive consumption of micro-credit has the potential to increase household real income, its consumption to smoothen individual consumption leads to the depletion of real income due to repayment of principal amount and costs. Reduced real income negatively affects the quality of social reproduction of households when there is no collective consumption to bridge the gap in individual consumption needs as a result of low wage from the capital–labor nexus (Heinrich 2012; Altman 2007). Micro-credit consumption is often used to smoothen individual consumption in South Africa, rather than the promotion of micro enterprise (Calvin and Coetzee 2010).

The dimension at which credit is consumed is also important in shaping its effect on household quality of social reproduction. It emphasizes the degree of drive to consume credit. The study reveals three dimensions of desperation-need-choice on a continuum of highest to lowest drive to consume credit. The higher the drive to consume credit, the lower is consumer power to negotiate positive terms in a credit relationship. The dimension at which a household consumes micro-credit is an indication of its location in her social reproduction needs. For instance, when micro-credit is consumed at the desperate dimension, such as for food or transport to get to work, households might have no leverage of time to consider alternative or negotiate favorable terms.

The granting of micro-credit in South Africa is focused on the affordability of monthly repayment installments, credit history and formal employment. Purpose is not given much attention, except in house mortgage. Vangile, a query line manager, did not mince her words about the priority micro-credit institutions placed on affordability when she said:

> It's just plain simple, if you can afford it we will give it to you. For whatever reason that you take it up for, it is your baby (Vangile: MC 8, P 17–10/09/2011).

Henry is a branch manager of in one of the big micro-credit granting institutions in South Africa. He stressed the importance of affordability, employment and credit history—in his words:

> So affordability plays a major role in giving the client the product or not … There are other stuffs that we look at, employment, how long the client has been employed … the client needs to be employed, minimum a year with the same institution. So those are the specific criteria that we look at; affordability, credit name and employment (Henry: MC 3, P4–07/06/2011).

It was inferred from the study that a focus on purpose and dimension is important because it can inform the architecture of collective consumption, in the form of social policy to advance social well-being. This approach to poverty could target those living close to poverty, which are not often included in the poverty discourse, and uncover social institutions that might subtly create poverty. The dimension at which households consume credit determines its urgency and importance in their social reproduction. Credit consumption purpose and dimension are connected. For example, purpose can reflect dimension. The consumption of credit for food and medical care reflects a desperate situation that must be satisfied urgently. The study revealed that credit is consumed for food, electricity, transportation, tuition fees, medical bills, debt consolidation, school uniform, clothing and the payment of existing credit monthly instalments. Teballo's, Ma Ntombi's, Lerato's and Lebo's words show their desperation for micro-credit to fill their social reproduction needs gap thus:

> I only survive when I go and borrow money from a 'mashonisa' [informal moneylender] … I have Mr. Price account on which I pay R150 every month. I bought a fridge, on which I am paying R150 per month as well, and I have to eat and send some of the money home (Teballo: SR 9, P2, 3, 4–24/03/2011).

> Like when the kids are sick because we don't have a medical aid … We go to a 'mashonisa' [informal moneylender] and loaned the money because we must take the kids to the hospital … Sometimes we don't have electricity because we can't buy enough electricity for the whole month … then we go to 'mashonisa' or there is something that is an emergency (Ma Ntombi: MC 10, P9–16/04/2012).

> Sometimes we don't manage to buy uniform for our young children, so we have account to buy uniforms for school at Ackermans … R200 every month … No, not only uniforms, sometimes it is for winter clothes, sometimes for Christmas (Lerato: SR 30, P8–06/09/2011).

> Last year I took my son to the … skills college … he did what, boiler making. So I went to African Bank to borrow the money. African Bank gave me 5.5 [R5500] … they are still taking that money, R383.05 … I took 5½ thousand … now I owe the bank 11000, which means the interest is maybe 6000 (Lebo: SR 29, P4 – 03/09/2011).

The various needs for which credit is sought reflect different dimensions. The credit consumer is powerless at the desperate dimension, with no time to compare alternatives. While needs might be satisfied in desperation, the cost might be huge for households in the long run. The need dimension is when credit is used to close the income–need gap. There is little time to consider alternatives. It is also a position of powerlessness because in order to socially reproduce the needs not covered by income must be satisfied. There is ample time to consider alternatives at the choice dimension. Credit is used for non-compulsory needs, therefore the household can decide to consume credit or not. There were clear indications that credit consumption at the desperate and need dimensions can push the household into poverty in the long run due to the repayment of principal debt and costs, causing continuous reduction in households' real income. Credit consumption by people living in the poverty range at these dimensions could lead to over-indebtedness, bad debt, credit administration, garnishee orders and attachment of property. Tebogho clearly expresses her over-indebtedness when she said:

> I'm sinking in a 'titanic' … I was paying this furniture there, the divider there, the fridge, the mirror and the machines … Then I decided in January this year to borrow a loan from African Bank to settle all of my accounts. I had a loan [from] African Bank; they are disturbing me now … Then I have to settle that one as well in January. It was R22,000 and some odds … I was also having the one for the fridge and the one for the machine and other shops now for the clothes. But applying for a loan at African Bank is very easy, but it's so frustrating because you'll pay until I don't know, 5 years … and their interest is sky-high … I decided to go to Capitec because I was so fed-up of having those phone calls from the shops like RCS and Joshua Doore and stuff … then Capitec settled that African Bank loan, the big one that I have. It was like now R38,000 that they settled for me. And then they settle that Joshua Doore and RCS … Capitec said they are not going to settle the credit card that I have at African Bank. So I am left with that credit card at African Bank (Tebogho: SR 14, P2, 3 – 03/07/2011).

Refilwe is under debt administration due to over-indebtedness:

> It is hard men because of now we are at … administration … I ended up at credit bureau, those people ended up interfering with my salary because I'm the one who is working. The lawyers wanted to deduct my money so I ended up going to administration to help me. They call it debt counselling. I am paying those people R750 … to pay lots of accounts, ABSA loan, Foschini, and Truworths. So they ended up making it one credit … those administrators, and then paying those debts (Refilwe: SR 31, P4 – 07/09/2011).

According to Nicole, when people are desperate the cost of credit is rarely taken into consideration when they are making micro-credit consumption decisions:

> You see, if you are desperately in need of money, you just sign and … because you want the money, you don't check what … is the interest. So … last month I said … no man, something is not right, let me just check … it comes out like R475 on R300 (Nicole: SR 8, P4 – 22/03/2011).

The entanglement in debt cycle is clear as Teballo's experience shows she survives by consuming micro-credit repeatedly:

> I'm renting a room in Mamelodi, I am the one paying the rent, I buy food worth R200, train is R100 and taxi I spend R200 per week on taxi. Still I only survive when I go and borrow money from a 'mashonisa'. I borrow from them; I do what I needed to do. At the end of the month they take their money from my salary. I take the money, they deduct it, I take the money again, they deduct it again, and on and on like that (Teballo: SR 9, P3 – 24/03/2011).

The study therefore shows that micro-credit institutions, which seem remote to the discourse of poverty, can actually push households that are living just above poverty into poverty when they try to solve their individual consumption challenges with credit consumption. The argument here is that where the structure of the political economy is weak on collective consumption, individual households that use micro-credit to solve the challenge of individual consumption might be gradually pushed into poverty in the long run. It is therefore imperative that the study of poverty in Africa should transcend description and obvious structural causes to uncovering remote social institutional practices that might cause or aggravate poverty. Such is the case of the consumption of micro-credit by those living in the poverty range in South Africa. In addition to economic growth, comprehensive social policy on collective consumption might be important to deal with the prevalence of poverty in Africa. Such policy has the capacity to raise the socioeconomic floor and build individual capabilities to convert resources to high quality functioning.

Conclusion

The prevalence of poverty in Africa means that how it is treated is unique to the African context. About 50% of Sub-Saharan Africans (as well as North Africa) are poor using the $1.90 per day international poverty line at 2011 PPP (World Bank 2016). In excess of 50% of the populations in most African countries are poor using their local poverty lines and the $1.25 a day international poverty line (African Development Bank 2015). The figures are worse at the $2.00 and $3.10 2011 PPP. Though Africa has achieved an average 5% growth rate in the past decade, the level of poverty reduction achieved is not significant. This situation is accompanied by diseases, conflict, hunger and lack of proper shelter (Ikejiaku 2009a). Therefore poverty can better be conceived as a development challenge in Africa. The targeting of social welfare is not likely to be effective in a context where a significant proportion of the population is poor. A universal social policy is needed to complement economic policy in order to deal with Africa's development (poverty) challenge (Ikejiaku 2009a; Ali 2003; Mafeje 2001; White et al. 2001).

In view of these contextual realities, it is pertinent to talk about the structure of poverty in Africa as a relational phenomenon. The structure of Africa's relationship with the rest of the world, which is capable of causing or aggravating poverty, is imperative. Also, the structure of poverty can be considered as contextual institutional practices that are capable of causing or aggravating poverty. What is more important for the way poverty is viewed in this chapter is the study of institutions that appear remote to poverty, yet a closer interrogation could uncover that they are capable of causing and aggravating poverty in Africa. This is important if we have to move from description to an explanation of poverty (Jones 2006).

There are many causes of poverty in Africa if it is approached by means of structural institutional practices; hence, the approaches applied should differ from country to country. It is the position here that the poverty eradication agenda, as proposed in Africa's Agenda 2063 and the SDGs, must complement economic growth with human capabilities development policies. The socioeconomic floor must be raised broadly in order for targeted social protection policy to have any meaningful effect on poverty eradication. Therefore comprehensive social policy must be considered to unlock human potential. Social policy should not be treated as residual, but as a complement to economic policy.

The complementary relationship between economic and social policy in the treatment of poverty is vivid within the framework of the political economy that speaks to how a society satisfies productive, individual and collective consumptions through the institutions of the economy, family/household and the state. Within this frame, poverty is a challenge of individual consumption within the family/household as a result of human capabilities and entitlements (Sen 2009), which merge claims to wage funds in the capital–labor nexus (Heinrich 2012) and claims on social provisions and collective consumption often led by (but not limited to) the state. Both sites (the economy and state/social cooperation) of entitlements, defined by human capabilities, must complement each other to foster social well-being. When individuals' entitlements are inadequate to facilitate absolute and relative socially acceptable functioning (living) or quality of social reproduction, they are deemed to live in poverty. Therefore, a poverty reduction or eradication agenda must target economic and social policies simultaneously. Both possess the tools to enhance human capabilities to increase their entitlements so as to foster improved social well-being. In the African context, where poverty is overwhelming and the social floor is very low, human capabilities improvement through comprehensive social policy (seen as social investment) can increase economic participation and foster growth and distribution, which are all important for development.

References

Abrams, D., & Christian, J. (2007). A relational analysis of social exclusion. In D. Abrams, J. Christian, & D. Gordon (Eds.), *Multidisciplinary handbook of social exclusion research*. West Sussex: Wiley.

African Development Bank. (2014). *African Development Report 2014*. Abidjan: African Development Bank.

African Development Bank. (2015). *Annual Report*. Abidjan: African Development Bank.

African Union. (2015). *Agenda 2063: The Africa we want*. Addis Ababa: African Union Commission.

Ali, A. A. G. (2003). Structural adjustment and poverty in sub-Sahara Africa: 1985–1995. In T. Mkandawire & C. C. Soludo (Eds.), *African voices on structural adjustment: A companion to our continent, our future* (pp. 189–228). Trenton: Africa World.

Altman, M. (2007). *Low wage work in South Africa*. Pretoria: Human Science Research Council.

Barrett, C. B., Carter, M. R., & Little, P. D. (2006). Understanding and reducing persistent poverty in Africa: Introduction to special issue. *Journal of Development Studies, 42*(2), 167–177.

Barrett, C. B., Carter, M. R., & Little, P. D. (2008). Understanding and reducing persistent poverty in Africa: Introduction to special issue. In C. B. Barrett, M. R. Carter, & P. D. Little (Eds.), *Understanding and reducing persistent poverty in Africa* (pp. 1–11). London: Routledge.

Baulch, B. (1996). The new poverty agenda: A disputed consensus. *IDS Bulletin, 27*(1), 1–10.

Bigman, D. (2011). *Poverty, hunger, and democracy in Africa: Potential and limitations of democracy in cementing multiethnic societies*. Basingstoke: Palgrave Macmillan.

Blakemore, K., & Griggs, E. (2007). *Social policy: An introduction* (3rd ed.). Berkshire: Open University, McGraw-Hill.

Budowski, M., Tillmann, R., Keim, W., & Amacker, M. (2010). Conceptualizing 'precarious prosperity': Empirical and theoretical elements for debate. *International Journal of Comparative Sociology, 5*(4), 268–288.

Burgess, R. (1984). *In the field*. London: Routledge.

Calvin, B., and G. Coetzee (eds.). 2010. A review of the South African microfinance sector, 2009: Success, challenges, and policy issues. Pretoria: FinMark Trust and the Centre for Microfinance, University of Pretoria.

Charmaz, K. (2006). *Constructing grounded theory: A practical guide through qualitative analysis*. London: Sage.

Danermark, B., Ekström, M., Jakobsen, L., & Karlsson, J. C. (2002). *Explaining society: Critical realism in the social sciences*. London: Routledge.

Dey, I. (1999). *Grounding grounded theory: Guidelines for qualitative inquiry*. London: Academic.

Dickinson, J., & Russell, B. (1986). Introduction: The structure of reproduction in capitalist society. In J. Dickinson & B. Russell (Eds.), *Family, economy and state: The social reproduction process under capitalism* (pp. 1–20). London: Croom Helm.

Glaser, B. G., & Strauss, A. L. (1967). *The discovery of grounded theory: Strategies for qualitative research*. London: Weidenfeld and Nicolson.

Gordon, D. (2002). The international measurement of poverty and anti-poverty policies. In P. Townsend & D. Gordon (Eds.), *World poverty: New policies to defeat an old enemy* (pp. 53–80). Bristol: Policy Press.

Heinrich, M. (2012). *An introduction to the three volumes of Karl Marx's Capital*. New York: Monthly Review.

Hope, K. R. (2008). *Poverty, livelihoods, and governance in Africa: Fulfilling the development promise*. New York: Palgrave Macmillan.

Hulme, D., & Shephered, A. (2003). Conceptualizing chronic poverty. *World Development, 31*(3), 403–423.

Ikejiaku, B. (2008). African debt crisis and IMF with a case of Nigeria: Towards theoretical explanation. *Journal of Politics and Law, 1*(4), 2–7.

Ikejiaku, B. (2009a). The concept of 'poverty' towards understanding in the context of developing countries 'poverty qua poverty': With some comparative evidence on Britain. *Journal of Sustainable Development, 2*(2), 3–13.

Ikejiaku, B. (2009b). The relationship between poverty, conflict and development. *Journal of Sustainable Development, 2*(1), 15–28.

Jencks, C. (1992). *Rethinking social policy: Race, poverty, and the underclass*. Cambridge, MA: Harvard University.

Jencks, C. (1996). Can we replace welfare with work? In M. R. Darby (Ed.), *Reducing poverty in America: Views and approaches*. Thousand Oaks: Sage.

Jones, B. G. (2006). *Explaining poverty: A critical realist approach*. Oxford: Routledge.

Kanbur, R. (2000). Aid, conditionality and debt in Africa. In F. Tarp (Ed.), *Foreign aid and development: Lessons learnt and directions for the future* (pp. 409–422). London: Routledge.

Kumar, R. (2005). *Research methodology: A step-by-step guide for beginners*. London: Sage.

Kumar, S. (2002). Round pegs in square holes: Mismatches between poverty and housing policy in urban India. In P. Townsend & D. Gordon (Eds.), *World poverty: New policies to defeat an old enemy* (pp. 271–296). Bristol: Policy Press.

Levitas, R., Pantazis, C., Fahmy, E., Gordon, D., Lloyd, E., & Patsios, D. (2007). *The multi-dimensional analysis of social exclusion*. Bristol: Department of Sociology and School of Social Policy, Townsend Centre for the International Study of Poverty and Bristol Institute for Public Affairs, University of Bristol.

Lister, R. (1996). Introduction: in search of the 'underclass'. In R. Lister (Ed.), *Charles Murray and the underclass: The developing debate*. London: The IEA Health and Welfare Unit.

Lister, R. (2004). *Poverty*. Cambridge, MA: Polity.

Mafeje, A. (2001). Conceptual and philosophical predisposition. In F. Wilson, N. Kanji, & E. Braathen (Eds.), *Poverty reduction: What role for the state in today's globalized economy?* (pp. 15–32). London: Zed Books.

Martins, J. H. (2007). Household budgets as a social indicator of poverty and inequality in South Africa. *Social Indicators Research, 81*, 203–221.

Mbaku, J. M. (2014). The rule of law and poverty eradication in Africa. *African and Asian Studies, 13*, 530–557.

Millar, J. (2007). Social exclusion and social policy research: defining exclusion. In D. Abrams, J. Christian, & D. Gordon (Eds.), *Multidisciplinary handbook of social exclusion research.* West Sussex: Wiley.

Miller, S. M. (1996). The great chain of poverty explanations. In E. Øyen, S. M. Miller, & S. A. Samad (Eds.), *Poverty: A global review: handbook on international poverty research* (pp. 569–586). Oslo: Scandinavian University.

Ministry of Finance, Planning and Economic Development. (2014). *Uganda poverty status report 2014*. Kampala: Ministry of Finance, Planning and Economic Development.

Mkandawire, T., & Soludo, C. C. (2003). Introduction: Towards the broadening of development policy dialog for Africa. In T. Mkandawire & C. C. Soludo (Eds.), *African voices on structural adjustment: A companion to our continent, our future* (pp. 1–16). Trenton: Africa World.

Murray, C. (1996). The emerging British underclass. In R. Lister (Ed.), *Charles Murray and the underclass: the developing debate*. London: The IEA Health and Welfare Unit.

Mwega, F. M. (2003). Financial sector reform in Eastern and Southern Africa. In T. Mkandawire & C. C. Soludo (Eds.), *African voices on structural adjustment: A companion to our continent, our future* (pp. 353–382). Trenton: Africa World.

Noble, M., Ratcliffe, A., & Wright, G. (2004). *Conceptualizing, defining and measuring poverty in South Africa: An argument for a consensual approach*. Oxford: CASASP.

Noble, W. J. M., Wright, G. C., Magasela, W., & Ratcliffe, A. (2007). Developing a democratic definition of poverty in South Africa. *Journal of Poverty, 11*(4), 117–141.

Nussbaum, M. C. (2003). Capabilities as fundamental entitlements: Sen and social justice. *Feminist Economics, 9*(2–3), 33–59.

Nussbaum, M. C. (2011). *Creating capabilities: The human development approach*. Cambridge, MA: Belknap.

Omomowo, K.E. 2015. *The lords of poverty? Micro-credit institutions and social reproduction in South Africa*. Dissertation, University of the Western Cape.

Ravallion, M. 1998. *Poverty lines in theory and practice* (LSMS Working Paper No. 133). Washington, DC: World Bank.

Sen, A. K. (1997). From income inequality to economic inequality. *Southern Economic Journal, 64*(2), 384–401.

Sen, A. (1981). *Poverty and famine: An essay on entitlement and deprivation*. Oxford: Clarendon.

Sen, A. (1999). *Development as freedom*. New York: Anchor Books Random House.

Sen, A. 2000. *Social exclusion: Concept, application, and scrutiny*. Social Development Papers No 1. Manila: Asian Development Bank.

Sen, A. (2008). Capability and well-being. In D. M. Hausman (Ed.), *The philosophy of economics: an anthology* (3rd ed., pp. 270–294). Cambridge, MA: Cambridge University Press.

Sen, A. (2009). *The idea of justice*. Cambridge, MA: The Belknap Press.

Soludo, C. C. (2003). Industrialisation and growth in sub-Saharan Africa: Is the Asian experience useful? In T. Mkandawire & C. C. Soludo (Eds.), *African voices on structural adjustment: A companion to our continent, our future* (pp. 103–160). Trenton: Africa World.

Stats, SA. (2015). *Methodological report on rebasing of national poverty lines and development of pilot provincial poverty lines*. Pretoria: Stats, SA.

Stewart, F., Saith, R., & Harriss-White, B. (2007). *Defining poverty in the developing world.* New York: Palgrave Macmillan.

Townsend, P. (1979). *Poverty in the United Kingdom: A survey of household resources and standards of living*. Berkeley: University of California Press.

Townsend, P. (1987). Conceptualising poverty. In S. M. Miller & Z. Ferge (Eds.), *Dynamics of deprivation* (pp. 31–44). Aldershot: Gower.

Townsend, P. (1993). *The international analysis of poverty*. Hemel Hempstead: Harvester Wheatsheaf.

Townsend, P. (2009). Three models of social security in the history of the industrialized countries. In P. Townsend (Ed.), *Building decent societies: Rethinking the role of social security in development* (pp. 169–189). Basingstoke: Palgrave Macmillan.
United Nations. (2013). *The millennium development goals report 2013*. New York: United Nations.
United Nations Development Programme (UNDP). (2015). *MDG report 2015: Assessing progress in Africa toward the millennium development goals*. Addis Ababa: United Nations Economic Commission for Africa.
White, H., Killick, T., Kayizzi-Mugerwa, S., & Savane, M. (2001). *African poverty at the millennium: Causes, complexities, and challenges*. Washington, DC: World Bank.
Wilson, W. J. (1987). *The truly disadvantaged: The inner city, the underclass, and public policy*. Chicago: University of Chicago.
World Bank. (2016). *World development indicators 2016*. Washington, DC: World Bank.
World Economic Forum. (2015). *The Africa competitiveness report 2015*. Geneva: World Economic Forum.
Yin, R. K. (2009). *Case study research: design and methods* (4th ed.). Los Angeles: Sage.

Kolawole Emmanuel Omomowo is a Postdoctoral Fellow at Archie Mafeje Research Institute, College of Graduate Studies, University of South Africa. Kolaskysy11@gmail.com.

Chapter 6
Education in Africa

Chizoba Vivian Nwuzor

Introduction

Talking about education and development together might be easier to approach if one starts on an individual level. What readily comes to mind on speaking or hearing about them is one being well informed and having an all-round 'good' living, mentally and physically, which issue from a good learning and a good earning, both from good work. While 'good' may be relative, taken objectively, an educated and a developed person has the ability to use available information to provide and sustain comfortable shelter, food, clothing, healthy living and peace of mind every day for himself/herself and family (where it applies). Sustaining all this implies security of the person and the process of good living.

Sustaining these require understanding the need to do so, while understanding is achieved by information. Information is knowledge acquired through observation, experience and instruction. It provides one with an opportunity to have different experiences, which should help in making the most of the choices. This implies informed decisions, which from empirical experience we can all agree with pay, perhaps reaffirming Sir Francis Bacon's conclusion that 'knowledge is power'. Power is the possession of a controlling ability and influence to face and surmount life challenges. Invariably, it takes a well-informed, educated mind to surmount life challenges and consequently to make a developed human and material output. A developed mind continues learning, informing itself to adapt to evolving challenges in its environment. Thus, education and development are positively and cyclically correlated.

Certainly, education is central to human and material development. Africans, like other people, by natural instinct educated their people and evolved their respective indigenous education. As accounted by historians, Africa's indigenous education encouraged skill, and moral and intellectual development and served their needs

C.V. Nwuzor (✉)
Ann's Indulgence Limited, Abuja, Nigeria
e-mail: chizobanwuzor@yahoo.co.uk

O. Akanle, J.O. Adésìnà (eds.), *The Development of Africa*, Social Indicators Research Series 71, DOI 10.1007/978-3-319-66242-8_6

(Fafunwa and Aisiku 1982, 10, 14). Their respective societies train generations to integrate well. These are what education does. The coming of their colonial masters and the missionaries brought an imposition of Western/foreign, Christian and Islamic education that Africans integrated with their indigenous education. The British colonial masters' education prepared their colonies for future self-administration. That of the French colonies comprised mostly French life-oriented education, in Fafunwa and Aisiku's word a "frenchifying" that majorly neglected African indigenous education (Fafunwa and Aisiku 1982, 22–26; Rayfield 1983, 5–6). Colonization also brought cultural, philosophical, religious, socio-political and economic reorientation, and the ongoing technological revolution together with globalization. These contributed to the demanding all-round reorientation of Africa and the world over. These pose challenges for societies that need to be surmounted.

However, for the past five decades, since most African countries gained independence to run their economies and education, most Africans have shown an inability to integrate well in life and provide for their needs. Most African countries still have the challenge of breaking away from poverty (Deininger and Okidi 2003; Hill 1998) and are so not developed.

Following propounded growth theories in various fields of knowledge and sectors, several efforts have been made by the countries of the continent to generate and sustain growth to attain development (ECOWAS 2015). These efforts include the increasing use of education to seek growth (Nwaobi 2007; Nwuzor 2008; Stroombergen et al. 2002).

These countries have over the years, especially with the introduction of Universal Basic Education (UBE) in the 1990s and the Millennium Development Goals (MDGs), which terminated in 2015, increased enrolment in education, and continuously used and evolved both their indigenous and foreign education in order to meet the changing demands of the societies. These suggest more education amidst supposedly improved indigenous, adapted foreign and modern education. However, it is worrisome that despite the undisputed theoretical conclusion and empirical realization of the effectiveness of education in poverty reduction, as seen with developed countries and more especially with the Asian Tigers' experience in lifting their economies from poverty in the 1990s, Africa, especially the Sub-Saharan, despite its education reforms remains overly poor (Fig. 6.1).

It is observable, without rigorous research, that high income economies with higher literacy rates (Figs. 6.2 and 6.3) still rely on improving education further to sustain their development. Thus, the enthusiasm for reinforcing education in Africa is well warranted. Nwuzor's (2008) study of 22 African countries and several other studies found that education is a significant factor that Africa needs to attain growth. These suggest increasing attention to education. They raise the following questions:

- What is the nature and state of education in Africa?
- How critical is education for Africa's development and/or underdevelopment?
- Can the current education scenario drive growth and development in Africa?
- What is in African countries' education and development experiences that they have not used education to drive development?

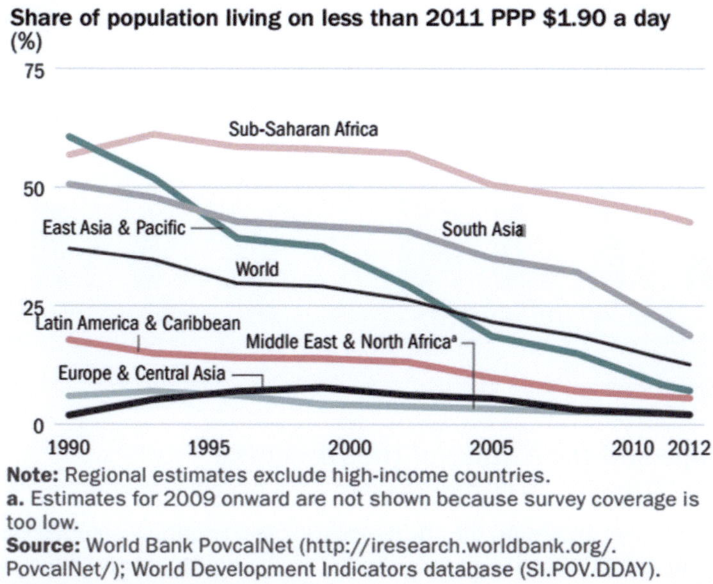

Fig. 6.1 Share of population living on $1.90 a day (%)

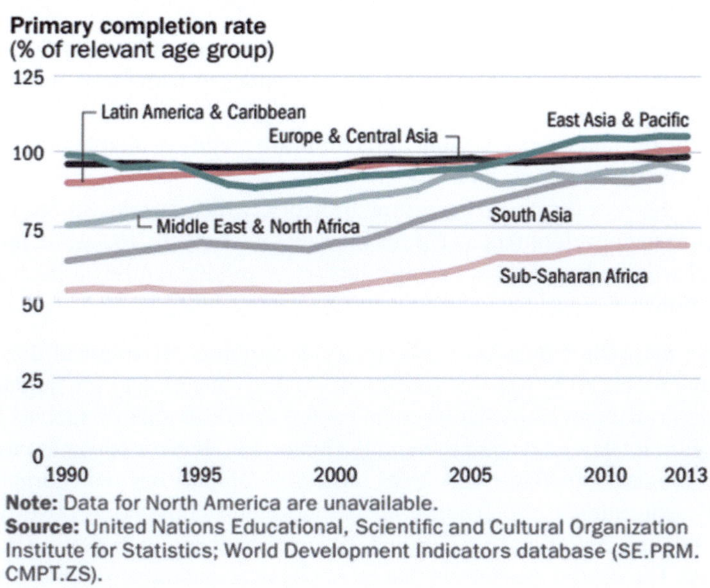

Fig. 6.2 Primary completion rate

- Are there case studies in education and development experiences of Africa and developed countries that Africa needs learning to achieve development?
- What is the solution for Africa to drive development through education?

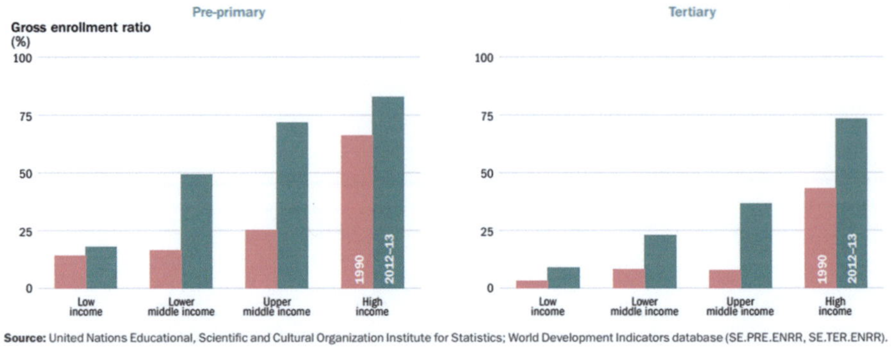

Fig. 6.3 Gross enrollment ratio

The Scope and the Nature of the Discourse

In answering these questions, the efforts seek a sound empirical approach to making education in Africa effective in contributing to the development of the continent. Education should serve the needs of the individual(s) and the nation(s). To achieve this, it must be evolving and development-oriented. Thus, the approach relies extensively on the facts:

- Firstly, human capital theory, which is relevant for individual development and plays an important role in the model of endogenous growth for an individual and a nation,
- Secondly, the abundance of labor, a factor more readily available than other factors in African countries, and
- Thirdly, the postulation of new growth theory, which is relevant for economic and all-round development as it points out that the capacity to sustain production given the limited capacities of other factors of production lies in technological innovation.

To have these three facts used effectively in bringing development they have to be directly influenced by *applied* education. It takes education to use human capital to produce growth beyond what physical capital and other factors such as land and capital could. It takes education to build the labor skill. It takes education to achieve the technological breakthrough that increases output beyond normal skills. Invariably, education's effectiveness in reducing and eliminating poverty in line with the human capital and new growth theories happens with the application of knowledge. The central message is that mere physical and human capital accumulation, increased enrolment in education and education policy changes, which Africans have done, cannot just bring the vast growth, over time, in output per person, needed to develop an economy (Romer 2003, 28).

Also, the introductory micro-level analogy on taking education and development together with an individual is to be replicated on a macro-level in looking at education in Africa with respect to answering questions on achieving and sustaining Africa's development. Ideally, when more people (and households) in an economy are able to have more access to information and apply it, it is likely[1] to translate to growth and, consequently, development.

In essence, education policies that affect the 'quantity and quality of labor' should affect the incomes of individuals and consequently the national output, reducing the poverty gap. The application of positive realistic changes in not just quantity but quality education should significantly reflect positively in the developing economies' poverty reduction efforts.

Specifically, the discourse aims to provide a solution on 'How to make education in Africa effective to drive development for the continent.' In doing so, it is pertinent to understand the themes; development, growth, human capital, education and poverty reduction while exploring the link among them with respect to African countries' experiences. Subsequently, the history, core and contemporary issues in education in the continent are recapped. Expectedly, the analyses of the issues guided the proffering of a conclusive solution to the quest.

Linking Development, Growth, Human Capital, Education and Poverty Reduction

Our world is, all the more, becoming globalized such that cultural, social, political and economic experiences are becoming somewhat unified. This is in the sense that humans, the world over, are all the more learning from and living with similar experiences with just, so to say, a very insignificant difference. Humans are the same in basic features of living. We all breathe and eat to live and also seek to live and adapt to our environment. As individuals and countries we all desire growth. We all engage our human capital for productivity. We all receive a form of education in our lifetime. The themes mean virtually the same to all humankind; only the means, the approach and the depth of seeking growth, using human capital, getting educated and certain gestures may vary with cultures and economies. For instance, what the Africans made as objects of worship kept in sacred places, their Western colonial masters made objects or artefacts viewed in the museums for socioeconomic and intellectual purposes. While to an African and a Jew, the use of the left hand to give and receive gifts matters, to some other cultures it means nothing. In Africa, looking straight into the eyes of an elder may be interpreted as rude and disrespectful; the Western cultures see it as a sign of speaking with confidence and telling the truth. This is usually due to the concerns and depths in beliefs, social and cultural understanding, experiences, purposes and available information each has.

However, we seek to live with one another beyond our communities, states and countries. We have nations and continents coming together to be guided by the same

[1] Not all growth might mean development when it is not (re)distributed. An economy can record a substantial growth in its GDP while both inequality in income and poverty remain or increase.

rules and even unified laws as sought by world organizations such as the United Nations (UN), the World Bank, the Economic Community of West African States (ECOWAS) Commission and several other multinational organizations.

These are all efforts in integrating living, investing in people and resources to meet the challenges of globalization (Cammack 2004, 192), making living more meaningful and better, which every rational individual and country desires. It is a result of information, which as earlier said enables making the most of options. For instance, some Africans gave a spiritual interpretation to having twins, saw it as evil and so killed such children. However, their encounter with Western/Christian missionary educationist, Mary Slessor, made them learn the scientific explanation (cell division) to it. Today the Africans cherish multiple births. African indigenous education accepts physical discipline like gentle smacking for children. Western education discourages it. Yet, some ongoing research and debate are revisiting the issue and advocating for that. This is likely to lead to reform in discipline if given a conclusive stance in the future. In this way, people relearn and improve life issues over time, which become a way of life.

We keep learning and evolving education in order to live better. It is inherent in humans to consciously or unconsciously learn by theorizing, following the observation of their environment. Theories often incorporate facts, laws and tested hypotheses that with time become beliefs that guide peoples' living. They form a supposition or a system of ideas to explain and surmount life challenges. This goes on, a continuous process, and is one of the features of education.

Given these, the link among the themes follows. This will guide the analysis of education in Africa and provide answers to the fundamental questions sought by this discourse.

Development and Growth

While development is variously defined, it has a general connotation of all-round growth—increase and strength—in virtually everything. With reference to a country's development, it readily suggests big and strong economic status alongside that of other spheres; the cultural, political and social spheres of the country. *Sensu lato*, it is usually talked about alongside growth. *Sensu stricto*, it is often discussed through growth. This is not surprising since development is achieved through a process of accumulated and sustained growth.

Unlike the economists' point of view, some other definitions of it do not necessarily point to development as different from growth. They seem to be used interchangeably. However, despite the complexity surrounding the definition, in analyzing development as all-round growth, abundant literature on various fields of knowledge focuses majorly on economic factors with an emphasis on macroeconomic data. For instance, the book, *Growth and Development in West Africa*, which contains a discussion on the terms 'growth' and 'development' by a collection of African researchers in various fields such as psychology, sociology, philosophy, economics, anthropology and geography, essentially used economic data and aligned their subject analysis to economic growth. In the call for contributions for this book, *The Development of Africa: Issues, Diagnoses and Prognoses*, which sought to have researchers from various disciplines explore the depth and breadth of Africa's development trajectories and provide practical solutions to achieving development in Africa, references were mostly on economic and growth data to project the book's title and research relevance.

Hence, to narrow down the complexity, this discourse will use 'growth' in approaching development. Development is a sustained stage of growth with reduced poverty. It takes a sustained and distributed growth to reduce and/or eliminate poverty. As further established by the World Bank (2007), economic growth is a clear marker of development. Invariably, reduced and/or eliminated poverty is a state of development.

Many theories have been propounded on growth following the foremost establishment of land, labor, capital and entrepreneurship as factors of production that influence economic growth. In a concise treatment of the popular theories of economic growth:

Nwuzor (in ECOWAS 2015) notes that all the theories including other means of growth such as trade openness, the international flow of financial resources, foreign finance and investment and so on build on the foremost established factors. None of the theories is necessarily new. Rather, each merely emphasized, at a particular time and for a particular challenge, the application of a particular factor in a different way to sustain growth given the limits found in other factors. Our life challenges, noted earlier, from early to modern humans, are the same. It is only the means of surmounting them that change. In essence, what Africa needs to attain growth will require emphasis on applying certain option(s) differently. The solution is neither beyond its reach nor magical.

Human Capital and Education

Recent growth theories accord a large role to human capital. Human capital is the skill found in labor, which is a factor of production. It is a stock of knowledge and skill embodied in the population of an economy acquired through informal and/or formal experiences and training that make individuals and societies productive.

According to Lucas's (1988) model, everything else – capital, output – adjusts endogenously to the accumulation of human capital, the factor that drives growth. Thus, every other factor is enhanced depending on the extent of human capital. It takes human capital to make good use of land, physical capital and technology. The more developed human capital becomes, the more room there is to manipulate [vary] ideas (technical expertise) and to enhance the performance of land, capital, entrepreneurial and all other growth resources. This obviously suggests investing in human capital to enhance productivity and growth.

In the imitation model of Rivera-Batiz and Romer (1990), human capital drives the imitation of technology, which ultimately determines the speed of convergence to the technological frontier (Pissarides 2000). Technical knowledge, which new growth theory projects, is enhanced through increased training and learning. It is what human capital relies on to achieve increased differences (variations) in output, which all other factors of production fail to do given their fixed, incapable nature to keep *multiplying* (not just increasing, but rather exceptional addition in quantity and quality) output.

So far, the words 'information', 'training', 'instruction', 'observation', 'learning', 'knowledge' and 'technology' keep recurring. Inarguably, they all are required in improving human capital and are attributes of education. Education links up with human capital. Gary Becker, Mark Blaug and many others on human capital theory assert that education creates skills, which facilitate higher levels of productivity amongst those who possess them in comparison with those who do not. Correspondence theory further implies that increasing levels of schooling in the labor force is likely to be functional to the process of employment growth. Increasing employment will increase income, which should reduce poverty.

Skill acquisition and improved knowledge, the practical application of which is technology, are gained through informal and formal education. Education comprises information, training, instruction, observation and learning applied for a better living, and relates directly to human capital and vice versa. Hence, in order to avoid a separate repetitive treatment of education, the next section looks at education in connection with growth, development and poverty reduction.

Education, Growth, Development and Poverty Reduction

Education is defined as learning through a 'process' of deliberate informal (unorganized and occurring through the family, peer group, mass media, religious bodies) and formal (organized and occurring through the school) settings. It is a 'product' of what one receives and a 'discipline' of a systematic body of knowledge. In this sense, education is intended to act with people in order to bring out or develop their potential, which implies quality education that should translate into a range of personal, communal and developmental benefits (Dewey 1916) including a learnt orderly behavior (Nwuzor and Ocho 1988). It aims at the all-round development of individuals and society.

Sustained growth, as earlier pointed out, connotes an all-round development. Thus, education and growth are factors in development. Education is a means of poverty reduction. The relationship of education to growth, which brings poverty reduction, is set in the links that human capital theory draws between education and poverty. In essence, influencing (investment in) education (of humans) influences growth such that continued growth results in poverty reduction and the development of individuals and the economy as a whole. Conversely, the poverty of individuals and an economy as a whole poses a constraint on their education. This throws a big challenge to the mostly poor African economies. Growth also requires monitoring because some growths may not result in increased welfare for the poor. Some rather increase the poverty gap among the population. Effectively reducing poverty requires good and *exceptional* work given the constraint that it could face at the expense of growth.

Having linked the themes to enable the approach of using the facts of human capital, labor and new growth theory to achieve the aim of the discourse, the effort now explores issues in making education effective.

Making Education Effective in Bringing Development

Education is effective in bringing development, as over the past decades several studies such as that of Schultz (1961), Psacharopoulos (1994) and the World Bank (1995), as well as the Asian Tigers' experience, have proved. The challenge is how to make it effective in developing Africa. The compelling issues in making education effective in bringing development are discussed in the following sections:

Education Quantity, Quality and Demand

The trend in the literature is the debates beyond the issue of the quantity or amount of schooling. Enrollment in education could generally increase without increasing the output. In a survey by Colclough (1994), it was found that some extremely poor African countries, such as Lesotho, Madagascar and Togo, have primary gross enrolment ratios in excess of 100%. Yet they are still poor. Such a record has shifted emphasis to the quality of schooling, the institutional framework in which the education takes place and, more recently, the utility in terms of the outcome of education. This refers to the issue of the applicability and effectiveness of skills that are purported to be acquired through education. In this regard, high-quality education is not always effective. For instance, poor families are not only 'sensitive to cost' and quality but are also interested in the utility they get from education. The poor have agriculture (small farmers and farm workers), crafts, trades and small trading businesses (informal sector) as their primary source of income. Instruction that does not prepare these people for these activities can seem superfluous (Morrisson 2002).

Education, Physical Capital, Infrastructural and Institutional Set-Up

The World Bank (1995, 3) states that education alone will not generate growth but rather requires investment in other factors such as physical capital and infrastructure. In a similar notion, the environment external to the learning system may be unconducive to the application of some acquired skills and so the people concerned are not able to lift themselves from poverty. The dearth of complementary investments in electricity and other infrastructure and persistent civil strife affect the outcome of education.

Given these, the next section recaps and analyses education in Africa. It does so with respect to the issues of debate in making education effective in bringing development.

A Recap on History and Contemporary Issues in Education in Africa

Education is a universal phenomenon, a general feature of human life (Nwuzor et al. 2010). It is our everyday activities and experiences, within or outside of both home and classroom, through which we unconsciously or consciously, informally or formally acquire knowledge for application in our living. This discourse stresses that education requires the 'application' of learnt skills and behaviors. Rationally, we all seek to acquire knowledge of what is 'good'. While 'good' may differ with individuals and among people, it is suggestive of what is 'positive' and 'beneficial'. Education is, and gives, what is generally accepted.

The history of education in Africa, like that of any other country, dates back to its early life. The early humans wherever they existed were predominantly agriculturists. By natural instinct, they learnt to adapt and lived in their environment. They consciously and unconsciously transferred the knowledge about their environment to their offspring by direct observation, guidance, participation, exploration and discovery. They evolved their activities and occupation following their discoveries and experiences.

Humans, being rational with the changing social structure, evolved education from the preliterate form to proto-literate education around 3000–1800 BC. At that point, nomadic hunting moved to a more settled life in agriculture as the dominant occupation of humanity. As accounted by Fafunwa and Aisiku (1982) and Nwuzor and Ocho (1988), African countries like all other countries of the world had predominantly used informal education. This was from the Stone Age to the preliterate (the primitive) stage of education. They were predominantly agriculturists (Faure 1972, 5; Nwuzor et al. 2010; Nwuzor and Ocho 1988) who produced mostly at subsistence level like every other early human.

Much later, the emerging economic, political, religious and social forces could no longer sustain an informal education process alone (Nwuzor and Ocho 1988). Humans began to leave impressions on the walls of caves. This brought the development of temples as forerunners of schools and also marked the beginnings of reckoning, writing and seeking a means of livelihood beyond one's immediate environment and the search for converts to beliefs.

Records show that Mesopotamia and Egypt (an African country) were notably among the earliest civilizations to have organized education through their temples. Temples served as agents of control over society and its institutions. Organized education was also seen with the emergence of the oriental schools, and with the

Jews, the Greeks, the Western, Christian and Islamic education that to date education, both informal and formal, have deepened in their scope, breadth, discipline and modifications in curriculum and methodology, all in an effort by humanity to live better with its environment.

In primitive times, most of Africa had no documented records.[2] While there were no primitive documented records, people developed and worked with theories in virtually all spheres of their life. This is evident in their rich social, cultural, political and religious set-up, which adopted certain rules and practices. They also relied and still rely on proverbs and wise sayings, which guided their living in much the same way as modern theories guide humans' living today.

For the majority of Africans, education took place through observation, storytelling, instruction and participating in domestic, social, cultural and religious activities. Neither a particular time nor place was needed. Africans have similar features in living. They value their culture, family, communal life and health. They mostly believe in a Supreme Being, gods and spirits. These are reflected in and guide their indigenous education content, which is:

- **Vocational training—**agriculture, trade, craft, family crafts, secret and religious organizations, priesthood, divination, medicine and surgery
- **Moral education—**conforming to the wishes of the gods, humans and parents, and learning to respect, greet, sympathize, empathize, cooperate, tolerate and other societal values
- **Intellectual education—**learning family and local history, nature study, religious, social and political education
- **Physical education—**for physical fitness and skills development in competitive and non-competitive games such as wrestling, running, role playing, acrobatics, masquerade displays, tree climbing and dancing (Nwuzor et al. 2010).

Formal education was recorded in most of Africa when the white people came to their countries between the 1870s and 1900. The British and French colonial masters brought Western and Christian education to them. Islamic education was mostly in North Africa. Africa's indigenous education has many features in common with foreign education. They both have a given process of education, methodology, staffing, content and curriculum, discipline, apprenticeship/on-the-job learning, free and guided exploration, and targeted objectives. The objectives for both are in the main the integration of their people in the society and for human and economic development. Foreign education, however, unlike indigenous African education were distinguished as compartmentalized and more organized.

Apart from learning done at home, at church, in the mass media, and suchlike, with the increasing complexity of the society and the educational process which required special handling, school was invented (Nwuzor et al. 2010). While the

[2] In the Stone Age, virtually all humanity had no record of writing while in the primitive era (the time after the Stone Age) some people began to keep records in the form of writings with signs or letters and pictures as found on the caves. Most of Africa, apart from Egypt, have no written records of the primitive period.

formal education process is, notably, the most important form of educational process and the major form of education for promoting growth, informal education is still relevant to growth. This is because schooling alone does not mean education but is just a medium devised to carry out the process of education. The primary function of the school is to educate the society. Thus, education, including informal education, deals with society such that changes in society affect education and vice versa.

Africans adopted foreign education systems, which their colonization greatly influenced. To this day, they combine them along with their indigenous education and continue to modify and develop them through policies and reforms.

With regard to the modification, African's indigenous education, like all cultures and societies, has continually evolved and reflected the changing values and demands of the socio-political, religious, economic and global systems. Globalization has also necessitated the changes. As regards formal education, African economies have over time instituted various reforms; thus both informal and formal education change with the demands of the times.

Issues on Education in Africa

Africa instituted various education reforms such as UBE, national policies on education, and MDGs education-targeted policies, among others. All of these were in the quest to improve Africa's human capital, in essence to improve education and consequently effect an overall development. According to the ECOWAS Commission, investment in education was an integral part of each of its Poverty Reduction Strategy Papers (PRSP) and Regional Poverty Reduction Strategy (RPRS), which as their names clearly depict are projects to reduce poverty. The justification for these is established from the microeconomic level as increased education increases income and wellbeing and offers skills for greater productivity. It implies that a greater distribution of education can serve as a means for reducing poverty and income inequality on the macroeconomic level.

However, in adopting foreign education systems Africa has failed specifically to align most of their goods in relation to societal needs. For instance, most Africans adopted their colonists' language as the mode of instruction leaving their native languages undeveloped such that some are becoming extinct. Language has often been cited as one of the issues affecting schooling in Africa.

In adopting foreign education, most Africans have also jettisoned their cultural, political and religious values, merely copying the 'white people'. Learning should have a positive influence—when one learns better (efficient) ways of doing things, it is rational to drop the bad/cumbersome (inefficient) ways. However, Africans often seem to do just the opposite. Using food, a necessity of life, as an example, most Africans opt for imported foreign foods to the extent of neglecting production of the same food locally. Africa has numerous hospitals and physicians and yet many Africans seek medical assistance in foreign lands. Another instance is the *nouveau riche*; the moneybags in tropical Africa who install and turn on air conditioners to a low temperature and cover themselves with blankets to keep warm.

Nigeria, the most populous country on the continent, as well as over 90% of the other African countries, is plagued with poor power supply (World Bank 2016). For someone with, say, carpentry or hairdressing skills acquired during his/her secondary school education, applying these skills is often affected by inefficient power supply. Productivity is greatly affected by regular power failure. When power fails costs are incurred, for example paying rent and wages without having clients. This renders people vulnerable to remaining in poverty. Stopping at the secondary education level may have been a result of poverty, making the person unable to further his/her education. This micro-level illustration is analogous to the macro-level reality. Such an economy is susceptible to remaining in a poverty trap.

Poverty exposes people with a poor education to unemployment, underemployment, non-functioning institutions, poor/failed/absence of infrastructure, double-digit inflation, hunger/starvation, poor sanitation, diseases/disabilities, crime, suicide, discrimination, lower life expectancy, depression, abuse, coups, corrupt practices, terrorism, war, homelessness, migration (to seek better education and living) and many other bad effects. These factors are also the very causes of poverty (Hill 1998) and have characterized African economies. Poverty, thus, recycles poverty.

These examples readily depict Africa's underdeveloped educational systems. An effective education should promote and enhance the values, local products and services while adopting better foreign ones. To date, African education systems face a myriad of problems, which have been the same set of problems since the past five decades. These include

- lack of finance for training, remuneration of teachers and for research and development
- over-centralized control in most economies' federal set-up
- corruption and politics in university education
- poor educational environment
- the absence of moral education in schools
- strikes and student unrest
- cultism
- examination malpractice
- fall in quantity and quality in the education system and
- poverty.

This complicates the issues further. It shows that the less developed countries cannot 'just' break away from poverty. If total output is low then income is low, making for little investment in education, infrastructure and its maintenance, no reserve stock and no strong institutional set-up. There is no surplus for capital accumulation. This reduces the hopes of getting a good education, health services and infrastructure and increasing output. This causes continued deterioration of African economies, institutional failure, corruption and the poverty cycle. Yet some economies like the Asian Tigers and Botswana, an African country, despite having similar characteristics (trap) before the 1990s, have recorded and sustained growth of over 5% in their GDP. What efforts have the rest of Africa made or could make to leave their trap of these perennial problems?

An Analytical Comparison of Means to Growth Through Education

The possibility of leaving the trap is through the technological innovation advocated by the new growth theory. Exceptional skills and ideas for the rapid technological innovation and adaptation needed for growth come from research and development, an important aspect of education, which yield ideas of doing everyday tasks better. Ideas translate into multiplied, improved and limitless productivity where factors of production may have been limited by their ordinary capacity to sustain increased output.

Education should also inculcate a positive change and discipline in the people who receive it. This enables dogged adherence to applying ideas and strong will against practices that inhibit individual and societal growth. It was discipline in the management of institutions and social cohesion that enabled Asian Tigers and Botswana to consistently apply sound macroeconomic ideas (policies) that promote rural development and prudent investment in basic education and health (ADB 2017; Cammack 2004). This implies that the performance of education is very much determined by the existing structure of the society's institutions.

Hence, this discourse considers the foremost concern of Africa's education to be not about the subjects. Notably, Africa has very similar subjects to the subjects included in the foreign education they adopted. Many Africans who completed their secondary education in Africa and did undergraduate and graduate courses in Western and developed countries have not only seen the same subjects but have also performed excellently. Africa has also undergone several reforms to improve the content and focus of subjects. For instance, Nigeria's National Policy on Education has interesting implications designed to enable a secondary school leaver to make a living if he/she is not able to go on to higher education. It emphasizes mathematics to develop numeracy skill; English as a language option to communicate ideas; and reinforced (building laboratories for) vocational subjects such as agriculture, introductory technology and home economics. However, many leave school without these achieved. Indeed, many of those who, obtained higher education remain jobless and cannot create jobs due to the failure of the system to use education to make them creative, disciplined and able to reserve capital to fund available investment ideas.

Moreover, and regrettably, in the Organization for Economic Co-operation and Development (OECD) 2009 World Ranking on education, Tunisia was the only African country that made the list on reading, maths and science scores and even that country recorded below average scores. On the UN database (http://data.uis.unesco.org/), as at January 2017, apart from South Africa which has data for 2001–2014, the rest of Africa has scant data (two to five-year period) for education attainment of ages above 25 years and incomplete data over the years for subject performance. Hence there is inadequate data to make a conclusive quantitative subject analysis. This is a concern as data is needed for research, development and planning.

This informs the option for a qualitative issue analysis. This is done by conducting a comparative view of the past and present status of African and foreign education with respect to the new growth theory. Like growth theories discussed in the Development and Growth subheading of this discourse, education systems (see Table 6.1) evolved over time with different regions adopting and/or influencing systems of others. The objective of education remains the same for all humankind with slight differences in approach and coverage depth.

Indigenously, African economies exhibited popular growth theories in their productive activities. Historical accounts show that Africans, in the primitive era and to date, had people in certain geographic locations known for one form of production; agriculture, trade, crafts and religious professions. They also had roles allocated to them, given their understanding of gender capabilities, where the females did less strenuous work and the males the more strenuous work. This, obviously, is specialization and division of labor.

They also went as far as reinvesting their productive capital. Despite being predominantly subsistent agriculturists, they did not consume all their produce but kept some of it and replanted/bred (reinvested) it in subsequent seasons. They also continually sought to increase and improve the human capital invested in production. This is evident in the intermarriages and polygamy practiced by many Africans, the reasons being to repopulate (increase) the workforce needed for their farms and trades. Learning socioeconomic, cultural and religious values by observation and participation, despite their informal approaches, improved the skills of its people from childhood to adolescence when people take on greater responsibility, contributing to society starting with their families. Some bought and used slaves, and warlords expanded their territories to add human capital to their workforce and took up more land to add to their physical capital, all making for more resources to pursue growth.

While some of these practices—slavery, wars, conquests and taking other peoples' territory—are amoral, they have the attributes of the capitalist and communal approaches/theories to wealth production. Right from the primitive age, African economies practiced the conclusion of the Human Development Report, 2010, which emphasized human capital, pointing out that "[p]eople are the real wealth of nations." Africans reckon in their various languages that 'a collection of people is strength'. In essence, Africans have never been oblivious to the fact that how differently (variedly) one works determines the level of output. However, the extent and magnitude of application of that consciousness is the extent of growth, the core concern.

Indigenous African education was functional. The curriculum, despite not being formerly compartmentalized like the colonial Western/foreign systems, was relevant to the needs of society (Fafunwa and Aisiku 1982; Moumouni 1968). With the adoption of foreign education, which has the same objective as Africa's indigenous education, the expected improvement in the overall development seems to have eluded Africa. Some African economies such as Botswana, Algeria and recently, in 2014, Nigeria, have recorded up to 5% growth in their GDP. However, the performance in terms of improving their living standards is poor. This means that, even for those countries that have shown a reasonable growth rate, like the 5% recommended

Table 6.1 World education that directly influenced African education

Region/Type	System	Objective	Curriculum	Method of teaching/ learning	Agent	Evaluation
African	**Pre-colonial** **Indigenous** Informal, not compartmentalized	Formative effect on the way one thinks, feels and acts, targeted from childhood Integrate one with the society, and with modern direction of living with the world as a whole Formative effect on the way one thinks, feels and acts Integrate one with the society formative effect on the way one thinks, feels and acts integrate one with the society	Everyday living: Moral, vocational, intellectual, religious, social studies, science & technology Emphasize skillfulness and good character	Observation, instruction, storytelling, participation, exploration, experiment	Parents, relatives, elders, peers, skilled ones in various vocation, priests/ spiritual guides	Agents' oral approval, society's honor and investiture (with title)
	Postcolonial **Indigenous/foreign/ Western** Informal and formal		Indigenous plus foreign formal content Emphasize intellectualism	Indigenous plus foreign methods	Indigenous plus foreign education agents	Indigenous plus foreign education evaluation
Western/foreign	**British** Formal **French** Formal		Everyday living: Classified subject areas; maths, English, French, reading etc. emphasize intellectualism	Majorly schooling plus emphasis on technology and industry	Majorly trained teachers (as instructors) and in classroom, majorly state controlled	English/ French influenced by the Greeks'
Religious	**Christian** Formal **Islamic** Formal		Emphasize belief in god, the trinity and learning the Bible Emphasize belief in Allah and learning the Koran	Influenced by the Romans' Methods Influenced by the Greeks' methods	Trained priests, missionaries in church/classroom Imams in mosque/ classroom	Reflect roman approaches that influenced modern education
The world as a whole	**Stone age** **Indigenous/informal** No specific time/place, interplayed in everyday living activities, not compartmentalized **Proto-literate** **Indigenous/formal** Early alphabets, the oldest found with **Mesopotamia** and **Egypt**		Everyday living: with early humans predominantly agriculturists	Observation, instruction, storytelling, participation, exploration, experiment	Parents, relatives, elders, peers, skilled ones in various vocation, priests/ spiritual guides	Oral approval and recognition in the society

	Greek (and the **oriental;** Babylon, Egypt, Assyria, Persia, China, India and the Jews)		Indigenous, plus introduction of writing and reading (the beginning of reckoning)	Indigenous methods plus writing and reading in an organized gathering of scribes, thinkers, philosophers and scholars in the temple, city square, hall and then classroom	Indigenous agents plus those who are seen as wise thinkers and scribes and controlled majorly by the state and recognized institutions The emergent of schools	Written, oral and practical tests, at specified times/places with awarded marks, honors, certification and/or move to other levels of education and vocation in the case of religious education
	Roman (colonized by the Greeks) **Modern** **Formal/indigenous:** Romans and Greeks influence led to **Western civilization** and **modern** day education embraced the world over		Birth of educational disciplines; sociology, psychology, curriculum, astrology, methodology Emphasized oratorical and military training	Inherited Greco-Roman methods that influenced Western education plus research & development	Majorly trained teachers/skilled persons as instructors, mostly in classroom and by correspondence, online and media	Mostly the Western education evaluation approach
			Emphasized mentally and physically well balanced individuals			
			Indigenous plus reading, writing and numeracy skills with emphasis on technology and globalization			

by the World Bank to attain development, the achieved growths were not fairly (re) distributed in the economies and even not sustained. If both the Asian economies and Botswana, which adopted the same system, have succeeded in sustaining growth from the 1990s, then Africa should look at the conscious implementation of its education policies, which greatly helped the Asian Tigers and Botswana.

To summarize, the discourse on growth theories alongside issues on African education, which analyzed Africa's inability to effectively use education to create and apply ideas to match the challenges of globalization, explain the cycle of poverty in African countries. Their perennial problems are mostly a result of corruption. Corruption led to the mismanagement of their resources. It brought incompetent and unqualified personnel and soldiers, who interfere(d) with and mismanage(d) education; even the low funds allocated for education are embezzled (Nwuzor 2002). This has greatly affected education administration, effectiveness and consequently the development of Africa.

Conclusions

Nothing is necessarily new on the face of the earth. All humanity seeks to live well and in harmony. The means for living well change over time and/or with people. Thus with the developed economies reinforcing their modern education, which emphasizes technology and the increasing inclination towards globalization and the experiences of the Asian Tigers and Botswana, education is unquestionably critical for African development. It takes education to generate the required technical knowledge in all spheres of knowledge and living. The current state of education in Africa, however, given the problems of education in Africa listed in the section of this work that discussed Issues on Education in Africa, is not fit to drive development.

It is time Africa moved from the idea that a collection of people is strength to the development of actual strength and the application of technical knowledge for the collective individuals. Skill enhancement should not just be for the arts and sciences or for white-collar jobs but also for the carpenter, cook, hairdresser, mason, mechanic, shoemaker and tailor, to spur their productivity and creativity. Technology is not just about machines but also about better ways of teaching and learning as well as simple acts of communication that yield development.

Education should not only target equipping individuals with skills to be adopted for innovation and technical progress in primary, secondary and tertiary productive education and activities. There is need for an emphasis on moral education. Education should help to make people behave positively, reject corrupt practices and engineer positive ideas.

The power of technical idea improved through education, when not undermined, as Nwuzor (2008) concluded, can drastically minimize and/or eliminate corruption, which has been one of the long-standing impediments to implementing robust education policies and Africa's development course. For instance, while teaching and 'encouraging' good morals, creativity and patriotism in children and youths, project ideas on reputable lifetime societal and intellectual awards could be engineered to positively 'entice' the inherent human inclination to self-glorification and make leaders and followers invest public funds prudently.

Curbing corruption will help the implementation of policies, some of which have the established infrastructure needed for development. While policies are fully implemented, simultaneous monitoring of their outcomes will guide further improvement of different levels of formal education and approaches to informal education and the emphasis of subjects. Otherwise, until knowledge is applied and corruption curbed, no matter how effective a growth option is, the course of Africa's development will remain a 'seeming' mystery.

References

African Development Bank (ADB). (2017). https://www.afdb.org/en/countries/southern-africa/botswana/botswana-and-the-afdb/

Cammack, P. (2004). What the World Bank means by poverty reduction, and why it matters. *New Political Economy June, 9*(2), 189–211.

Colclough, C. (1994). *Under-enrolment and low quality in African primary schooling: Towards a gender-sensitive solution* (IDS Working Paper 7). Brighton: IDS.

Deininger, K., & Okidi, J. (2003). Growth and poverty reduction in Uganda, 1999–2000: Panel data evidence. *Development Policy Review, 21*(4), 481–509.

Dewey, J. (1916). *Democracy and education: An introduction to the philosophy of education.* New York: Free Press.

ECOWAS. (2015). Growth and development in West Africa. In C. V. Nwuzor (Ed.), *Social dimensions of economic growth* (pp. 156–192). Berlin: Verlag Dr. Koster.

Fafunwa, A. B., & Aisiku, J. U. (Eds.). (1982). *Education in Africa: A comparative survey*. London: George Allen and Unwin.

Faure, E. (Ed.). (1972). *Learning to be: The world of education today and tomorrow*. Paris: UNESCO force surveys. Research Information, Department for Education and Skills, England.

Hill, L. E. (1998). The institutional economics of poverty: An inquiry into the causes and effects of poverty. *Journal of Economic Issues, 32*, 279–285.

Lucas, R. E. (1988). On the mechanics of economic development. *Journal of Monetary Economics, 22*, 3–42.

Morrisson, C. (2002). Health, education and poverty reduction. *OECD Policy Brief No. 19.*

Moumouni, A. (1968). *Education in Africa* (N. Phyllis, Trans.). London: Deutsch.

Nwaobi, G. C. (2007). *Educational [work] performance in African countries: Problems, policies and prospects*. Nigeria: Quantitative Economic Research Bureau.

Nwuzor, R. A. (2002). *Educating for democracy in Nigeria*. Enugu: Future Tech.

Nwuzor, C. V. (2008). *The effectiveness of education in the context of poverty reduction: A panel analysis with twenty-two African countries*. Unpublished MSc thesis, University of Sheffield.

Nwuzor, R. A. and Ocho, L. O. (1988). *History of education* (Revised ed.). Anambra, Nigeria: Pacific Publishers.

OECD (2009). Annual Report.

Nwuzor, R. A., Igboabuchi, B. O., & Ilorah, B. C. (2010). *Education in Nigeria: A historical account* (Revised ed.). Onitsha: Lincel.

Pissarides, C. (2000). *Labour markets and economic growth in the MENA region*. Princeton: Global Development Network.

Psacharopoulos, G. (1994). Returns to investment in education: A global update. *World Development, 22*, 1325–1343.

Rayfield, J.R. 1983. *The legacy of colonialism in education in West Africa.*. Mimeo paper. Toronto: York University.
Rivera-Batiz, L. A., & Romer, P. M. (1990). Economic integration and endogenous growth. *The Quarterly Journal of Economics, 106*(2), 531–555.
Romer, D. (2003). *Advanced macroeconomics* (4th ed.). New York: McGraw-Hill.
Schultz, T. P. (1961). Investment in human capital. *The American Economic Review.*
Stroombergen, A., Rose, D., & Nana, G. (2002). *Review of the statistical measurement of human capital, infometrics.* New Zealand: Consulting Limited.
World Bank. (1995). *World development report: Workers in an integrating world.* Geneva: World Bank.
World Bank. (2007). *World development report: Development and the next generation.* Geneva: World Bank.
World Bank. (2016). *World development report: Digital dividends.* Geneva: World Bank.

Chizoba Vivian Nwuzor is a teacher, and the Chief Executive Officer of Ann's Indulgence Limited, a research and events management consultancy. She worked with Economic Community of West African States (ECOWAS) Commission as a research staff. She enjoys tennis, ideation (especially adapting education and economics principles for solutions to everyday problems) and contributing to Africa's development. She is a member of American Economic Association (AEA). She holds a master's degree in economics from The University of Sheffield, United Kingdom. She obtained her first degree in economics from Nnamdi Azikiwe University, Nigeria, where she is pursuing a PhD in development economics.

Chapter 7
The Land Question, Agriculture, Industrialization and the Economy in Zimbabwe: A Critical Reflection

Busani Mpofu

Introduction

The land question in Zimbabwe is very relevant in understanding agricultural, industrialization and economic trajectories, and the prospects and challenges of development in Africa. Common narratives and interpretations of Africa's development and underdevelopment hinge on the roles of agriculture and industrialization in the economy. At the same time, the land question has become the most important factor in the agricultural performance of Zimbabwe since the 1998 land occupations. Thus, this chapter adopts the Zimbabwean realities and experience relative to land, agriculture, industrialization and economy to theoretically and pragmatically interrogate Africa's development issues. This is important as many accounts of development are centered on the state of the economy and many African economies are still agrarian based. This chapter therefore seeks to understand the interface between land reform, agriculture, industrialization and the economy in Zimbabwe, especially since the beginning of the 2000 Fast Track Land Reform Programme (FRLRP). In the process, it seeks to invoke more debate on the following questions: Can land reform and agriculture drive the economic development of Zimbabwe? Can agriculture lead the industrial paths in Zimbabwe? What is the state of agriculture and industrialization in Zimbabwe? What is the missing link in the economy and can agriculture and industrialization reconnect the severed chain of Zimbabwe's development? What is the state of Zimbabwe's economy and the role of agriculture and industrialization? Are there specific Zimbabwean issues that can drive home the points and trajectories of Africa's development? What are the prospects and challenges in Zimbabwe's development? What are the policy issues and what are the solutions? What lessons can be drawn from the Zimbabwean type of development?

B. Mpofu (✉)
Archi Mafeje Research Institute, University of South Africa (UNISA), Pretoria, South Africa
e-mail: Mpofub@unisa.ac.za

O. Akanle, J.O. Adésìnà (eds.), *The Development of Africa*, Social Indicators Research Series 71, DOI 10.1007/978-3-319-66242-8_7

This is because apart from ordinary Zimbabweans citizens, who have borne the major effects of the country's economic decline since 2000, there have been widespread negative regional economic and political repercussions.

What Is the State of Zimbabwe's Economy and the Role of Agriculture and Industrialization?

Spontaneous land invasions protesting the government's failure to implement meaningful land reform occurred in June 1998, and were hijacked by some veterans of Zimbabwe's liberation war and other government supporters in 2000 when they began invading farms owned by white farmers and forced them off the land. The government immediately followed in with the FRLRP in February 2001 (Mlambo 2014, 236). The ruling ZANU PF party argued that the land invasions were meant to consolidate economic independence as part of the Third *Chimurenga*[1] (Mlambo 2005; Tendi 2010, 73–107), hence the Government's slogan, "The land is the economy: The economy is the land" (Mlambo 2005, 1). So if 'the land is the economy: the economy is the land', what impact did the land reform have on the economy?

The FRLRP severed the strong supply linkages between commercial agriculture and manufacturing, and industrial production collapsed (Timmer 2016). Farm invasions and the violence that accompanied them had far-reaching socioeconomic and political effects that consequently made the country a pariah state in the international community (Mlambo 2014, 236). For example, in 2001 and 2002 the US and the EU respectively imposed 'targeted' sanctions against key individuals in the Zimbabwe African National Union-Patriotic Front *(*ZANU-PF) accused of human rights abuses. These measures, according to Mlambo and Raftopoulos (2010), combined with the cessation of Zimbabwe's relations with the international financial institutions since the late 1990s, effectively cut the Zimbabwean government off from any development assistance other than humanitarian aid. The invasions severed the economy by disrupting normal agricultural activity and eventually ruining the agricultural sector. Since agriculture had always been the backbone of the country's economy and the major foreign currency earner, apart from the heavy reliance of the local manufacturing sector on agriculture, the damage was immediate and catastrophic (Mlambo and Raftopoulos 2010, 8).

As most of the manufacturing industries were dependent on the agricultural sector for inputs and markets, its collapse had numerous negative ripple effects throughout the national economy. The effects included factory closures, declining outputs and foreign currency earnings and massive unemployment (Mlambo and Raftopoulos

[1]The Third *Chimurenga* was thus seen as a further advancement of the struggle, but this time to achieve economic independence. The term *Chimurenga*/Umvukela refers to the African armed uprisings that occurred in resistance to colonial rule in Zimbabwe. The First Chimurenga/Umvukela occurred in 1896, while the Second occurred from the 1960s to 1979.

2010, 3). That is, the decline in agricultural production crippled milling companies, bakeries, leather goods manufacturers, clothing and textile manufacturers and other industries that relied on agricultural products. In December 2002, for example, the Confederation of Zimbabwe Industries (CZI) reported that 400 companies had shut down in 2000, leading to a loss of 10,000 jobs. One hundred manufacturers had been liquidated by 2001, with 3500 jobs lost in the process. In November 2002, the CZI reported that 540 engineering companies had to reduce their workforce to minimize operational costs because of a shrinking demand for their products due to the disruption in the agricultural sector (Mlambo 2014, 236–237).

By 2008, the Zimbabwe economy had almost totally crumbled. According to Mlambo and Raftopoulos (2010, 3):

> [I]nflation rates were estimated in percentages of hundreds of millions, with the country's currency, now denominated in quintillions, becoming virtually worthless. Indeed, by 2007, per capita GDP was estimated at $200, compared to $900 in 1990, while over 80% of the Zimbabwean population was reported in 2005 to be living on less than $2 a day. Exports, which in 1997 had accounted for 33.5% of the country's GDP, were worth only 9.9% of the GDP in 2007. Unemployment at 2008 stood at 90%... According to the World Bank, Zimbabwe had "the world's fastest shrinking economy for a country not at war".

Zimbabwe is currently suffering from what Tony Hawkins has described as "premature de-industrialisation". The country's manufacturing sector expanded in the 1960s and 1970s when the colonial government of Prime Minister Ian Smith imposed blanket import controls to counter mandatory UN economic sanctions after its unilateral declaration of independence in 1965. These boosted the local import substitution industrialization pursued by the Smith government. The manufacturing industry accounted for 22% of GDP at the peak of the 'sanctions boom' in the mid-1970s, climaxing to 27% at the start of the 1990s, 10 years after independence (Hawkins 2014).

Currently, Zimbabwe has become a basket case in Africa as it is increasingly relying on food aid and imports to feed its population. For example, by November 2002, it was reported that more than 6 million people in the country were in need of food aid and the country was no longer able to produce for export to earn the much needed foreign currency (Mlambo 2014, 237). And history shows that no country has ever mounted a successful development program while dependent on food aid (Timmer 2016). Writing in 1991, Samir Amin argued that the African state in general faced the dilemma of economic development characterized by an urbanization crisis and mass unemployment, agricultural stagnation, soil deterioration, famines and massive imports of food products, among others (Amin 1991, 554). These same challenges have festered now, including in Zimbabwe. Worse still, it is widely believed that no further stage of development can be considered before Africa has started an agricultural revolution. The general rural–urban migration in Africa is not due to overpopulation caused by some agricultural progress, but migration in search of greener pastures causing an urbanization without any prospect for industrial employment (Amin 1991, 555).

What Is the Missing Link in the Economy, and Can Agriculture and Industrialization Reconnect the Severed Chain of Zimbabwe's Development?

Timmer posed the question of whether it was possible for Zimbabwe to 'destroy' its agricultural sector and still develop its economy. His answer to the above question is no, precisely because, historically, "No country has been able to sustain a rapid transition out of poverty without raising productivity in its agricultural sector." This involves a successful structural transformation whereby agriculture, through higher productivity, provides food, labor and savings that will boost urbanization and industrialization. In the end, modernized agriculture raises labor productivity, and while the importance of agriculture in the overall economy may decline, industrial and service sectors grow rapidly to boost the economy (Timmer 2016). With sufficient food supplies in world markets and with increasingly open borders for trade, what can the role of agriculture in development in Zimbabwe be? Can Zimbabwe invest in agriculture to feed its population or can it invest to produce for the world through the economies of scale to earn foreign currency? As the Chief Executive Officer of Dairibord Holdings Limited, Anthony Mandiwanza, rightly argues, Zimbabwean companies should strive to produce for export to boost liquidity in the economy and to create jobs, as concentrating on supplying the domestic market only has very limited prospects of improving the Zimbabwean economy which is relatively small and not competitive at the moment (Ndlovu 2016a).

The immediate objective of Zimbabwe's land reform was not increased productivity, but transfer of ownership. As a result, the success of the land reform, according to the government, was to be measured in terms of the transfer of ownership in the short term; increased production was to be attended to in the long term (Tekere et al. n.d.). It is this long-term objective that has now become the government's Achilles' heel. Maximizing agricultural production and productivity is the missing link in the re-industrialization efforts that are crucial for the revival of the economy. This is because if production is low, companies across all the value chains in the agricultural sector are automatically affected in terms of their manufacturing capacity (Kazunga 2016). Barclays Zimbabwe Managing Director George Guvamatanga called for the setting up of minimum production levels for landholders so that agriculture can reclaim the position it occupied before 2000 as the country's top foreign currency earner, as failing to do so was compromising the economy. To revive the Zimbabwean economy, Guvamatanga noted that the right thing to do is to ensure the availability of raw materials:

> The biggest issue we must do in this economy is production. Unless we want to change the model of this economy, Zimbabwe has always been agricultural driven economy … to be importing maize, wheat, beans, sweet potatoes, things that we never used to import before, … means we have not yet started doing the right things…" … we are just a non-productive lot. Some of the people who have land do not have the capacity, knowledge or commitment to produce … we have killed the agriculture value chain (Harare Bureau 2016).

Any re-industrialization prospects in Zimbabwe are dependent on a robust agricultural revolution. CZI President, Busisa Moyo, argued that "[o]ur industries rest on the bedrock of agricultural production, without agricultural output there are no industries to talk about" (Business Reporter 2016). The Zimbabwe Revenue Authority (ZIMRA) also believes that the economic recovery of Zimbabwe lies in the farming sector. According to the ZIMRA board chair, Willia Bonyongwe, the country's economy is based on agriculture, its economic recovery "will always lie in this sector", as such any increase in agricultural production will boost industrial capacity and commercial activity (Business Editor 2016a). As a result, in 2016, the CZI, under its theme for the congress of the year, 'Strengthening value chains for sustainable industrialization and economic development', identified 18 value chains that needed to be prioritized to revive the country's economy. A number of them are linked to the agricultural sector, including the cotton clothing, beef to leather, juice to can, horticultural farm to juice value chain and the fish to fork, among others (Business Reporter 2016).

What Are the Challenges in Zimbabwe's Development? Factors Behind Low Agricultural Production

The unresolved land question, the worst excesses of political patronage and land grabbing, unutilized farms, lack of funding and security of tenure issues all contribute to low agricultural production in resettlement areas. Since the land occupations in 1998 and the eventual evictions of most white commercial farmers in Zimbabwe that followed, the country has been experiencing very low agricultural production that cannot sustain the revival of the manufacturing sector in the medium term at least. Currently, agricultural production is affected by a number of factors which are highlighted below.

Since 2000, there has been no political will within the national government to redress the imbalances of the land grab and the ruling party political elites still use land for patronage purposes. Strong political cronyism has been at the forefront of resisting a much needed genuine land audit to reduce the worst excesses of political patronage and land grabbing, as well as new legislation to forestall land acquisition by elites through corrupt processes, and the setting up of an independent land commission (Mpofu 2011a, 673–675; Scoones et al. 2010, 241). This, together with the initial refusal by the government of Zimbabwe to compensate evicted white farmers, has contributed to security of tenure disputes and lack of funding, making it difficult to promote sustainable production on the distributed farms. As a result, the current Reserve Bank of Zimbabwe (RBZ) Governor John Mangudya, when addressing the 75th annual congress of the Zimbabwe Farmers Union, argued that Zimbabweans needed to separate politics from farming, saying: "We need to remove politics from farming if we are to re-energize the sector: Zimbabweans tend to mix the two." Mangudya added that the country does not need thousands of farmers to feed itself and produce a surplus, which could be exported; but only "need[s] about 2000 serious farmers who are adequately funded to produce food for the country at just 1000 hectares each" (Manicaland Correspondent 2015).

Governor Mangudya also highlighted that the country had a lot of farms which were lying idle because of what he termed 'a culture of laziness on the farms' and the abuse of the government's free input scheme whereby seed, fertilizer and implements supplied by the state are often quickly resold for quick cash by the new farmers. As a result, Zimbabwe's fields were 'brown with weeds and grass.' On top of that, new farmers who accessed credit lines from the government or banks often refuse to repay loans. According to Governor Mangudya, agriculture can only recover in the country if new farmers operated like entrepreneurs with better planning. As an example of poor agricultural practices, he highlighted that during the 2014–15 agricultural season, the government provided \$60 million, micro financial institutions provided about \$9.4 million, contract farming provided \$24 million and \$48 million was provided by other partners and NGOs. But in the end, farmers failed to produce harvests that could feed the country (Manicaland Correspondent 2015).

Governor Mangudya advocated that Zimbabwe needed a new land policy with a clear 'use it or lose it' emphasis (Manicaland Correspondent 2015). This was also reiterated by the Deputy Minister of Agriculture, Mechanisation and Irrigation Development, Davis Marapira, who stated that the government is currently crafting a 'use or lose it policy' to make it mandatory for authorities to repossess and redistribute underutilized land. Marapira argued that if every farmer who benefited from the land redistribution exercise were utilizing his or her land the country would not be having a deficit necessitating the importation of maize now (Chitumba 2015).

The official concern that some beneficiaries of land redistribution were not utilizing the land was first revealed by the former RBZ Governor, Gideon Gono, whose bank spearheaded the national government's quasi-economic activities to finance the FRLRP. In 2011, Governor Gono complained that the economy was littered with farms lying idle, "farms which have been turned into grasslands instead of maize lands, soya lands and so forth, yet we need to be utilising the available resources … to advance our national economic fortunes" (Nyambabvu 2011).

In March 2015, President Mugabe also highlighted that A2 farmers have been problematic as most of their farms were lying idle. He accused some A2 farmers of using land as a kind of status symbol. Mugabe noted: "We want to carry out an audit on A2 farms because some people are having farms for status. They tend to say that I have a farm; I am a farmer. But the question is what are you doing in those farms" (Harare Bureau 2015). President Mugabe also noted that farms required huge capital and good management, which many new farmers did not have, and they (farms) had just become a status symbol to many. Some resettled farmers had turned their farms into ordinary pasturelands for their cattle, which they were not even looking after (Harare Bureau 2015). In June 2015, Vice President Emmerson Mnangagwa also threatened that "[t]imes have changed. Anyone given land and doesn't utilise it, we will give warnings for three years. After three years lapse when someone has been sleeping on the land, we will ask him to go and sleep somewhere and leave the land" (Manyukwe 2015a).

The remarks by President Mugabe followed his admission previously that most resettled black farmers were ill equipped to operate viably the vast tracts of farmland they were given. In an interview with the state-owned Zimbabwe Broadcasting Corporation on 26 February to mark his 91st birthday on 21 February 2015, Mugabe noted that he thought that "the farms we gave to people are too large. They can't manage them. You find that most of them are just using one third of the land" (Interview between President Mugabe and the Zimbabwe Broadcasting Corporation, 26 February 2015).

Not surprisingly, in early March 2015, the national government announced that more than 50 resettled black farmers in the Midlands province were set to lose their land after recommendations to downsize the farms for resettlement. This was because, according to the provincial chief lands officer, Joseph Shoko, many irregularities had been discovered on the leased farms (*NewZimbabwe* 2015). In June 2015, Vice President Mnangagwa also revealed that "[t]here are people who were given farms—more than one per person, per family. We will take some and you'll be left with one … The one you're left with must be the agreed size" (Manyukwe 2015a, b).

The threat of eviction of unproductive resettled farmers and the unresolved ownership disputes raise security of tenure issues among resettled farmers. Zimbabwe Commercial Farmers Union director, Jeremiah Tevera, argued that "everybody who is a beneficiary of the land under the FRLRP is said to be on disputed land." Tevera welcomed the government's new resolve to compensate former white farmers as he felt that this move would eliminate the current land disputes, unlock the value of land and make it possible for new farmers to access loans cheaply (Gumbo 2016).

Worst Excesses of Political Patronage and Land Grabbing: Unutilized Farms

While the national government's rhetoric emphasized 'one man one farm policy' during the FRLRP, several political elites possess more than one farm, a fact that makes them resist a genuine land audit. For example, in December 2014, after former ZANU-PF Secretary for Administration and former minister in the President's Office Mutasa was sacked by the President, it was alleged that since 2005 he had allocated A2 farms illegally to his girlfriends and relatives when he was still Minister of State for National Security, Lands, Land Reform and Resettlement in the President's office. Manicaland Provincial Affairs Minister Chimene's office and other departments repossessed 12 farms that Mutasa had fraudulently allocated to white farmers who paid rent directly to him (Mazire 2015).

In 2015, the state owned *Chronicle* newspaper reported that ZANU-PF and government bigwigs who had seized vast pieces of land during the FRLRP which they were not utilizing fully were set to have their farms reduced at the beginning of June that year. Most farms exceeded the recommended sizes gazetted in different provinces. For example, in the Midlands province, a land audit committee established that more than 70 farms far exceeded the maximum recommended sizes of 500 hectares while the list of people in need of land kept growing. The Minister for Lands and Rural Resettlement, Douglas Mombeshora, also noted that about 40 farms in Mashonaland East province were set to be assessed with a view to downsizing them. Under the proposed new policy, the government will no longer issue offer letters to farm or plot holders whose land exceeded the recommended sizes set by the government for each province (Share and Musiiwa 2015). In June 2014, Minister Mombeshora also highlighted that a preliminary audit of the database of land reform beneficiaries done by his ministry revealed that some undeserving people benefited from the program and exposed the fraudulent acquisition of farms on behalf of children as one of the factors behind lack of productivity on some farms (Mugabe 2014).

The Impact of the Unresolved Land Question: Lack of Funding to Boost Agricultural Production in Resettlement Areas

Successful agricultural transformations have always been subsidized by massive state or donor funding.[2] Because of the contentious nature and lack of transparency of Zimbabwe's land reform, donors and banks have not been forthcoming to support the FRLRP. The Zimbabwe Commercial Farmers Union (ZCFU) director, Jeremiah Tevera, argued that resettled farmers found it difficult to get loans from financial institutions because the ownership of their land is still regarded as in dispute, and international financiers regarded the country as a risky investment destination. Local banks willing to offer loans charged exorbitant interest rates pegged at 23%, which is unsustainable for many farmers (Gumbo 2016). This has been exacerbated by the failure by the government so far to conduct a much needed genuine land audit.

In early 2015, Minister Mombeshora highlighted that a national land audit to address issues of multiple farm ownership and underutilized land was due to commence in April in Mashonaland East province which had been specifically targeted because of numerous anomalies in land ownership.[3] Mombeshora revealed that his

[2] White farmers became firmly established in colonial Zimbabwe because of massive national government funding between 1908 and 1914, a period dubbed as white agricultural policy; see Palmer (1977). On the success of former Zimbabwean white farmers in Nigeria, see Raufu (2011:535–561).

[3] Apparently, this is the province that President Mugabe blamed in early 2015 for continuing to harbour the highest number of white commercial farmers in the country. The President noted that these white farmers should be removed and blamed the former ZANU-PF chairperson, Mashonaland East Ray Kaukonde, for protecting them (*NewZimbabwe* 2015).

ministry had received $7 million from the European Union (EU) and the United Nations Development Program (UNDP) to carry out the program. However, by the end of August 2015 the exercise was yet to commence as the government had failed to raise the $35 million required for the exercise. This was happening at a time when there were widespread reports of illegal land sales, reports of double allocations by the Ministry of Lands and reports of vulnerable, landless people being duped by land barons (Mashonaland East Correspondent 2015). To raise the money needed for the audit, the Cabinet in 2015 approved new rentals of $3 and $2 unit tax per hectare annually for A2 farmers. A1 farmers are now obliged to pay $10 land rental and $5 unit tax per year (Share and Musiiwa 2015). The tax, according to Finance Minister Chinamasa, is one way of raising money to pay compensation to white farmers who have been evicted from their farms since 2000. ZCFU President Wonder Chabikwa reported that resettled farmers have been failing to repay the loans they accessed between 2009 and 2012 due to poor agricultural conditions and the high interest rates (as high as 35%) that banks have been charging borrowers (Kazunga 2016).

The Zimbabwe government, RBZ-sponsored farm mechanization scheme (under its quasi-fiscal activities) failed to empower the thousands of resettled small-scale peasants. For example, under this scheme, the RBZ contracted a local agro-equipment supplier, Farmtec Spares and Implements, to supply 150 tractors. Farmtec supplied 60 of the 150 tractors and billed the RBZ US$2.1 million. The RBZ, however, failed to pay Farmtec and the deal collapsed. Those tractors were not distributed to ordinary peasants. The current ZANU-PF government has since adopted the RBZ debt meaning that those who were given the tractors and for free would never pay anything (*NewZimbabwe* 2015). This is another example of why Governor Mangudya complained that some new farmers who accessed credit lines from the government or banks often refuse to repay loans. He thus argued that if agriculture is to recover in the country, the new farmers need to operate like entrepreneurs (Manicaland Correspondent 2015). In this case, the land reform is detrimental to the manufacturing sector of the economy; especially the sector that produces farming implements as the government wants to take the implements without paying for them. This could see more engineering companies imploding due to lack of demand for their products.

As a result of funding deficiencies, in March 2015, the Midlands Lands Committee resolved to spare 30 white commercial farmers from eviction, indicating that they (farmers) were contributing significantly to the province. A report by the Committee revealed that a resolution was passed to spare 16 dairy farms, seven of them in Gweru and another seven in Kwekwe and another two located in Shurugwi and Mvuma respectively. Of the 14 other white farmers that were spared eviction, 10 specialized in cattle ranching while four of them produce soya beans on a commercial scale. This was because it has been noted that “there has been a drastic decline of milk production since the beginning of the land reform programme.” The Cabinet approved that the white-owned dairy farms be spared eviction. This came after the realization that viable and sustainable dairy production required intensive and heavy capital outlays and investments and experience, which newly resettled black farmers did not have (*NewZimbabwe* 2015). Defending this logical move that appears to be a major climb-down by the Zimbabwean government, in March 2015 Minister Mombeshora argued that the government can exempt farms engaged in operations considered strategic to national development, especially those involved in dairy farming, seed producing including tobacco seed producers. According to Mombeshora, "a farmer's stay (whether black or white), may depend on the community in the province." Those farmers who fail to co-exist with others may have their farms targeted for acquisition.

In June 2015, Minister Mombeshora officially asked provincial leaders in the country to draw up a list of white farmers they wanted to remain on their farms, especially those considered to be of strategic economic importance. The farmers, according to Mombeshora, will then be given security of tenure documents to enable them to plan their operations properly (*NewZimbabwe* 2015). In another wrangle over the allocation of part of Barquest Farm owned by Mrs. Hellen Mitchell to the Minister of Tourism and Hospitality Walter Mzembi, the Masvingo Provincial Lands Committee recommended a withdrawal of the offer letter to Mzembi because the farm was considered strategic to the province as it supplied 100,000 day-old chicks a week and eggs to the Masvingo, Manicaland and Midlands provinces. The Provincial Affairs Minister, Shuvai Mahofa, argued that the provincial leadership would not allow the takeover of productive farms that benefit the majority of the population. Mahofa asked the Ministry of Lands and Rural Resettlement to identify another farm for Mzembi, but only after investigating reports that he already owned two farms including a conservancy of the outskirts of the province (Manyukwe 2015a, b; Maponga 2015).

In a case similar to the one cited above, Vice President Mphoko intervened to stop a Central Intelligence Officer (CIO) allocated a Maleme farm in February 2015 from evicting a white farmer Cunningham in Matobo, Matabeleland South province. Three traditional chiefs and hundreds of villagers opposed the taking over of the farm because it was benefitting at least 800 families, and Cunningham was assisting locals with various projects that included chicken breeding and teaching them modern methods of farming. Vice President Mphoko asked the Ministry of Lands and Rural Resettlement to identify another farm for the CIO operative. Mphoko argued that taking a farm with projects benefiting the community worked against government policy. The chiefs and villagers celebrated Vice President Mphoko's reversal of the decision to allocate the farm to a new owner, indicating that the projects carried out on the farm had enabled them to become self-sufficient in food supplies and to be able raise money to send their children to school (Katongomara 2015). This is also in line with Vice President Mnangagwa's statement in June 2015 in White City Stadium in Bulawayo that white farmers in Matabeleland North and South provinces who would survive the repossession of land would be those that communities recommended to be spared (because they are running projects that are beneficial to those communities) (Manyukwe 2015a, b).

This contradicted President Mugabe's statement during the celebration of his 91st birthday in February 2015 at Victoria Falls that "the remaining whites must go" and that "no white-man should own land in the country" (*NewZimbabwe* 2015).

Mugabe was also once quoted as saying, "Don't be too kind to white farmers … They can own industries and companies, or stay in apartments in our towns but they cannot own land. They must leave the land to blacks" (*NewZimbabwe* 2015). Contradictory messages from different government officials create a lot of uncertainty and confusion with regard to ownership and security of tenure issues, leaving the land question unresolved. In June 2016, Finance Minister Patrick Chinamasa argued that for Zimbabwe's economy to recover, "the land question should be brought to finality." This includes the question of compensating white farmers who were evicted from farms. This is because since 1998, the land question has become the most important factor in the agricultural performance of Zimbabwe (Tekere et al. n.d.). As Sara Berry has aptly argued, if the 2000 land occupations saved President Mugabe's political career, they did little to clarify the land question (Berry 2002:661). In fact, the 2000 land invasions have shown that land is always a deeply political issue, involving highly disputed and very dangerous terrain (Palmer 2004).

A similar argument was raised by the EU envoy to Harare Philip Van Damme, who argued that finalizing the land question would help facilitate Zimbabwe's agricultural exports to the European Union. Van Damme clarified that by this he did not mean a reversal of the land reform, but referred to the contested implementation and accompanying measures. For example, he highlighted that small farmers still needed to be supported to make them more competent and to develop productive farming. However, as has become the norm with some government officials who want to presume that anybody highlighting irregularities in the land reform process suggests a reversal of the process, Agriculture Minister Joseph Made responded arguing that "[t]he issue of land reform in Zimbabwe is irreversible … totally irreversible." He continued, "We do not want anybody to enter our land reform debate". This attitude is retrogressive in attempts to solve the land question in the country, which also affects the productivity of the sector and its overall contribution to industrialization and the economy as a whole. This confirms that the pre-2000 land disparities along racial lines cannot be taken as a suggestion that the corresponding wholesale land transfers (from whites to blacks) after the introduction of the FRLRP would automatically solve the agricultural transformation challenges faced by small-scale farmers in Zimbabwe.

To address low agricultural output concerns, the government of Zimbabwe is currently working towards introducing a $500 million command agricultural program to produce 2 million tons of maize on 400,000 hectares of land. Under the program, identified farmers will be given inputs, irrigation and mechanized equipment, and will be required to commit five tons per hectare to the government annually as repayment for the inputs and agricultural equipment (Share 2016). Whether this will succeed or not, will only be evaluated after the implementation of the program which is very similar to another one called Operation Maguta, which failed to address the country's low agricultural output after the introduction of the FRLRP. To revive the livestock industry, Agriculture, Mechanisation and Irrigation Deputy Minister Paddy Zhanda recently hinted that the government planned to repossess underutilized ranches so as to encourage fruitful utilization (Business Editor 2016a, b).

Development for Whom and by Whom: What Are the Policy Issues and What Are the Solutions?

Development strategies implemented in postcolonial Africa did not priorities an agricultural revolution or any significant industrialization other than extending the colonial pattern of integration into the world capitalist system. Achieving an agricultural revolution requires an industrial revolution, but one that delinks from the global economic capitalist expansion as the seeds for underdevelopment were first sown when the African economy was integrated into the international division of labor (Amin 1991, 551). The national liberation movement was a bourgeois one even though it succeeded in mobilizing peasant masses. Its petty bourgeois component had, of course, given the illusion of a possible socialist prospect (Amin 1991, 554). As a result, they cannot be trusted to implement development policies beneficial to the majority of the population in their countries.

According to Mlambo and Raftopoulos (2010, 12), in Zimbabwe there has been an "intense struggle between an authoritarian nationalist party attempting to extend its class-economic agenda and patronage network through a renewed 'indigenization' programme". This includes new ownership regulations introduced in 2010 as an extension of the land occupations that characterized the last decade. Mpofu (2011b) reported "a massive attempt by the country's ruling elites to 'blacken' the ownership of the country's economic resources through dubious indigenization and economic empowerment legislation." This process began with the land occupations but soon spread to other sectors of the economy, including banking, manufacturing, retailing and mining, which essentially ensured that ZANU-PF elites controlled the economy for their own benefit, not for the benefit of the country.

Some failed farmers, including government officials, also stampeded to gain access to other economic assets targeted for indigenization like mines, banks and industries, in a primitive accumulation style of grabbing the means of production. Former RBZ Governor Gono, who was at the helm of the central bank when it embarked on quasi-fiscal activities that helped to sustain ZANU-PF in power, however, encouraged the government to re-think this indigenization program by blocking failed farmers that he labelled 'economic non-performers'. Gono argued that:

> Where an individual has benefited from the historic Land Reform Programme, and was allocated a farm(s) which they are not making full use of, those people, in our view, should not be allowed to go and multiply that failure into other sectors such as mining, manufacturing and many others (Nyambabvu 2011).

As noted in some sections of this chapter, it was known that some government officials owned more than one farm each, against the government's one man one farm policy. With these acts of 'economic banditry' or expropriation of farms that end up underutilized also reported in the agricultural sector, the country may still be a long way off from achieving satisfactory agricultural production and productivity that will ignite the re-industrialization of the country.

Are There Specific Zimbabwean Issues That Can Drive Home the Points and Trajectories of Africa's Development?

Development economists follow Zimbabwe's experience with considerable interest for a number of reasons. Firstly, according to Timmer (2016), this is because "rarely has a controlled experiment of this magnitude been carried out on a country's entire development strategy". Secondly, a common belief is that secure property rights are essential to agricultural modernization, and for a country such as Zimbabwe, such modernization will be crucial to further development of the country's entire economy. Tony Hawkins argues that perhaps policymakers across sub-Saharan Africa, including Zimbabwe should now consider that for industrialization late-starters, the African development path has to bypass manufacturing altogether and leapfrog from dependence on agriculture, mining or oil to a service-driven economy. That is, it is time policymakers and entrepreneurs looked for new development models instead of trying to replicate what worked in Asia decades ago (Hawkins 2014). This is not possible at the moment. As Timmer (2016) rightly argues, Zimbabwe's development path cannot "leapfrog agriculture", and historically, "[n]o country has been able to sustain a rapid transition out of poverty without raising productivity in its agricultural sector."

What Are the Prospects and Challenges of Development in Zimbabwe?

According to Manjengwa et al. (2014), while the newly resettled farmers are not yet maximizing the use of land and are still in need of support, production is increasingly steadily with very limited support given by the government. This may take time though as it takes about 20 years for a new farmer to dominate the farm and maximize production. Increased agricultural output can certainly boost industrial productivity. In 2014, the CZI estimated the capacity utilization of Zimbabwe's manufacturing industry to be at 36% in the country. The revival prospects of the manufacturing industry were described as bleak because the country's infrastructure was in a deplorable state and in need of massive investment to sustain any economic growth over the medium term (Hawkins 2014). Prior to 2014, the government increased import tariffs to protect local manufacturers by taking a number of products off the open general import license list. This meant that importers were now obliged to obtain a license to be allowed to import those products. This protective measure, according to Hawkins, was unlikely to lead to industrial revival in the country. This is basically because the domestic market is small and had been forecast to grow at around 3.5% for the rest of the decade. At the same time, as a landlocked country, Zimbabwe's industry was poorly located geographically in comparison to South Africa whose manufactured goods accounted for 48% of Zimbabwe's imports. Furthermore, the investment climate is poor in Zimbabwe's rankings of 171st out of 189 countries in the 2015 World Bank/International Finance Corporation Doing Business Report (Hawkins 2014).

The government, however, proceeded to introduce import restrictions in 2016 under Statutory Instrument (SI) 64 of 2016. Vice President Mnangagwa argued that this was part of the country's import substitution strategy meant to increase local industrial productivity and in the process create more jobs (Ndlovu 2016a, b). Products which were removed from the Open General Import License for business importers included bottled water, salad cream, jams, peanut butter, canned fruits, maheu, vegetables, yoghurts, pizza, flavored milks, dairy fruit blends, ice creams, cultured milk, cheese, coffee creamers, camphor creams, body creams, white petroleum jellies, plastic pipes, second-hand tires, urea and ammonium nitrate fertilizers, tile adhesives and tylon, shoe polish, synthetic hair products, wheelbarrows, roofing frameworks, pillars, columns, balustrade, shutters, towers and matts among others. The CZI supported SI 64 of 2016, highlighting that imports had contributed to the country's de-industrialization and the manufacturing sector's low capacity utilization which stood at 34% in 2015 (Dube 2016). The imports ban was, however, met with violent protests by Zimbabwean cross-border traders, travelers and transporters, and resulted in the burning down of a ZIMRA warehouse at the Beitbridge border post.

Worse still, improving competitiveness in Zimbabwe's dollarized economy (since 2009) is a difficult task because it is expensive now to do any business using the strong US$ as the main currency. Zimbabwe's manufacturing sector suffers severely from a lack of working capital to invest in new machinery, coupled with the high cost of borrowing and weak demand linked to the prevailing liquidity constraints (Kazunga 2016). For example, Zimplow Limited, a farm implements manufacturer, recently lobbied the government to introduce import restrictions on agricultural equipment and machinery to protect it from competition from cheaper imports. Their ploughs cost $58 each while the imported ones cost $35 each. As a result, because of the high cost of producing their ploughs, and low internal demand, between January and July in 2016, they had only produced 7000 of the estimated 26,000 ploughs they usually produce within this period (Mlilo 2016). Zimra board chair Bonyongwe also pointed to the high costs of doing business in the country as a major hindrance to attracting foreign direct investment (Business Editor 2016a, b). This led the CZI and other economists in Zimbabwe to call for the internal evaluation of the US$ and for the adoption of the South African rand as an alternative currency. This suggestion has, however, been shot down by the RBZ Governor Mangudya, who correctly believes that Zimbabwe's problems are not a currency issue but one caused by low productivity (Ndlovu 2016a, b).

Conclusion

This chapter used the Zimbabwean realities and experience relative to land, agriculture, industrialization and economy to theoretically and pragmatically interrogate Africa's development issues because, since 1998, the land question has become the most important factor in the agricultural performance of Zimbabwe (Tekere et al. n.d.). The FRLRP severed the strong supply linkages between commercial agriculture and manufacturing, leading to the collapse of industrial production. In other words, the decline in agricultural production crippled the clothing and textile manufacturers, leather goods manufacturers, milling companies, bakeries, and other industries that relied on agricultural raw materials. As the immediate objective of Zimbabwe's land reform was not increased productivity, but transfer of ownership, its success, according to the government, was therefore measured in terms of the transfer of ownership in the short term; increased production was to be attended to in the long term (Tekere et al. n.d.). It is this long-term objective that has now become the government's Achilles' heel.

Increased agricultural production is the missing link in the re-industrialization efforts that are crucial for the revival of the Zimbabwe economy. While the government continues to be frustrated by low agricultural production levels and has expressed its desire to address them to boost the country's re-industrialization efforts and revive the economy, it is doubtful whether it has enough resources and political will to do so. The unresolved land question, the worst excesses of political patronage and land grabbing, unutilized farms, lack of funding and security of tenure issues all contribute to low agricultural production in resettlement areas. These development challenges in Zimbabwe present Africa with a unique development challenge, especially because the land reform left the country a pariah state in the international community (Mlambo 2014, 236). This negative image may mean that Zimbabwe has to rebrand itself (Mugobo and Myles 2014) to enhance its prospects for re-industrialization and economic revival.

Zimbabwe's land reform process is one that highlighted the visibility of the constitutional dimensions of land questions in contemporary Africa and had far-reaching public debates about both democracy and development (Boone 2007). As such, development economists follow Zimbabwe's experience with considerable interest for a number of reasons (Timmer 2016). Firstly, this is because it still remains to be seen how Zimbabwe's land reform experiment, which disregarded property rights laws, will fare and what impact this will have on the agricultural modernization which is crucial to further development of the country's entire economy. Most crucially, the land issue currently determines the agricultural performance of the country and in the process the prospects of its re-industrialization and economic growth. Hawkins believes that policymakers across Sub-Saharan Africa, including Zimbabwe, should now consider that for indust y hinted that the government planned to rialization late-starters, the African development path has to bypass manufacturing altogether and leapfrog from dependence on agriculture, mining or oil to a service-driven economy (Hawkins 2014). This seems impossible at the moment. As Timmer (2016) succinctly argues, Zimbabwe's development path cannot "leapfrog agriculture", and historically, "[n]o country has been able to sustain a rapid transition out of poverty without raising productivity in its agricultural sector."

Currently, the revival prospects of the manufacturing industry are bleak because its infrastructure is in a deplorable state, and in need of massive investment to sustain any economic growth over the medium term (Hawkins 2014). Improving competitiveness in Zimbabwe's dollarized economy is a difficult task because it is more expensive to do business in the country using the strong US$ as the main currency. As a result, the country's manufacturing sector suffers severely from a lack of working capital to invest in new machinery, coupled with the high cost of borrowing and weak demand linked to the prevailing liquidity constraints.

References

Amin, S. (1991). The interlinkage between agricultural revolution and industrialization: Alternative strategies for African development. In A. Adedeji, O. Teriba, & P. Bugembe (Eds.), *The challenge of African economic recovery and development* (pp. 551–563). London/Oregon: Frank Cass.

Berry, S. (2002). Debating the land question in Africa. *Comparative Studies in Society and History, 44*(4), 638–668. doi:10.1017/S0010417502000312.

Boone, C. (2007). Property and constitutional order: Land tenure reform and the future of the African state. *African Affairs, 106*(425), 557–586. doi:10.1093/afraf/adm059.

Business Editor. (2016a, August 1). Economic recovery lies in the farming sector. *Chronicle*. http://www.chronicle.co.zw/economic-recovery-lies-in-farming-sector/

Business Editor. (2016b, July 19). Govt to repossess underutilised ranches. *Chronicle*. http://www.chronicle.co.zw/govt-to-repossess-underutilised-ranches/

Business Reporter. (2016, August 3). CZI conducts manufacturing survey. *Chronicle*. http://www.chronicle.co.zw/czi-conducts-manufacturing-survey/

Chitumba, P. (2015, September 7). Use it or lose it land policy on the cards. *Chronicle*. http://www.chronicle.co.zw/use-it-or-lose-it-land-policy-on-the-cards/

Dube, Y. (2016, July 28). Import restrictions meant to revive the economy. *Chronicle*. http://www.chronicle.co.zw/import-restrictions-meant-to-revive-industry/

Gumbo, L. (2016, August 2). Expedite compensating white commercial farmers: Govt urged. *Chronicle*. http://www.chronicle.co.zw/expedite-compensating-white-commercial-farmers-govt-urged/

Harare Bureau. (2015, March 23). President slams 'status symbol' land holders. *Chronicle*. http://www.chronicle.co.zw/president-slams-status-symbol-land-holders/

Harare Bureau. (2016, July 21). Call for minimum production levels for landholders. *Chronicle*. http://www.chronicle.co.zw/call-for-minimum-production-levels-for-land-holders/

Hawkins, T. (2014). *Zimbabwe ponders the struggle to industrialise*. http://blogs.ft.com/beyond-brics/2014/11/03/zimbabwe-ponders-the-struggle-to-industrialise/

Katongomara, A. (2015, March 16). Maleme victory: VP Mphoko orders CIO chief out. *Chronicle*. http://www.chronicle.co.zw/maleme-victory-vp-mphoko-orders-cio-chief-out/

Kazunga, O. (2016, August 4). Indebted farmers seek Zamco bailout. *Chronicle*. http://www.chronicle.co.zw/indebted-farmers-seek-zamco-bailout/

Manicaland Correspondent. (2015). RBZ Chief: Politics, lazy new farmers destroy Zim agriculture. *NewZimbabwe*. http://www.newzimbabwe.com/news-24622-RBZ+Lazy+new+farmers+destroy+agriculture/news.aspx

Manjengwa, J., Hanlon, J., & Smart, T. (2014). Who will make the 'best' use of Africa's land? Lessons from Zimbabwe. *Third World Quarterly, 35*(6), 980–995. doi:10.1080/01436597.2014.907722.

Manyukwe, C. (2015a, June 10). VP warns bigwigs. *Chronicle*. http://www.chronicle.co.zw/vp-mnangagwa-warns-bigwigs/

Manyukwe, C. (2015b, March 14). Mzembi defies Mahofa. *Chronicle*. http://www.chronicle.co.zw/mzembi-defies-mahofa/

Maponga, G. (2015, April 1). Mzembi loses farm battle. *Chronicle*. http://www.chronicle.co.zw/mzembi-loses-farm-battle/

Mashonaland East Correspondent. (2015, August 31). Land audit fails to kick off as government fails to raise $35. *NewZimbabwe*. http://www.newzimbabwe.com/news-24565-Govt+fails+to+raise+$35m++for+land+audit/news.aspx

Mazire, I. (2015, January 25). Murder, underage sex, and fraud: 'Mafia boss' Didymus Mutasa faces a slew of charges. *The Sunday Mail*. http://www.sundaymail.co.zw/murder-underage-sex-and-fraud-mafia-boss-didymus-mutasa-faces-a-slew-of-charges/

Mlambo, A. S. (2005). Land grab or taking back stolen land: The fast track land reform process in Zimbabwe in historical perspective. *History Compass, 3*(1), 1–21. doi:10.1111/j.1478-0542.2005.00150.x.

Mlambo, A. S. (2014). *A history of Zimbabwe*. New York: Cambridge University Press.

Mlambo, A., & Raftopoulos, B. (2010). *The regional dimensions of Zimbabwe's multi-layered crisis: An analysis*. Election processes, liberation movements and democratic change in Africa conference, Maputo 8–11 April. CMI and IESE.

Mlilo, B. (2016, August 4). Zimplow seeks products protection. *Chronicle*. http://www.chronicle.co.zw/zimplow-seeks-products-protection/

Mpofu, B. (2011a). Zimbabwe's land reform: Myths and realities – Book review. *African Affairs, 110*(441), 673–675.

Mpofu, B. (2011b, September 16). Some perceptions on the poverty question in Zimbabwe. http://www.solidaritypeacetrust.org/1109/some-perceptions-on-the-poverty-question-in-zimbabwe/

Mugabe, T. (2014). Land audit exposes anomalies. *Chronicle* 10 June. http://www.chronicle.co.zw/land-audit-exposes-anomalies/

Mugobo, V. V., & Wakeham, M. (2014). *Rebranding Zimbabwe: A transformative and challenging process*. Cape Town: Cape Peninsula University.

Ndlovu, P. (2016a, August 3). Let's produce for export. *Chronicle*. http://www.chronicle.co.zw/lets-produce-for-export/

Ndlovu, P. (2016b, July 4). VP Mnangagwa urges import substitution. *Chronicle*. http://www.chronicle.co.zw/vp-mnangagwa-urges-import-substitution/

NewZimbabwe. (2015, September 7). RBZ buys 60 tractors under infamous farm equipment programme, refuses to pay. http://www.newzimbabwe.com/news-24691-RBZ+buys+60+tractors,+refuses+to+pay/news.aspx

Nyambabvu, G. (2011, August 1). Block failed farmers from mines: Gono. *New Zimbabwe*. http://www.newzimbabwe.com/news-5711-Block+failed+farmers+from+mines+Gono/news.aspx

Palmer, R. (1977). *Land and Racial Domination in Rhodesia*. London: Heineman.

Palmer, R. (2004, October 28). Struggles over land: Central to the fight for global justice. Issue 180. http://pambazuka.org/en/category/comment/25381

Raufu, A. M. (2011). Zimbabwean farmers in Nigeria: Exceptional farmers or spectacular support. *African Affairs, 110*(441), 35–561.

Scoones, I., Marongwe, N., Mavedzenge, B., Mahenehene, J., Murimbarimba, F., & Sukume, C. (2010). *Zimbabwe's land reform: Myths and realities*. Oxford/Harare/Johannesburg: James Currey, Weaver Press and Jacana Media.

Share, F. (2016, July 26). $500m agric programme mooted. *Chronicle*. http://www.chronicle.co.zw/500m-agric-programme-mooted/

Share, F., and Musiiwa, M. (2015, June 1). Crackdown on bigwigs' oversize farms. *Chronicle*. http://www.chronicle.co.zw/crackdown-on-bigwigs-oversize-farms/

Tekere, M., Hurungo, J., & Rusare, M. (n.d.). *WTO agreement on agriculture: The implementation experience*. http://www.fao.org/docrep/005/y4632e/y4632e0y.htm

Tendi, B. M. (2010). *Making history in Mugabe's Zimbabwe: Politics, intellectuals and the media*. Oxford: Peter Lang.

Timmer, P. (2016). *Why Zimbabwe cannot leapfrog agriculture*. http://www.cgdev.org/page/why-zimbabwe-cannot-leapfrog-agriculture

Busani Mpofu is a senior researcher at the Archie Mafeje Research Institute (AMRI), College of Graduate Studies, University of South Africa and a former Research Fellow in the Human Economy program, University of Pretoria. His current research interests include Land reform and agricultural development, urban 'citizenship' and the history of African cities, and development, inequality and poverty. He has published on urban housing, social history and land reform. Email address: Mpofub@unisa.ac.za.

Chapter 8
Africa's Governance Travails After More Than Two Decades of Democratic Experiments

Madalitso Zililo Phiri

Introduction

The end of the Cold War signaled the beginning of a new era in democratic experiments across the world and particularly for African countries. Yet for millions of Sub-Saharan African citizens the gains of democratic governance have not resulted in the realization of freedom, justice and equality. This chapter answers the following question: What conditions and ideas have led to Sub-Saharan Africa's failure to deliver on a new social contract for its citizens? The anti-colonial struggles against colonial and imperial rule degenerated into one-party states, extra-judicial killings, violent civil conflicts and coup d'états. Taking into consideration development and socioeconomic indicators, most African countries lost the economic prowess that had pioneered growth and development between the 1960s and 1970s (see Cooper 2002). Scholarly literature on Africa's governance trajectory caricatured the continent as 'neopatrimonial', confirming the failure of Africa to adapt to conditions of modernity. This theoretical framework misses out on foundational ideas, historical events, and the constraints of the global imperial knowledge regime that have played a significant role in shaping Africa's democratic governance debates. This chapter departs from the neopatrimonial school because, as Mkandawire has argued, "the language of neopatrimonialism has permeated news coverage of African affairs so much that the flow of ideas and 'facts' between research results and the media has created a self-reinforcing discourse" (Mkandawire 2015). Governance is defined as the provision of the political, social and economic goods that a citizen has the right to expect from his or her state, and that a state has the responsibility to deliver to its citizens (Mo Ibrahim Foundation 2016a).

M.Z. Phiri (✉)
Archie Mafeje Research Institute (AMRI), College of Graduate Studies, University of South Africa (UNISA), Pretoria, South Africa
e-mail: madalitsophiri1@gmail.com

O. Akanle, J.O. Adésìnà (eds.), *The Development of Africa*, Social Indicators Research Series 71, DOI 10.1007/978-3-319-66242-8_8

Throughout the 2000s the discourse around democracy and development fitted the neoliberal paradigm which championed the effectiveness of policy implementation through Poverty Reduction Strategy Papers (PRSP); 'good governance', managing debt through the Heavily Indebted Poor Country (HIPC) initiatives; sound management of fiscal and monetary policies; and deregulation of the state (Collier 2007; Sachs 2005). It came as no surprise that even under the guise of these 'democratic values' donor governments supported pseudo-democratic regimes, and authoritarian politics in the name of promoting good governance, i.e. Mozambique and Angola (see Hanlon and Mosse 2010; Hanlon 2009; Vines and Campos 2010). In the last 15 years of the twentieth century African countries like Zambia, Nigeria and Angola saw a resurgence of growth dubbed the 'Africa rising'. Powered by a commodity boom and China's growing influence across the continent some African countries sustained positive economic growth rates, attracted venture capitalists, and experienced a slight increase in infrastructure investments (Cheru and Obi 2010), although slowing growth in China and sluggish European recovery has also led to recessions across the continent. As the African Development Bank (2016) suggests, the continent's economic performance held firm in 2015, amid global headwinds and regional shocks. Growth in real gross domestic product (GDP) in 2016 was estimated at 3.6%, higher than the 3.1% for the global economy and 1.5% for the Euro area. Africa remained the world's second fastest growing economy after East Asia. In 2015, Sub-Saharan Africa (excluding South Africa) grew faster than the continental average, at 4.2%, with East Africa leading the way at 6.3%.

Simultaneously, millions of people across Sub-Saharan Africa have not benefited directly from these growth spurts as the negative effects of poverty, inequality, social exclusion, violent civil conflicts, terrorist attacks, internal and external refugee crises and new territorial contestations are evident (Hammar 2014; Murungu 2014; Sembene 2015). Between 1999 and 2011, the increase in the number of poor was barely 30 million, equivalent to only 5% of the total population increase that took place in the region over the same period (Sembene 2015). Poverty headcount ratios have continued to decline since the mid-1990s after reaching a record high of 60%. However, this change has also taken place at a time when poverty incidence still remains high with almost one out of every two Africans living below the poverty line. In pursuit of alternative development paradigms the World Bank also experimented with social policies aimed at reforms that led to Africa's lost decades during the 1980s and 1990s (World Bank 2009); yet the ubiquitous nature of policy failures is currently manifest in almost all African countries. Policy analysts have argued that although African countries have reduced the number of people living in absolute poverty, simultaneously inequality had been on the increase (Sembene 2015; Bigsten 2014).

Taking into account international instruments agreed to reduce poverty, most African countries did not meet the Millennium Development Goals (MDGs) as had been envisioned, in spite of the adoption of the PRSP, casting doubt on whether the Sustainable Development Goals (SDGs) will also be met (Sembene 2015; Bigsten 2014). Ravallion and Chen (2012) computed estimates of inequality on the basis of 850 household consumption surveys for 1979–2008, covering 125 developing countries. They show that Sub-Saharan Africa has higher inequality than other regions with the exception of Latin America and the Caribbean. However, according to Sembene (2015), inequality increased in about half of the sample of PRSP and non-PRSP countries, even though the latter experienced relatively more cases of improved Gini indices. Greater income inequality thus appears to be associated with higher poverty incidence in PRSP countries. At the same time, only modest increases in the income share were secured for the poorest quintile in less than half of these countries (Sembene 2015).

The Arab Uprisings that began at the beginning of the decade highlighted neglected questions of whether authoritarian governments in the Maghreb region and democratic polities across the African continent could coexist with inequality. Inspired by new social movements and citizenship demands, the ideas of the imagination of a new social contract became central to the overthrow of totalitarian regimes that had been in power for almost four decades (Khatib and Lust 2014; Achar 2013). For some scholars the Arab Uprisings signaled a new era where first impression suggested that what happened may not have overturned the political order of the MENA region but was nonetheless profound; as the fall of these *ancien regimes* would have consequences for the future of the region, and beyond (Pollack et al. 2014). This chapter aims to analyze these developments through a historical framework of an African theory toward democratic governance. Key to unlocking these debates is that democracy and development have always been central to Africa's intelligentsia even before the wave of democratization in the 1990s. The political transformations across the African continent need to be understood through the lenses of history and analogy, as Mamdani (1996) has argued. It is impossible to comprehend democratization and development without a re-examination of the postcolonial state as a creation of colonial violence and domination that is tied to the teleological goal of Western modernity. As Mamdani (2003, 132) suggests that "the modern political sensibility sees political violence as necessary to historical progress. Ever since the French Revolution, moderns have come to see violence as the midwife of history".

The first section of this chapter provides a conceptual framework for understanding the intellectual discourses of colonial violence (Cesaire 1972; Mamdani 2003) juxtaposed with neopatrimonialism. This section further locates the Arab Uprisings in their conceptual framework as they pertain to debates on democratization across the Sub-Saharan continent. The second section traces the ideas of democracy and development across the African continent by engaging the ideas of pan-Africanists like Mafeje (1995, 2002), Mamdani (2003) and Mkandawire (1989, 2015) to neglected dimensions of African voices on the democratization process on the continent. The third section follows the evolution of discourses on democracy and development in three countries across Sub-Saharan Africa: South Africa, Mozambique and Rwanda. All three countries have encountered different levels of violence that are birthed in a global imperial and colonial imagination. Further, the three countries have moved from violent civil conflicts to forge 'democratic governments' that champion equality, freedom and justice, yet these yardsticks are questioned. The chapter concludes that crucial to the reconfiguration of discourses on democracy and development is to understand the political economy of colonialism's physical and epistemic violence, whilst simultaneously committed to principles of an New African Democracy premised on a 'radical humanist' agenda. As Mamdani (2003, 132) further suggests, "what horrifies modern political sensibility is not violence per se, but violence that does make sense. It is violence that is neither revolutionary nor counter-revolutionary, violence that cannot be illuminated by the story of progress that appears senseless to us. Not illuminated paradigmatically, non-revolutionary violence appears pointless".

Towards an African Revolutionary Theory of Democratic Governance

There is a singular narrative that attempts to understand the process of democratization and development on the continent. As Hammar (2014, 12) has suggested from assertions of 'its' historical and continued marginalization and 'failure' (Van de Walle 2001); to culturalist presentations of a socially embedded 'moral economy' of different shades (Olivier de Sardan 1999), marked not least by pervasive neopatrimonialism (Chabal and Daloz 1999; Kelsall 2008); to images of a continent whose economic form and fate are largely defined by violence, war, chaos and criminalization (Bayart et al. 1999); to the recent more optimistic soundbites of 'Africa rising' and its new value in the global economy linked to growth in (China-led) demands for natural resources and for land for biofuel and food production. Whichever position is adopted, little importance is placed on Africa's democracy and development discourse which focuses on the evolution of the continent's historical sociology that has shaped past and contemporary democratic trajectories. The struggle to topple imperialist and colonial governments, predicated on democratic aspirations degenerated into one-party states, totalitarian rule leading to social and economic malaise. The late 1980s and 1990s witnessed the resurgence of democratic aspirations, powered by global events and local conditions that were ripe for multiparty politics (see Bratton and Van de Walle 1994; Chabal and Daloz 1999; Van de Walle 2001). Although the Western mantra of supporting authoritarian politics as a Cold War tactic evolved to a recognition and promotion of human rights, 'good governance', rule of law, civil liberties and democratic aspirations based on the concept of liberal democracies, democracy has been imposed at gunpoint across the world, and some scholars have suggested that international pressure can help to create more stable democratic institutions (Carter 2016). It is assumed, as had been predicated by the neoconservative theorist Fukuyama (1992), who declared the 'end of history', that democratic institutions modeled on Western 'egalitarianism' would usurp traditional African values and bring about a homogenous world order.

In contemporary times the same democratic experiments that had been envisioned to deliver on a new social contract have also produced and reproduced several crises; political, social, economic, environmental, rooted in residues of colonial and postcolonial state configurations. The neopatrimonial school, as it became commonly understood, vilified and caricatured the African leader and state, arguing that African societies were incapable of achieving a rules-based liberal democracy. Yet neopatrimonial theorists exaggerate institutional malaise, and fail to theorize to understand the binaries of authoritarian and progressive politics across the continent. The argument is simple, just as the African continent has produced dictators like Mugabe and Idi Amin, it has also produced progressive politics through Mandela and OR Tambo. It is pivotal to understand the evolution of state relations and the quest for progressive politics in the historical and sociological contexts in which both leaders and states have been produced. This, however, requires a rejection of the imperial and colonial theories that have given distorted views of the African continent in general. It is also important to turn to the Arab Uprisings as a significant moment where discourses around democracy and democratization have been brought to the fore.

The Arab Uprisings that began in Tunisia, spreading to Libya, Egypt and parts of the Middle East, reinvigorated debates on freedom, equality and justice. However, there have been several revolts and 'revolutionary processes' for example in Egypt that can be described more as a revolution than present events. The 1952 coup of the Free Officers led by Gamal Abdel-Nasser unquestionably led to a transformation of Egypt much more radical than anything that has so far resulted from the Revolution of 2011 (see Achar 2013; Hanieh 2013; Mitchell 2011). Indeed, we might go so far as to say that the passive counterrevolution led by Anwar al-Sadat after Nasser's death in 1970 also brought about deeper socioeconomic changes than those seen in Egypt since the downfall of Hosni Mubarak on 11 February 2011. Yet the immense uprising that began on 2011 constitutes a bursting of the masses onto the political stage that had no precedent in the very long history of the land of the pyramids (Achar 2013). The following is further proposed, providing a different account of revolutionary violence:

> The 1952 coup led to the overthrow of a dynasty, the abolition of the monarchy and parliamentary regime, the creation of a republican military dictatorship, the nationalization of foreign assets, the subversion of the old regime's property-holding classes (big landed property, commercial and financial capital), a major drive to industrialize, and far-reaching progressive social reforms. These changes certainly better deserve to be called a 'revolution' than do the results of the uprising set in motion in January 2011, which so far has led only to the overthrow of the small clan that dominated the state, and the democratization of the semi-presidential regime, pending a change in the constitution by means that seek to maintain juridical continuity with the old institutions (Achar 2013, 16).

Western media treated these events and transformations, which are also desperately needed across the African continent, as pivotal moments that would redefine social and political conditions. Some pundits have predicted an Egyptian-style revolution in light of rising inequalities and state repression in South Africa in 2020 and the overthrow of Mugabe in Zimbabwe. However, as Achar (2013) has argued, "the Tunisian and Egyptian political revolutions have, nevertheless, left the state apparatuses of the fallen regimes essentially intact; only in Libya was the old state machine largely dismantled by a civil war." These sweeping generalizations do not pay attention to history and analogy and thorough theoretical attempts to understand the course of revolutionary violence on the continent. Mamdani (2003) suggests, "faced with political violence that arises in a modern context but will not fit the story of progress, theory has tended to take refuge in theology by branding violence as evil to be understood outside historical time." He further suggests that "there is a huge resistance, moral and political, to thinking through this violence by locating it in a historical context". In retrospect, as Achar has argued, none of the Arab countries has yet experienced a social revolution in the sense of a thorough transformation of its social structure. Only factions at the pinnacle of the social hierarchy—big or small, depending on the case—have been affected. Nowhere has that hierarchy itself been modified.

In a similar vein the democratic transformations that swept across Sub-Saharan countries in the 1990s produced and reproduced despotic regimes, pseudo-democracies and unconstitutional changes of power that at times failed to deliver on citizenship demands for most citizens. It is tempting to accept the imperial and colonial theories like neopatrimonialism to explain de-democratization, social alienation, de-development and all kinds of crises. However, state formation on the African continent was predicated on the imagination of colonial violence which produced an anti-democratic, anti-human, anti-development state artifact. The anti-colonial leaders were therefore products of a violent state, whereby the rubrics of society were predicated on exclusive citizenship rights for the European to the exclusion of the native. If this is the case, how is it possible then that an anti-democratic, anti-human project state and leader would be expected to bring about a more just, fair and equitable society?

In order to arrive at a revolutionary theory on democracy, Cesaire's (1972) *Discourse on Colonialism* is crucial to the arguments. The modernist concepts were predicated on violence and the elevation of the European as the 'total human' in its civilizing mission. Cesaire argues that a clinical account of the colonizing mission should be taken to understand the very contradictions of Euro-modernity. He suggests that the steps taken by Hitler and Hitlerism reveal to the very distinguished, very humanistic, very Christian bourgeois of the twentieth century that without his being aware of it, he has a Hitler inside him, that Hitler inhabits him, that Hitler is his demon; what he cannot forgive Hitler for is the crime against the white man, the humiliation of the white man, and the fact that he applied to European colonialist procedures which until then had been reserved exclusively for the Arabs of Algeria, the coolies of India, and the blacks of Africa. Cesaire therefore deals with these binaries, how is it possible that a civilization that purports itself to be the 'total human' revives itself to make universal democratic claims about belonging to the civilized world. As Cesaire himself notes that to gain a clear picture of our modern conditions, we must study how colonization works to *decivilize* the colonizer, to brutalize him in the true sense of the word, to degrade him, to awaken him to buried instincts, to covetousness, violence, race hatred, and moral relativism. Recognizing the wanton destruction that Europe inflicted on the psyche of the colonized Africa, Cesaire concludes that the only hope lies in the death of a world that is predicated on anti-black racism or in other words, class suicide. He suggests the following:

> … and since you are talking about factories and industries, do you not see the tremendous factory hysterically spitting out its cinders in the heart of our forests or deep in the bush, the factory for the production of lackeys; do you not see the prodigious mechanization, the mechanization of man; the gigantic rape of everything intimate, undamaged, undefiled that, despoiled as we are, our human spirit has still managed to preserve; the machine, yes, have you never seen it, the machine for crushing, for grinding, for degrading peoples? … which comes down to saying that the salvation of Europe is not a matter of a revolution in methods. It is a matter of Revolution- the one which, until such a time as there is a classless society, will substantiate for the narrow tyranny of a dehumanised bourgeoisie the preponderance of the only class that still has a universal mission, because it suffers in its flesh from all the wrongs of history, from all the universal wrongs: the proletariat (Cesaire 1972, 23)

The anti-colonial leaders were therefore incapable of producing a 'radical humanist society' as the system that birthed them is predicated on colonial violence. There were attempts to transcend colonial violence and imaginations; Nkrumah's call for African unity, Kaunda's African humanism, Nyerere's Ujamaa projects, and Machel's '*Novo Homem*'. With noble intentions, these democratizing projects degenerated into authoritarian politics and the vilification of dissidents. To understand the mindset that conceived the postcolonial state we need to return to political identities crafted by modern imperialism, the settler and the native, as Mamdani (2003, 1996) has argued.

Until recently, emphasis was placed on the agency of the settler, but not on the agency of the native. It is not just the settler; the native too is a product of imperial imagination. Framed by a common history, they define two sides of a relationship. Unless they are transcended together, they will be reproduced together (Mamdani 2003). Fanon in the *Wretched of the Earth* (1967) noted the contradictions that would engulf the 'anti-colonial' ruling elite as being trapped in the state apparatus of the colony. As Mamdani himself has noted, while Fanon was recognized as the prophet of decolonization on the publication of this monumental study, he was also a critique of decolonization. Fanon (1967) argued that "[t]he colonized man liberates himself in and through violence". Mamdani's expository account therefore becomes central to understanding the violence for Fanon's thesis was at the same time a description, a claim and a problematization. As Mamdani (2003) suggests, firstly Fanon's thesis was a description of the violence of the colonial system, of the fact that violence was key to producing and sustaining the relationship between the settler and the native. Second, it was a claim that anti-colonial violence is not an irrational manifestation but belongs to the script of modernity and progress, that it is indeed a midwife of history. Thirdly, it was a problematization, of a derivative violence, of the violence of victims turned into killers. As Mamdani (2003, 135–136) further suggests:

> It is in Fanon himself that one finds the premonition of the native turned perpetrator, of the native who kills not just to extinguish the humanity of the other, but to defend his or her own, and of the moral ambivalence this must provoke in other human beings like us. Native violence, Fanon insisted, was the violence of yesterday's victims, the violence of those who had cast aside their victimhood to become masters of their own lives. He of whom they have never stopped saying that the only language he understands is that of force, decided to give utterance by force … The argument the native chooses has been furnished by the settler, and by an ironic turning of the tables it is the native who now affirms that the colonialist

understands nothing by force. For Fanon, the proof of the native's humanity consisted not in the willingness to kill settlers, but in the willingness to risk his or her own life. If the outcome was death, natives killing settlers, that was still a derivative outcome. The native who embraces violence to safeguard his and her freedom is the victim-turned-perpetrator.

Neopatrimonialism theorists seeking to understand the democratic trajectory of African countries undermine the extent to which colonial modernity was predicated on the decimation of the natives. Colonial genocide is the foundational philosophy of the state itself. In other words, colonial state configuration is anti-democratic as the native existed as a figment of its imagination, to serve a violent state that had rendered ideas of inclusion, belonging and citizenship exclusively reserved for the European. Mkandawire (2015) suggests that most scholars agree with Clapham's (1985) concise definition of neopatrimonialism as "a form of organization in which relationships of a broadly patrimonial type pervade a political and administrative system which is formally constructed on rational-legal lines. Officials hold positions in bureaucratic organizations with powers which are formally defined, but exercise those powers … as a form of private property". Neopatrimonialism is, then, a marriage of tradition and modernity with an offspring whose hybridity generates a logic that has had devastating effects on African economies (Mkandawire 2015). The past therefore becomes central to understanding the present especially postcolonial predicaments that engulf our world as Said (1993) argued. Further, Mafeje (2002) also noted that "while in reality there cannot be any clean break with pre-existing forms of social organization, politically it is arguable that the present states in sub-Saharan Africa (excluding Ethiopia which fits in the Oriental model) are a derivation of the colonial state *par excellence*".

Liberalism or New African Democracy on the Continent

So far the argument that has been made is that state configurations across the African continent are predicated on colonial violence that produces an anti-human, anti-democratic, and anti-development postcolonial project. A cursory examination of colonial violence therefore demystifies 'Arab exceptionalism' that had been propagated by Western pundits. Most Maghreb countries are even latecomers to the discourses on democratization if followed from the teleological goal of building Western democratic institutions since the inception of the Third Wave. As a point of correction, it was the Maghreb countries that had a lot to learn from Sub-Saharan Africa discourses, especially on how fragmented states that had dealt with democratic polities after the 1990s could coexist with religious difference, tolerance and inclusivity. Yet, these lessons are couched in universal experiences that perpetuate the myth of Sub-Saharan Africa as a dark region, where despotic governments have thrived and failed to build democratic institutions that safeguard the interests of its citizens. This too is theoretical imperialism, which was concretely dispelled in Said's (1978) initial laments in "*Orientalism*".

It was Mafeje (1995, 1999, 2002) who raised pertinent theoretical questions on the meaning of democracy across the continent. Mafeje's exposition asked "does democracy mean freedom; or is it 'human rights', a celebration of anthropology of all humanity, or is it self-glorification by the West at its moment of absolute triumph, an affirmation of its discretionary power which allows it to pick and choose in Bosnia, Somalia, Rwanda, South Africa, the Congo, Nicaragua, Ecuador, Palestine, Afghanistan, and Kosovo?" In asking this question he was bringing an indictment on the continued colonial violence of modern state crafting which disguises itself in forms of universalism. Since the inception of Euro-modernity a universalism paradigm defines all experiences of the 'human' to be Western. In this teleological goal, Western concepts can give full expressions of liberty, fraternity and equality as enshrined in the French Revolution, yet the framings of these allude to the human as a 'Western subject'. Even when one takes it further to the American Revolution, 'all men are created equal, to pursue life, liberty and happiness', the liberal values and ideals are hypocritical. This is not a polemical statement, for at every stage of the evolution of Western ideas of inclusion, they coexisted with social and political exclusion; women, non-property owners and the descendant of slaves.

When Mafeje raised the questions above, he was in effect asking where the 'human' is in the democracy discourse. This therefore requires a rejection of the very liberal ideas and the values it purports. It is not enough to suggest liberalism has self-correcting mechanisms, for in this philosophy lies the ideas that can enslave, justify democratic imposition and moral superiority. As Mafeje (1999, 2) further noted:

> [A]part from the obvious political implication and unmistakable cynicism, this is an indication that these concepts, despite their universalistic pretensions are subject to more than one interpretation i.e. they are subject to manipulation … Fraudulent and hypocritical interventions must be exposed for double standards cannot at the same time serve as the basis for universal claims. Indeed, even without such duplicity, it is very doubtful philosophically if at the level of values there can be any universalism. It is significant that the leaders of the "free world" namely, the Americans, unabashedly justify committing atrocities outside the West by putting a premium on their values and way of life. Far from affirming any kind of universalism, this pits one universalism against all other … While purporting to represent universal moral principles, even such codes of conduct are not by any means an epitome of universalism … The West (Americans in particular) does not only treat its type of democracy as a universal principle but also arrogates itself the moral right to impose it on others when it suits it politically.

In retrospect, if liberalism, and the democratic values and principles it purports are problematic, it requires a rejection of imperial theories and ideas that have sustained it. Liberalism is couched in a theoretical imperialism which has constructed the modern world as it is to benefit the West. Mudimbe in both the *Invention of Africa* (1988) and its sequel, *The Idea of Africa*, tasked himself with understanding the colonial imagination and noted that "the colonising structure undertook the domination of space, the integration of local economies into the capitalist system, and the re-forming of the natives' minds". This was further elucidated by Said (1993) who noted "'imperialism' means the very practice, the theory, and the attitudes of a dominating metropolitan centre ruling a distant territory." Against this background most pan-African scholars like Mafeje, Anyang'

Nyong'o and Mkandawire committed themselves to finding heuristic models to explain democratic conditions on the continent. After a preoccupation with debates on dependency theories, capitalism versus socialism, the African intelligentsia sought to articulate its own voice on democratic processes. It became obvious that African countries not only failed to deliver, but also after decades of independence their economies had overwhelmingly fallen into a political abyss. It is fair to say that these scholars, as Mafeje (1999) suggests, were not unduly worried about the 'one party state' or *parti unique*, but more about the failure of African states to deliver what had been promised at independence, namely, freedom from the oppression and exploitation that were the hallmark of the colonial state. However, there were diverging voices within these discussions which become pivotal to this conceptualization.

Mafeje (1999) suggests that Anyang' Nyong'o's positions were interrelated. First, he noted that the disintegration of the national alliance that led to independence ushered in a phase of dictatorships. Second, the resultant lack of democracy in Africa is the root cause of the lack of development, that is, there cannot be democracy in Africa without development. Mafeje further elaborates that in the spirit of independence, Anyang' Nyong'o (1988) was less interested in elaborating a formal definition of 'democracy' than in determining the extent to which the general populace was free to participate in national reconstruction and thus guarantee development. Anyang' Nyong'o was accused by Mkandawire of instrumentalism, who argued instead that democracy is an absolute value. Mkandawire (1989) succeeded in undermining Anyang' Nyong'o's position by citing historical cases such as Germany, Japan and, more recently, the South East Asian countries, where development occurred without any real democracy—meaning vaguely liberal democracy. Yet, in Mkandawire's (1989) rebuttal as Mafeje (1999) has suggested, he relativized his concept of democracy by submitting that liberal democracy is better than nothing—a not uncommon argument but mistaken in principle. It becomes clear in these debates that what was at stake were the very ideas that constitute 'democracy'. As Mafeje himself had noted, instead of maintaining the discourse on the conceptual plane, a number of protagonists began to fasten on single items such as the four classical freedoms, the right to opposition and the rule of law. Involved in this juristical liberalism were noted radical African scholars such as Mkandawire (1989), Mamdani (1990) and Mandaza (1991). The debates were inconclusive as they represented in actuality a disagreement within the left about political realities and strategies rather than ideological preferences (Mafeje 1999).

It was Shivji (1980, 1989) who contemptuously referred to "compradorial democracy" to the irritation of his more pragmatic colleagues, who in his opinion were being influenced by the "fashionable bandwagons" of the West. Shivji's case was vindicated by the fact that in the new "democratization" in Africa the popular masses who initiated the process were usurped or their movement was hijacked by their class enemies and liberal democracy remained a sham. Further debates saw those on the left as radical African nationalists. Ake (1996), for example, rejected the liberal thesis. He further articulates this rejection in his last testimony that Africa requires something more than the impoverished liberal democracy that prevails in the industrialized countries. As Mafeje (1999) argues, his outright rejection of liberal democracy is "inimical to the idea of the people having effective decision making power". In contradistinction, Ake advocated: "a social democracy that places emphasis on concrete political, social and economic rights, as opposed to liberal democracy that emphasizes abstract political rights." However, it was left to Wamba dia Wamba (1992) to carry his Afrocentric perspective to its logical conclusion by calling for an African democracy that relied on traditional mechanisms such as village palavers and lineage assemblies. Mafeje (1999) rebuts by suggesting that we need to guard against reversion to the past with its pitfalls or relapse into uncritical cultural revivalism.

The discussion above seems to suggest that what African countries face is an impasse to theoretical alternatives. In search for alternatives it is not enough to think only theoretically, but to think with theory, or what Adesina (2006, 2008) termed "epistemic rupture". There can be no reversion to a romanticized African past and yet the liberal ideas present existential difficulties for continental realities. However, for the African scholar this requires a new imagination beyond liberalism, as a sociologist like Rabaka (2010) has called it, *Against Epistemic Apartheid.* A new theoretical paradigm in Africa's democracy needs to be cognizant of both the physical and 'epistemic' violence that were the hallmarks of colonial modernity on the African psyche; in conjunction with the substantial freedoms, justice that goes beyond the parameters of colonial territorial constructions like states. In other words, the emergence of a 'new African humanity' can only be achieved once imperialist theories that make universal claims about Africa's ontological, existential, social and political realities have been transcended. It was Mafeje (1995, 1999, 2002) who insisted that African people should be their own "theoretical interlocutors."

In his critique of the neopatrimonial school that views Africa as prone to dictatorship because of an authoritarian past, Mafeje (1995, 2002) notes that this is anthropologically at variance with facts—African societies featured kingdoms, chiefdoms, uncentralized societies or the so-called 'acephalous' societies, clan and lineage societies—there is no political mode that could be described as having been characteristic of its historical past, as Africa has more than one past.[1] Yet a new theoretical paradigm would also need to transcend state configurations of the African state imagination itself. Mafeje engages with the basic presupposition that the African

[1] Cheik Anta Diop (1981) wrote a monumental treatise to usurp imperial historiography that views Africa as having one past. In *Civilization or Barbarism*, he makes a strong case for the blackness of the Egyptian civilization. His thesis moves from the negated history to an affirmation of Egypt's place in the history of Africa. His point is not that Africa should return to this romanticized past, rather he points out that Africa's rebirth will require the centrality of Egypt in its ontological imaginations. He argued that since the birth of Egyptology, most Egyptologists committed their well-known crime against science by becoming guilty of a deliberate falsification of the history of humanity. The new Egyptological ideology, born at the opportune moment, reinforced the theoretical bases of imperialist ideology. These positions drowned out the voice of science by throwing the veil of falsification over historical truth. Imperialism first killed the being spiritually and culturally, before trying to eliminate it physically. The negation of the history and intellectual accomplishments of Black Africans was cultural, mental murder, which preceded and paved the way for their genocide in Africa and the world.

state and economy are a continuation of the colonial state and as such can deliver neither political democracy nor social democracy. The colonial and postcolonial states are therefore antithetical to the existence of democracy, as both present contradictions that need to be overcome. With regard to the colonial state, Mafeje (2002) asserts that it was a creation of the colonial powers for their purposes. As such it exhibits specific characteristics that are not found in the metropolitan state, which are (i) an imposition from outside; (ii) contrivance meant to administer not citizens but colonial peoples or natives, i.e. to administer not subjects but objects; (iii) not accountable to those who are administered but to itself and ultimately to the metropolitan power; (iv) arbitrary use of power and lack of transparency; (v) highly extractive, especially with regard to the peasants; and (vi) disregard of all civil liberties in the colony.

The violent colonial state therefore produced and reproduced its violent other, the postcolonial state. After an expository account of the postcolonial state, Mafeje concludes that the neocolonial African state is characterized by authoritarianism and callous disregard for civil liberties and, further, is a degenerate derivative or poor reproduction of the colonial state mechanism. He suggests that given that no prototypical state model exists in Africa, then the question that has to be answered is whether or not the neocolonial state in Africa can be democratized. While this chapter partially agrees with this argument, this paradigm may also limit other dimensions. Mafeje suggests Africans should not do away with idea of the state in Africa, as it is still potentially the most important single actor in the political and economic arena in Africa, especially under threat of globalization. He suggests that the problem is how to reconcile democratic pluralism with the integrity of the state, however defined. The argument in this chapter is that the whole world is predicated on anti-black racism and extermination. It therefore calls for a re-imagination of the only way out of the trappings of colonial modernity as its own death, as Cesaire suggests.

While Mafeje's ideational sophistication is cognizant of no permanency in the history of the world his paradigm is still trapped in colonial modernity. This is not an indictment of Mafeje as "colonial"; rather he exists in the "colonising structure" as Mudimbe (1988, 1994) noted; a reality that confronts both past and present pan-African scholars. Mafeje (2002) notes the contradictory ideas of the 'good governance' debates across the African continent as he argues that on the one hand this paradigm called for democracy and 'good governance' while it fought battles with governments that were supposed to be democratizing in Tanzania, Zambia, Nigeria, and Ghana. On the other hand, he also notes that this paradigm demanded that African states take a back seat in development as it wanted 'strong states' or authoritarian governments to implement its unpopular programs. It is a contention of mine that liberalism cannot address its contradictions; it is ethically, spiritually, morally and politically bankrupt. A more democratic world requires the death of the nation-state mentality, whose thought has evolved to privilege the West's existential, ontological and political aspirations as universal realities, and in doing so the primacy of the state as a monopoly of violence. This requires a social death of anti-democratic, anti-human, anti-development articulations, which are deeply embedded in the idea of the state and can therefore not be democratized. Mafeje (2002) falls back on the concept of a "social democracy" for Africa, which he argues can be subsumed under the "New Democracy". He concludes that while the former cannot be used as a basis for national liberation, the latter can; this confronts the African with an awkward question. In our circumstances, would this constitute a radical departure from what came to be popularly known as 'independence' or a continuation of an unfinished revolution? Africa is pregnant with new meanings but its problem is agency, Mafeje (2002) suggests. For a further application of this, the three case studies of South Africa, Mozambique and Rwanda need to be considered.

Democracy and Development in Comparative Perspective: South Africa, Mozambique and Rwanda

The 'democratic' transitions that swept most African countries in the 1990s had different effects on the polities of South Africa, Mozambique and Rwanda. Through a negotiated settlement, in 1994 South Africa embarked on the path of overcoming violent conflict to build a more inclusive and tolerant democracy that would do away with racial hierarchies (Bond 2000, 2001). Mozambique overcame two conflicts, one against colonial domination and a civil conflict rooted in Cold War rivalries; culminating in a peace agreement in 1992 that led to democratic elections in 1994. Rwanda embarked on democratic reforms after a brutal civil conflict between 1990 and 1994, which culminated in the genocide of 1994 (Melvern 2000). In all three countries, 'liberation parties' that saw themselves as safeguarding the interests of all their citizens won contested elections to become governing parties in their own right, the African National Congress (ANC) in South Africa, the Frente de Libertação de Moçambique (FRELIMO) in Mozambique and the Rwandan Patriotic Front (RPF) in Rwanda. While literature has concentrated on understanding the nature of these transitions in their global importance, more attention needs to be paid to the sociological dimensions that have raised questions on how to make sense of the governance of 'post-genocidal democratic' polities.

All three countries became the beacon of hope for most African countries. There was a sense of triumphalism and belief in the forging of new democratic institutions that could overcome civil conflict to build tolerant and inclusive societies. In a continent-wide analysis between 2000 and 2015, the Mo Ibrahim Governance report (2016a, b, c) found that ten countries out of 54 moved up a band of "overall governance"; five from "medium-low" in 2006 to "medium" in 2015 (Congo, Côte d'Ivoire, Guinea-Bissau, Togo and Zimbabwe); four from "medium" to "medium-high" (Kenya, Morocco, Rwanda and Uganda); and one – Seychelles – from "medium-high" to "high". These countries cover 15% of Africa's population and 18% of Africa's GDP. Rwanda, one of the ten countries mentioned, under the leadership of the RPF has aimed at sustaining growth, becoming a leader in telecommunications and agriculture. Kagame has made it a priority for Rwanda to become a middle-income country by 2020. In South Africa, the 'rainbow nation' project dominated the myth of transition in the first decade of democratization. In Mozambique, donor governments promoted the mantra of 'a development miracle', where before the meltdown in 2015, economic growth was seemingly trickling down to reduce poverty and underdevelopment. Figure 8.1 below illustrates overall governance[2] across the three countries. The highest score that was captured for South Africa was 71.5 which is a record since the inception of the Mo Ibrahim Index in 2000. While the country still ranks in the top ten for 'overall governance', the average rating in the last 5 years has been deteriorating. Between 2010 and 2015 the average rating for 'overall governance' captured was 69.5, a score which was last recorded in 2002. In a similar vein, 'overall governance' in Mozambique has deteriorated since 2000 with two consecutive record lows of 52.1 in both 2013 and 2014. Average 'overall governance' between 2010 and 2015 was 53, which was last captured in 2001.

On the other hand, Rwanda has seemingly made progress, recording its highest score for 'overall governance' in 2015 at 50. Between 2000 and 2015 the increment in shift of score was minute, calculated at 1% in the entire period. Between 2000 and 2015, Rwanda's 'overall governance' in terms of ranking saw a recorded increase of 3.3%. However, average 'overall governance' between 2010 and 2015 was 49.7, which is equal to the continental average of 49.7, as reported in the Mo Ibrahim Governance Report. In actuality, 'overall governance' has deteriorated in six countries to a downward movement in band: Algeria, Libya, Madagascar, Mali, Mozambique and South Africa. Of these, South Africa has fallen from the "high" into the "medium-high" band of countries; Algeria, Mali, Madagascar and Mozambique from "medium-high" to "medium"; and Libya from "medium" into the "medium-low" band (Mo Ibrahim Foundation 2016a, b, c).

These achievements mask the failures of the three countries as 'democratic polities' to imagine a new social contract. Under the leadership of the ANC, South Africa has birthed political, social and economic crises. The party has been criticized for an authoritarianism from below that has defined state, economy and party relations (Southall 2013). Some on the left have characterized South Africa as a 'suspended revolution' (Habib 2013). Economically, South Africa moved from being Africa's largest economy to witnessing little or no growth, a global ratings downgrade, high inflation zone, unresolved labor disputes and high unemployment rates. Socially, South Africa has witnessed levels of intolerable state violence as exemplified in the Marikana massacre of 2012, student protests for free education and decolonization, and rising inequality. The ANC prides itself on being a vibrant democratic institution within all echelons of the party, yet it is increasingly difficult

[2] Given that the data utilized in the construction of the Ibrahim Index of African Governance (IIAG) come from 34 separate data providers that present their data on different scales, all data are standardized. This is done through a statistical process called normalization whereby raw data for each indicator are transformed by the min-max normalization method. This process allows all scores to be published in common units and within the same bounds of 0–100, where 100 is always the best possible score. The application of this normalization method means that a score of 100 relates to the best possible score within the group of 54 African countries between 2000 and the latest data year. The Foundation publishes standard errors and confidence intervals alongside the composite IIAG and category scores to reflect degrees of uncertainty, which are available on the Foundation's website (Mo Ibrahim Foundation 2016a, b, c).

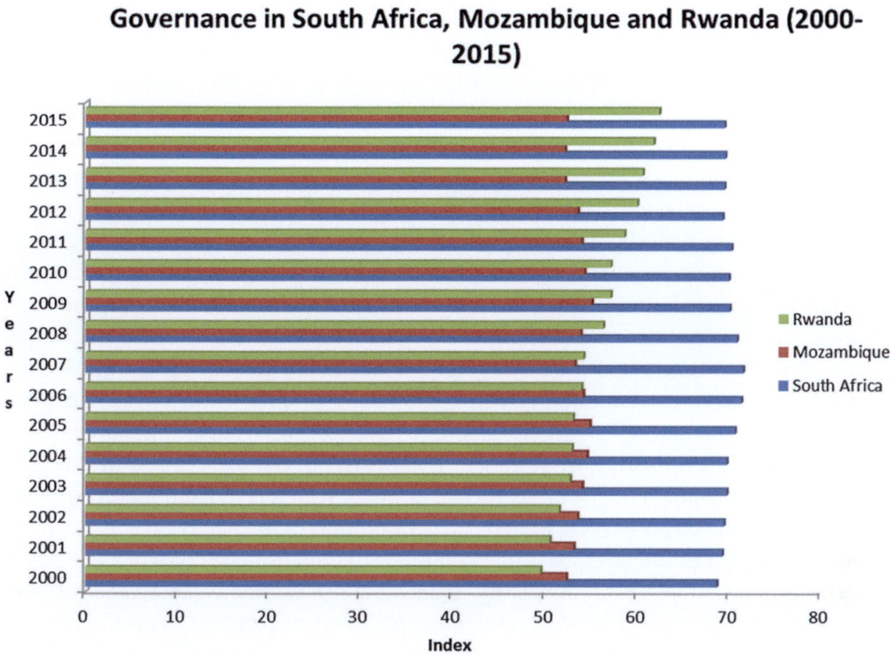

Fig. 8.1 Governance in South Africa, Mozambique and Rwanda (2000–2015) (Source: Mo Ibrahim Foundation (2016b))

to ascertain whether it still represents the political aspirations of working class communities. South Africa is overdue for a credible leftist party (Phiri and Macheve 2014) and a true democratic revolution that will deliver on a democratic polity not predicated on coercion, violence and torture and a classless society. It will not come in self-proclaimed Marxist-Fanonist parties like Malema's Economic Freedom Front (EFF). The EFF's rise has added vibrancy to South Africa's nascent democracy, promoting the idea that coalition politics will be possible (Phiri and Macheve 2014). However, the party remains an opportunist pseudo-democratic movement in South Africa's turbulent political dispensation. South Africa needs a democratic revolution that is committed to social justice and humanism, which will mean going beyond the 'politics of anger' to the 'politics of the governed'. In the realms of the economy, given its turbulent history and the aspirations of its labor and citizens, nationalization may be a necessity. However, the country can learn from a myriad global successes and failures, like the Norwegian oil miracle, Brazil with Petrobras and the role of the Workers Party (PT), and the Chinese Communist Party's insistence on growing their economy under state owned enterprises (SOEs). The answer lies in between these examples, it is not an either or question.

In times of crisis, it is tempting to see forms of 'developmentalism' in Rwanda as a model for development and democracy across the continent. South Africa, Mozambique, and Rwanda oscillate between institutional inertia and a failure to transform colonial states predicated on violence to postcolonial political aspirations of a more humane social contract. For critics the transformation to a democratic polity that is more human remains an abstract political and social reality. The antidote, however, is that 'democratic politics' premised on force, coercion and the exclusion of weaker members of society is anti-human. Figure 8.2 below illustrates how 'political violence' has been on the increase in the past 5 years, especially since the 1994 post-conflict settlements. South Africa recorded its worse rating since the inception of democracy at 33.5 in 2012. Between 2010 and 2015 the average score for 'political violence' stands at 57.5 which is almost the same as the 2014 figure of 56.9. The average score over a 15-year period between 2000 and 2015 is 67.5 which is equal to the 2001 score. Rwanda's worse score was captured in 2011 at 39.8. Mozambique's highest score was 75 which is higher than the average score that South Africa has been rated over a 15-year period. These scores explain the broken social contract where a dehumanized citizenry has resorted to violent acts, xenophobic attacks, 'fees must fall', and pre-election violence in 2016. Simultaneously, the state apparatus has resorted to violence, manifested in the vilification of political dissidents and the silencing of oppositional politics, which is in itself a failure of the postcolonial state to go beyond the artefacts of colonial violence itself.

Mozambique's political, social and economic structure remains broken. The peace agreement has come under attack by Dhlakama's RENAMO. FRELIMO under Chissano and Guebuza, and now Nyussi, three pertinent stakeholders, party, civil society, and the economy (see Phiri and Macheve 2014; Hanlon 2009; Hanlon and Mosse 2010), are in perpetual conflict. Mozambique's social pact also remains fragmented, where growth that was fueled by a mineral resource sought by China has not directly resulted in the equalization of the social contract for all its citizens (Hanlon and Cunguara 2010; Hanlon and Mosse 2010). Inequality is on the increase, and government has attempted to adopt 'progressive social policy' reforms in the form of cash transfers to reduce inequality (Hanlon and Cunguara 2010). There are similarities between South Africa and Mozambique as citizens' demands have become the 'poli-

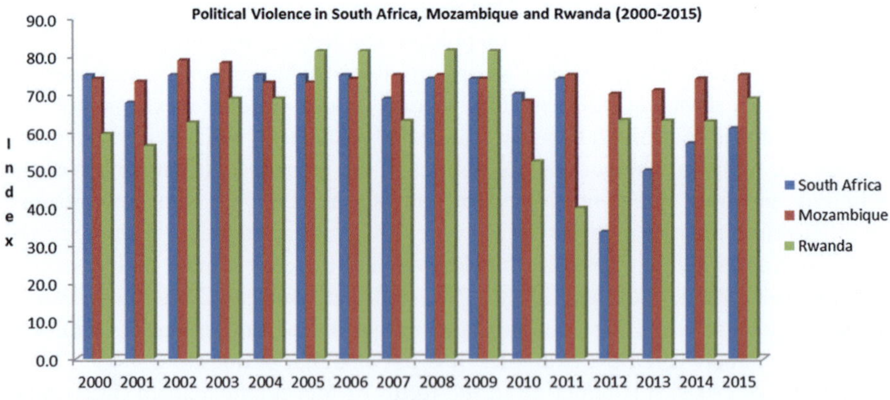

Fig. 8.2 Political violence in South Africa, Mozambique and Rwanda (2000–2015) (Source: Mo Ibrahim Foundation (2016c))

tics of the ungoverned', a trend that has defined Southern Africa's liberation movements like the Zimbabwe African National Union (ZANU) in Zimbabwe. Undoubtedly, Rwanda has managed to achieve stable economic growth rates and has banned the use of colonial ethnic identification (Hutu/Tutsi) in its constitution, yet the latter is questionable. The resort to non-ethnic identification may seem to be progressive; however, it masks the theoretical dimensions of post-conflict reconstruction and the reconfigurations of the postcolonial state. A careful consideration of colonial cartography to understand present-day predicaments becomes key. As Mamdani (2003) has suggested the colonialists did not identify "tribes" but races—Hutu as Bantu and Tutsi as Hamites. The Bantu were presumed to be uncivilized, and the Hamites a civilizing agent.

Throughout the twentieth century, academic writing on Rwanda had been dominated by sympathy with the Rwandan Revolution of 1959, as several authors have argued (Melvern 2000; Mamdani 2001, 2003; Desforges 1999). Mamdani further suggests that "unable to see the dark underbelly of the Revolution, and thus to grasp the link between the 1959 Revolution and the 1994 genocide, this kind of writing portrays the genocide as exclusively or mainly a state project of a narrow ruling elite." It is unquestionably the case that under the leadership of Kagame, aspirations for a 'new Rwanda' remain committed to a politicized, factionalized, Tutsi project to usurp the Hutu nationalism that dominated politics throughout the twentieth century. This is not an attempt to create a new postcolonial state project that goes beyond the ethnic categories of colonial modernity. This could be the reason why even under the guise of developmentalism, an authoritarism from below has emerged to vilify political dissidents and those on the margins of this social project. There are little or no guarantees that developmentalism will not use extractive means to safeguard its own constituency especially in a context where political leadership is embedded in a personality cult. The imagination of a new social contract needs to be understood in these racialized identities. In portraying racism and racial identities as exclusively state defined and state enforced, these positions fail to explain how the same identities became socially embedded and were reproduced socially (Mamdani 2003).

The three examples expounded above point to a failure of political projects, under the guise of 'liberation parties', to imagine a 'New African Democracy'. As Mafeje (2002) noted, Mbeki's inaugural speech as ANC president proclaimed that in South Africa "the revolution is as yet incomplete". After recent reversals in Egypt, Ethiopia and Zambia and upheavals in Zimbabwe, the same could be said. In the next round, what is it going to be? What is to be done or can be done under the determinate conditions in Africa?

Conclusion

This chapter has attempted to offer explanations why Sub-Saharan Africa has failed to re-imagine the ideas of the social contract for its citizens. Present democratic struggles ought to be anchored in both the theoretical and empirical discourses of democracy and development across the continent. Democracy and development cannot be framed in the universal experiences of imperial theories. At the same time, Africa as a continent cannot be studied, let alone understood, outside imperial and colonial imaginations. The Arab Uprisings brought to the fore democratic debates across the continent, yet these transformations left most of the state apparatuses intact. Since the coining of the 'Africa rising' narrative there has been a wave of optimism that economic growth would trickle down, leading to the equalization of the playing field for all citizens across Sub-Saharan Africa. However, millions of people across the region continue to be poor, and the neoliberal policy agenda emphasizes poverty reduction to the neglect of inequality. In a true sense, poverty and inequality are produced and reproduced by forms of physical, epistemic and structural violence that are embedded in the imaginations of colonial and postcolonial statecraft. Africa is in desperate need of a social revolution as the three case studies of South Africa, Mozambique and Rwanda have shown; this needs to be predicated on transcending imperialist theories and imaginations and the realization of substantial freedoms, justice and equity.

The democratic transitions of the Third Wave have in retrospect produced and reproduced different crises in contemporary times. This chapter has argued that to understand the crises that engulf the democratization project(s) across the African continent, scholars and practitioners alike should reconsider the theoretical paradigms that have been adopted to understand democratic relations across the continent. Discourses on democracy and development ought to incorporate both the physical and colonial violence that produced and reproduced a postcolonial state that mimicked its colonial other. As Mamdani (2003) suggests, you can turn the world upside down, but still fail to change it. To change the world you need to break out of the worldview of not only the settler but also the native. Unless we break away from this worldview postcolonialism will remain a purgatory punctuated by non-revolutionary violence. More than any other contemporary event, the genocide in Rwanda poses this dilemma more sharply than ever before. The colonial state was therefore anti-human, anti-democratic and anti-development. The reconfiguration of democratic relations will require an epistemic death of imperialist theories like the neopatrimonial school that has been popularized for over two decades to understand governance, state relations and development on the continent. As Mkandawire (2015, 598) has suggested,

> … the policy failures of African states are never inadvertent or the by-product of diffusion; they are ineluctably linked to rent seeking and neopatrimonialism, which leaves no room for learning or the interplay of ideas. However, the neopatrimonialism school of thought seeks to give agency to Africans by permitting them choice about development trajectories, its approach is predisposed to downplay ideas (Mkandawire 2015).

References

Achar, G. (2013). *The people want: A radical exploration of the Arab uprising*. Berkeley: University of California Press.

Adesina, J. (2006). Sociology, endogeneity and the challenge of transformation. *African Sociological Review, 10*(2), 133–150.

Adesina, J. (2008). Archie Mafeje and the pursuit of endogeny: Against alterity and extroversion. *Africa Development, 33*(4), 133–152.
African Development Bank (AfDB). (2016). *African economic outlook: Sustainable cities and structural transformation*. http://www.africaneconomicoutlook.org/. Accessed 7 Oct 2016.
Ake, C. (1996). *Democracy and development in Africa*. Washington, DC: Brooking Institution.
Anyang' Nyong'o, P. (1988). *Popular struggles for democracy in Africa*. London: Zed Books.
Bayart, J. F., Ellis, S., & Hibou, B. (Eds.). (1999). *The criminalization of the state in Africa*. Oxford: James Currey.
Bigsten, A. (2014). *Dimensions of African inequality* (WIDER Working Paper 2014/050). Helsinki: World Institute for Development Economics Research.
Bond, P. (2000). *Elite transition: From apartheid to neoliberalism in South Africa*. London: Pluto Press.
Bond, P. (2001). *Against global apartheid: South Africa meets the World Bank, IMF and international finance*. Cape Town: UCT Press.
Bratton, M., & van de Walle, N. (1994). Neopatrimonial regimes and political transitions in Africa. *World Politics, 46*(4), 453–489.
Carter, B. L. (2016). The struggle for term limits in Africa: How international pressure can help. *Journal of Democracy, 27*(3), 36–50.
Cesaire, A. (1972). *Discourse on colonialism*. New York/London: Monthly Review Press.
Chabal, P., & Daloz, J.-P. (1999). *Africa works: Disorder as political instrument*. London: James Currey.
Cheru, F., & Obi, C. (Eds.). (2010). *The rise of China and India in Africa: Challenges, opportunities and critical interventions*. London/Uppsala: Zed Books/Nordiska Afrikainstitutet.
Clapham, C. (1985). *Third world politics: An introduction*. London: Croom Helm.
Collier, P. (2007). *The bottom billion: Why the poorest countries are failing and what can be done about it*. Oxford: Oxford University Press.
Cooper, F. (2002). *Africa since 1940: The past of the present*. Cambridge: Cambridge University Press.
Desforges, A. (1999). *Leave none to tell the story: Genocide in Rwanda*. New York: Human Rights Watch.
Diop, C. A. (1981). *Civilization or barbarism: An authentic anthropology*. Paris: Presence Africaine.
Fanon, F. (1967). *The wretched of the earth*. London: Penguin.
Fukuyama, F. (1992). *The end of history and the last man*. New York: Penguin.
Habib, A. (2013). *South Africa's suspended revolution: Hopes and prospects*. Johannesburg: Wits University Press.
Hammar, A. (2014). Displacement economies: Paradoxes of crisis and creativity in Africa. In A. Hammar (Ed.), *Displacement economies in Africa: Paradoxes of crisis and creativity*. London/Uppsala: Zed Books/Nordiska Afrikainstitutet.
Hanieh, A. (2013). *Lineages of revolt: Issues of contemporary capitalism in the Middle East*. Chicago: Haymarket Books.
Hanlon, J. (2009). *Mozambique's elite: Finding its way in a globalised world and returning to old development models*. Paper presented at a Crisis States Research Centre Seminar. London: London School of Economics.
Hanlon, J., & Cunguara, B. (2010). *Poverty is not being reduced in Mozambique* (Working Paper no. 74, Crisis States Working Paper Series No. 2). London: Crisis States Research Centre, London School of Economics.
Hanlon, J., & Mosse, M. (2010). *Mozambique's elite: Finding its way in a globalized world and returning to old development models*. Helsinki: UNU-WIDER (United Nations University – World Institute for Development Economics Research).
Kelsall, T. (2008). Going with the grain in African development? *Development Policy Review, 26*(6), 627–655.
Khatib, L., & Lust, E. (Eds.). (2014). *Taking to the streets*. Baltimore: Johns Hopkins University Press.

Mafeje, A. (1995). Theory of democracy and the African discourse. In E. Chloe & J. Ibrahim (Eds.), *Democratization processes in Africa: Problems and prospects*. Dakar: CODESRIA Book Series.
Mafeje, A. (1999). *Democracy, civil society, and governance in Africa*. Addis Ababa.
Mafeje, A. (2002, April 26–29). *Democratic governance and new democracy in Africa: Agenda for the future*, Prepared for presentation at the African Forum for envisioning Africa, Nairobi, Kenya.
Mamdani, M. (1990). *Reconceptualising the birth of state nationalism and defeat of popular movements*. Proceedings of the sixth general assembly of CODESRIA.
Mamdani, M. (1996). *Citizen and subject: Contemporary Africa and the legacy of late colonialism*. Princeton: Princeton University Press.
Mamdani, M. (2001). *When victims become killers: Colonialism, nativism, and the genocide in Rwanda*. Princeton: Princeton University Press.
Mamdani, M. (2003). Making sense of political violence in post-colonial Africa. *Socialist Register, 39*, 132–151.
Mandaza, I. (1991). Democracy in the African reality. *SAPEM* 11 September.
Melvern, L. (2000). *A people betrayed: The role of the West in Rwanda's genocide*. London: Zed Books.
Mitchell, T. (2011). *Carbon democracy: Political power in the age of oil*. London: Verso.
Mkandawire, T. (1989). Comments on democracy and political instability. *CODESRIA Bulletin* 1.
Mkandawire, T. (2015). Neopatrimonialism and the political economy of economic performance in Africa: Critical reflections. *World Politics, 67*(3), 563–612.
Mo Ibrahim Foundation (MIF). (2016a). *2016 Ibrahim Index of African Governance: A decade of African Governance, 2006–2015*. http://mo.ibrahim.foundation/iiag/. Accessed 4 Oct 2016.
Mo Ibrahim Foundation (MIF). (2016b). *Governance in South Africa, Mozambique and Rwanda, 2000–2015*. http://mo.ibrahim.foundation/iiag/downloads/. Accessed 4 Oct 2016.
Mo Ibrahim Foundation (MIF). (2016c). *Political violence in South Africa, Mozambique and Rwanda, 2000–2015*. http://mo.ibrahim.foundation/iiag/downloads/. Accessed 4 Oct 2016.
Mudimbe, V. Y. (1988). *The invention of Africa: Gnosis, philosophy, and the order of knowledge*. Bloomington: Indiana University Press.
Mudimbe, V. Y. (1994). *The idea of Africa*. Bloomington: Indiana University Press.
Murungu, C. B. (2014). International crimes that trigger article 4(h) intervention. In D. Kuwali & F. Viljoen (Eds.), *Africa and the responsibility to protect: Article 4(h) of the African Union constitutive act*. London: Routledge.
Olivier de Sardan, J. P. (1999). The moral economy of corruption? *The Journal of Modern African Studies, 37*(1), 25–52.
Phiri, M., & Macheve, A. (2014). Mozambique's peace decades since the end of the conflict: Inclusive or managed democracy? *African Journal on Conflict Resolution, 14*(1), 37–62.
Pollack, K., Byman, D. L., Al-Turk, A., Baev, P., & Doran, M. S. (2014). *The Arab awakening: America and the transformation of the Middle East*. Washington, DC: Brookings Institution.
Rabaka, R. (2010). *Against epistemic apartheid: W.E.B. Du bois and the disciplinary decadence of sociology*. Lanham: Lexington Books.
Ravallion, M., & Chen, S. (2012). *Monitoring inequality*. Mimeo. https://blogs.worldbank.org/developmenttalk/files/developmenttalk/monitoring_inequalit y_table_1_.pdf. Accessed 7 Oct 2016.
Sachs, J. (2005). *The end of poverty: Economic possibilities of our time*. New York: Penguin Books.
Said, E. W. (1978). *Orientalism*. London: Penguin.
Said, E. W. (1993). *Culture and imperialism*. New York: Vintage Books.
Sembene, D. (2015). *Poverty, growth, and inequality in Sub-Saharan Africa: Did the walk match the talk during the PRSP approach* (IMF Working Paper, WP/15/122). Washington, DC: International Monetary Fund.

Shivji, I. (1980). The state in the dominated social formations of Africa: Some theoretical issues. *International Social Science Journal, 32*(4), 730–742.
Shivji, I. (1989). The pitfalls of the debate on democracy. *CODESRIA Bulletin*, p. 13.
Southall, R. (2013). *Liberation movements in power: Power and state in Southern Africa.* Woodbridge/Scottsville: James Curry and the University of Kwa-Zulu Natal Press.
Van de Walle, N. (2001). *African economies and the politics of permanent crisis, 1979–1999.* New York: Cambridge University Press.
Vines, A., & Campos, I. (2010). China and India in Angola. In C. Fantu & C. Obi (Eds.), *The rise of China and India in Africa*. London: Zed Books.
Wamba dia Wamba, E. (1992). *Africa in search of a new historical mode of politics*. Proceedings conference on democratization process in Africa of CODESRIA, Dakar.
World Bank. (2009). *Conditional cash transfers: A World Bank policy research report*. Washington, DC: World Bank.

Madalitso Zililo Phiri is a Doctoral Research Fellow in Sociology at the University of South Africa's (UNISA) DST/NRF SARChI Chair in Applied Social Policy, College of Graduate Studies. He is also a Dissertation Completion Fellow (2016–17) through the Social Science Research Council (SSRC), New York, United States of America (USA); Dissertation Completion Laurate through the Council for the Development of Social Science in Africa (CODESRIA), Dakar, Senegal; and a recipient of the African Pathways Doctoral Scholarship through the National Institute for the Humanities and Social Science (NIHSS) and CODESRIA. His publications include book chapters and refereed journal articles in Innovation and Development, the Journal of Conflict Resolution (AJCR) and the South African Journal of International Affairs (SAJIA).

Chapter 9
The Limitations of Peace Negotiations and Identity Constructs in Conflict-Prone Countries in Africa: A Focus on the Central African Republic (CAR)

Wendy Isaacs-Martin

We will respect human rights when we have the means.

(Noureddine Adam, minister of public security, Seleka General, 2013)

Introduction

The African continent is plagued by the continuous failure of peace agreements. These agreements follow a standard model which includes Demobilization, Disarmament and Reintegration (DDR) initiatives, transitional governments, cease-fires, reforms and elections (De Zeeuw 2008). These agreements are supposed to be implemented or monitored by peacekeeping forces from regional or international stakeholders. These initiatives based on the agreements are repeated continuously but they fail to have long-term, or even relative short-term, effects (Alden et al. 2011). This is due to several reasons: the lack of support from stakeholders, the lack of commitment by interested parties to the negotiations, the absence of mechanisms to support any investigations and bring perpetrators to justice, skewed attitudes that allow certain groups to escape arrest and prosecution, and finally delayed implementation of these peace agreements that indirectly exacerbate residual tensions and allow the conflict to continue if not escalate.

Numerous African countries have negotiated peace agreements since the end of the Cold War but the majority have failed and have led to further conflicts, to the detriment of their economies, their armies (Ferreira 2014) and their civilian populations (Vinck and Pham 2010). These peace agreements have instead become part of

W. Isaacs-Martin (✉)
Archi Mafeje Research Institute (AMRI), University of South Africa (UNISA), Pretoria, South Africa
e-mail: isaacw@unisa.ac.za

O. Akanle, J.O. Adésìnà (eds.), *The Development of Africa*, Social Indicators Research Series 71, DOI 10.1007/978-3-319-66242-8_9

the endgame of many warlords and governments in order to negotiate better personal terms. Warlords are known for using fighters to delay entering the DDR programs or to apply to several programs in order to receive the financial rewards which are then redistributed rather than used by the intended recipient.

This demonstrates that the manner in which peace agreements are designed and implemented is flawed. Yet the same process is implemented over and over again rendering the same results. Agreements such as MONUC (United Nations Mission in the Democratic Republic of Congo) and the Lusaka Ceasefire Agreement signed in 1999 did not bring about peace or stability. Often the same parties are brought into negotiations over a number of peace agreements and the number of signatories is few rather than a representative number of the parties participating in the conflict. Militias claim to represent rural or oppressed populations who are marginalized by the national government but on closer investigation the role of militias is varied.

Warlords, or regional strongmen, enjoy control over a small region and create a hierarchy of clientelism (Marten 2012). Warlords are often former bureaucrats within the state institutional structures, former cabinet ministers or rural leaders with traditional authority or claiming such authority. These individuals, while claiming to espouse a particular ideology in defense of their communities, seek financial assistance from government or external stakeholders in order to maintain control over particular areas. Warlords are seldom interested in assuming national political leadership but instead are focused on controlling a small region in order to access and extract mineral resources. They are opportunistic and will often eliminate any economic incentives in areas under their control in order to control the population. The question posed is *whether the manner in which militia leadership is targeted for negotiation offers the best manner in which to facilitate peace and nation building in a war-torn country?* The aim of this chapter is to demonstrate that without understanding the motivation of governments, particularly state leaders, or those of warlords and strongmen, it is unlikely that peace agreements can work effectively. Rather, these individuals recognize that maintaining conflict is a source of personal enrichment and grants them social and political power (Isaacs-Martin 2015). In such an environment of limited economy the warlord and those in political power are able to strengthen clientelistic relationships. This creates a pyramid of dependence and loyalty and is not the mutualistic benevolent relationship as often portrayed (Marten 2012).

This chapter does not intend to unpack all peace agreements signed in Africa or even in a particular region but rather an attempt is made to offer a cursory explanation. The Central African Republic (CAR) is demonstrated here as a case of how several peace agreements have failed to deliver on the articles presented and as signed by those attending the negotiations. This is not an exhaustive search and analysis of all the agreements but rather a focus on four intra-state negotiations. The conclusions drawn are that these agreements proved ineffective because of their generalized nature and the fact that they served to provide rewards for the participants rather than a method by which to seek effective solutions.

Methodology

Africa is confronted with persistent and recurring small wars and rural conflict, with occasional rather than continuous peaceful periods (Ferreira 2014). Even with the intervention of international stakeholders to implement peaceful transitions and the attempted restoration of normative society the trend remains a default to violence. The overwhelming ideology of these peace agreements is to implement democratic processes, in particular hosting general elections and bringing about governments of national unity. Yet countries such as the CAR have rarely experienced democracy and certainly the institutions of governance are ill equipped to facilitate democratic processes and transition but rather ensure employment, and enrichment, for particular ethnic groups aligned to political leadership interests.

The chapter attempts to scrutinize intra-state peace agreements. Owing to similarities in the content of these agreements it was decided to limit the explanation to four CAR agreements and ceasefires in understanding attempts to restore peace, ensure democratic elections, install representative government and create institutions that ensure human rights and uphold democratic processes. The four peace agreements include the Bangui Agreement of 1997, the Birao Peace Agreement signed in 2007, the Libreville Ceasefire and Peace Agreement signed in 2008, the National Reconciliation Pact of 1998 and the Transitional Government and the Armed Groups on the Principles of Disarmament, Demobilization, Reintegration and Repatriation Agreement signed in 2015.

Using a desktop literature review, documentary sources were extensively scrutinized with the main premise being that peace agreements are ineffective, and that indirectly these processes exacerbate the proliferation of warlords. In creating such generic agreements the mandate is flawed and rather than 'contributing to the development and promotion of survival of societal systems' it becomes an effective tool that warlords and strongmen can use to ensure their movement towards political power, maintenance of their rural political fiefdoms and further financial enrichment (Ferreira 2014; Kaplan 1994).

While peace agreements and DDR programs are negotiated and signed, the length of time in terms of implementation and the required funding often leads to resentment amongst militias and communities. Many are not punished or held accountable for their actions and this adds to an already volatile situation (Mudge and Le Pennec 2013). Armed groups are unwilling to admit to or be held accountable for the atrocities they stand accused of committing. Often the accusations are also one-sided and prejudicial in favor of a particular group so this undermines the peace treaties. Often atrocities continue once the agreements are signed and according to international law governments are required to prosecute perpetrators.

Literature Review

Weak governments deliberately sabotage their own bureaucracies in an attempt to reduce expenditure on state institutions. As a result of the poor economies, low employment and insufficient tax revenues, many governments in Africa were, or remain, dependent on the aid provided by international entities. These resources are then channeled into the armed forces, to main clientelism, and to reward strongmen and warlords in order to gain better traction with foreign stakeholders (Reno 1997). Because of the insecurities faced by bureaucrats many resort to plundering what little state resources exist, alternatively they become patrons to ethnic or regional group interests or they resort to becoming warlords (Mann 2005).

Warlordism and militias in Africa are widespread and demonstrate the crisis of the nation state (Lemarchand 1972). Warlords challenge the stable institutional structures and thus the motivations of warlords vary according to their ambitions, resources and political will. It is not the intention of all warlords to gain national political leadership and power but rather regional influence and control of populations and resources. In Africa, many fragmented unstable states underwent devolution of power, where power is delegated from the central government political authority to the peripheral regional administration. The militias that operate under the warlord, together, exploit this state fragility and its inability, or unwillingness, to exert control over the peripheral areas (Marten 2012). Often governments relinquish their socio-political governance of these regions and surrender it to the warlords (Mumford 2013). Governments believe that the warlords are able to control these problematic outlying regions but often, owing to the autocratic and corrupt practices of the warlord, usurpers challenge his position leading to conflict. Militias, under the leadership of commanders and warlords, claim to represent rural or oppressed populations who are marginalized by the national government (Hoffman 2007). Often these groups challenge the status quo and demand access to political power and resources, but it is civilians who are the casualties in these confrontations. It is often with the high mortality rate amongst civilians that international actors are eager to draft peace agreements.

Protecting civilians remains the primary reason that peace agreements are initiated yet they are seldom the beneficiaries. Rather civilians find themselves in a situation where criminality continues unabated; those who terrorize their communities continue to do so without being arrested and often act as a law unto themselves (Vinck and Pham 2010). Often peace agreements include the deployment of peacekeepers that do not quell violence but rather exist as a precursor to civil functionaries to engage in reform rather than enforcing law and order and resuscitating justice mechanisms to ensure peace and stability. The inclusion of all parties in the transitional government does not necessarily bring peace but rather creates political fiefdoms (Pouligny 2004). It has been shown that the parties (and individuals) selected to the transition governments have personal interests that do not extend to governance and socioeconomic growth.

Peace agreements in Africa, and particularly in the CAR, are a repetitive process. Seldom do these agreements acknowledge the political complexities of specific countries, rather a generic draft is put forward that only accommodates certain strongmen at the negotiating table (Daley 2006). Existing government leaders and warlords who have control over and access to economic resources are invited to participate in these processes (Debos 2008). Opposition political parties that do not engage in violent activates and many smaller rebel groups are often excluded from these negotiations (Reno 1997). This ensures that only those who have already benefited from the conflict will continue to benefit from these negotiated settlements. DDR programs that form part of these agreements are manipulated by warlords to benefit themselves personally rather than their fighters or the general population. Warlords, those who have previously served as strongmen in rural areas or as state bureaucrats, are able to further secure senior positions in government (Mehler 2011).

Governments of national unity, or transitional governments, in an attempt to include all warring sides, do not solve the complex political issues nor do they address the issues that led to the conflict. Rather the agreements address issues that are standardized in terms of demobilization, disarmament and rehabilitation. Yet seldom is it considered that many warlords do not wish to cease fighting as the rewards of economic extraction in the regions under their control offer greater financial rewards. Secondly, these resources have to be surrendered to the government, undermining the possible influence, position and authority of the warlord over the region (Hills 1997; Reno 1999). Those who have served in these militias, or state forces, are manipulated into either giving any apportioned benefits they received to their commanders (in a clientelistic relationship) or they resume fighting if they have not received any financial reward (Debos 2008).

Fighters have little in common with professional soldiers and mercenaries so the armed groups are not homogenous (Pouligny 2004). Often fighting is not a fulltime occupation so there is diversity within the groups (Gerlach 2010). Initially, villages and communities create self-defense movements as government authority does not extend to these areas. In response to attacks, theft and intimidation, farmers form armed groups to defend their limited assets, usually grain or animals. These isolated groups eventually form allegiances with other armed groups, state and non-state, to secure better weaponry and other resources. Often these low-level fighters are not considered a central part of the conflict and they are not included in the programs. Funding needed for the demobilizing process is seldom forthcoming or it is delayed. Often women and children, who may be very loyal to their groups, may be fighters and are excluded from these programs as well (for example in countries such as Sierra Leone) (Kaplan 1994; Sullivan and Bunker 2002).

Warlords and Strongmen in Africa

Warlords and strongmen are not a simplistically defined group of individuals. Rather it should be considered that these are individuals who exert control over a small area using a "combination of force and patronage" (Marten 2012). Yet although a warlord exerts this control, his authority, as this is a male socio-political space, requires external financial support either from the government or elsewhere to sustain his control and maintain his control (Aapengnou 2010). Therefore for him to maintain this control there must be collusion with state institutions. However, warlords in Africa must have financial support, often from external stakeholders such as nationals living abroad and donors, in order to maintain clientelistic relationships (Davis 2009).

As African states are weak and seldom meet the Weberian notion of an autonomous sovereign state, they are unable to exert legitimate force over their territorial space. As such the responsibility to maintain political control over the space is relegated to clients. However, as foreign governments no longer provide weaponry in terms of proxy wars this has reduced the influence that African political leaders had over the regional leaders. These leaders were not necessarily traditional leaders but they attributed such characteristics to themselves (Sambanis 2004). Rather warlords are manipulative of not only those whose services they utilize, such as the youth, unemployed men and peasant farmers, but also of NGOs and external stakeholders. Warlords seek out stakeholders who are able to finance their interests, and therefore their ideological interests change in accordance with their sponsors. Therefore a state with weak or failed institutions provides these individuals with access to weaponry and funding with the opportunity to become warlords.

In order to gain attention from the international sponsors and donors, warlords make agricultural activity difficult by chasing farmers off the land or by recruiting them into militias. Warlords require two levels of civilians within their territory (Fearon and Laitin 2003). On one level they require supporters who are recipients of the warlord's largesse who are relatives and/or clients and the second level are the impoverished civilians. By undermining the agricultural processes in their area, the warlord through violent means moves the population within his area and through the lack of resources to sustain the amassed group who fled areas of violence and lost many of their assets. These areas draw the attention of donors who are quick to negotiate with warlords to alleviate the refugee problem (Fearon and Laitin 2010). Warlords can thus gain significantly from these negotiations by creating social instability and manipulating the donors and NGOs.

Warlords are thus able to play various contributors and gain from various stakeholders that include the state, external investors and donors. The persistent state instability through weak governance and inept bureaucratic institutions allows the warlords to gain popularity in their areas. Civilians are led to believe that the warlord has assisted them and many men within camps then established by the donors join the militias to assist the warlord.

Warlords are not uniform in character; their ideology, beliefs and political intentions vary, depending on the relationship to the existing government along with their ability to resource funding to accumulate and maintain power (Reno 1998). The devolution of power at the center results in warlords claiming authority, although illegitimate, due to the lack of state security in rural areas (Hills 1997). Perceptions of traditional authority allow these individuals to validate their presence and their claims to authority, which allows them to recruit individuals for their own limited interests.

Individuals are recruited into militias which are universally defined as armed groups operating under the instruction of a 'leader', although it is argued that in

Africa, unlike militias located on other continents, there is a distinct lack of political will (Hills 1997). This suggests that there are variations of militias which may either be clan, private or freelance aligned. A central factor is that militias extort cash, often to supplement their stipend from the warlords, or as a new breakaway group claiming to protect particular areas.

African political leadership is fraught with individuals who serve in political institutions but are also involved as strongmen and eventual warlords (Mehler 2011). Mehler further asserts that violence is an established mode of competition. Often these individuals recognize that they will not succeed in elections and opt for violent confrontation instead. Utilizing their rural social linkages they offer resources to impoverished villagers to participate in violence. Using the path of legitimacy, political parties, particularly in states such as the CAR, receive less attention from the media and external stakeholders. However, former bureaucrats, and many strongmen are within the government structure, utilize militias in order to receive media coverage, sympathy from citizens and supporters living abroad, and support from external stakeholders. Mehler (2011) suggests that legitimate political parties are marginalized by international mediators in terms of conflict and therefore lose out in the negotiations in peace processes. Therefore any attempt to create democratic governance is marginalized by warlord transition.

In many African countries elections and political leadership are done along ethnic and regional cleavages. Due to the clientelist relationship that exists within African societies and the lack of will to operate and maintain strong state institutions it is easier to secure political longevity through patronage to strongmen in the regions (Marten 2012). Marten asserts that declining revenues from state institutions and the increasing financial assistance from foreign interests, usually in the natural resources, allow rural-based strongmen the option to detach from a dependent relationship with government leadership to assert their own cantons and establish their own unidirectional client relations. This process allows them to assert social and security dominance in their regions by arming the youth and other impoverished individuals. As Mehler (2011) argues, exerting violence garnered international attention particularly when civilians were targeted rather than government forces and opposing militias.

This external support creates state weakness and instability, whether the support originates from NGOs or investors in economic extraction. It is further problematized in that many African governments do not exercise control or authority over many regions, particularly the rural areas (Marten 2012). Weak states create opportunities for warlords to arise. This is not to suggest that all warlords seek national authority, rather warlords and strongmen are most effective in smaller locations where they can exercise control, and manage and monitor the population.

In the African context conflict begins at a higher level and trickles down into the population. Fear within a political environment leads individuals to seek methods to maintain and gain access to political power. Through this process of incorporating armed groups the conflict is transferred from the political sphere to the social civilian environment and (re)interpreted into identity concerns (Francis 2005). When governments promote and are eventually dominated by a single ethnic group it may purposely exclude other groups from accessing state institutions. The perception created is that prosperity is linked to ethnic identity. Those currently accessing the material benefits associated with the state groups in turn support the political identity of the government to the exclusion of others. In such countries where economies are state monopolies and access to employment and economic opportunities are limited, usurping control of the state becomes a goal, or 'the' goal (Mann 2005). The result is an increase in the formation of militias and therefore an increase in violence against state institutions particularly state employees and eventually against civilians.

Repetitive Agreements, Continuing Violence and Identity Salience in the Central African Republic

The CAR descended into violence soon after independence (Vinck and Pham 2010). To maintain relative regime and government stability, political authority mutated into an institution of personal power rather than institutional leadership. As leaders use ethnic and religious affiliations, in the form of client relationships, to maintain political power, this process has undermined the potential for nation-building and patriotism. It is a fragile state like numerous other states in Africa where internal and external influences resulted in a series of governments unable (or unwilling) to protect its citizens. Instead there has been a retreat to using and manipulating identities to maintain positions of power.

The CAR has experienced four violent changes in political leadership, often the result of coups. Ange-Félix Patasse was elected democratically in 1993 but the election came about as a result of an earlier coup in 1981 by General André-Dieudonné Kolingba, against the first president of the CAR, David Dacko. Patasse was then ousted by François Bozizé in 2003. Bozizé in turn was ousted by Michel Djotodia who claimed the presidency in 2013. Only Catherine Samba-Panza, a non-partisan who was appointed interim president, had no known links to militias or defense units. Therefore, since 2000, and within little over a decade, CAR has witnessed violent coups from within, either by the military or militias. During this period an increasing number of militias were observed in the various prefectures, initiated by government and non-government forces, and either in partnership or in conflict with government forces, other militias or civilians.

The conflict in the CAR was and continues to be portrayed as a simplistic bifurcated war between Muslims and Christians. It is simplistically stated that this particular conflict began in December 2012 with the attempt of the Seleka coalition to overthrow President Bozizé's government (Isaacs-Martin 2016). Ignoring the complex political developments and the proliferation, and sustainability, of militias in the CAR, the narrative created of the conflict ignores the competition for political, national and regional control. The country lacks visible policing or effective institutions and this facilitates violence and attacks by the militias, encouraging those seeking access to political power and resources to use violence without negative repercussions for themselves (Isaacs-Martin 2015). Porous borders add to the complexity of upholding peace agreements and DDR programs (Ferreira 2014). When peace programs recommend investigations into violence against civilians such initiatives are undermined as they receive little if any funding. Also the efforts are biased, and serious crimes such as extrajudicial killing, torture and rape are overlooked.

An established pattern of conflict is the movement of people, often other/competing ethnic identities, into agricultural areas particularly for grazing. One such example is a claim made by villagers in relation to the Mbarara community, part of the Peuhl cultural group from Chad, that includes other communities of tension such as the Mbororo and the Fulata (Vinck and Pham 2010; Dunn and Tian 2014). A common trend in competing for arable land is that civilian groups attack each other not under the auspices of identity but rather to access resources such as water and space for animals. Later the identity aspect is manipulated by interest groups and individuals seeking political traction (Scherrer 2003). The tension is heightened when bandits steal cattle and kidnap individuals, then communities attempt to arm themselves. This has led to an alignment with militias such as the coalition Seleka and the continued ethnic tensions that may initially not have been violent but tense and which gradually took on confrontational overtones.

In general, ethnic groups are defined, either within or outside the groups, as sharing a common descent, history, culture, language, religion or territory (Mann 2005). These traits are often internalized and considered natural and ascribed by many within the group identity. This belonging implies an extension of kinship and community linked to a distinct identity with distinct boundaries (Cohen 1985). These boundaries define the characteristics and the sentiment of those within the community. According to prevailing theories, this creates an emotional connection in which certain members are willing to kill those who are outside of the group and even those within the group who are seen to be traitors to the identity structure. Leaders, in particular, use these sentiments to evoke images of unity and blood connections to raise hostilities towards outsiders (Hughey 1998). History demonstrates that it requires little effort for these sentiments to be translated into issues of self-defense, preservation and opportunism (Weber 1998). While ethnic groups remain distinct with underlying tensions, the CAR has not had a lengthy history of ethnic conflict and almost no religious conflict, even as the country has faced continuous economic difficulties, deprivation and marauding bandits in the rural areas. Since 2002 much of the conflicts and violence has been attributed by the population to competing political elites rather than to strife between communities of different ethnic identities.

Using these sentiments and traits of identity, ordinary civilians are capable of murder if such behavior is supported by institutions seen as legitimate (Isaacs-Martin 2016). Often this behavior is interpreted as self-defense and ironically it is often the perpetrators that consider themselves the victims. Alternatively the ethnic tensions are such that perpetrators consider their violence to be a necessary preemptive attack as they perceive, or are led to believe through actors, that their lives are inevitably in danger (Mann 2005). Civilians receive information through government sources or the militias that certain groups are being favored or targeted. As identities are embedded in ethnicity, religion, or tribal allegiances people are easily convinced that their group is exploited, excluded, targeted, or condemned. These sentiments have political and social consequences that in their extreme form can result in cleansing and expulsion (for ethnic cleansing in general, see Mann 2005).

Militias are not homogenous or cohesive in terms of structure or motive. They are comprised of, although not always, a dominant ethnic or religious group and members, particularly rank-and-file, consist of a motley crew of ex-soldiers, mercenaries, unemployed youth with guns and bandits. These groups form and disintegrate quickly after seeking access to material gains, first in the locality in which they often originate where they monopolize violence (Alden et al. 2011; Gerlach 2010). This use of identity allows the militia to claim ideological control over a region to the exclusion of competitor militias such as loyalists and government troops.

Farmers form self-defense units in the rural areas to protect their villages from looting, attacks and assaults by armed groups and bandits. Farmers, as with members of the military, are more traditional in thinking and therefore more ethnically aligned. While there are militias who claim to embrace an ideological standpoint, most exist for the extraction of resources and extortion from the population. An example is the UFDR, claiming to represent the grievances of the Gula ethnic group (Vinck and Pham 2010) but maintained control of the diamond trade in the Haute-Kotto prefecture (Mudge and Le Pennec 2013). Similarly, the CPJP formed in 2008 claiming to represent the Runga ethnic group and yet also gained control of diamond mines in the Haute-Kotto prefecture. These groups eventually merged into the Seleka.

The Seleka became a coalition militia composed primarily of the Convention of Patriots for Justice and Peace (CPJP), the Patriotic Convention for the Salvation of Kodro (CPSK), the Union of Democratic Forces for Unity (UFDR), Union of Republican Forces (UFR) and the Alliance for the Rebirth and Rebuilding (A2R) as well as self-defense units that join the other militias to access weapons, resources and protection (Mudge and Le Pennec 2013).

The Seleka coalition seized control of 15 out of the 16 prefectures, taking control of the capital Bangui and suspending the Constitution where Michel Djotodia, a Muslim, proclaimed himself interim president in 2013. Due to the successful yet violent momentum of Seleka, and the perceived religious element, at best marginally relevant to the participants in government and the militias, became salient once the conflict escalated and incorporated the anti-Balaka forces. However, once Seleka gained control of Bangui they began to attack all the neighborhoods as well as the FACA (Forces Armees Centra Africaines), demonstrating the factionalism within militia structures and the lack of central coalition leadership authority over the fighters (Isaacs-Martin 2016). Seleka became notorious for attacking and razing villages in the rural areas of the CAR and targeting young men. Such behaviors also heightened ethnic and religious tensions between communities as happened with the Mbarara ethnic group (see Mudge and Le Pennec 2013).

Almost all those who claim leadership have utilized violence in the form of militias to secure their positions. It must be noted that prior to the claims of a bifurcated conflict in the CAR there were several militias. Also armies from neighboring countries, most notably Chad, are said to contribute to the instability in the northern prefectures of the CAR (Debos 2008). Chadian soldiers even formed part of the presidential guard under Bozize.

In the course of the conflicts and political turmoil, CAR is a fertile ground for the development of a number of militias and armed groups, and various more or less fragile coalitions among these. These armed groups controlled areas within particular prefectures, and therefore the militia coalition Seleka exercised virtually full control of the northern and eastern prefectures to the exclusion of the government. The fragility of these relationships and the instability of the militias were illustrated by segments of the CPJP militia defecting to support the government troops. These armed groups in the CAR exhibit loose social affiliations and shared ethnic, religious and regional identities. The origins of the anti-Balaka armed group are like those of any militia. It is reported that it was created by Bozizé, but its origins are most likely to have begun in the 1990s as a self-defense group responding both to attacks by bandits from the north of CAR and to the Armée pour la Restauration de la République et al. Démocratie (APRD). The removal of Bozizé in 2013, many ex-government troops and ex-presidential guards joined the anti-Balaka in the hope they could regain their state employment. Like the Séléka, the anti-Balaka became, and remains, a coalition of interest groups. These associations are more about convenience and pursuing a particular aim than acknowledging conscious identity: there does not appear to be an ideology other than material gain and access to political power for the leaders of these groups.

Within such a complex morass of conflict the notion of peace agreements as they currently exist is not an effective solution in returning the country to social, political and economic stability. Peace agreements do not necessarily appeal to all the invited parties; often militia and government leaders do not accept or adhere to agreements. An example of such behavior is that of a CPJP commander, Mohamed Moussa Dhaffane, who rejected the terms of the 2012 peace agreement and created his own rebel group, the CPSK. Although he later merged his militia with the Seleka he was appointed as a minister in the transitional government but was later accused of recruiting mercenaries hence repeating a cycle of violence to gain more power (Mudge and Le Pennec 2013). The proliferation of non-state actors in the country, overwhelmingly led by former bureaucrats and government ministers, has challenged the power and authority of existing government leadership. The reason for this is that many challengers would be unable to secure leadership through a democratic elective process. Political parties in the CAR (Mehler 2011) are often marginalized in conflict and do not receive the support, or resources, that are allocated to warlords, strongmen, militias and governments. Therefore external stakeholders and donors exacerbate the continued use and existence of non-state armed actors through the methods used that benefit the combatants more than civilians.

Ineffectiveness of Peace Agreements in the CAR

The Ariadne thread present in all the peace agreements signed in the CAR is the general amnesty granted to military personnel, combatants and civilians from recognized militias who are present in the negotiations. While for the international stakeholders it suggests the quickest solution to the conflict, it indirectly creates an environment where greed, revenge and power are sought. Militias become a tool used to manipulate populations, stakeholders and donors. The constant changing of allegiances is indicative that smaller groups utilize identity in order to coalesce while the larger groups, which often incorporate other armed actors, are most concerned with resource extraction and financial incentives. This makes lasting peace impossible due to the limited opportunities available to men and women that are indirectly impacted upon by militia behaviors.

Peace agreements dictate that militia troops must be confined to particular regions to undergo DDR programs and that these sites will be determined by mutual agreement between the negotiating parties. This demonstrates a lack of understanding of how militias operate and their fluid associations and allegiances. Promises are also made that various militias, such as with the Birao Agreement the APRD, FDPC and UFDR fighters, will be placed under the protection of the national armed forces, FACA. A common characteristic of militias is that fighters are seeking entry or re-entry into the military because it is seen as an opportunity of secure employment. Yet conflict has arisen, as seen with the Bagui Accords, because the failure to pay soldiers also leads to them deserting the ranks and forming militias (Pouligny 2004).

The National Reconciliation Pact noted the recurring problems of nepotism, tribalism, political patronage and the misappropriation of funds. Much of the state appointments in CAR happen through a process of clientelism and group familiarity. State institutions serve predatory functions rather than to benefit civilians. Bureaucrats learnt to utilize their positions in order to secure themselves as patrons and thus establish themselves as pseudo leaders in the rural areas. This is often how warlords establish themselves by making claims to traditional leadership. As long as the state institutions that monitor graft are ineffective, this avenue remains open to abuse and the continued cycle of violence. Therefore the state becomes an enemy upon itself and forms the location where non-state actors are initiated.

Peace agreements are limited in their effectiveness due to the limited number of signatories. One such example was the Birao Agreement, a committee comprised of one representative from Gabon, three from the CAR government, three from the militias referred to as politico-military movements, a special representative of the UN secretary-general and a representative of the International Organization of La Francophonie. The militias that are invited to these agreements are often coalitions and although there is a central leadership, they do not have effective control over the organization. Because these coalitions are loosely affiliated, each militia has its own command structure and the fighters are loyal to that particular commander. Also this is linked to patrons that transcend conflict so individuals and communities remain loyal to them even if they join coalition forces.

A consistency in the agreements is strengthening democratic processes and respecting human rights; that differences between parties must be settled by non-violent means (United Nations 2008a, b). The National Reconciliation Pact highlighted that signatories could only use elections to access political power not violence. Mehler (2011) noted that when individuals realize they have little chance of success in using elections as a means to access political power, they resort to violence and the use of armed groups to further their political agenda. This has been a procedure utilized for decades in the CAR and without effective institutions to override this behavior it will persist as an effective method. Another concern is that government itself is a problem in terms of limiting and restricting candidates to run for political office (Reno 1998). By arresting opposition or competitors the government itself limits opportunities for political access and forces former bureaucrats to use violence to access, and eventually control, political institutions.

Noted in the National Reconciliation Pact of 1998 there is an overarching theme of national unity and sovereignty (United Nations 2008c; 2013). The Pact highlights the complexities in the CAR at present, including the persistent socioeconomic crisis, resulting in escalating poverty, declining purchasing power, reduced food production resulting in famine and widespread malnutrition, as well as the breakdown of family and social ties. These social and economic concerns elevate social conflict. The proliferation of weapons, banditry and common criminality led to an upsurge of insecurity in the capital Bangui as well as the interior (United Nations 1998). The Pact has the largest number of signatories including the Armed Forces, the Association of Mayors, 29 political parties, five trade unions and a number of civil society and religious organizations. The 2013 signing of the Libreville Agreement included the Seleka coalition, representatives of other militias and political party representation. This agreement gives a general mention of returning the country to peace and the rule of law. It includes the need for cooperation. The Libreville Accord, as signed on 11 January 2013, incorporated the CAR government, the Seleka (UFDR, CPJP, CPSK, UFR), political parties, civil society groups and other militia groups (United Nations 2015).

While in principle these agreements seem inclusive, the problem is the shortsightedness of those seeking political power. In 2014 it was noted that when the Seleka negotiated it wanted access to portfolios that were resource driven such as mining, lumber extraction and defense. The notion of creating a cohesive society and the creation of a viable inclusive economy seemed to be of little interest to the group. Therefore if the parties to negotiations are not themselves invested in creating national unity but rather enrichment the purpose of the peace agreements is void.

The initial Libreville Peace Agreement of 2008 focuses on the APRD and the need to rehabilitate the civilian population as well as to implement DDR programs. It also speaks of the need to incorporate combatants and provide amnesty to the fighters and civilians involved in the conflict. Because the conflict was concentrated in the north, north-east and center of the country, there were two parties engaged to sign the Agreement, namely, three representatives of the CAR government and three representatives of the APRD (United Nations 2008a). In the Accord signed in June 2008 the signatories were government and three representatives of the various militias.

The 2015 Agreement between the Transitional Government and armed groups was the first document that incorporated the role played by women and children in the conflict. Women are to receive the same treatment and rewards as men. Combatants are provided with the opportunity to be absorbed into the state forces or be reintegrated back into their communities and provided with a 'basic support package' that includes reskilling to provide individuals with alternative opportunities and choices. This package, which is often delayed due to the bureaucratic processes and conditions that external donors seek, complicates the aim of preventing fighters from resorting to arms again.

Common to all the agreements is the notion to respect law and order and particularly the civilian population with the assistance of the international community. In order for the agreement to be realized one of the shared aims is to reduce weapons in the affected country as this contributes to criminality and intimidation but also serves as an avenue to continue violent attacks and warfare.

More than 50% of conflicts that have entered into peace agreements have erupted again in civil wars (Ferreira 2014). This can be attributed to weak governments as well as existing ethnic and religious tensions. Also combatants who are trained by international teams assisting governments also find the fighters defecting to militias which further highlights the fluidity of these armed associations. Peace agreements need to be country specific rather than generic in their character. Without understanding the complexity of a state and particularly the manner in which state and non-state actors behave, these agreements will only serve as platforms for opportunism. While governments and militias use rhetoric to defend their positions and highlight their ideological underpinnings, their actions reveal a lack of interest in creating democratic processes and effective governance. This is most evident in the composition of the motley crew of fighters and, secondly, violence and intimidation seem to be the only purpose of these armed groups.

Conclusion

Persistent conflicts in Africa result in a cyclical proliferation of peace agreements, accords and ceasefires. While these documents attempt in good faith to bring about peace, restore government and manifest democratic processes, they fail more than they actually succeed. This is due to the generic expectations set out in these documents that do not address the socio-political and economic complexities in many of the affected states and regions. Often these documents do not consider that there are external and internal factors that bear directly on the conflict and that negotiations between invited parties do not necessarily quell these hostilities.

This chapter attempted to point out that these documents do not offer targeted solutions but rather overarching solutions that are deemed appropriate to end conflict. These include that the parties to the agreement should cease fighting and violence against each other and the civilian population. Secondly, that once all the parties have agreed to the conditions set out for achieving peace, which is to stop the violence, then elections can be held, a government of national unity can be established, democratic government institutions can be (re)constituted and the civilian population are granted their human rights. While these generic suggestions can assist with nation building these processes include problematic initiatives as well.

The peace agreements targeted in this chapter recommend that all combatants who are signatories to the negotiations are to be granted amnesty. Thereafter many of the fighters are to be drafted into DDR programs in which they can choose to be reintegrated into their communities or become part of the state armed forces. These are complicated by actors not often considered within these processes such as militia commanders, warlords and strongmen. Often DDR programs are manipulated by signatories along with the networks of militias and ordinary fighters find themselves disadvantaged by programs meant to assist them. However these are very complex processes and they are further complicated by issues of clientelism and ethnic and cultural identities.

Although identities are not considered the primary reason for the conflict, often these issues are located in economic and employment concerns (De Zeeuw 2008). Fighters are often recruited into militias from former self-defense units along with unemployed youth, ex-soldiers, ex-policemen and professional mercenaries (Pouligny 2004). Although a motley crew of combatants their primary concern is financial, although their ultimate motivations vary for example ex-soldiers and farmers do not share the same basic interest in joining militias – ex-soldiers wanting to return to the state forces and farmers seeking financial gain to supplement their limited resources. It is within the structure of these groups that identity becomes a salient feature in terms of the actions of the militias and the civilians that are directly affected by the violence.

In the CAR, as with many other states, the violence takes on secondary identity concerns in which ethnicity and religion become a salient feature. This leads outsiders to believe that the conflict is purely directed at ethnic or religious groups. Yet it is seldom considered that this is a consequence of the conflict and it provides a motivation to participants. It is within this environment that the violence escalates and more civilians become victims to criminality that is disguised as ethnic or religious conflict.

Peace agreements do not take these complexities into account particularly in an environment such as the CAR where ethnicity and now religion always become an issue on which militias justify their actions. Their behavior polarizes the social fabric, allowing for personal interests to take precedent among warlords, bureaucrats and strongmen and making it more difficult for generic agreements and accords to be effective in the long term.

References

Aapengnou, C. M. (2010). Misinterpreting ethnic conflicts in Africa. *Africa Security Brief: A Publication of the Africa Center for Strategic Studies, 4*, 1–4. http://www.africacenter.org. Accessed 20 June 2016.

Alden, C., Thakur, M., & Arnold, M. (2011). *Militias and the challenges of post-conflict peace*. London/New York: Zed Books.
Cohen, A. (1985). *The symbolic construction of community*. London/New York: Tavistock Publications.
Daley, P. (2006). Challenges to peace: Conflict resolution in the great lakes region of Africa. *Third World Quarterly, 27*(2), 303–319.
Davis, D. E. (2009). Non-state armed actors, new imagined communities and shifting patterns of sovereignty and insecurity in the modern world. *Contemporary Security Policy, 30*(2), 221–245.
De Zeeuw, J. (2008). *From soldiers to politicians: Transforming rebel movements after civil war*. Boulder: Lynne Rienner.
Debos, M. (2008). Fluid loyalties in a regional crisis: Chadian "ex-liberators" in the Central African Republic. *African Affairs, 107*(427), 225–241. doi:10.1093/afraf/adn004.
Dunn, J. P., & Tian, N. (2014). Conflict spillovers and growth in Africa. *Peace Economics and Peace Science, 20*(4), 539–549.
Fearon, J. D., & Laitin, D. D. (2003). Ethnicity, insurgency and civil war. *American Political Science Review, 97*(1), 75–90.
Fearon, J. D., & Laitin, D. D. (2010). Sons of the soil, migrants and civil war. *World Development, 39*(2), 199–211.
Ferreira, R. (2014). South Africa's participation in the Central African Republic and Democratic Republic of Congo peace missions: A comparison. *Politiea, 33*(4), 4–27.
Francis, D. J. (2005). *Civil militia: Africa's intractable security menace?* Hants: Ashgate.
Gerlach, C. (2010). *Extremely violent societies: Mass violence in the twentieth century world*. New York: Cambridge University Press.
Hills, A. (1997). Warlords, militia and conflict in contemporary Africa: A re-examination of terms. *Small Wars and Insurgencies, 8*(1), 35–51.
Hoffman, D. (2007). The meaning of a militia: Understanding the civil defence forces of Sierra Leone. *African Affairs, 106*(425), 639–662.
Hughey, M. W. (1998). *New tribalisms: The resurgence of race and ethnicity*. New York: New York University Press.
Isaacs-Martin, W. (2015). The motivations of warlords and the role of militias in the Central African Republic. *Conflict Trends, 14*, 26–33.
Isaacs-Martin, W. (2016). (Re)creating political identity, (re)creating spaces: Similar enemies, different victims in the Central African Republic (CAR) conflicts. *International Journal of Conflict and Violence, 10*(1), 25–39.
Kaplan, R. (1994). The coming anarchy. *The Atlantic Monthly, 273*(2), 44–76.
Lemarchand, R. (1972). Political clientelism and ethnicity in tropical Africa: Competing solidarities in nation-building. *The American Political Science Review, 66*, 68–90.
Mann, M. (2005). *The dark side of democracy: Explaining ethnic cleansing*. Cambridge, MA/New York: Cambridge University.
Marten, K. (2012). *Warlords: Strong-arm brokers in weak states*. Ithaca/London: Cornell University.
Mehler, A. (2011). Rebels and parties: The impact of armed insurgency on representation in the Central African Republic. *Journal of Modern African Studies, 49*(1), 115–130.
Mudge, Lewis & E. Le Pennec. (2013, September 18). *I can still smell the dead: The forgotten human rights crisis in the Central African Republic*. https:www.hrw.org/report/2013/09/18
Mumford, A. (2013). *Proxy warfare*. Cambridge, MA/Malden: Polity.
Pouligny, Beatrice. 2004. *The politics and anti-politics of contemporary disarmament, demobilisation and reintegration programs/Les anciens combattants d'aujourd'hui désarmement, démobilisation et réinsertion*. Programme for Strategic and International Security Studies. Centre d'Etudes et de Recherches Internationales Sciences Po/CNRS (CERI). Secrétariat Général de la Défense Nationale (Services du Premier Ministre, France [SGDN]).
Reno, W. (1997). African weak states and commercial alliances. *African Affairs, 96*, 165–185.
Reno, W. (1998). *Warlord politics*. Boulder: Lynne Rienner.
Reno, W. (1999). *Warlord politics and African studies*. Boulder: Lynne Rienner.

Sambanis, N. (2004). What is civil war? Conceptual and empirical complexities of an operational definition. *Journal of Conflict Resolution, 48*(6), 814–858. doi:10.1177/0022002704269355.

Scherrer, C. P. (2003). *Ethnicity, nationalism and violence: Conflict management, human rights and multilateral regimes*. Hants/Burlington: Ashgate.

Sullivan, J. P., & Bunker, R. J. (2002). Drug cartels, street gangs and warlords. *Small Wars and Insurgencies, 13*(2), 40–53.

United Nations. (1998). *National Reconciliation Pact (Bangui National Reconciliation Conference)*. http://peacemaker.un.org/carnationalreconciliationpact98. Accessed 20 June 2016.

United Nations. (2008a). *Accord de cessez le feu et de paix entre le Gouvernement de la Republique Centrafricaine et le mouvement politique et militaire Centrafricain APRD.*. http://peacemaker.un.org/carceasefireaprd2008. Accessed 20 June 2016.

United Nations. (2008b). *Accord de paix global entre le Gouvernement de la Republique Centrafricaine et les mouvements politico-militaires APRD, FDPC, UFDR.*. http://peacemaker.un.org/centrafriqueaccordglobal2008. Accessed 20 June 2016.

United Nations. (2008c). *Déclaration de principe des parties aux négociations de Libreville sur la crise Centrafricaine.*. http://peacemaker.un.org/cardeclarationofprinciples2013. Accessed 20 June 2016.

United Nations. (2013). *Accord politique de Libreville sur la résolution de la crise politico-sécuritaire en République Centrafricaine.*. http://peacemaker.un.org/centrafriqueaccordpolitique2013. Accessed 20 June 2016.

United Nations. (2015). *Agreement between the transitional government and the armed groups on the principles of disarmament, demobilization, reintegration and repatriation and of integration into the uniformed state forces of the central African Republic.*. http://peacemaker.un.org/node/2742. Accessed 20 June 2016.

Vinck, P., & Pham, P. (2010). *Building peace, seeking justice: A population-based survey on attitudes about accountability and social reconstruction in the Central African Republic*. Berkeley: Human Rights Centre.

Weber, M. (1998). Ethnic groups. In M. W. Hughey (Ed.), *New tribalisms: The resurgence of race and ethnicity* (pp. 17–30). New York: New York University.

Wendy Isaacs-Martin is an associate professor in the Archie Mafeje Research Institute at the University of South Africa. Her fields of research include identities – gendered, ethnic, religious – and scapegoating in conflict with regard to nation building and national consciousness. Central to her research is the construction of communities and how violence is linked to the memory, development and sustainability of group identity central and peripheral to political dynamics. Contact details: isaacw@unisa.ac.za.

Chapter 10
Africa and the Media

Damilola Adegoke

Introduction

The name 'Africa' elicits unpalatable images of depressed people regularly inundated with tribal conflicts and wars over minerals; this bias is further entrenched in media representation that quite often portrays Africa as a backwater continent ravaged by people with no development agenda; perpetually in need of paternalistic intervention from the more developed countries of the West. The narratives garishly feature disease-stricken infants tied to the back of bone-bare mothers with flies feasting their battered frames. Aid agencies use some of these pitiful images for their fund-raising appeals for saving the vulnerable people of the *helpless continent*. Michira (2002) captures these conditions thus: "The African continent is depicted as the 'dependent Africa', 'crisis driven Africa' and 'hopeless' or 'pitiable Africa'". The images have largely portrayed the continent negatively and they tend to exaggerate the 'dark' side of Africa. Some of these warped representations of Africa are carry-over from slavery and colonial episodes of the continent; unfortunately, these perceptions still remain the same till date. Powerful media houses, editors, journalists, politicians and scholars have helped to solidify these obvious misrepresentations or jaundiced view of the continent and its people.

Success stories, home-grown indigenous-led innovations are rarely covered by these media outfits who will fly in a heartbeat to the continent to report epidemic and war outbreaks. These biased representations have been criticized by scholars, media analysts and development strategists as negatively impacting on the image of the continent (Mahadeo and McKinney 2007). The colonial narrative of the dark continent still dominates several media portrayals of Africa; underneath most pretentitious liberal 'objective' view of Africa are several silent instances of discriminative depiction of a hopeless continent of conflictual people. Media representations

D. Adegoke (✉)
African Leadership Centre, Kings College, London, UK
e-mail: damilola.adegoke@kcl.ac.uk

O. Akanle, J.O. Adésìnà (eds.), *The Development of Africa*, Social Indicators Research Series 71, DOI 10.1007/978-3-319-66242-8_10

are about the West and the Rest, with contrasting stories of western progress against non-functional, retrogressive countries of Africa. Nyabola (2014) also observed this betraying overgeneralization, according to her, "The Rest is necessarily set up in opposition to The West in resulting coverage, and issues or situations are rarely, if ever, analysed for their intrinsic impact or worth. Events or situations are therefore analysed as what the West is not.

There are magazine programs and documentaries about Africa which paint glooming pictures of squalor, poverty and lack of agency; this is in contrast with a more progressive programming of the West as innovative, idyllic and cosmopolitan (Kenney 1995). This further accentuates the negative stereotypes about the continent. African media organizations depend largely upon foreign news corporations for information about Africa - these media organizations are usually more funded than their African counterparts; it is not too uncommon to read news about Africa reproduced by local stations from these western big media organizations. This dependency extends to the proliferation of Africa-focused documentaries in various communication media across the continent. Africa is not all wars, gloom and doom. There are outstanding innovative ideas in different sectors which are underreported or omitted by the media behemoth.

The impacts of the media on development across the continent is immeasurable. Both traditional and the new media have played significant roles in revamping development initiatives and discourses across the different countries on the continent. Internet digital technologies just like its predecessors – radio, television and the print media, have contributed to large paradigmatic shifts in various aspects of the social-economic experience of the people of the continent. The pivotal roles played by development internet communication ranging from the fields of health, agriculture and development financing, to mobile banking have been discussed in several scholarly publications (Ojo 2006; Awuor et al. 2016). The opportunities provided by internet technologies have enhanced development engagements with different people thinking up solutions to diverse challenges; there are applications developed to address health issues; expand commerce, and provide accessible information on weather and new agricultural practices to farmers who needed information for yield increase. The democratic, participatory nature of the internet, most importantly the social media, exposed several sustainable development interventions undertaken by Africans for Africa as against the old perception of a needy continent with no agency. The superlative contributions of the new media to development in Africa is no doubt inspiring, but the reach and extent of such impacts are limited due to several factors to be discussed in this chapter. However, there is still more to be done to address the several emerging problems.

It is not an overstatement to affirm the contribution of the media to democratic governance. Social media in recent times has helped to mobilize activists against dictatorship and ant-democratic forces - a ready case in point is the July 2016 foiled coup attempt in Turkey, where the President enjoined Turkish and pro-government forces to quell the coup (Aribogan 2016). The media also helped in mobilizing the people of Tunisia and Burkina Faso to unseat their unpalatable government; a similar transformational experience occasioned by the new media has been reported in Ivory Coast.

The internet combines all the elements of the other traditional print and electronic media. It makes interconnectivity possible across different locations, provides a broad platform for the other non-electronic media to easily disseminate information while looping back-and-forth feedbacks between communicators and their targets. The different internet versions of the existing media empower development agencies, governments and democratic interests to engage actively with the community in a return path approach for their advancements.

There are inventive media programs which diverse development themes and agenda including; mass mobilization programs at elections, child immunization campaigns, health awareness or disaster information management amongst other initiatives. There are several media and communication theories which help explain the roles of development communication and media. These theories include development communication theory, social responsibility theory, and democratization/democratic-participant media theory. Others are dominant theory, self-reliance theory, diffusion theory, and dependent and interdependent theory. This chapter focuses on the first three theories because this work is not a treatise on development communication per se. These theories shall be discussed because they provide explanatory models and templates for understanding issues and challenges surrounding the role of media in development; especially as regards the African continent. The impacts of new media—the internet technologies on development in Africa shall be discussed alongside the selected theories.

Development Media and Communication Theories

The emergence of development communication theory could be linked with the evolution of the modernization theory of development of the 1950s and 1960s. This model is predicated on the assumption that development is synonymous with industrialization and westernization; a society without a vestige of Western modernization is considered underdeveloped while those who chose to emulate the western template are categorised as 'developing'. This may not be too far from the colonial impression of previous centuries, when natives were called pagans in need of the illuminating light of the gospel. Missionaries had to be sent to civilize the savage; this undergird several evangelization motives of the colonial Africa era.

The index for measuring countries' development is the gross national product (GNP)—the sum total of the market value of all goods and services produced by a country and for final sale in an economy. Closely related to GNP is the gross domestic product (GDP), which is restricted to the measure of the values of goods and services produced within a country. It differs from GNP which includes the country's owned entities outside of its shore (James 2011). This reduces development measures to economic development only. This biased approach favors the West because of their mass production capabilities which trump those of the developing countries. Countries in the Global South, particularly Africa, will find it difficult to make the criteria because of some inhibitors which affect their production capabilities. Most of these developing countries are mere raw materials exporting countries whose major foreign exchange earnings come from feeding big production factories of more industrialised Europe and America. Non-Processed products of the rubber plantations of Liberia; the unrefined Niger-Delta oil, raw Ghana's cocoa, and tea leaves of Kenya are ferried to service big factories of the industrialised West. These are then processed into different finished goods that are exported back to the developing countries at far greater price more than the value of the raw products they got form these countries. As a result of these unbalanced development matrices, real development should not be restricted to economic advancement alone but must include social justice, transparency in governance and other forms of ethical practices that will assure equity in the distribution of the countries' wealth amongst their citizens.

The previous assumption influenced the top-down mass communication approach of the 50s and 60s that development information dissemination must be about prompting less developed countries to adopt and emulate the Western modernized model. People became masses to be programmed and manipulated into following particular behavioural pattern; to be spoon-fed with perceived panacea for development. This top-down hierarchical development communication approach was promoted by UNESCO for Third World countries; they were inadvertently or deliberately encouraged to adopt the process of mass media influenced largely by David Berlo's Sender–Message–Channel–Receiver (SMCR) model of communication which was derived from the Shannon Weaver model of communication of the 1940s. This particular model of communication considers mass communication as the transmission of information from a particular point to the other; that is, the sender to the final receivers though specific channels—the aim is to influence change in the targeted masses towards particular goals (Berlo 1960). It was a favoured approach of the modernization theorists, as less developed countries were encouraged to copy the 'developed' West. TV and radio became means of fostering particular views of development as the standard textbook practises for development – Westernization became synonymous with development.

Modernization theory also known as the dominant paradigm of development in development communication is influenced by the scholarly works of Daniel Lerner (1958), Wilbur Schramm (1962) and Everett M. Rogers (1962). Lerner posited that mass media seems to correlate with increased urbanization and political participation. He observed that wealthy countries do have more mass media than poor countries; hence the submission that for poor countries to attain development, they must embrace mass media. In Lerner's words (1958, 52) "[a]s people are more exposed to media, the greater is their capability to imagine themselves as strange persons in strange situations, places and time than did people in any previous historical epoch." Wilbur Schramm submits that mass media is a tool for mass mobilization for development. Mass media should be a platform for motivating social change in the different social and economic lives of people in developing countries, including but not limited to health, urbanization, literacy and agriculture. Like Lerner, Schramm presented examples of the correlation between these mass media campaigns and development (Schramm et al. 1997). Everett Rogers' "diffusion of innovations" characterizes a process of transmission or communication of innovations across social systems over time. Innovation is necessary for the sustenance of societal development; the resultant effects of innovation adoption would be felt when it reaches critical mass among adopters who are grouped into five categories, namely, the innovation itself, communication channels, time, and a social system (Rogers 1962, 150). The ease or otherwise of the diffusion of innovation across the different structures of society through communication would decide the development or underdevelopment of that society.

All the positions expressed above are somewhat illustrative of the correlation versus causation argument of Thomas Friedman's McDonald's Peace Theory, also known as the Golden Arches Theory of Conflict Prevention, which argues that countries with McDonald's within their territories have never gone to war against each other, thereby tending towards a certain warped conclusion that McDonald's correlates with peace (Friedman 1999). Similarly, it would be erroneous to conclude that the modernization process of mass media propagation will definitely lead to development. There are other extraneous, latent factors which must be taken into consideration which also play significant roles in development other than the obvious factors.

A new theory emerged challenging the modernization theory. This new theory emerged from the influence of Raúl Raúl Prebisch, the Argentine director of the United Nations Economic Commission for Latin America and his colleagues; different variants of the theory feature emerged in the late 50s and early 60s, they include liberal reform—the Marxist approach of Andre Gunder Frank, and Immanuel Wallerstein's world systems theory. These theories were widely adopted by members of the Non-Aligned Movement which includes countries categorized as underdeveloped or less developed. Raúl Prebisch proposed a radical departure from the trade-and-export orientation favored by developed countries which hampers the economic growth of the less developed states to an import-substitution industrialization (ISI) model; this model is more like the Prebisch-Singer hypothesis, jointly promoted together with Hans Singer, which suggests that the terms of trade between developed and underdeveloped countries positioned the former more advantageously to be able to exchange more valuable finished goods for cheap raw materials from underdeveloped countries, thereby making the developed countries richer than their less fortunate trading partners (Singer 1998; Toye and Toye 2003; Reinsdorf 2010).

Neoclassical modernization theory does not favor the interests of the less developed states because of some intrinsic flaws in the theory. According to dependency theorists, the world is divided between the rich core developed states and the periphery poor countries exploited by the former. It has been observed that there is an unfair trade balance between the dominant countries and their dependencies (Reyes 2001). Dependency theory suggests a more participatory and inward-looking development communication approach. Unlike the rigid, mass media approach of communication, which often portrays the West in a better light than the impoverished periphery countries, dependency theory advocates for more participatory, community-driven development communication. This horizontal approach is a communication for development (C4D) approach with more focus on everyone which is a far departure from the top-down approach. It enables citizens of the developing countries to tell their own stories. They do not have to fit into predetermined mould and they are people; and not just objects to be used.

It is in consonance with the prevailing narrative to represent the negative side of Africa socio-political life. The focus is usually on the negative; remarkable achievements are underreported. From the media representation of the continent, Africa is a continent in perpetual debt, ravaged by internecine conflicts; with the countries ruled by corrupt dictators. They rarely provide objective analysis of the root causes of these negative experiences. Some of these dictators are stooges of Western imperialist interests; Africa's stolen wealth are banked in the West; this part of the ugly narrative is omitted by western media. Western democracies bolster oppressive regimes and even overthrow legitimate leaders; they sell arms to rebels in troubled regions. The debts allegedly owed the 'pristine' West are usually forced on these countries to support irrelevant elephant projects which are contracted to Western companies. These are few of the imbalances which necessitate the call for a more locally-driven, community-based communication approach.

Though favoured above the modernization theory, dependency theory is faced with several challenges which include the difficulty of its applications to real life challenges which portend serious setbacks for its applicability; another major factor which affect the popularity of the alternative theory is the fall of communism. Capitalism and crass consumerism which glorify Western lifestyles dominated media across the globe, and its impact resonate more in developing countries of Africa and the global south. Though Community radio is favored above mass media of communication, because of its inherent advantages such as cost-effectiveness and its focus on providing general information on various social as well as community interests; the more market-driven mass media is prevalent across the continent.

Social Responsibility Theory of the Media

The media is pivotal to democracy. Freedom of expression is enshrined in several legal documents of countries of the world. Freedom of expression and information is taken to be a defining factor in determining the openness of a country; it is the basis upon which some nations are considered free while others are termed dictatorial. Social responsibility is a term used in different sectors of human endeavors to describe professional, organizational or individual ethical expectations. Social responsibility theory of the media is a media ethics theory which sits between normative and prescriptive ethical lines. In media and communication discourses, social responsibility theory is used to describe the fourth theory of the media which is preceded by the authoritarian, the liberal and the soviet theories of the media.

Authoritarian theory favours government or state control of the media. Contents are subject to regulation and practitioners are subject to directives or guidelines stipulated by the state. It is a state-centric approach with the main aim of regimepreservations in some case. Less democratic countries adopt this tight-knitted media approach because it helps to consolidate power in the hands of the dictators (who are beneficiaries of this approach). It is a centralised system and largely paternalistic. Political theorists such as John Locke and other libertarians who were ill-disposed to the monarchical absolutism of their time influence advocates of the independent media. With the birth of new democratic nations such as the United States and the French Republic, freedom of expression became the maxim of most of the political leadership over time. The need for a media that is free from government interference and control led to the firming up of the libertarian media theory view that assumes that media practitioners and organs should be free to publish news without fear of sanction or intimidation.

The soviet theory of media is similar to the authoritarian theory but with a slight ideological bent. The area of departure is the role of the media as an integral part of state machinery for ideological propaganda. Private ownership of media is not permitted and the entire contents are subject to the approval or disapproval of the politburo. It is a soviet-style, communist and paternalistic media approach; the aim is to control narratives without allowing for individual expression since the greater preservation of state is considered far above the individuals within the state.

The liberal theory of the media has larger following than the previous autocratic and soviet-style theories; but there are concerns about the nature of what constitutes liberty, especially in relation to responsibility and accountability because absolute freedom is just the extreme opposite of absolute dictatorship. The need to address the controversy attached with yellow journalism led to the search for a better alternative. The ethical demands of media and communication deeply rooted in western thought system represented in Jürgen Habermas's discourse ethics in moral consciousness and communicative action. Habermas's position on media ethics is somewhat related to Immanuel Kant's categorical imperative which sought a form of universal ethics where morality should be universally applicable and not subjective. A street moral ethics which succinctly captures Kant's ethical imperative is that oft-quoted maxim "do unto others, what you will have them do to you." Habermas's position is about media responsibility; both the senders and receivers must understand the extent of their message (Habermas 1990). Absolute freedom is as dangerous as absolute censorship; a responsible, free media that is accountable to societal values is considered better by advocates of this alternative theory than any of the last three preceding theories.

Social responsibility theory of the media, though rooted in classical ethical theories, gained currency in modern times through the report of the Hutchins Commission, officially named the Commission on Freedom of the Press. The Commission was composed of several scholars led by Robert Hutchins and funded by Henry Luce the publisher of Time during the Second World War. It was formed to address emerging criticism of Western media and their ownership. The mandate of the Commission was to identify the proper role of the media in a modern democracy (Pickard 2014). It was an attempt at reinvention of the image of the media. The social responsibility media theory prescribes the responsibility of media and journalists to society (Nerone et al. 1995). However, while pretending to implement some of the recommendations of responsibility theory, several African governments clamp down on media organizations; they attempt to gag the media.

Nigeria, Kenya and Uganda have attempted at different times to enact media gag laws under the guise of ensuring socially responsible media. There are obvious debasements of the term; the confusion often unfolds from the meaning of the word "responsible"; responsible to whom? If it is responsibility to society, these draconian leaders believe they possess the mandate of society to determine what is socially appropriate. Since the term society in itself is also subject to diverse interpretations.

Without playing hard at sophistry, social responsibility theory sought a media that is beneficial to the general society and not just to a section of the society. Another subject of concern is whether society could be trusted with the determination of ethics/morality because what is moral in one society may be considered immoral in others. Despite these problematics, social responsibility theory seems to promote democratic ideals more than the more centralised and anachronistic theories.

Democratization/Democratic-Participant Media Theory

By the 1960s, the media took a huge leap with the sporadic rise in big media corporations. These big media organizations were owned by big governments and private interests. The ownership of the media raised several questions about media freedom; the implication of the emergence of these media behemoth challenged the libertarian and social responsibility models. The last two theories originally sought to combat authoritarian and Soviet style mass media, but the consequences of the adoption of some of the models led to big media, top-down hegemonies with more power to the senders while the receivers got neglected or excised from media decisions. It is almost taken as a given that the telling sign of a truly democratic society is a vibrant and open media; several scholars have researched this trend (Baker 2002; Dahlgren 2009; Curran 2011).

The command model of previous theories needed to give way for a more associative model which is similar to the libertarian and social responsibility models' preference for freedom of the media, but unlike the libertarian view of media, the democratic-participant theory advocates a more participatory model where everybody- citizens inclusive, participated in media contents decision programming. The participation may be active or passive. The idea of a monolithic, unidirectional, centralized media had to give way for a more pluralistic, multi-directional, looping approach to enhance democratic participation. The major demand of democratic-participant theory is summarized in the quest for a more democratic approach to the media without leaving out any nodes (senders and receivers).

The democratization theory of the media provides opportunities for non-institutionalized entities such as individuals, communities and social interest groups to own their own communication processes and to tailor their content to their needs and demands. They have true freedom to choose and design their information channels to suit their needs without the stiff bottle-neck of the other media processes. Ghana, Kenya. Nigeria and some other countries in Africa have benefited from this model of communication; the advent of internet radio further enhances media democratization. There are now community-based radio and online media platforms focusing on rule of law, health awareness, voters' participation and political engagements.

While there are several theories and models of media and communication, the three pivotal theories above help to properly identify some of the opportunities and challenges militating against the impacts of conventional media and the new social media on development in Africa. While acknowledging the skewed media presentation or underreporting of Africa's true development strides by journalists outside the continent, a lot still has to be done by policymakers, African journalists, and African-owned media organizations in promoting the positive image of Africa.

Digital Media, Social Media and Development: Opportunities and Challenges

New technologies do not completely displace preceding technologies; they are innovations for newer opportunities. Digital broadcast technologies and social media technologies have not totally displaced or totally eradicate challenges of older technologies; instead, these newer technologies present a more robust approach to doing things differently. Whereas the communication media of the pre-digital era favors centralized control which empowers big businesses and governments with the capabilities to regulate the message and transmission media; newer digital communication technologies including the internet have drastically reduced that capabilities. In the past, it was expensive to set up a radio, print or television media outfit. There were strict government regulations and bureaucracies which made establishments of media outfits challenging. This is no longer the case, because of the democratization of the internet which made user-generated content possible; individual enthusiasts can now stream live videos and broadcast radio contents all over the internet with little or no government control. This chapter will address some associated socio-thematic issues which define the opportunities and challenges surrounding new media technologies. They include the nature of open governance and participatory democracies; civic engagements and agenda setting; economy and trade.

Open Governance and Participatory Democracies

Media and Information and communication technology (ICT) have aided plurality and transparency in governance—two key ingredients for progressive democracy. That claim has formed the subject of several discourses around media and development (Carpentier 2011). In recent years, several countries have witnessed significant political change which would not have been possible decades ago before the coming of social media. Governments in developing countries, including those in Africa, have always enjoyed large media control; the emergence of the new media is preserved as an active threat against this hegemony. The features of open governance which include citizens–leaders' interactions, social-driven legislation and mass political engagement through debates on media has contributed to the entrenchment of democracy in some countries of the continent. Politicians now set up Twitter and Facebook pages to engage with their constituents thereby enhancing feelings of inclusivity unlike in the past when politicians only meet with their constituents during electioneering periods.

The inclusivity preached by the democratization theorists is apt here in this case because of the many politically active internet users who constantly use social media to interact with political leadership. The United Nations recently passed a resolution affirming that the same offline freedom of expression human rights enshrined in Article 19 of the Universal Declaration of Human Rights and the International Covenant on Civil and Political Rights should be extended to include online expressions (United Nations 2016). Nigeria and Senegal are parties to this resolution. Kenya, the Republic of Congo, Burundi and South Africa voted against the resolution with Togo, Cote D'Ivoire, Ethiopia and Algeria abstaining. This resolution will protect online social and political activists from repressive government legislation aimed at shutting down political dissent.

Results of these internet democratization can be observed in the various political experiences across countries of the continent in recent times. The Tunisian revolution which saw the ousting of Ben Ali was partly made possible by the new media. The Egyptian revolution is another example of the effects of the people's power; though it would be too optimistic to credit the success of these political changes solely to the social media; but the new media enhanced and empowered citizens to take on big powers.

Aside from regime change, new media and digital technologies have also helped to ensure open elections across the continent. Politicians now deploy verified fan pages through which they present manifestos and address the public without having to rely on state media which may not be favorable to opposition parties. The Ushahidi and Frontline SMS platforms have been used to monitor elections in Mozambique, Kenya and Nigeria using crowdsourcing techniques.

The 2030 Agenda for Sustainable Development acknowledges certain fulcra points which include access to justice, financial transparency, and rule of law demands that signatory countries provide transparency and social inclusion in their policies. In pursuit of the ideals included in the several conventions and resolutions to which member states are signatories, the African Union declared 2016 as the Year of Human Rights and member states have perhaps, recognized the need to allow for more inclusion in political affairs.

It is not an exaggeration to state that transparency in governance can boost development. In 2011, Kenya adopted an open budget policy which gives citizens the opportunity to monitor government spending and to track budgetary allocations; this makes Kenya the first country to do so (World Bank 2012). Liberia, Sierra

Leone and to some extent Nigeria have also seen the need to allow open budgeting in parliamentary, states or executive spending, a good example is Kaduna State of Nigeria with its recent open budget policy (Adelana 2015). Tanzania's use of open data to guarantee transparency over land access and distribution has been applauded because it could increase citizens' confidence in government (Taylor 2014). All these gains have been made possible through the thriving democratization of the media and the influences of other development media theories.

It must be noted however, that there have been several attempts by governments to stifle the new media Africa because of the threat to hegemonic powers which they enjoyed but which now seem threatened. The power of the media to expose corruption and illegal conduct have not served the interests of the ruling African elites well, hence attempts have been made by several governments including those of Nigeria, Kenya and Tanzania to promulgate media gag bills'.

Civic Engagements and Agenda Setting

Maxwell McCombs and Donald Shaw's agenda setting theory of the 1970s accentuates the need to dwell more on salient media contents and representation as well as the effects they have on the audience (McCombs and Shaw 1972). It is now taken for granted that the media help shape popular perceptions and set agenda for public discourses, debates and eventual policy formulations. The crucial role of the media to development comes into play in this regard because in recent times both the traditional and the new digital media interface by making certain issues prevalent in the public domain; the consequence of which is response from government. The triads—agenda setting, priming and framing—are central to policy and development communication.

In 2014, schoolgirls were abducted in Chibok. The incident did not receive the expected reactions from the government of Nigeria until a tweet by Ibrahim Abdullahi went viral leading to a massive movement now known as the #BringBackOurGirls movement; the hashtag caught the attention of several celebrities and global leaders leading to global pressure on the Nigerian state to do more for the abducted girls. The issue of the Nigeria girl child became the subject of several media engagements following this awareness.

Prior to the Chibok abduction, another issue which dominated the media was the #ChildNotBride hashtag war which led to several interrogations on the status of the Nigerian girl child. Senator Sani Yerima was called out for what was perceived as his attempt to slip in child marriage into Nigeria's constitution through the backdoor. The reason behind the media uproar was a widely-supported argument for the removal of section 29 (4)(b) of Nigeria's constitution which states that "any woman who is married shall be deemed of full age." Retention of that section of the constitution would legalize child marriage because any girl below 18 could be regarded as a woman by the reason of marital status (Shantel 2014). This position was resisted vehemently by Nigerians across different strata. The social media provided a crucial platform for collectivising and aggregating opinions for active citizenship engagements and agenda setting in both cases.

Most Westerners have not been to Africa, yet they have media-primed images of a dark continent where people go about shooting each other; these images are bolstered by films and camera shots of major news channels depicting gross poverty-stricken people led by rogue leaders (Dijkstra 2014). The dire situations in selected parts of Africa are generalized for the entire continent. Some erroneously have this conjured image, naively induced by media props that make them assume that Africa is a country and not a continent.

African countries need to harness the full potential of the media, especially the movie industry, to influence behavior and to sway public opinion towards development ends. Hollywood has helped to promote American culture in idyllic ways and these movies largely influence several immigrants from developing African countries to attempt ardours journey to European countries where the streets are thought to be 'paved with gold.' These characterizations have become ingrained on the minds of youths in developing countries who want to emulate the lifestyle of the West through the purchase of several goods which are considered sleek and trendy from these countries. New African music productions copy western styles just like the movie industries.

In Africa, the Nigerian movie industry, also known as Nollywood, is serving the same purpose but not to the extent of America's Hollywood. These movies have spread Nigerian culture across the continent, though much still needed to be done in the area of content improvement because the stories in the movies portray Africans as fetish, ritualistic, superstitious, and ignorant. Inspired by the Nollywood's success stories, some African countries have invented their own version of the local movie industry; there is the Ghallywood in Ghana and Riverwood in Kenya.

Infusion of Development themes such as women and gender issues, poverty eradication, health, ethnic integration, cooperative living, environmental sustenance into these local productions could positively impact the people. Aside from public opinion manipulation for political gains, a media agenda for development is benevolent if properly employed to serve beneficial ends such as conflict prevention, conflict management, peacebuilding and peacekeeping.

African countries have to tap into the immense potentials of the new media. Social media opinion mining and sentiment analysis algorithms have been implemented by western countries to measure and map people's opinions in real time; these machine learning procedures have contributed immensely to policy formulation, civic engagement and conflict prevention (DARPA 2016; Lambert 2016). The emotional contagious influence of social media have been widely studied by scholars; it has been proven that verbal and nonverbal expressions do influence behaviors of online users. According to a study, exposure to positive expressions on social media produced fewer negative posts; while the reverse produced converse behavior (Ferrara and Yang 2015; Lewis 2014). This could be observed in online philanthropic donations, fundraising for poor patients, and mobilizations for disaster relief efforts. People replicate popular culture and opinions; this basic human nature have helped marketers to sell products in large numbers. The usual assumption is that if others are doing it, why should I be left out; that feeling could be deployed to positive and negative use. Governments can use the social media to counter hate speeches, fake news and misinformation.

Economy and Trade

The media has contributed to economic development across the continent; more could be done but it must be acknowledged that the film production industry alone has accounted for trade and economic growth in some countries of Africa. An example is Nigeria, where Nollywood (Nigeria's version of Hollywood) is rated as the second biggest employer of labor after agriculture. It is reputed to be capable of generating at least 8.5 billion in 2018, from 7.3 billion Nigerian film industry has engaged more than 1 million people; if well tapped, the film industry as a subsector of the larger media and entertainment industry is capable of grossing more income for the country (Okeke 2016). To combat revenue loss to piracy, several companies have emerged to handle the distribution sector of the Nigeria's film industry. A leading Nollywood distribution channel is iROKOtv, an online movie content distribution company like Netflix. This company pays filmmakers about 25,000 for the digital rights to stream their content for a period of time, and it claims to be the world's largest online distributor of African contents with a catalogue of 5000 Nollywood films (Oladipo 2014).

South Africa's film industry is another success story with more than 35,000 people employed in the sector alone. According to South Africa's National Film and Video Foundation, the industry's contribution to the GDP of the country is around £ providing jobs for 250,000 Kenyans (Okulo 2015). There are rooms for improvement to achieve the success recorded by Nigeria and South Africa. Apart from generating employment, film locations also attract some economic benefits; an estimated 250 films are shot yearly in Morocco. Popular films like Troy, Gladiator, and Black Hawk Down were shot in Morocco. Mozambique gained million from distributing digital music in Africa from January to June 2016 through MP3, ringtones, caller ring back tones, music on demand and music subscriptions (Lourie 2016). There are huge economic and trade benefits derived from the media which can provide alternative sources of income outside of the mineral exploitations.

Media productions have contributed to transnational trade and more boundaries are beginning to open up through the influence of the media; it is not uncommon these days to experience Nigerian hip-hop music blaring from loudspeakers in Cameroon, Liberia, Uganda and other countries of Africa. Digital Paid TV such as DSTV has linked many homes across the continent with several programs promoting cross-continental interests. Most Africans get to watch the Big Brother Africa production and other country-specific productions.

The story of mobile phone-based money transfer platforms is encouraging, especially as the continent has experienced increased internet and mobile telephony penetrations in the last decade. M-Pesa, an innovative platform grew from a simple application in 2007 to a behemoth by 2013 servicing about 43% of Kenya's GDP with over 237 million person-to-person transactions. It is not limited to money transfer; it has been extended to include money deposits, bill payment, microcredit schemes and remittances (Rounde 2015).

Summary, Recommendations and Conclusion

Africa's story is not often judiciously presented in the largely Western dominated media. It is not that African media organizations are any better as noted in the early part of this chapter. The jaundiced and ill-informed mediation of Africa as a backward continent reflects negatively on her image. The various media and development theories presented in this chapter help to understand the relationships between media and development while situating these relationships in the larger development theories. African countries and governments must be more open and media-gag laws should be repealed to provide more opportunities for participatory governance.

Participatory governance is necessary for development. Governments of African countries must ensure the full democratization of the media so that more benefits may accrue to the continent from active citizens' participation in governance and information access. These progressive gestures will stimulate effective interactions between leaders and followers. Efforts should be made to invest more in infrastructure for improving media penetration and accessibility across the continent; rural areas should be connected with urban areas for wider coverage. No community no matter how remote should be left behind.

References

Adelana, O. (2015). Kaduna state declares its finances open. *Naij*. https://www.naij.com/472283-kaduna-state-declares-its-finances-open.html. Accessed 25 May 2016.

Aribogan, D. (2016). Why Turkey's coup failed. *The Nation*. https://www.thenation.com/article/this-is-why-i-come-to-work-every-day. Accessed 20 July 2016.

Awuor, F., Raburu, G., Onditi, A., & Rambim, D. (2016). Building e-agriculture framework in Kenya. *Journal of Agricultural Informatics, 7*(1), 75–93.

Baker, E. C. (2002). *Media, markets, and democracy*. Cambridge: Cambridge University Press.

Berlo, D. K. (1960). *The process of communication*. New York: Holt, Rinehart, & Winston.

Carpentier, N. (2011). *Media and participation: A site of ideological-democratic struggle*. Bristol: Intellect.

Curran, J. (2011). *Media and democracy*. London: Routledge.

Dahlgren, P. (2009). *Media and political engagement: Citizens, communication, and democracy*. Cambridge: Cambridge University Press.

DARPA. (2016). DARPA Goes 'meta' with machine learning for machine learning. *DARPA*. http://www.darpa.mil/news-events/2016-06-172. Accessed 8 June 2016.

Dijkstra, J.R. (2014). 100 years of photographic misrepresentation. *This is Africa*. http://thisisafrica.me/lifestyle/100-years-photographic-misrepresentation. Accessed 9 July 2016.
Ferrara, E., & Yang, Z. (2015). Measuring emotional contagion in social media. *PloS One, 10*(11). doi:10.1371/journal.pone.0142390.
Friedman, T. L. (1999). *The Lexus and the olive tree*. New York: Farrar, Straus, Giroux.
Habermas, J. (1990). *Moral consciousness and communicative action*. Cambridge, MA: MIT Press. http://www.tc.umn.edu/~rbeach/teachingmedia/student_units/module5/images_of_africa_michira.pdf.
James, J. (2011). Pros and cons of GDP as a measure of economic development versus Human Development Index. *Blog Nang Joseph*. http://josephjames007.blogspot.com.ng/2011/12/pros-and-cons-of-gdp-as-measure-of_5743.html. Accessed 3 August 2016.
Kenney, K. R. (1995). Images of Africa in news magazines: Is there a black perspective? *International Communication Gazette, 54*(1), 61–66.
Lambert, L. K. (2016). Machine learning is reshaping security: Maybe, but what the heck is it anyway? *CSO*. http://www.csoonline.com/article/3046543/security/machine-learning-is-reshaping-security.html. Accessed 28 June 2016.
Lerner, D. (1958). *The passing of traditional society: Modernizing Middle East*. New York: Free Press of Glencoe.
Lewis, T. (2014). Facebook emotions are contagious, study finds. *Live Science*. http://www.livescience.com/46609-facebook-emotions-contagious.html. Accessed 28 June 2016.
Lourie, G. (2016). MTN has been quietly conquering Africa's digital music. Does it want to be Apple Music of Africa? *The Tech Financials*. http://techfinancials.co.za/2016/08/mtn-quietly-conquering-africas-digital-music-want-apple-music-africa. Accessed 9 July 2016.
Mahadeo, M., & McKinney, J. (2007). Media representations of Africa: Still the same old story? *Policy & Practice: A Development Education Review, 4*, 14–20.
McCombs, M. E., & Shaw, D. L. (1972). The agenda-setting function of mass media. *Public Opinion Quarterly, 36*, 176–187.
Michira, J. (2002). *Images of Africa in the Western media*. Accessed 19 Aug 2016.
Nerone, J. C., Braman, S., Christians, C. G., Guback, T. H., Helle, S., Liebovich, L., Berry, W. E., & Rotzol, K. B. (1995). *Last rights: Revisiting four theories of the press*. Urbana: University of Illinois Press.
Nyabola, N. (2014). Why do Western media get Africa wrong? *Al Jazeera*. http://www.aljazeera.com/indepth/opinion/2014/01/why-do-western-media-get-africa-wrong-20141152641935954.html. Accessed 25 June 2016.
Ojo, T. (2006). Communication networking: ICTs and health information in Africa. *Information Development, 22*(2), 94–101.
Okeke, I. (2016). Nigeria's $7 billion film industry gains traction in Europe. *Asoko Insight*. https://asokoinsight.com/news/nigerias-7-billion-film-industry-gains-traction-in-europe. Accessed 3 Aug 2016.
Okulo, L. (2015). Lights, camera, action! Filming in Kenya. *Daily Star*. http://allafrica.com/stories/201504171237.html. Accessed 20 June 2016.
Oladipo, T. (2014). 'Nigeria's Netflix' takes Nollywood to a global audience. *BBC News*. http://www.bbc.com/news/business-28528396. Accessed 29 July 2016.
Pamoukaghlian, V. (2015). Rising African film industries: The Nollywood–South Africa axis. *AFK Insider*. http://afkinsider.com/84131/rising-african-film-industries-nollywood-south-africa-axis/#sthash.Tfth0v4f.acHLStMf.dpuf. Accessed 25 June 2016.
Pickard, V. (2014). *America's battle for media democracy: The triumph of corporate libertarianism and the future of media reform*. Cambridge: Cambridge University Press.
Reinsdorf, M. B. (2010). Terms of trade effects: Theory and measurement. *Review of Income and Wealth, 56*(1), 177–205. doi:10.1111/j.1475-4991.2010.00384.x.
Reyes, G. E. (2001). Four main theories of development: Modernization, dependency, world systems, and globalization. *NOMADAS, 4*, 1–12.
Rogers, E. M. (1962). *Diffusion of innovations*. New York: Free Press of Glencoe.

Rounde, D. (2015). M-Pesa and the rise of the global mobile money market. *Forbes*. http://www.forbes.com/sites/danielrunde/2015/08/12/m-pesa-and-the-rise-of-the-global-mobile-money-market/#680b5c6923f5. Accessed 3 Aug 2016.

Schramm, W. (1962). Mass communication. *Annual Review of Psychology, 13*(1), 251–284.

Schramm, W., Chaffee, S. H., & Rogers, E. M. (1997). *The beginnings of communication study in America: A personal memoir*. Thousand Oaks: Sage.

Shantel, O.E. (2014). Child is not bride! *Nigerian Observer*. http://nigerianobservernews.com/14012014/14012014/features/features8.html#.V7l4lq22GyE. Accessed 9 July 2016.

Singer, H. (1998). The terms of trade fifty years later-convergence and divergence. *The South Letter, 30*(1), 1–5.

Sunday, E. (2015). How Nigeria's film industry contributes to national economy. *Peoples Daily*. http://www.peoplesdailyng.com/how-nigerias-film-industry-contribute-to-national-economy. Accessed 25 May 2016.

Taylor, B. (2014). Tanzania's second Open Government Partnership (OGP) Action Plan published. *Twaweza*. http://www.twaweza.org/go/tz-ogpplan2. Accessed 20 May 2016.

Toye, J., & Toye, R. (2003). The origins and interpretation of the Prebisch-singer thesis. *History of Political Economy, 35*(3), 437–467. doi:10.1215/00182702-35-3-437.

United Nations. (2016). *Promotion and protection of all human rights, civil, political, economic, social and cultural rights, including the right to development, A/HRC/32/L.1*. http://ap.ohchr.org/documents/E/HRC/d_res_dec/A_HRC_32_L1.docx. Accessed 18 July 2016.

World Bank. 2012. *Open budgets portal: Kenya*. http://wbi.worldbank.org/boost/country/kenya-0. Accessed 9 July 2016.

Damilola Adegoke is a Research Associate/Doctoral Fellow, African Leadership Centre, Kings College, London. damilola.adegoke@kcl.ac.uk.

Chapter 11
Retooling Africa's Development: Child and Youth Inclusion in the Development Agenda

Victor Ogbonnaya Okorie

Introduction

If childhood and youth are a mistake, then adulthood will be a struggle while old age will be regretted. Invoking this modified quote of Benjamin Franklin seems most appropriate at the beginning of this chapter: it aptly articulates not only the complex connections among the concepts of interest but also appositely echoes the cannon warning informing the chapter. The unfolding argument is that the lines etched in childhood certainly draw the wrinkles of adulthood. The chapter therefore makes a claim of causality in the nexus between Africa's development and the situations of its children and youth; indicating however that causal links between the state and the situations are not always linearly unidirectional and explicit. They are sometime nonlinearly bidirectional and implicit, visible and invisible, as well as blurred and bolded. The state of Africa's development and the situation of its youth are infinitely entwined, reflecting the relationship between a chicken and its egg (Odoh et al. 2014). As such, they mutually reinforce and simultaneously weaken each other, while their effects are seen not only in the present but also in the future. If the purpose of development is articulated in consonance with the Cocoyoc Declaration (1974), that is, to develop human beings not things by granting all humans access to food, shelter, clothing, health, education and freedom, then any society without a conscious and conscientious plan to include all its youths and children in its development agenda has already lost the essence of development (Sen 1999).

Adulthood and childhood are contextualized, respectively, as the today and tomorrow of any society, while 'youthhood' is the bridge between them. Accordingly, the inclusion of child and youth in development agenda is a sure path to continuous

V.O. Okorie (✉)
Department of Urban and Regional Planning, Faculty of Natural and Agricultural Sciences, Bloemfontein 9300, South Africa
e-mail: vicokoria@yahoo.com

O. Akanle, J.O. Adésìnà (eds.), *The Development of Africa*, Social Indicators Research Series 71, DOI 10.1007/978-3-319-66242-8_11

and sustainable improvements in human progress and well-being for any society. Non-inclusion of young people in development agenda is a proven recipe for perpetual underdevelopment and crises. Effective linkages between the past, the present and the future of Africa are achieved chiefly through enculturation, socialization and the proper integration of children and youth into the formal structures, thereby harnessing and unleashing their youthful energy in the growth and development process of the continent. The mandate of this chapter is to articulate how to achieve child and youth inclusion in Africa's development. As a result, the chapter interrogates the following: Who is a child and who is a youth in social, economic, cultural, physical and development terms? What are the experiences of children and youths within Africa's development realities? Are there different development and survival experiences for children and youths across Africa? How can/should children and youths in Africa be more included in policy and development processes and outcomes?

The chapter addresses these questions with a affirm conviction that critical factors such as Africa's youth bulge are an investment to be leveraged and not a cost to be justified. This thrust is in consonance with the emergent view about child and youth: youth is an explosive force; whether it becomes a curse or a blessing depends on how it is treated now (Farinde et al. 2008). To this end, the chapter is divided into five sections: The first section explores issues of inclusive development paying attention to ideas about growth, equal opportunity, and equal outcome. The second section presents a definitional discourse on the youth and the child, focusing various markers of child and youth, as well as identifying diverse categories of children and youth to be included in development agenda. The third examines the situations and struggles for survival of some African children and youths, using case studies from Sub-Saharan Africa; and the fourth narrates strategies for child and youth inclusion in development agenda, presenting some success stories from two African countries. The fifth section concludes the chapter.

Conceptual Framework

The framing and formation of this chapter is rooted in the concept of inclusive development. It is apparently a sympathetic concept for inclusive education, which has been reconfiguring access to formal education since the 1950s. Inclusive development perhaps owes its emergence to the growing dissatisfaction of some pundits, policymakers, and epistemic communities with other concepts, such as inclusive growth and pro-poor growth, which tend to substitute an increase in per capita income for improvement of human well-being. The concept has multiple dimensions, which make it more heuristic and popular among its rival terms in the literature. It, thus, enjoys more followership from the World Bank, the Asian Development Bank and the African Development Bank. Although there is no definition commonly agreed on among scholars (Ali and Zhuang 2007; Kozuka 2014), there are some common threads that run through various definitions of inclusive development. To illustrate, Oxfam (n.d.) says that inclusive development is "a pro-poor approach that equally values and incorporates the contributions of all stakeholders—including marginalized groups—in addressing development issues. It promotes transparency and accountability, and enhances development cooperation outcomes through collaboration between civil society, governments and private sector actors." Kozuka (2014) defines the concept as development that enhances people's well-being by advancing the equality of opportunity for all members of society, with particular attention to the poor, the vulnerable, and those disadvantaged groups normally excluded from the process of development. As such, inclusive development promotes efficient and sustainable economic growth; ensures a level political playing field; strengthens capacities; and provides for social safety nets. For the United Nations Development Programme, development can be inclusive "only if all groups of people contribute to creating opportunities, share the benefits of development and participate in decision-making". Inclusive development thus reflects ideas about human security and follows a human development approach, as well as integrates the standards and principles of human rights—participation, non-discrimination and accountability—which UNDP advocates.

Each of these definitions explicitly endorses the inclusion of every segment of society in development agenda. All the definitions advocate the contribution of everyone, especially those at the margins, to human progress. Both the similarities and variations among the definitions indicate that inclusive development is a multidimensional concept, covering almost every aspect of human life and experience. Its economic and humanistic dimensions that deal with economic growth and equal opportunity respectively are highly important in the context of child and youth inclusion in development. These dimensions emphasize issues of income, human capital development, cultural capital acquisition, social capital development, gender and development, and social protection for all categories of children and youths, since childhood and youthhood do not imply a form of homogeneity. Rauniyar and Kanbur (2010) say that human capital development refers to access to education, primary health care and other essential services, while social capital development means increasing the opportunity of the poor to participate in decision-making and self-managed community services such as creating community-based groups in microfinance, health and natural resources management. Gender and development, the authors argue, involve improving the status of women through health and welfare programs and promoting their participation in the development of society, just as social protection addresses the vulnerabilities and risks of age, illness, disability, natural disasters, economic crises, and/or civil conflict. Cultural capital deals with issues of etiquette, ethics and other non-monetary assets that make an individual culturally and socially acceptable in a given society. It promotes social mobility. The capital includes but is not limited to style of speech, dress or physical appearance and greeting.

These capitals collectively constitute the bases for positive youth development, which emerges "when the potential plasticity of human development is aligned with developmental assets" (Lerner et al. 2005). Positive Youth Development (PYD) according to Lerner and colleagues comprises competence, confidence, connection, character and caring. Or as Guerra and Bradshaw (2008) explain: it consists of a positive sense of self; self-control; decision-making skills; a moral system of belief; and prosocial connectedness. PYD has implications for community programs and social policies pertinent to children and youth in the context of inclusive development. Therefore, child and youth inclusion in development agenda is not only about making the aforementioned capitals available and granting young people's right to them. Rather it implies guaranteeing all categories of children and youth what I call 'fair equality of access' to the economic and non-economic capitals. The word 'access' is contextually used in line with Ribot and Peluso's (2003, 153) notion, which depicts access as "the ability to derive benefits from things", rather than the right to things or property. In this sense, inclusion of children and youth in development agenda addresses issues of equal opportunity, equality of opportunity, equal outcome, and equality of outcome.

Equality of opportunity is conceptualized and contextualized following the suggestions of modern egalitarian philosophers, such as Ronald Dworkin and John E. Roemer, who have explicitly added the perspective of individual responsibility to the theory of equal opportunity (Roemer 2009). Metaphors associated with their views are "leveling the playing field and "starting gate of equality" (Roemer and Trannoy 2016) and stand in contrast to equality of outcome. The critical difference being that the latter secures an equal outcome for all individuals without questioning the choices they made to affect that outcome. In contrast, equality of opportunity holds individuals responsible for the actions under their control and compensates only for the disadvantages beyond their control, so that all have the potential to achieve the same outcome (Roemer and Trannoy 2013). For Roemer, equal opportunity means guaranteeing that those who apply equal degrees of effort end up achieving equal results, regardless of their circumstances. To form an equal opportunity policy, he proposes that the population be partitioned into several types according to their circumstances. Then, a policy should be chosen that maximizes the minimum level of advantage of individuals, across all types, who expend the same degree of effort (Roemer 2009).

These views are very telling in the context of child and youth inclusion in development agenda in Africa. Many children and youths live under different conditions and with diverse clusters of disadvantages (Honwana 2014). Child and youth inclusion in development agenda implies factoring the circumstances into development policies with a focus on removing the disadvantages. Based on Roemer's suggestion, children and youths in Africa can be classified, for policy purposes, into the following: children and youth living with disabilities; children and youth in dysfunctional families; out-of-school and unemployed children and youth; children and youth in violent situations, child laborers; teenage parents (Okorie et al. 2015); children and youth living on the streets; children and youth living with HIV and AIDS or other life-threatening diseases (Okorie 2014). Others include but are not limited to orphans (Timaeus and Boler 2007); children and youth sex workers (Foster and Williamson 2000); children and youth in remote areas (Porter et al. 2007); illiterate youth juveniles; adolescent caregivers; rural farm youth (Bezu and Holden 2014); youth in conflict with the law and youth alcohol and substance abusers (Parry et al. 2004). Inclusion of these categories of children and youths in development agenda requires a clear definition of the concept of youth and child. Accordingly, the next section addresses the definitions of child and youth paying attention to social, economic, cultural, physical and development contexts from which the definitions emerged and the problems associated with them.

Child and Youth: A Social Shifter and an Anti-structure?

In the field of child and youth studies, the first approach to definitions of a child or a youth has always been to draw from chronology, culture, the Constitution, and economic and political dynamics, while the second tends toward viewing youth as a metaphor for the general condition and the future of a given society (Honwana 2011). The first approach gives multiple definitions; the second produces a homogenous child and youth, albeit a problematic one. Based on the first approach, there are no globally accepted definitions of child and youth. Child and youth are both relational and culturally constructed concepts (Durham 2000). A sexagenarian remains a child to his/her parents just as a teen parent is an adult to his/her children. Child and youth as concepts are thus a social shifter or a deictic. They indicate shifting relationships of power and authority, responsibility and capability, agency and autonomy, and the moral configurations of society (Durham 2000). Whether one refers to another as a child or a youth depends on who is speaking as well as the context. Cultural variations; diverse religious beliefs; varied political factors; variations in economic realities; variations in the Constitutions and laws of various nations; and variations in social norms and values are responsible for the non-existence of a universally accepted definition. Determinants of personhood, childhood and youthhood in some African cultures are shown in Box 11.1:

Box 11.1: Cross-Cultural Determinants of Childhood and Time of Youth in Some African Countries

Amongst the Maasai of East Africa, boys become adults through the ritual of circumcision. They are incorporated into a generational category or age-set, whereas girls join the age grade of their husbands. Each age-set is expected to evolve from uninitiated through to warrior (*moran*) to Ol Ngesher ('legs drawn astride'); that is, a circumcised boy and his cohorts pass through the stages of warrior (*moran*), junior elder, senior elder and retired elder—each stage lasting about 15 years. The senior elder age-set had primary responsibility for the traditional administration in Maasai land. Junior elders carry out the instructions of the senior elders. While decision-making is by consensus, those who occupy higher up the chain command relatively more respect and make a greater impact on the tribe (Okorie et al. 2017).

For the Nuer of Sudan, a female remains a child until she gives birth (Hutchinson 1996).

Similarly, among the Ibibo, Igbo and Yoruba of Nigeria a married male is considered an adult. Among the Yoruba of Nigeria, personhood and childhood of any individual is recognized and affirmed through the rituals of the naming ceremony, which occurs 8 days after delivery (Ekong 2003; Jibowo 2000).

Table 11.1 Ten notions that differentiate youthhood from adulthood

Youthhood	Adulthood
Not adult/adolescent	Adult/grown up
Becoming	Arrived
Pre-social self that will emerge under the right conditions	Identity is fixed
Powerless & vulnerable	Powerful & strong
Less responsible	Responsible
Dependent	Independent
Ignorant	Knowledgeable
Risky behaviors	Considered behavior
Rebellious	Conformist
Reliant	Autonomous

Source: Sciology Australia Website (n.d)

For statistical purposes the United Nations has however used age a parameter for conceptualizing youth. It defines youths as young people between 15 and 24 years of age. This definition has equally been critiqued as it could not serve as a universal definition because of the variations in law, customs and Constitution governing the age consent, age of maturity or age of full social responsibility from one country to another. However, age category appears to be the most widely adopted marker, although in this sense it is expected that different countries may categorize the age group for the youth based on their socio-cultural and economic realities. In Nigeria, for instance, some scholars categorize youths as young men and women between the ages of 13 and 30 (Torimiro and Okorie 2009). This was informed by the fact that the expected age of entry into primary education or vocational apprenticeship training is 13, that is, the age of entry into the youthhood, while individuals above the age of 30 are not expected to participate in the country's National Youth Service Corps (NYSC)—a youth program for graduates from either universities or polytechnics. This age bracket is however at variance with similar youth program in Ghana, which includes graduates who are 39 years old. For the African Youth Charter, 'youth' is a social, as well as a biological, construct—a process of 'becoming' as well as a category marked by the age boundaries of 15 to 35. Tanzania and South Africa, on the other hand, define the youth population as those between 15 and 35 years of age just as Swaziland defines it as those between 12 and 30 years; and Botswana and Mauritius define it as those between 14 and 25 years (Odoh et al. 2014). These definitions differ from what the United Nations claimed should be the age range of youths. Besides age, behavior is considered another marker of child and youth. The use of behavior is no less problematic. It overtly suggests the linear evolution of an individual from childhood through youthhood to adulthood. Cases of child marriage and teen parents arguably defeat the classification. A summary of these behaviors is given in Table 11.1.

While 'Sociology Australia Webstie's description is quite interesting, it is important to remember that good behavior and manners are not the exclusive property of any category of individual: even among supposed adults, foolishness may not be absent. Hence child and youth is a problematic category. The second approach is to

Box 11.2: The Usage of the Phrase "Children of Nowadays" Elicited from Google Scholar Search

'But, she told me, **children of nowadays** look after themselves only' (Werbner 2010).

'**Children of nowadays** need a lot of food and nutrients that mother's breast-milk production cannot keep up with' (Davies-Adetugbo 1997).

'The **children of nowadays** do not want to engage themselves in anything that involves hard work, they just want quick access to everything' (Chinweoke 2015).

'Actually the **children of nowadays** make us parents cry, because the child doesn't listen, even if you' (Wamoyi and Wight 2014).

view children and youth collectively as an idiom for imminent social change and radical reconfigurations of values, social orders and norms. They are an avatar of disorder, unordered and out of order. This framing describes children and youth not only as a problematic category but also as a problematic population. This view is reflected in discourses employing phrases such as 'children of nowadays' in their descriptions of children and youth. Box 11.2 shows the usage of the phrase elicited from Google Scholar Search by the author on 19 January 2017. The usage of the phrase-children of nowadays-addresses all categories of young people including newborns.

This is well articulated in Davies-Adetugbo's (1997) and Werbner's (2010) articles wherein unweaned babies and individuals already working in the formal sector were both referred to as children of nowadays and respectively accused of demanding more nutrients and of being stingier than previous generations. Also in Chinweoke's (2015) and Wamoyi and Wight's (2014) studies, the phrase describes young people in different social situations. To illustrate, while Davies-Adetugbo's (1997) usage of the phrase emanates from her key informant's narration of social cultural factors influencing breastfeeding in Nigeria, Werbner's (2010) comes from the lamentations of a mother over her impoverished condition, although her children work and earn money in Botswana's formal sector. Chinwoke's (2015) "children of nowadays" simultaneously reflects the perceived youth's abandonment of dignity in labor for the pursuit of quick wealth in Nigeria. In Wamoyi and Wight's (2014) study, the phrase describes parents' moral indignation towards children who have taken full control of their sexual life in Tanzanian. Although these contexts vary, the phrase explicitly indicates that children and youth are completely out of order. To invoke the foremost symbolic anthropologist, Victor Turner, they are 'anti-structure' (1967).

Framing children and youth as an anti-structure is both instrumental and symbolic. The concept embodies the manifold failings of agents of socialization and acculturation processes and their imminent maleficent consequences. In this sense, ideas about children and youth tend to address issues at the heart of the social imagination. Such issues have always been at the root of major revolutions, with the youth as the major actors.

The anti-structure also symbolizes the transitory nature of childhood and youthhood, which is defined by diverse rites of passage. A rite of passage comprises three phases, namely, separation, liminality (anti-structure) and reintegration (Turner 1967). The liminality constitutes a big threat to the order of things and the social structure because the adepts are at 'transitional limbo'. Frustrations and other problems arising from the limbo make the youth bulge a symbolical time bomb. Its explosion either makes or mars the society depending on extant policies on children and youth as well as their implementations. Absence of clear policies on facilitating children's and youth's transitional limbo in the periods of kingdoms and empires contributed to the demise and dissolution of such socio-politico-cultural and economic structures. Accordingly, there is a palpable fear that a higher percentage of child and youth in a society is a harbinger of doom, war and conflict.

While this youth-bulge-nation-break thesis appears incontrovertible, worthy of note is the fact that its fulfillment is dependent on extant policies and their implementation. Importantly, the availability of viable child and youth development policies could transform the youth-bulge-nation-break syndrome into a youth-bulge-nation-boom scenario. This is because proper transitions in childhood and youthhood ensure that children and youth are properly integrated into the formal structure of the society and empowered to pursue their society-given cultural and market mandates. Actualization of these mandates is sine qua non for their transition from childhood and youthhood to adulthood and very fundamental to the well-being of the nation. The next section examines the transition, paying attention to varying experiences of children and youths as they purse their societal-given mandates within the context of Africa's development realities.

Children's and Youths' Multiple Mandates in Africa: Situations, Struggles and Survivals

Transition from childhood and 'youthhood' to adulthood is mediated by several factors. To transit, young people are expected by default to fulfill their societal-given mandates. The mandates are diverse yet interdependent. They are the societal expectations of young people as well as crucial criteria they must meet to qualify as adults. These mandates include but are not limited to market and cultural mandates, which are deeply inscribed in and transmitted through various institutions instrumental to the identity formation, enculturation and socialization processes of young people. The market mandate refers to societal expectations of the young people to move from financial dependence to independence. According to the World Bank (2007), young people need to transit from learning to work. This type of transition has become the most difficult mandate for a majority of young people in the context of emergent economic realities in Africa.

The arrival of the forces of the free market on the African shore has reconfigured the educational and economic landscape of Africa. More than ever before, child and youth poverty is on the increase as a result of the inability of young people to move from learning to work (Banks 2016). At the time of the collapse of colonialism on the

African continent, Nkrumah, one of the foremost Africanists, was quoted to have said: "seek ye first the Western education and everything other thing shall be added unto you." This suggests a quick transition from classroom learning to earning a living. From the colonial period up to today, functional literacy has improved remarkably in Africa, yet many educated young people or 'the schooled' as they were called in colonial and apartheid South Africa, are yet to transit to the world of work. Youth unemployment has remained high, although the economy of Africa has shifted from concession through state-led capitalism/socialism and nationalization to free market, defined by privatization and deregulation. Nevertheless the invisible hand of the market has failed to give many educated young people jobs in the formal sector. Worse still, war and HIV and Aids have vitiated the effectiveness of economic safety nets hitherto provided by family and kinship networks for children and youths in many African communities. Rural and urban areas are disgracefully littered with children and youths whose rags of clothing are so inadequate that their bare buttocks literally scream the message of poverty to an insensitive world (Torimiro and Okorie 2009).

The inability of many young people to be integrated into formal institutions of politics, education and employment (economic) has led to the availability of a surplus army of able-bodied men and women who are integrated into various shadow networks (Okorie 2013). Others have taken to migration through dangerous and treacherous desert and stormy seas. As a result, the printed media are daily awash with stories of young helpless African immigrant youths drowning in the Mediterranean Sea; cases of serial shooters and suicide bombers; and the scourge of xenophobic and racism attacks (Charman and Piper 2012). Images of young Africans' violent deaths resulting from child and youth poverty, which are frequently commoditized and consumed through the ubiquitous airwaves, are idioms for the inability of young people to fulfil their market mandate. A majority seeks solace in the informal sector, where some are turned into sex slaves and machines, under poor working conditions (Fitzgibbon 2003). In these sites, the labor power of the youths is highly malleable and fluid: their masters set both the work hours and wage. They always willing, trusting that the goodwill of their masters will turn the tide one day. But for a majority, the tide never turns. Instead they are thrown out of the sites immediately the economic calculus of capitalist's logic finds their labor power wanting in terms of profit maximization (Torimiro and Okorie 2009).

Other young people have found employment on warfronts and in torture centers, where they wage war as work (Hoffman 2011; Okorie 2013). This claim was evident in the rupturing of societal fabric by internecine civil conflicts in Liberia and Sierra Leone, where Charles Taylor deployed his infamous Small Boy Unit (Hoffman 2011). This also currently exists in the conflict-ridden Niger Delta of Nigeria, where some soldiers operate Torture Centers, employing young men for the violent labor (see Box 11.3). Okorie (2013) shows that the identities of young violent laborers are highly fluid, flexible and comfortably conflictive, while their violent labor is malleable and highly fungible as they navigate and negotiate the landscape of inequality, unemployment and insecurity in the context of politics of loss and plunder in the Niger Delta. The overall socioeconomic and political disempowerment of youths has given them dangerous coping mechanisms and alternatives, which are presented in Boxes 11.3 and 11.4.

Box 11.3: Situations and Struggles of Youths in Chad, Mali and Nigeria

Chad: *Human Rights Watch also documents the huge humanitarian crises in eastern Chad as a result of armed attacks by youth militias (allied to Chadian rebels) especially from November 2006. It is noted that "some towns in eastern Chad have increased ten-fold in size due to the influx of displaced rural villagers due to massive internal displacement", thereby exacerbating the existing humanitarian challenges occasioned by refugees from Sudan. Apart from inflicting considerable human and material damage on civilians, the groups have destroyed socioeconomic infrastructure, endangered the physical security of citizens, and made overt threats to regime stability*. Source: Jaye et al. (2011)

Mali: *Early September another event reached the headquarters of the international press: Boni, a small town in central Mali, was occupied by 'jihadists'. The story is a little fuzzy. Apparently the military had retreated from Boni, leaving it in the hands of the population. The youth groups, so-called Jihadists, who have their camps in the region, took their chance to manifest their power and 'conquered' Boni … for a few days. The military finally took it back. Instead of questioning what happened and who these young military, associating clearly with jihadist movements are, they are coined as terrorists and will be trailed if they can be arrested. But indeed, who are these young men, part of the youth population of Mali?* Source: mirjamelisabethdebruijn (2016).

Nigeria (Fig. 11.1)

Fig. 11.1 A young violent labourer at work in a Torture Center while his colleague watches on just as the owner of the means of production is in his official uniform getting ready to go to his duty-post (Photo by the author, Victor Okorie)

From both Boxes 11.3 and 11.4, children and youth confront different situations with respect to survival in Africa. Based on Sen's (1980) capability approach, child and youth poverty is the deprivation of child and youth's capability to live a good life. Children and youths living in poverty are those who experience deprivation of the material, spiritual and emotional resources needed to survive, develop and thrive, leaving them unable to enjoy their rights, achieve their full potential or participate as full and equal members of society' (UNICEF 2011). Some qualitative and pictorial descriptions of child and youth poverty conditions due to lack of access to decent work are presented in Box 11.4.

Box 11.4: The Conditions and Struggles of Child and Youth in Ethiopia and South Africa

Ethiopia: "Young men's inability to experience progress and take on the normative responsibilities of adults is conditioned by economic policies associated with structural adjustment and local values surrounding occupational status. Young men construct international migration as a solution to their temporal problems ... Disempowered youth have come to symbolize the collective shame of not having proper functioning states, and there seems to be a global moral panic" (Mains 2007).

South Africa (Fig. 11.2)

Fig. 11.2 Children scavenging for food at a waste dump in Grassland, Bloemfontein, Free State, South Africa: The older child is sucking a discarded Coca-Cola can while the younger is yet to find anything, Source: photo by the author, Victor O Okorie

Box 11.5: Youths: Negotiating the Marriage Market

Zimbabwe: *A 60 year old Masvingo woman in Eastern Zimbabwe, Dorothy Mwanyisa, was thoroughly beaten by her son for denying him a portion of his sister's lobola. Aspinas Masaze was charged with domestic violence for the assault after his mother told him she had little to spare after giving a portion of the cash to his late father's elder brother as required by traditional custom.*

Cameroon: *Women's respectability in southern Cameroon has long depended on proper marriage, but marriage is increasingly vexed. Marriage rates have fallen, the rituals marking the transition to marriage have been altered and reordered, and women's expectations of marriage have changed. Over the last two decades, transformations in cultural meanings and in population rates in southern Cameroon have reinforced one another, and marriage has gone from a prerequisite for female adulthood to a sign of pecuniary honor. Nonetheless, marriage retains its symbolic centrality, and marriage to a European man has come to be viewed by many women as a viable 'modern' substitute—perhaps even the best substitute—for what is locally construed as 'traditional' bridewealth marriage*. Source: Johnson-Hanks (2007).

The foregoing discussion indicates that many youths have not achieved the market mandate. Besides the market mandate, there are other factors that influence transition. For many cultures in Africa, the transition to adulthood is not necessarily determined by age but marriage. With the exception of celibates, many youths want to fulfill their marriage mandate. The inability of these youths to gain financial independence has however continued to reconfigure the shifting contours of the marriage market, especially for male youths. Banks (2016) indicates that male youths' inability to secure decent work has reduced the number of married male youths relative to their female counterparts in urban Arusa, Tanzanian. In South Africa, young men are expected to pay *lobola* (bridal wealth) worth up to 11 cows if the bride is a virgin or less if otherwise. The *lobola* is approximately US$7000.

Lobola and similar factors have barred many, especially male youths, from getting married. Some African youths are however consistently contesting both cultural and economic barriers to the actualization of their marriage mandate. Such a struggle is not a new phenomenon in the history of marriage in Africa. In colonial Kenya for instance, youths contested the colonizers' attempt to stop female circumcision, which most Kenyians beleived to be the gateway to marriage. They also publically enacted rituals of vengeance and rebellion against men who sided with the Crown. The public performance of the rituals included but was not limited to songs: "Elder of the Church, your uncircumcised daughter is pregnant and she will give birth to dogs" (Thomas 2003, 46). In postcolonial Africa, the reconfiguration of the global space by internet technology has opened a new space not only for identity construction but also for marriage redefinition and negotiations. In view of the lack of available partners in their vicinity, some youths seek virtual spouses through virtual communities. In so doing, they reconstruct marriage, and reform and reformulate the cultural norms and values underlying it. Box 11.5 shows varied experiences of some African youth with *lobola* and spouses.

Schemata that link marriage to honorable forms of self-mastery and honorable forms of consumption have been transposed onto the dream of Internet-mediated marriages.

New forms of marriage and family life emerge, such as the 'Come we Stay' partnership that rests on an agreement between partners on living together and establishing a family with mutual obligations with the common understanding that the union may be temporary. This arrangement, well known in Europe and the US, is widespread among young people in East Africa's urban centres (Christiansen et al. 2006; Spronk 2005).

Doing the Inclusion: Do Basic Need, Right-Based and Capability Approaches Count?

Inclusion of child and youth into development agenda may take diverse approaches; nonetheless only three are highlighted in this chapter. They are the human rights-based, basic needs and the capability approaches. The basic need approach focuses on addressing basic necessities. Ideas about basic need have been around from the end of the Second World War, but it became popular in the 1970s when it was published by ILO. ILO applied the concept to formulate employment policies. The origin of basic need stems from Maslow's publication of the hierarchy of human needs, starting with physiological and ending with self-actualization needs (1942). Ideals of basic need found expression in a flurry of initiatives focusing on remedying the carnage of the Second World War. The central idea here is that life is not sustained by extravagant needs but by the essentials. The need approach was evident in the operation of Freedom from Hunger in the 1940s as well as in the multi-sectoral Nutrition Planning Approaches and Conceptual Framework of the United Nations International Children Emergency Fund in the 1970s. Policies underlying free school meals and free clothing programs perhaps originated from the basic need approach. In Africa, few countries have embraced such policies. The Nigerian government, for instance, is experimenting with school feeding programs in some primary schools. A basic needs approach, while not sufficient is at least necessary (Galtung 1980). African leaders should factor in the basic needs of children and youths into development agenda. The African Union and its Regional Economic Blocks should champion this course because it is fundamental to other achievements. For instance, school enrolments and class attendance increased with the introduction of food programs in some states in Nigeria (Akanbi 2011).

The term 'capability approach' was coined by Amartya Sen, an acclaimed economist. For Sen (2001) "poverty" is "deprivations in the capability to live a good life", and "development" is "understood as capability expansion". In this thinking, child and youth poverty is a deprivation of children's and youths' capability to live a good life where youth development is an expansion of the capability. Sen's capability approach contributed to the evolution human development index, which addresses capabilities in health, education and income. Inclusion of child and youth development entails enhancing capability by eliminating factors that could deprive children and youths of such capabilities. Such factors include but are not limited to ignorance, government oppression, lack of financial resources, or false consciousness. Policies and programs that offer unemployment benefits, free immunization, and free education for the youth are in line with the demands of capability approach. According to European Youth Forum (2014, 1), a rights-based approach to youth development

> … integrates the norms, standards and principles of the international human rights system into the development, implementation and evaluation of youth policy. A rights-based approach implies empowering young people to claim, exercise and defend their rights and fulfil their responsibilities through their active participation in society; encouraging mutually accountable partnerships between young people and duty bearers responsible for validating youth rights; actively working against the discrimination of young people on age or any other grounds, and towards ensuring the full inclusion of youth within society (European Youth Forum 2014).

Youth development may be conceptualized as "the ongoing growth process which all the youths in the rural communities are engaged in, attempting to (1) meet the basic personal and socio-economic needs to be safe, feel cared for, be valued, be useful, and be spiritually grounded, and (2) to build skills and competencies that allow them to function and contribute in their daily lives" the (Putnam 2000). It should also transform institutional arrangements that impinge on rights of children and youth. Based on the foregoing, African institutions such as the African Union (AU) and the regional economic blocs should take more interest in youth development than they have done in the recent past. Games and sport have been the main areas wherein the continent has shown some degree of commitment to youth development. Growing evidence affirms that commitment to child and youth development is an investment to be leveraged and not a cost to be justified. Evidence from Nigeria and Ghana's graduate youth programs confirms this claim. In Nigeria and Ghana, National Youth Service Corps (NYSC) and the National Service Scheme (NSS) have both contributed to immense economic growth and democratic governance in both countries (Enegwea and Umoden 1993). The NYSC and NSS are partially rooted in prescriptions found in basic need, rights-based and capability approaches to youth development. Graduates in Nigeria and Ghana who are below 30 and 40 years of age in these respective countries are employed at least for 1 year where they serve their nation in both the public and private sectors. The graduates provide an array of services in the agricultural, health, education and economic sectors of their nation.

In Ghana, Fleischer says that the benefit of the program is about $USD296 million while the cost is about $USD262 million, which implies that every $USD 1 invested into the program the government earns $USD1.13. Similarly, the involvement of these institutions in democratic election has brought more transparency to democratic governance in the country. It has also reduced ligation from 600 cases to 400 in the 2015 general election (Harris 2015). Thus, engaging the youths in this way and in related programs is an investment to be leveraged and not a cost to be justified. The following policy options and implementations strategies in Boxes 11.6 and 11.7 may be of help to the AU and its economic blocks:

Box 11.6: Some Policy Options for the AU

- Involving and ensuring the participation of youth in the socio-politico-cultural and economic development of Africa
- Fostering local, national and international understanding and unity among African youths
- Inculcating the virtues of discipline, selfless service, honesty and leadership in African youths with a view to ensuring peaceful coexistence and a purposeful sense of direction for the continent
- Providing opportunities for vocational training for schooled and unschooled African youth oriented primarily towards self-employment and self-reliance
- Encouraging an active complementary role for voluntary youth organizations in the overall development of African youths
- Making deliberate efforts on a continuous basis to understand, prevent and provide solutions to pressing youth problems such as drug abuse and addiction, and unemployment
- Cultivating in the African youth, leadership values, tendencies and capacity for positive role models and role taking
- Organizing and committing the energies of the African youth to serve their neighborhoods and community in their respective nations
- Encouraging the development of talents in gifted youth; and involving the youth in decision-making at all levels in matters affecting them.

Box 11.7: Guidelines for the Implementation of Youth Development Policies

1. Create a structural and legal framework for the execution of youth development programs.
2. Establish and maintain an International Advisory Committee to advise the AU and its economic blocs on youth development matters. Such committees should include representatives of the various AU members to establish a national youth development centre in each state of the federation.
3. Create a favourable environment beginning with the home to the community to make for the healthy development of our youth.
4. The relevant staff of state and local government should intensify the monitoring of the activities of the youth social clubs and associations in order to make such clubs/associations more effective.
5. Create social awareness on the need for youth participation in nation building by preparing documentaries, lectures, seminars, workshops, posters and other visual aids.
6. Educate youth on morality, religious harmony and tolerance to foster better understanding and appreciation of the views and beliefs of others.
7. Encourage the youth to join youth clubs, associations and other voluntary organizations.
8. The AU should introduce encourage its member States to the teaching of political and citizenship education at all levels of education.

Conclusion

This chapter presents a conceptual basis for the inclusion of children and the youth into development agenda in Africa. It shows that inclusion does not only imply granting young people the right to appropriate the capital they need to be integrated into the formal structures of the society but rather giving them fair access to such capital. The chapter documents diverse meanings of child and youth in different countries in Africa, indicating that the meanings are a product of cultural variations; diverse religious beliefs; varied political factors; variations in economic realities; variations in Constitutions and laws of various nations; and variations in social norms and values. It identifies various categories of child and youth to be included in development agenda as well as their struggles for transition. The chapter argues that the palpable fear about the youth bulge in Africa is driven in part by the transitional limbo status of many children and youths. Finally, the chapter presented some success stories from the continent and demonstrated why and how the youth bulge in Africa can become an investment to be leveraged and a not cost to be justified.

References

Akanbi, G. O. (2011). Home grown school feeding and health programme in Nigeria: An approach to boosting enrollment in public primary schools: A study of Osun state 2002-2010. *African Symposium, 11*, 20–28.

Ali, I., & Zhuang, J. (2007). *Inclusive growth toward a prosperous Asia: Policy implications* (ERD Working Paper Series 97). Manila: ADB.

Banks, N. (2016). Youth poverty, employment and livelihoods: Social and economic implications of living with insecurity in Arusha, Tanzania. *Environment and Urbanization, 28*(2), 437–454.

Bezu, S., & Holden, S. (2014). Are rural youth in Ethiopia abandoning agriculture? *World Development, 64*, 259–272.

Charman, A., & Piper, L. (2012). Xenophobia, criminality and violent entrepreneurship: Violence against Somali shopkeepers in Delft South, Cape Town, South Africa. *South African Review of Sociology, 43*(3), 81–105.

Chinweoke, F. U. (2015). Recovery of human values through mathematics education for social and economic development in Nigeria. *International Journal of Science and Research (IJSR), 4*(11), 2474–2476.

Christensen, A., Atkins, D. C., Yi, J., Baucom, D. H., & George, W. H. (2006). Couple and individual adjustment for 2 years following a randomized clinical trial comparing traditional versus integrative behavioral couple therapy. *Journal of Consulting and Clinical Psychology, 74*(6), 1180.

Cocoyoc Declaration. (1974). http://helsinki.at/projekte/cocoyoc/COCOYOCDECLARATION_1974.pdf

Davies-Adetugbo, A. A. (1997). Sociocultural factors and the promotion of exclusive breastfeeding in rural Yoruba communities of Osun State, Nigeria. *Social Science & Medicine, 45*(1), 113–125.

Durham, D. (2000). Youth and the social imagination in Africa: Introduction to parts 1 and 2. *Anthropological Quarterly, 73*(3), 113–120.

Ekong, E. E. (2003). *Rural sociology: An introduction and analysis of rural Nigeria Uyo*. Nigeria: Dove Edu.

Enegwea, G., & Umoden, G. (1993). *NYSC: Twenty years of national service*. Lagos: National Youth Service Corps Directorate Headquarters.

European Youth Forum. (2014). http://www.youthforum.org/assets/2013/07/0334-14-RBA-definition-YFJ1.pdf

Farinde, A. J., Okorie, V. O., & Lukman, Y. (2008). Evaluation of child and youth programme: A case study of nomadic education programme in Niger State, Nigeria. *The African Symposium: Journal of the African Educational Research Network, 8*(1), 165–176.

Fitzgibbon, K. (2003). Modern-day slavery? The scope of trafficking in persons in Africa. *African Security Studies, 12*(1), 81–89.

Foster, G., & Williamson, J. (2000). A review of current literature on the impact of HIV/AIDS on children in sub-Saharan Africa. *Aids-London-Current Science, The Rapid Science Publishers, Lippincott Raven, 14*, S275–S284.

Galtung, J. (1980). *The basic needs approach*. Cambridge: Cambridge University Press.

Guerra, N. G., & Bradshaw, C. P. (2008). Linking the prevention of problem behaviors and positive youth development: Core competencies for positive youth development and risk prevention. *New Directions for Child and Adolescent Development, 122*, 1–17.

Harris, S. B. (2015). *Assessing the participation of youth corps members in the 2015 electoral processes*. http://www.inecnigeria.org/wp-content/uploads/2015/07/Conference-Paper-by-Shehu-Bello-Idris.pdf

Hoffman, D. (2011). *The war machines: young men and violence in Sierra Leone and Liberia*. Duke University Press.

Honwana, A. (2011, September). Youth and the Tunisian revolution. In *Conflict Prevention and Peace Forum policy paper*

Honwana, A. (2014). Waithood: Youth transitions and social change. In D. Foeken, T. Dietz, L. De Haan, & L. Johnson (Eds.), *Development and equity: An interdisciplinary exploration by ten scholars from Africa, Asia and Latin America* (pp. 28–40). Leiden: Brill.

Hutchinson, S. E. (1996). *Nuer dilemmas: coping with money, war, and the state*. University of California Press.

https://mirjamdebruijn.wordpress.com/2016/09/17/poverty-and-youth-a-recipe-for-change-in-mali/

http://thisisafrica.me/lobola-bride-price-custom-gone-bad/

http://www.greatweddings.net/2014/08/the-anatomy-of-lobola-lobola-bride.html

Jaye, T., Garuba, D., & Amadi, S. (Eds.). (2011). *ECOWAS and the dynamics of conflict and peace-building*. Oxford: African Books Collective.

Jibowo, G. (2000). *Essentials of rural sociology*. Gbemi Sodipo Press.

Johnson-Hanks, J. (2007). Women on the market: Marriage, consumption, and the Internet in urban Cameroon. *American Ethnologist, 34*(4), 642–658.

Kozuka, E. (2014). Inclusive development: Definition and principles for the post-2015 development agenda. In JICA Research Institute (Ed.), *Perspective on the post-2015 development agenda* (pp. 109–122). Tokyo: JICA-RI.

Lerner, R. M., Almerigi, J. B., Theokas, C., & Lerner, J. V. (2005). Positive youth development a view of the issues. *The Journal of Early Adolescence, 25*(1), 10–16.

Maslow, A. 1942. A theory of human motivation. *Psychological Review* 50(3, March): 370–396.

Odoh, E., Chukwuma, J., Egwuma, R., & Eme, O. I. (2014). Role of the youths in national development. *Singaporean Journal of Business Economics, and Management Studies 3*(2):164–181.

Okorie, V. O. (2013). *Living with oil: Pollution and politics of loss and plunder in postcolonial Nigeria*. PhD dissertation, The Concil for Social Science Research Development in Africa, Book Series, Dakar Senegal (inpress).

Okorie, V. O. (2014). An assessment of rural farm youths' vulnerability to HIV/AIDS in Osun State. *Annals of Child and Youth Studies, 5*(1), 67–87.

Okorie, V. O., Torimiro, D. O., & Makinde, A. A. (2015). An analysis of correlates of educational aspiration among in-school teenage mothers: Empirical evidence from southwestern Nigeria. *African Journal of Gender and Development, 2*(1), 13–22.

Okorie V.O., Adzande, P.T., & Shmonde, S.R. (2017). *Peacebuilding between herders and farmers in East and West Africa: Does local institution count?* (CODESRIA Book Series).

Oxfam. (n.d.). https://www.oxfam.org/sites/www.oxfam.org/files/inclusive_development.pdf. Accessed 12 Jan 2017.

Parry, C. D., Myers, B., Morojele, N. K., Flisher, A. J., Bhana, A., Donson, H., & Plüddemann, A. (2004). Trends in adolescent alcohol and other drug use: Findings from three sentinel sites in South Africa (1997–2001). *Journal of Adolescence, 27*(4), 429–440.

Porter, G., Blaufuss, K., & Acheampong, F. O. (2007). Youth, mobility and rural livelihoods in sub-Saharan Africa: Perspectives from Ghana and Nigeria: Poverty, development and livelihoods. *Africa Insight, 37*(3), 420–431.

Putnam, R. (2000). *Youth service and social capital.* Opening plenary of the worldwide Workshop on Youth Involvement as a strategy for Social, Economic, and Democratic Development, sponsored by the Ford Foundation, San Jose, Costa Rica.

Rauniyar, G., & Kanbur, R. (2010). Inclusive growth and inclusive development: A review and synthesis of Asian Development Bank literature. *Journal of the Asia Pacific Economy, 15*(4), 455–469.

Ribot, J. C., & Peluso, N. L. (2003). A theory of access. *Rural Sociology, 68*(2), 153–181.

Roemer, J. E. (2009). *Equality of opportunity*. Boston: Harvard University Press.

Roemer, J. E., & Trannoy, A.(2013). *Equality of opportunity* (Cowles Foundation Discussion Paper no. 1921). New Haven: Cowles Foundation for Research in Economics, Yale University.

Roemer, J. E., & Trannoy, A. (2016). Equality of opportunity: Theory and measurement. *Journal of Economic Literature, 54*(4), 1288–1332.

Sen, A. K. (1980). Equality of what? In S. McMurrin (Ed.), *Tanner lectures on human values*. Cambridge: Cambridge University Press.

Sen, A. (1999). *Development as freedom*. New York: Knopf.

Sen, A. (2001). *Development as freedom*. Oxford: Oxford Paperbacks.

Sociology Australia Website. (n.d). *The Concept of youth*. http://sociologyaustralia.allenandunwin.com.s3-websiteap-southeast-2.amazonaws.com/files/RETHINK.PDF

Spronk, R. (2005). Female sexuality in Nairobi: Flawed or favoured? *Culture, Health & Sexuality, 7*(3), 267–277.

The World Bank (2007). *Globalization and Employment Conditions Study*. http://documents.worldbank.org/curated/en/947881468141552096/pdf/396000SP00708.pdf

Thomas, L. M. (2003). *Politics of the womb: Women, reproduction, and the state in Kenya*. University of California Press.

Timaeus, I. M., & Boler, T. (2007). Father figures: The progress at school of orphans in South Africa. *AIDS, 21*, S83–S93.

Torimiro, D. O., & Okorie, V. O. (2009). Globalization and African youth exploitation: The needs for good governance. *Journal of Youth Studies, 3*, 235–259.

Turner, V. (1967). Betwixt and between: The liminal period in rites de passage. In*Forest of symbols: Aspects of the Ndembu ritual* (pp. 23–59). Ithaca: Cornell University Press.

UNICEF. (2011). *Child Poverty | UNICEF NZ*. https://www.unicef.org.nz/learn/our-focus-areas/child-poverty

Wamoyi, J., & Wight, D. (2014). 'Mum never loved me': How structural factors influence adolescent sexual and reproductive health through parent–child connectedness: A qualitative study in rural Tanzania. *African Journal of AIDS Research, 13*(2), 169–178.

Werbner, P. (2010). Appropriating social citizenship: Women's labour, poverty, and entrepreneurship in the manual workers union of Botswana. *Journal of Southern African Studies, 36*(3), 693–710.

Victor Ogbonnaya Okorie holds a joint PhD in development and anthropology, as well as a Master of Arts in cultural anthropology from the University of Wisconsin-Madison, USA. He also holds a Master of Philosophy in agricultural extension and rural sociology and a Bachelor of agriculture from Obafemi Awolowo University, Ile-Ife, Nigeria. Okorie is a Senior Lecturer at Obafemi Awolowo University, Nigeria, and also a Postdoctoral Fellow in University of the Free State, South Africa. Some of his awards are:MEO Scholarship, USA; BIARI Fellowship and Alumnus's Grant, USA; Social Sciences Research Council (SSRC) Grant, USA; and CODESRIA's CRN Grant, Senegal. Email: vicokoria@yahoo.com.

Chapter 12
Health and Diseases in Africa

Benjamin Anaemene

Introduction

One conspicuous development challenge in Africa is the health and disease burden. It is undeniable that Africa faces more health challenges when compared with other regions of the world. Of greater concern is the fact that African health indicators lag behind those of the rest of the world including the poor countries of South Asia and South East Asia that were lagging behind Africa when measured on these metrics a few decades ago (KPMG Africa 2012). According to the World Health Statistics (WHO 2015), life expectancy for the African region is 58 years, which is lower than the 68 years for the South East Asia region. Infant mortality and under-five mortality are 59.9 and 90.1 respectively (per 1000 live births) which are also higher than the figures for South East Asia – (37.3 and 46.9 respectively).

Much of this gap, which has widened since the 1980s, is the consequence of emerging and re-emerging diseases, such as HIV and Aids, tuberculosis, malaria, Ebola, hepatitis, meningitis, sleeping sickness, SARS and others. HIV and Aids, in particular, has affected Africa more than any other region on earth. Yet another concern is that Africa bears a significant proportion of the global burden of chronic diseases (Zondi 2010). The World Health Organization has projected that by 2020 the continent will experience the highest increase in death rates from cardiovascular disease, cancer, respiratory disease and diabetes (WHO 2005). This state of affairs has been exacerbated by recurring natural disasters, poor economic performance and military conflicts. All these problems have posed serious development challenges for Africa.

Health and disease are related concepts. Yet, health is not synonymous with disease. Disease refers to "any deviation from or interruption of the normal structure or function of any part, organ or system (or combination thereof) of the body that is

B. Anaemene (✉)
Redeemer's University, Ede, Nigeria
e-mail: anaemeneb@run.edu.ng

O. Akanle, J.O. Adésìnà (eds.), *The Development of Africa*, Social Indicators Research Series 71, DOI 10.1007/978-3-319-66242-8_12

manifested by a characteristics set of symptoms and signs" (*Dorland's Illustrated Medical Dictionary* 1994), whereas health refers to "a state of complete physical, mental and social wellbeing and not merely the absence of disease or infirmity" (WHO 1948, 1). Health is a more encompassing phenomenon, as it emphasizes the significance of social welfare of populations and not merely the medicalization of diseases and allows for the consideration of the complex set of cultural, social political and environmental factors as well as biological and genetic components that influence the health and well-being of populations. Since health is a state of complete, physical, mental and social well-being of an individual, it is important in the development of every society (US National Intelligence Council 2008). The importance of health as a developmental issue is better understood in terms of the components of good health. These include peace, freedom from violence, freedom from pain, discomfort, boredom and stress, absence of illness, infirmity and diseases, balanced nutrition, qualitative and quantitative housing, water supply; good working and living conditions, access to educational resources (Bircher and Kuravilla 2014). Health and wellbeing also require social justice, a stable ecosystem and sustainable resources.

Several scholars have argued that there is a strong and reciprocal relationship between health and development. The WHO has also attested to the linkage between health and development, when it stressed:

> Any social and economic development program is primarily based on the availability and potential of human capital which is needed for developing various sectors of a country's economy; its industry and its agriculture productivity depends to a considerable extent on the health and wellbeing of the labour force, because in order to mobilise human resources, there must exist the precondition that they are physically fit to be mobilised. Ill health, undernourishment, poor environmental conditions and debility affect the development process (WHO para doc: AS/EC/TR. 22).

Improved health has been one of the main benefits of development. Fogel (1991) argued that Britain's early industrial breakthrough was largely due to the mastering of high mortality and morbidity as a result of improvements in nutritional status and the conquest of many contagious diseases from the late eighteenth century onwards. Similarly, it has been estimated that between 1965 and 1990, about 30 to 50% of overall economic growth was actually attributable to investments made in the health sector. Good health strengthens development because it increases productivity. It also strengthens people's capabilities, increases savings and investments, and promotes positive behavior.

Conversely, economic development can also facilitate financing of environmental, health and sanitation campaigns for education, immunization and screening (Mills and Cult 2004). Moreover, social development, especially in the field of education, has been associated with improved health status through improved nutrition and reproductive health. However, it has been argued that macroeconomic changes may not filter down to benefit the whole population. Scholars have shown that many sound policies in economic terms, notably structural adjustment policies, have had devastating human effects in increasing poverty and maladministration of resources (Muiu 2002).

Despite the recognition of these health challenges in Africa, an understanding about what must be done to improve the health and wellbeing of Africans remains a largely unfinished agenda in today's development process. This chapter therefore analyses the health and disease trajectories in Africa with a view to demonstrating and documenting their development implications. It also examines the various global and regional health initiatives adopted over time for improved health in Africa, as well as interrogates the constraints for achieving health and development in Africa. The study also proffers solutions for improved performance.

Historicizing Health and Disease in Africa

Three important periods are discernible in the history of health and disease in Africa. First is the Paleolithic period, which began about 2 million years ago up to about 8000 BC (Adegbulu and Faseke 2014). During this period, African populations were hunter-gatherers; depending for their subsistence on hunting wild animals and birds, fishing and collecting wild fruits, nuts and berries. These hunting and gathering societies were known for their small size and their mobility. Available evidence suggests that these societies had few epidemic diseases largely because of their nomadic life (Mckeown 1988). Second, is the Neolithic period, which began with the invention of agriculture (Adegbulu and Faseke 2014). The domestication of animals and growing of crops were major steps in creating settled agricultural societies. Domestication meant more contact between humans and cattle, chickens and goats, resulting in increasing vulnerability to animal diseases. Viruses that previously affected by animals were given multiple opportunities to mutate and transition from being purely animal diseases to human ones. The practice of agriculture also changed the disease environment in Africa through the changes associated with the clearing of land and the cultivation of wild grains in a single area, creating places for vectors to breed and places for people to be exposed to those vectors (Mckeown 1988). Agriculture brought about the development of permanent shelters. Thus, with the gathering of people in a particular location it can be said that the agricultural societies experienced more endemic contagious diseases than the hunter-gathering societies.

Another way that the disease environment changed in Africa was through contact with the outside world. Africa has had a long history of intercontinental exchange with Europe and Asia including the exchange of disease. On the west coast of Africa, there was regular and sustained contact with Europeans from the 1500s for the purpose of trade. Similarly, the east coast was also a destination for traders and travelers from the Middle East, Oman and India. With this long-standing and continuous exchange in commodities and culture, no doubt diseases were transmitted as well. As Patterson (1981) states, "these early contacts almost certainly introduced some of the major infections of the Eurasian land mass, such as smallpox, measles and perhaps gonorrhea and others in pre-European times." However, early epidemics were probably milder than those that came in the nineteenth and twentieth centuries, as low population densities and limited mobility probably made most outbreaks local and sporadic.

It must be emphasized that Africans in the pre-colonial period remained much more isolated in general compared to the colonial and postcolonial eras and as a corollary epidemics were likely less destructive in pre-colonial times and the human capacity to transmit these diseases across long distances was low due to poor transportation methods and generally low traffic between points (Heaton 2005). This trend changed with the expansion of roads and rail in the late nineteenth and early twentieth century with the attendant growth of urbanization. The development of urban areas and new modes of transportation contributed to the spread of European diseases into Africa.

There were pre-existing strategies and practices that Africans had adapted to guard against certain diseases. In the pre-colonial era, most communities had some form of organized social structure, an important component of which was the health care system. Attention for the provision of personal health usually centered on individuals with expertise in preventive, curative and rehabilitative medicine. Some of these traditional medicine practitioners specialized in midwifery (traditional birth attendants), treatment of psychiatric disorders, orthopedics among others. Others were generalists to whom clients turn for a variety of ailments ranging from infertility and impotence to persistent fever, loss of weight and chronic ulcers. The indigenous healers have adopted two major approaches to healing, namely, the pragmatic and the symbolic aspects (Barnett 2000). The pragmatic aspect involves examination of patients in order to diagnose, treat and prevent disease using their clinical judgment. On the other hand, the symbolic aspect is used when the healers attribute illness to societal imbalances rather than to biological causes. Although these precolonial communities were not conversant with modern germ theory of disease causation or the fundamental scientific basis of such complex issues like genetics and immunology, they established and were governed by set of rules and regulations (Health Reform Foundation of Nigeria 2006).

Unfortunately and inevitably, some of the socio-cultural practices and taboos were injurious to personal health – such as the practice of female circumcision and the use of non-sterile instruments. Uninformed postnatal care contributed to high maternal mortality while high infant mortality rates induced families to have more children to make up for the attendant wastages. The contact with Europeans led to the introduction of modern medicine in Africa. It delivered modern medicine via two main factors. Foremost is the role of Christian missionaries from Europe and North America, who took the gospel to Africa along with modern medicine. The missionaries used medical care both as a reward for acceptance of the new faith and as an incentive for the doubtful (Mburu 1981). Second, the colonization of Africa by European countries was an important factor in the emergence of and development of modern medicine in Africa.

The imposition of European colonial rule and African responses to it provoked important changes in the disease burdens of African peoples. It will be recalled that after the establishment of colonial rule, the Europeans extracted resources and labor to boost their metropolitan economies. In many of the new colonies, the Europeans forced their subjects to gather wild rubber or to work on plantations or in mines. These working conditions as well as African flight from colonial labor demands heightened colonial subjects' exposure to infectious disease. In terms of health interventions, until the 1920s colonial authorities confined their health services to settler populations and combating epidemics of infectious and tropical disease that threatened native labor and economic productivity (Lyons 1992). Colonial administrations gave more attention after the First World War but were particularly concerned with the reproduction of a healthy workforce, because the greater exposure to disease and poor nutrition of populations under colonial rule became apparent in high mortality and low birth rates. In the late 1920s and in the 1930s, some progressive voices called for improvement in socioeconomic conditions and for a focus on African welfare. However, these initiatives were not sustained due to lack of political will. In the 1940s, particularly after the Second World War, the development of vaccinations and antibiotics as well as the increasing agitation of nationalist movements for better living standards and for political participation, led to efforts by colonial administrations to extend some health care services to broader populations (Packard 1997). However, interventions to improve living conditions remained patchy, unfinished and focused mainly on political vocal groups, such as the nationalist class and the urban wage laborers.

The attainment of independence by African countries coincided with the period when long-term planning and state direction was acknowledged as the most promising route to modernization and development. Frederick Cooper (2002) argues that "no word captures the hopes and ambitions of Africa's leaders, its educated populations and many of its farmers and workers in the post-war decades better than development." As a result, the first generation of African governments was committed to fostering a developmental state (Nkandiwire 2001). During this period, the African developmental state sought to intervene to accumulate surpluses from the agricultural sector and use them to find import substitution-driven industrialization (Saul and Leys 1999). This accounted for the rapid annual growth rates experienced by African countries during this period. As Thandika Nkandiwire (2001) rightly argued, in the period between 1967 and 1980, no fewer than 10 African countries enjoyed annual growth rates of more than 6%, with Kenya and Nigeria, for example, outperforming Malaysia and Indonesia (Nkandiwire 2001).

Similarly, available evidence also indicates greater improvements in Africa's health during the first decades of independence, suggesting that African crises in health are of more recent origin. Interestingly, between 1960 and 1980, most African countries made significant advances in extending health care coverage. In addition, larger scale campaigns were launched against specific infectious diseases, health facilities were expanded and there was a significant increase in the number of trained health workers. For instance, in 1960 tropical Africa had one qualified doctor for every 50,000 people; by 1980, this has become one for every 20,000 (Illiffe 1995).

The period of the developmentalist state was ephemeral. The auspicious beginning in terms of health care delivery was halted by the global economic recession in the 1980s. It would be recalled that in the heyday of economic growth, most African countries obtained loans from Western commercial banks. Unfortunately, the economic crisis in the 1980s made it virtually impossible for most African countries to redeem their debts. It was in the bid to contain the crisis in the economy that most African countries began to obtain loans from the international capital markets (World Bank and IMF). This led to the introduction of Structural Adjustment Programs (SAPs), formulated to ensure that the developing countries including Africa that were entangled in external indebtedness were able to save funds towards fulfilling their obligations.

The implementation of the SAP with its harsh conditionality negatively affected the health sector and the health status of Africans (Loewenson 1993). This included a shift from direct provisioning by government, which essentially entails greater reliance on private voluntary services, instituting a number of financial measures like introduction of user fees and contracting out to the private sector as a way of improving efficiency and patient satisfaction. As a corollary, government expenditure on health in sub-Saharan Africa declined from an average of 6.2% of GDP in 1972, and 5.3% of GDP in 1982 to 1.6% in 1995 (World Bank 2000). Consequently, health care systems became dysfunctional across the continent creating near catastrophic conditions. More than 200 million Africans have no access to health services because of the near collapse of acute hospital services, characterized by frequent drug shortages, run-down physical structures and the efflux of highly skilled but demotivated medical specialists. This has left diseases to rage unchecked. The successes recorded during the early 1970s were followed after 1980 by a major slowdown in the decline of mortality rates. The past two decades have witnessed the emergence of new infectious diseases, Aids and Ebola, and the recrudescence of old scourges like tuberculosis and malaria as well as non-communicable diseases like diabetes, cancer, hypertension among others. Consequently, there has been an erosion of capacity in virtually all African states. State failure led to the externalization of responsibility for social services.

Exploring Global and Regional Initiatives for Addressing Africa's Health Development Challenges

This section examines the various policies and initiatives adopted over time, both at the global and international levels, geared towards addressing the health and disease burden in Africa. As shown in the discourse below the persistent health and disease burden may not be blamed on the dearth of policies or initiatives. Some selected policies and initiatives are presented in the following analysis.

Alma Ata Declaration 1978

The Alma Ata Declaration of 1978 is a health initiative developed through the efforts of the World Health Organization (WHO) and the United Nations Children Education Fund (UNICEF), which focused on primary health care. It had its background in the problems associated with the health care systems of many developing countries, which emerged from the colonial medical services and emphasized costly high technology and curative care. It was also urban biased (Werner 1997). Another factor is the problem that arose from the implementation of the vertical health approach of international development agencies including the WHO (Magnussen et al. 2004).

In the 1950s and 1960s, vertical disease-oriented programs were the major form of cooperation targeted at eradicating specific diseases. A typical example was the WHO Global Malaria Eradication Program launched in 1955 and the Global Smallpox Eradication Program in 1959. Each disease eradication program operated autonomously with its own budget without any integration into the larger health system (Ehiri and Prowse 1999). It has been argued that although there were successes during this period, these short-term interventions were not addressing poor populations' overall disease burden. It was realized that despite the fact that one disease might be controlled or eliminated, recipients of that intervention might die of another disease or its complications (Gadomski et al. 1990). Consequently, between the late 1950s and early 1970s, the vertical health approach was subjected to serious criticism. Thus by the mid-1970s, international health agencies began to examine alternative approaches to health improvement in developing countries.

The Alma Ata Declaration called for strengthening health care infrastructure, health workers' training, redistribution of health resources to rural areas and building of existing community strengths such as traditional midwives. It also emphasized preventive health care through a focus on immunization, reproductive health, contraception, sanitation and the promotion of safe motherhood. It also encouraged community participation as the means through which public health efforts would be responsive to local needs.

It cannot be denied that some progress was made with the health services. For the first time, the needs of the larger rural population were being met and after a while people began to see the results particularly in immunization programs, diarrhea in children, malaria treatment and acute respiratory infection. In Nigeria, for instance, primary health care formed an integral part of Nigerian social and economic development. It became the first level of contact of the individual and community in the national health system thus bringing health care closer to the people and contributing the first element of a continuing health care process. However, the early advance lost momentum. The Alma Ata vision of primary health care (PHC) was criticized for being ambitious and expensive. Several forces disrupted the PHC strategy including the continuing economic recession in the 1980s, the rise of neoliberalism, market ideologies and structural adjustment policies and new epidemiological challenges like the emergence of HIV/ and Aids. It was replaced in the 1980s by selective PHC, which focused on a few cheap and effective interventions requiring little investment in infrastructure – such as oral dehydration therapy for diarrheal disease in children and growth monitoring, breast feeding and immunization programs.

Nevertheless, the Alma Ata declaration was remarkable as it was the first time the health care problems of the poorest countries were seriously taken into consideration, both health needs and development issues were strongly linked. It also marked a paradigm shift, establishing the notion of international responsibility for health, the idea that rich countries should help poorer ones to achieve health goals.

Bamako Initiative

The Bamako Initiative (BI) was launched in 1987 in an attempt to meet the growing crisis of scarcity of drugs and reduced access to quality health care, as well as to counter the negative impact of the SAPs (WHO 1987). It was introduced against the background of the problem of financing health services experienced in the 1980s in many countries especially in Sub-Saharan Africa. Despite the fact that they accepted the core tenets of comprehensive primary health care, they were burdened by lack of resources and practical implementation strategies. In particular, many health facilities lacked the resources and supplies to function effectively. As a result, health workers were sometimes merely prescribing drugs to be bought from private outlets, usually unlicensed and unsupervised. Moreover, many patients lost confidence in the inefficient and underresourced public health facilities. All these developments, threatened to reverse the gains of the 1980s. The core challenges were to promote additional donor investment, and stop and reverse the decline of government expenditure on social spending in general and health in particular.

It was in recognition of this dismal situation that the WHO African Region in collaboration with UNICEF in September 1987 proposed measures at its annual meeting of African Ministers of Health in Bamako, Mali, for providing the necessary resources to deal decisively with the problem of health care delivery in many parts of Sub-Saharan Africa. These measures formed the basis of what has been described as the 'Bamako Initiative (BI).' The Bamako Initiative sought to accelerate and strengthen the implementation of comprehensive primary health care with the goal of achieving universal accessibility to these services. The Bamako Initiative was built on eight principles: improving PHC services for all; decentralizing management of PHC services to district level; decentralizing management of locally collected patient fees to community level; ensuring consistent fees are charged at all levels for health services, whether in hospitals, clinics or health centers; high commitment from governments to maintain and expand PHC services; national policy on essential drugs should be complementary to PHC; ensuring the poorest have access to PHC; and monitoring clear objectives for creative health services (WHO 1987).

In 1988, Nigeria adopted the Bamako Initiative as a strategy for strengthening PHC with five major components. These include community participation through a variety of local government, district and village level committees; improvement of maternal and child health (MCH) services; the provision of essential drugs, cost recovery and enhanced management, supervision and monitoring systems (Ogunbekun et al. 1996). In 1995, of the 589 local government areas in Nigeria, 53 were responding to the Bamako Initiative (Ehimwenma 1996), and by 1997 about

60 out of the 774 local governments in Nigeria covering approximately 10% of the population had adopted the Bamako Initiative (Shehu 1997).

The Bamako Initiative was not without its limitations. The application of user fees to poor households and the principles of cost recovery drew strong criticism. In most African countries where the Bamako Initiative has been deemed a success, poor people viewed price as a barrier. Consequently, a large share did not use essential health services despite exemptions and subsidies. It also gave rise to multi-drug prescribing, some of which is irrational. The initiative was donor driven with limited coverage.

World Development Report 1993

The inability of the PHC and Bamako Initiative and other international initiatives to improve access and quality of healthcare in Sub-Saharan Africa led to the search for alternatives to health policymaking (Oluwole 2008). Viewed against this background, the interest began to shift from 'Health for All' towards what became known as 'Health Sector Reform'. Andrew Green and Ann Matthias (1997) reaffirmed this when they wrote, "if primary health care was the talking point in the early 1980s, health sector reform has replaced it a decade later as the major policy thrust occupying donors." The major precursor of health sector reforms was the World Bank through its several publications particularly the 1993 World Development Report (World Bank 1993). This report demonstrated that investing in health is a prerequisite for sustained development. Another publication 'Better Health in Africa' (World Bank 1994) set forth a vision of health improvement that was achievable through health sector reform.

The United Nations Millennium Development Goals/Sustainable Development Goals

Another global initiative was the United Nations Millennium Development Goals. These goals were first agreed at a summit by virtually all leaders at the UN in 2000. The MDGs were meant as a major motivational device to increase development efforts particularly in developing countries including Africa. Three of the eight MDGs were directly related to health. These include Goal 4: Reduce child mortality, Goal 5: Improve maternal health, and Goal 6: Combat HIV/AIDS, malaria and other diseases. Other MDGs indirectly relate to health. African countries made significant progress towards achievement of MDGs, although the progress was highly variable across goals and countries. Africa for instance witnessed a marked reduction in under-five mortality rates and the maternal mortality rate has halved during this same period. There was also increased life expectancy. The shortfall in the attainment of health MDGs is attributable to operational failures that implicate many stakeholders in Africa and in the developed rich countries. Promises of official development assistance by rich countries for instance were not kept.

In September 2015, the world unanimously declared their support for the newly adopted Sustainable Development Goals at a summit of world leaders. The newly adopted goals are much broader and comprehensive than the MDGs they replaced. Health is covered under SDG-3: 'Ensure healthy lives and promote wellbeing for all at all age', and has nine proposed targets. It has been argued that the SDGs and their new targets are windows of opportunities to accelerate the development trajectory of Africa, because many of the challenges (including health and disease) that the new goals seek to address have a particular reference to Africa. It should be noted that the 2030 Agenda, among other things: "reaffirms the importance of supporting the African Union's Agenda 2063 and the program of the New Partnership for Africa's Development (NEPAD), which are both integral to the new Agenda.".

US Global Health Initiatives

African countries have also benefitted from the US global health initiatives – US President's Emergency Fund for AIDS Relief (PEPFAR), and the US President's Malaria Initiative. Presidential Emergency Plan for HIV/AIDS Relief is a 5-year bilateral commitment by the United States Government to support HIV/AIDS prevention, care and treatment programs in developing countries (Sessions n.d.). Apart from providing the general policy framework, the law outlines PEPFAR funding priorities. The majority of the PEPFAR resources are dedicated to focus-country programs and 12 African countries are beneficiaries. In all 15 focus countries, PEPFAR supports a comprehensive program in HIV/AIDS prevention, care and treatment, as well as limited activities in health system strengthening as it relates to HIV/AIDS monitoring and evaluation and policy reform. An assessment of the progress of PEPFAR on HIV/AIDS indicates that it has achieved encouraging results and has also made significant contributions to Nigeria's HIV response. For instance, in 2014, PEPFAR supported the following achievements in Nigeria: life-saving antiretroviral treatment (ART) for 610,599 people; testing and counselling for more than 8.6 million people; care and support for 698,408 orphans and vulnerable children affected by HIV/AIDS; and antiretroviral treatment (ART) for 55,703 pregnant women living with HIV/AIDS to reduce the risk of mother-to-child transmission (PEPFAR 2014).

In May 2009, President Barrack Obama announced the Global Health Initiative (GHI), a multi-year comprehensive effort to reduce the burden of disease and promote healthy communities and families around the world. The President's Malaria Initiative (PMI) is a core component of the GHI. The PMI was launched in June 2005 as a 5-year, $1.2 billion initiative to rapidly scale up malaria prevention and treatment interventions and reduce related mortality by 50% in 15 high burden countries in Sub-Saharan Africa (President Malaria Initiative Nigeria 2015). With the passage of the Lantos-Hyde Act, funding for PMI was extended to 2014 and as part of the GHI, the PMI goal was adjusted to reduce malaria-related mortality by 70% in the original 15 countries by the end of 2015. While the US assistance has been beneficial in these areas, its performance in terms of overall health impact has been limited. This is attributable to several factors, namely, poor aid harmonization, limited support for general budget support, a vertical disease approach among others.

Regional Initiatives

The AU has since its inception developed several initiatives to address the health problems in the region. In April 2001, the AU Heads of state adopted the Abuja Declaration on HIV/AIDS, Tuberculosis and other Related Infectious Diseases, pledging to make fighting against HIV/AIDS their highest priority in respect to national development plans (African Union 2001). They also pledged to set a target of allocating at least 15% of their annual budget to the improvement of the health sector. They called for international resources and collaborations between the WHO, UNAIDS, other UN and regional organizations, and monitored the implementation of the outcome of the summit. In 2006, the AU adopted the Abuja Call for Accelerated Action towards Universal Access to HIV/AIDS, Tuberculosis and Malaria Services by 2010.

Another AU health initiative was the African Health Strategy (AHS) 2007–2015, which was recently revised as African Health Strategy 2016–2030 (African Union 2016). Against the backdrop of Africa's increasing disease burden, despite good plans, strategies and progress, the African Union developed the Africa Health Strategy (AHS) 2007–2015 endorsed by the 3rd Conference of African Ministers of Health in 2007 and the 11th Session of the Ordinary Executive Council in 2008. The goal of the strategy was to enrich and complement Member States' strategies by adding value in terms of health systems strengthening from the unique continental perspective. The AHS 2007–2015 provided strategic direction to Africa's efforts in creating better health for all and had recognized that Africa had previously established health goals in addition to the Millennium Development Goals (MDGs) to which it has committed.

The AHS 2007–2015 explored challenges and opportunities related to efforts that can decrease the continent's burden of disease, strengthen its health systems and enhance human capital by improving health. It highlighted strategic directions that can be helpful if approached in a multi-sectoral and multi-stakeholder fashion that adequately resourced, implemented and monitored Africa's efforts in creating better health for all, and recognized that Africa had previously established health goals in addition to the Millennium Development Goals (MDGs) to which it has committed.

The AHS 2016–2030 is similar to some extent to its predecessor in that it also seeks to provide strategic direction to Africa's efforts in creating better performing health sectors, recognizes existing continental commitments and addresses key challenges to reducing the continent's burden of disease, while also drawing on lessons learned and existing opportunities. Its strategic directions require multi-sectoral collaboration, adequate resources and leadership to champion its implementation coupled with effective accountability frameworks. In this light, the AHS 2016–2030 seeks to complete the unfinished agenda, adjust the course based on lessons learned from implementing AHS 2007–2015 and build on member states' and RECs' achievements.

There is no doubt that a number of these initiatives are progressively being achieved. However, the challenges to progress on health include resource limitations and the non-implementation of health initiatives in member states.

Challenges of Sustainable Health Development in Africa

The above analysis has demonstrated that there is no dearth of initiatives or policies adopted both at the global and the regional levels to improve the parlous health situation in Africa. However, such policies and initiatives are stymied by several problems. One such problem is the weak and inappropriate health systems in Africa. The health systems as organized today are not adequately addressing the increasing burden of health and disease. New and emerging diseases have created a scenario in service delivery as many diseases have defied conventional medical technology. Health systems in most African countries are ill equipped to adequately address their health problems.

Improvement in health is also affected by the lack of access to health facilities in Africa. More than 50% of African populations do not have access to modern health facilities and 40% has no access to safe drinking water and sanitation. In Nigeria, for instance, the national accessibility to health facilities is about 54.1%, while the percentage of those who attended public health institutions in Nigeria was 59% in 2007 (Alabi 2007). The 54.1% accessibility to health facilities in Nigeria is below the 65% accessibility to health services estimated by UNICEF for African countries (UNICEF 2000).

Worse still, the health facilities in Africa have been concentrated in the urban areas. Thus, where the urban access to health facilities was 69.7%, the rural areas had a rate of 46.8%. The urban bias in health resources and facilities distribution in Africa has been noted by the WHO (2003). These inequalities in the distribution of health care resources may affect the pattern of its demand. Although there has been a marked improvement in health infrastructure since the 1990s, whenever medical facilities exist in the rural or urban areas, such facilities are usually short staffed, poorly maintained and inadequately supplied with drugs, especially those located in the rural areas. The equity implications of user fees have not been adequately addressed. A large share, particularly among the poor does not use essential health services because of the price barrier. There is also the lack of complementary infrastructure to health services delivery, such as access roads, constant electricity supply and so forth.

Most African countries are constrained by resource scarcity. In terms of allocation of scarce resources, the health sector is usually ranked very low in national development priorities. The average expenditure in the health sector in Africa rarely exceeds 5%, with most African countries spending less than US$34 overall including financing from government and household sources. African countries have failed to fulfil Abuja pledge to commit 15% of their national budgets to health spending. According to a WHO report, only four countries (Rwanda, Botswana, Zambia and Togo) were compliant with the Abuja pledge (WHO 2011). Another 22 countries spent between 10% and 15% of their budgets on health, but 25 countries spent less than 10%, and five spent less than 5%. Today, a number of countries now allocate a lower portion of their budgets to health care than before Abuja.

The poor health status of the population is mirrored by the crisis in human resources for health. With 24% of the world's disease burden, Africa has only 3% of the world's health professionals, with massive shortages of physicians, nurses, technicians, health managers and administrators and planners. In addition to emigrating to better paying employment in the developed world, health professionals are being drawn from rural to urban areas, from the public to the private sector and from lower income to higher income countries within Africa.

Health improvement in Africa is largely constrained by corruption. Corruption is the misuse of entrusted power for private gain (Transparency International 2011). It occurs when public officials, who have been given the authority to carry out goals, which further the public good, instead use their position and power to benefit themselves and those close to them. Corruption is a pervasive problem affecting the Nigerian health sector. Evidence abounds on the negative impact of corruption on health and welfare of Nigerians.

There is no doubt that corruption remains an enormous drain on the resources needed for developmental programs including health. The Nigerian health sector is particularly vulnerable due to several factors. These include the uncertainty surrounding the demand for services; many dispersed actors including regulators, payers, providers, suppliers interacting in complex ways; and asymmetric information among the different actors making it difficult to identify and control for diverging interest. In addition, expensive hospital construction, high tech equipment and the increasing arsenal of drugs needed for treatment, combined with powerful vendors and pharmaceutical companies present risks of bribery and conflict of interest in the health sector. Government officials use discretion to license and accredit health facilities, providers, services and products, thereby opening the risk of abuse of power and use of resources. The resulting corruption problems include among others, inappropriate ordering of tests and procedures to increase financial gain, absenteeism and the use of government resources for private practice.

The implication of corruption problems is that not all the money appropriated for health programs in the country ends up being spent effectively. About half of the funds and materials provided for health efforts in the country never reached the lowest levels where they are needed most. For instance, the mosquito treated nets, which are meant to be given out free, are sold to the patients in some health institutions in the country. This has brought to the fore the issue of accountability and transparency. There is no doubt that lack of accountability and transparency creates opportunity for corruption. There are three components of accountability, namely, a measurement of goals and results, the justification or explanation of those results to internal or external monitors and punishment or sanctions for non-performance or corrupt behavior (Vian 2008). Unfortunately, these components are either lacking or are not strictly adhered to in Africa's health sector. This can be attributed to the fact that several actors are involved in the provision of health care, which results in chaotic coordination, communication and poor accountability.

Another serious challenge is the proliferation of external actors in Africa's health sector. The growing number of external actors has been accompanied by an increasingly fragmented aid architecture and diversity of governance arrangements at the country level that is challenging national systems and management capacity in African states (USAID 2008). In addition, many of the initiatives also lack mechanisms of accountability, transparency and evaluation in the way they operate in African countries. There is a disjuncture between the issues that external actors and African recipients prioritize. While attention to priority diseases has initiated much needed increases in external assistance for health, these priorities are not necessarily in line with the recipient country government's overall plan for the health sector. In Rwanda, for instance, donors earmarked $46 million for HIV/AIDS in 2005, when the country had a 3% prevalence rate, and only $18.3 million for malaria, which was the biggest cause of mortality (Ntawukuliryayo 2006). Likewise, a significant portion of health aid is tied in many cases to short-term numerical targets such as increasing the number of people receiving specific drugs, decreasing the number of pregnant women diagnosed with HIV, or increasing the quantity of bed nets handed out to children to block disease-carrying mosquitoes. They tend to be 'top down' in nature and are largely driven by donor agendas rather than the country's own needs and priorities.

Another problem is attributable to the web of global institutional arrangements, which perpetuates massive poverty in African countries. The introduction of the SAP, the World Bank ideological framework based on neoliberal policies, affected and has continued to affect health care delivery in most African states (Loewenson 1993). While the SAP affected the delivery of health care directly through budget cuts and privatization, it also made an impact indirectly by contributing to poverty. The macroeconomic changes from the SAP resulted in reduced incomes and unemployment. Another significant example is the activities of powerful transnational economic forces that have stymied national revenue generation and delivery of services essential for the protection of health. In Sierra Leone, for instance, structural adjustments imposed by the International Monetary Fund to reduce fiscal deficits and cut government spending since 1990s reduced civil service wages (Kentikelenis et al. 2015). Consequently, by 2004, the country spent about 1.2% of its GDP or less on civil service wages. The country also loses about US$244 million in annual revenue through tax waivers for transnational corporations and organizations that it cannot afford (O'Hare 2015). Likewise, the WTO Agreements, particularly the General Agreement on Trade and Services (GATS) since 1995, have further undermined the already precarious health sector in most African countries resulting in the migration of African health professionals to the West (Aginam 2007).

The Ebola crisis in 2014 revealed the challenge of neglected diseases concentrated among the poor. Since 1976, more than 20 Ebola outbreaks have occurred in Sub-Saharan Africa, yet so little has been done to combat the virus, especially as it relates to drug and vaccine development, until now. There are two reasons for this neglect. First, past outbreaks were usually confined to rural areas in some of the world's least developed countries. Indeed, such diseases concentrated among the poor, no matter how widespread and severe, are not attractive targets for pharmaceutical research. This is so because the demand for such a medicine drops off sharply. Moreover, there is the further risk that a successful effort will be greeted with high demands to make the medicine available at marginal cost or even for free, which will force the innovator to write off its initial investment as a loss. In view of such prospects, biotechnology and pharmaceutical companies would prefer even the trivial ailments of the affluent. This problem of neglected diseases is also known as 10/90 gap – alluding to only 10% of all pharmaceutical research being focused on disease that account for 90% of the global burden of diseases. Second, international donors devoted their aid to disease with larger burdens (Global Forum for Health Research 2013).

The net result of all these challenges is the inability of Africa to sustain the laudable health initiatives, as manifested by its unsatisfactory performance in essential health indicators. In the final analysis, these factors have combined to foreclose the attainment of optimal benefits from the various health sector initiatives.

Conclusion and Policy Recommendations

This chapter has analyzed the health and disease trajectories in Africa. It found that health and disease are major obstacles to Africa's development for several decades. Nevertheless, the parlous health situation in Africa can be salvaged if the following policy recommendations can be adhered to. One potential way to enhance the health status of African populations would be for future global actions to address the global political and economic determinants of health inequities, which cannot be addressed in isolation through technical solutions, the health sector or national governments alone but need global level solutions with an emphasis on reducing global inequalities. Future global health initiatives should concentrate on mitigating the problem of neglected diseases concentrated among the poor by supplementing the patent regime with a complementary source of incentives and rewards for developing new medicines. The proposal for a Health Impact Fund—a global agency financed mainly by governments—that would give pharmaceutical innovators the option to register any new product is instructive (Hollis and Pogge 2011).

African countries should implement programs that are geared towards the attainment of universal health coverage. Health sector reforms should be explicit about reducing inequality in access to health services and ensuring that public health systems mitigate the impact of socioeconomic inequalities. Experience has shown that prioritizing for-profit private healthcare delivery is extremely unlikely to deliver better health outcomes for poor people thereby frustrating the attainment of universal health care. Private health systems have been shown to be highly regressive, serving the rich far more than the poor. Several studies have also demonstrated higher levels of exclusion of poor people from treatment and care while the wealthy receive the best available medical care. The poor are excluded from most privately funded health insurance schemes. Many poor people are forced to rely on low quality health care administered by unqualified staff and make out-of-pocket payments for treatments or 'simply do without' and this has had significant access implications particularly in developing countries.

Notwithstanding their numerous challenges, publicly financed and delivered health care services offer higher performing, more equitable health systems. For instance, research conducted in Asia found that no low or middle-income country in the region has achieved universal or near universal access to health care without relying predominantly on tax-funded public sector delivery. A case in point is Nepal, where significant improvements in access to health care were achieved after user fees were removed for primary health care services in public services in 2008 (Witter 2011). There is no doubt that universal public services are critical in the fight against inequality. They mitigate the impact of skewed income distribution and redistributive wealth by putting virtual income into the pockets of the poor. Thus, in the face of the growing inequality in low and medium income countries, urgent and dedicated action is needed to strengthen public health systems. The international community, realizing that African countries have been the victim of the highly uneven global income and wealth, should not merely help more, but also harm less. They should focus, in subsequent years, on supporting governments in African countries to expand publicly provided health care—a proven way to save millions of lives worldwide and drive down inequality. They should also assist them to abolish user fees and strengthen their capacities to regulate the private sector.

Primary health care should be revitalized as a strategy for health improvement and the struggle for social justice. There should be the steady rolling out of primary health care to remote areas, providing vaccinations, clean water, midwife assistance and basic health advice to larger numbers of people. There should be efforts to establish complementary infrastructure to health services delivery, such as access roads and electricity, among others. This is imperative, as available health centers are too far away from vulnerable people and those who actually need Medicare.

In proposing a sustainable African health system, it is important to appreciate the fact that a human resources issue is both a quantitative (appropriate numbers) and quantitative (appropriate skill, mix, motivation) issue. Focusing on such issues as the shortage of the right people, in the right place, with the right attitudes and skills mix must be addressed in order to produce professionals with skills that are not only technical but also managerial and relational. Health professionals in Africa should be able to see beyond the direct causes of ill health to indirect and proximate determinants of health such as poverty, disparity, ignorance and marginalization. They should be able to facilitate, mobilize, organize, discuss, work and provide feedback with people as partners.

Furthermore, there is need to emphasize disease prevention in Africa. Capacity building for disease prevention should be a major concern of the government. Therefore, greater consideration should be given to developing capacity to report, detect and investigate suspected infectious disease outbreaks and prevent sporadic cases, especially of known disease, from escalating to epidemics, and more resources for training, supplies, funds and foreign expertise should be provided for establishing and maintaining a sustainable disease surveillance system in Africa.

African states can maximize their gains from external assistance for health if they take leadership in coordinating health activities in their countries within the context of a comprehensive national health plan. Experience to date in Rwanda lends credence to this view. The Rwanda health sector is dominated by donor project support, with donors contributing 43% of all health sector funding and government 32%. Unlike, many African countries, where such donor assistance has contributed to the verticalization and fragmentation of services, the Rwandan Ministry of Health has managed to direct donors to align their contributions with national policies through a donor mapping study and a systematic costing of the health sector strategic plan. Each year all donors meet with government to evaluate progress made and plan for future activities. As a result, Rwanda has become the only African country with near universal health coverage. Immunization rates at 95% are among the highest in Sub-Saharan Africa. The proliferation of new aid mechanisms should not detract from African governments' commitment to finance health care for their citizens. This is because a population's health is principally a national responsibility. African countries owe their citizens a comprehensive package of essential health goods and services under its obligations to respect, protect and fulfill the human right to health.

It must be emphasized, however, that all these measures are destined to fail if the issue of corruption in the health sector is not tackled. The government should institute reforms to address endemic corruption in Africa's health sector. This is imperative to ensure transparency and accountability in the disbursement of funds meant for the health sector.

References

Adegbulu, F., & Faseke, B. (2014). Origins and early centres of civilization in Africa. In J. Osuntokun (Ed.), *African peoples, cultures and civilization* (pp. 13–26). Ede: Redeemer's University.

African Union. (2001). *Abuja declaration on HIV/AIDS, Tuberculosis and other related infectious diseases* (OAU/SPS/ABUJA/3).

African Union, African Health Strategy. (2016–2030). http://www.au.int/en/document/africa-health-strategy-2016-%E2%80%93-2030. Accessed 20 May 2016.

Aginam, O. (2007). Predatory globalisation? The World Trade Organization, GATS, and migration of African health professionals to the west. In T. Falola & N. Afolabi (Eds.), *The human cost of African migrations* (pp. 65–67). New York: Routledge.

Alabi, R. (2007). Estimating the cost in urban and rural area of Edo state. *Journal of Human Ecology, 2*(2), 15–32.

Barnett, W. (2000). Medicine, science and technology. In T. Falola (Ed.), *African cultures and societies before 1885* (pp. 189–215). Durham: Carolina Academic Press.
Bircher, J., & Kuravilla, S. (2014). Defining health by addressing individual social and environmental determinants: New opportunities for health care and public health. *Journal of Public Health Policy, 35*(3), 363–386.
Copper, F. (2002). *Africa since 1940: The past of the present*. Cambridge: Cambridge University Press.
Dorland's Illustrated Medical Dictionary. 1994. 28th edition. Philadelphia: Saunders.
Ehimwenma, P. (1996). Drug power to the people. *World Forum, 17*, 386–388.
Ehiri, J., & Prowse, J. (1999). Child health promotion in developing countries: The case for integration of environmental and social interventions. *Health Policy and Planning, 14*(1), 1–10.
Fogel, R. (1991). The conquest of high mortality and hunger in Europe and America: Timing and mechanisms. In H. Patrice, D. Landes, & H. Rosovsky (Eds.), *Favourites of fortune: Technology, growth and economic development since the industrial revolution*. Cambridge, MA: Harvard University Press.
Gadomski, A., Black, R., & Mosley, M. (1990). Constraints to the potential impact of child survival in developing countries. *Health Policy and Planning, 5*(3), 235–245.
Global Forum for Health Research. (2013). *The 10/90 report on health research 2003–2004*. http://announcementsfiles.cohred.org/gfhr_pub/assoc/s14789e/s14789e.pdf. Accessed 13 May 2016.
Green, A., & Matthias, A. (1997). *Non-governmental organisations and health in developing countries*. London: Macmillan.
Health Reform Foundation of Nigeria. (2006). *Nigerian health review 2006*. Lagos: Health Reform Foundation of Nigeria.
Heaton, M. (2005). African cities and the globalisation of disease: The influenza pandemic of 1918–1919. In T. Falola & S. Salm (Eds.), *Urbanisation and African cultures* (pp. 433–450). Durham: Carolina Academic Press.
Hollis, A., & Pogge, T. (2011). *The health impact fund: Making new medicines accessible for all*. http://healthimpactfund.org/wp-content/uploads/2012/11/hif_book.pdf. Accessed 20 Apr 2016.
Illiffe, J. (1995). *Africans: The history of a continent*. Cambridge: Cambridge University Press.
Kentikelenis, A., King, L., Mckee, M., & Stuckler, D. (2015). The international monetary fund and the Ebola outbreak. *Lancet Global Health, 3*, 69–70.
KPMG Africa. (2012). *The state of healthcare in Africa*. KPMG.
Loewenson, R. (1993). Structural adjustment and health policy in Africa. *International Journal of Health Services, 23*(4), 717–730.
Lyons, M. (1992). *The colonial disease: A social history of sleeping sickness in northern Zaire*. Cambridge: Cambridge University Press.
Magnussen, L., Ehiri, J., & Jolly, P. (2004). Comprehensive versus selective primary health care: Lessons for global health policy. *Health Affairs, 23*(3), 167–176.
Mburu, T. (1981). Sociopolitical imperative in the history of health development in Kenya. *Social Science Medicine, 15A*, 521–527.
Mckeown, T. (1988). *The origin of human diseases*. Oxford: Basil Blackwell.
Mills, A., & Cult, S. (2004). Communicable diseases. In B. Lomburg (Ed.), *Global crisis, global solutions* (p. 62). Cambridge: Cambridge University Press.
Muiu, M. (2002). Globalization and hegemony: Which way Africa? *The Journal of African Policy Studies, 8*(1), 68–88.
Nkandiwire, T. (2001). Thinking about development states in Africa. *Cambridge Journal of Economics, 25*(3), 289–314.
Ntawukuliryayo, J. (2006, June). *Scaling up to reach the health MDGs in Rwanda*. Presentation delivered at the follow-on meeting to the post-high-level meeting on the health MDGs. Tunis, Tunisia.
O'Hare, B. (2015). Weak health systems and Ebola. *Lancet Global Health, 3*, e71–e72.

Ogunbekun, I., Adey, O., Wouters, A., & Morrow, R. (1996). Cost and financing of improvements in the quality of material health services through the Bamako initiative in Nigeria. *Health Policy and Planning, 11*, 369–384.
Oluwole, D. (2008). Health policy developments in Sub-Saharan Africa: National and international perspectives. http://www.transparency.org. Accessed 20 Sept 2011.
Packard, R. (1997). Visions of postwar health and development and their impact on public health interventions in the developing world. In F. Cooper & R. Packard (Eds.), *International development and the social sciences: Essays on the history and politics of knowledge* (pp. 93–115). Berkeley: University of California.
Partnering to Achieve Epidemic Control in Nigeria (PEPFAR). (2014). http://www.pepfar.gov/countries/nigeria/. Accessed 20 July 2016.
Patterson, D. (1981). *Health in colonial Ghana: Disease, medicine and socio-economic change*. Waltham: Crossroads Press.
President's Malaria Initiative, Nigeria Malaria Operational Plan. (2015). http://www.pmi.gov/docs/default-source/default-document-library/malaria-operational-plans/fy-15/fy-2015-nigeria-malaria-operational-plan.pdf?sfvrsn=6. Accessed 6 Sept 2015.
Saul, J., & Leys, C. (1999, July/August). Sub-Saharan Africa in global capitalism. *Monthly review*.
Sessions, M. (n.d.). *Overview of the President's emergency plan for HIV/AIDS relief (PEPFAR)*. Center for Global Development, http://www.cgdev.org/page/overview-president%E2%80%99s-emergency-plan-aids-relief-pepfar. Accessed 20 Aug 2015.
Shehu, M. (1997). Overview of the Bamako initiative programs in Nigeria: Progress made and problems encountered. Conference paper on Bamako Initiative, Federal Ministry of Health, Abuja.
The Abuja Declaration: Ten years on. (2001). http://www.who.int/healthsystems/publications/abuja_report_aug_2011.pdf?ua=1. Accessed 20 July 2016.
Transparency International. (2011). http://www.transparency.org/cp2011/indetail. Accessed 10 June 2015.
UNICEF. (2000). *Annual report*. Lagos: UNICEF country office.
US National Intelligence Council. (2008). *Strategic implications of global health*. http://www.dni.gov.nic/NIC/_specialproducts.html
USAID. (2008). *Health financing in Africa today: Challenges and opportunities*. Washington, DC: USAID.
Vian, T. (2008). Review of corruption in the health sector: Theory, methods and interventions. *Health Policy and Planning, 28*, 83–94.
Werner, D. (1997). *Questioning the solution: The politics of primary health care and child survival*. Palo Alto: Health Wrights.
Witter, S. (2011). The national free delivery policy in Nepal: Early evidence of its effects on health facilities. *Health Policy and Planning, 26*(2), 1184–1191.
World Bank. (1993). *The world bank report*. New York: Oxford University Press.
World Bank. (1994). *Better health in Africa: Experience and lessons learned.* Washington, DC: World Bank.
World Bank. (2000). *World development report*. Washington, DC: World Bank.
World Health Organization (WHO). (1948). Constitution of the world health organization. Geneva: WHO.
World Health Organization (WHO). (1987). *Women and children's health through funding and management of essential drugs at community level: The Bamako initiative* (WHO /AFR/R37/4). Brazzaville: WHO.
World Health Organization (WHO). (2003). *The African malaria report 2003* (WHO/CDS/MAL-Report). Geneva: WHO.
World Health Organization (WHO). (2005). *Chronic disease: A vertical investment*. Geneva: WHO.
World Health Organization (WHO). (2011). *The Abuja declaration: Ten years on*. http://www.who.int/healthsystems/publications/abuja_report_aug_2011.pdf?ua=1. Accessed 28 May 2016.

World Health Organization (WHO). (2015). *World health statistics 2015*. Geneva: WHO.
Zondi, S. (2010). *Overcoming Africa's health burden: Challenges and prospects*. Pretoria: Africa Institute of South Africa.

Benjamin Anaemene holds a Ph.D in diplomatic history from the Department of History and Strategic Studies, University of Lagos, Nigeria. He is currently a Postdoctoral Fellow at the United Nations University International Institute for Global Health, as part of the Governance for Global Health programme. Prior to joining the UNU-IIGH, he has been teaching and conducting research in diplomatic history, global health governance and health diplomacy at both Redeemer's University and the University of Lagos, Nigeria. He spent some time at the WHO headquarters, Geneva conducting research on the role of the WHO in the development of Nigeria's health sector. Dr. Anaemene has carried out several studies, which include the impact of health diplomacy on regional integration particularly in West Africa and the influence of health diplomacy on public policy in Nigeria. His research interests are mainly on global health governance, health diplomacy and health policy. He has published several articles in peer reviewed journals. Email: benjaminanaemene@gmail.com or anaemene@unu.edu.

Chapter 13
Corruption and Africa

Richard A. Aborisade and Nurudeen B. Aliyyu

Introduction

At the point of independence, African countries were largely offered new opportunities to chart new directions in their development agenda for the improvement of the livelihoods of their people. During this period, the policy agenda of most African countries was to combat poverty, ignorance and disease. To date however, it is remarkable that most of these countries continue to experience low levels of development with unemployment, insecurity, poverty, and general moral and social decadence. These challenges, which hinder the development of the continent, are in part blamed on bad governance and more particularly on misrule and the high levels of corruption on the continent (Lumumba 2011; Ijewereme and Dunmade 2014; African Development Bank, United Nations Development Program and Organization for Economic Cooperation and Development 2015; Akanle and Adesina 2015; Alliyu 2015; Nwabughiogu 2015). Indeed, Africa's case is one of paradox, in the sense that it is the richest continent in the world in terms of natural resources, yet it stays at the very bottom of the development and global governance prism.

It is indeed a truism that corruption exists all over the world, however, its seriousness is fully recognized by African countries while questions have continued to be raised over the genuineness of efforts made to tackle it. The enormous economic costs that corruption poses to developing countries have been well documented (Abraham 2008; African Development Bank 2014; Asongu and Jellal 2015; AlixPartners, LLP 2015). This includes the diversion of resources that would have been better invested in societal development, creating poverty, exclusion and conflict, subversion of development plans and programs, impeding the structural

R.A. Aborisade (✉) • N.B. Aliyyu
Department of Sociology, Faculty of Social and Management Sciences, Olabisi Onabanjo University, Ago-Iwoye, Ogun, Nigeria
e-mail: ra.aborisade@gmail.com

O. Akanle, J.O. Adésìnà (eds.), *The Development of Africa*, Social Indicators Research Series 71, DOI 10.1007/978-3-319-66242-8_13

transformation of Africa and endangering the lives and wellbeing of the citizenry (African Development Bank, UNDP and OECD 2015; African Peer Review Mechanism 2015; African Union Commission 2015). It is worth noting at this juncture that corruption distorts the African market to the extent that it remains the strongest factor inhibiting investment in the continent. An environment where corruption thrives is bad for society because "the real development priorities of a country are often neglected in favour of those that generate personal gains of the decision makers" (Samura 2009, 1).

Although corruption existed in varying degrees prior to the colonial period, its growth and effects in postcolonial Africa has been quite phenomenal. At present, Africa represents one of the typical cases of regions of the world whose development has been undermined and truncated by the menace of corruption (Chipkin 2013). Efforts to tackle the problem of corruption have seen the formulation of several reforms by many African countries and governments with little success recorded (Kimenyi et al. 2011). Consequently, extant literature has asserted that corruption has permeated African society to the extent that it will require significant concerted effort and social revolution for the menace to be effectively tackled (Otusanya et al. 2012; Luminita 2013; Mohammed 2013; Kararach 2014). Although it is incontrovertible that corruption has direct grave consequences for the economy of African countries, especially in respect of revenue loss and diversion of funds from their intended use, the indirect costs of corrupt practices as they applies to profligacy, waste of resources, economic distortions, inefficiencies and moral panic are enormous and create problems that are difficult to address on the long run.

In several African societies, the culture of corruption pervades and appears in many forms. Like the heads of Hydra dragon, corruption presents itself in different forms in society from the home front, streets, highways, workplaces to the corridors of powers. In Nigeria, hardly anything can be achieved in the public service without money (or other forms of gratification) exchanging hands (Alliyu 2015), while endemic police corruption in the country has continued to undermine the rule of law (Aborisade and Fayemi 2015). In Kenya, motoring offences necessitate turning up at a court and the payment of bail. However, those that can pay a few thousand shillings (about $30) will avoid going to court (*The Economist* 2015). Similarly, in Zimbabwe the police secretly released a suspect that raped a 9-year old girl and infected her with HIV just because he paid a bribe (Transparency International 2015). In some Cameroonian public hospitals, BBC News (2004) reported that patients have to put some money in the doctor's consultation book before they are able to receive medical attention. Transparency International (2015) stated that about 75 million people in Sub-Saharan Africa volunteered that they had paid a bribe within the previous year in order to escape punishment by the police or courts, while many were forced to pay bribes to get access to the basic services that they need.

This chapter examines the origins of corruption in Africa, its causes and its consequences for political, economic and social development in Africa. A comparative analysis of how various forms of corruption have ravaged various African countries will be presented. A critical examination of efforts and measures put in place by different African governments to check the menace of corruption is equally contained. The chapter ends by offering practical remedies that can be used to reinforce the combatting of corruption, to improve governance, renew growth and put the continent back on the path towards development.

Conceptualization of Corruption

Corruption is quite dynamic as a concept, making it challenging to come to a precise definition for it. There are varying degrees of complexity of the corruption phenomenon in all countries of the world as no single clear internationally accepted definition for corruption exists. This, without doubt, is responsible for the definitional ambiguity that affects international rankings and efforts at conducting cross-country comparisons (Cobham 2013). In cases where such comparisons are done, there are limitations on the usefulness of the conclusions drawn. Although what constitute corruption in terms of meaning has remained controversial, the depth and magnitude of the socioeconomic devastation caused by it is consensually agreed (Carnegie Endowments for International Peace 2014; Escresa and Picci 2015; Engjell 2015).

Transparency International (2015) describes corruption as "the abuse of entrusted power for private gain." It then classifies corruption into petty, political and grand, depending on the value of money stolen and the sector in which it happens. Petty corruption is one that is used to describe the abuse of power entrusted to low and mid-level public officials in their dealings with ordinary citizens, whose are usually interested in accessing basic goods or services in places like schools, police stations, hospitals, ministries and other agencies. Political corruption on the other hand happens when institutions, policies and rules of procedures are being manipulated in the allocation of resources and financing. Decision-makers engage in the abuse of their position in order to sustain their status, wealth and power (Transparency International 2015). Finally, grand corruption includes the acts committed at a high level of government that obstruct policies or the central functioning of the state, which enables the leaders to benefit to the detriment of the masses.

Origin of Corruption in Africa

Today, administrative corruption may be rampant in Africa; however, extant literature has posited that corruption is indeed alien to African culture (Freund 1984; Mazrui and Tidy 1984; Ayittey 1992; Makumbe 1994; Hope 1997; Mulinge and Lesetedi 1998). According to Ezeanya (2012), most of pre-colonial Africa was founded on strong ethical values sometimes packaged in spiritual terms, mainly targeted at ensuring social justice and compliance. Colonialism has been pointed to as a source of grand scale systemic corruption in Sub-Saharan Africa. The indigenous standards, values, checks and balances were repudiated and clandestine superimposition of Western structures destabilized the existing bureaucratic machinery that was ongoing in pre-colonial Africa (Freund 1984; Mazrui and Tidy 1984; Ayittey 1992; Makumbe 1994; Hope 1997; Mulinge and Lesetedi 1998).

Corruption in Pre-colonial Africa

Governance in both centralized and decentralized pre-colonial communities in Africa was conducted with high degree of seriousness. Though laws were basically unwritten which made them easily forgotten, they were usually situated around supernatural premise in a way that drove fear and reverence in the subconscious of the people (Johnson 2010). There are a number of examples of such high degree of emphasis on good governance and accountability in most pre-colonial communities in Africa. In the western part of Africa, strict rules and regulations are recorded to have thrived among the Asante confederation in Ghana (Ayittey 1992). The Kingdom was believed to be held together by the symbolic Golden Stool of Ashante-Heneis established by seven clans near the city of Kumasi. Similarly, among the Yoruba people of western Nigeria there was the institution Oyo-*mesi* which is a body that acted as a check against the abuse of power by the Alaafin (the Oyo King) (Johnson 2010). Consequently, there were constraints on the exercise of power by the Alaafin who could be reprimanded if found to have miscarried justice for personal gains.

In pre-colonial Rwanda, there was high level of organization and efficiency and a centralized system of administration. There were equally well-established systems of checks and balances among those who ruled at the clan level, even in the relatively hierarchical and autocratic system that was presided over by the king (Ezeanya 2012). The land ownership structure of *Ubukonde* reigned supreme within pre-colonial Rwanda. This is a custom of mutually beneficial exchange of labor that existed between the Twa, Tutsi and Hutu founded on agreed principles. There were equally several examples across the Sub Saharan Africa of communities that held strong values of social justice and accountability. These meant that administrative corruption was limited to the barest minimum in traditional African societies, basically as a result of the consensus of principles, rules and regulations, and moral values that guided human interactions in such communities.

Colonial Origins of Corruption in Africa

The contributions of colonialism which led to the emergence of administrative corruption in Africa have been captured in a number of ways. Let us examine some of these ways:

Direct and Indirect Rule System

The direct and indirect rule system adopted by the colonialists to govern most African communities turned leadership in the continent into an enterprise of corruption where power was held in trust for the colonial authorities as against being held in trust for the people (as it was in pre-colonial Africa). The machinery of governance was abused and used as an instrument to extract obedience forcefully from the people. Often, the social misfits or dregs of society were employed by the British authorities as warrant officers to govern over their communities (Mulinge and Lesetedi 1998). At some point corruption was entrenched within this system as some agents of British authorities demanded for money in exchange for manipulating the colonial masters (Mulinge and Lesetedi 1998; Ezeanya 2012). Gradually, a culture developed where people started seeing bribery as a first and last resort in order to avoid arrest and punishment or to gain access to some basic rights.

Taxation

The taxation system of the colonialists contributed in no small measure to the emergence of corruption in Africa. Without adequate information on the economic earnings of potential taxpayers, the colonial masters imposed flat rates of tax on the colonies. The mode of collecting tax was often steeped in violence, in which the warrant officers and district commissioners were given the power to arrest those that defaulted on payment (Ezeanya 2012).

The colonialists used the tax collected mainly for the payment of emoluments and salaries as well as running their offices. The people that paid tax were unable to see much of the benefits that accrued from the payments they made in the form of social services. Consequently, the willingness to continue paying such exorbitant taxes dropped gradually leading to the evolution of a latently corrupt system (Mazrui and Tidy 1984). This situation culminated in a system that negated accountability, which pitched the ruling class against the citizens and the citizens against themselves.

The Police and Military

Globally, the history of the formation of police and military forces has been connected with the need to protect citizens and ensure territorial integrity. However, this belief is slightly different in the case of Africa as the establishment of the police and the military was primarily to meet the need of the colonialists to crush civilian opposition (Aborisade and Fayemi 2015). In Nigeria, during the colonial period, both the local police forces and the Nigeria Police Force were implicated in numerous acts of abuse and corruption (Human Rights Watch 2012). The engagement of the police with the populace was based on the need to enforce colonial laws that attracted debilitating and hateful reactions from the people, including segregation, forced taxation, and the crushing of anti-colonial uprisings. With the end of colonial government, the newly formed African government took over institutions that had internalized a culture of extortion and oppression of citizens (Human Right Watch 2010).

Conspicuous Consumption

Prior to the colonialization of Africa, the emphasis on moral values was profound, as earlier pointed out. The people who were weak in society as a result of being physically impaired, suffering ill health, or old age received adequate care and support. However, this practice was destabilized by the colonialists who forcefully made people work, irrespective of their condition, as miners, houseboys and clerks and in other menial capacities (Ezeanya 2012). The colonial master also introduced a culture of consumerism, and acquisition of alien tastes, rather than production. The farming activities that were mainly focused on food crops were changed to cash crops as more emphasis continued to be placed on material wealth. Rather than the hard work and moral uprightness that pervaded in the pre-colonial society, the colonial masters who lived in 'big' houses, drove exotic cars and treated African with disdain redirected the taste of Africans by their show of wealth.

The Monetization of Africa's Economy

In most African communities, prior to the invasion of the colonialists, work and other economic activities had more social relevance than the mere acquisition of wealth (Ocheni and Nwankwo 2012). People engage in work-related activities to solidify the bond of friendship and social relationships between them. However, this notion largely changed upon the intrusion of the colonialists as work and other economic activities were largely monetized. This introduced a culture of greed and lack of compassion in business dealings which was alien to African society prior to colonialization (Ezeanya 2012). The emphasis placed on monetary incentives as a reward for work ignited corrupt practices as people gradually became reluctant to do favors without financial gratification. The drive to amass wealth as enshrined by the colonialists changed the face of African economy and raised the desperation of the populace for material gain. Several years on and Africa has remained enchanted with the trappings of modernity without the character to cultivate it.

Manifestation and Prevalence of Corruption in Africa

Measuring corruption has remained cumbersome due to the fact that corruption exists in many facets and is often conducted in secrecy, making it inherently challenging to be precise and objective in measuring it or determining its prevalence. This accounts for a measure of skepticism that often trails any results that emanate from empirical measurements of corruption. Consequently, the use of perceptions of corruption as against acts of corruption per se is widely adopted for the measurement of the prevalence of corruption. This has been reported to include increased cost of doing business, misallocation of scarce resources, reduction in the quality of services, shrinking the revenue of governments on tax and discouraging foreign investments (African Development Bank, UNDP and OECD 2015). It is estimated that African countries lose about US$148 billion per annum in corruption (African Development Bank 2014).

There is no doubt about the varying nature of corruption, especially across borders, and the challenges that it poses to precision in measuring the phenomenon; however, the number of indices for measuring it has grown exponentially over the years, mainly to raise awareness among policymakers and the general public (United Nations Economic Commission for Africa 2016). These indicators range from Corruption Perceptions Index (Transparency International) to the Worldwide Governance Indicators (the World Bank). Meanwhile, there are indices that fall within the 'newer generation' which include the Global Integrity Index (Global Integrity), the Index on African Governance (Mo Ibrahim) and the Global Corruption Barometer (Transparency International).

Figure 13.1 contains an analysis of relative median rankings in perceived corruption and shows that Africa is perceived to be significantly corrupt, with a median ranking around the 65th percentile, when the largest group of countries in the continent (52) was ranked. A comparison is drawn between 2007 and 2014. If one takes a closer look at a reduced set of countries (14 out of 54) that were measured by the Corruption Perception Index from 1998, it shows a rising rate of corruption up to 2008, which then improves. In the ranking involving a higher number of African countries, for which data is continuously available, for a shorter period of time, no significant changes over time in the perceptions of corruption, in relation to the remaining parts of the world, have been noted. Irrespective of the significant efforts that have been made in controlling corruption in Africa, there has been no improvement, based on what is presented in the Corruption Perception Index.

The relative median ranking for the five sub-regions in Africa is presented in Fig. 13.2, showing the performance of only the group of 52 countries the data for which are continuously available from 2007 onward in the Corruption Perceptions

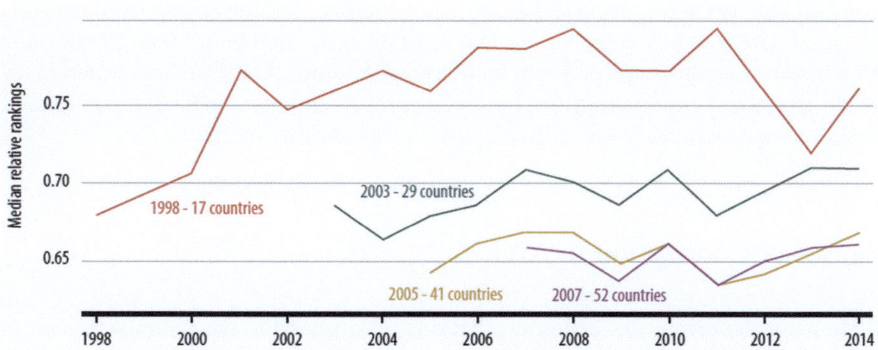

Fig. 13.1 Transparency international's corruption perception index: comparable median relative rankings in Africa (Source: United Nations Economic Commission for Africa 2016)

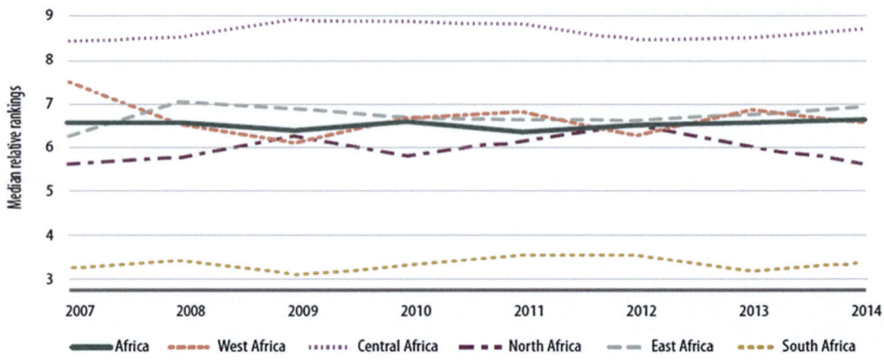

Fig. 13.2 Corruption perception index: comparative relative rankings of Africa sub-regions (Source: United Nations Economic Commission for Africa 2016)

Index. The relative median ranking for Africa as a whole is shown by the thick line, corresponding to the line starting in 2007 in Fig. 13.1. The different vertical scale of Fig. 13.1 in comparison with that of Fig. 13.2 shows that the time series looks remarkably smoother in Fig. 13.2. The relative median rankings of West, North and East Africa are very similar to that of the whole of Africa—with North Africa coming up in most years as marginally less corrupt than the rest of the continent. The present report, on the other hand, notes that Central Africa is perceived to be remarkably more corrupt and Southern Africa less corrupt, than the rest of the continent.

There was little remarkable variation between 2007 and 2014 in the entire trend. As has already been observed in respect of Fig. 13.1, there has been a minor dip in perceptions on the entire continent of Africa since 2011. In taking a look at the subregions of Africa, one can observe that perceptions of the level of corruption in North Africa somehow improved in 2013, and again in 2014.

In Fig. 13.3, a comparison of the Index relative median ranking for the whole of Africa is presented, with a selection of other regions of the world. The figure is based on the very high levels of perceived corruption. An illustration of the performance of Africa as presented shows that the continent fared better than South Asia, but worse when compared to South and Central America. Only Central America, of all the selected regions, exhibits a marked degree of improvement, as the continent moved up approximately one decile in the 5 years starting in 2009.

Causes of Corruption in Africa

Aside from the origin of corruption that has been traced to the colonial period in Africa, there are a number of reasons why corruption thrives in the continent. The major causes to be discussed in this section include bad governance, greed, poor accountability, high quest for wealth and unemployment.

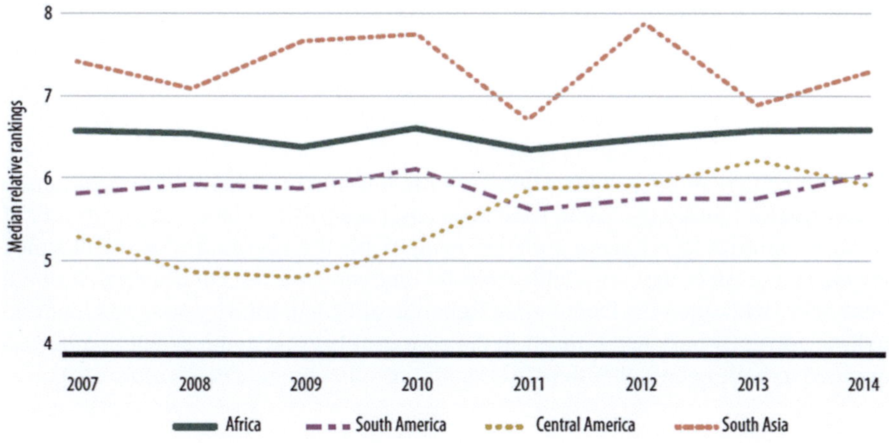

Fig. 13.3 Transparency international's corruption perception index: comparable relative rankings of Africa and other regions (Source: United Nations Economic Commission for Africa (2016))

Dictatorial Leadership and Bad Governance

It is common knowledge that Africa has been plagued with leadership problems since the end of colonialism in the continent. Through improper governance African leaders have consciously or inadvertently empowered corruption to thrive in the continent. Leaders in most African countries hold discretionary powers and control all relevant branches of their economy—civil service, electoral commission, security forces, media and the central bank (Ayittey 2012). Furthermore, Ayittey asserts that the endemic corruption in Africa is an outcome of long-term tenures of dictatorial and bad leadership in the continent.

Examples of past dictators that prolonged their rule in Africa include Ethiopia's Emperor Selassie, who ruled for 44 years, Gabon's Omar Odimba Bongo (42 years), Libya's Mommar Gaddafi (42 years), Togo's Gnassingbe Eyadema (37 years), Cote D'Ivoire's Felix Houphouët-Boigny (33 years) and Egypt's Hosni Mubarak (31 years) (Ayittey 2012). Similarly, there are some current dictators that have already spent more than three decades in power, including Angola's Jose dos Santos, Equatorial Guinea's Teodoro Mbasosgo, Zimbabwe's Robert Mugabe, and Cameroon's Paul Biya. Studies have shown that these leaders or dictators spent their long stay in power enriching themselves, intimidating political opponents, actively frustrating movements towards constitutional rule, and failing to submit to true democratic processes in their governance.

Greed as a Cause of Corruption in Africa

Greed is one of the major factors and causes of the growth of corruption in the African continent. In spite of the fact that democracy in Africa is very expensive as a result of the high allowances that political office holders allocate to themselves, they still engage in gross embezzlement of public funds in their bid to continue to amass wealth limitlessly. There have been cases where presidents and governors of African countries have been reported as being richer than the entire society that they govern as a result of their insatiable thirst for amassing wealth. For example, Mobutu Sese Seko, who ruled the Democratic Republic of Congo for 31 years, was reported to have corruptly enriched himself in the course of his rule to the extent that he was reported to have been richer than his country at some point (*The Guardian* 2013).

Lack of Accountability

Accountability is one of the fundamental prerequisites for the prevention of power abuse and for ensuring that the direction of power is towards the achievement of efficiency, transparency and effectiveness. However, this is lacking in most African communities as many government officials govern with bold disregard for the rule of law. Public officials that are fully aware that there is no firm mechanism for accountability on how they run their expenses and income abound (Okekeocha 2013). Evidence of Nigeria's political elites taking advantage of the accountability problem in President Jonathan's administration is to be found in the $2.2 billion arms deal fraud that had a good number of political leaders in the country indicted. The country's former national security adviser, Sambo Dasuki, was arrested for allegedly diverting funds meant to procure equipment to fight Boko Haram Islamist militants through the award of phantom contracts to his political associates.

Socio-cultural Underpinnings: High Quest for Wealth

The prevailing values of most African communities pay more importance to the acquisition of success, making money and wealth at all costs. A syndrome of 'do what you have to do but just get the money' abounds. Well-known deviants and criminals are celebrated and accorded honors and chieftaincy titles once they have successes and wealth to show for their criminal exploits. African youths are ready to kill and commit any crime because they are seriously hungry for money. This explains why many youths in the continent are engaging in criminal activities and are willing parties in acts of corruption.

Unemployment

The rate of unemployment in Africa is very high. This leaves a high population of people that are ready to do anything to make a living. In order to secure jobs, applicants are willing to pay bribes (Abraham 2008). These job seekers who offer bribes before they secure their jobs will likely continue to offer and demand bribes in their workplace (Adesina 1998). Also, during electioneering campaigns, jobless electorates are often more than willing to sell their votes for money and so on. Unemployment also drives youths to engage in nefarious and corrupt activities like internet fraud, selling of fake or adulterated drugs, piracy and so on (Alliyu 2015).

Cases of Grand Corruption in Africa

Guinea (1990s) one of the largest mining projects in Africa (worth $20 billion) is that of the Simandou iron-ore project which included railway construction and exploration of four mining blocks located in the Simandou region. The award of the four blocks contract was initially made in favor of Rio Tinto; afterwards, two blocks were withdrawn from the company and given to another company BSG Resources who did not go through any tender process (United Nations Economic Commission for Africa 2016). There have been a series of allegations of how substantial bribes were given to facilitate the splitting up of the blocks, leading to a massive scandal. The conclusion of the inquiry by the Federal Bureau of Investigation revealed that BSGR was awarded the contract after paying bribes (*The Economist* 2014).

Kenya (2005) the country was in the news for negative reasons as a result of the fall-out of the so-called Anglo Leasing Scandal which was based on the abuse of lease financing for the funding of security-related projects. In particular, the scandal exposed corruption that surrounded the awarding of the contracts (worth $100 million) for a new passport printing system. The contract was found to have been awarded to non-existent companies with several members of the government involved. Kenya's minister in charge of the project, Chris Murungaru, was subsequently banned from travelling to the UK by the UK government, on the grounds that it would serve the public no good (BBC News 2015).

Uganda (2010) a contract was awarded to a German firm Muhlbauer Technology Co. Ltd. for the printing of national identity cards through a single source contracting process that was questionable and in spite of the Public Procurement Authority advising against it. Although the company was given well over $100 million, the number of cards produced as at 2012 was fewer than 500 and these only went to top politicians (The Monitor 2014).

Malawi (2012) the original design of the Integrated Financial Management Information System (IFMIS) was to ensure that governments are able to monitor the position of their cash and budget. The role of IFMIS is to review identified important control weaknesses in the Malawian system (Combaz 2015). This is based on the government's realization that a number of people are able to take advantage of these weaknesses to transfer funds from government bank accounts to vendor accounts for goods and services that were never supplied and without authorization, and thereafter delete the transactions. The National Audit Office of Malawi stated that up to 6,096,490,705 Malawi kwacha (about $15.5 million) had been classified as theft as at 20 February 2014 (United Nations Economic Commission for Africa 2016).

South Africa (1999/2000) the country was jolted by the political corruption that raised some dust in the US$5 billion Strategic Defence Procurement Package (known as the 'arms deal'), which was contracted in 1999/2000. By the year 2003, there were surprises that sprang up in the case, as it revealed that the financial advisor of Deputy President Jacob Zuma had been charged with corruption relating to the arms deal (Ikejiaku 2009).

Nigeria (2013) the former governor of the Nation's apex bank, Mallam Sanusi Lamido informed the then President Goodluck Jonathan that the state oil company, NNPC, had failed to remit US20 billion to the coffers of the government (*Nigerian Bulletin* 2015). This claim was however dismissed by the president and the governor was subsequently replaced for mismanaging the central bank's budget. Furthermore, a Senate committee investigated and found Sanusi's claim to be lacking substance. At the end of the account audit of NNPC in January 2015, it was concluded that the outfit's non-remitted revenue was actually US$1.48 billion (Cocks and Brock 2015). Meanwhile, based on the report by both Deloitte and PwC on the eve of the exit of the last administration, the auditors found close to $20 billion missing or misappropriated or spent without appropriation (Aguntansoolo 2015).

Corruption as an Albatross for African Development

Though corruption has been adjudged to affect all countries of the world, evidence has shown that poor people are more affected than others. Corruption stifles economic growth and diverts funds that are desperately needed for healthcare, education, infrastructural development and other public services. The World Bank estimates the amount that is annually siphoned through bribes at one trillion US dollars. According to Yury Fedotov, the Executive Director of the United Nations Office on Drugs and Crime (UNODC), "[c]orruption is a global threat. It is a serious roadblock to economic development, it aggravates inequality and injustice, and undermines stability, especially in the world's most vulnerable regions" (UNODC 2011). The large-scale occurrences of corruption are evident in many areas of development and are intrinsically connected with underdevelopment (Akanle and Adesina 2015).

Corruption and Poverty

Though corruption conjures up images that people are rich, empirical studies have established the strong connection between corruption and poverty (Forbes 2009; Kararach 2014; African Union Commission 2015; Akanle and Adesina 2015). Economic growth has been adjudged to be delayed, distorted and diverted by corruption. It can affect income inequality and poverty through various channels, including biased tax systems, overall growth and poor targeting of social programs, as well as through its impact on asset ownership, education inequalities, human capital formation and factor accumulation uncertainties (Gupta et al. 1998). There are two reasons that account for the connection between high corruption and poverty in any given society. First, there is empirical evidence that points to the association between a higher growth rate and a higher rate of poverty reduction (Ravallion 1997; Abraham 2008), and that corruption impedes the speed of poverty reduction by reducing growth. Second, there is equally evidence that indicates that income inequality is harmful to growth (Alesina 1998; Samura 2009; Kimenyi et al. 2011), and if inequality is increased by corruption, then it will also reduce growth and consequently impede poverty reduction (Ravallion 1997).

Poor Infrastructural Development

Corrupt practices generally impact negatively on infrastructural development in Africa as corrupt officials often accept kickbacks from contractors and thus a substandard quality of service. This eventually deprives the community of value-added services which ultimately lead to the building of water washed roads, the importation of fake drugs, clearing of sub-standard products at border posts, and so on. In Africa, public procurement systems have increasingly been the target of corrupt practices (Ayittey 2012). Corruption entrenched in the process of public procurement of goods and services remains a major impediment to economic growth and development.

Misplacement of Government's Priorities

One of the key effects of corruption is evident in the misplacement of government's priorities or choices when corruption sets in. This happens when the real development priorities of a country are neglected in favor of those projects that will potentially generate personal gains for the decision-makers. This is particularly common in Nigeria where governments both at the state and federal levels approve contracts that promise greater kickbacks and for which they will score higher political points than providing basic amenities for the people. In Africa, many such projects end up being white elephants and an easy route for personal enrichment (Abraham 2008; Ijewereme 2015).

Local, Regional and International Efforts to Curb Corruption in Africa

Consequent upon the increased realization of the devastating effects of corruption and the detrimental consequences it has on development, strategies to combat the scourge have become top priority in policy circles all over the world. As a matter of fact, in recent years, we have witnessed the speedy development of the fight against corruption into a major industry which involve most international organizations, including Transparency International (TI), the United Nations (UN), the European Union (EU), the European Bank for Reconstruction and Development (EBRD), the International Monetary Fund (IMF), the World Bank (WB), the World Trade Organization (WTO) and the Organization of Economic Cooperation and Development (OECD) (Mungiu-Pippidi 2015). Without doubt, most of the efforts of these movements in quelling corruption have been targeted at the African continent (Kpundeh 2014).

Africa doubles as home to most corrupt countries in the world and the largest number of 'losers of corruption' in the world. As a result of this, in the past 15 years most African countries have embarked locally on a number of reforms to fight corruption. A good number of studies on the anticorruption fights of African countries have indicated that the theoretical approach of principal–agent is often adopted (Andvig and Fjeldstad 2001; Johnston 2005; Ivanov 2007; Lawson 2009). As a result, the policy instruments that are used have been primarily designed to influence the number of transactions over which public officials at various levels have discretion, the value of the offered bribes (i.e. the scope of gains from each transaction), the probability of being caught, in addition to the loss that the person caught will suffer (i.e. the penalties for corrupt practices) (Kpundeh 2014).

Specifically, the target of reforms in African countries is the reduction of discretion of public officials through privatization and deregulation; reduce monopoly through the promotion of economic and political competition, increasing accountability by supporting democratization (for political accountability) and bureaucratization (for administrative accountability); improving public officials' salaries, as this will increase the opportunity cost of corruption for those that are corrupt; improving the rule of law in order for corrupt bureaucrats and politicians to be prosecuted and punished accordingly, and strengthening transparency in the decision-making process of government by deepening democratization and decentralization, in addition to creating and encouraging civil society watchdogs (Ivanov 2007; Lawson 2009; Akanle and Adesina 2015).

The international community, in their specific prescription of "closing the loopholes for corruption in Africa" (United Nations Development Programme 2014, 9), stated the need for a "holistic anticorruption strategy" (Carnegie Endowments for International Peace 2014) which should increase public awareness; ensure the reduction of rent seeking as a means of economic liberalization, tax simplification, deregulation, de-monopolization, and macroeconomic stability; reduce discretion through administrative and civil service reforms, encouraging meritocratic recruitment and decentralization; and increasing accountability through the building up of institutions like accountancy and auditing units, through legal reforms like strengthening the judicial arms, and by boosting public oversight through parliament, a media that is truly independent, and a more vibrant civil society (World Bank 2000; Transparency International 2000; United Nations 2004; UNDP 2014).

In Kenya, the efforts of the ruling National Rainbow Coalition government in curbing corruption involved a comprehensive strategy of establishing a number of institutional and legal reforms designed to promote good governance and check malfeasance (Persson et al. 2010). The instruments deployed include encouraging an active culture of parliamentary, constitutional reforms, the reorganization of the public service, the decentralization of decision-making and service delivery, deploying means of encouraging the participation of civil society and an active media, and the implementation of radical privatization programs. In respect of the legal reforms adopted by Kenya, the country also enacted the Anticorruption and Economic Crimes Act and the Public Officers Ethics Act. In addition to the creation of new laws, the country also established institutions for the prevention of corrupt practices in the country. Among these institutions are the Ministry of Justice and Constitutional Affairs, Kenya Anticorruption Commission (KACC), the Steering Committee on Corruption, Office of the Permanent Secretary for Governance and Ethics and the Office of the Auditor General.

In Uganda, an elaborate legal and institutional effort at fighting corruption was established. The 1995 constitution made provisions for the Inspectorate General of Government (IGG), as the national ombudsman and leader of the anticorruption agency. The strategy of the country's anticorruption fight consists of three components—prevention, enforcement and institution building. The country also created additional institutions for the fight against corruption which include the Auditor General (AG), which oversees the auditing of all government income and expenditure; the Directorate of Ethics and Integrity (DEI); the Criminal Investigation Department under the police; the Director of Public Prosecution; the Public Accounts Committee of Parliament (which is saddled with the responsibility of reviewing the annual report of the AG on public accounts of government organizations); the Public Procurement and Disposal of Public Assets Authority and the Parliament and the newly established Anticorruption Court (Persson et al. 2010). In addition, a number of special tribunals were established among which is the recently created Judicial Commission of Inquiry into Corruption in the Uganda Police Force (Africa News 2016).

Though it is fair to acknowledge the effort of African governments and the support provided by the international community in the fight against corruption in the continent, these efforts have not met with remarkable success. It is noteworthy that the international community has been quite successful in drawing attention to the problem of corruption that was hitherto neglected, in addition to promoting formal institutional and legal reforms in a number of developing countries; however, there remains a consensus that these anticorruption efforts are not on a par with the successes recorded so far (Johnston 2005; Kpundeh 2014). In spite of the huge resources committed to the fight against corruption, there is still little success to show for it in

3 BEST PERFORMERS Lowest percentage saying corruption has increased		3 WORST PERFORMERS Highest percentage saying corruption has increased	
Burkina Faso	28%	South Africa	83%
Mali	31%	Ghana	76%
Cote D'Ivoire	32%	Nigeria	75%

Fig. 13.4 The perception of citizen of changes in corruption in the last 12 months (Source: Transparency International 2015)

most African countries when it comes to actual implementation of the numerous anticorruption reforms (Lawson 2009; Ittner 2009; Akanle and Adesina 2015; Alliyu 2015). According to the Afrobarometer survey of Transparency International (2015), there is no government in Africa that is positively rated by its citizens in its anticorruption effort. In fact, 18 out of 29 governments are perceived by a large majority of citizens to be failing to address corruption in their countries. As a result of this, corruption remains rampant in Africa today.

Figure 13.4 shows the perception of citizens of Sub-Saharan Africa on how corruption has changed over the past 12 months, as reported by Transparency International (TI) (2015). The figure shows that citizens of Burkina Faso have the highest belief in the reduction of corruption in their country, as only 28% of the citizens still hold that corruption has increased as against South Africa where 83% of the citizens believe that corruption is on the increase in the country.

In respect of the efforts of the governments of Africa in fighting corruption, the ratings show that the citizens of Madagascar have the lowest belief in the efforts of their government in fighting corruption (see Fig. 13.5). Figure 13.5 shows ten Sub-Saharan African countries with the least vote of confidence by the people in terms of their government's performance in fighting corruption. Meanwhile, in the second part of Fig. 13.5, African countries whose citizens have the highest confidence in their government's effort in fighting corruption are presented. Lesotho emerged as the country with the highest level of confidence in government's anticorruption performance.

Governments' Challenges in Fighting Corruption in Africa

There have been a number of measures put in place by different African countries to combat the problem of corruption across the continent. However, these efforts are yet to effectively materialize as the scourge of corruption has continued to grow in leaps and bounds across the continent. The following are some of the challenges faced by governments in their efforts to fight corruption in Africa:

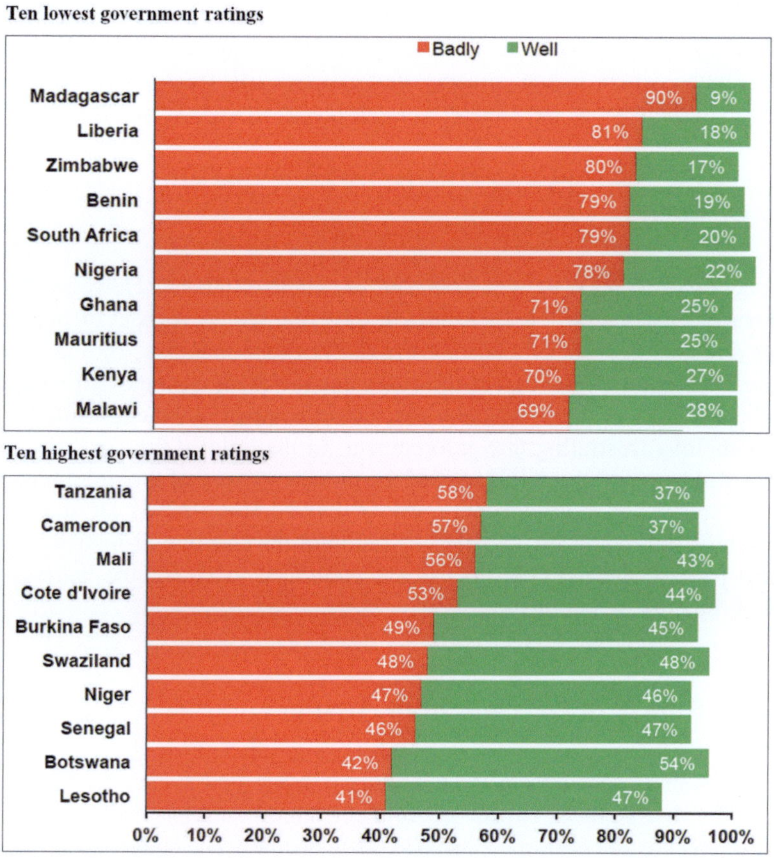

Fig. 13.5 Response to survey on how well government is doing in fighting corruption (Source: Transparency International 2015)

Socio-cultural Challenge

One of the key challenges that confront different efforts targeted at fighting the scourge of corruption in Africa is the cultural dimensions to the problem of corruption in the continent. In Africa, there is the 'big man' syndrome which indicates that the society places high emphasis on material wealth and flamboyance.

Poor Demand for Accountability

A large number of Africans are either illiterate or not politically conscious. This explains why there is a low level of demand for accountability from political office holders by the governed. There is little awareness of the public's right to demand better goods and services. The public also does not have the information available to hold the government accountable. This degree of ignorance is exhibited during elections where voters accept monetary and material gifts from political aspirants in exchange for their votes.

Legal Obstacles

The judiciary provides oversight for the enforcement of the law. However, there are a number of issues with legal systems in the continent in respect of prosecuting corrupt officials. Corrupt officials are usually buoyant enough to hire lawyers that help them to prolong hearings of the cases against them with the ultimate aim of subverting justice. This allows many cases to be trapped in the convoluted judicial process, thereby frustrating law enforcement. In the light of this, the President of Nigeria, Muhammadu Buhari, identified the judiciary as one of the stumbling blocks of his administration's anticorruption war (*Premium Times* 2016). He stated that in spite of reforms brought by the Administration of the Corruption Justice Act 2015, the slow pace of the judicial process has continued to hinder the anticorruption stance of the present administration.

Complex Nature of Corruption in Africa

The fight against corruption in the continent is made problematic by the complex nature of the scourge itself. Higher levels of corruption, such as grand corruption, are complex in nature and need specialized skills to uncover. The budget padding case in Nigeria is an example of the complexities of corruption in the continent. The speaker of the House of Representatives, Yakubu Dogara, who was accused of padding the budget, defended his action by stating that "[b]udget padding is not an offence. What is padding? I studied Law and I have been in the legislature and all this period I have never heard of the word padding being an offence under any law" (*The Punch* 2016).

Corruption Flourishes in Secrecy

Corruption is a practice that is not often perpetrated in the open. This makes it difficult not only to measure its actual prevalence but to also effectively arrest it. Meanwhile, those who are aware of corrupt activities going on in their organization rarely report it for fear of reprisal. Consequently, the rate of reporting of corruption is very low across the African continent, making it difficult for anticorruption agencies to address the trend effectively. The low rate of report of corruption cases is also due to the low level of trust that people have in the criminal justice system and the rule of law across the continent.

Corruption Is Transnational

High profile corruption cases usually involve individuals of different nationalities and residing in different jurisdictions that have different provisions in their criminal justice system. Cross-border corruption and money laundering are becoming common, yet are rarely curtailed because of jurisdictional and sovereignty issues. Most African leaders that engage in embezzlement, money laundering and other corrupt practices are in the habit of transferring such funds into foreign accounts.

Theories of Corruption

In this chapter, an eclectic theoretical approach was adopted in order to present a multidisciplinary analysis of corruption and anticorruption, as well as acknowledging the multidimensional studies conducted in understanding the phenomena. Theories with roots in economics, sociology, political science and criminology were deployed in a theoretical triangulation targeted at harmonizing the various perspectives on corruption.

Rational Choice Theory: The Principal–Agent Model

Several researchers have pointed out that the anticorruption fight of most African government has usually followed the logic of principal–agent theory (Andvig and Fjeldstad 2001; Johnston 2005; Ivanov 2007; Lawson 2009). Though the principal–agent model was originally designed to model economic relations, such as the relationship between managers and the owners of a company, it was later extended to political science to model bureaucratic relations within public institutions. Basically, the concern of the model is the design of rules by the principal "which are directed at assigning tasks to the agent, and intended to regulate exchange with a client" (Lambsdorff 2006, 15). For instance, a principal can be the government that sends an agent, an ambassador, to the United Nations to deal with a client, other ambassadors (Lambsdorff 2006). However, as a result of the problems associated with the design of principal–agent relations, a number of challenges emanate, which are usually known as 'the agency problem.' The principal is challenges by limited resources, which include time, making him delegate some tasks to an agent.

There are two assumptions upon which the principal–agent problem is based: that the agent and the principal have diverging interests and that the agent has more information than the principal (information asymmetry) (Persson et al. 2013). The agent, based on his responsibilities, is availed of a surplus of information as against the principal. The problem is that the principal cannot effectively observe, control or even evaluate whether the agent did his job openly, consequently he is confronted with enormous monitoring problems (Lambsdorff 2006). Even in cases where the principal bases his evaluation on the outcomes of what an agent comes up with in a certain action, he cannot be sure that this outcome was definitely produced by his agent and not by someone else, for example a client.

Consequently, moral hazards occur when the interests of the principal and the agent do not agree, making the agent to pursue his own interests at the expense of the interests of the principal (Rose 1973; Harris and Raviv 1979). Often, corruption is described as existing in society as a double principal–agent problem. In this scenario, a political leader is considered as a 'principal'; saddled with the responsibility of monitoring the activities of the bureaucrat's 'agents' so as to keep them accountable. In situations where the principals are unable to properly monitor the activities of the bureaucrats, the rationally minded bureaucrats will make use of their discretion to administer the resources and extract rents when given such opportunities.

Collective Action Theory

The collective action approach to understanding the problem of corruption was adopted as a response to the criticisms that trailed principal–agent theory (Bauhr and Nasiritousi 2011; Persson et al. 2013). More attempts have therefore being made to viewing corruption as well as governance more broadly. Dozens of studies have focused on the factors that impact on people's perceived interests and calculations to contribute towards the common good of society. One cogent factor that has been pointed out is the influential role that perceptions on how other group members act or speak plays (Seabright 1993). This has largely informed the inspiration that authors had in rooting the application of collective action to the conceptualization of corruption.

Booth and Cammack (2013) posit that corruption should be viewed as a problem of collective action, especially in the context of systemic corruption as it is evident in Africa. As they argue, viewing corruption from a collective perspective will express the nature of the scourge better and the difficulty in the anticorruption measures taken in changing levels of distrust in society and norms that reinforce persistent patterns of systemic corruption. Theorists of collective action have pointed out, however, that there are several other variables that play an important role in influencing whether a group acts collectively (Bauhr and Nasiritousi 2011).

In the use of collective action theory for the conception of corruption, corruption is considered to be a manifestation of free-riding itself, as one's motivation to engage in corruption is believed to have emanated from putting personal interests ahead of the interests of the larger group. In this case, the collective benefit of the group can be depicted as being either quite concrete or abstract (Persson et al. 2010). In the case of the group interest being perceived as abstract, the choice to engage in corruption denies the group a 'corruption-free environment' or a good quality of government. Rothstein (2011) describes good quality government as one in which all citizens are given equal treatment in accordance with the dictates of the rule of law. A good quality of government has positive associations with a number of tangible economic, health and other social outcomes; however, it also means something more abstract, which is an environment of governance that both citizens and (foreign) investors trust to be reliable and fair, and is connected with greater life satisfaction. Corruption has been charged as causing the depletion of tangible resources in Africa, negating the realization of a good quality of government and an environment that is fair to both citizens and foreigners.

General Strain Theory

Agnew's general strain theory has been tested on a number of populations and across a wide range of crimes (Agnew 1992). The generality status of a theory on crime is more accepted if it is applicable to both street and white collar crimes. However, only a few scholars have bothered to relate the theory to white collar crimes like bribery and corruption. The initial strain theory was confronted with a number of criticisms which hinders its applicability in explaining delinquency other than among young, urban, lower-class groups.

In 1992, Robert Agnew remarkably renewed and extended the classic strain theories of Merton (1938) and Sutherland (1940) with his general strain theory. To Merton, an integrated society maintains a balance between social structure (approved social means) and culture (approved goals). Anomie is what results from societal mal-integration when there is dissociation between valued cultural ends and legitimate societal means to those ends. The African theme and principle of equity promotes equality among tribes, sex and religious affiliations. This principle is supported by the educational system which welcomes all and sundry to receive formal skills in order to enhance one's chances of making a success of life. However, in reality, disadvantaged people on the lower rung of the social ladder do not have access to such legitimate opportunities. It is obvious that the African values attribute more importance to the acquisition of success, making money and wealth at all costs. Modern African society celebrates well-known corrupt officials as long as they are able to benefit from the person's loot.

Agnew (1992) postulated that strain need not be specifically tied to economic status since it actually operates through negative emotions instead of simply rejecting the negative means or definitions of success. As a result, individuals from all social classes can engage in criminal behavior due to their experience of negative emotions that arises from strain, and this modification helped to restore strain theory to a place of theoretical importance within criminology. He then went further to argue that an important type of strain occurs when one is unable to legitimately achieve one's desired monetary success. Finally, Agnew was cautious in acknowledging that "certain types" of white-collar crime could be solutions to the strain of excessive demands, connected with conventional pursuits like a well-paid job (Agnew 2001, 168). Therefore, Agnew created the foundation for general strain theory to be applied to white collar crime outcomes.

Anticorruption: The Big Bang Theory

Two different ideas are mainly used by social scientists in examining and understanding human agency. These are either that agents are more or less absolved in their culture and history and are thus historically and/or structurally determined to act the way they do, or they are rational agents using utility-maximizing calculations to engage in frequent cost-benefit analyses of various incentive systems that they encounter. As a result of the limitation of theories that examine how culture or incentive-inducing institutions change, these human agency ideas do not provide much room for explaining change. In fact, the two of them are very improbable descriptions of how the minds of humans are made up about 'how to play' or 'what they can expect.' In his evolutionary game theory, Peyton Young (1998) offers a more realistic picture of how human agency can be understood. Theory like this is of particular interest for anticorruption research rather than merely focusing on 'one-shot' interactions. This type of game theory thinks of development as an (endless) set of consecutive forms of small and big strategic interactions. A more realistic and useful notion of human agency then evolves with this. The first is that "agents are not perfectly rational and fully informed about the world in which they live," rather, "they base their decisions on fragmentary information" and "they have incomplete models of the process they are engaged in."

Consequently, policy implications of the theory portend a holistic change in all institutions within the society as being important. In situations where one institution, say the court, is reformed, while the civil service, civil society, mass media or the integrity of the politically elected are neglected, then corruption is likely to creep in from the other ignored institutions. Therefore, instead of selective reforms, a total reform is preferred in order for the powerful networks to realize that everywhere they turn there is a new practice in town that is devoid of corruption. Second, a simultaneous approach at changing everything should be deployed as much as possible. If the anticorruption policy measures are constrained to the introduction of small measures ('entry points'), enough agents will not be convinced that the continuation of their corrupt practices is no longer a viable option and the most probable outcome is that the system will not get to the desired change but slide back into its old practices of systemic corruption. Hence, the theory posits that the change in the society from corruption should not be gradual but total and all encompassing. This theory gave credence to the failure of several anticorruption measures adopted by many African countries that have appeared to be selective and gradual. The lack of sincerity of purpose of these governments is part of the factors responsible for the failure of the anticorruption drive.

Conclusion and Recommendations

Neither corruption nor its study is new. However, as long as the problem of corruption continues unabated, the significance of studies conducted on the phenomenon will continue to be acknowledged. Consequently, interest in corruption has remained central to the discussion of economic performance and development over the last two decades. This chapter, in contributing to the bourgeoning body of knowledge on the corruption menace in Africa, has x-rayed the origins, causes, and consequences of corruption in the continent. The chapter has further joined ranks with similar studies to emphasize the need for concerted efforts and strong-willed resolution to curb the problem of corruption in the African continent. Indeed, the fight against corruption requires multifaceted and multidisciplinary approaches that will be targeted at the economic, political, legal, social, moral and administrative levels. This therefore requires broad-based, consistent and coherent measures with long-term focus.

First and foremost, it is important for corruption to be declared a continental disaster. This is a clear strategy for eliciting collective action against the scourge. There is a need for all governments in Africa to offer leadership by inviting national, regional and international responses to corruption with the use of sound educational, enforcement, administrative and preventive mechanisms.

Another important step towards a sustainable anticorruption drive for Africa is to intimately examine the funding and management of political parties. This is because political parties are strong instruments for fostering corruption within the continent based on their direct involvement in the business sector, and their lack of transparency and accountability for funding the parties.

The structuring of political parties is imperative to ensure they are well governed and positioned to lead the quest for transparency and accountability in governance. In order for this to be done, political parties should be mandated to adhere to the established laws, norms and rules of society or a nation. African countries that are yet to establish a fair legal and political system that can enable political parties to follow best practice of effective representation, regulation of party funding and streamlining of party management should do so with the urgency that the situation deserves.

Whistleblowing is a responsibility that many people are not ready to accept in Africa due to the fear of retribution as information about the whistleblowers is often not held in confidence. This trend must change as invaluable information that can be obtained from whistleblowers will only be available if adequate legislative protections are provided.

Though some countries already have fully operational anticorruption agencies, some other African countries are yet to establish theirs. These countries should be enlightened and encouraged to set up anticorruption agencies in the countries to spearhead the fight against corruption. In addition, it is imperative for such agencies to be truly independent in their operations and devoid of any political interference. This is one of the factors impeding the smooth and unbiased operations of most anticorruption agencies in Africa, as the ruling governments often use the agencies as an instrument to subdue their political enemies.

The traditional African values that abhor corrupt practices have been neglected at the altar of wealth, status and power. Consequently, corruption can only be effectively quelled in the continent if there is social rejuvenation that fosters the indigenous values of African community and of the constitutions. There is a need for honesty to be rewarded as punishment is meted to deviants.

Developing a culture of merit-based appointments to jobs within the public service is one of the measures that can put paid to corruption in the continent. In environments where clearly stated qualifications are not the main criterion used to determine employability, corruption is usually difficult to curb.

African countries that are multi-ethnic and multiracial have the challenge of making corruption fights as objective as possible. Sentimentalism is a serious challenge that could render fights against corruption ineffective. In order for fights against corruption to be totally committed, citizens should be able to condemn corrupt practices and actors irrespective of their ethnic or racial affiliations.

Finally, there is no gainsaying the fact that the corrosive effect of corruption needs urgent and sustained action that requires Africa to strengthen governance to combat the scourge. It is dangerous for this social menace to continue to be allowed to be hidden under the carpet of equivocal and wavering legal technicalities and political will.

References

Aborisade, R., & Fayemi, J. (2015). Police corruption in Nigeria: A perspective on its nature and control. *Nigerian Journal of Social Sciences, XVII*(2), 245–262.

Abraham, J. (2008). *Corruption, social inequality and poverty in Mano River Union states of West Africa*. http://repository.uneca.org/bitstream/handle/10855/3685/bib.%2029122_I.pdf?sequence=1. Accessed 11 July 2016.

Adesina, A. (1998). The political economy of stabilizations and income inequality: Myths and reality. In V. Tanzi & C. Ke-young (Eds.), *Income distribution and high-quality growth*. Cambridge, MA: MIT Press.

Africa News. (2016, June 23). Ugandans believe police are 75% corrupt: Survey. *Africa News*. http://www.africanews.com/2016/06/23/ugandans-believe-police-are-75-percent-corrupt-survey/. Accessed 11 Aug 2016.

African Development Bank. (2014). *Governance Strategic Framework and Action Plan II (GAP II): Promoting good governance and accountability for Africa's transformation*. http://www.afdb.org/fileadmin/uploads/afdb/Documents/Project-and-Operations/Governance_Strategic_Framework_and_Action_Plan__GAP_II___2014-2018_-_Appraisal_Report.pdf. Accessed 11 July 2016.

African Development Bank, UNDP and OECD. (2015). *African economic outlook: Structural transformation and natural resources*. www.africaneconomicoutlook.org/en/theme/structural-transformation-and-natural-resources. Accessed 10 July 2016.

African Peer Review Mechanism. (2015). *Democracy and good political governance*. http://aprm-auorg/democratic-and-political-governance. Accessed 10 July 2016.

African Union Commission. (2015). *Agenda 2063: The Africa we want*. http://agenda2063.au.int/en/sites/default/files/agenda2063_popular_version_05092014_EN.pdf. Accessed 10 July 2016.

Agnew, R. (1992). Foundation for a general strain theory of crime and delinquency. *Criminology, 30*(1), 47–87.

Agnew, R. (2001). An overview of general strain theory. In R. Paternoster & R. Bachman (Eds.), *Explaining criminals and crime*. Los Angeles: Roxbury.

Aguntansoolo. (2015, April 29). *This yam, this goat, this country: PwC on NNPC*. https://aguntasolo.com/2015/04/29/this-yam-this-goat-this-country-part-1/. Accessed 7 Aug 2016.

Akanle, O., & Adesina, J. (2015). Corruption and the Nigerian development quagmire: Popular narratives and current interrogations. *Journal of Developing, 31*(4), 421–446.
Adesina, A. (1998). The political economy of stabilizations and income inequality: Myths and reality. In V. Tanzi & C. Ke-young (Eds.), *Income distribution and high-quality growth*. Cambridge, MA: MIT Press.
AlixPartners, LLP. (2015). *Cross-border M&A: Bribery and corruption issues in international transactions*. http://www.alixpartners.com/en/Publications/AllArticles/tabid/635/articleType/ArticleView/articleId/1699/Cross-Border-MA.aspx#sthash.oyOSQbze.dpbs. Accessed 12 July 2016.
Alliyu, N. (2015). Leadership, followership and corruption in Nigerian society. In N. Alliyu (Ed.), *Sociological issues in industry and Nigerian society* (pp. 145–165). Ibadan: Ibadan University Press.
Andvig, J., & Fjeldstad, O. (2001). *Corruption: A review of contemporary research reports*. Buegen: Michelsen Institute.
Asongu, S., & Jellal, M. (2015). *On the channels of foreign aid to corruption*. Cameroon: African Governance and Development Institute.
Ayittey, G. (1992). *Africa betrayed*. New York: St Martin's Press.
Ayittey, G. (2012, May 24). *Defeating dictators. Speech given at the Oslo Freedom Forum*. Retrieved 5 August, 2016, from https://oslofreedomforum.com/speakers/george_ayittey.html
Bauhr, M., & Nasiritousi, N. (2011). *Why pay bribes? Collective action and anticorruption efforts*. QOG Institute: Goteborg.
BBC News. (2004, June 18). *How deep is corruption in Africa?* United Kingdom. http://news.bbc.co.uk/2/hi/africa/3819027.stm. Accessed 16 July 2016.
BBC News. (2015, March 4). *Kenyan officials charged over Anglo leasing scandal*. http://www.bbc.com/news/world-africa-31733052. Accessed 9 Aug 2016.
Booth, D., & Cammack, D. (2013). *Governance for development in Africa: Solving collective action problems*. New York: Zed Books.
Carnegie Endowments for International Peace. (2014). *Corruption: The unrecognized threat to international security*. New York: Working Group on Corruption and Security.
Chipkin, I. (2013). Whither the state? Corruption, institutions and state-building in South Africa. *Politikon, 40*(2), 211–223.
Cobham, A. (2013). Corruption perceptions: Why Transparency International's flagship, corruption index falls short. *Foreign Policy*. http://foreignpolicy.com/2013/07/22/corrupting-perceptions/#sthash.ojqUB9aA.dpbs. Accessed 13 July 2016.
Cocks, T., & J. Brock. (2015). Special Report: Anatomy of Nigeria's $20 billion "leak". *Reuters*. http://www.reuters.com/article/us-nigeria-election-banker-specialreport-idUSKBN0LA0X820150206. Accessed 7 Aug 2016.
Combaz, E. (2015). *Implementing integrated financial management information systems*. Applied Knowledge Services. GSDRC. http://www.gsdrc.org/wp-content/uploads/2015/06/HDQ1229.pdf. Accessed 8 Aug 2016.
Engjell, P. (2015). The impact of good governance in the economic development of Western Balkan countries. *European Journal of Government and Economics, 4*(1, June), 50–62.
Escresa, L., & Picci, L. (2015). A new cross-national measure of corruption. *The World Bank Review*. doi:10.1093/wber/lhv031.
Ezeanya, C. (2012, August 12). *Origin of corruption in Africa and the way forward*. https://chikaforafrica.com/2012/08/21/origin-of-corruption-in-africa-and-the-way-forward/Accessed. 6 Aug 2016.
Forbes. (2009, January 22). *Corruption and poverty*. http://www.forbes.com/2009/01/22/corruption-poverty-development-biz-corruption09-cx_mj_0122johnston.html. Accessed 24 July 2016.
Freund, B. (1984). *The making of contemporary Africa: The development of African society since 1800*. Bloomington: Indiana University Press.
Gupta, S., Davoodi, H., & Alonso-Terme, R. (1998). *Does corruption affect income inequality and poverty?* Fiscal Affairs Department. International Monetary Fund. https://www.imf.org/external/pubs/ft/wp/wp9876.pdf. Accessed 21 July 2016.

Harris, M., & Raviv, A. (1979). Optimal incentive contract with imperfect information. *Journal of Economic Theory, 20*, 231–259.
Hope, K. (1997). *African political economy: Contemporary issues in development*. London: M.E. Sharpe.
Human Rights Watch. (2010, August 17). *Everyone's in on the game: Corruption and human rights abuses by the Nigerian Police Force*. New York. www.hrw.org/reports/2010/08/17/everyone-s-game-0. Accessed 12 Dec 2015.
Human Rights Watch. (2012). *Everyone's in on the game: Corruption and human rights abuses by the Nigerian police force*. New York: Human Rights Watch.
Ijewereme, O. (2015, April–June 1–16). Anatomy of corruption in the Nigerian public sector: Theoretical perspectives and some empirical explanations. *Sage Open*.
Ijewereme, O., & Dunmade, E. (2014). Leadership crisis and corruption in the Nigerian public sector: Implications for socioeconomic development of Nigeria. *International Journal of Public Administration and Management Research, 33*(1), 24–38.
Ikejiaku, B. (2009). 'Crime', poverty, political corruption and conflict in apartheid and post-apartheid South Africa: The implications on economic development. *African Journal of Political Science and International Relations, 3*(10), 451–459.
Imhonopi, D., & Ugochukwu, M. (2013). Leadership crisis and corruption in the Nigeria public sector: An albatross of national development. *The African Symposium: An Online Journal of the African Educational Research Network, 3*(1), 78–87.
Ittner, S. (2009). *Fighting corruption in Africa: A comparative study of Uganda and Botswana*. PhD thesis, Deutschen Hochschule für Verwaltungswissenschaften.
Ivanov, K. (2007). The limits of a global campaign against corruption. In S. Bracking (Ed.), *Corruption and development: The anticorruption campaigns* (pp. 28–45). Basingstoke: Palgrave Macmillan.
Johnson, S. (2010). *The history of the Yorubas: From the earliest times to the beginning of the British protectorate*. Cambridge: Cambridge University Press.
Johnston, M. (2005). *Syndromes of corruption: Wealth, power, and democracy*. Cambridge: Cambridge University Press.
Kararach, G. (2014). *Development policy in Africa: Mastering the future?* Basingstoke: Palgrave Macmillan.
Kimenyi, I., Mwangi, S., & Mbaku, J. (2011). *Africa's war on corruption in foresight Africa: The Continent's greatest challenges and opportunities for 2011*. Washington, DC: Brookings Institution.
Kpundeh, S. (2014). *Building state capacity in Africa*. Washington, DC: World Bank Publications.
Lambsdorff, J. (2006). What is bad about corruption? The contribution of the new institutional economics. In H. R. Hemmer (Ed.), *Good governance* (pp. 11–55). Frankfurt: Kreditanstalt für Wiederaufbau.
Lawson, L. (2009). The politics of anticorruption reform. *Journal of Modern African Studies, 47*(1), 73–100.
Luminita, I. (2013). The role of technology in combating corruption. *Journal of Economics, Management and Financial Markets, 8*(3), 101–106.
Lumumba, P. (2011). *Corruption: The bane of Africa. SAPICS 33rd Annual Conference and Exhibition 26 to 28*. Sun City, South Africa. http://www.eacc.go.ke/docs/Corruption%20the%20bane%20of%20Africa.pdf. Accessed 12 July 2016.
Makumbe, J. (1994). Bureaucratic corruption in Zimbabwe: Causes and magnitude of the problem. *Africa Development, 19*(3), 45–60.
Mazrui, A., & Tidy, M. (1984). *Nationalism and new states in Africa from about 1935 to the present*. New Hampshire: Heinemann.
Merton, R. (1938). Social structure and anomie. *American Sociological Review, 3*, 672–682.
Mohammed, U. (2013). Corruption in Nigeria: A challenge to sustainable development in the Forth Republic. *European Scientific Journal, 9*, 118–137.
Mulinge, M., & Lesetedi, G. (1998). Interrogating our past: Colonialism and corruption in Africa. *African Journal of Political Science, 3*(2), 15–28.

Mungiu-Pippidi, A. (2015). Corruption: Diagnosis and treatment. *Journal of Democracy, 17*(3), 86–99.
Nigerian Bulletin. (2015, February 6). Politics NNPC Audit: No Missing $20 Billion – Bloomberg. https://www.nigerianbulletin.com/threads/nnpc-audit-no-missing-20-billion-%E2%80%93-bloomberg.107644/. Accessed 7 Aug 2016.
Nwabughiogu, L. (2015, August 20). Over 100m Nigerians living below poverty line: Osinbajo. *Vanguard Newspapers*, pp. 22–23.
Ocheni, S., & Nwankwo, B. (2012). Analysis of colonialism and its impact in Africa. *Cross Cultural Communication, 8*(3), 46–54.
Okekeocha, C. (2013). A case study of corruption and public accountability in Nigeria. Dissertation, Kennesaw State University, Department of Political Science and International Affairs, Kennesaw.
Otusanya, O., Lauwo, S., Adeyeye, G. (2012). *A critical examination of the multinational companies' anticorruption policy in Nigeria.* Accountancy Business and the Public Interest. http://visar.csustan.edu/aaba/Otusanya2012.pdf
Persson, A., Rothstein, B., & Teorell, J. (2010). *The failure of anticorruption policies: A theoretical mischaracterization of the problem.* Gothenburg: University of Gothenburg, Department of Political ScienceThe Quality of Government Institute.
Persson, A., Rothstein, B., & Teorell, J. (2013). Why anticorruption reforms fail: Systemic corruption as a collection action problem. *Governance, 26*(4), 449–471.
Premium Times. (2016, July 18). *How lawyers, judges are slowing down Nigeria's anticorruption war: Buhari*, p. 21. http://www.premiumtimesng.com/news/headlines/207102-lawyers-judges-slowing-nigerias-anticorruption-war-buhari.html. Accessed 10 Aug 2016.
Ravallion, M. (1997). Can high-inequality developing countries escape absolute poverty? *Economics Letters, 56*, 51–57.
Rose, S. (1973). The economic theory of agency: The principal's problem. *The American Economic Review, 63*(2), 134–139.
Rothstein, B. (2011). Anticorruption the indirect 'big bang' approach. *Review of International Political Economy, 11*(2), 228–250.
Samura, B. (2009). *The negative effects of corruption on developing nations.* http://www.carl-sl.org/home/articles/125-the-negative-effects-of-corruption-on-developing-nations-a-perspective-on-sierra-leones-effort-to. Accessed 12 July 2016.
Seabright, P. (1993). Managing local commons: Theoretical issues in incentive design. *Journal of Economic Perspectives, 7*(4), 113–134.
Sutherland, E. (1940). White collar criminality. *American Sociological Review, 5*, 1–12.
The Economist. (2014, December 6). Mining and Corruption: Crying Foul in Guinea. *The Economist*. http://www.economist.com/news/business/21635522-africas-largest-iron-ore-mining-project-has-been-bedevilled-dust-ups-and-delays-crying-foul. Accessed 10 Aug 2016.
The Economist. (2015, December 3). *The scale of corruption in Africa.* http://www.economist.com/news/middle-east-and-africa/21679473-gloomy-news-transparency-international-scale-corruption-africa. Accessed 15 July 2016.
The Guardian. (2013, October 25). *Mobutu Sese Seko's body to be returned to Democratic Republic of the Congo*. New York. https://www.theguardian.com/world/2013/oct/25/mobutu-sese-seko-remains-repatriated-congo-zaire. Accessed 22 July 2016.
The Monitor. (2014, April 20). *Will Gen Aronda finally deliver ID cards for Ugandans?* http://www.monitor.co.ug/Magazines/PeoplePower/The-search-for-identity-/689844-2285514-11i2m90z/index.html. Accessed 8 Aug 2016.
The Punch. (2016, August 7). Budget padding is corruption, SERAP tells Dogara. *The Punch Newspapers*. http://punchng.com/budget-padding-corruption-serap-tells-dogara/. Accessed 7 Aug 2016.
Transparency International. (2000). *TI sourcebook. Confronting corruption: The elements of a national integrity system.* Berlin: Transparency International.

Transparency International. (2015, November 30). Corruption in Africa: 75 million people pay bribes. http://www.transparency.org/news/feature/corruption_in_africa_75_million_people_pay_bribes. Accessed 15 July 2016.

United Nations. (2004). *Anti-corruption toolkit*. New York: UN.

United Nations Development Programme. (2014). *Anticorruption practice note*. New York: UNDP.

United Nations Economic Commission for Africa. (2016). *Measuring corruption in Africa: The international dimension matters*. African Governance Report IV, Addis Ababa. http://www.uneca.org/sites/default/files/PublicationFiles/agr4_eng_fin_web.pdf. Accessed 14 July 2016.

UNODC. (2011). *Impaect of corruption on development and how states can better tackle corruption under the spotlight at UN Anticorruption Conference in Morocco*. The Fourth Session of the Conference of the States Parties to the United Nations Convention against Corruption. Marrakech.

World Bank. (2000). *Anticorruption in transition: A contribution to the policy debate*. Washington, DC: World Bank.

Young, P. (1998). *Individual strategy and social structure: An evolutionary theory of institutions*. Princeton: Princeton University Press.

Richard A. Aborisade is a Senior Lecturer and acting Head of the Department of Sociology, Faculty of Social and Management Sciences, Olabisi Onabanjo University, Ago-Iwoye, Ogun State. He holds degrees from the University of Ibadan, Nigeria (BSc, MSc, and PhD Sociology) and Coventry University, UK (MBA, Information Technology). Dr. Aborisade has published in both local and international journals in the areas of security management, criminal justice, criminology, victimology, and penology. His most recent work includes *The Essentials of Sociology*, (co-edited) and *Crime and Delinquency: A Sociological Introduction*; both published by Ibadan University Press. He can be reached via email: aborisade.richard@oouagoiwoye.edu.ng.

Nurudeen B. Aliyyu, Ph.D trained as a Sociologist at the University of Ibadan, Nigeria. He is an Associate Professor of Sociology at Olabisi Onabanjo University, Ago-Iwoye, Nigeria. He has conducted (with other researchers) empirical social and marketing researches that enjoyed support from both local and international donor agencies such as Family Health International (FHI) Lagos; Pathfinder International (PI) Lagos; Liverpool Associates in Tropical Health (LATH) UK, African Development Foundation (ADF), Washington DC and Tertiary Education Trust Fund TETfund, Nigeria. He was pioneering Consultant with Communication and Marketing Research Group Limited (CMRG) Lagos, Nigeria. Dr. Adetola has published in both local and international journals in the areas of gender and development. His research interests include Sociology of Development and Development Studies especially Gender and Women Studies, Social Theory and Research Methods. He is the Lead Researcher in a recently awarded small grants funded by Tertiary Education Trust Fund (TETfund), Nigeria on waste generation, management and wealth creation in Ogun State, Nigeria. His latest edited work published by Ibadan University Press is Sociological Issues in Industry and Nigerian Society. E-mails: Obatunde.adetola@oouagoiwoye.edu.ng & octomay07@yahoo.com

Chapter 14
Africa and Climate Change Refugees' Quandary: Kenya Perspectives

Joseph M. Karanja and Zakaria Abdul-Razak

Introduction

Climate change holds a great threat to the survival of humankind and ecosystems. The Intergovernmental Panel on Climate Change (IPCC) warned that a temperature rise beyond the 2 °C threshold will likely cause climate disruption for several decades (IPCC 2007). With leading pollutant countries showing little commitment to reducing carbon emissions and emerging economies expected to follow suit, there is a discernible need to protect susceptible communities living in environmentally fragile areas. There is clear evidence that the effects of climate change are felt today and the impacts are unavoidable tomorrow (Global Leadership for Climate Action 2009). African countries, in particular, are perceived to be the most vulnerable even though they have contributed least to greenhouse gas emissions. Although the rich countries dominate the current greenhouse gas emissions, the developing countries emission contribution is expected to increase rapidly (Costello et al. 2009; Stern 2006). What does this mean for developing countries?

They must not only prepare to adapt to the current changes but also must take a different development route. The advocacy of green development especially by industrial countries is alleged by developing countries as neocolonialism strategy. Developing countries are confronted by climate change dilemmas that are compounded by financial constraints. How do they curb the effects of climate change? How do they cut their emissions while promoting economic growth and eradicating poverty? Will climate change beget poverty traps? Considering that the most advanced countries are the largest contributor of this menace, are they obligated to assist the developing countries? As we ponder about these questions, it is clear that a 'business as usual' approach will render developing countries more susceptible. Given that past emissions are already causing changes, developing countries must

J.M. Karanja (✉) • Z. Abdul-Razak
University of Tsukuba, Tsukuba, Japan
e-mail: josentokaranja@gmail.com; nurazak830@gmail.com

O. Akanle, J.O. Adésìnà (eds.), *The Development of Africa*, Social Indicators Research Series 71, DOI 10.1007/978-3-319-66242-8_14

act now. Nevertheless, coping with the challenges of climate change (particularly the irreversible ones) is a daunting task especially for the African countries.

Stern (2006) argues that climate change adaptation (CCA) is essential for sustainable development. Nonetheless, how do African countries adapt to irreversible changes? There are several studies examining the impacts of climate change in Africa. Nonetheless, there are relatively limited studies investigating the dilemma of climate change refugees. In this chapter, we analyze the implications of climate change and climate change effects on environmental refugees, by giving empirical evidence from Kenya.

Climate Change Refugees

Climate change will exacerbate the already complex refugee crisis. In 2015, approximately 28 million people were displaced globally as a result of wars, conflicts and disasters (IDMC 2016). The contributions of climate change to refugees can be threefold, that is, natural, conflict-induced and economic. First, global warming is expected to increase the return period and severity of water hazards such floods, drought, heat waves and storms (Costello et al. 2009), as well as escalate the frequency and magnitude of extreme events (IPCC 2007). The hazards will severely affect people and regions in susceptible areas. Weather-related disasters displaced 14.7 million people globally, and 1.1 million people from Sub-Saharan Africa (IDMC 2016). The report does not account for displacement triggered by slow-onset disasters such as drought and desertification. In addition, rising temperature and sea levels are likely to make some places uninhabitable. Temperature and rainfall in Kenya are expected to increase at a range of 2.5 °C to 30 °C, and 5% to 20% respectively by the end of the century. Moreover, research shows that a 30 cm sea-level rise would submerge 17% of the Kenya coastal region (Awuor et al. 2008).

According to Antwi-Agyei (2012), the temperature in Ghana has increased by about 1°C and rainfall and run-off have decreased by approximately 20% and 30% respectively. He predicts that the country's temperature will rise by 0.6°C, 2.0°C and 3.9°C by the years 2020, 2050 and 2080 respectively. Rainfall, on the other hand, has been predicted to decrease by 2.8%, 10.9% and 18.6% during the same period. In 2007 the northern part of Ghana, particularly communities located along the White Volta Basin, was reported to have been affected by floods. More than 275,000 people were affected and the majority were displaced from their homes. This flooding incident also destroyed farmland and resulted in the total loss of harvest. More than 12,200 ha of farmland and about 160,000 metric tons of food were reported lost as a consequence. Climate variability in the form of erratic rainfall influence not only livelihoods and food security but also economic development. Future forecast is that climate change coupled with increasing population would worsen the situation (Mul et al. 2015).

Climate change will likely disrupt source of livelihoods of vulnerable people. The economies of most African countries tend to rely on ecosystems and ecosystem services such as agriculture, forests, water, health and coastal zones. These sectors are under serious threat of climate change (Global Leadership for Climate Action 2009). For instance, agriculture is the backbone of Kenya's economy with an estimated direct and indirect gross domestic product (GDP) contribution of 24% and 27% respectively. The sector provides 75% of industrial raw materials, 45% of government's revenues and is responsible for more than 50% of export earnings. It accounts for 60% of the total employment (Kenya Agricultural Research Institute 2012) and provides livelihoods to 75% of the national population (Ministry of Agriculture, Livestock and Fisheries 2015). The majority of the farmers depend on rain-fed agriculture. Some crops and livestock might not survive in certain regions due to the changing climatic conditions. As result, climate change will threaten food security, given that erratic and/or short rains significantly reduce agricultural production (Ministry of Agriculture, Livestock and Fisheries 2015). This will also have serious repercussions for agricultural dependent industries and will stagnate the national economy, not to mention the millions of people who will be rendered jobless. The jeopardized agriculture sector in Kenya might compel millions of people to look for an alternative source of livelihood.

In the Upper East region of Ghana, farmers along the Volta River Basin lose their harvest to floods caused by erratic rainfall and the spillage of the Bagre Dam located upstream in Burkina Faso, sometimes experiencing total crop loss. Free range livestock are also carried away by the flood. Some farmers migrate to the southern part of Ghana in search of work as a result. On 20 August 2016 for instance, the *Daily Guide*, a Ghanaian newspaper, reported on the Bagre Dam spillage, under the headline: "Farmers cry out over Bagre Dam spillage". It reports that 63 communities in the Bawku West, Bawku East, Binduri and Talensi districts of the upper east region of Ghana are very likely to be affected when the spillage occurs. It has become a yearly ritual that communities situated along the Volta River Basin suffer from crop loss due to climate hazards and the Bagre Dam spillage that is not properly managed. This generates hundreds of climate refugees every year and has increased tension between affected communities and local government authorities (*Daily Guide* 2016).

There has been a contentious debate about the effects of climate change on conflict (empirical evidence will be provided in results section). This brings us to the third climate change refugee phenomenon, conflict-induced refugees. Climate change impacts will induce migration and violent conflict especially in the least developed countries (Barnett 2003; Raleigh and Urdal 2007; Reuveny 2007). In 2015, 2.2 million people in Sub-Saharan Africa were displaced by conflicts (IDMC 2016). As the migrants settle down in safer and more habitable regions, competition over scarce resources (such as water, pasture, land) might spark conflict in the newly settled territory.

However, it is very hard to distinguish climate change refugees from the prevailing conflict-induced and economic refugees. Even the term 'climate change refugee' is debatable. Boateng (2014) defines a climate refugee as a person or group of persons who are displaced by environmental conditions which are influenced by climate hazards like droughts, cyclones/monsoons, rainfall-induced floods, climate-induced sea-level rise and intense icy winters and can no longer gain a secure livelihood in their homelands/habitats and are obliged to leave their habitual homes, or choose to do so, either temporarily or permanently and within their country or abroad. We define climate change refugees as people who are forced to leave their homes because of the effects of climate change. These includes short and long-term effects as well as slow and rapid onsets ones. There is no standard definition of the term ‘climate change refugees’, which makes it harder to recognize and protect the victims. Migrants displaced across national borders due to climate change and environmental factors are not legally recognized as legitimate refugees. How do we then recognize and protect millions of potential climate change refugees? This research aimed at understanding the dilemma of potential climate change refugees by examining vulnerable semi-arid regions in Kenya.

Kenya is both a victim and a host of refugees. Prolonged drought and famine often displace residents of northern Kenya. In 2011, East Africa recorded the worst drought in 60 years, affecting 13 million people in Djibouti, Ethiopia, Kenya, and Somalia. This caused massive movement of victims especially from Somalia to Kenya (BBC 2011). Early in 2017, the Kenya National Drought Management Authority warned that the country would experience another severe drought similar to that of 2011 (Standard Digital 2017). Since independence, Kenya has been home to thousands of refugees mainly from Somalia, Ethiopia and South Sudan. Nonetheless, the Kenya government is committed in closing Dadaab camp, the world’s largest refugee camp, and resettling approximated 600,000 refugees (CNN 2016). The government has cited security and economic concerns as the reasons behind this move. Initially, the camp was officially supposed to be closed by the end of November 2016, but Kenya’s government delayed the closure for 6 months after an appeal from the United Nations (Aljazeera 2016; Daily Nation 2016). Given the current scenario, the research will examine the impacts of climate change and conflict and political stability in Kenya. The research first examined the climate change dilemma and a synopsis of climate change refugees was given. The following sections will discuss the materials and methods employed in this research. The research findings and results will be presented and later discussed in detail.

Materials and Methods

Study Site

The research was conducted in the semi-arid region of Kenya. Two-thirds of Kenya’s landmass comprises semi-arid areas. Since independence, people living in semi-arid areas have struggled to cope with drought, famine and water shortages. The study aimed at understanding the implications of climate change for the current predicaments and potential new threats. Two semi-arid counties, namely, Mandera and Turkana were surveyed. The selection of the counties was based on administrative

Table 14.1 Study counties and their distinct characteristics

Counties	Population	Neighboring countries	Average temperature (°C)	Annual rainfall (mm)	Study site	Sample population
Mandera	1,025,756	Ethiopia, Somalia	28	255	Kotulo	95
Turkana	855,399	Uganda, South Sudan, Ethiopia	25–35	300–400	Lokitaung	75

Source: Soft Kenya (2012), Turkana County Government (2016)

boundaries, geographic location, economic activities, climatic conditions and vulnerability levels (Table 14.1). These counties are neighboring on more than one country. During the dry season there is frequent movement across national borders especially by the nomadic pastoralists (Fig. 14.1).

Mandera borders on Somalia to the east and Ethiopia to the north. It is one of the poorest, hottest and driest counties in Kenya, with an annual rainfall of approximately 255 mm (Soft Kenya 2012). The research was conducted in Kotulo region in the southern part of Mandera close to neighboring Somalia. Turkana, on the other hand, borders Uganda to the west, South Sudan to the north and Ethiopia to the northwest. The region is usually hot and warm and experiences unreliable annual rainfall ranging between 300 mm and 400 mm annually. Nomadic pastoralism and fishing are the main economic activities practiced in this county (Turkana County Government 2016). Turkana county is home to the Kakuma refugee camp, which houses approximately 180,000 refugees, although the Kenyan government has threatened to shut down the camp (*The Guardian* 2016). The research was specifically conducted in the town of Lokitaung, which is one the most remote regions near the Ethiopian border.

Ninety-five and 75 questionnaires were administered in Kotulo and Lokitaung respectively in order to understand the local people's perceptions of climate change. Key interviews were held with county government representatives and with NGO project coordinators operating in the area. The collected data was coded and analyzed using Stata.

Results

Socio-demographic

Of the 170 respondents in both the Kotulo and Lokitaung areas, 52% were male and 48% female (Table 14.2). Men are usually the head of the house and are responsible for the major decision-making both at the household and the community level. The majority of the respondents fell between the age of 20 and 49, hence they were relatively young and energetic. The literacy level is generally low given that 42% of

Fig. 14.1 Map of Kenya counties

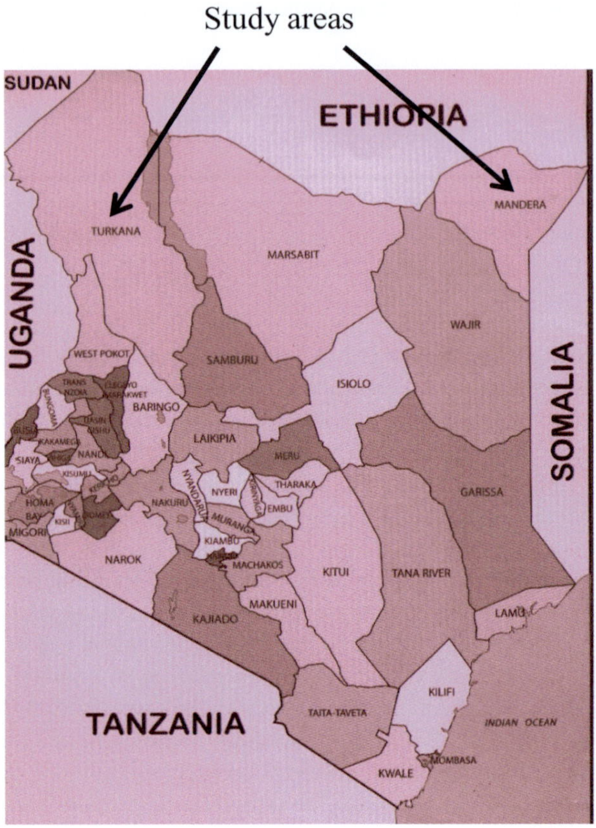

the respondents had no formal education and roughly 36% had only attained primary level education. This might explain why unemployment levels are high, since around 20% had no stable annual income. Due to unreliable rainfall (Table 14.1), crop cultivation is practiced on a small scale by 18% of the respondents. The majority of the respondents (89%) are nomadic pastoralists. The most common domestic animals include cattle, goats, camels, donkeys and dogs. The harsh climatic conditions (Table 14.1) and constant water and pasture shortages compel residents to trek for long distances.

Drought, Conflict and Migration Nexus

In a marginalized and semi-arid region, drought, conflict and forced migration are inextricably linked. The majority of the residents in northern Kenya are nomadic pastoralists. Livestock keeping is entwined with the cultural settings of the local

Table 14.2 Socio-demographic features of the respondents

	Characteristics	Kotulo (95)	Lokitaung (75)	Total (170)
Gender	Male	49 (52%)	39 (52%)	88 (52%)
	Female	46 (48%)	36 (48%)	82 (48%)
Age	< 20	2 (1%)	1 (1%)	3 (2%)
	20–29	22 (23%)	15 (20%)	37 (22%)
	30–39	31 (33%)	27 (36%)	58 (34%)
	40–49	21 (22%)	17 (23%)	38 (22%)
	50–59	13 (14%)	11 (15%)	24 (14%)
	> 59	6 (6%)	4 (5%)	10 (6%)
Education level	None	39 (41%)	33 (44%)	72 (42%)
	Primary	34 (36%)	27 (36%)	61 (36%)
	Secondary	18 (19%)	13 (17%)	31 (18%)
	University	4 (4%)	2 (3%)	6 (4%)
Annual income (USD)	< 100	6 (6%)	4 (5%)	10 (6%)
	100–200	53 (56%)	45 (60%)	98 (58%)
	201–300	23 (24%)	19 (25%)	42 (25%)
	301–400	7 (7%)	3 (4%)	10 (6%)
	401–500	3 (3%)	2 (3%)	5 (3%)
	< 500	3 (3%)	2 (3%)	5 (3%)
Occupation	Livestock keepers	82 (86%)	69 (92%)	151 (89%)
	Crop cultivators	15 (16%)	16 (21%)	31 (18%)
	Entrepreneurs	10 (11%)	11 (15%)	21 (12%)
	Civil servants	2 (2%)	1 (1%)	3 (2%)
	NGO staff	4 (4%)	3 (4%)	7 (4%)

residents. Many are the times that the respondents or their immediate relatives have put their life on the line for the protection of their domestic animals. The number of livestock is often regarded as a measure of wealth or social status in this community. Domestic animals are largely used in the dowry payment process by many tribes in Kenya, including the nomadic pastoralists. Owing to their socioeconomic importance and the high dependence on livestock, cattle rustling is often the norm in the arid and semi-arid lands (ASAL) of Kenya (Kaimba et al. 2011; SRIC 2016). According to the village elders in both Kotulo and Lokitaung, traditionally cattle rustling was a festival and a competition between communities. There was direct communication and agreements on the period of cattle raids. The cattle raids at the time were well organized for the benefit of the community. The youths were trained with raiding and protection skills. Simple weapons such as arrows were used.

However, cattle rustling has been now been highly politicized and commercialized. The politicization and commercialization of cattle rustling have not only increased raid attacks and retaliations but also significantly increased illegal firearms, thus threatening the regional security. This has led to several attacks on innocent civilians and police officers, which culminated in the Barogoi massacre in

Turkana County. This started as a government security operation in 2012, with the aim of curbing Samburu-Turkana tribal clashes over stolen cattle. Unfortunately, the cattle raiders ambushed and killed over 40 police officers (*The Star* 2015). Two years later (2014), an attempt to recover the stolen cattle in Kapedo, Baringo, led to the killing of over 20 police officers (*The Star* 2015). The stolen police firearms were used to carry out more raids. NGO staff have reported that sometimes illegal firearms find their way to terrorist groups and poachers. Kaimba et al. (2011) found that cattle rustling and drought have a significant influence on the migration of pastoralists in ASAL. According to the survey we conducted, famine and drought determine the intensity and frequency of cattle raids. The survey revealed that 67% and 64% of cattle raids are conducted during extremely dry periods in Kotulo and Lokitaung respectively. The pastoralist communities are compelled to move from one place to another not only in search of water and pastures but also to minimize the probability of raids. In Kotulo and Lokitaung, 26% and 23% respectively of cattle raids are conducted immediately after the rains. This is usually done in an attempt recover lost domestic animals (during the dry period), either through death and/or cattle rustling. Cattle raids are at their lowest levels during the rainy seasons (i.e. 7% in Kotulo and 13% in Lokitaung).

Kenya as a Recipient of Refugees

Since the 1990s (Fig. 14.2), Kenya has been a leader in hosting thousands of refugees, particularly of Somali origin. The civil war and the state of statelessness in Somalia in the early 1990s led to an influx of refugees into Kenya's territory, reaching a maximum of 402,194 in 1992 (Fig. 14.2). By 2015, Kenya was estimated to be host to approximately 553,912 refugees (World Bank 2016a). It is important to note that these figures only account for documented refugees, residing mainly in Dadaab and Kakuma refugee camps, which are located in Wajir (neighboring Mandela county) and Turkana counties. Interviews with the local residents revealed that due

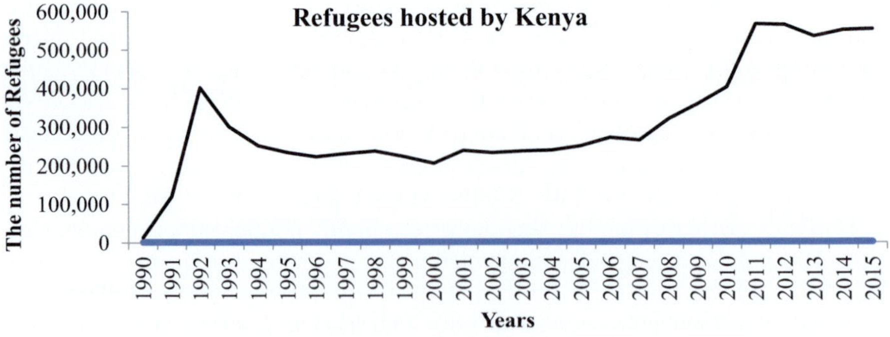

Fig. 14.2 The number of refugees hosted by Kenya (Source: World Bank 2016a)

to the porous border between Kenya and Somalia and Kenya and Ethiopia, coupled with corruption expedited by border control and security officers, illegal immigrants roam around like local residents. Following Kenya's decision to close Dadaab camp (Aljazeera 2016; *Daily Nation* 2016), the current and immediate fate of refugees fleeing particularly from Somalia is uncertain. The provision for climate change refugees from the neighboring countries is even more uncertain.

Discussion

Nomadic pastoralists who are the dominant residents in ASAL suffer from water insecurity, hunger, famine, cattle raid conflicts and malnutrition. We noted that the drought-conflict and migration relationship is deeply rooted. On average, there is a two-thirds probability for cattle raids to happen during the prolonged dry period as opposed to the other seasons. Climate change, land degradation, desertification and extreme weather events in ASAL are likely to skyrocket the cattle raids. Increased cattle raids will further threaten security in the currently fragile region, hence exacerbating the refugee crisis.

An understanding of the climate change dilemma and the need to urgently address current vulnerabilities and enhance the coping capacity of the most susceptible groups ought to advocate for political change in Africa. To mitigate and adapt to the effects of climate change, African countries must pave the way for inclusive governance. Addressing the needs of climate change refugees demands the effective collaboration of all key stakeholders, including different sectors of national government, local governments, private organizations, NGOs, civil societies, local people, and researchers. The limited resources and competing needs should also promote partnerships and collaboration at all levels. For instance, Costello et al. (2009) stress that low capacity in research institutions in developing countries is likely to deepen the vulnerability of the community. As a result, African research institutions and universities ought to collaborate in research so as to share their resources, expertise, technology and information. Sharing of technology is essential for boosting agricultural productivity, addressing food insecurity, enhancing climate change modeling, and mapping potential climate change refugees. We recommend the establishment of a portal for sharing climate change data and efficacious adaptation strategies employed by different countries. The forecast and findings of climate change refugees must be promptly and clearly disseminated to the policymakers, implementers and the potential victims. Given that climate change is very complex and characterized by a lot of uncertainties, the African Union, African governments, and other funding organizations must expand climate change research funding. Research findings ought to create a better foundation for the development of CCA scenarios and also ensure timely and effective early warning and comprehensive preparedness measures.

The continuous population growth in Africa poses a great challenge to climate change mitigation and adaptation. Given that 40% of Kenyans are under the age of

15, Kenya's population is projected to increase from the current 44 million (World Bank 2016b) to 82 million under the current fertility or to 65 million with a fertility of 2.1 by 2040 (National Coordinating Agency for Population and Development 2010). Unsustainable population growth is likely to overwhelm efforts to curb poverty, food insecurity, water insecurity and unemployment and minimize disaster impacts. According to the 2005 Millennium Ecosystem Assessment report, 60% of ecosystem services are degraded or used unsustainably. Population growth is likely to exert more pressure on the natural resource base thus threatening the continuous supply of ecosystem services for future generations. Additionally, environmental degradation increases the vulnerability of communities by deteriorating ecosystems' hazard defense (Krishnamurthy and Shaw 2009). Development initiatives must take into account national and regional population projections.

Large-scale internal displacement of people might threaten national and regional political stability. The climate change refugee issue is very complex and ought to be viewed as a political and development concern, not as a humanitarian issue. This perspective will promote proactive actions aimed at addressing the root causes and underlying vulnerability conditions. Internationally displaced persons must be protected in line with the 1998 principles on internal displacement and related domestic and regional instruments, as well as the African Union Convention for the Protection and Assistance of Internally Displaced Persons, known as the Kampala Convention.

Legal and Protection Gap

Human rights have witnessed an unprecedented change in the international arena. Classical international law focused mainly on the rights of states; however the establishment of the United Nations led to the widespread growth of human rights that culminated with the adoption of the Universal Declaration of Human Rights. Since then many conventions supporting human rights have been adopted such as International Convention on the Elimination of All Forms of Racial Discrimination in 1965, the International Covenant on Economic, Social and Cultural Rights in 1966, the Convention on the Rights of the Child in 1989, and the International Convention for the Protection of All persons from Enforced Disappearance in 2006. However, the effects of climate change are likely to deprive some fundamental human rights, hence undermining the significant achievements in this discourse. Climate change refugees will probably pay the highest price for climate change since they are not recognized or protected under international refugee law. International refugee law defines a refugee as "someone who is unable or unwilling to return to their country of origin owing to a well-founded fear of being persecuted for reasons of race, religion, nationality, membership of a particular social group, or political opinion" (UNHCR 2001, 8–9). The African Union Convention Governing Specific Aspects of Refugee Problems in Africa defines refugees on the basis of fear of persecution (OAU Convention 1969). Therefore, people who are compelled to move from their country of origin due to environmental pressures exacerbated by climate change are not legally recognized as refugees. This raises concerns about the resilience of vulnerable communities such as those living on remote islands who are likely to be displaced by a rise in sea level.

Therefore, the current definition of refugees is limiting and needs to be expanded so as to ensure people seeking asylum for climate change reasons are identified as legitimate refugees. However, this is more difficult than it sounds since it is extremely challenging to verify whether someone is moving because of environmental pressures exacerbated by climate change. Some people might take advantage of the situation and start seeking asylum in advanced countries even where there are no real environment pressures. One way to overcome these bottlenecks is to ensure that all people seeking asylum as a result of environmental pressure are backed by credible published papers and should also be approved by credible, transparent and impartial international organizations such as the UNHCR or the UNEP. A special climate change refugee committee should be established under the UNHCR to investigate, oversee and guarantee the rights of these refugees. There should be a supporting document that validates the fact that the affected country does not have enough capacity to support and provide for the needs of the people seeking asylum because of environmental pressures. With the current geopolitical situation, this is unlikely be welcomed, let alone be approved in the international arena. As a result, regional and national agreements regarding the protection of climate change refugees should be developed and, hopefully, in the future will set the scene for a universal protection protocol.

Conclusion

The research observed that there is a very strong link between drought, armed conflict and forced migration. Most of the cattle raids are conducted during the prolonged dry seasons. Climate change and land degradation are expected to increase the frequency of cattle rustling, thus threatening the regional security. Climate change research and the dissemination of research findings, multilevel governance and efforts to reduce current vulnerabilities will generate dividends in reducing the number of climate change refugees. The research also observed that there is a protection gap in relation to climate change/environmental refugees internationally. Given the current debate, an international convention recognizing and legalizing climate change refugees is unlikely to be introduced owing to the complex issues surrounding climate change refugees. The research recommends national and regional agreements protecting the rights of climate change refugees, which should set the foundation for an international convention.

References

Aljazeera. (2016, November 17). *Kenya delays Dadaab refugee closure by six months*. http://www.aljazeera.com/news/2016/11/kenya-delays-dadaab-refugee-camp-closure-months-161116130647820.html. Accessed 23 Jan 2017.

Antwi-Agyei, P. 2012. Vulnerability and adaptation of Ghana's food production systems and rural livelihoods to climate variability. Thesis for the degree of Doctor of Philosophy at the University of Leeds School of Earth and Environment, UK.

Awuor, C. B., Orindi, V. A., & Adwera, A. O. (2008). Climate change and coastal cities: The case of Mombasa, Kenya. *Environment and Urbanization, 20*(1), 231–234.

Barnett, J. (2003). Security and climate change. *Global Environmental Change, 13*(1), 7–17.

BBC. (2011, June 28). *Horn of Africa sees worst drought in 60 years*. http://www.bbc.com/news/world-africa-13944550. Accessed 17 Jan 2017.

Boateng, I. (2014, June 16–21). *Assessing climate change induced displacements and its potential impacts on climate refugees: How can surveyors help with adaptation?* FIG Congress 2014. Engaging the Challenges, Enhancing the Relevance Kuala Lumpur, Malaysia. www.fig.net/pub/fig2014/papers/TS01J/TS01J_boateng_6779.pdf

CNN. (2016, May 7). *Kenya to close refugee camps, displacing more than 600,000*. http://edition.cnn.com/2016/05/06/africa/kenya-closing-refugee-camps/. Accessed 23 Jan 2017.

Costello, A., Abbas, M., Allen, A., Ball, S., Bell, S., Bellamy, R., ... & Lee, M. (2009). *Managing the health effects of climate change*. The Lancet. doi:https://doi.org/10.1016/S0140-6736(09)60935-1

Daily Guide. (2016, August 20). *Farmers cry out over Bagre Dam spillage*. http://dailyguideafrica.com. Accessed 27 Dec 2016.

Daily Nation. (2016, November). *Kenya delays closure of Dadaab camp for six months*. http://www.nation.co.ke/news/Dadaab-closure-delayed-by-six-months/1056-3454406-byljwr/16. Accessed 23 Jan 2017.

Global Leadership for Climate Action. (2009). *Facilitating an international agreement on climate change: Adaptation to climate change*, pp. 6–10. http://www.unfoundation.org/assets/pdf/adaptation_to_climate_change.pdf

IDMC. (2016). GRID 2016. *Global report on internal displacement*. http://www.internal-displacement.org/globalreport2016/

IPCC. (2007). *Climate change 2007: Synthesis report*. Contribution groups I, II and III to the fourth report on the interngovernmental panle on climate change. IPCC, Geneva, Switzerland. ISBN 92-9169-122-4. https://www.ipcc.ch/pdf/assessment-report/ar4/syr/ar4_syr_full_report.pdf

Kaimba, G. K., Njehia, B. K., & Guliye, A. Y. (2011). Effects of cattle rustling and household characteristics on migration decisions and herd size amongst pastoralists in Baringo District, Kenya. *Pastoralism: Research, Policy and Practice, 1*(1), 18.

Kenya Agricultural Research Institute. (2012). *Food security report*. Food Security Portal. http://www.foodsecurityportal.org/kenya/food-security-report-prepared-kenya-agricultural-research-institute.

Krishnamurthy, R. R., & Shaw, R. (2009). *Disaster management: Global challenges and local solutions, 400*. India: University Press.

Millennium Ecosystem Assessment. (2005). *Ecosystems and human wellbeing*. http://www.millenniumassessment.org/documents/document.356.aspx.pdf. 29/06/2017

Ministry of Agriculture, Livestock and Fisheries. (2015). *Economic Review of Agriculture (ERA) 2015*. http://www.kilimo.go.ke/wp-content/uploads/2015/10/Economic-Review-of-Agriculture_2015-6.pdf

Mul, M., Obuobie, E., Appoh, R., Kankam-Yeboah, K., Bekoe-Obeng, E., Amisigo, B., Logah, F. Y., Ghansah, B., McCartney, M. (2015). *Water resources assessment of the Volta River Basin*. Colombo, Sri Lanka: International Water Management Institute (IWMI). 78p. (IWMI Working Paper 166). [doi:https://doi.org/10.5337/2015.220]

National Coordinating Agency for Population and Development. (2010). *RAPID Population and Development*. http://www.healthpolicyinitiative.com/Publications/Documents/1095_1_Kenya_booklet_3_31_10_sglepg_LOW_RES_PDF_for_INTERNET_acc.pdf

OAU Convention CAB/LEG/24.3. (1969, September 10). *Governing the specific aspects of refugees problems in Africa*. http://www.achpr.org/files/instruments/refugee-convention/achpr_instr_conv_refug_eng.pdf

Raleigh, C., & Urdal, H. (2007). Climate change, environmental degradation and armed conflict. *Political Geography, 26*(6), 674–694.

Reuveny, R. (2007). Climate change-induced migration and violent conflict. *Political Geography, 26*(6), 656–673.

Soft Kenya. (2012). *Mandera County*. http://softkenya.com/county/mandera-county/. Accessed 11 July 2016.

SRIC. (2016). *Security research and information center*. Cattle Rustling. http://srickenya.org/index.php?option=com_content&view=article&id=134:cattle-rustling-&catid=39:news. Accessed 23 Dec 2016.

Standard Digital. (2017, January 12). *Kenyans bracing for tough times as worst drought in 5 years looms*. https://www.standardmedia.co.ke/article/2000229540/kenyans-bracing-for-tough-times-as-worst-drought-in-5-years-looms. Accessed 23 Jan 2017.

Stern, N. (2006). What is the economics of climate change? *World Economics-Henley On Thames, 7*(2), 1.

Turkana County Government. (2016). *Turkana County*. http://www.turkana.go.ke/. Accessed 11 July 2016.

The Star. (2015, May 13). *The history of inter-communal conflicts among pastoralist communities*. http://www.the-star.co.ke/news/2015/05/13/history-of-inter-communal-conflicts-among-pastoralist-communities_c1133600. Accessed 22 Jan 2017.

The Guardian. (2016). *Refugees urge Kenyan leaders to rethink closure of Dadaab camp*. https://www.theguardian.com/global-development/2016/may/13/refugees-urge-kenyan-leaders-to-rethink-closure-of-dadaab-camp. Accessed 8 Aug 2016.

UNHCR. (2001). *Refugee protection: A guide to International Refugee Law* (pp. 8–9).

World Bank. (2016a). *Refugee population by country or territory of asylum*. Kenya. http://data.worldbank.org/indicator/SM.POP.REFG?end=2015&locations=KE&start=1990&view=chart. Accessed 21 Jan 2017.

World Bank. (2016b). *Total population*. http://data.worldbank.org/country/kenya. Accessed 28 July 2016.

Joseph M. Karanja A doctoral candidate at the University of Tsukuba, Japan, pursuing Sustainable Environmental Studies. He holds a masters of science in Sustainability from the United Nations University, Japan. He also has bachelor's degree in Disaster Management and International Diplomacy from the Masinde Muliro University of Science and Technology, Kenya. Mr. Karanja is a co-founder of, and a Director of Research in Novelty Intervention Kenya. Research Interests: Climate Change, Ecosystem Services, Disaster Risk Reduction, Environmental Governance, and Environmental Justice. Email: josentokaranja@gmail.com

Zakaria Abdul-Razak An Agricultural Extension Officer with the Ministry of Food and Agriculture of Ghana. He is currently studying Master's degree in Environmental Sciences in the University of Tsukuba, Japan. He also holds a Bachelor's of Science in Agricultural Technology, from the University for Development Studies, Ghana. Research interests: Climate Change, Adaptation Strategies, Sustainable Agriculture, Value Chain Development, Agribusiness and Environmental Policy. Email: nurazak830@gmail.com

Chapter 15
Gender in Africa

Olabisi Sherifat Yusuff

Introduction

Around the world, gender implies the primary division of roles between people. Every society sorts men and women into separate groups and gives them different access to property, power, and prestige (Henslin 2010). Gender is widely agreed to be a construct that arises out of culture. It is not seen as being biologically determined. However, Akanle and Adejare (2016) note that the term 'gender' has enjoyed frequent usage, but has also been subjected to diverse definitions and interpretations among scholars and non-scholars. For instance, in African culture and traditional life, gender is defined according to roles and functions in the society. It is what it means to be male or female in a certain society that shapes the opportunities one is offered in life, the roles one may play, and the kinds of relationships one may have. The World Health Organization (WHO 2012) defines gender as the result of socially constructed ideas about the behaviors, actions and roles a particular sex performs. Ferrante (2011) defined gender as a socially created and learned distinction that specifies the ideal physical, behavioral, mental and emotional traits characteristics of males and females. Ideal in this context according to Ferrante (2011) means a standard against which real cases can be compared. Although 'gender' is commonly used interchangeably with 'sex', within the academic fields of gender studies and the social sciences in general, the term 'gender' often refers to purely social rather than biological differences.

Humankind has for long created roles in which males and females must fit and must play diligently. Traditionally, the male is the provider, holds the power and makes important decisions on issues affecting the lives of members of his household.

O.S. Yusuff (✉)
Department of Sociology, Faculty of Social Sciences,
Lagos State University, Lagos, Nigeria
e-mail: soyusuf@yahoo.co.uk

O. Akanle, J.O. Adésìnà (eds.), *The Development of Africa*, Social Indicators Research Series 71, DOI 10.1007/978-3-319-66242-8_15

Women, on the other hand, are submissive nurturers. Women are socialized from youth to believe that their primary existence in life is to marry and give birth. Thus, this creates a mindset which paints the repression and subjection of women's role as acceptable Musau (2015). Consequently, when women step out of their prescribed gender role, society views it as challenging the male's exercise of authority. The male then feels an innate need to push the female back into her gender role(s) in any way deemed acceptable. There are several mechanisms that perpetuate gender ideals in society. One such mechanism is the socialization process of girls. Socialization theorists argue that an underdetermined yet significant portion of male–female differences are products of the ways in which males and females are socialized (Ferrante 2011).

However, in developing countries, traditional gender roles are gradually changing; especially in matters relating to household welfare (Yusuff and Ajiboye 2014). But it is more difficult to break down women's roles completely due to several factors such as the patriarchal nature and culture of most developing countries and the inadequate access of girls to formal education and socialization processes. Why, then, do these stereotypes persist? Largely because we do not differentiate between sex and gender, and many of us believe that 'anatomy is destiny'. As a result we ignore the importance of the social context that produces and maintains these stereotypes. All of these promote and sustain cultural gender myths that are detrimental to both men and women in African societies. The aim of this chapter is to holistically examine gender in Africa. How does society construct gender? What are the gender roles in Africa? How and in what ways does gender inequality manifest itself in the lives of African women? What strategies have been adopted by African governments to end gender inequality? And what are the pressing problems that hinder the achievement of gender equality? The next section examines how gender roles are constructed.

Understanding the Social Construct of Gender

A social construct is a concept or practice that is a construct (or artifact) of a particular group (Berger and Luckmann 1991). A social construct is something that does not exist; this means that its meaning, use and definition are contingent on culture. Social constructs are generally understood to be by-products of countless human choices rather than laws resulting from divine will or nature (Hacking 1999). Gender is one such construct. The idea that gender is socially constructed is a view presented in many philosophical and sociological theories (Jost and Kruglanski 2002). According to Jost and Kruglanski, society and culture create gender roles, and these roles are prescribed as ideal or appropriate behavior for a person of that specific gender. A social constructivist framework holds that there is no essential, universally distinct character that is masculine or feminine. According to Anderson (2000), behaviors are influenced by a range of factors such as class, culture, ability, religion, age, body shape and sexual preference.

In the opinion of Giddens (2004) the principal self-identification of an individual as a man or a woman, with ideas and desires that accompany that identification, depends largely on what label is attached to that individual in childhood. The ways in which we were socialized into gender begin from a very early age. For example, studies of mother–infant interaction reveal distinct differences in the ways in which boys and girls are treated, even in situations where the parents believe their reactions to both are the same. In addition, male and female adults usually handle infants differently and by age two children have a partial understanding of what gender is. Gender roles then, can be understood as those sets of norms that communicate what is generally considered appropriate for each sex (Burns 1996).

Ferantee (2011), in explaining the construct of gender, noted that there are gender ideals in almost every society in the world, which shape practically every aspect of life-influencing, among other things how people dress, how they express emotions and what occupations they choose. This has led to gender polarization which is the organization of social life around male and female ideals, so that people's sex influences every aspect of their life. This includes the way they dress, the way they pose for photographs, and all the social roles they take on, even the way they express emotions and experience sexual attraction. Decisions and viewpoints about any aspect of life are considered gender schematic if they are influenced by a society's polarized definition of masculinity and femininity rather than by criteria such as self-fulfillment, ability, interest or personal comfort (Ferantee 2011). The most important insight on the construct of gender is that because boys and girls are treated differently and put into different learning environments, they develop different needs, wants, desires, skills and temperaments. In short, they become different types of people—men and women—who hardly question why they are different and how they ended up being different. Society treats them differently and gives them different opportunities for development. This differential treatment promotes certain behaviors and self-images that recreate the preconceived cultural stereotypes about gender. The process repeats itself over and over in an unending spiral across the generations, so that although gender stereotypes are being constantly re-created and modified, they seem natural and impervious to change. The next section examines gender roles across Africa. This is to buttress the fact that gender roles are socially created and vary from one country to another.

Variations in Gender Roles in Africa

Each culture has its own gender-role norms and values, and the degree of equality between men and men differs across African societies. Ferrante (2011) notes that gender inequality exists between men and women when one category relative to other (i) faces greater risks to physical and emotional well-being; (ii) possesses a disproportionate share of income and other valued resources; and/or (iii) is accorded more opportunities to succeed. In Africa, there are several areas in the developmental process where women as a group are disadvantaged more than men.

North Africa

In Islamic societies in North Africa, there is a great deal of variation across Islamic societies concerning women's roles in the family, education, politics, and employment opportunities. Each country in North Africa interprets women's rights under Islam somewhat differently Sabban (1995). However, social class and religious laws often play an important role in defining women's educational and employment opportunities. Haq (1996) argued that Islamic women's roles are complex. On the one hand, some women's organizations have been challenging some of the most repressive Islamic laws and practices of Muslim fundamentalists that limit women's participation in education, politics and the economy. On the other hand, many women often reject the West's permissive sexual attitudes and what they see as a lack of cooperation between males and females in the family. Sabbagh (1996) reiterated this when he pointed out that many Islamic women feel safe and protected by being 'veiled' and clothed in garments that cover the woman's entire body. In Arab countries, Muslim fundamentalist men compete with educated urban women over limited educational resources and shrinking employment opportunities (Haq 1996).

In Sudan, there are clearly defined gender roles. Men make decisions, but also bear the responsibility of providing financially for their mothers, sisters and aunts. Women take care of children, the sick and the elderly, as well as running the household. Gender relations in South Sudan are complex: the roles and responsibilities of women, men, boys and girls are clearly delineated. Women and girls have responsibilities related to farming, collecting water and firewood, cooking, cleaning, childcare, and brewing beer. Men and boys have responsibilities as decision-makers for the community and their families, cattle (boys in particular tend to be cattle-herders), hunting, fishing and charcoal making. In times of crisis, gender roles and responsibilities change to take account of the context, the needs and the different coping strategies families and individuals adopt (Ali 2011).

In general, South Sudanese women from rural villages are treated as second-class citizens. They do not hold roles of authority or have any esteemed significance in their families or communities. They are obligated to marry a man chosen by the family in line with the dowry system, a system that treats women as a commodity to essentially be bought or sold. Rural South Sudanese women have no voice regarding their own rights, and are unable to participate in any major decision-making processes regarding themselves or their families (Kuanyi 2010). Gender-based violence and protection violations in South Sudan are driven by a culture of silence and stigma, masculine identity tied to cattle-raiding, bride-price, a lack of access to legal recourse, and customary practices that favor compensation for crimes (Ali 2011). In some tribes, such as those in the Dinka and Nuer regions, women are regarded solely as a source of income for the family's benefit. Rarely is the importance of designating resources to send a wife or daughter to school to receive an education considered. In these male-dominated cultures, women are to be submissive and subservient to their family-in-laws and to their husbands (Care 2016).

West Africa

Ghana

Ghana's ethnic, cultural and agro-ecological diversity make generalization about gender relations and their consequences for women's access to resources, decision-making and status extremely difficult. Different ethnic groups are characterized by a variety of kinship systems with different implications for access to resources and decision-making power by gender (Adama 2016). Combined with this is the strong patriarchal family structures, which influence women's lack of influence in decision-making (Basden 1999).This results in generally more limited options for women. The Akan ethnic group constitutes the largest ethnic group residing mainly in the southern part of Ghana. The Akan are organized along matrilineal lines but most other ethnic groups, in the North and the East, are organized along patrilineal lines. The Ga, who are concentrated around Greater Accra, are somewhat anomalous in having bilateral inheritance and kinship structures. However, matrilineal systems may give women greater access to resources outside marriage than patrilineal systems although they are characterized by a weaker nuclear household offering little economic security to women. Patrilineal systems do not necessarily imply significantly greater access to resources and/or higher status for women (Quartey and Martin 2008).

Gender division of labor in Ghana is highly segregated by sex in both the traditional and modern wage sector. Only a very small number of women have broken through into modern sector occupations and even fewer into managerial positions (Global Gender Report 2013).Women's labor participation rates are generally high throughout Ghana. There is some regional diversity and variation in socioeconomic opportunities for women from different backgrounds. The most striking feature, however, is that about 99% of women are self-employed or work as unpaid labor in agriculture, agro-based enterprises and commerce or small-scale manufacturing in informal sector activities with low productivity which on average yield low incomes (Ofosu-Baadu 2012). Osei-Boateng and Ampratum (2011) noted that women predominate in the trading sector, mainly in petty trading, although a small minority of women had gained substantial market power. Women's trading activities according to Osei-Boateng and Ampratum (2011) are hindered by poor infrastructure, bad road conditions, weak marketing channels, limited storage facilities, and a lack of other facilities at marketplaces such as water and toilets. The continuing gender imbalance in access to education in Ghana limits women's access to employment and productivity. For instance, in urban areas, lack of qualifications and a narrow range of skills limit female access to formal employment. Also, in rural areas, lack of female education limits farm productivity (FAO 2012). Currently, Ofosu-Baadu (2012) points out that three-quarters of female farmers have no education, and inadequate literacy and numeracy skills are also reported to limit the efficiency of female traders.

Nigeria

There are two main religions in Nigeria, Islam and Christianity, and a variety of indigenous beliefs across the country that have a significant impact on gender roles, apart from culture. The 1999 Constitution of Nigeria prohibits discrimination on the grounds of gender, but customary and religious laws continue to restrict women's rights. The gender roles among Nigerians of different ethnic group vary, and this can be viewed from the aspect of the major constraints women face in public/private and traditional positions: their overall workload and the moral pressures and negative attitudes of both men and women towards women. Prior to now, the traditional and social practices as well as role stereotypes have confined women to the home as housewives and child bearers, hence they were largely economically dependent on their husbands, and by implication subservient to them (Odeyemi 2013).

Yoruba culture does not discriminate against women participating in decision-making within the home and in the political or public sphere. Although, Yoruba culture is hierarchically based with men on top of the ladder, respect is reciprocal and understood to work for the preservation of the community. Differentiation is more likely to be viewed from age or position (respect) rather than gender in the traditional Yoruba society. However, Azuh et al. (2015) noted that the hierarchical nature of Yoruba society in Nigeria relegates women to a subordinate position in matters of family planning and otherwise. Makama (2013), in a study among the Hausa of Northern Nigeria, found that the most important factors contributing to maternal deaths is Islamic culture that undervalues women; a perceived social need for women's reproductive capacities to be under strict male control; the practice of purdah (wife seclusion), which restricts women's access to medical care; almost universal female illiteracy; marriage at an early age and pregnancy often occurring before maternal pelvic growth is complete; harmful traditional medical beliefs and practices; and responsibilities of husbands among others. The keeping of women in seclusion (purdah) is another perceived area of female subjection among the Hausa ethnic group. In the practice of purdah, women's movement outside the house is severely circumscribed and public forms of physical labor are associated with considerable shame and insecurity for women (Zakaria 2001). In Northern Nigeria, this practice is coterminous with the introduction of Islam. Today, Hausa-land is a major area in the whole of Africa where the seclusion of adult females is strictly practiced as a cultural norm (Mudiare 2013).

Gender roles defined the place of the male and female in Igbo society. The female is seen as being subordinate to her male counterpart, which was how it was defined by the traditional setting in Igbo society. Igbo traditional society attaches much importance to this gender issue, where men and women operate in separate practices, albeit in the same culture gender functions have been so arranged and segregated that men arrogate superior functions to themselves and inferior functions to women. Over the years, these roles have been tolerated and assimilated by people and have become part of the people's customs and traditions. Discourse on the role of women in Igbo traditional society by many scholars who examined the economic role of Igbo women established that such revolves around agriculture, manufacturing and trading (Ezuma 2003). In agriculture, for instance, Igbo women fill a substantial role in decision-making and execution in the production process and the associated food processing activities (Ikpeze 2000). In the area of trade, women dominate the marketplace in traditional Igbo society where they sell agricultural products as well as handicrafts and other manufactured goods; however, the men engage in long distance trading (Ikpeze 2000).

East Africa

Pankhurst (2002) claims that Uganda's gender relations remain "highly unequal by any standard measure." In Uganda, women's rights or equality is more talked about than are a reality at different levels. Within education, women's participation remains below that of men, with a net enrolment rate of only 21% of girls in secondary school (UNICEF 2011). In university education, women have remained a minority as students and staff, and especially as academics and managers (Yusuff 2014). Kasente (2003) points out that men have a clear advantage over women in access to and control over resources, while cultural practices also bestow more power on men than on women in various aspects. In Kenya, gender roles tend to vary by ethnic group and by rural-urban settlement. Gender equity is highest in Nairobi and the areas around it and lowest in the northeastern part of the country. However, 60% of the land is owned by women (CEDAW 2011). Land is the primary asset in Kenya and 70% of livelihoods are in agriculture. Patrilineal inheritance traditions mean that men own all but a small portion of the land. In 2010, it became legal for women to have their name on a land deed but women's access to land is controlled by men (Ndiritu and Nyangena 2010). In Malawi, the government is trying to discourage traditional practices where girls are married before the legal age. Despite these attempts, girls as young as 13 are often married off (FAO 2011).

South Africa

In South Africa:

> Culture plays an undeniable part in traditional gender roles. Within South Africa, there is a specific atmosphere which reinforces traditional gender roles. In general, all racial and ethnic groups in South Africa have long-standing beliefs concerning gender roles, and most are based on the premise that women in South Africa are less important, or less deserving of power, than men. Most African traditional social organizations are male centered and male dominated (Hutson 2009).

Much of the problem in South Africa lies within the African women themselves. Because the young men played such a crucial role in the collapse of apartheid, they are eager to collect their dues, and the women understand and respect such a notion.

Therefore, the constraints that emanated from the post-apartheid society were to give priority to the full employment of young men. These are supported by the women in South Africa who believe that the young men need the jobs more than women (Meer 2007).

The Rise of Feminism

For the past few decades the world has witnessed a resurgent interest in feminist jurisprudence. This interest has culminated in the emergence of numerous global strategies geared towards women empowerment and emancipation. Examples of such strategies are the Vienna Declaration Programme and Action; Nairobi Forward-looking Strategies for the Advancement of Women: The ICPD Programme of Action; the Beijing Conference among others. This global feminist interest has also given birth to a catalog of international and national instruments aimed at protecting and promoting the rights of women. The instruments in question include the Convention on the Elimination of All Forms of Discrimination Against Women (1979), the Declaration on the Protection of Women and Children in Emergency and Armed Conflict (1974); the Optional Protocol to the Convention on the Elimination of Discrimination Against Women (2000); and the African Charter on Human and Peoples Rights (1986). These legal instruments unanimously affirm the fact that all human beings are born free and equal in dignity and rights without any distinction of any kind, including distinction as to sex. They recognize the fact that discrimination against women is incompatible with human dignity and with the welfare of the family and of society, prevents women's participation on equal terms with men in the political, social, economic and cultural life of their countries and is an obstacle to the full development of the potentialities of women in the service of their countries and of humanity. There is, however, contention over the applicability of Western feminists' ideologies in Africa, bearing in mind the culture and colonial experiences of Africans (Yusuff 2013).

Manifestation of Gender Inequality in Areas in African Countries

In simple terms, 'gender equality' is equality for all, where one group of people are not preferred or discriminated over others in the distribution of food, shelter, healthcare, education, job training and professional opportunities. It is where every group or individual is subject to the same laws, with no individual or group having special privileges. It means equal rights under the law, such as security, voting rights, access to education and healthcare, safety, respect, assembly and property rights. It also means that everyone regardless of human limitations and circumstances of birth should enjoy the same rights and privileges as all others in the society. There are several areas where gender inequality manifests itself, but only three areas will be discussed here.

Female Unemployment in Africa

Women continue to face considerable barriers in African labor markets as a result of lack of education, inadequate access to training, discrimination, and cultural attitudes about their role in the workplace. However, official figures provided by UNESCO (2010a) indicate that there is very little difference between the unemployment rates of adult women and men in Sub-Saharan Africa. In contrast, young women are less susceptible to unemployment in Sub-Saharan Africa. This does not imply, however, that young women in this region have better access to the labor market; rather, they do not have the 'luxury' to actively search for a job and hence take up employment in the informal sector or remain outside the labor force. Although the female employment rate for some African countries has increased, since 1990 none of the countries for which recent data are available has reached 50% gender parity in wage employment (IFAD 2011a). The countries that were closer to reaching the parity target of 50% in 2004 are South Africa (45.9), Botswana (43) and Ethiopia (40.6). Namibia scored 48.8 in 2000 and may have reached parity if such trend has been sustained. The major challenges affecting the achievement of gender parity in formal employment include the low educational level of women and girls; lack of skills; labor laws that still disadvantage women in most countries and the continuous heavy burdens of unpaid domestic work, childbearing and childcare, which restrict the time and energy available for income-earning activities (UNESCO 2006).

Political Participation

Women's representation in the national parliament has improved in the majority of African countries. This section reviews the participation of women in decision-making at different levels: the executive, the judiciary and the legislature. Recent data collected by the Division for the Advancement of Women in collaboration with the Inter-Parliamentary Union (IPU) provides a summary of the overall presence of African women at the highest levels of national level politics.

Several countries have significantly increased the level of women's representation in parliament, with one country reaching an impressive 49% (Rwanda) and four at 30% or more (Mozambique, South Africa, Tanzania and Burundi). Africa has the highest reported rate of progress over the period 1990 to 2007. But the story is not altogether cheerful as 17 countries have shown only a slight improvement over the period 2003–2007 (UNECA 2008).

Women are under-represented in all political decision-making bodies. In Nigeria, the participation of women in politics still falls short of the desired 30% by international standards and 35% as entrenched in the National Gender Policy 2006. Current statistics indicate that in the 2007 election, only 516 women sought elective positions to state Houses of Assembly, the National Assembly, Governorship and the Presidency. In 2011, however, 921 women contested elections to these offices and the percentage generally increased, although only by just 8.4% during the period. Although African countries have made some progress in women's representation and participation, it is important to note that this higher representation of women has not yet systematically led to adequate budgets, institutional frameworks and policies for implementing gender programs for gender equality (UNECA 2007). The major challenges affecting the effective political participation of women, according to Olurode (2013), can be located at two levels. These are the level of ideas and social values, that is, ideology, and at the level of material relationships.

Education

In spite of the efforts of national and international organizations in developing countries, gender inequality still exists. The considerable importance that has been attached to education in Africa is based on the assumption that education plays a crucial role in promoting social and economic development (Nwomonoh 1998; World Bank 1988). Education also enables one to make informed decisions in such areas as health and nutrition, family planning, water and sanitation, food production and its management. The education of girls and women in particular has cascading benefits, including helping to decrease poverty, prevent disease, eradicate violence and deter political instability. It is also a means of securing intergenerational transfers of knowledge, and providing the substance of long-term gender equality and social change. Sub-Saharan Africa has registered profound change in both participation and educational expansion in all levels of education since independence.

The number of children enrolled in primary education grew from 12 million to almost 61 million (excluding South Africa) between 1960 and 2000 (UNESCO 2009). The net enrollment ratio (NER) for primary education climbed from 56% in 1999 to 70% in 2006. In 2006, more than 23 million of the region's children entered a classroom for the first time—an increase of some 7 million over the level in 1999 (UNESCO 2009). The region accounted for the world's highest increase in total primary enrollment, which rose by 42% between 1999 and 2006. This increase enabled countries such as Botswana, Cape Verde, Congo, Malawi, Mauritius, Namibia, South Africa, Swaziland, Togo and Zimbabwe to achieve a primary gross enrollment rate of 100% (UNESCO 2008). While the number of primary school aged children out of school has dropped by 10 million since 1999, 35 million children of primary school age were still not enrolled in 2006, about one-third of this area's population. The region accounts for 47% of the world's out-of-school population, with 54% of this being girls (UNESCO 2009). The average primary school completion rates for boys stands at 56%, but only 46% for girls (low in both cases). Countries such as Burkina Faso, Guinea, Madagascar, Mozambique and Niger have less than 15% of girls completing primary school. Girls make up more than half of the school-age population in most Sub-Saharan African countries and accounted for only 44% of primary school enrollments in the 1980s.

At the secondary level, enrollment increased by 15 times between the 1960s and the 1990s. The number of students enrolled jumped from almost 800,000 to 12 million in the same period. Girls accounted for 34% only of secondary school enrollments in 2008, and few African countries will achieve the gender parity target by 2015 at the secondary level if the current trends continues (UNESCO 2008). Tertiary enrollment increased by 20 times with the number of those enrolled rising from 21,000 to 600,000 between 1999 and 2006 (UNESCO 2006). Females comprised 21% of university level enrollments in the 1980s. They constituted less than two-fifths of the population, with only 38% enrolled in tertiary education in 2007. Furthermore, those female students enrolled in postsecondary education were concentrated in the Humanities, Arts and Social Sciences, with a weaker presence in scientific and technological subjects. For example, female students constituted a mere 40% of total enrollments in Sub-Saharan Africa in technical and vocational education in 2005 (UNESCO 2009).

The factors behind the gender inequity and inequality in education in Africa are driven by socioeconomic and political factors that include political instability and violence, poverty and economic challenges, negative cultural values, attitudes and practices that foster female genital mutilation, early marriage and sexual harassment. These are some of the leading contributors to gender inequity and inequality in education. There is also a lack of gender responsiveness among teachers and in the curriculum, teaching methodology, teaching and learning materials, school management systems and the overall school environment (Ombati and Ombati 2012).

The Effects of Gender Inequality on African Development

Women in Sub-Saharan Africa still often lack access to the same chances for economic success as their male counterparts. While there has been some progress on the third Millennium Development Goal to "promote gender equality and empower women," as indicated in the 2013 Millennium Development Goals Report, there is still a long way to go when it comes to equal education and economic opportunities for women. The African Human Development Report (2016) found that economic and social discrimination against women cost African countries more than US$100 billion per year. The report finds African women across the board are denied the same kind of economic, social and political opportunities men enjoy. It says women lose out when it comes to education, work and health. It notes that fewer girls than boys go to school, women earn less money than men for paid labor, harmful traditional practices affect their health, and certain cultural norms act as a hindrance to women moving ahead in society. A complete picture of how discrimination against women is affecting national development may not be available but some issues are stated below (UNESCO 2010b):

- Owing to the lack of women in decision-making positions, there is low investment in sectors such as health and education that are crucial to human development outcomes.
- The limitation of women's choices and options is hampering the achievement of economic growth and development.
- Women are reluctant to take on responsibilities in politics owing to a lack of economic empowerment to actualize their ambitions.
- The increasing incidence of insecurity, violence and crime such as armed banditry, kidnapping, prostitution, child trafficking, cultism, increasing culture of begging are the result of poverty in society, which women's empowerment could ameliorate.

The African Gender and Development Index

After over 15 years since the implementation of the Beijing Platform for Action, African states have certainly become more aware of the need to eliminate gender inequality. This is evidenced by the numerous legal, policy, institutional, communication and other programmatic initiatives which have evolved over the years. Nevertheless, governments have found it difficult to assess the actual extent of gender inequality in their societies, whether progress is being made and if so to what extent. The African Gender Development Index (AGDI) is a composite index made up of two parts. The first, the Gender Status Index (GSI), measures relative gender inequalities based on readily available quantitative indicators of education and health: income time use, employment and access to resources; and formal and informal political representation. The African Women's Progress Scoreboard (AWPS), which is the second, measures progress in women's empowerment and advancement. To facilitate an effective monitoring mechanism on gender equality and women's advancement, the ECA introduced the African Gender and Development Index (AGDI), which is designed to measure the gap in the status of women and men in Africa and to assess the progress made by African governments in implementing the gender policies they have developed World Women Report (2016).

As an index, it gives a clear political message and allows for easier comparison between countries. The AGDI is constructed as a tool for women's empowerment and gender equality and is based on an analysis of gender gaps and the underlying gender relations in Africa. Effective gender policies can work towards greater gender justice and equality. Gender equality does not mean same-ness of men and women, but refers to equality of rights, participation, opportunities, voice and access, and control over resources. Gender relations are relations of social inequality. They are present in all aspects of life. Gender is related both to the use of public space and the domestic domain.

The Interface Between the MDGs and the AGDI

The Millennium Development Goals (MDGs) form the world's major commitment to the promotion of an action agenda which emphasizes sustainable human development as the key to fulfilling social and economic progress. All 191 Member States of the United Nations have pledged to achieve these goals by the year 2015. Addressing poverty and the other goals outlined is only possible if a holistic, gender-sensitive approach is adopted. Although only one goal explicitly addresses gender equality and women's empowerment (MDG 3), and MDG 5 addresses maternal mortality, gender issues are key to achieving success on the other MDGs as well. For ease of appreciation of the interface between the AGDI and the MDGs, the latter are listed as follows:

1. Eradicate extreme poverty and hunger
2. Achieve universal primary education
3. Promote gender equality and empower women
4. Reduce child mortality
5. Improve maternal mortality
6. Combat HIV/AIDS, malaria and other diseases
7. Ensure environmental sustainability
8. Develop a global partnership for development.

These goals are accompanied by concrete targets and indicators, both in a direct sense, where indicators such as income, education, child health and HIV/AIDS are concerned, but also in a more holistic way, where issues such as violence against women and customary laws in which gender inequality are entrenched, are addressed. Women, half of the world's population, can only be empowered to participate fully in the immense effort needed to eradicate poverty and ensure environmental sustainability when they can act in an environment without fear and are provided with access to adequate resources.

Progress Made So Far in Achieving Gender Inequality in Africa

The Millennium Declaration of 2000 resolves to promote gender equality and the empowerment of women as effective ways to combating poverty, hunger and disease and to stimulating sustainable development. By implication, it recognizes the centrality of gender equality and empowerment of women to the achievement of all international development goals and also has a goal specifically addressing gender equality. In 2005, the UN World Summit recognized the importance of achieving MDG3 through gender equality in education, non-agricultural employment and participation in decision-making. In addition, the Summit reiterated the importance of promoting women's right to own and inherit property; ensuring tenure of property and housing, and equal access to productive assets and resources, including land, credit and technology; ensuring universal access to reproductive health; and eliminating all forms of discrimination and violence against women and girls. The Summit noted significantly that failure to make any meaningful strides in these areas would not only result in imbalances in the distribution of the opportunities and benefits of development, but also hamper the achievement of all the MDGs.

According to World Women Report (2013), the following progress was recorded in an effort to achieve gender equality in Africa

- In developing regions, the proportion of people living on less than $1.25 a day fell from 47% in 1990 to 22% in 2010. About 700 million fewer people lived in conditions of extreme poverty in 2010 than in 1990. Over 2 billion people gained access to improved sources of drinking water. Over the last 21 years, more than 2.1 billion people have gained access to improved drinking water sources. The proportion of the global population using such sources reached 89% in 2010, up from 76% in 1990. This means that the MDG drinking water target was met 5 years ahead of the target date, despite significant population growth.
- Remarkable gains were made in the fight against malaria and tuberculosis between 2000 and 2010; mortality rates from malaria fell by more than 25% globally. An estimated 1.1 million deaths from malaria were averted over this period. Death rates from tuberculosis at the global level and in several regions are likely to be halved by 2015, compared to 1990 levels. Between 1995 and 2011, a cumulative total of 51 million tuberculosis patients were successfully treated, saving 20 million lives.
- The proportion of slum dwellers in the cities and metropolises of the developing world declined between 2000 and 2010. Over 200 million slum dwellers benefitted from improved water sources, sanitation facilities, durable housing or sufficient living space, thereby exceeding the 100 million MDG target. Many countries across all regions have shown remarkable progress in reducing the proportion of urban slum dwellers. A low debt burden and an improved climate for trade are levelling the playing field for developing countries. The debt service to export revenue ratio of all developing countries stood at 3.1% in 2011, down from nearly 12% in 2000. Their duty-free market access also improved in 2011, reaching 80% of their exports. The exports of least developed countries benefitted the most. Average tariffs are also at an all-time low.
- The hunger reduction target is within reach. The proportion of undernourished people in developing regions decreased from 23.2% in 1990–1992 to 14.9% in 2010–2012. Given reinvigorated efforts, the target of halving the percentage of people suffering from hunger by 2015 appears to be within reach. Still, one in eight people in the world today remain chronically undernourished. Gender-based inequalities in decision-making power persist whether in the public or private sphere, from the highest levels of government decision-making to households; women continue to be denied equal opportunity with men to participate in decisions that affect their lives

Problems in Africa in Achieving Gender Equality

At their annual summit in 2014, African Union leaders declared 2015 as the Year of Women's Empowerment. After 20 years of intense advocacy for women's rights, there is a palpable feeling of disenchantment with the slow pace of progress on the challenges women faced in 1995 (UN Women 2015). The global body dedicated to gender equality and women's empowerment pointed out that progress towards fulfilling commitments made in Beijing has been painfully slow and uneven. Although, the number of women in parliament has doubled globally in the last 20 years, in Africa only one in every five members of parliament is a woman, which is still below the 30% threshold for minimum representation from either gender. Although Africa has some of the top performers in women's representation, it also has the highest number of countries that are underperforming. In agriculture, about 70% of the crops are produced by women, yet they still own only 2% of the land. In addition, women earn 30% less than men for the same work. Violence against women has reached alarming proportions, with one in every three women in Africa experiencing some form of violence in her lifetime. Many girls still face the threat of female genital mutilation, early or forced marriages and unwanted pregnancies. Extremists also threaten to turn back the few fragile gains women have made. Despite these obstacles, important advances have been made, including bridging the gender gap in primary education, improving maternal health, fighting HIV/AIDS and new laws to fight discrimination and harmful cultural practices enacted. Between the establishment of the Millennium Development Goals in 1990, and the transition to the Sustainable Development Goals last year, the gap between girls' and boys' primary school enrollment was dramatically narrowed, the average rate of maternal mortality was almost halved, the ratio of women to men in the labor force increased so that it is now greater than in any other region of the world, and the average representation of women in national parliaments more than doubled—with Rwanda and Senegal topping the list of countries with the highest proportion of women in parliament (in Cabo Verde, gender parity at the cabinet level has prevailed for over a decade). Part of the reason for this progress is that countries all across Africa have turned the depressing statistics into a surprising advantage (African Human Development Report 2016).

Evidence from Africa also shows us that, sometimes, simply making the economy work better can disproportionately benefit women, even without an explicit focus on gender. Some recent experiences with land tenure reform provide one such example. Improving tenure security can increase incentives to invest in land by giving land owners greater confidence that they will reap the benefits of whatever investments they make. Evidence suggests that the impacts of such improvements are greater for women, who tend to have less access to land and weaker tenure security. This is an important issue for economic growth in Africa, where so much economic activity is concentrated in the agriculture sector. In Rwanda, improving land owners' tenure security caused women to increase investments in their land by 19% points, which had double the impact on men (African Human Development Report 2016).

Conclusion and Recommendations

Achieving gender equality is key to releasing vital growth potential for the continent (IFAD 2011a; b). The empowerment of women and girls is a crucial element in Africa's quest for inclusive, sustainable growth and development. Africa must close its gender gaps in order to succeed. Many African countries have made great progress through the MDGs in the enrollment of girls and boys for primary school education and increased enrollment at secondary level. It is important to build on this good start and close the considerable gaps that still remain, including poor quality of education, teacher shortages and high dropout rates—especially amongst girls. Those dropout rates reflect the prevalence of forced and early marriages and teenage pregnancies; the confines of unpaid care work; and obstacles such as lack of feminine hygiene infrastructure for adolescent girls at schools.

Without full and equal rights to land, economic opportunity, finance, and services to help relieve the care burden, women's contributions to food security, development, and national—and personal—growth are inhibited. In Africa, most women's jobs are informal. As a result they are not covered by labor relations laws, have no minimum wage and no social protection, no maternity benefits and no old age pension. Ultimately, bringing new light and resources to the informal sector, strengthening social services, upholding women's rights and breaking access barriers will not only make economies work for women but will also benefit societies as a whole by creating a more sustainable future for Africa. Agriculture, in which almost all employment is currently informal, can be a key contributor in Africa to growth and poverty reduction. As a major employer, transformation of agricultural activities into a formal sector would be influential. Agricultural development should be seen as a priority for creative and innovative action by both governments and the business world. Women's productivity could be multiplied through the design of agricultural technologies that are specifically suitable for women and that free up their time, currently so constrained by infrastructural limitations such as water and fuel. Improved post-harvest storage facilities would preserve farm yields, and improved access to markets would allow more efficient distribution.

Business is a big part of the solution, with the power to pay equal wages, remove glass ceilings, and offer wages and opportunities for women in the work and marketplace that will help to reduce the 30% average gender pay gap for Sub-Saharan Africa (World Report 2013). Small and medium enterprises are vigorous engines of job growth in the world economy, accounting for 80% of jobs worldwide. Investing in women-owned firms will pay dividends in terms of job creation and development. New technologies such as mobile banking can be key facilitators and drivers of business development for women. Together, with clear leadership on these aspects from the business sector, we can ensure concerted investment in expanded employment options, with education, training and mentorship so that women are properly equipped to work, advance and excel in all sectors, including as entrepreneurs. Efforts to achieve a world of prosperity, equity, freedom, dignity and peace will continue beyond 2015. The United Nations in concert with governments, civil society and other partners has built on the momentum generated by the MDGs to craft an ambitious, yet realistic, post-2015 development agenda known as the Sustainable Development Goals (SDGs). Gender equality is not only a fundamental human right, but a necessary foundation for a peaceful, prosperous and sustainable world. Providing women and girls with equal access to education, health care, decent work, and representation in political and economic decision-making processes will fuel sustainable economies and benefit societies and humanity at large. The following recommendations are made in this regard:

1. **An urgent review of all gender discriminatory laws in Africa**
   African governments should collaborate with traditional rulers in Africa and other stakeholders to ensure that all harmful and traditional practices which target only women are uprooted. This could be advanced through dialoging with traditional rulers who are the custodians of culture; they should be made to outlaw all oppressive customary practices in their domain.
2. **Economic empowerment of women**
   It is high time African governments increased women's presence at the labor market. African governments should embark on initiatives to get more women into top jobs in economic decision-making. Furthermore, female entrepreneurship should be promoted by making loans available to women on lenient terms. Economic empowerment of women is imperative if any headway is to be made in this struggle for gender equality. An economically dependent woman is powerless and voiceless, and cannot assert her rights, not to speak of seeking legal redress in courts.
3. **Educational empowerment of women**
   Compulsory girl-child education is a useful strategy that should be adopted to bridge gender gaps in Africa. Currently, laws against the trafficking of young girls as domestic servants and prostitutes should be strictly enforced. Education of a girl-child, in the long run, would equip her for future participation in key decision-making in government and also enable her to influence gender-friendly policies.
4. **More political appointments for women**
   African governments should beef up their political appointive positions for women. The present appointments still fall short of the international expectation, that is, 35% of all political appointments should be reserved for women. The need to integrate women into the mainstream of decision-making in government can never be over-emphasized.
5. **Overhauling of social institutions**
   It is evident that inequalities are often rooted in social institutions. African governments should therefore endeavor to overhaul and reform all institutional frameworks that limit the development of women's potentials and skills. A leaf should be taken from Tunisia's book, where such efforts are paying off. In Tunisia today, 30 to 50% of judges, physicians and school teachers are now women. Similarly, in India, women have risen to the highest levels of politics and business in recent times. African governments should endeavor to review all gender discriminatory laws and practices.

6. **The role of the media**

   African government media should devise more effective awareness raising programs especially at the grassroots level. The media should henceforth desist from portraying women in a negative and degrading manner such as 'sex objects' and 'housewives'.

7. **Establishment of more internet portals to foster dialogue for the promotion of gender equality**

   The establishment of this portal will create an avenue of reaching out to the public by fostering dialog on the importance of gender equality. Websites such as Wikigender provide an open forum to share and exchange information on the situation of women and also encourage frank discussion on the factors that impede women's social, political and economic empowerment. It is believed that such forums will reveal people's personal experiences on gender rights violations, and will definitely help to deal with stubborn social attitudes and mind sets, while enabling policymakers to tailor their strategies to the specific situation in a country or community.

References

Adama, J. S. (2016). *Gender equality and women's rights in modern Ghana.*

African Human Development Report. (2016). www.report.hdr.undp.org. Accessed 7 June 2016.

Akanle, O., & Adejare, G. (2016). Towards understanding gender and sexuality: Transgender relation relations shifts in contemporary Nigeria. In E. O. Wahab, O. E. Ajiboye, & O. S. Yusuff (Eds.), *Essentials of sociology: A brief introduction* (pp. 73–85). Festac: Department of Sociology, Lagos State University.

Ali, N. M. (2011). *Gender and state building in South Sudan: Special Report.* United States Institute of Peace. http://www.usip.org. Accessed 10 Aug 2016.

Anderson, M. (2000). Shifting the centre and reconstructing knowledge. In M. I. Anderson & P. H. Collins Race (Eds.), *Class and gender: An anthology* (4th ed., pp. 40–48). Belmont: Wadsworth Thomas Learning.

Azuh, D., Fayomi, O., & Ajayi, L. (2015). Socio-cultural factors of gender roles in women's health utilization in south west Nigeria. *Open Journal of Social Sciences, 3*, 105–117. http://www.Scrip.org/Journal/JSS. Accessed 7 July 2016.

Basden, G. T. (1999). *Niger ibos.* London: Frank Cass.

Berger, P. L., & Luckmann, T. (1991). *The social construction of reality: A treatise in the sociology of knowledge.* Garden City: Anchor Books.

Burns, S. (1996). *The social psychology of gender.* New York: McGraw Hill.

Care. (2016). *Gender in brief: South Sudan.* http://www.Care.org. Accessed 4 Aug 2016.

CEDAW. (2011). *CEDAW 7th country report Kenya.* Ministry of Gender, Child and Social Development. http://www.gender.go.ke/index.php/downloads1/viewdownload/9-gender-mainstreaming/7-cedaw7th-country-report-kenya. Accessed June 2016.

Ezuma, N. N. (2003). *Perception of womanhood in Nigeria and the challenge of development.* http://www.gwsafrica.org/know. Accessed May 2016.

Ferrante, J. (2011). *Sociology: A global perspective* (7th ed.). Belmont: Wadsworth Cengage Learning.

Food and Agriculture Organization (FAO). (2011). *The state of food and agriculture report 2010–2011.* Women in agriculture: Closing the gender gap for development. http://www.fao.org/docrep/013/i2050e/i2050e.pdf

Food and Agriculture Organization (FAO). (2012). *Gender inequalities in rural employment in Ghana: Policy and legislation*. http://www.Stasghana.gov.gh/docfiles/gender/FAO-Ghana
Giddens, A. (2004). *Sociology*. London: Polity Press.
Global Gender Report. (2013). *The centre for commonwealth education* (CCE Report No. 8).
Hacking, I. (1999). *The social construction of what?* Cambridge, MA: Harvard University Press.
Haq, F. (1996). Women, Islam and the state in Pakistan. *Muslim World, April*(86), 158–175.
Henslin, J. M. (2010). *Sociology: A down to earth approach* (10th ed.). New York: Pearson.
Hutson, S. (2009). *Gender oppression and discrimination in South Africa*. ESSAI 5.
IFAD. (2011a). *Rural poverty report*. http://www.ifad.org/documents/10180
IFAD. (2011b). Gender inequalities in rural employment in Malawi: An overview.
Ikpeze, N. (2000). Post-Biafran marginalization of the Igbo in Nigeria. In I. Amadiume & A. An-Na'im (Eds.), *The politics of memory: Truth, healing and social justice* (pp. 90–109). London/New York: Zed Books.
Jost, J. T., & Kruglanski, A. W. (2002). The estrangement of social constructionism and experimental social psychology: History of the rift and prospects for reconciliation. *Personality and Social Psychology Review, 6*(3), 168–187.
Kasente, D. (2003). *Gender and education in Uganda* (Background paper for EFA Global Monitoring Report).
Kuanyi, M.A. (2010). *Women and culture: Role of women in development of Southern Sudan*. Gurlong. Bring South Sudanese together. http://www.gurlong.net. Accessed 15 July 2016.
Makama, G. A. (2013). Patriarchy and gender inequality in Nigeria: The way forward. *European Scientific Journal, 9*(17), 115–145.
Meer, F. (2007, March 30). The future for women. *The Unesco Courier*, *2*, 30–32. History Study Center. College of DuPage Library, Glen Ellyn.
Mudiare, P. U. (2013). The perception of gender violence and its implication for spousal violence in Kaduna metropolis, Kaduna State, Nigeria. *European Scientific Journal, 9*(23). ISSN: 1857 – 7881.
Musau, Z. (2015). *Gender equality still within reach*. Africa Renewal. http://www.un.org. Accessed 23 June 2016.
Ndiritu, S. W., & Nyangena, W. (2010). Environmental goods collection and children's schooling: Evidence from Kenya. *Regional Environmental Change, 11*(3), 531–542.
Nwomonoh, J. (1998). *Education and development in Africa: A contemporary survey*. London: International Scholars Publication.
Odeyemi, J. S. (2013). Gender issues among Yorubas. *The International Journal of African Catholicism, 4*(1, Winter), 1–8.
Ofosu-Baadu, B. (2012). *Women in rural Ghana*. Ghana statistical services. 4th Global forum on gender statistics. http://unstats.un.org. Accessed 3 May 2016.
Olurode, L. (2013, April). *State and political participation: Women in Nigeria's 2011 elections* (Discussion paper No. 4). Friedrich Ebert Stiftung.
Ombati, V., & Ombati, M. (2012). Gender inequality in education in Sub-Saharan Africa. *Journal of Women Education and Entrepreneur, 3–4*, 114–136.
Osei-Boateng, C., & Ampratum, E. (2011). *The informal sector in Ghana*. Friedrich Ebert Stiftung Ghana Office. http://www.fes.de/pdf/files/Ghana
Pankhurst, D. (2002). Women and politics in Africa: The case of Uganda. *Parliamentary Affairs, 55*(1), 119–128.
Quartey, O., & Martin, A. (2008). *Gender and diversity report: Ghana*. C:AVA. Cassava: Adding value for Africa. Natural Resources Institute.
Sabbagh, S. (1996). Introduction: The debate on Arab women. In S. Sabbagh (Ed.), *Arab women: Between defiance and restraints*. Brooklyn: Olive Branch Press.
Sabban, W. (1995). *The conceptualization of gender, perspectives on gender discourse: Gender and constitution-making in Kenya*. Heinrich Boll Foundation, Regional Office, East and Horn of Africa.
UNECA. (2007). *A human rights -based approach to education for "All"*. United Nations Children's Fund. Available at http://www.Unicef.org/publications/files. Accessed 20 Jan 2016.

UNECA. (2008). *Regional overview: Sub-Saharan Africa, overcoming inequality* (EFA. Global Monitoring Report). Paris: UNESCO.
UNESCO. (2006, 2008). *Meetings of experts on women in informal sector*. United Nation 2009.
UNESCO. (2009). *Regional overview: Sub-Saharan Africa; overcoming inequality* (EFA Global Monitoring Report). Paris: UNESCO.
UNESCO. (2010a). *Africa human development report. 2012*. Towards a food secure future.
UNESCO. (2010b). *School fees for Africa: Coming to grips with an elusive promise*. New York: United Nations Children's Fund.
UNICEF. (2011). *The state of the world's children: Adolescence an age of opportunity*. New York: UNICEF.
UNWomen. (2015). *Rural women, their contribution and challenges to be highlighted at UN commission on the status of women*. http://www.unwomen.org. Accessed 6 Apr 2016.
World Bank. (1988). *Education in Sub-Saharan Africa: Policies for adjustment, revitalization and growth*. Washington, DC: World Bank.
World Health Organization (WHO). (2012). *A World Bank policy research report*. New York: Oxford University Press. 2001. Engendering development: though gender equality in rights, Resources, and voice.
World Women Report. (2013). *Human rights watch*. http://www.hrw.org. Accessed 20 June 2016.
World Women Report. (2016). *Human rights watch*. http://www.hrw.org. Accessed 20 June 2016.
World Report. (2013). *World report 2013: Nigeria human rights watch*. Available at http://www.hrw-org/worldreport/2013/country/chapters/Nigeria. Accessed 30 Nov 2016.
Yusuff, O. S. (2013). Feminism: An African perspective. In A. O. Olutayo & O. Akanle (Eds.), *Sociological theory for African students* (pp. 209–230). Nigeria: University of Ibadan Press.
Yusuff, O. S. (2014). Gender and career advancement in academia in developing countries: Notes on Nigeria. *International Journal of Sociology of Education, 3*(3), 269–291.
Yusuff, O. S., & Ajiboye, O. E. (2014). Social change and traditional gender roles in Lagos state. *African Journal of Psychological Study of Social Issues, 17*(3), 58–68.
Zakaria, Y. (2001). Entrepreneurs at home: Secluded Muslim women and hidden economic activities in Northern Nigeria. *Nordic Journal of African Studies, 10*(1), 107–123.

Olabisi Sherifat Yusuff, holds a PhD and lectures in the Department of Sociology, Lagos State University, Nigeria. Her research interests include: Gender/Women Studies, Sociology of Development and Family Studies. She has published in reputable journals, including among others, International Journal of Sociology, Akademia, South East Journal of Social Sciences and Humanities. E-mail address:soyusuf@yahoo.co.uk.

Chapter 16
Non-state Actors as the Strategic Realm in Africa's Development

Olayinka Akanle

Introduction

A major problem confronting most countries in Africa is underdevelopment. Even though a little variation may exist among nations on the continent, the reality is that countries on the African continent are relatively underdeveloped (Akanle 2013). Regrettable still is the fact that most African countries continue to go deeper into underdevelopment while the hitherto promising ones are losing such promise due to terrorism, corruption, patrimonialism, weakened global demand for natural resources and generalized misgovernance. Included in this category, for example, are Egypt, Tunisia and, to some extent, South Africa. Underdevelopment on the African continent has worsened since the 1980s and even though most African nations are now democratic and consolidating their democracies, most have not been able to sustainably jumpstart development and many have over time fallen deeper into underdevelopment—Sudan and Somalia for instance to the point of near failed statehood. While there have been many explanations for continued and aggravated underdevelopment of African nations, old and recent events suggest the need for a fresh examination of the development realities of Africa. This is especially through accounting for hitherto unaccounted for key players in the development space of the continent—non-state actors (NSAs). Hence, the underdevelopment realities on the Africa continent call for the need for fresh narratives and accounting relative to key actors in the African development marketplace.

There is thus the need to rethink, redirect and better interconnect, normatively, theoretically and practically, Africa's underdevelopment through the windows of NSAs as the strategic realm in Africa's development. This is important because most narratives on development in Africa either do not account at all or mis-account for the roles of these actors. Most narratives are too state-centric to the extent that

O. Akanle (✉)
Department of Sociology, University of Ibadan, Ibadan, Nigeria
e-mail: yakanle@yahoo.com; yk.akanle@ui.edu.ng; akanlo@unisa.ac.za

O. Akanle, J.O. Adésìnà (eds.), *The Development of Africa*, Social Indicators Research Series 71, DOI 10.1007/978-3-319-66242-8_16

the roles of NSAs are taken for granted. Unfortunately, given what is now known about the roles of NSAs in developed countries and other developing continents like Latin America and the Middle East, there is a need to better examine the roles of NSAs in the development equations of African countries to make development feasible on the continent. It can therefore be hypothesized that a positive relationship may likely exist between NSAs' roles and development in developing countries, and until the trajectories of these roles are sufficiently appreciated and factored into development processes on the continent, development may remain elusive in Africa. NSAs are critical change and development agents and there is the need for better analysis and understanding of their contours on the African continents.

Even though NSAs are not new to Africa in terms of their contribution to development, many extant narratives have reduced their *interventions* to emergency/disaster management and there has been over-emphasis on their political economy (Steer et al. 2015; Weiss et al. 2013). It is therefore evident that there is need for a more recent and practical consideration of their development contributions in Africa, beyond existing political and international relations repertoires, which have remained fixated at the level of the state, as the suprarelational institution responsible for driving development, even when recent occurrences appear to be proving otherwise, as many NSAs are now setting nations' development agenda, driving such agenda and determining the outcomes of such agenda either equally with the state or even outside the state (Valensi 2015; Ewumbue-Monono 2006). Cases abound but examples include the armed non-state actors in the Middle East/North Africa (Islamic State), East Africa (Al-Shabab) and West Africa (Boko Haram) (Akanle and Omobowale 2015; Ewumbue-Monono 2006).

This chapter seeks to contribute to the understanding of development on the African continent with a focus on the roles of NSAs as critical and important actors in the development field. This is particularly important as the significance of NSAs has increased dramatically in the last 20 years even when the legitimacy and capabilities of states to drive development have continued to be challenged and undermined within the same period. Hence, while states have continued to witness resistance and lose popular support and legitimacy, NSAs have continued to proliferate and, sometimes, enjoy goodwill, and their structures often make them less amenable to the political and diplomatic problems states often confront. More players in the development sectors—including sovereign nations—now sometimes prefer to contribute to development in developing countries through NSAs to avoid diplomatic complications, political backlashes, prohibitive bureaucracies, ethnic sensationalism/sentimentalism and corruption. This has contributed to the significance and rise of the NSAs in the development space. According to Weiss et al. (2013), due to the realization of the importance of NSAs in the development of developing nations, the second half of the twentieth century saw an astronomical increase in the numbers of NSAs in the development space of many developing countries. There is thus the need to understand the dynamics, implications, drivers, trajectories and contours of these existentialities and increase of NSAs in Africa, particularly in relation to the development of countries on the continent.

Non-state Actors: Conceptualization and Characterization

Given the dynamism, multifariousness and multidimensional functions of NSAs, it is difficult to arrive at a universally acceptable definition. A common intersection in existing definitions and conceptualizations is however discernable. NSAs are commonly defined and conceptualized around what they do, how they do what they do and structures of their operations. NSAs can be broadly described as organized groups with a basic structure of command functioning and operating outside state control that often use force to achieve their political and allegedly political objectives (Valensi 2015; Maseng 2014; Hofmann and Schneckener 2011). In a related version, NSAs can be defined as organizations largely or entirely independent of the state/central government funding and control emanating from civil society or from the market economy or from political impulses beyond state control and direction (Malka 2015; Briscoe 2013; Bruderlein 2000). Hence, NSAs are summarily change agents and their processes and outcomes are usually direct and indirect, intended and unintended. Their objectives and processes affect socioeconomic and political arrangements and outcomes of societies and states, while international institutions and territories are not immune to the objectives and outcomes of NSA activities whether partly or wholesale.

It is common to identify two broad types of NSA and the major difference in the existence and characterization of these broad typologies is their mode of operation. Sometimes, even their objectives and outcomes overlap even though this is indirectly and unintentionally. The two broad types of NSAs are armed non-state actors (ANSAs) and unarmed non-state actors (UNSAs). It is noteworthy that these two broad categories are in themselves not entirely homogenous. They sometimes also still have variants but these broad categorizations suffice based on the primary strategies they commonly adopt as their flagships of existence. ANSAs describes a variety of bodies and entities that engage in armed conflicts for the main purpose of religious, political, social, economic and cultural goals/reasons (Briscoe 2013; Hofmann and Schneckener 2011). UNSAs on the other hand are entities that are motivated by social, cultural, religious, economic and political reasons but achieve or set to achieve goals without overt physical weapon wilding conflict of violence. Unlike ANSAs, UNSAs do not engage in armed conflict but often deploy lobbying and diplomacy. When conflict becomes imminently apparent, UNSAs suspend operations until the situation improves and peace is restored. The motivations of NSAs drive their philosophies and their philosophies drive their approaches, strategies and tactics.

While both ANSAs and UNSAs operate outside the state, at least largely overtly, they both also have something in common—they both have objectives which they strategize to achieve either through violence or otherwise. The ultimate focus of NSAs is their beneficiaries and they circumvent all other interests for the benefit of the 'focus' (beneficiaries). Examples of ANSAs are armed militias, terrorist organizations, armed bandits, rebel groups, armed freedom fighters and armed liberation movements. All these use force to propagate and achieve force and collateral damage as objects of negotiation, voice gathering and attention drawing. The more violent, the more destructive and the more undermining the better it is for ANSAs. ANSAs are usually not recognized by states and are not widely recognized internationally. UNSAs, on the other hand, broadly include multinational corporations (MNCs), non-governmental organizations (NGOs), intergovernmental organizations (Valensi 2015) and extra-ordinarily influential individuals (E-OIIs[1]). These UNSA actors are both territorial and extra-territorial and their modus operandi is non-violence, at least in the overt sense, even though they use diplomatic, intellectual and relational pressures that many in international relations may consider as systematic violence which is commonly inevitable. This includes lobbying states and international organizations to impose sanctions, deploy overt force, freeze assets and impose travel bans on targeted individuals and organizations.

MNCs as NSAs are important because of their private identities and economic capabilities. Even though they are non-state, they often have state relationship capital that they often deploy for other private and non-private purposes because they are multinational, operating in at least two countries—the first country being their home country and other countries being destinations of their companies and operations. NGOs, like MNCs, are voluntary, private, but not profit making, unlike MNCs, and self-governing. Like MNCs, however, even though NGOs are autonomous of the state governments in which they operate, there are state instituted regulatory frameworks guiding their operations. Generally, therefore, while ANSAs are forcefully out of state control, NGOs and other UNSAs are not entirely out of states' control. While ANSAs overtly undermine the state and its interests, UNSAs are seen as complementing the development efforts of the state and are commonly seen as partners in progress with the state. Generally, by their objectives and strategies, they are overtly free from government and external control and influences.

E-OIIs are individuals with huge socioeconomic, political, cultural and religious capital. These capitals are very variable, enduring and massive yet very fragile, depending on the prevailing circumstances in the state and the world. Examples of E-OIIs are past political leaders like heads of state, successful industrialists, philanthropists and financiers, media personalities/celebrities and religious leaders. Popular examples may include Kofi Anan, Bill and Melinda Gates, Thabo Mbeki, Aliko Dangote, Bill Clinton, Tony Blair, Oprah Winfrey and Banki Moon. E-OIIs accumulate their capital over time through past successful public engagements and they remain largely independent of current overt political/state activities. Intergovernmental organizations (IGOs) are interstate/across sovereignties. IGOs are established through national/international understandings and partnership agreements for common purposes, usually around peacebuilding and sustainable

[1] E-OII is my original concept created to accommodate what the NCI described as the *super-empowered individuals*. I consider the concept of E-OIIs more appropriate because the nucleus of strength of such *larger than life individuals* in the NSA marketplace is the resource of influence which they deploy as an object of negotiation. This influence thus becomes very variable and dynamic to the extent that it translates to empowerment but the main essence, structure and element of the empowerment is the extraordinary influence that may have come from previous socio-economic, political, religious, diplomatic and other powers.

development of nations and the world. The essence of IGOs is collective galvanization of resources for the achievement of common interests. Generally, IGOs include official arrangements and connections to states through interstate political agreements and interactions. A very popular example of IGOs is the United Nations which is an amalgamation of sovereign nations for the protection of common world interests.

Generally, NSAs contribute directly and indirectly to the development of nations, continents and the world. The impact NSAs' activities have on any space at any particular point in history is, however, noticeable through their implications for the institutions and people of that society. Broadly, NSAs serve positive and negative purposes depending on which side of the divide and observatory point the issues and outcomes of actions of NSAs are being described. That is, whose interest is at stake? Whose interest is being protected? Who are the gainers and who are the losers? Who is doing the observation and who is doing the analysis? What strategies are being deployed by the stakeholders? What is the long-term implication of the action or inaction? What strategy has been deployed and is being deployed? And what is the motive of engagement? These are critical key questions that can be used in characterizing the nature, existence, strategies, tactics, objectives and outcomes of NSAs, particularly in relation to development in developing countries.

Non-state Actors and Development in Africa

This section examines the role of NSAs in contributing, or otherwise, to the development of Africa. This is very important as a major problem that has an overarching effect on Africa today is underdevelopment. While many angles have been explored in scholarship and practice relative to issues of development in Africa, more is needed in accounting for development of Africa through the (in)activities of NSAs. As already demonstrated in the previous section, there are two broad categories of NSAs—Armed and Unarmed NSAs. These both play critical roles in affecting development in Africa. These two broad categories are therefore examined in this section. Although many existing works on NSAs often unbundle their analysis when addressing NSA issues, the two broad categories will be examined together for complete analysis in this chapter. The relationships of NSAs with development are explored through major clusters of development indicators of Africa to understand their significance and the dynamics of Africa's development. The four broad sectors/indicators adopted systematically for analysis in this chapter are health, human rights, poverty and humanitarian aid (general development/aggregate development). NSAs play diverse roles based on different interests which have the capabilities to affect development ultimately on the African continent. Often, these roles are driven and moderated within the world system to the extent that global interests, national interests, local interests, institutional interests and even personal interests may constellate to determine eventual continental development interests. The intensity and dynamics of these constellations of interests ultimately determine the development outcomes of nations and continents.

Globalization and the political economy of international development somewhat affect the (in)activities of NSAs and their development outcomes. The massive reduction in space of interactions among institutions, nations, groups, governments, cultures and individuals through technology (Akanle and Taiwo 2013) means NSAs can now share strategies and resources more easily to affect development especially in developing countries. Particularly, globalization has made it far easier, cheaper and faster for people, organization and NSAs to reach nations and communities even in previously unreached/unreachable places. It is now possible and easier for NSAs as key actors in the development marketplace to exchange ideas and other resources within themselves and across the broader spectrum of the relational and development interface. Globalization for NSAs means they can now leverage more resources, engage with more issues, relate with more stakeholders, cover more spaces and make a greater impact relative to development. Globalization enables NSAs to affect more norms, values, principles and practices and drive development ideals in Africa through global governance. This is why more NSAs are now engaging broader issues of development like climate change, HIV/AIDS, poverty, gender equality, peace building, maternal health, child rights protection and human rights in Africa.

NSAs participate in Africa's development and this is very important as Africa's development questions remain massive, multidimensional and essentially unanswered. There have been aggravated government failures in Africa to the extent that many Africans no longer trust their states and governments to drive development sustainably. Common reasons for this are corruption, nepotism, tribalism, favoritism, conflict, political instability, ethnic cleansing, terrorism, compromised military systems, crime and weak institutions among others. NSAs are noted to intervene in the cases of state deficits and social malaise driven by compromised systems in Africa, like many other developing countries, to make a difference and drive development. NSAs enjoy goodwill among many Africans given their independence from government, and their simplicity, transparency, non-involvement in local social problems and detachment from politics and the state. Whether ANSAs or UNSAs, depending on the context of actions and the social relations of engagements, NSAs tend to have local support and sympathy which often makes their development contributions noteworthy. While many African nations have become democratic and some have consolidated their democracies with evident increasingly transparent elections, for instance Nigeria and Ghana, and there has been reduction in coups d'état and flagrant human rights abuses, the roles of NSAs actors is significant in achieving these.

Many NSAs monitor elections and fund election observations just as many institute observatory for human rights watch and build local capacities to deploy monitoring technologies including very simple ones. Many NSAs also checkmate the state through effective subtle diplomacy, advocacy and lobbying (in the case of UNSAs) and/or through negotiations or violent coordinated resistance to get the attention of the state (in the case of ANSAs). For the ANSAs, violent resistance thus becomes the object of negotiations for the interests of regions or perceived marginalized groups. The perceived development contribution of NSAs and their impacts, however, largely depend on the perspectives of the observers and the contexts of analysis. While there may be a difference in the strategies, tactics, motives and impacts of ANSAs and UNSAs, depending on the socioeconomic systems and the political economy of existence and objectives, all NSAs are now important forces in development decision-making in Africa. In addition, they are now recognized stakeholders in driving development on the continent, as can be seen in political conscientization and participation and advocacy around human rights and sexuality, religious tolerance, campaigning for more inclusive ethno-religious and political space, public policy and education. For example, the role of NSAs in galvanizing human rights (Maseng 2014) of for instance the LGBT (lesbian, gay, bisexual and transgender) is particularly noteworthy, as can be seen in Uganda and South Africa. The role of NSAs in protecting the education rights of the girl child in Northern Nigeria and North Africa is also worthy of note. NSAs also play important roles in relief, aid and emergency management in Africa, especially in war zones and conflict areas involving ethnic and religious militias—terrorist organizations—in the Democratic Republic of Congo, Sudan, Nigeria, Somalia, Chad, Cameroun, Tunisia, Egypt among others.

Non-state Actors and Health

A sector that demonstrates the development roles of NSAs in Africa is health. The important roles of NSAs (UNSAs) in Africa can be seen and felt in the areas of access to health, preferences/choices, quality and affordability/economics of health care. World leaders have long recognized this even at the level of the United Nations to the extent that the Millennium Development Goals (MDGs) and the Sustainable Development Goals (SDGs) factored the NSAs in principle into the achievement of these two overarching development frameworks. Health as a complete positive state of wellbeing is central to the achievement of all other SDGs in Africa and the NSAs must play a central role in this regard in terms of managing, implementing, harnessing and mobilizing critical health facilities and systems. NSAs are central to strengthening both state and non-state health structures and institutions to make them more amenable to the needs of Africans in terms of governance, regulation, funding and quality service delivery. NSAs often have critical networks, strategies, capacities, goodwill and frameworks to drive investments, performance and accountability in the health sector of Africa. This is critical given the governance and infrastructural gaps on the continent.

Like in many other developing countries, many NSAs in Africa were formed and now exist, at the turn of the millennium and earlier, to contribute to the health sector of Africa. Many NSAs directly fund the health systems of Africa through direct funding in critical sectors of the health systems while many inject resources to address specific health crises like malaria, Ebola, HIV/AIDS, and sickle cell anemia amongst others. Examples of NSAs in this health marketplace include the Bill and Melinda Gates Foundation, the Global Fund and the World Health Organization

(WHO). Broadly, the NSAs in the health sector fall into the categories of private institutions, NGOs, community-based organizations (CBOs), faith-based organizations (FBOs) and international/multinational organizations like the WHO. A significant proportion of Africans relies on the NSA actors to meet their unmet health needs. For example, according to the World Bank (2011), across Africa as many as 52% of low income people obtain health care services through the NSAs. This is, however, not limited to the poor African households, as a nearly equal proportion can be found even among Africans in the top income class. Locality in terms of rurality and urbanity is also not a major factor because as many people in both rural and urban centers rely on NSA services, structures, systems and networks for their health care needs (WHO 2008).

Particularly, data suggests that as much as 50–95% of children with respiratory tract infections in 42 countries (in the categories of low and middle income countries) look towards NSAs for their medical needs (World Bank 2011; WHO 2008). The number is far higher among populations with heart and renal/organ diseases. Examples of NSAs in these areas include, for example, the Kanu Heart Foundation in Nigeria, the Red Cross and Doctors Without Borders. Generally, common endemic and fatal diseases that confront Africans which have made NSAs critical to health care on the continent include HIV/AIDS. The Sub-Saharan African region is among the worst hit and about 68% of HIV-infected persons live on the African continent. According to data from UNAIDS this goes as far back as 2010, even though the region accounts for barely 12% of the world population. Other prevalent diseases in Africa include malaria, tuberculosis, sleeping sickness, Lassa fever, elephantiasis, leprosy (which causes disfiguring skin sores and nerve damage), helminthiasis and trachoma (a bacterial eye infection which can lead to blindness).

Even though Africa is commonly regarded as a continent given the geography and identical rate of underdevelopment, there are remarkable differences in the healthcare infrastructure, policies, funding and capabilities of African countries. Many African countries lack the capability to meet their health obligations making NSAs essential to health care on the continent. There are also rural–urban differentials in access to healthcare. Urbanites tend to have better access to health care and NSAs tend to concentrate more in the urban centers. Yet most Africans live in the rural areas; common diseases in Africa are found in rural areas and cultural infrastructure that rationalizes ill health is more profound in the rural areas and many rural dwellers lack access to clean water and sanitation (leading to poor hygiene) and making them more prone to diseases like cholera and diarrhea. These contradictions often limit the impact of NSAs in health interventions and result in many Africans suffering debilitating health consequences.

Budgetary allocation and spending on healthcare in Africa are comparatively low, necessitating NSAs as key players. Against the background of the African Union (AU) 2001 agreement that countries in Africa should allocate up to 15% of budgetary spending to healthcare, very few African countries—Botswana, Burkina Faso, Malawi, Niger, Rwanda and Zambia—have been able to deliver on this continental agreement regardless of the smallness of this percentage in meeting the healthcare needs of Africans. Reasons for this failure are myriad but lack of resources, mismanagement, corruption and lack of political will to prioritize health-care finance from the state are key reasons. Although the training of health officials does occur in African countries, Africa is one of the most brain-drained continents with many of its health personnel seeking better paying healthcare jobs in Europe, America and the Middle East. This leaves most African countries understaffed with as few as 1.15 health workers to 1000 population (even though variation exists by country[2]) and leads to massive loss of life even from very curable and preventable diseases, as many Africans lack access to important lifesaving drugs.

NSAs broadly shape health agenda and programs through multiple stakeholder partnerships and mechanisms for better health in Africa. NSAs leverage on multi-sectoral and cross-industry partnerships and engagements to address Africa's new and old health gaps and wellness deficits, particularly with the increasingly popular challenge of non-communicable diseases (NCDs) like the spread of polio to Central Africa. Unfortunately, against the gargantuan health deficits in Africa and the need for NSA optimization, NSAs still function at the margins of the healthcare market-place in Africa. NSAs' engagement with local populations, key national actors, the WHO and other key agencies is at suboptimal level. This limits the extent of functionality of NSAs and compromises the extent to which Africans can use the NSAs' advantages in the Africa's health sector. While NSAs have the capacity to be critical assets in the health care systems of Africa, if they are not decidedly appropriated and optimized by local, national and global stakeholders, the benefits will be undermined. People across classes in Africa use the health systems of NSAs owing to their cost, availability, structure and organization. There is thus a need for better appreciation and inclusion of NSAs in the health arrangements of Africa. Global, continental and national agencies and institutions must begin to better acknowledge the gaps being filled by the NSAs in the health sector of Africa.

Unfortunately, in many instances, governments and political institutions in Africa view the operations of NSAs with skepticism and often even see them as rivals as NSAs' performances usually indict state lethargy. Major challenges of NSAs in the healthcare systems of Africa are excessive fragmentation, weak coordination of activities and poor regulation. There is also no sufficiently reliable data in most African countries to reliably manage, monitor and evaluate health interventions and diseases. There is also excessive overlap in the operations of NSAs and these often lead to a waste of time and resources. There is also internal competition among NSAs in the sector as NSAs work to appear to be more relevant than others. This is to get credibility from stakeholders and attract greater funding. The performance of NSAs in the African health sector is thus intrinsically very competitive in both positive and negative ways.

---

[2] For example, according to data from the United States Center for Global Development, countries like Mozambique and Angola have more doctors abroad than are resident in the countries. The case is not entirely different in Nigeria and Zimbabwe, although South Africa and North Africa are to some extent exceptions.

Non-state Actors and Human Rights

Until the increasing democratization of African countries, human rights violations were prevalent on the continent. Even with increasing democratization, however, human rights violations have not totally disappeared. From Tunisia to Egypt to Somalia and Burundi to Nigeria, for example, human rights protection is not total with high levels of extrajudicial killings and incarceration and assassination of political opponents in many African countries. Human rights protection is therefore a major area of operation for NSAs in Africa. The roles of NSAs are particularly important in Africa because most human rights violations in the continent are perpetrated by governments through state security agencies and the political class, as well as significant others at the family and community level. NSAs, like NGOs, FBOs, IGOs and philanthropic individuals play an important moderating role. It is, however, noteworthy that the role of NSAs in human rights is not entirely positive, especially in relation to the environment and human rights at the grassroots. NSAs play both a positive and negative human rights role in Africa. Examples of the positive human rights role of NSAs include intervening in human rights violations through advocacy, litigation, lobbying and education. NSAs play a negative human rights role when they abuse human rights through their operations/activities and inactivity.

In fact, there have been attempts in the past to bring NSAs to account for violations of human rights. An example of this was the African Commission on Human and Peoples' Rights (the African Commission). In its 39th Ordinary Session in Banjul, The Gambia, a decision was made to conduct a study on human rights violations by NSAs in African countries. This was to document issues that could be used to jurisprudentially hold NSAs liable for human rights violations within a broader framework of the African Charter on Human and Peoples' Rights (the African Charter). Human rights issues concerning NSAs range broadly from the political, the girl child, women, extractive industries and environmental issues, among others. In these sectors, the responsibilities and liabilities of NSAs are constantly brought to bear. Many NSAs are accused of cultural, traditional and physical environmental destruction of indigenous communities as they attempt to drive development which sometimes comes from above. Human rights violations in such instances intersect with the social, economic and environmental rights of locals and often indigenous marginalized groups. Resources extracted from local populations' communities are also often expropriated leaving indigenous people impoverished.

Apart from the exploitation of local environments and the expropriation of capital from local populations, some NSAs cause divisions and conflicts in host communities to perpetuate and service their interests. Interestingly, many African states have a head in the sand attitude to the human rights implications of NSA activities. In many instances, African governments are accomplices in this situation. NSAs also fuel corruption across spaces in African countries. Even when laws and regulatory frameworks exist to address human rights issues relating NSAs, such laws and regulations are never enforced sufficiently as the NSAs bring state officials on board their operations and proceed directly or indirectly. Through their international networks, resources and political economic resources, some NSAs blackmail and threaten state governments in Africa with reports to home countries and legal action to sustain operations. These are effective strategies and tactics in Africa given legitimacy and capacity issues with many African governments and political elites who constantly look towards the West for assistance and legitimacy.

Hence, even some African elites may be either shareholders or stakeholders in the resources of many NSAs. These resources include economic and non-economic ones like being part of the same social and/or kinship networks. This is why even though many African countries have potent and world class environmental laws and policy frameworks, there is often a lack of political will and moral capability to activate and apply those laws. Many African political elites are themselves rent seekers either from the NSAs or their mother countries mostly in the West. Also, many governments in Africa consider NSAs as important development partners who they feel bring important investments and capital into the country. Therefore, even though NSAs sometimes flout environmental and human rights laws, there is often unwillingness on the part of African governments to bring them to account. In cases of mounting pressure from African countries for NSAs to be more accountable in terms of human rights, they threaten African governments with either lawsuits or mass relocation or both. For many African countries with nascent democracies, weak foreign exchange, poor economies and massive legitimacy deficits, these are largely unaffordable conditions.

This is largely the case across Sub-Saharan Africa where many NSAs operate far below global best practices and outside the social responsibility and human rights code obtainable in their home countries. Apart from local inability to hold NSAs to account, global and international legal frameworks are also liable. For example, NSAs have sovereign immunity within their local operational environments and international arbitrators are often reluctant to indict NSAs who they see as *helping Africa develop,* especially in the face of the declining state authority and weakening international trade of African countries. Considering the importance of NSAs in Africa's development, a need exists for more responsibility from the NSAs, particularly relative to human rights. More strategic and tangible obligations need to be attached to NSAs and more workable policy and legal frameworks must be put in place to make NSAs more accountable for more sustainable development and socio-political stability in the Sub-Saharan African region. NSAs have to be made to act more appropriately in a manner that can better enhance human rights in Africa.

NSAs have also played a positive humanitarian role in Africa and beyond. Important examples of such humanitarian roles are collective engagements to mount pressure on ANSAs to disarm, respect and adhere to national and global humanitarian norms (The Geneva Call). This includes advocacy for the ban on anti-personnel (AP) mines. These advocacy efforts of the NSAs have been widely acknowledged even by the European Union (EU) and the African Union (AU) as the advocacy not only involves benefits for humanitarian efforts but also peacebuilding and human security in Africa and around the world. NSA efforts thus promote the struggle for compliance with international humanitarian laws and policies for the ultimate protection of human rights for the common good and continental development and for the world at large.

Poverty and Non-state Actors

Arguably, the single most important development problem facing Africa is poverty. Africa is virtually synonymous with poverty. Poverty has an overarching influence on every other development problem in Africa be it health, human rights or even armed conflict. Many ethnic militias and terrorists in Africa, for example, cite socio-economic marginalization (poverty) as their main reason for taking up arms against the state. Even though Africa is heavily endowed with resources (it is the world's second largest continent only second to Asia, with a huge population and extensive natural resources), it is the poorest continent. The single most definitive underdevelopment identifier in Africa is poverty. From Nigeria to Malawi, Ghana, Sudan, Kenya, Zimbabwe, Congo, Burundi, Mozambique and Uganda and across the continent, poverty is preponderant and successive efforts to eradicate it have largely failed over the years. Around 70% of Africans live in poverty. In some countries like Zimbabwe, the figure is higher. Many in Africa, unlike Europe and America, live in extreme poverty with poverty outrunning the population and available resources. Over the years, overseas development assistance to the continent has fueled corruption, violence/conflict and aggravated poverty and built super rich political class amidst extraordinarily poor populations (Easterly 2007).

While most African countries depend on primary products like crude oil for foreign exchange, the continual decline in global prices has meant poor foreign exchange and aggravated poverty. Unfortunately, income from such primary products over the past years of favorable high prices was never wisely invested but rather embezzled. Most Africans live in rural areas making the continental average rurality about 70%. Although urbanization is increasing in places like Nigeria and Egypt, rural dwelling holds sway generally across Africa—rural dwelling is as high as over 80% in Ethiopia for example. The case is no different in East and Southern Africa which have the highest numbers of rural poor in the world. Most rural dwellers are poor, depending on subsistence agriculture and unfortunately local and international development assistance to agriculture has continued to decline. Development problems like deforestation, climate change, land degradation, overgrazing and erosion have also reached crisis levels and this has aggravated poverty in Africa especially as it co-relates with other crises on the continent.

It is against this background that NSAs become key actors in the development marketplace of Africa. It is apparent that governments in Africa lack the capacity and will to end poverty on the continent without any external partnerships. Such external assistance and partnerships include direct funding, technical assistance and oversight. For instance, United States Landsat Earth observation satellites have collected data that will help reduce hunger and poverty in Africa. This has also assisted Africa in harnessing technology for environmental management and poverty redress. The US Agency for International Development (USAID) and the UK Department for International Development (DFiD) have also been assisting African countries since the 1980s in the fight against poverty. The Swedish and Canadian governments through the Canadian International Development Agency (CIDA) and the Swedish International Development Cooperation Agency (SIDA) have also been at the forefront of NSAs' fight against poverty in Africa through capacity building, policy development, program funding, technical partnerships and experience sharing. This is in order to drive economic growth pragmatically and holistically and make governments work for everybody to reduce poverty in Africa through interventions in critical sectors of the countries. Such mutually reinforcing poverty-impacting areas include capacity building, climate change, agriculture, good governance, consolidated democracies and free and fair elections, health and natural resource management.

Local and international assistance and pressure in relation to poverty in Africa may have yielded some positive results over time. For example, poverty has responded slightly to interventions in Sub-Saharan Africa over the last two decades: while as many as about 56% of Sub-Saharan Africans lived in poverty in 1990 (by the less than $1.90 a day measure), this number declined slightly to 43% in 2012. This figure remained stable at slightly below 50% in 2016. Rapid population increase in the face of dwindling resources and increased unemployment, however, mean that difficult living conditions and poverty remain very high on the continent and in Sub-Saharan Africa particularly. Poverty remains a problem in Africa as more people are poor in Africa than in any other continent in the world.

Even when there have been some gains in education and health, gains in these sectors have not translated to widespread development, unlike in Brazil, India and China. While marked disparities exist in proportion and experiences of poverty in Africa, the high continental poverty burden overshadows pockets of poverty reduction success stories. For example, Ghana, has reduced its poverty burden by more than half in the last 26 years and Ethiopia, Rwanda, Botswana, Tanzania and Senegal have done well in reducing poverty by increasing agricultural investments and outputs as well as the adoption of some innovative poverty-reducing innovative policies like giving non-financial aid to poor families (an initiative borrowed from Brazil). An important point in this regard is that NSAs play an important role in these poverty-reducing efforts even though more is still needed from the NSAs to continue to fight poverty in Africa. Perhaps it can become history in the near future.

Armed Non-state Actors and Development in Africa

Issues around ANSAs are the most controversial in Africa as well as globally. ANSAs are major impediments to growth and development in Africa. From Al-Shabab (Kenya/Somalia) to Boko Haram (Nigeria), the Party for the Liberation of the Hutu People – National Liberation Forces (Palipehutu-FNL) (Burundi), Alliance des Patriotes pour un Congo Libre et Souverain (APCLS) (Congo), Forces

Démocratiques pour la Libération du Rwanda (FDLR) (Congo), Puntland State of Somalia (PSS) (Somalia) and so on, ANSAs have an impact on the peace and development infrastructure of the affected African states and the continent at large. Since development can only thrive in an atmosphere of peace, it is understandable that development remains elusive in spaces affected by ANSAs in Africa. Unfortunately, the development implications of ANSAs are wide ranging and critical. This is because local, national and international rules that regulate governments and other NSAs even in conflict situations appear not apply to ANSAs.

ANSAs often operate outside all laws and rules. They actually set their own rules outside the state and international frameworks to legitimize their interests and activism. Even when some ANSAs make efforts to comply with international human rights laws (IHLs) and cooperate with humanitarian organizations like the Geneva Call on humanitarian grounds in Africa, such cooperation is piecemeal, always concessionary and not enforceable as agreements are broken at will unlike when states are involved.

Many ANSAs take up arms against the state and deliberately undermine the state and state efforts to achieve group interests. While ANSAs fight the common enemy—the state—they also fight inwardly against themselves further making the implications and development deficits of ANSAs complicated and wide ranging. It is thus very difficult to regulate the destructive activities of ANSAs. For example, while it is possible to charge a government or president for crimes against humanity in cases of genocides and abuse of human rights of a group of people, it is practically impossible to apply such rules to ANSAs who do this regularly as a sign of their potency and capacity to undermine the state for their own interests. Destruction of lives and property are common objects of operations and negotiations of ANSAs. The more collateral the damage, the better for ANSAs and this has been demonstrated by the many ANSAs in Africa through hostage taking, suicide bombing, non-suicide bombing and random attacks on soft targets like crowded open markets, schools, hostels, shopping malls, stadiums and so on in Kenya, Somalia, Nigeria, Mali and Sudan among others. Unfortunately, African countries have not developed enough infrastructural and intelligence capacities to counteract ANSAs on the continent. This is why many of the ANSAs on the continent have continued to threaten development and have grown consistently in numbers and operations to the extent that some have graduated to the level of pledging allegiance to the Islamic State in Iraq and Syria (ISIS) to fortify, professionalize and globalize their operations.

As conflicts, wars and violence remain aggravated in Africa, poverty, hunger, internal displacement, ethnic cleansing and general underdevelopment hold sway on the continent. This is not surprising because conflicts, wars and violence are proven drivers of underdevelopment wherever they operate including the more developed systems. In Nigeria, for example, owing to the activities of Boko Haram, the northeastern part of the country, the epicenter of Boko Haram's operations, has one of the highest numbers of internally displaced persons in the world, as well as the most shut down schools, closed businesses, destroyed government infrastructure and abandoned private offices. Many of the local government areas and villages also remain deserted. How can development thrive in such a sociopolitical space? Boko Haram, by implication, not only affect northeastern Nigeria but also the entire country in development terms and the whole sub-region of West Africa as a whole, as Niger, Chad and Cameroun also directly bear the brunt of the terrorist group's venom. The case is similar in Burundi for example. The number and proportion of people living in poverty increased by 43% (21–64%) in Burundi as a result of the 13 years of war (1993–2006) in the country.

While many African countries are rich in resources, including but not limited to crude oil, diamonds and gold, conflicts and terrorism have made it impossible for these nations to peacefully translate the benefits of these resources to development. The resources actually partly fuel the conflict, militancy and terrorism. The now popular cliché of 'blood diamond' and 'oil curse' are relevant to this analysis. While conflict and violence through ANSAs in Africa may not necessarily be sufficient factors for the underdevelopment of Africa, they are nevertheless important. Other factors include corruption, misgovernance, external connivance, poor value addition to primary products, declining global prices of resources and technological advancement in providing alternatives globally. Armed struggles and conflicts through NSAs are, however, necessary and important factors in Africa's underdevelopment. Armed conflicts in NSA domains have translated to comparatively less competitive and less attractive investment climates, high insecurity, lower life expectancy, illiteracy, higher malnutrition and poverty and increased domestic violence. Cases abound but aggravated examples of these situations can be found in Kenya, Nigeria, Sudan, Democratic Republic of Congo, Somalia and the South-Botswana, Lesotho, Namibia, South Africa, Swaziland and Zambia. Africa can now be described as a continent under siege to violence, terrorism and ANSAs. Based on recent events, it can be submitted that ANSAs are on the increase and terrorism is on the rise in Africa with about 200 violent attacks between 2015 and 2017. Interestingly, these attacks are well planned, very focused and determined, well-coordinated and increasingly sophisticated. ANSAs are also quick to claim responsibilities on the continent to show their invincibility and supremacy to the state in terms of capacity to deploy violence as the object of negotiation and statement issuance.

There has been consistent violent extremism in North and West Africa and the Sahel. Terrorist threats are severe in Sudan, Mali, Niger, and Libya and international terrorist groups (like al-Qaeda and the Islamic State) have continually made these African countries their battle ground on the continent thereby undermining the socioeconomic growth of the continent. The Niger Delta and the Horn of Africa also present a rising and consolidated case of local terrorism and violent extremism in Africa. Of interest here are Niger Delta Avengers (NDA), the Movement for the Emancipation of the Niger Delta (MEND) and the rise of Al-Shabaab in Somalia and beyond to Kenya and Ethiopia for example. Of note generally is the fact that these ANSAs are the products and consequences of poor governance, weak and irresponsible state and continental security systems and apparatuses, poor coordination and deployment of anti-terrorism policies and structures in Africa. The attitude of many African nations and leaders is that if it is not affecting my country and it is not happening in my country, it is their problem not mine. This attitude is deep-rooted in Africa and it is affecting collective efforts against violence, terrorism and ANSAs on the continent. Until these problems are seen as collective ones to be collectively fought, they will proliferate and affect the continent as a whole. This is particularly so as most African countries lack the resources and capacity to fight ANSAs on their own. Collective, broad-based, multi-stakeholder approaches are thus key and the right way to go.

Many African countries also politicize and sensationalize the activities and threats of ANSAs. They erroneously describe such groups as 'disgruntled elements', 'political opponents', 'opposition groups', 'criminals', 'powerless troublemakers', 'mischief makers' and so on. Underrating ANSAs is the greatest undoing of African nations. It is these years of underestimation that have allowed most ANSAs to thrive and undermine development and states in Africa. Most African governments do not even take the time to understand the trajectories and drivers as well as root causes of ANSAs' extremism and violence. They disregard them and dispel their threats with a wave of hand yet the ANSAs remain potent. A good case in point is the case of Boko Haram in Nigeria. Boko Haram started as a simple, harmless, small religious group in Borno state Nigeria until it became violent, political and indoctrinated. When the sect was preaching radical Islam, political actors simply condoned this and used them for political gains against opponents. When it became national threats, the then President Goodluck Ebele Jonathan of Nigeria blatantly refused to recognize their destructive terrorist capabilities as he described them as a ploy of his northern opposition groups to blackmail his government. Not even the abduction of over 200 schoolgirls in Borno convinced the president of the serious threat posed by Boko Haram to Nigeria and Africa. He continued to make use of denial, politics and blame game narratives in relation to Boko Haram until the 2015 general elections. At that point, he suddenly realized how much damage his poor handling of the Boko Haram problem had done to his chances and his political credibility.

It is thus not surprising that President Goodluck Jonathan suffered a massive loss in the election to his rival. He became the very first sitting president to ever lose elections in the history of Nigeria. The two most important campaign points his opponent used to gather votes against him were promises to defeat Boko Haram and corruption—two extreme issues that were also traceable to terrorism in Nigeria. To check the proliferation of ANSAs in Africa and put the continent of the path to growth, it is important for states and continental/global stakeholders to check and counteract radical education, create more inclusive socioeconomic systems and deglamorize terrorism (NSAs). The media—both old and new—have a critical role to play in this regard. Long-term strategies must also be put in place to disarm and rehabilitate the ANSAs but both local/national and international development partners must be involved in this as no single African country has the capacity and resources to defeat violence, extremism and terrorism as core approaches of ANSAs on the continent. It is not until this is done that growth and development can be achieved in Africa.

Conclusion

This chapter has examined NSAs and their implications for development in Africa. The chapter triangulated academic and practice approaches to make the important subject covered relevant to broader users and increase its value across a broad spectrum of experts. The gap in the literature on Africa's development relative to the roles of NSAs was first engaged and a case made for the need to better factor NSAs into the development processes and narratives of Africa. The chapter also engaged the conceptualization and characterization of NSAs for a better understanding of their development trajectories and implications. Four critical areas of development were systematically adopted to demonstrate the dynamics and contours of the NSAs' role in the development marketplace of Africa. The areas adopted included health, human rights, poverty and humanitarian/general development of Africa. These four broad clusters of development indicators were presented in ways that demonstrate the strengths and weaknesses of the NSAs so the implications are clearer.

This chapter, unlike many others, boldly engaged the two core types of NSA to have a clear and harmonized perspective and understanding of the NSAs as they affect development in Africa. From the foregoing, it can be maintained that NSAs are very important to Africa's development and they play uniquely critical roles. They often fill the gaps in development where governments have failed and they hold important positive promises and prospects for the development of Africa. More coordination, monitoring, evaluation and political will are, however, needed on the part of African states and international partners to make all NSAs more transparent, more accountable, more synergistic and more responsible. Only then will NSAs be able to contribute positively to the sustainable development of Africa by reducing threats, minimizing waste and optimizing strengths and opportunities on the African continent for the continent of Africa.

References

Akanle, O. (2013). The development exceptionality of Nigeria: The context of political and social currents. *Africa Today, 59*(3), 31–48.

Akanle, O., & Omobowale, A. O. (2015). Trans-border banditry and integration in the ECOWAS region. In A. O. Olutayo & I. A. Adeniran (Eds.), *Regional economic communities: Exploring the process of socio-economic integration in Africa* (pp. 101–110). Dakar: CODESRIA.

Akanle, O., & Taiwo, P. A. (2013). Globalization and inequality. In R. Aborisade, A. O. Omobowale, & O. Akanle (Eds.), *Essentials of sociology* (pp. 283–294). Ibadan: Ibadan University Press.

Briscoe, I. 2013. Non-conventional armed violence and non-state actors as challenges for mediation and humanitarian action. Norwegian Peacebuilding Resource Centre Report. Oslo: Noref.

Bruderlein, C. (2000). *The role of non-state actors in building human security: The case of armed groups in intra-state wars*. Geneva: Centre for Humanitarian Dialogue.

Easterly, W. (2007). *The white man's burden: Why the West's efforts to aid the rest have done so much ill and so little good*. Camberwell: Penguin Books.

Ewumbue-Monono, C. (2006). Respect for international humanitarian law by armed non-state actors in Africa. *Review: Reports and Documents, 83*(864), 905–924.
Hofmann, C., & Schneckener, U. (2011). NGOs and nonstate armed actors: Improving compliance with international norms. *United States Institute of Peace Special Report, 284*, 1–13.
Malka, H. (2015). *The challenge of non-state actors*. In*Global Forecast, Centre for International Studies* (pp. 1–2).
Maseng, J. O. (2014). *State and non-state actors in South African public policy*. In*Policy Brief*. Pretoria: Africa Institute of South Africa.
Steer, L., Gilliard, J., Gustafsson-Wright, E., & Latham, M. (2015). *Non-state actors in education in developing countries: A framing paper for discussion*. Paper prepared as background to the Annual Research Symposium of the Centre for Universal Education held 5–6 March. Washington, DC: Centre for Universal Education at Brookings.
Valensi, C. (2015). Non-state actors: A theoretical limitation in a changing Middle East. *Military and Strategic Affairs, 7*(1), 59–78.
Weiss, T. G., Seyle, D.C., & Coolidge, K. (2013). *The rise of non-state actors in global governance: Opportunities and limitations* (Discussion Paper). One Earth Foundation, pp. 1–13.
World Bank. (2011). *Healthy partnerships: How governments can engage the private sector to improve health in Africa*. http://www.ifc.org/wps/wcm/connect/industry_ext_content/ifc_external_corporate_site/industries/health+and+education/news/features_health_healthypartnerships. Accessed 10 Aug 2016.
World Health Organization (WHO). (2008). *Capacity building to constructively engage the private sector in providing essential health care services*. http://apps.who.int/gb/archive/pdf_files/EB124/B124_18-en.pdf. Accessed 10 Aug 2016.

Olayinka Akanle, PhD, is a Lecturer in the Department of Sociology, University of Ibadan, Nigeria. He has received many scholarly awards like been a Postdoctoral Fellow at the South African Research Chair Initiative (SARChI) in Social Policy, College of Graduate Studies, University of South Africa (UNISA), South Africa; World Social Science Fellow (WSSF) of The International Social Science Council (ISSC), Paris, France, Laureate of Council for the Development of Social Science Research in Africa (CODESRIA) and University of Ibadan Postgraduate School Prize for scholarly publication awardee. He has published many articles internationally and he has co-edited many books. He is the author of Kinship Networks and International Migration in Nigeria (2013). His research interests include: Sociology of Development and Development Studies, Social Theory, Social Policy, Sociology of Religion, Migration and Diaspora Studies, Child, Youth, Gender and the Family in Post-Colonial Africa. E-mails: yakanle@yahoo.com, yk.akanle@ui.edu.ng.

Chapter 17
Globalization and Africa's Development

Olanrewaju Emmanuel Ajiboye

Introduction

We live in a globalizing and increasingly interdependent world. For instance, in developing societies in Africa and Asia, among others, dependence on the developed and industrialized rich nations remains a stark fact of economic life. The so-called developing countries are becoming even more economically dependent on the developed nations (Todaro and Smith 2009). In the last three decades or more, globalization has not only become a major topic of discussion both in academic and business circles but also a source of concern in economic circles. The integration of various communities, villages, towns and countries into the global markets has created a wide range of opportunities for greater growth, and presents a potential opportunity for developing countries to improve their economy as well as their living standards (Todaro and Smith 2001; Todaro 2000). However, this comes with its attendant problems as most developing countries of the world are focusing attention on the downside risks of this emerging new phenomenon with concerns arising over the risks of marginalizing the less industrialized countries of the world. This in itself has given rise to a sense of misgiving and anxiety, particularly among developing countries over the consequences of the globalization phenomenon on various developmental strategies and policies. Having said this, this chapter will briefly examine the historical and developmental specificities of globalization. The theoretical contours of globalization will also be critically reviewed. The impact of globalization on Africa's development from its inception to date will be reviewed. The role that Africa played in the globalization processes and the extent to which Africa benefited/did not benefit from globalization will be focal points of discussion in the chapter.

O.E. Ajiboye (✉)
Department of Sociology, Faculty of Social Sciences,
Lagos State University, Ojo, Lagos, Nigeria
e-mail: oeajiboye@yahoo.com; olanrewaju.ajiboye@lasu.edu.ng

O. Akanle, J.O. Adésìnà (eds.), *The Development of Africa*, Social Indicators Research Series 71, DOI 10.1007/978-3-319-66242-8_17

In view of the forgoing, it is necessary to say that so much has been written about globalization that it is really of no use to start seeking definitions. For instance, at the level of the daily lives of ordinary citizens, it is even doubtful whether our people are really interested in one way or the other in what intellectual ideas on the topic may be. Rather, this is a manifestation of their collective cynicism toward this concept. Unless we are able to capture the reasons for this drift, we run the risk of merely speaking to ourselves.

In spite of the position above, it would be germane to examine a few of the various definitions of globalization as given or defined by various writers. However, before considering the various definitions, we must make it abundantly clear that the concept of globalization is a complex one therefore it has not lent itself to one particular definition. The simple reason for this may not be unconnected with the multidisciplinary status of the phenomenon of globalization. Hence, globalization has been defined from many disciplinary points of view such as Economics, Political Science, Sociology, Humanities, Arts, Music, and so forth. Globalization has become the defining process of contemporary society. According to Khor (1996), globalization is a polarized concept and paradigm which means different things to different people, depending on their worldview, orientation and perspectives. Globalization is multifaceted with a multiplicity of interpretations. Put differently, globalization means different things to different people across cultures. Some describe it as the movement of people, language, ideas and products around the world. Others consider it as the dominance of multinational corporations and the promotion of ethnocentrism with its attendant socially destructive consequences for the cultural identities of the developing societies. Globalization broadly refers to the expansion of global linkages, the organization of social life on a global scale, and the growth of a global consciousness, hence to the consolidation of world society. This definition expresses both the scope and context of what globalization means or refers to in most literature. However, in spite of this there is still no consensus or universal agreement on its meaning. It encompasses several large processes hence definitions differ in what they emphasize. Globalization is historically complex; definitions vary in terms of the particular driving force they identify. The meaning of the term is itself a topic of global discussion; it may refer to 'real' processes, ideas that justify them, or to a way of thinking about them.

Finally, in the most basic terms, the globalization of the world economy is the weaving together of the economies of the various societies through trade, financial flows, technology and information, and the movement of people. The rising importance of world trade and capital flows in the world economy today can be attributed to the extent of the trend towards integration of the world economy. This has contributed to increased gross domestic product (GDP) through international trading activities across the world. These are seen in the growth experienced in cross-border financial flows, particularly in the form of private equity and portfolio investment, compared with the past. Furthermore, the revolution in communication and transportation technology and the much improved availability of information have allowed individuals and firms to base their economic choices more on the quality of the economic environment in different countries. As a result, economic success in today's world is less a question of relative resource endowments or geographical location than it used to be in the past. Now, it is more a question of the market perception of the orientation and predictability of economic policy. The main objectives of this chapter are to investigate the nexus of interaction between the phenomenon of globalization and Africa's development. However, to achieve this, other specific objectives include:

- examining the various drivers of globalization in Africa.
- investigating the various forces and elements of globalization in Africa.
- determining the impact of globalization on Africa's development.
- examining critically the roles Africa has played in the globalization process.
- determining the extent to which Africa is benefiting/not benefiting from globalization.
- suggesting how Africa can better appropriate globalization.

Theoretical Understanding of Globalization

Theory of Globalization

The theory of globalization emerges from the global mechanisms of greater integration with particular emphasis on the sphere of economic transactions. In this sense, this perspective is similar to the world-systems approach. However, one of the most important characteristics of the globalization position is its focus and emphasis on cultural aspects and their communication worldwide. Rather than economic, financial and political ties, globalization scholars argue that the main modern elements for development interpretation are the cultural links among nations. In this cultural communication, one of the most important factors is the increasing flexibility of technology to connect people around the world (Adorno 2000, 2003).

The main aspects of the theory of globalization can be delineated as follows:

- The recognition that global communication systems are increasing in importance every day, and through this process all nations are interacting much more frequently and easily, not only at the governmental level, but also within the citizenry.
- Even though the main communication systems are operating among the more developed nations, these mechanisms are also spreading in their use to less developed nations. This fact will increase the possibility that marginal groups in poor nations can communicate and interact within a global context using the new technology.
- The modern communication systems imply structural and important modifications in the social, economic and cultural patterns of nations. In terms of the economic activities the technological advances in communications are becoming more accessible to local and small business. This situation is creating a completely new environment for carrying out economic transactions, utilizing productive

resources, equipment, trading products, and taking advantage of the "virtual monetary mechanisms". From a cultural perspective, the new communication products are unifying patterns of communication around the world, at least in terms of economic transactions under the current conditions.
- The concept of minorities within particular nations is being affected by these new patterns of communication. Although these minorities are not completely integrated into the new world systems of communication, the powerful business and political elites in each country are a part of this interaction around the world. Ultimately, the business and political elite continue to be the decision-makers in developing nations.
- Cultural elements will dictate the forms of economic and social structure in each country. These social conditions are a result of the dominant cultural factors within the conditions of each nation.

The main assumptions which can be extracted from the theory of globalization can be summarized in three principal points. First, cultural factors are the determining aspect in every society. Second, it is not important, under current world conditions, to use the nation-state as the unit of analysis, since global communications and international ties are making this category less useful. Third, with more standardization in technological advances, more and more social sectors will be able to connect themselves with other groups around the world. This situation will involve both the dominant and non-dominant groups from each nation.

Globalization theories emphasize cultural factors as the main determinants of the economic, social and political conditions of nations, which is similar to the 'comprehensive social school' of Max Weber's theories. From this perspective, the system of values and beliefs, and the pattern of identity of dominant groups (or hegemony) and alternative (or subordinate) groups within a society are the most important elements in explaining national characteristics in economic and social terms (Adorno 1992). It is obvious that for the globalization position this statement from 1920s Weberian theory must apply to current world conditions, especially in terms of the diffusion and transference of cultural values through communication systems, which are increasingly affecting many social groups in all nations.

Theory of World Systems

A central element from which the theory of world systems emerged was the different form that capitalism has taken around the world, especially since the 1960s. Beginning in the emerging period, the theory provides a premise for new conditions in Third World countries to elevate their standards of living and improve social conditions and the overall well-being of the citizenry. These new conditions were related to the fact that the international financial and trade systems began to take on a more flexible character, in which national government exerted less and less influence. Basically, the new economic conditions provided a motive for a group of radical researchers led by Immanuel Wallerstein to conclude that there were new activities in the capitalist world economy that could not be explained within the confines of the dependency perspective (Unerman 2003).

This group of researchers found that there are worldwide conditions that operate as determinant forces especially for small and underdeveloped nations, and that the nation-state level of analysis is no longer the only useful category for studying development conditions, particularly in Third World countries. The various factors which had the greatest impact on the internal development of small countries were the new global systems of communication, the new world trade mechanisms, the international financial system, and the transference of knowledge and military links. These factors have created their own dynamic at the international level, and at the same time these elements are interacting with the internal aspects of each country.

The tenets of the world-systems theory include that (i) there is a strong link between social sciences—especially among sociology, economics and political disciplines. This school recognizes that more attention is usually given to the individual development of each of these disciplines rather than to the interaction among them and how these interactions affect in real terms the national conditions of a given society; (ii) instead of addressing the analysis of each of the variables, it is necessary to study the reality of social systems; and (iii) it is necessary to recognize the new character of the capitalist system. For example, the approach followed by the classical political economy perspective was based on the conditions of the capitalist system during the Industrial Revolution in the United Kingdom. There was concrete evidence to support open competition, more productive patterns in the industrial sector, and large groups of the population which provided labor for the newly established factories (Wallerstein 1974a, b).

Today this is not the situation especially when we consider the important economic role of transnational corporations, the international political climate, the interdependence that affects the governments of poor nations, and the role of speculative investments. For the world systems school, current economic conditions are not fully explainable by traditional development theories. This criticism of the capitalist system has been present since its emergence. Under current international conditions, there are specific features of monopoly capital, its means of transaction, and its concrete operations worldwide which have affected international relations among nations to a considerable degree. From the analysis of the various characteristics of world systems theory, it becomes evident that the main unit of analysis is the social system, which can be studied at the internal level of a country, and also from the external environment of a particular nation. This social system affects several nations and usually also an entire region.

The world systems most frequently studied in this theoretical perspective are systems concerning the research, application and transference of productive and basic technology, the financial mechanisms, and world trade operations. In terms of financial resources, this development position distinguishes between productive and speculative investments. Productive investments are financial resources which reinforce manufacturing production in a particular nation, while speculative investments normally entail fast profits in the stock market; they do not provide a country with a sustainable basis for long-term economic growth and therefore are more volatile (Wallerstein 1979, 1999). When world systems theory considers trade mechanisms, it distinguishes between the direct transactions, which are those that have a greater, more significant and immediate effect on a country, and those operations which are indirect trade transactions, such as future trade stipulations, and speculation on transportation costs and combustibles prices and forecasts on agricultural crops when they depend on weather conditions to obtain their productivity and yield.

Conspiracy Theory

Conspiracy theory is a term used to explain a situation that clashes with what people believe in, or have believed in any given society for a long period of time (Perez 2001; Kotilainen and Katila 2002). Accepting new information that runs counter to a current practice or belief system may not be easy and can cause feelings of cognitive dissonance, which is a term used in modern psychology to describe the feeling of discomfort that arises from being confronted with two or more conflicting ideas, beliefs or values. Sociologically, where this happened it results in what has been described as cultural lag. It therefore suggests that we have an inner drive to hold onto all our beliefs and attitudes, avoiding the feelings of discomfort and instability that accompany new ideas, regardless of whether those ideas are backed by evidence and sound logic. Most intellectual works in conspiracy theories and conspiracism present a range of assumptions as a basis for studying the phenomenon of globalization. Conspiracism serves the needs of diverse political and social groups anywhere in the world. It identifies elites, blames them for economic and social catastrophes, and assumes that things will be better once popular action can remove them from positions of power. As such, conspiracy theories do not typify a particular epoch in history or ideology of a particular groups or individuals.

The history of African societies has shown that African political and economic leaders have genuinely been the cause of enormous amounts of death and misery, and they sometimes have engaged in conspiracies while at the same time promoting conspiracy theories about their targets. When examined critically within the nexus of globalization and African's development, it is found that the role played by political and economic elites in Africa, particularly as when it comes to the impact of globalization on African's development, is enormous. For instance, while the political elite in the former colonies was constituted as the new leadership to run the states as a bureaucratic comprador bourgeoisie, the business elite known as the national elite was to serve as the agents of foreign capital, in other words as petty bourgeoisie. Thus what emerged from the compromise was known as neocolonialism.

Furthermore, although independence was granted to the former colonies, the structural and institutional foundations of imperialist exploitation were strengthened through the accommodation of the national elite and the accentuation and internationalization of imperialist exploitation through the accommodation of the new exploiter powers. The political elite took over power to consolidate the previous policies and programs of the imperial powers. The rise of the new colonial system, which was characterized by (i) exploitation and direct political control and (ii) the involvement of new powers such as the United States, Japan and Germany in the economies of the former colonies, has been associated with more vigorous advocacy of liberalization. Hence, African's development predicament may not be unconnected with the roles played by African elites in conspiring against their own people and maintaining the structure of inequality between the African economy and that of the rest of the world. A critical review of our theories indicates clearly that globalization and world systems theories take a global perspective in determining the unit of analysis, rather than focusing strictly on the nation-state as was the case in the modernization and dependency schools. The contrasting point between world systems theory and globalization is that the first contains certain neo-Marxist elements, while the second bases its theoretical foundations on the structural and functionalist sociological movement. Therefore the globalization approach tends more toward a gradual transition rather than a violent or revolutionary transformation. For globalist authors, the gradual changes in societies become a reality when different social groups adapt themselves to current innovations, particularly in the areas of cultural and technological communication. On the other hand, conspiracy theory emphasizes that the rise of the new colonial system was characterized by (i) exploitation and direct political control and (ii) the involvement of new powers such as the United States, Japan and Germany in the economies of the former colonies has been associated with more vigorous advocacy of liberalization.

Definition of Terms

Development

The concept of development means different things to different people or societies. It is a relative term that describes different situations in different epochs. Development in human society is a multifaceted phenomenon. At the level of the individual it implies increased skill and capacities, greater freedom, creativity, self-discipline, responsibility and material well-being. At the level of countries, development implies an increasing capacity to regulate both internal and external relationships. Much of human history has been a fight for survival against natural hazards and against real and imagined human enemies. Development was universal because the conditions leading to economic expansion were universal; however, development cannot be seen purely as economic affairs, rather it is an overall social process which is dependent upon the outcome of man's efforts to deal with his natural environment. The first sociological account of the development was modernization theory, which held that the less developed countries would eventually catch up with the industrialized world, provided they emulate the economic and social systems of Western capitalism. Modernization theory conceptualized development as a staged transition from tradition to modernity brought about at the economic level by the operations of the market and foreign investment; at the social level by the adoption of appropriate Western institutions, values and behavior; and at the political level by the implementation of parliamentary democracy. There has also been a renewed analytic emphasis on the interdependency and integration among nations, not just in term of economic processes, but also at the level of culture and ideology. This premise has significant and growing overlaps with sociological debate about globalization and the environment.

Sustainable Development

Evidence abounds that the most critical debate in the intellectual arena in the contemporary world is to bring about the most beneficial aspects of the two dominant global issues preceding the globe into the new millennium, namely, sustainable development and globalization. These two important concepts appear to occupy two polar opposites. Put differently, the two concepts tend to have two opposing tendencies within them which this section of this chapter tries to address by balancing the demand for sustainable development and the goal. The definition of sustainable development varies from one society to another. However, the internationally accepted definition emphasizes the need for a long-term planning horizon, and the adoption of a development path that improves the quality of life of the current generation, while leaving future generations with at least the same capacity and option for development. Sustainable development reflects the process that meets the needs of the present without compromising the ability of future generations to meet their own needs. In other words, sustainable development is the ability to achieve today's development by all standards and not compromise future development. This is often called intergenerational equality—the ideas is that we should share natural resources not just with people who are alive on the planet today but also with inhabitants in future generations. The realization of this has impelled both national and international organizations to embark on various efforts to bring about measures to achieve development today without compromising the future of others.

Globalization

Globalization in simple terms denotes the expanding scale, growing magnitude, speeding and deepening impact of transcontinental flows and patterns of social interaction. It refers to a shift or transformation in the scale of human organization that links distant communities and expands the reach of power relations across the world's regions and continents. Globalization can be examined from two different but interdependent points of views. The first viewpoint is to examine globalization as an inevitable effect of economic growth which includes industry, technology, communication, and so on. As we experience growth in the economy, it is natural and expected for a global market to become established in previously local areas. While we look forward to the establishment of global markets in previously local areas, free trade and the free movement of capital are important and a crucial part of the processes. Globalization is not just an expansion but an increasingly integrated global economy. Therefore, to achieve integration of the global economy, economic freedom is necessary. The second point of view is to examine globalization as a deliberate process, and this is almost certainly more accurate. Yes, there is a degree of inevitability involved, but this is due in large part to the agreements made between nations, between corporations, among others. Business wants globalization and it has almost single-handedly caused it to happen. The emergent globalization in human society was not a humanitarian effort but rather a vision of business opportunities. And these visions become grander and more easily conceived as technological and political progress, globalization also progresses.

Drivers of Globalization in Africa

The phenomenon of globalization can be said to be driven by many factors. There is not just one driver of globalization but rather several drivers which could be summarized into five major areas as discussed below. The media and almost every discussion on globalization by international business speak about different drivers of globalization. These can basically be separated into five different groups: namely, technological drivers; political drivers; market drivers; cost drivers; and competitive drivers. The first and the most talked about is the commoditization of information and communication technology (ICT) infrastructure—computers, software and the internet.

The first two drivers above are now fueling the third driver, economic expansion of emerging markets and new business venturing. Entrepreneurial capitalism is expanding around the world. For example, the Global Entrepreneurship Monitor reports that there are more than 500 million adults actively involved in entrepreneurial activities around the world. China and India are two countries leading this pervasive adoption of free-market ideology and the introduction of free enterprise, entrepreneurial capitalism into their societies. In fact, there are more than 100 million entrepreneurs in each of these two countries. As domestic markets become more and more saturated, the opportunities for growth are limited and global expanding is a way most organizations choose to overcome this situation. Common customer needs and the opportunity to use global marketing channels and transfer marketing to some extent are also incentives to choose internationalization. Sourcing efficiency and costs vary from country to country and global firms can take advantage of this fact. Other cost drivers to globalization are the opportunity to build global scale economies and the high product development costs nowadays (Ferrier 2004).

With the global market, global inter-firm competition increases and organizations are forced to 'play' international. Strong interdependencies among countries and extensive two-way trade and FDI action also support this driver.

Elements of Globalization in Africa

The increase in the volume, scale, and velocity of social interactions has been a force behind globalization in Africa. Globalization has many detractors, who claim that global capital privileges profit over local interests and deplore the 'Westernization' of local cultures and what they see as the negation of local identities and autonomies. Others suggest that globalization is a dialectical process; although it invades local contexts of action, it doesn't destroy them. Instead, new forms of local existence and expression emerge. Local products can be globally advertised via the World Wide Web, and emerging agricultural countries of Africa can begin to sell to Western supermarkets through global commodity chains, which have lowered the threshold of entry for smaller enterprises. Basically, globalization rests on a tripod of elements, namely:

1. The expansion of markets (economic), challenges to the state and institutions (political), and the rise of new social and political movements (cultural). Economically, technological changes and government deregulation have permitted the establishment of transnational network in production, trade, and finance, creating what is referred to as a 'borderless world.'
2. The political power—political power and activities extend across the boundaries of nation-states while policymaking on issues such as human rights, environmental degradation and nuclear safety have required global consensus.
3. The cultural element—the third element of globalization affects more than markets and states. It is altering the lives of people across the globe.

Historical Development of Globalization

Globalization as a phenomenon is not a new concept. History has revealed how national borders had been forcibly broken and left wide open by our colonial masters prior to the amalgamation experiences of most Africans. The origin of globalization can be traced back to the early fifteenth century which was the era of European expansion, settlement and colonialization of most African countries. What this translates to mean is that the current globalization is not the first in history. History equally reminds us how many able-bodied forebears, men and women, were taken as slaves by the European to work in their various plantations to develop their economy. This era can be termed the era of mercantilism. Most of our local produce was condemned and described as inferior and substandard; however, it was later carted away as raw materials to feed their companies producing refined products. This was an era during which the industrial expansion campaign by Britain, France, Portugal, Spain and Germany among many other nations was driven by the spirit of imperialism aimed at the accumulation of capital. The famous Trans-Atlantic trade was part of the mercantilist globalization. The founding of Latin America by Portugal and Spain through its discovery by Christopher Columbus and others was part of the mercantilist movement. Although the term globalization had not been coined during this era of discovery, the period could be said to be characterized by mercantilist activities that indirectly began in all the continents in the name of searching for markets and raw materials.

It is a known fact that the goals of globalization cannot be achieved without removing all obstacles to the free movement of capital and labor and implementing liberal policies. However, this may not have been possible if Africans had not played key roles in the globalization process. The policies that integrated African countries into the world economy were necessitated by the Industrial Revolution in Britain which called for human and raw materials to be used in the industries (Todaro 1981). From the 16th to the early nineteenth century, Africa played an important part in the growth and development of the world economy. It served as a source of slaves and raw materials for the white settler plantations and the mines in the New World. Britain began to preach the gospel of 'free trade' following her emergence as the first industrialized capitalist power. This she did with the aim of removing the mercantile barriers to her manufactured products that were exported to other countries. In the last quarter of the nineteenth century and the first decade of the twentieth century, France, the United States, Germany, Belgium, Italy and Japan joined the industrialist capitalist race (Todaro 1981, 1997). The resultant effect of this race was the industrial carving up of the world which began a new phase of globalization, encapsulated in the colonization of Africa, Asia and Latin America.

Thus, during the nineteenth century, the continent was progressively transformed as an additional source of raw materials for European factories and also, by the end of the century, as a market for goods from their factories. The famous Berlin Conference led to the partition of Africa while Asia and Latin America were also shared among the leading imperial powers. This period marked the era of colonialism in which these continents were invaded by the European countries for human and raw material resources for their industries. This was mainly done through the slave trade, colonialism, neocolonialism and now globalization. The period of colonialism marked the emergence of new industrialized powers that were not part of the old system, for example the United States, Japan and Germany began to show interest as a means of advancing their economic strength. This generated rivalries among the new economic powers and the traditional economic powers. As colonial imperialism developed, the contradiction generated gave rise to the growth and development of nationalism within the colonies. There was compromise in which the new economic power and the traditional economic power, which included firstly the investment and other economic interests of the traditional colonial power in each colony, were to be left untouched. Secondly, the new powers were allowed free access to the former colonies, in other words the former colonies were to be open to the new powers.

Finally, the political elite in the former colonies were constituted as the new leadership to run the states as a bureaucratic comprador bourgeoisie, and the business elite known as the national elite served as agents of foreign capital, in other words as petty bourgeoisie. Thus what emerged from the compromise was known as neocolonialism. In addition, the independence which was granted to the former colonies had the structural and institutional foundations of imperialist exploitation strengthened through the accommodation of the national elite and with the accentuation and internationalization of imperialist exploitation through the accommodation of the new exploiter powers. The political elite took over power to consolidate the policies and programs of the imperial powers. The rise of new colonial system was characterized by (i) exploitation and direct political control and (ii) the involvement of new powers such as the United States, Japan and Germany in the economies of the former colonies and has been associated with more vigorous advocacy of liberalization. It should be mentioned here that the fact that Africa became the supplier of the industrial raw materials and energy needs of developed countries while the Africans themselves stood at the receiving end was made possible because of the roles played by the African socio-political and economic elites.

Impact of Globalization on Africa's Development

Globalization holds wide ranging improvements particularly for the economic state of a country. According to Adedeji (2012), globalization should benefit all countries and should raise the welfare of all people. This implies that it should raise the rate of economic growth in poor countries and reduce world poverty (Ravillion 2003). It should not increase inequalities or undermine socioeconomic security within countries. Added to this, the real test for globalization is whether it significantly speeds up development and the reduction of absolute poverty in the world, and whether it ensures economic, social and environmental sustainability. Hence, the impact of globalization should not be confined to poor countries that have been marginalized from the process.

For people in richer countries, the information revolution is helping to forge a sense of global community and transnational solidarity. This is visible in the growth of global coalitions of non-state actors around issues of universal concern such as globalization itself, the environment, human rights, humanitarian aid and labor exploitation. In addition, Adedeji (1981; Ogunsola 2005) emphasized that the global information revolution has also clearly affected cultures and social values. The fear contemporarily is that constant exposure of the images of Western life styles and role models could lead to tensions and gross diffusion both culturally and socially, and it has been experienced as divisive by developing nations. For instance, in Nigeria the main mode of dress among the youth (aged 15–35 years): males wear earrings and draw their trousers down below their waist (fondly called 'sagging') and the female dress similarly. These, to mention just a few, are considered strange to Africa culture (Tebin and Estabrooks 1995; Tendon 1998a, b). On the aspect of growth of illicit cross-border activities, Khor (1996) remarked that global interconnectivity, which facilitates legitimate cross-border economic transactions, has helped to increase tax evasion, money laundering, trafficking in people and trade in sex and drugs. In this regard, such nefarious activities caused a great setback to developing nations, in particular to Nigeria over the years based on serial activities of political stooges to the West and some sycophants that have arm-twisted the development of the country.

Benefits of Globalization to Africa

Globalization is the term used to describe the trend towards countries joining together economically, through politics and education. Countries joining together economically view themselves not just through their national identities, but as part of the world as a whole. The dynamism of globalization is engineered by the rate of development and the level of intensified interdependence which makes it almost impossible for any nation to isolate itself if it is to develop. All nations have tendencies to benefit from the interdependence which is manifested in the increasing economic linkage among countries through trade, financial flow and so forth. Below is a list of a few of the many benefits of globalization to Africa's development. Firstly, globalization benefits certain countries more, such as those in the First World or the Global North. These advantages include:

- Resources of different countries are used for the producing goods and services they are able to do most efficiently.
- Consumers to get a much wider variety of products to choose from.
- Consumers get the product they want at more competitive prices.
- Companies are able to procure the input goods and services required at the most competitive prices.
- Companies get access to much wider markets.
- Globalization promotes understanding and goodwill among different countries.
- Businesses and investors get much wider opportunities for investment.
- The adverse impact of fluctuations in agricultural production in one area can be reduced by pooling the production of different areas.
- Globalization helps in bringing the whole world together as one village. Every consumer has free and frequent access to the products of foreign countries.
- Optimum use of natural resources is possible.
- Helpful in cost reduction by eliminating cross-border duties and fees.

However, as a result of globalization, many local brands and businesses in poorer developing countries go bankrupt and cannot survive the economic might of the rich countries. Local cultures and traditions change. People no longer wear national costumes because they all want to look like Hollywood stars and wear jeans, for example. People want to become 'American' and consume everything American. Also because of globalization, more and more people are learning and speaking English to the detriment of local languages. There are more international schools and the focus now is on the acquisition of this global language rather than their own mother tongue. The disadvantages of globalization include the following:

- Developed countries can stifle development of undeveloped and underdeveloped countries.
- Economic depression in one country can trigger an adverse reaction across the globe.
- Globalization can increase spread of communicable diseases.
- Companies face much greater competition. This can put smaller companies at a disadvantage as they do not have resources to compete on a global scale.
- Globalization increases the gap between the poor and the rich.
- Cultural convergence—more people are moving towards Western fashion.
- Environmental harm—resources are used up—scarcity creates externalities, pollution and waste products.
- Globalization demands more of skilled workers causing redundancy of skilled workers.
- Globalization is a direct attack on local small industry.
- Global companies with hi-fi infrastructure have almost ruined local traditional small and medium industries.
- Globalization increases cut-throat competition.
- Globalization increases monopolization by countries equipped with know-how and power.

Panacea to Africa's Development

In order for Africa to enjoy the benefits of globalization as enumerated above and achieve meaningful development, the various political dispensations of Africa must strive to tackle the intricacies that are bedeviling the continent. Accordingly, the following must be achieved:

- Corruption should be eliminated or at least reduced to the bare minimum.
- A strong message should be sent to the West not to provide of safe havens for Africa's economic looters.
- Military and other forms of assistance to combat insurgency must be intensified.
- Provision and assistance for the internally displaced persons (IDPs) within the continent which is increasing at an alarming rate, considering the sociodemographic characteristics involved.
- Trade – effective bilateral relationships must be pursued and sustained by all parties.
- Financial assistance 'grants' should be supplied to combat poverty and boost agriculture in order to enhance employment of the unemployed.

- Assistance in the area of security challenge(s) and aa host of other social problems.
- Improvement in political and democratization processes.
- Enthronement of rightful political leaders with appropriate will to galvanize the nation to development.

Conclusion

Globalization is a product of human processes, and the advantage belongs to those with adequate management of human resources. There is no doubt that the world is growing rapidly and developing into a single world unit, otherwise known as the 'global village'. Rapid movement in realizing the new and ongoing process of reforms and the effect of globalization is a direct function of (national) development. Africa, Nigeria in particular may in the near future begin to emerge as one of the leading active participants in the world economic order if the necessary conditions for rapid development are in place. These include:

- Gear towards formidable political leadership.
- Improved export capacity (agricultural produce, resourceful manpower etc.) and decreased importation.
- Reduction in volume of external debt in order to relieve the burden of debt servicing.
- Curb mismanagement and corruption.
- Re-invigorate absolute independence and tactical withdrawal from imperialism and neo-imperialism.

Thus, if the above recommendations as identified are put in place and instituted, Africa might be on the path of galvanizing development and benefiting from the advantages accruable from globalization.

References

Adedeji, A. (1981). *Indigenization of African economies*. New York: Africana Pub.Co.

Adedeji, A. (2012) Corruption and development in Nigeria: A psychological perspective. *Global Journal of Human-Social Sciences Research*, 12(9).

Adorno, T. (1992). *Notes to literature* (Vol. 2). New York: Columbia University Press.

Adorno, T. (2000). In B. O'Connor (Ed.), *The Adorno reader*. Malden: Blackwell.

Adorno, T. (2003). *Negative dialectics*. New York: Continuum.

Ferrier, W. J. (2004). *Drivers of globalization: Integration of theories and models*. Munich: GRIN, Verlay, Georgia.

Khor, M. (1996). *Globalisation: Implications for development policy*. A chapter delivered at the 8th general conference of the European Association of Development Research and Training Institutes at Vienna on 11–14 September.

Kotilainen, M., & Kaitila, V. (2002). Economic globalization in developing countries. *The Journal of Economics in Developing Countries, 3*, 70.

Ogunsola, L. A. (2005). Information and communication technologies and the effects of globalization: Twenty-first century "digital slavery" for developing countries—Myth or reality? *Electronic Journal of Academic and Special Librarianship, 2*, 1–2.

Pérez, E., & others. (2001). *Un análisis del Tratado de Libre Comercio entre el Triángulo del Norte y México*. Estudios y perspectivas series, no. 3 (LC/L.1605-P), Santiago, Chile, Economic Commission for Latin America and the Caribbean (ECLAC). United Nations publication, Sales no. S.01.II.G.145.

Ravillion, M. (2003). The debate on globalization, poverty and inequality: Why measurement matters. *International Affairs, 79*, 739–753.

Tebin, H. M., & Estabrooks, M. (1995). The globalization of telecommunications: Study in the struggle to control markets and technology. *Journal of Economic Issues, 29*(2), 535.

Tendon, Y. (1998a). Globalization and Africa options (part two) *AAPS Newsletter*, Harare African Association of Political Science, May–Aug, 3(1).

Tendon, Y. (1998b). Globalization and Africa options (part three). *AAPS Newsletter*, Harare African Association of Political Science, Sep–Dec, 3(1).

Todaro, M. (1981). *Economic development in the third world*. New York: Longman.

Todaro, M. (1997). *The urban informal sector in developing countries: Employment, poverty and environment*. Geneva: International Labour Office.

Todaro, M. P. (2000). *Economic development*. New York: Longman.

Todaro, M. P., & Smith, S. C. (2001). *Economic development*. Essex: Pearson Education.

Todaro, M. P., & Smith, S. C. (2009). *Economic development* (10th ed.). Harlow: Pearson Addison Wesley.

Unerman, J. (2003). Enhancing organizational global hegemony with narrative accounting disclosures: An early example. *Accounting Forum, 27*(4), 425–448.

Wallerstein, I. (1974a). The rise and future demise of the world capitalist system: Concepts for comparative analysis. *Comparative Studies in Society and History, 16*(4), 387–415.

Wallerstein, I. (1974b). *The modern world system*. New York: Academic Press.

Wallerstein, I. (1979). *The capitalist world-economy: Essays*. London: Cambridge University Press.

Wallerstein, I. (1999). Globalization or the age of the trajectory of the world-system. Online chapters.

Olanrewaju Emmanuel Ajiboye joined the service of Lagos State University, Ojo, Lagos about a decade and half ago where he currently teaches and carries out researches in Social Gerontology, Gender, Theories and Research Methodology. He holds Ph.D in Sociology with specialization in Gender and Social Gerontology from University of Lagos, Akoka, Lagos, Nigeria. He has taught courses at both undergraduate and postgraduate levels. He has held various academic and administrative positions in the University. His research articles have appeared in learned journals, locally and internationally. Contact Emails – oeajiboye@yahoo.com & olanrewaju.ajiboye@lasu.edu.ng.

Chapter 18
Breaking the Incubus? The Tripartite Free Trade Agreements and the Prospects of Developmental Integration in Africa

Samuel O. Oloruntoba

Introduction

Since gaining political independence from the late 1950s, political leaders have recognized the imperative of cooperation through the integration of institutions, policies and strategies as a means of achieving development. Leading post-independent political leaders like Kwame Nkrumah of Ghana, Julius Nyerere of Tanzania, Nnamdi Azikiwe of Nigeria, Modibo Keita of Mali, among others, emphasized the necessity of unity and integration to the search for development on the continent. This perspective is informed by the logic of shared experience of oppression, brutality and exploitation which Africans have suffered in their relations with former colonial masters such as Germany, France, Britain, Belgium and Portugal. The expectation that the political and economic integration of the continent can lead to development was informed by the historical trajectories of the continent, the collective struggle to end official colonialism and the continuing unequal power relations between Africa and the former colonizers. Historically, scholars have argued that Africans related among themselves before the forceful and artificial bifurcation of the continent at the Berlin Conference of 1884/1885. For instance, Zeleza (1993) argues that precolonial African kingdoms and societies developed strong networks of trade relations and routes through which they traded with one another. At the political level, Nkrumah's famous aphorism that the independence of Ghana would mean nothing without the independence of other African countries reinforced the high level of collaboration that existed among African countries in the struggle to decolonize the continent.

Scholars like Ndlovu-Gatshenie (2013) and Ki-Zerbo (2005) show how Pan Africanism provided the rallying point for anti-colonial struggles until the last vestige of colonial control was upended in apartheid South Africa in 1994. Paradoxically,

S.O. Oloruntoba (✉)
Thabo Mbeki African Leadership Institute, University of South Africa, Pretoria, South Africa
e-mail: soloruntoba09@gmail.com

O. Akanle, J.O. Adésìnà (eds.), *The Development of Africa*, Social Indicators Research Series 71, DOI 10.1007/978-3-319-66242-8_18

the high hope for freedom and liberation that informed the anti-colonial struggles has been conflated with emancipation in the sense that the political freedom was not backed up by economic power or freedom for Africans. As Mazrui (1999) argues, the economic challenges faced by the majority of African countries after independence undermined Kwame Nkrumah's euphoria of 'seek ye first the political kingdom and all other things shall be added to it'. Indeed, in what will pass for the continuity of colonial economic structures in which African countries are trapped in an unequally designed international division of labor, the composition and direction of trade and investment on the continent remain tied to the former colonial masters. To elaborate, five decades after gaining political independence, imports and exports in Africa have been geared toward satisfying the markets of the developed countries both in terms of exporting raw materials and importing manufactured products.

The overall result of this unequal exchange has been a disarticulated economic structure whose health and vitality are determined by what happens in the developed economies. These challenges have been worsened by the weakening capacity of the state, which the neoliberal globalization processes fostered in Africa from the 1980s (Ajulu 2010). To be sure, the state in Africa was not designed with any inherent capacity to foster development. Rather, by its violent, statist, autocratic and dependent nature, it was created by the colonialists as an institution of extraction, exploitation and domination (Ake 1980). The purpose of the colonial state was in synchronization with the logic and philosophy of colonialism as a system of exploitation of the periphery by the metropoles. An irrefutable justification of this logic was the manner in which the colonialists organized the economy of the colonies in ways that ensured that the latter are designed to permanently export raw materials to the former. At the political level, the use of force to force people into wage labor and pay colonial tax, the perfection of divide and rule were other clear manifestations of the anti-developmental objectives of the colonialists (Mamdani 1996). Although the formal colonial structure of governance appeared to have ended with independence, the neocolonial state continues to manifest all the features of the logic of colonialism (Ndlovu-Gatsheni 2013; Amin 2002; Gana 1985; Ake 1985). This peculiar nature of the state in Africa has affected its capacity to formulate and implement development strategies that have bearing on the aspirations of the majority of the citizens for a better life. Paradoxically, with very few exceptions, postcolonial African leaders have continued in the trajectory of the colonialists of using the state as a means of personal accumulation. Scholars such as Taylor (2014), Ake (1996) and Shivji (1980) argue that the postcolonial elites in Africa lack hegemony, coherence, imagination and ideology of development. Although there are a few instances such as in Tanzania under former President Julius Nyerere, and Kwame Nkrumah of Ghana and Thomas Sankara of Burkina Faso, where deliberate efforts were made to pursue an indigenous developmental approach, many leaders on the continent only see politics as a means of survival.

The failure of leadership at the national level and the continued revolutionary pressures from below necessitate the search for alternative or complementary governance architecture for development in Africa. Other than the ideational and political considerations that informed efforts at regional integration, the need to foster economic agglomeration through the creation of market access, as well as security concerns, have been critical factors.

Major continental development agendas such as the Lagos Plan of Action and Final Act of Lagos of 1980, the Abuja Treaty of 1991 and the New Partnership for African Development, 2001 all had regional integration as major planks on which development processes should rest. However, owing to a combination of several factors such as the paradox of narrow nationalism and pan-Africanism, which fuel divisions among African political elites on the best approach and sequence of integration, overlapping membership of regional economic communities (RECs), bondage of boundaries, preoccupation with the European integration theoretical approach and active efforts by Western powers to undermine the best efforts, regional integration has not taken root, neither has it delivered on its potentials for development in Africa (Oloruntoba 2016a; Ndlovu-Gatsheni 2013; Draper 2013; Adedji 2012; Gibb 2009). The implications of the above is that even though there are huge informal trade volumes across the various regions of the continent, formal intra-Africa trade remains a paltry 13% and remains the lowest among other regions in the world (UNECA 2013). As the multilateral governance architecture for the conduct of international trade continues to falter and regional trade agreements proliferate, African leaders have continued to increase the tempo of either negotiating new trade agreements or concluding new ones. The African Union has also continued to support initiatives toward reaching the goal of a Continental Free Trade Area and an eventual African Economic Community by 2017 and 2028, respectively.

One of the ongoing processes of regional integration in Africa is the RECs on the continent, namely, the Southern African Development Community (SADC), the Common Market for Eastern and Southern Africa (COMESA) and the East African Community (EAC). In June 2015, these RECs signed an agreement to form a TFTA, geared to fostering higher intra-Africa trade. With a population of about 632 million people, gross domestic product of about $1.2 trillion and a large land mass four times the size of Europe, the TFTA holds a huge but challenging potential for economic development on the continent. Based on the review of extant literature, this chapter employs the theory of development cooperation at the regional level to analyze the new dimension in regional integration in terms of the prospects, challenges and the implications for full integration in Africa.

Given the sheer scope of the agreement, I examine the extent to which the TFTA can have a spillover effect on other processes toward integration in Africa. Beyond the creation of market access, this chapter also interrogates the development potentials of the new agreements. After this introduction, the next section examines the conceptual underpinnings and contending theories of regional integration, with special focus on Africa. This is followed by past and previous integration efforts as well as the challenges that have affected their optimal performance in fostering closer trade and investment relations across the various regions of the continent. The penultimate section examines the TFTA in terms of its prospects and challenges for integration while the last section concludes the chapter.

Regional Integration: Concept and Theories

Regional integration connotes various meanings depending on the spatial consideration and the disciplinary context of usage. The divergences in the meaning and usage of regionalism or integration pose both epistemological and ontological problems for the concept. Thus among geographers and urban planners, it could be viewed from the perspectives of unifying processes in levels of government within a national border such as provincial and regional governments. Among scholars of political science, economics and international relations, regionalism includes both the integration of institutions and governance processes among geographically contiguous countries and non-contiguous countries that seek cooperation on issues of trade, security and development (Oloruntoba 2016b; Vayrynen 2003; Lee 2003; Mansfield and Milner 1997). Lee (2003, 1) explains regionalism as an arrangement that "encompasses efforts by a group of nations to enhance their economic, political, social or cultural interaction".

Efforts geared towards these objectives can take the form of regional cooperation, market integration, development integration and regional integration. To a certain degree, the ontological foundation for regional integration varies between the old and new regionalism. While the former was essentially informed by security considerations, especially in Europe, the latter considers economic cooperation as imperative for both security and development. In this connection, Harrison (2006, 23) notes that "the new regionalism has undoubtedly emerged with an overt economic focus, drawn out through its close links with institutional economics, economic sociology and evolutionary political economy." Nye (1987) provides a more nuanced conceptualization of regionalism, when he argues that integration groups too many disparate phenomena to be helpful. In order to ensure its conceptual clarity, he recommends that regionalism should be broken down into various dimensions such as economic integration (the formation of a transnational economy), social integration (the formation of a transitional society), and political integration (the formation of a transnational political system) (Nye 1987).

Regionalization has been distinguished from regionalism to mean "an activist element and denotes the empirical process which be defined as a process of change from relative heterogeneity and lack of cooperation towards increased cooperation, integration, convergence, coherence and identity in a variety of fields such as culture, security, economic development and politics, within a given geographical space" (Schulz et al. 2001, 5). What this distinction implies is that regionalization appears to be embracing and encompassing than regionalism. The differences also relate to the scope of the two concepts which have been located within the broad theoretical constructs developed by scholars from various fields. While regionalism may refer to the process of integration, regionalization relates to the outcome.

Apart from the conventional idea of integration in which contiguous states pool institutions and remove barriers to trade, integration has increasingly been defined by the formation of integration agreements by non-contiguous states as a way of creating market access and facilitating non-people factors of production. In this regard, the formation of free trade areas between developed economic blocs such as the European Union and African countries as well as between United States of America and Asian countries is an example of regional integration. Previous engagements with the study of regionalism and regional integration were focused on the role of state actors. These studies also focused on the establishment of institutions in the process of fostering both horizontal and vertical relationships among sovereign states. These early theories were based on the European experience of regional integration. According to Schulz et al. (2001, 7) "theories of regional integration can be grouped into three sets, namely: neorealism; functionalism and institutionalism; and regional economic integration." Realist theory views the interstate relations essentially within the prism of power and interests in which strong states have their way at the expense of weaker ones. Realist and neorealist scholars like Mongenthau (1948) and Buzan (1986) underscore the importance of security and the role of state in using power to project and protect its interests in the comity of nations. As Buzan (1986 cited in Schulz et al. 2001, 8) argues:

> A group of weak states forming a security regime because they realised that such an arrangement would strengthen the domestic legitimacy of their regimes, whereas pursuing conflicts among themselves was likely to exacerbate divisions within their fragile domestic structures

This theory underpins the formation of security alliances like the North Atlantic Treaty Organization (NATO) and the Organization of America States, among others. Functionalist theorists like David Mitrany emphasize the importance of functional cooperation among states on a sectoral basis in such a way that will minimize costs while ensuring equitability in sharing of benefits among member states in the integrative arrangement. Such cooperation will also lead to avoidance of conflict in the distribution of benefits while leading to gains and economies of scale within given sectors of the economies of the countries involved (Mitrany 1966). Development integration theory differs from market integration in that it sees integration as a means of fostering socioeconomic development with the active involvement of the state. Such involvement will result in the redistribution of income and benefits to those who are previously excluded (Lee 2003). Regional integration theory has also been developed to explain regionalism. It differs from market integration in that

> … while formal institutions are necessary to oversee the linear progression of the various phases of integration, regional integration does not necessarily require formal institutional structures, nor is there necessarily a linear progressions of integration. In the case of the latter, integration is assessed by the amount of economic, political. Social and cultural interaction transpires between member states. It does not require all member states to share these activities simultaneously (Haarlov 1997 cited in Lee 2003, 4–5).

Notwithstanding, changes in the process of integration across the world, especially the involvement of civil society actors have spurred new thinking on the multidimensionality of integration. In particular, the New Regionalism Approach (NRA) transcends the traditional state-centric approach to the understanding of integration processes to incorporate the civil society and other informal networks of interactions across regions. It also goes beyond trade integration to incorporate other forms of integration, including cultural interactions, cross-border cartels and criminal networks as parts of the features of regional integration, which dominant literature appears to have neglected. The NRA has been complemented by Networked Political Economy, Private Authority and Regional Identity approaches to the understanding of the emerging dynamics of regional integration and global governance. These approaches were developed by scholars like Cutler et al. (1999),[1] Nye and Donahue (2000),[2] and Lake (2010)[3] to help our understanding of the roles of non-state actors such as civil society, intergovernmental organizations and corporate organizations, as legitimate agents and actors in global governance. Private authority is often referred to as 'governance,' that is, the exercise of authority by an actor over some limited community or issue that often involves multiple authorities (states, civil society, international NGOs, etc.), horizontal networks, and voluntary rules[4] (Iheduru 2012).In the case of West Africa, for instance, Iheduru provides empirical evidence that supports the theoretical standpoint of Networked Political Economy by showing how indigenous African banks are indirectly promoting the pan-Africanist ideal of an integrated continent through the establishment of banks in countries within the sub-region outside the countries of origin. Apart from state actors, these financial institutions exercise some kind of authority and promote regional integration on the continent.

These new approaches to the explanation of integration flows outside the structures of the state could provide deeper illumination of the trajectories of regional integration, especially in Africa where the grand ambition of integration which was promoted by some early post-independence leaders like Kwame Nkrumah has suffered a setback through a combination of domestic and external factors. The debilitating effects of these factors have been exacerbated by the dependent nature of the state and the ethnocentric base of many of the post-independent political leaders whose claim to a pan-Africanist ideal is at best suspect (Ki-zerbo 2005). Lacking in capacity to deliver public good to the majority of their starving citizens, ensconced as peripheral entities within an unequal global division of labor, these political elites have taken refuge in populist nationalistic politics under which they persistently castigate other Africans as undesirable elements who steal local jobs and opportunities that belong to the locals (Nyamnjoh 2006). Recent research has shown that despite the seeming lack of knowledge about the processes of integration at the institutional level, Africans who are not within the elite bracket express interest in

[1] This relates to work on the private authority of the state.

[2] The work of these authors highlights the importance of non-state actors in the process of building regional integration. This is very important as this adds a new dimension to the study.

[3] Beyond the general narrative that global governance is essentially the preserve of state actors, this work shows that non-state actors play very important roles in the global governance. This perspective provides insight to the role of private institutions in global governance.

[4] This work also shows that private companies can function to achieve political ideologies of the state actors, in this case, the regional expansion of Banks in West Africa are framed within the political ideology of pan-Africanism https://www.tralac.org/images/Resources/Tripartite_FTA/Third_Tripartite_Summit_Communique_10062015.pdf [Accessed 22 September 2016].

an integrated continent (Oloruntoba, Gumede and Kamga, Mokoena, forthcoming). The research shows that regardless of the official obstructions, cross-border flows continue across the various artificial borders created by the colonialists. Non-economic forms of integration have also increased in the form of inter-state marriages and the diffusion of music, dress, food and entertainment across the continent.

Regional Integration: History and Contexts

Integration processes in Africa date back to the pre-colonial times, when European imperial powers, especially Britain and France, forcibly stuck together previously autonomous nations and kingdoms. As Adedeji (2012, 87) argues,

> … almost all the fifty four African states and territories are the product of some form of integration brought about by European colonial rule. Nigeria for instance, was an integrative arrangement championed by British Governor Lord Lugard, who in 1914 amalgamated the protectorate of Northern and Southern Nigeria into a single political entity. Similar and even more grand forms of integration were adopted by the French colonial government which 'grouped its twelve territories into two federations—the French West Africa Federation (Afrique Occidentale Francaise, AOF) and the French Equatorial Africa (Afrique Equatoriale Francaise, AEF).

In Southern and Central Africa, the colonial settler governments also formed the federation of central Africa as well as Rhodesia and Nyasaland (Oloruntoba 2016b). There is no doubt that these groupings facilitated easier administration and cheaper costs for the colonialists. However, regardless of the political and economic potentials that the groupings had for socioeconomic development of post-independent Africa, the colonialists, on the eve of their departures, dissolved these integration arrangements by returning the arbitrary borders drawn at the 1884/1885 conference in Berlin. As Ki-Zerbo (2005) argues, the artificial borders have led to wars, conflicts and crisis since independence.

Post-independent African leaders have not lacked initiatives towards regional integration. In the 1960s, British West African countries planned various integrative schemes including the aborted federations of Senegambia. In 1960s, West African leaders such as Eyadema of Togo and Yakubu Gowon of Nigeria also worked with other leaders in the sub-region to establish Economic Community of West African States in 1975 (Oloruntoba 2016b). Before this, the United Nations Economic Commission for Africa had mobilized African leaders towards forming integration arrangements that could give African countries a basis for achieving greater volumes of trade and greater voice at the multilateral level of negotiations. Thus, in the 1980s, African leaders met in Lagos to adopt the Lagos Plan of Action and the Final Acts of Lagos, with regional integration and self-reliance as key strategies for the socioeconomic development of the continent. As Adedeji further notes, the Lagos Plan of Action specifically called on African leaders to establish their own RECs (2012, 96).

The Lagos Plan of Action of 1980 was followed by the Abuja Treaty of 1991 which established the African Economic Community (AEC) was to be achieved by building on the regional economic communities. In order to achieve this objective, eight RECs were recognized by the leaders. These included the Common Market for Eastern and Southern Africa (COMESA, 19 states), the Economic Community of Central and Eastern African States (ECCAS, 11 states), the Southern African Development Community (SADC, 15 states), the Community of Sahel-Saharan States (CEN-SAD, 24 states), the Economic Community of West African States, ECOWAS, 15 states), the Inter-Governmental Authority on Development (IGAD, seven states), the Arab Maghreb Union (AMU) and the East African Community (EAC). The formation of the African Union in 2002 and the New Partnership for African Development (NEPAD) also consider regional integration as necessary for achieving socioeconomic development on the continent.

These initiatives were part of the processes of seeking to transform the continent from its parlous conditions into a more relevant actor in the international community. Given the peculiar conditions of the continent in terms of underdevelopment and the micro nature of the state after independence, regional integration was considered to be a strategic approach to addressing these challenges and bringing about development. Adedeji (2012, 98) puts it in proper perspective thus:

> It will be clear … that the experiences to which Africa was subjected by Europe—particularly the continent's partition, and the century of colonialism; the persistence and pervasiveness of separatism and irredentism that made it easy for colonialism to exists and thrive as well as to divide and dominate Africa and deepen its Balkanization; the pervasive underdevelopment of Africa; and the emergence of large number of miniscule states, many of which are also landlocked—all rendered regionalism in Africa a strategic tool for survival, revival and transformation

What emerged from the preceding session is that regional integration has been on the agenda of African leaders since independence. However, the lofty objectives, which it was meant to achieve, have not been achieved. Several scholars such as Oloruntoba (2016a), Ndlovu-Gatsheni (2013), Asante (1995) Draper (2013) and Adedeji (2012) among others have argued that the failure of regional integration initiatives in Africa is informed by a plethora of both domestic and external factors. These factors can be further categorized as economic and political. The economic factors include the disarticulated economic structures (defined by small and underdeveloped markets), lack of agglomeration, low level of cross-continental infrastructure, overlapping membership (with one country belonging to at least two RECs) over-emphasis on raw material export and external orientation of economic activities. The political factors are both internal and external. The former include lack of genuine commitment to regional integration by political leaders due to the consideration for narrow nationalism and appeal to populist sentiments (Prah 1999).

This singular factor has been responsible for the failure to implement most of the protocols and treaties that have been agreed upon at various summits on boosting regional integration on the continent. The political differences that have existed since the early 1960s when the political leaders were divided into three groups, namely, the Casablanca, Monrovia and Brazzaville, on the basis of the speed and sequence of unification of Africa are also borne out of the lack of genuine commitment to the integration and unity of the continent. Paradoxically, this half-hearted commitment continues today as many of the countries not only fail to ratify or implement agreed treaties, but are in arrears on the payment of annual dues to both the African Union, which superintends the continental integration, and the RECs (Asante 1995; Nabudere 2001). Lack of contributions from member countries has resulted in a situation in which donors are responsible for over 50% of the budget of both the African Union Commission and some RECs, with the result that the interests of such donors receive priority on trade and other matters.

The low capacity of the RECs, in which mostly junior political officers are posted to represent member countries, further shows that while there is so much talk about regional integration, the commitment at the state level has continued to be an issue. Perhaps this lackluster approach is largely responsible for the ease with which the external powers, especially France, have continued to exercise the practice of divide and rule on the continent. More than half a century after gaining political independence, the Francophone countries appear to be more inclined to relating with France on economic and political issues than with their African counterparts. Although the European Union would appear to be helping and facilitating regional integration on the continent, the actual operations of this very influential economic bloc appear to be further fragmenting the continent. For example, even though it was one of the stated intentions of the EU that negotiations of the economic partnership agreements will be done on a regional basis as a means of promoting regional integration in Africa, the actual negotiation process has only led to further bifurcation of the continent as bilateral EPA negotiations eventually replaced regional EPA negotiations in quick succession (see Meyn 2012). Given the above mentioned challenges, meeting the goals of an African Economic Community and Common Market of Africa by 2017 and 2028, respectively, appears to be unlikely. It is in the context of the contradictions of expectations and realities that the signing of the TFTA by three of the largest RECs in June 2015 merits a close interrogation.

Tripartite Free Trade Agreements: A New Hope on the Horizon?

The signing of the TFTA by the three regional economic groupings in June 2015 could represent a new dimension in the integration agenda of Africa. Indeed, viewed within the broader integration objectives of the African Union, the TFTA could be a building block for establishing the long-expected Continental Free Trade Area by 2017 and the common market by 2020 (Erasmus and Harzenberg 2012). The decision to form the TFTA under the Cape to Cairo initiative was taken at the Kampala Tripartite Summit of October 2008 by the Heads of State and Government. In 2011, the leaders of the three RECs also met and signed a declaration launching negotiations for the establishment if the COMESA-EAC-SADC Free Trade Area. The 2011

Summit made a declaration which emphasized that member states had "adopted a developmental approach to the Tripartite integration process that will be anchored on three pillars namely, market integration based on the Tripartite Free Trade Area; infrastructure Development to enhance connectivity and reduce costs of doing business as well as Industrial Development to address the productive capacity constraints" (Erasmus and Harzenberg 2012, 3).

As stated above, the TFTA was adopted by the Heads of State and Government or their authorized representatives during the Tripartite Summit on 10 June 2015 at Sharm El Sheikh in Egypt. Article 3 of the Tripartite Agreement states its general objectives to include the following:

1. To promote the rapid social economic development of the people of the region through job and wealth creation and the elimination of poverty, hunger and disease, through building skills, innovativeness and hard and soft infrastructures and through improving the locations of factors of production for sustainable generation of local, regional and foreign investment and trade opportunities
2. To create a larger single internal market with free movement of goods and services and business persons and eventually to establish a customs union and a common market
3. To mitigate the problem of multiple membership and expedite the regional and continental integration process
4. To build a strong people-based Tripartite Community, and
5. To promote close cooperation in all sectors of economic and social activities (Tralac 2015).

Although there are other specific objectives of the Tripartite Community, which deal with issues of tariff removal, rules of origin, market access and so on, my analysis is limited to the above general objectives in terms of the possible prospects and challenges of using the TFTA as a springboard for fostering continental integration on the continent. To start with, out of the 26 member states, 24 have ratified the declaration (the only exceptions being Eritrea and Libya), while 17 have signed. It is significant that most of the countries that have signed cut across the three regional economic communities. The general objectives of the TFTA are central to the realization of the African Economic Community as well as the common market as envisaged by the Abuja Treaty of 1991 and the Constitutive Act of African Union of 2002. For instance, the issue of infrastructure is critical to fostering integration on the continent. Lack of good transportation networks in terms of rail, air and road has hindered the ease with which goods and services flow across the continent.

Recognition of the importance of infrastructure and a general commitment to funding can help to accelerate the pace of integration in Africa. Creation of markets, which is the second objective of the TFTA, also strikes at the heart of one of the challenges of integration. Scholars like Draper (2013) and Collier and Venables (2008) have argued that the small markets in African countries are disincentives to vertical integration. They argue that African countries should rather continue to trade with the West as the latter has wider and deeper markets. The argument that the market in Africa is small flows from official statistics which mask the huge volume of trade that takes place at the informal sector. Thus, a commitment by political leaders and in this case the private sector[5] to integrate a market that consists of over 600 million people could be a step in the right direction towards harnessing the over 1 billion market that the whole continent has grown to become. Rather than the external orientation of exports and imports which have defined the structure of trade in Africa since colonial times, this new agenda to create an internal market could yet change the direction of trade and the impacts that trade could have on the overall economic development of the participating countries.

The three other objectives, which deal with addressing overlapping membership, building a strong people-based Tripartite Community and fostering sectoral cooperation both in the economic and social spheres, are critical to successful integration of the continent. Their uniqueness is in their departure from the previous integration arrangements which were only concerned with removal of tariffs on imports (UNECA 2012). By promoting people to people integration and mainstreaming the social with the economic, the TFTA may be leading the way to the ideals of pan-Africanism on which the eventual renaissance and transformation of Africa tenuously hangs (see Prah 2006, 2001; Ki-zerbo 2005; Nkrumah 1963).

While these objectives and the well-targeted actions hold strong potential and give cause for optimism, greater challenges lie ahead on the actual implementation of the agreements. Apart from the need to ensure continuous political commitment, the huge requirements in terms of funding, especially infrastructure; concern over transfer of sovereign control of exchange rate and trade policy, complementarity of institutions, adjudicatory and enforcement capacity of regional courts, building institutional capacity, harmonizing monetary systems, rule of origin and managing the disparity in the cost and benefits among member states are capable of stifling the possibilities of fully implementing the agreements. As Erasmus and Hartzenberg (2012, 5) caution, "the establishment of the T-FTA will have to accommodate separate legal and institutional arrangements (including secretariats and regional courts) as well as national designs for domesticating and implementing existing legal instruments on regional trade." Also in view of the overt declaration that the T-TFTA has industrialization as one of its key components, how the member states carry out the harmonization of the various industrial policies to a regional one will be a task that must be given due consideration.

Conclusion

This chapter has examined the travails and the prospects of regional integration in Africa within the context of the TFTA. I argue that regional integration arrangements in Africa predate political independence as the colonialists formed various

[5] The private sector from the three Regional Economic Communities met in Rwanda in February 2016 to express the view and recommendations on how the Tripartite Agreements can be of benefit to them.

integration schemes as means of reducing the cost governance. The chapter also showed that, among others, lack of political commitment among African leaders has contributed to the delay in achieving integration not only because of the refusal of many of them ratify agreements but also because they willingly become tools in the hands of neo-imperial forces that are bent on keeping Africa divided. Despite the challenges, it is heartening that regional integration has remained on the agenda since independence. In what UNECA (2013) would refer to as new momentum in this process, the African Union Commission has put in place various initiatives which are geared towards achieving an African Economic Community and a Common Market by 2017 and 2028 respectively.

Among the ongoing processes is the TFTA, which involves the formation of a Free Trade Area and eventual common market among three RECs, namely, COMESA, SADC and EAC. Given the general and the specific objectives of the TFTA, there are high prospects that it may be able to break the incubus of failed integration arrangements in Africa. Although the challenges remain huge, the involvement of the private sector and civil society organizations can bridge the gap in the previous integration Schemes. I also argue that the inclusion of a social element in the TFTA may well be the key to making it different from past integrative processes on the continent. Beyond market access, which has been the preoccupation of previous regional integration efforts, a commitment to industrialization and developmental regionalism under the TFTA could help in ensuring a successful integrative outcome. Lastly, the sustenance of the current political commitment, effective communication of the benefits of integration to the various segments of the society, large financial outlay (which can come from the private sector and multilateral financial institutions) and the alignment of institutions are key requirements for the success of regional integration in Africa. In other words, if the TFTA is to succeed, the above-mentioned recommendations should be taken seriously by all the stakeholders in Africa's development.

References

Adedji, A. (2012). The travails of regional integration in Africa. In A. Adebajo & K. Whiteman (Eds.), *The EU and Africa: From Eurafrique to afro-Europa* (pp. 83–104). Johannesburg: Wits University Press.

Ajulu, E. (2010). Introduction: A region in transition: Towards a new integration agenda in East Africa. In R. Ajulu (Ed.), *A region in transition: Towards a new integration agenda in East Africa*. Midrand: Trust Africa and Institute for Global Dialogue.

Ake, C. (1980). *The political economy of Africa*. London: Longman.

Ake, C. (1985). The state in contemporary Africa. In C. Ake (Ed.), *Political economy of Nigeria* (pp. 1–15). Lagos: Longman.

Ake, C. (1996). *Democracy and development in Africa*. Dakar: CODESRIA.

Amin, S. (2002). Africa living on the fringe. *Monthly Review, 53*, 41–50.

Asante, S. (1995). Pan Africanism and regional integration in Africa. In A. Mazrui (Ed.), *General history of Africa* (pp. 724–743). Oxford: James Currey.

Buzan, B. (1986). A framework for regional security analysis. In L. Ohllson (Ed.), *Case studies of regional conflict and conflict resolutions resolution*. Goteberg: Padrigu Paper.
Collier, P., & Venables, T. (2008). *Trade and economic performance: Does Africa's fragmentation matter?* Cape Town: Annual World Bank Conference on Development Economics. June.
Cutler, A., Haufler, V., & Porter, T. (Eds.). (1999). *Private authority and international affairs*. New York: State University of New York Press.
Draper, P. (2013). Breaking free from Europe: Why Africa needs another model of regional integration. In L. Fioramonti (Ed.), *Regionalism in a changing world: Comparative perspectives in the new global order*. London/New York: Routledge.
Erasmus, G., & Harzenberg, T. (2012). Introduction. In G. Erasmus & T. Harzenberg (Eds.), *The tripartite trade area: Towards a new African integration paradigm?* Stellenbosch: Trade Law Centre for Southern Africa.
Gana, A. (1985). The state in Africa: Yesterday, today, and tomorrow. *International Political Science Review, 6*(1), 115–132.
Gibb, R. (2009). Regional integration and development trajectory: Meta-theories, expectations and reality. *Third World Quarterly, 30*(4), 701–721.
Harrison, J. (2006). Re-reading the new regionalism: A sympathetic critique. *Space and Polity, 10*(1), 21–46.
Iheduru, O. (2012). Regional integration and the private authority of banks in West Africa. *International Studies Review, 14*, 273–302.
Ki-Zerbo, J. (2005). African intellectuals, nationalism and pan Africanism: A testimony. In T. Mkandawire (Ed.), *African intellectuals: Rethinking politics, language, gender and development*. Dakar/London: CODESRIA and Zed Books.
Lake, D. (2010). Rightful rules: Authority, order, and the foundations of global governance. *International Studies Quarterly, 54*, 587–613.
Lee, M. (2003). *The political economy of regionalism in Africa*. Cape Town: UCT Press.
Mamdani, M. (1996). *Citizens and subjects: Contemporary Africa and the legacy of late colonialism*. New Jersey: Princeton University Press.
Mansfield, H., & Milner, H. (Eds.). (1997). *The political economy of regionalism*. New York: Columbia University Press.
Mazrui, A. (1999). Seek ye first the political kingdom. In A. Mazrui (Ed.), *General history of Africa* (pp. 105–126). Oxford: James Currey.
Meyn, M. (2012). In A. Adebajo & K. Whiteman (Eds.), *An anatomy of the economic partnership agreements in The EU and Africa: From Eurafrique to Afro-Europa*. Johannesburg: Wits University Press.
Mitrany, D. (1966). *A working peace system*. Chicago: Quadrangle Books.
Mongenthau, H. (1948). *Politics among nations: The struggle for power and peace*. New York: Alfred A. Knopf.
Nabudere, D. (2001). The African renaissance and globalisation: New perspectives on African unity and integration. In I. Mandaza & D. Nabudere (Eds.), *Pan-Africanism and integration in Africa*. Zimbabwe: SAPES Trust.
Ndlovu-Gatsheni, S. (2013). Decolonial epistemic perspective and pan-African unity in the 21st century. In M. Munchie, P. Lukhele-Olorunju, & O. Akpor (Eds.), *The African union ten years after* (pp. 385–409). Pretoria: African Institute of South Africa.
Nkrumah, K. (1963). *Africa must unite*. London: Panaf Books.
Nyamnjoh, F. (2006). *Insiders and outsiders: Citizenship and xenophobia in contemporary Southern Africa*. Dakar: CODESRIA.
Nye, J. (1987). *Peace in parts: Integration and conflicts in regional organization*. New York: Little, Brown and Co..
Nye, J., & Donahue, J. (Eds.). (2000). *Governance in a globalizing world*. Washington, DC: Brookings Institution Press.
Oloruntoba, S. (2016a). *Regionalism and integration in Africa: EU-ACP economic partnership agreements and euro-Nigeria relations*. New York: Palgrave Macmillan.

Oloruntoba, S. (2016b). ECOWAS and regional integration in West Africa: From state to private authority. *History Compass, 14*(7), 295–303.
Prah, K. (1999). In M. Malegapuru & W. Makgoba (Eds.), *African renaissance or warlordism? In: African Renaissance* (pp. 37–61). Cape Town: Mafube.
Prah, K. (2001). African unity, pan-Africanism and the dilemmas of regional integration. In D. Nabudere & I. Mandaza (Eds.), *Pan Africanism and integration in Africa*. Harare: SAPES Books.
Prah, K. (2006). *The Africa nation*. Cape Town: CASS.
Schulz, M., Soderbaum, F., & Ojendal, J. (2001). Introduction. In M. Schulz, F. Soderbaum, & J. Ojendal (Eds.), *Regionalization in a globalizing world: A comparative perspective on forms, actors and processes* (pp. 1–17). London/New York: Zed Books.
Shivji, I. (1980). The state in the dominated social formations of Africa: Some theoretical issues. *International Social Science Journal, 32*(4), 730–742.
Taylor, I. (2014). *Africa rising? BRICS-diversifying dependency*. London: James Currey.
United Nations Economic Commission for Africa (UNECA). (2012). *Assessing regional integration in Africa*. Addis Ababa: United Nations Economic Commission for Africa.
United Nations Economic Commission for Africa (UNECA). (2013). *Eighth session of the committee on trade, regional cooperation and integration. Report on international and intra-Africa trade*. UNECA: Addis Ababa.
Vayrynen, R. (2003). Old and new regionalism. *International Studies Review, 5*(1), 25–51. https://www.tralac.org/images/Resources/Tripartite_FTA/Third_Tripartite_Summit_Communique_10062015.pdf. Accessed 22 Sept 2016.
Zeleza, P. (1993). *A modern history of Africa Vol. 1: The nineteen century*. Nairobi: East African Educational Publishers in association with CODESRIA.

Samuel O Oloruntoba is a Senior Lecturer at the Thabo Mbeki African Leadership Institute, University of South Africa, Pretoria, South Africa. He was a Post-Doctoral Fellow at the same Institute from August 2013 to October 2014. He obtained his PhD in Political Science with specialization in International Political Economy of Trade from the University of Lagos, Nigeria, where he is tenured a Faculty member. He was previously a Visiting Scholar at the Program of African Studies, Northwestern University, Evanston and Brown University in United States of America. He has published in local; and international journals. His single-authored book on regionalism and Integration in Africa: EU-ACP Economic Partnership Agreements and Euro-Nigeria Relations was published by Palgrave Macmillan, New York, United States of America in January, 2016.

Chapter 19
Peace and Security in Africa: United Nations Challenges

Primus Fonkeng

Introduction

International organizations have played and continue to play an important role in the development and evolution of the international community. During the twentieth century two major experiments in global organizations were attempted, namely, the League of Nations in the aftermath of the First World War and the United Nations (UN) after the Second World War. Ever since its creation in 1945, the UN has addressed a wide range of issues which affect international wellbeing and political, economic and socio-cultural problems. The UN deals with those issues in various dimensions in accordance with the provisions of the organization's Charter. In Article 55 of that Charter the UN committed itself to the promotion of higher standards of living, full employment, political progress and the development of member countries. Africa as a whole began to make significant economic and political progress in recent years, but in many parts of the continent, progress remained threatened or impeded by conflict. There was no higher goal for the UN, no deeper commitment and no greater ambition than preventing armed conflict. The prevention of conflict begins and ends with the promotion of human security and human development. Ensuring human security is the cardinal mission of the UN.

In the first few years of its existence, the major task with which the UN was confronted was the economic reconstruction of war-torn Europe after the devastating effects of the Second World War. As European economies gradually became revived, the political and socioeconomic problems of less developed countries or the Third World became its preoccupation. Since the early 1990s, Africa has been swept by a proliferation of armed conflict as many of the continent's established military and one-party regimes were undercut by the end of the Cold War. This further led to the

P. Fonkeng (✉)
University of Buea, Buea, Cameroon
e-mail: primusf2000@yahoo.com

O. Akanle, J.O. Adésìnà (eds.), *The Development of Africa*, Social Indicators Research Series 71, DOI 10.1007/978-3-319-66242-8_19

growth of pro-democracy movements and eruption of ethnic and other social tensions. From Somalia and Rwanda to Liberia, Sierra Leone, Ivory Coast, Burundi, Sudan and the Democratic Republic of Congo (DRC), hundreds of thousands of Africans were killed and millions more succumbed to war-related epidemics and starvation. The difficulties confronting international efforts in Africa were dramatically demonstrated by the losses suffered by US forces in Somalia in 1993, prompting that country's unilateral withdrawal. This seriously weakened the UN Peacekeeping Mission, which ultimately ended without restoring national political order. The Somalia effect combined with the preoccupation of the US and other NATO powers with events in the Middle East and the Balkans led to a decline in international participation in UN Peacekeeping Missions especially in Africa. When the Rwandan genocide erupted in 1994, the small UN Mission already there was far too weak to stop it.[1]

Nevertheless, in assessing the challenges of the UN experience in the African continent, it is important to recognize that the UN is not a supranational governmental organization with independent goals and interests, nor is it a legal institution that develops and implements programs and policies it considers beneficial to global society. The UN does not transcend world politics, rather it is an organization based on the interests and will of its sovereign member-states. When the UN takes action, it does so because its members agreed to a shared objective. The UN was not created to modify the sovereign power of states but to promote transnational cooperation and strengthen inter-state relations. Its aim was to enable states to realize their objectives and to facilitate international problem-solving. Indeed, its success or failure ultimately depends on the level of cooperation and coordination that states voluntarily place on her to achieve. The study recommends that countries should reduce their demands on the UN, giving it a decent chance of carrying out policies, or recognize the necessity of improving its capacity and granting it greater resources, functions and coordinating powers as established in its Charter.

United Nations Charter's Provisions on Peace and Security

The UN was created to fulfill a variety of objectives, which have not changed fundamentally. The primary objective of the UN is the maintenance and building of peace in the world. Other objectives of the UB include to maintain international peace and security through the process of collective security (Adigwi 1981, 76); to develop friendly relations among nations; to achieve international cooperation in solving economic, social, cultural and humanitarian problems and to promote and encourage respect for human rights and fundamental freedoms for all people without distinction as to race, sex, language or religion.

[1] The private sector from the three Regional Economic Communities met in Rwanda in February 2016 to express the view and recommendations on how the Tripartite Agreements can be of benefit to them.

Maintenance of International Peace and Security

One of the fundamental objectives of the UN is the maintenance of international peace and security in the world. This entails acting collectively to prevent or suppress any threat to peace. The UN has used, to that effect, a series of mechanical methods, depending on the nature of the situation and context. One of them has been through Article 33 of the UN Charter, which specifies that the parties to a dispute shall first of all seek a solution by negotiation, enquiry, mediation, conciliation, arbitration, judicial settlement, resort to regional agencies or arrangement or other peaceful means of their own choice (Elisha 2006). If the parties fail to observe their obligation or are not successful in settling their disputes through any of these traditional methods of peaceful settlement they can have recourse to the UN.

The UN uses coercion through force to check confrontation of situations of insecurity. Such actions, with varying degree of success, were carried through the use of peace-keeping in the Middle East in 1948, Pakistan 1949, Cyprus 1964, Syria 1974, Lebanon 1978, Western Sahara 1991, Georgia 1993, Kosovo 1999, Sierra Leone 1999, Democratic Republic of Congo 1999, Ethiopia and Eritrea 2000, East Timor 2002, Liberia 2003, Ivory Coast 2004, Haiti 2004, Burundi 2004, and Darfur 2006 (Basic Facts About the United Nations, 2004). The UN has also used coercion through military group observers and truce supervisors. Some examples include the fielding of the UN truce supervision organization in Palestine in 1948, Lebanon and Yemen between 1964 and 1965, Suez Canal in 1967, India and Pakistan 1971, Syria 1974, Ivory Coast 2004, Haiti 2004, Burundi 2004, and Darfur 2006.

Besides coercion, the UNO also exercised pressure on parties in conflict such as between Iran and Iraq, Morocco and Western Sahara, Democratic Kampuchea and Vietnam, Cameroon and Nigeria. The pressure was exercised through good offices, special representatives and commissions (Teng 1968, 62). This type of diplomacy could be carried out in collaboration with other regional organizations concerned. The UN also organized international conferences on some crises. Examples include the situation in Palestine in 1947 and an international conference on Kampuchea in 1980, followed by declarations. The organization also drew up and executed humanitarian programmes to cater for victims in crisis, such as in the Congo, Cyprus and Palestine.

Promotion of Cordial Relations Between States

The UN serves as a forum for the harmonization of views and action of states.[1] Participants therein seek to reach agreement of opinion and interest after mutual exchange of views in general discussions, formal negotiations and recommendations. Again, the various universal and regional organizations might be involved in efforts of harmonizing opinions. This objective applies to wide ecological, scientific and other problems. Mandi (1970) describes this function as one of integration in the sense that it leads to gradual change in some attributes of sovereignty by relying on the UN forum where and when states failed (Elmanjra 1971, 113–114). It is not necessarily incompatible with national strategies; it is rather about where they decline and seeks integrated and coherent actions with states and other actors.

The UNO in accordance with the provisions of the Charter tries to promote international peace by regulating relations between states in certain crucial areas of international relations. It regulates the relations mainly by setting values.[1] Some of the remarkable actions by the UN in this area include the regulation of good neighborliness between states in 1957 and 1970, the declaration of the principle of self-determination and equality in 1960, the declaration of the inadmissibility of intervention in the domestic affairs of states and the protection of independence and sovereignty of each country in 1965 and 1981, and the declaration on the reinforcement of international security in 1970. It also codified laws on the definition of aggression in 1974, of war and the consolidation of international dètente in 1977, prepared a declaration on the prevention of nuclear catastrophe in 1981, and the peaceful settlement of international deputes in 1982 (Ewang 1987, 42–43).

The UN promoted these principles by declaring international days and years as well as organizing international conferences on them. It has gone further to implement some of the resolutions and declarations. Its efforts have been spectacular in the implementation of the principle of self-determination, leading to the decolonization of more than 75 countries between 1945 and 1984.[1] It has generally developed specific measures and procedures to meet such problems. The UN has also attempted to regulate the process of disarmament between states. It has encouraged and initiated collateral measures intended to decrease international tension in this issue.

The UN efforts in regulating friendly relations between states involved the promotion and respect for human rights and fundamental freedom. The organization gradually expanded human rights law to encompass specific standards for women, children, persons with disabilities, minorities, migrant workers and other vulnerable groups, who now possess rights that protect them from discriminatory practices that had long been common in many societies. Rights have been extended through ground-breaking General Assembly decisions that have gradually established their universality, indivisibility and interrelatedness with development and democracy. Education campaigns have informed the world's public of their inalienable rights, while numerous national judicial and penal systems have been enhanced through UN training programs and technical advice. The UN machinery to monitor compliance with human rights treaties has acquired a remarkable cohesiveness and weight among member states.

The UN has also laid down regulatory norms in the area of natural space and climatic changes. It has, for instance, sponsored legal principles on outer space through an accord on the activities of astronauts in 1967, a convention on International Liability for Damages caused by Spatial Objects in 1971, a Convention of Immatriculation in 1974, a Convention on States Activities on the moon as well as rules on terrestrial telediction (United Nations 1979, 364–370). Scientific and technical activities and programs have been carried out and exchange of information on education and training in these problems has taken place. The organization has codified rules on the use of sea beds, ocean floors and other water bodies to meet human, commercial and agricultural needs. The 1977 UN Water Conference, the International Conference on Water and the Environment and the Earth Summit in 1992, and the International Drinking Water Supply and Sanitation Decade in 1981–1990, all focused on these vital resources. The Decades helped some 1.3 billion people in the developing countries gain access to safe drinking water. The United Nations International Year of Fresh Water organized in 2003 aimed at raising public awareness on water crises in the world, while the first UN World Water Report in 2003 analyzed data and trends affecting the world's fresh water resources.[1]

Promotion of Economic Development and Social Welfare of Mankind

Although most people associate the UN with issues of peace and security, the vast majority of the organization's resources are in fact devoted to advancing the Charter's pledge to promote higher standards of living, offer full employment to people and improve on conditions of economic and social progress and development. The UN development efforts have profoundly affected the lives and wellbeing of millions of people in the world. Guiding the UN endeavors is the conviction that lasting international peace and security are possible only if the economic and social wellbeing of people everywhere is assured. Most of the economic and social transformation that has taken place globally in the last six decades has been significantly affected in its direction and shaped by the work of the organization. As the global center for consensus building, the UN set priorities and goals for international cooperation to assist countries in their development efforts and to foster a supportive global economic environment.

The work of the UN for economic and social progress covers a wide area. The activities of the Economic and Social Council and its subsidiary bodies includes transport and communications, fiscal and statistical questions, population and migration problems, social welfare question, human rights and freedom of information, refugees, child welfare, the status of women and narcotics In the beginning the UN was mainly concerned with the urgent post-war problem. For instance, the need for reconstruction of the devastated areas, the world shortage of food, the question of refugees and the special needs of the children of countries which had been the victim of aggression. Later, as the economies of the devastated developed countries began to recover, attention was increasingly directed towards the need of less developed countries. Technical assistance was given to countries by the UN and its specialized agencies in the course of their regular program.

In December 1948, the General Assembly voted a special fund for this purpose, and in 1949 agreed that these technical assistance activities be expanded to all nations. As a result of the first United Nations Technical Assistance Conference held in June 1950, a total of 54 countries pledged over 20 million dollars to finance the program during its first 18 months. Other economic questions considered by the UN included international and national measures to promote and maintain full employment on which basic recommendations were made on the basis of the report of a committee of experts; measure to develop world trade, resulting in the holding of multilateral tariff negotiations; the development of transport, including steps to create an inter-governmental shipping organization and the adoption of a new International Convention on Road Traffic and a protocol on Road and Signals; and the improvement of the comparability of statistics. Numerous economic, statistical and fiscal studies were undertaken and publications were issued, including annual surveys of world and regional economic conditions.

In the social domain, the UN took over and expanded the work of the League of Nations on the international control of narcotics. A convention for the suppressions of traffic in people and of the exploitation of the prostitution of others came into force in July 1951. Through the United Nations International Children Emergency Fund (UNICEF), food, clothing and medical suppliers were provided to aid needy children, pregnant women and nursing mothers. To complement governmental and other contributions, a worldwide appeal, by the United Nations Appeal for Children (UNAC), was conducted to secure voluntary contributions for such aid. The UN Assembly in 1950 decided that UNICEF should pay particular attention to the needs of children and women particularly in the less-developed countries.

Since the 1990s, the UN has provided a platform for formulating and promoting key new development objectives on the international agenda, through a series of global conferences. It has articulated the need for incorporating issues such as the advancement of women, human rights, sustainable development, environmental protection and good governance into the development paradigm. At the Millennium Summit in September 2000, member states adopted a set of wide-ranging Millennium Development Goals, supported by a series of specific, attainable targets.[1] The goals and targets aimed at eradicating extreme poverty and hunger; achieving universal primary education; promoting gender equality and the empowerment of women; reducing child mortality; improving maternal health, combating HIV/AIDS, malaria and other diseases, ensuring environmental sustainability, and developing a global partnership for development. International debate on economic and social issues has increasingly reflected the commonality of interests between rich and poor countries in solving the many problems that transcend national boundaries. These broad-based objectives of the UN have a considerable influence on peace and security in Africa. The objectives have been complemented with successful UN peace and security measures in the continent.

United Nations Achievements on Peace and Security in Africa

Crises in the Sahel Region

Africa's Sahel region faces many complex and interconnected challenges. Here are some of the major ones and how the UN is assisting the region in finding solutions. Political instability has plagued some of the Sahel's countries for years. In Mali, the military coup of March 2012 brought an abrupt halt to 20 years of the stable democracy. In its aftermath, terrorists who had occupied most of the Northern Region started heading south to control the whole country. In January 2013, a French-led and Chad-supported intervention stopped their advance. The conflict compounded the security and humanitarian crisis, in part by disrupting supply routes and causing food shortages. The crisis in neighboring Darfur, Sudan and the presence of an armed rebellion in the east did damage to Chad's security that lasted for many years. During Niger's 50 years of independence (International Crisis Group 2006) the country witnessed two armed rebellions, four coups, seven governments and periods of promising democratic change as well as reversals.

In a region with porous borders, a political or security crisis in one country is often a serious threat to its neighbors. These borders have benefited criminal networks and drug traffickers. The UN Office for Drug and Crime (UNODC) estimated that major illicit flows linked to criminal activities in the Sahel amounted to $3.8 billion annually. UNODC recently helped broker an agreement among Mali, Morocco, Niger, Burkina Faso, Chad and Algeria to address the problems caused by drug trafficking, organized crime and terrorism. In July 2013, the UN Security Council authorized the deployment of a peacekeeping mission to assist Mali on its way back to stability (Essoungou 2013, 23).

Historically the Sahel has been characterized by strong climatic variations and irregular rainfall, which posed two of the biggest obstacles to food security and poverty reduction in the region. According to UN Environment Program (UNEP), various factors account for the Sahel's environmental crisis; the combined effects of population growth, land degradation (deforestation, continuous cropping and overgrazing), reduced and erratic rainfall, lack of coherent environmental policies and misplaced development priorities, which contributed to transform a large proportion of the Sahel into barren land, resulting in the deterioration of the soil and water resources. Agriculture in the Sahel employs the majority of the region's workforce and contributes heavily to it gross domestic product (accounting for up to 455 in some countries of the region). It also plays a central role in food security. Yet it remains highly underdeveloped and it is characterized by an almost total dependency on three to 4 months of rainfall per year, as well as by low use of external inputs such as seeds and fertilizers, the absence of mechanization and poor links to markets. According to UNEP (2013), the recurrent droughts of the 1970s and 1980s caused massive losses of agricultural production and livestock, loss of human lives to hunger, malnutrition and diseases, massive displacement of people and shattered economies.

Among other recommendations, UN officials urged regional cooperation to defuse tensions between the countries of the region, and thereby reduce the risk of increased conflict and environmentally induced migration. Achim Steiner (2013), executive director of UNEP, called for the urgent need for scaled-up investments in adaptation, moving forward on the Green Fund and supportive measures such as reduced emissions from deforestation and forest degradation as well as realizing the climate finance of $100 billion a year by 2020. Throughout the lean season period between harvests from May to September 2010, the World Food Programme (WFP) gave food to between 5 and 6 million people each month through its nutrition and food security program. In 2012, the Food and Agriculture Organization (FAO) helped more than 5.2 million people through support to off-season food and crop production, soil and water conservation and rehabilitation projects, and desert locust control and monitoring. With its partners, the Office for the Coordination of Humanitarian Affairs (OCHA) also mobilized resources and assisted communities in need.

Peace Process in the Great Lakes Region

Five months after UN Secretary General Ban Ki-Moon and World Bank President Jim Yong Kim visited Africa's Great Lakes Region in 2013, a delegation of the UN Security Council followed suit. The delegation travelled to the region from 4 to 8 October 2013 and met with political leaders and local activists, displaced persons and refugees, as well as UN peacekeepers and diplomats. The visit was an attempt by the Council to get a better grasp of the complexities of a region where instability has persisted over the past two decades, with new waves of fighting observed in recent months. Since April 2012 and the creation of the March 23 armed movement (known as the M23), renewed fighting has forced up to 2 million people to flee their homes, mainly in the eastern region of the Democratic Republic of the Congo (DRC). The visit came 3 years after another Council trip to the same region that had modest ambitions: just a two country visit to the DRC and Uganda. This time, however, after stops in these two countries, the delegation went on to Rwanda before heading farther east to Ethiopia (Essoungou 2013, 3).

The council's busy agenda was an acknowledgement that a solution to the persisting instability in the Great Lakes region requires the active engagement and the commitment of key regional actors. On various occasions over the past years, the council has urged countries of the region to find a peaceful solution to the instability plaguing the DRC, mainly in the east. The latest of such calls came shortly after the M23 armed groups—allegedly supported by Rwanda—took up arms against the DRC government, plunging the region into one of its worst episode of instability in recent years. The M23 rebels were expected to sign a peace deal with the government in November after suffering defeats at the hands of government forces backed by a 3000-strong UN intervention brigade. In response, two political processes were initiated: a wide-ranging peace and security agreement among the countries of the region (DRC, Angola, Burundi, Central Africa Republic, Republic of Congo, Rwanda, South Africa, South Sudan, Tanzania, Uganda and Zambia), and peace talks in Kampala, Uganda's capital, between the DRC government and M23 leaders.

During its visit the council delegation was updated by regional leaders on the implementation of the agreement, and on the progress of the peace talks. On both issues the council urged the leaders not to repeat the mistakes of the past. The delegation informed presidents Joseph Kabila of the DRC, Paul Kagame of Rwanda and Yoweri Museveni of Uganda that unlike previous agreements, this one must be followed by action. On the Kampala talks, speaking to the press in Kinshasa on behalf of the delegation, the Security Council representatives for Morocco and France insisted that the past provides clear lessons about the consequences of integrating armed groups into national armies without rigorous vetting. They warned against repeating such mistakes. In the Council's view, they added, there could be no compromise on fighting impunity and no amnesty should be granted to M23 members who have committed serious crimes (Ochieno 2012, 17). Towards the end of the visit, the council members visited the African Union headquarters in Addis Ababa. In addition to addressing the situation in the Great Lakes region, they held discussions with AU officials on a wide range of issues related to peace and security in Africa.

Model of Peace and Security Along the Cameroon–Nigeria Border

Cameroon and Nigeria are separated by an 1800-kilometer long border zone which has witnessed insecurity and conflict for several years. Barely 6 years after independence, Nigeria was affected by a civil war, which lasted from 1967 to 1970. During this war, the Government of Cameroon played a supporting role by preventing the Biafran military from receiving foreign weapons through its border, which influenced the victory of the Nigerian Federal Government over the Biafran secessionists. The Cameroon Government refused to facilitate the independence of the break-away Eastern Region of Nigeria because of the devastating political effect that a successful secessionists Biafran state would have had on the territorial integrity and unity of the Federal Republic of Cameroon (Ngoh 1988, 296). This fear was well understood and expressed by Cameroon Government officials. A prominent Cameroonian ambassador said "Cameroon was threatened by divisive internal forces through domestic action." Thus, an independent Eastern Region from the Nigerian Federal Government would have encouraged secessionist tendencies in the former West Cameroon.

After the Nigerian civil war, President Ahmadou Ahidjo of Cameroon played the role of mediator between Nigeria and the African countries which had recognized the sovereignty of the Biafran state. As a result of the influential role played by

Cameroon in the Nigerian civil war, President Ahidjo of Cameroon and General Yakubu Gowon of Nigeria met in 1975 at Maroua, North Cameroon, and produced the Maroua Declaration (Aletum 1994). The Declaration was focused on the Cameroon–Nigeria border. In effect, Gowon made frontier concessions that recognized Cameroon sovereignty over a seabed rich oil deposit area around the Rio-del Rey region (the Bakassi Peninsula). The cordial relations between Cameroon and Nigeria, however, became strained after 1979 when some prominent Nigerians, including the Supreme Military Council (SMC), began criticizing Gowon's acceptance of the Maroua Declaration and advocated an outright rejection of its clauses. These conflicting views culminated in the first Cameroon–Nigeria border crisis in 1981.

Although the 1981 Cameroon–Nigeria border crisis was peacefully resolved, it left many Nigerians especially the Igbo dissatisfied. This was as a result of Cameroon's diplomatic and moral support to Nigeria during the 1967–70 civil war. The anti-Biafran stance which Cameroon adopted was a source of irritation to the Igbos. As a result, Dr. Okoi Arikpo and his supporters posited that Gowon's decision to recognize the Bakassi Peninsular as Cameroonian territory was to compensate Cameroon for the support she gave the Federal Republic of Nigeria during the war. They also asserted that the Cameroon–Nigeria boundary west of Rio-del-Rey, around the Bakassi Peninsula, had never been well defined and thereby encouraged Nigerian fishermen to settle in the area, which they believed was part of Nigeria. But when the Cameroonian authorities decided to tighten up tax payment and curb smuggling in this area, they stepped on the toes of Nigerian fishermen who neither accepted the paying of the taxes nor recognized Cameroon's sovereignty in the area.

On 21 December 1993, in defiance of the Charter of the Organization of African Unity (OAU) on inter-state relations, especially the principle of the respect of colonial boundaries and the peaceful resolution of disputes and also in defiance of agreements signed between the two countries concerning their border, Nigerian armed forces crossed the border and occupied the Bakassi Peninsula, in the localities of Jabane and Diamond Island. On 18 February 1994, Nigerian troops moved towards the villages of Archibong, Atabong and Akwa Bana on the Peninsula, maintaining that the villages belonged to Nigeria. In the quest for a peaceful settlement of this crisis, the Government of Cameroon took the matter to the International Court of Justice (ICJ) for arbitration. On 10 October 2002, the Court passed its verdict ceding the Bakassi Peninsula to Cameroon.

After the verdict of the ICJ, Cameroon and Nigeria intensified meetings to improve their bilateral relations through the influence of the UN. Under the auspices of the UN Secretary General, Kofi Annan, Presidents Paul Biya of Cameroon and Olusegun Obasanjo of Nigeria met on five occasions to foster the implementation of the ICJ verdict. During these meetings, the two heads of state resolved to establish a new form of cooperation, common undertaking in border areas and the promotion of initiatives that were aimed at building confidence between the two countries. To sustain these objectives, a Cameroon–Nigeria Mixed Commission was created by the United Nations to resolve the border disputes and improve relations between the two countries. From 2002 to 2006 some 19 sessions of the Mixed Commission were held, alternating between Yaounde and Abuja.

The Mixed Commission was very successful in its activities. It supervised the peaceful and orderly transfer of authority in some 40 villages around Lake Chad and along the land boundary. Some 460 kilometers of land boundary was demarcated. Agreements covering the four disputed sectors were realized. As a result of these UN initiatives, the Green Tree Accord was signed on 12 June 2006 and on 14 August, the Nigerian Government withdrew its forces from the Bakassi Peninsula. The Nigerian withdrawal was in respect of the 10 October 2002 ICJ ruling, which recognized the sovereignty of Cameroon over the Bakassi Peninsula. The peaceful resolution of the border dispute between Cameroon and Nigeria has been hailed in Africa and indeed worldwide as proof that it is possible for neighboring countries to solve their problems without resorting to war.

Challenges on United Nations Peace and Security Measures in Africa

Constraints on the United Nations Mixed Commission Over the Bakassi Conflict

During the resolution process over the Bakassi Conflict, the Cameroon-Nigeria Mixed Commission for the implementation of the ICJ judgment of 10 October 2002 had successfully held 16 meeting sessions by the end of 2006, including those of sub-commissions, but these meetings were plagued by several shortcomings which delayed the implementation process. One of the problems faced by the Mixed Commission was the non-respect of the withdrawal calendar by Nigeria. In the first phase of the withdrawal process in the Lake Chad area, things went smoothly as Nigeria withdrew its troops and administration without delay, and Cameroon did the same in the areas which were to be handed over to Nigeria. But when it came to the withdrawal of troops and administration from the Bakassi Peninsula, Nigeria used all measures to delay the process scheduled for 15 September 2004. Following Nigeria's refusal to respect the withdrawal and transfer of authority in the Bakassi Peninsula, meeting sessions were suspended for a period of 8 months between the 12th and 13th sessions, whereas official meeting sessions were to take place after every 2 months.

The activities of the Mixed Commission were foiled by some Nigerian officials who wanted to protect their interests in the Bakassi Peninsula. In August 2004, after the holding of the eleventh meeting, the technical team in charge of demarcation had to travel to the Bakassi Peninsula to prepare for the withdrawal process of Nigerian troops and administration, but the visit did not take place because the Nigerian population in the area protested against the withdrawal. These protests were orchestrated by politicians, who manipulated the population for their selfish interests. Among these politicians were the former Governor of the Cross-River State, Donald Duke and the Senator representing the Nigerian population in the Bakassi Area, Princess Florence Ita Giwa. Their aims were to preserve their political and economic interests in the area. Bakassi, being rich in oil, enabled them to receive enormous financial dividends from the Federal Government, depending on the oil productivity of their states. They believed that losing Bakassi would have a serious effect on the Cross-River State revenues and might influence the loss of the Senatorial seat in the area. These activities encouraged the population in the area to act aggressively towards the activities of the Mixed Commission. This dilatory strategy of the Nigerian politicians later resulted in a serious crime wave that included killings, burglary, piracy, hostage taking and requests for ransom, and total insecurity in the Bakassi Peninsula, which further paralyzed the activities of the Commission.

Within the Mixed Commission, the Nigerian delegation showed a tendency for bad faith by attempting to slow down its activities. Delays, contradictions and unprovoked aggression characterized Nigeria's responses during the deliberations. According to testimonies from some of the Cameroonian experts in the Mixed Commission, the representatives of the Nigerian Government in the Commission during meetings and/or in the field were always ready to contest or to call to question each boundary point which was to be marked. These Nigerian moves were aimed at renegotiating through the Commission the clauses of the ICJ ruling in their favor. In the same direction, Major Jean Nsola posited that Nigerians believed Cameroon was so attached to the Bakassi Peninsula that its government was ready to allow her maritime boundaries to be negotiated with Nigerian in exchange of the Bakassi Peninsula (Ebot 2006, 75). This view was buttressed by the fact that, during the preliminary session of the Joint Technical Team for demarcation in August 2004, the Nigerian delegation brought a new draft for the frontier that was not in conformity with the previous draft made by the ICJ. As a result, the draft was rejected by the Cameroonian and the UN delegations and the eleventh meeting which focused on that issue was suspended.

Furthermore, there was a scarcity of financial resources to facilitate the work of the Mixed Commission. According to the personal representative of the UN Secretary General, one of the reasons for the delay in the withdrawal and transfer processes in the Bakassi Peninsula was the scarcity of finances needed to carry on the demarcation activities.[1] The budgeted US$20 million needed to finance the demarcation process was not realized as Cameroon and Nigeria deposited the sum of US$4 million into the UN Trust Fund, the European Union donated 4 million euros, Germany and Britain also contributed, but the amount realized was not enough. To complete these funds, the two countries conjointly, with the UN Secretary General G, Kofi Atta Annan, reiterated their commitment to appeal to donors to raise additional funds for the demarcation activities. This situation seriously delayed the work of the subcommission on demarcation.

Multiplicity of Actors and the Fragile Peace Process in Burundi

A detailed examination of the Burundi peace negotiations and subsequent events (1996–2005) identify more specifically the inherent limitations in neoliberal conflict resolution.[1] This is achieved by constructing a narrative of the peace process that examines the impetus for peace, the key issues that stalled the talks and the contributions of a multiplicity of actors: regional states, mediators, especially the leadership (Julius Nyerere and Nelson Mandela), the protagonists (Burundi government, political parties, rebel movement, and their negotiating positions) and Western donors. The actualities of peace-making were investigated through a focus on the key issues debated and the tenets of the peace accord. Implementation of the accord, post-Arusha, reveals the temporality as well as the political space for marginalized ethnic elites and women; for example it eschews genuine public participation and institutionalizes violence as a mode of political contestation.

The anti-state critique at the foundation of neoliberalism manifests itself in the promotion of a multiplicity of actors in peace-making. In the case of the Burundi peace negotiations, states retained key roles in the procedures. Financial support for the talks came from international donors (the UN, EU, US, Canada etc.) and regional states (Uganda, Tanzania, Kenya, Zaire [DRC] and later South Africa) acted as overseers, supporting the mediatory roles of Julius Nyerere (April 1996–October 1999) and Nelson Mandela (1999–2000).[1] Regional states sought to define the nature of the peace process and to exert influence on the agreement. After regional summits in June and July 1996, they issued communiqués advocating a negotiated settlement to the crisis in Burundi and national reconciliation. They called for an arms embargo and the denial of visas to those opposed to peace. The Tutsi Officers' coup of 25 July 1996 that returned Pierre Buyoya, a former Tutsi president and coup leader, to power was condemned and regional states called for the immediate restoration of the national assembly and the lifting of the ban on political parties.

There were two mechanisms that regional states sought to use to exert influence over the peace process. The first was the proposal for the establishment of a regional peace-keeping force, which, although requested by the interim Burundian (Hutu) president, Syvestre Ntibantunganya, and his Tutsi prime minister, Antoine Nduwayo, met with considerable opposition from the military and the Tutsi-dominated parties (*Daily News* 1996; Bunting et al. 1999). Protests by members of the Tutsi political class and their supporters threw the country into the chaos that culminated in the July 1996 coup d'état.

The second mechanism by which regional states sought to exert pressure on the Burundi regime was regional sanctions. The economic embargo that was in place from October 1996 to January 1999 was not effective, in the sense that it was difficult to seal road, rail and air links to land-locked Burundi. Consequently, there was widespread violations and profiteering by regional elites (*The East African* 1998). Furthermore the lack of support from Western governments meant that goods and weapons continued to be transported via daily flights to and from Belgium, France and other EU countries.

The contradiction between the instant peace accord of neoliberal peace and the long drawn out concept of African peace was manifested in the establishment of the regional peace-keeping force. Despite considerable Tutsi opposition to the force of the African Union Mission to Burundi (AMIB), it started its operation on 18 October 2001 and was made up initially of 701 South African troops. Following UN Security Council Resolution 1554, AMIB was converted to the United Nations Mission in Burundi (ONUB) in June 2004 and increased to 5650, incorporating troops from Ghana, Nigeria and Senegal; all countries external to the region. ONUB's presences helped to maintain a semblance of stability during the implementation of the accord, but did not stop the flight and human rights violations by all sides.

Ceasefire negotiation between the traditional government and the Hutu rebel movement proceeded, with the facilitation team headed initially by the then deputy president of South Africa. The commitment of African leaders meant that what was a long and tortuous process ended with binding agreements. The lengthy process was due to the intervention of too many mediators (holding meetings in Rome, Libreville, South Africa and Dar es Salaam). Also, there was factionalism in the rebel movements; the Conseil National pour la Defence de la Democratie/Force pour la Defence de la Democratie (CNDD-FDD) had split into factions headed by Jean-Bosco Ndayikengurukiye and Pierre Nkurunziza, as did the Parti pour la Liberation du Peuple Hutu/Force National de Liberation (PALIPEHUTU-FNL) headed by Alain Mugabarabona and Agathon Rwasa. Finally, there was serious fighting by both the government and the rebels who used the post-accord period to rearm. Even the Front pour la Democratie au Burundi (FRODEBU), as late as November 2002, was reported to have established a rebel group, Ramico-pax.

A close examination of the procedures, actors and their positions during the Burundi peace negotiations reveals neoliberal peace-making as a contested terrain, in which long-term cessation of hostilities may not be top of the agenda. Thus, the commitment of many of the actors to the ending of direct violence appears questionable. The victory of CNDD-FDD reinforces the notion that the political kingdom can be won through violence. On the part of the belligerents, fighting intensified during and especially after the peace agreement. The Buyoya government used violence against civilians and, with the help of international actors, attempted to control the negotiations until the outcome was beneficial to the Tutsis and to the president.

Also, the asymmetrical power relations between Western donors and NGOs and regional and local actors, and their multiple and often competing interests, resulted in the Arusha Agreement reflecting only the minimal conditions for peace. It also institutionalized violence as part of the political discourse. Creating such spaces of peace requires a radical transformation of the state, much more than that envisioned in contemporary approaches to power-sharing and reconstruction programs. It is not just sufficient to ensure that peace remains on the agenda of regional and international organizations, a perspective on peace must be articulated, one which is long term in its outlook, opposed to all forms of violence, is inclusive and gives agency to a multi-voiced political community.

United Nations Failures During the Rwandan Genocide

The Rwandan genocide is a terrible drama that was experienced by the continent in the last century. It has been a difficult matter to allocate responsibility for the genocide and the interference of certain conflicting interests, both national and international. The responsibility of France which managed the situation until 1994 through Operation Noriot from October 1990, Operation Volcan from February 1993 and Operation Amaryllis in April 1994, gave rise to much debate. What is certainly true is that France, during this period intervened in an official framework of humanitarian operations. However, responsibility for the failure was largely attributed to the UN.

Many observers, during the last decade, highlighted several crucial mistakes made by the UN: mistakes in analysis at the regional level, likening the 'dispute' to a simple civil war which gave the UN a purely mediating role. The perpetuation of this mistake during the genocide was observed on 21 April 1994 when the UN Secretary General declared "that the most urgent task for UNAMIR was to seek a ceasefire, which could lead to positive political initiatives," whereas the real urgency lay in protecting the lives of tens of thousands of people in Rwanda (Soppelsa 2007, 166). Also, the vagueness of the missions assigned to UNAMIR which, according to reports, gave the impression of improvised activity driven more by the immediate interests of those who were making the decisions than by the security of the people of Rwanda.

A major failure was the obstinate refusal to have the genocide itself recognized by the Security Council. In this area, the prevarications of the Secretary General are also revealing: he initially proposed (after the Brussels decision to withdraw its contingent, following the massacre of 10 Belgian Blue Caps) to modify the mandate of UNAMIR and to authorize it to force the parties present to reach a ceasefire. Furthermore, he suggested a reduction of the said force, quartered in Kigali, in an effort to obtain the said ceasefire through meditation; this proposal was unfortunately put into effect, leaving the field open to the genocide killers. Finally, he tried to have the UN resolution implemented in order to envisage the possibility of the use of force. By contrast, however, the UN persisted at the time in refusing to use the term 'genocide,' under more or less silent pressure from Washington, in order to avoid the "legal consequences of such implementation", and in order not to be obliged to respect Article VIII of the 1948 Convention on the suppression of acts of genocide. We are only well aware of the consequences in Rwanda.

Today, the situation in the African Great Lakes Region in general and in Rwanda in particular, remains precariously balanced. Within the horn of Africa, the situation is even more dramatic: Somalia has been in the grip of civil war for several years, a war long aggravated by the increasing role of radical Islamism. The Somalian Islamist movement solemnly warned the international community that deployment of a peace force would be considered an act of provocation and would give rise to a fresh crisis. The radical Islamists are now advocating a holy war in an area of the world affected by a conflict which has led to some 500,000 deaths.

Flaws in United Nations Peacekeeping Mandates

Most early UN peacekeeping missions were so tightly circumscribed or left so vague and without support that they were doomed to ineffectiveness or failure from the very beginning. The financial situation of the UN may best be described as one of chronic financial crisis. Besides being generally underfunded, it has perpetual cash-flow dilemmas and is constantly off balance. The trouble in Rwanda, Burundi, Liberia and other countries was not properly addressed by the Security Council because of lethargy and ostensibly financial considerations with disastrous and tragic results. The following are some of the concrete financial problems of the organization: The big contributors on which the financial viability of the peace-keeping operations depends owe huge amounts. They use their powers to pursue policies where their interests are threatened and undermine the UN by withholding contributions. When they do not perceive the peace-keeping operations as of high priority in terms of their national interest, they simply neglect to pay (Mandez 2000, 43).

There are no penalties for late payment except the loss of their right to vote in the General Assembly if a government's arrears equal or exceed the amount it should have paid during the previous 2 years (Article 19 of the Charter). Penalties have been applied to small countries, but never to the big contributors. The UN reimburses governments that contribute troops and material to the peace-keeping operations or pays its missions directly, but payments are often late. Because cash-flow problems are typical and financial crises recurrent with the regular budget and the peace-keeping reserve fund is usually depleted early in the year, the UN has to dip into the peace-keeping special accounts to avert bankruptcy. There are so many UN peace-keeping operations and there will undoubtedly be so many more that for the system to have a special account for each one would be cumbersome and time-consuming.[1] The increasing costs of peace-keeping are the subject of complaints by both rich and poor countries and have been a factor in the Security Council's decisions to curtail operations in countries like Angola, Liberia and Rwanda. The present system obviously cannot support the establishment and maintenance of a standing military force for emergencies and prolonged operations.

Certain conventional proposals for reform have been presented and could possibly cover the short term. These can include charging interest or imposing fines for late payments, having a unified peace-keeping budget, authorizing the Secretary-General to obligate up to, say, one-third of the estimated cost of an operation once it is approved by the Security Council,[1] increasing the level of the Peace-Keeping Reserve Funds (and having it funded), exhorting the "deadbeat" countries—of which the US is the most notorious—to pay up their arrears, depriving delinquent countries of their rights to participate in the Security Council and General Assembly,[1] proposing that governments fund their contributions to peace-keeping budget from their national defense budget, and the like. Not only would it be difficult to obtain government agreement to such financial reforms but they would not address the basic problem of the UN's financial system: its complete dependence on dues from member governments, which have proven to be inadequate, unreliable, unpredictable and unassured. There is a crying need for radical surgery to place the UN's peace-keeping and other operations on a sound financial footing.[1]

Conclusion

Since its creation in 1945, the UN has played a significant role in maintaining peace and security, and the promotion of economic and socio-cultural development in the world. This study has argued that even though the UN has experienced several challenges in its objectives of maintaining peace and security in Africa, it has exhibited commendable efforts towards the promotion of peace and development in the continent. UN organizations played an important role in ending the Bakassi conflict between Cameroon and Nigeria. Solutions to the conflict went beyond the Bakassi Peninsula to other areas, which had been occupied by Nigerians along the border and also extended from a purely diplomatic solution to deal with security and developmental matters. Although the institution of the UN Secretary General was crucial in the resolution of the conflict, we however underscore the view that while peace can be achieved through the intervention of the UN, lasting peace can only be achieved through the collaboration and/or determination by the parties involved in the conflict.

Regional initiatives marked a significant and progressive step to the ending of genocide violence and the abuse of human rights in Africa, yet they did not have the full backing of international forces for peace. From the perspective of the Great Lakes Region, two lessons can be learnt from the Burundi peace negotiations. First, the potential exists for a major commitment by regional leaders to bring an end to protracted conflict in Africa, especially those that are genocidal and may have regionally destabilizing effects. Second, that with collective leadership, African leaders have the capacity to promote a new mode of politics, one that says no to coups and the overthrow of democratic regimes, and that this capacity can be mobilized and supported largely by African professionals. We acknowledge the efforts on the United Nations Office for Drugs and Crimes (UNODC) which in 2013 helped to establish an agreement in the Sahel Region between Mali, Morocco, Niger, Burkina Faso, Chad and Algeria to address the problem of drug trafficking, organized crime and terrorism. In the same year, a peace and security agreement was signed between the countries of the Great Lakes Region and peace talks held in Kampala, Uganda between the Government of the Democratic Republic of Congo and the M23 leaders all initiated by the United Nations.

This chapter revisited the Rwandan genocide to reveal that the failure of the UN to effectively implement peace in some countries could be due, to a great extent, to the unwillingness of states to support UN objectives. States are more concerned with their own national interests than with general interests of the global society. While governments regularly call for peace, justice and international cooperation, the particular interests of states often override their common goal. The challenges faced by the UN in implementing peace and security in the African continent lie in the self-interest and self-aggrandizement of African leaders. After 71 years of existence, the UN finds itself at a critical juncture that ought to be honestly confronted by the member states who are its proprietors and who endow it with its existing features. To reform the organization, two paths lie before the world community: countries should decide either to reduce their demands on the UN, thus giving it a decent chance of carrying out reduced policies, or recognize the necessity of improving its capacity and granting it greater resources, functions and coordinating power.

With the final winding down of the Cold War by the end of the 1980s, it was obvious to all that the UN would eventually embrace drastic reforms and changes if it was to remain relevant to the demands of the twenty-first century. Its structures and functions were determined by the victorious Allied Powers after the Second World War, but there was no doubt that it would continue that way with close to 60 member states at its inception in 1945. The organization has today grown into a truly universal organization with 194 members. Since many member states, especially those in Africa, gained independence after the organization was created, it now has to adapt to emerging geopolitical and geostrategic changes in the world. To remain static would render the organization ineffective to meet the aspirations of nation-states. Thus, the United Nations should carry out structural reforms in its major six organs and allow its member states especially from Africa to provide participatory functions.

The African continent is plagued with numerous conflicts, yet no African country is a member of the UN Security Council. The Security Council remains the exclusive monopoly of great powers who took decisions on African countries without their consent. Modern methods of conflict resolution involve an exclusive participatory function of the belligerents. This should be done not only at the level of the African continent but also at the UN Security Council. The implication was that the voices of those states that matter and of those regions, especially Africa, that were marginalized should be given their due recognition and importance in the Security Council. Those that contributed appreciably to the work of the UN should be rewarded with greater involvement in global governance as a measure to correct the injustices of the past and make the United Nations truly democratic and representative in the current global realities. In short, the institutional and structural inadequacies of the UN should be overhauled to enable the organization to face the challenges and collective threats in the world.

References

Adejumobi, S. (2000). Elections in Africa: A fading shadow of democracy. In O. Nnoli (Ed.), *Government and politics in Africa: A reader* (pp. 242–261). Harare: AAPS Books.

Adigwi, F. (1981). *Essentials of Government for West Africa*. Ibadan: Ibadan University Press.

Albert, T. (1979). *What kind of Africa by the year 2000?* Addis Ababa: Organization of African Unity.

Aletum, M. T. 1994. "Bakassi Conflicts: A Socio- Political Approach" in Jurisdis info, No. 21.

Aluko, O. (1997). *The foreign policy of African states*. London: Hodder and Stoughton.

Amstutze, M. (1995). *International conflict and cooperation: An introduction to world politics*. Madison: Brown and Benchmark.

Annan, A. K. (1998). *The causes of conflict and the promotion of durable peace and sustainable development*. New York: NGLC.

Annan, A. K. (2001). *Annual report on the works of the United Nations Organizations*. New York: NGLC.

Ayodele, A. (2001). *Africa women's forum: Women and conflict management in Africa*. Ogun State: Alf Publication.

Cruz, R. (1998). *Voices from Africa: Conflict, peace and reconstitution*. Geneva: NGLS.

Daley, P. (2007). The Burundi peace negotiations: An African experience of peace-making. In H. Graham & S. Colin (Eds.), *Review of African political economy* (pp. 333–352). United Kingdom: ROAPE Publications.

Denis Sassou, N. (2007). The African Union and the United Nations Organization. In L. Henry (Ed.), *African geopolitics: Africa in the United Nations system* (pp. 231–239). Brazzaville: Pasco Edition Publicite.

Ebot, D. T. (2006). *The Bakassi conflict resolution process from 1994 to 2005: Balance sheet and prospects*. DESS Dissertations in International Relations. Yaoundé: IRIC.

Elisha, B. M. (2006). *United Nations conflict resolution and management strategies: Rwanda, 1990-2004*. Ph.D Thesis, University of Calabar. Nigeria: University of Calabar.

Elmanjra, M. (1971). *The United Nations system: A critical analysis*. London: Faber and Faber.

Essoungou, A. M. 2013. "The Sahel: One Region, Many Crises", In AfricaRenewal , December.

Ewang, J. N. (1987). *Participation in the United Nations General Assembly: A study of Cameroons participation*. Doctoral thesis in International Relations. Yaounde: IRIC.

Francis, D. (2000). Anatomy of conflict in Africa. In O. Nnoli (Ed.), *Government and politics in Africa: A reader* (pp. 835–851). Harare: AAPS Books.

George, N. (2003). *The way forward for Africa*. Limbe: Design House.

Gerard, D. (2007). Lessons learned from the United Nations experience. In L. Henry (Ed.), *African geopolitics: Africa in the United Nations system* (pp. 181–189). Brazzaville: Pasco Edition Publicite.

Jacques, S. (2007). Two United Nations organization failures: Rwanda and Somalia. In L. Henry (Ed.), *African geopolitics: Africa in the United Nations system* (pp. 107–144). Brazzaville: Pasco Edition Publicite.

Mamdoni, K. (2000). Democratic theory and democratic struggles in Africa. In O. Nnoli (Ed.), *Government and politics in Africa: A reader* (pp. 220–239). Harare: AAPS Books.

Mandez, R. P. (2000). War and peace in the context of international public finance and globalization. In *Africa and the challenges of globalization*. Twenty-First Conference of Heads of State and Government of Africa and France. Yaounde.

Mandi, H. G. (1970). *The United Nations as a political institution*. London: Oxford University Press.

Moussounga, M. (2007). The cooperation between the United Nations and ECOWAS in Sierra Leone. In L. Henry (Ed.), *Africa in the United Nations system* (pp. 171–179). Brazzaville: Pasco Edition Publicite.

Ngoh, V. J. (1988). *Cameron 1884–1985: A hundred years of history*. Yaounde: Navi-Group Publications.

Rose frii, M. (2011). The conflict of civilizations: The case of the Arab and Western civilizations. In A. Daniel, A.-P. Temgoua, E. S. D. Fomin, & W. Dze-Ngwa (Eds.), *Boundaries and history in Africa: Issues in conventional boundaries and ideological frontiers* (pp. 259–269). Yaoundé: Department of History University of Yaoundé 1.

Shedrack, G. B. (2007). *Introduction to peace and conflict studies in West Africa*. Lagos: Spectrum Books.
Soppelsa, J. 2007. "Two United Nations Organizations Failures: Rwandan and Samalia" In African Geopolitics. No.25. January-March.
Steiner, A. (2013). Executive Director of UNEP.
Teng, C. C. (1968). *Synopses of United Nations cases*. New York: C.E.I.P.
United Nations. (1979). *Basic facts about the United Nations*. New York: United Nations Department of Public Information.
United Nations. (2004). *Basic facts about the United Nations*. New York: United Nations Department of Public Information.
United Nations. (2013). *United Nations Environmental Programme (UNEP)*. New York: United Nations Department of Public Information.
Yusuf, B. (2000). Perspectives on the politics of structural adjustment, informalisation and political change in Africa. In O. Nnoli (Ed.), *Government and politics in Africa: A reader* (pp. 771–798). Harare: AAPS Books.

Primus Fonkeng holds a Ph.D in History with specialization in the History of Cameroon and Nigeria and History of International Relations from the University of Yaoundé I, Cameroon. He is a Senior Lecturer with the Department of History, Faculty of Arts, University of Buea in Cameroon. He has published several Articles in Peer Reviewed Journals. His areas of research are Conflict Resolution and the Promotion of Peace, Human Rights and Governance in Africa and the World. Email: primusf2000@yahoo.com.

Chapter 20
African Development Initiatives

Peter Elias

Introduction

The state of economic and human development in Africa is a mirror of the continent's development initiatives. Such development in Africa has, compared to other developing regions, remained a dilemma in spite of various African development initiatives both domestic and foreign, before and after independence. Even though African development initiatives have come with clear development aspirations and milestones there continues to be profound, prevailing and increasing shortcomings that limit the capability to translate these aspirations into convincing achievements. It is interesting to note that the region has both the potential and prospects for economic and human development, as shown by recent indicators (Table 20.1) but the fluctuations and instability characterizing African development initiatives are indeed the major setbacks (Broadberry and Gardner 2013). For instance, in comparison with other developing regions (Table 20.1), population indicators in Africa offer both some prospects and possible challenges. The population growth rate and the proportion of urban dwellers as a percentage of the total population places a huge burden on urban governance for infrastructure delivery but also makes Africa a major attraction for labor and markets (Elias et al. 2016). Likewise, Africa's income indices including gross national product (GNP), purchasing power parity (PPP) and Gini levels show a big gap compared with other developing regions (Table 20.1), which is a measure of the performance of African development initiatives over the years. Also, in terms of economic outlook, including GDP per capita, investment per capita, exports per capita and savings per GDP, Africa lagged considerably in almost all, which points to the state of economic performance of various development initiatives. In like manner, the human capital indices as shown in

P. Elias (✉)
Department of Geography, University of Lagos, Akoka-Yaba, Lagos, Nigeria
e-mail: pelias@unilag.edu.ng

O. Akanle, J.O. Adésìnà (eds.), *The Development of Africa*, Social Indicators Research Series 71, DOI 10.1007/978-3-319-66242-8_20

Table 20.1 Development indicators in developing regions

Development indicators	Africa	South Asia	East Asia	Latin America
Population				
Population (millions), 1997	612	1281	1751	494
Population (millions), 2013	1216[a]	1670	2005[b]	588[c]U
Population growth (%), 1997	2.9	1.8	1.2	1.6
Dependency ratio (workers age per 15–64 per dependent), 1997	1.1	1.4	2.0	1.7
Urban population share (%) 1997	31.7	26.6	32.2	73.3
Urban population share (%) 2013	37	32	51	79
Urban population growth (%) 1997	4.9	3.3	3.7	2.2
Income				
GNP per capita (dollars at market exchange rate) 1997	510	380	970	3940
PPP GNP per capita, 1997	1460	1590	3170	6730
PPP GNP per capita, 2013	3314[a]	5031	10,729[b]	14185[c]
Gini index, latest year available	46.5	31.2	40.6	51.0
Economy				
GDP per capita, 1997	525	449	715	1890
Investment per capita, 1997	92	105	252	504
Exports per capita, 1997	163	51	199	601
Savings/GDP (%) 1997	16.6	20.0	37.7	24.0
Human capital				
Human development index, 1995	40.5	48.2	63.9	76.8
Life expectancy at birth (years) 1997	52.4	62.5	68.4	69.7
Infant mortality (per 1000 live births), 1997	89.9	70.5	37.8	31.8
Infant mortality (per 1000 live births), 2013	92	57	20	18
Adult literacy (%), 1997	43	51	17	13
Natural capital				
Land area per capita (hectares), 1997	3.85	0.37	0.91	4.06
GDP per hectare (1987 dollars), 1997	136	1214	786	466

Source: The World Bank Data
[a]Sub-Saharan Africa
[b]East Asia and Pacific
[c]Latin America and the Caribbean

Table 20.1 show that African development initiatives have not adequately supported improvement in critical aspects of human life and welfare.

Broadberry and Gardner (2013) give an historical insight into Africa's economic growth prospects using a European perspective. Their paper characterizes pre-independence and post-independence Africa's economic growth as the boom and burst periods and warns that the fluctuations will persist until a robust civil society is put in place in the region. Even though Broadberry and Gardner (2013) provided some development indicators to compare the pattern of African economic growth with other regions, especially Europe, but did not explicitly link these growth indices to any African development initiatives. Providing a link between African development initiatives and development indicators and/or performance will clearly explain the nature and role of African development initiatives in the economic and human development conditions of the region. It will also be easy to situate this within the context of Africa's development history and performance in the global context. This is the focus of this chapter.

A study of Africa's development initiatives will therefore be useful in providing answers to the frequently asked questions about the continent's checkered history, and its economic and human development trajectories. By using statistical facts, it will show the pattern of Africa's development through the various initiatives that have been largely influenced by different views, histories, regional alignments, and priorities. Rigorous analysis of the underlying philosophies, histories, perspectives and priorities is needed to connect our understanding of past, present and even future African development initiatives and performance indicators to the influence of global initiatives. This is also necessary to reconstruct Africa's past and future economic and human trajectories from past, present and future development initiatives. The evaluation also depicts the impacts of different development initiatives on African industrialization, entrepreneurship and institutions which enhance, limit or propel Africa to use the region's comparative advantage in global markets and for intraregional integration.

This chapter therefore characterizes African development initiatives by linking the economic and human development trajectories of Africa to development initiatives. It examines the proponents behind African development initiatives to show the various motivations and manipulations involved. The chapter also compares African development initiatives with their counterparts in other regions to see any similarities or differences in their essence, agenda and performances. The current debates on global and regional development initiatives are equally examined to note the recent priorities and pursuits that are shaping Africa's development processes, practices and experiences. Similarly, it assesses the constraints and opportunities associated with African development initiatives accounting for the past, present and future pattern of human and economic development. It makes practical suggestions on how African development initiatives can be strengthened to help development in the region.

The approach adopted for this chapter involves rigorous analysis of various African development initiatives with a view to increasing understanding of the past, present and possible future state of development in the region. It carefully analyzes existing facts and publications of UN development organizations, the World Bank, African national development agencies including the African Union (AU), the New Economic Partnership for African Development (NEPAD), the Economic Community of West African States (ECOWAS), Southern African Development Community (SADC), and other international development partners such as the European Union to establish some connections and expositions. After this introduction, the second section examines the historical pattern of African development initiatives, the third section focuses on the nature of African development initiatives, and in the fourth section, the chapter delves into the analysis of factors/considerations that form the underlying motivations for African development initiatives. The evaluation of African development initiatives and the strategies for strengthening them are presented in the fifth and sixth sections of the chapter.

Historical Construct of African Development Initiatives

African development initiatives have been viewed from many perspectives. Baah (2003) divides the history of African development initiatives primarily into two time periods; that is, the colonial and post-independence periods. The period before the 1960s is referred to as the colonial era characterized by imperialism and/or empire building. The post-independence period is further divided into three, namely, the 1960–70 period, which was termed the period of political freedom, self-realization, economic growth and increased standard of living; the 1970s, which were tagged the decade of political instability and the 1980s and 1990s which were dubbed the decades of decay. The paper contests that African development initiatives in colonial and post-independence Africa were times when the African region was 'raped' and robbed of its natural resources by the imperialists and empire builders. A similar study by Broadberry and Gardner (2013) groups the history of economic growth in Africa into two time periods. These are the pre-independence and the post-independence periods which are typified as the boom and burst periods respectively. In the context of African development initiatives however, this chapter adopts a historical timeline that is divided into three periods: (i) colonialism, (ii) pan-Africanism and (iii) globalism. This division reflects the core philosophies and policies which were fundamental to shaping African development initiatives. Colonialism spanned the period between the 1890s and the 1950s; pan-Africanism, which started as Africanism in the 1900s later crystallized into pan-Africanism around the 1960s and beyond; while the wave of globalization was noticeable by the turn of the century and is still very much with us, shaping the modern world and Africa in intricate ways.

According to the *Glossary of Sociology*, colonialism refers to the process whereby nations establish their political and economic rule over less powerful nations. In the period between the 1870s and the 1900s, the African region witnessed extraordinary European exploitation, political manipulation, forceful invasion and subjugation. The scramble for Africa was motivated by three factors, namely, economic, political and social (Iweriebor 2012). The economic considerations for the imperialist conquest of the region included the need to feed the expanding industrial establishments and firms with unfailing sources of raw materials, the availability of growing markets and the lucrative investment opportunities. Similarly, the inter-European rivalries and battle for supremacy also spurred the political dimension of the scramble for Africa. The acquisition of territories in Africa signaled national supremacy among powerful nations including Britain, France, Germany, Belgium, Italy, Portugal and Spain (Iweriebor 2012). Another factor was an array of social problems including unemployment, poverty, diseases, congestion and rural–urban migration which characterized the Industrial Revolution and left a sizeable proportion of the people in Europe largely uncared for. There was a need therefore to create and establish a number of settler colonies in different parts of Africa to absorb these surplus populations. The various colonialists introduced several policies that typified their philosophical orientations and priorities. In most of the English-speaking territories, the policy of indirect rule as a strategy of conquest was adopted which relied on traditional chiefs as intermediaries. The French territories on the other hand used the tactic of assimilation of a small population of Africans into French culture and citizenship.

Similarly, the colonial systems of governance were extremely centralized, resulting in mere political instruments rather than economic and human development strategies for African nations. It was a situation where certain people who had lived long in Africa were compelled to think about Africa in terms of Europe and for the interests of Europe. The two major colonial administrations in Africa were the British and the French, featuring clearly distinguishable development initiatives in their unique philosophies and policies on land, labor, commodity markets, social infrastructure and governance. The European appropriation and use of land varied between the British and French colonies using different strategies such as 'settlers', 'plantation' and 'peasants' involving land-extensive or labor-intensive cultivation (Iweriebor 2012). The characteristic nature of European farming techniques was both land-extensive and labor-saving which hindered productivity as a result of poor soil fertility (Austin 2008). This has a wide range of implications for productivity and incomes. According to Law (1995), this practice did enhance the potential comparative advantage of agricultural productivity for different nations from around 1880s.

On the other hand, Daron et al. (2009) have argued that the style of European colonialism accounts for Africa's relative poverty owing to the strategy of focusing on extraction rather than settling down in Africa to introduce durable institutions and policies for development, as was the case for economic development in Europe and the colonies of European settlement in North America and Australasia. Indeed, Palmer and Parsons (1977) argue further that European colonial extraction in Africa aimed to appropriate land or plantations for European settlers thereby providing investors and settlers with cheap and secure control over land; however, this compelled Africans to sell their labor to further European interests. This resulted in the absence of robust platforms for competition, an imperative for capitalism and self-sustained economic growth. Another feature of this period was the introduction of tariffs and the creation of marketing boards, which were allegedly a self-serving strategy rather than for the good of Africans, except a few who benefited and helped their principals to benefit from these arrangements. This situation pushed African nations and Africans to rigorously begin the campaign for inward development initiatives coined as Africanism.

The *Merriam-Webster Collegiate Dictionary* described the concept of Africanism as an allegiance to the traditions, interests or ideals of Africa. It suggests that the development philosophies of this tradition do not necessarily have to begin and end with Africans but a movement involving all pro-Africans. This gave birth to the pan-African movement around the 1900s whose foundation was laid abroad but was reinforced on African soil. This philosophy heralded a new wave of agitation and calls for the independence of African colonies from the European imperialists. So from around the 1960s and after, some previous European colonialists reluctantly granted their erstwhile colonies independence to create a new culture and philosophy of development initiatives. The whole scenario culminated in the formation of pan-Africanism focusing on issues of common interest in Africa and to Africans, including democracy, good governance, and human and economic development. Pan-Africanism was the bedrock for the formation of the Organization of African Unity in 1963 which later changed to the African Union (AU) in 2002. The AU which comprises 54 member nations was birthed to be the vanguard for a united continent to promote the realization of economic and political freedom from the colonialists and the integration of African nations. This has resulted in the creation and coordination of several institutions and initiatives for the economic, political and human development of Africa. The AU aims to introduce a single currency by 2023 through the establishment of a human rights court, a central bank and monetary fund. The Peace and Security Council was set up in 2004 to maintain peace and order in the region. For Africa's economic development, the AU in 2001 adopted the New Partnership for Africa's Development (NEPAD) with Africa's renewal strategies as a primary objective (AU/NEPAD 2010). It includes the eradication of poverty, the promotion of sustainable growth and development, and enhancing the integration of Africa into the global markets.

Thus, Africa's integration strategies aim at increased intraregional trade and improvement in international competitiveness. To achieve this goal, the sub-regional arrangements are being supported by a number of significant institutions and initiatives. These include several efforts to establish a single regional market such as the West African Economic and Monetary Union (WAEMU) established by ECOWAS; a free trade zone linking 11 countries in Central Africa and members of the Central African Economic and Monetary Community (CEMAC). Likewise in East Africa, the East Africa Community (EAC) established a customs union in 2005 known as Common Market for Eastern and Southern Africa (COMESA). There is also the Southern Africa Customs Union (SACU) which has been re-invigorated under a new agreement to galvanize its programmes. Part of the emerging strategies for the integration of African nations also include economic institutions and frameworks such as the African Common Market (2025), the Africa Monetary Union (2030), the Africa Customs Union (2019), the Africa Free Trade Areas (2017) and the United States of Africa. These institutions and initiatives have been buoyed by global events and policies under the influence of globalism.

Globalism marked the switch from national or regional thinking to global ideologies. It became popular around the 2000s and is considered to be a unique revolution whose far-reaching ideologies transcend state or regional borders. The *Merriam-Webster Collegiate Dictionary* defines globalism as a national policy of treating the whole world as a proper sphere for political influence. The increasing impact of globalism is witnessing the continued expansion of the global marketplace for goods, capital, labor, and ideas. This has necessitated states and regions experiencing a new fashion of integration. Globalism is affecting the world economic, political and cultural landscape in different but interconnected ways. The global markets remain the umbilical cord of economic growth in the modern world and particularly for Africa. Africa's economy shrinks or expands with fluctuations in the global markets. In the context of imperialism too, globalism is a marked feature of the African region whose economic and political history is dominated by influential nations. These nations have crafted and packaged very subtle financial inducements and policies to subjugate African nations. On the brighter side, however, in the era of globalism, low- and middle-income economies including Africa doubled their market share of world commodity exports from approximately 15% to almost 30% between 1990 and 2005. Likewise, during the same period, trade among developing nations increased even faster, at nearly 15% annually, to reach approximately 8% of world commodity exports. Similarly, international private financial flows tripled as a share of world GDP over the same period. In the meantime, international foreign direct investment flows by region in Africa grew unevenly between 2000 and 2014 as shown in Fig. 20.1.

The global integration of nations across borders has also resulted in a new wave of tourism and migration as shown by global facts (Elias and Babatola 2016). The available statistics show that international tourist arrivals in Sub-Saharan Africa almost doubled in 1990, which accounted for revenue of US$800 million in 2005. The fascinating feature of this national integration across borders is that the preferred destinations of almost 35% of the tourists are developing nations, which are even pulling new visitors at faster rates ahead of their developed counterparts. Similarly, the value of remittances repatriated by migrants from the developing economy in 2006 exceeded US$200 billion.

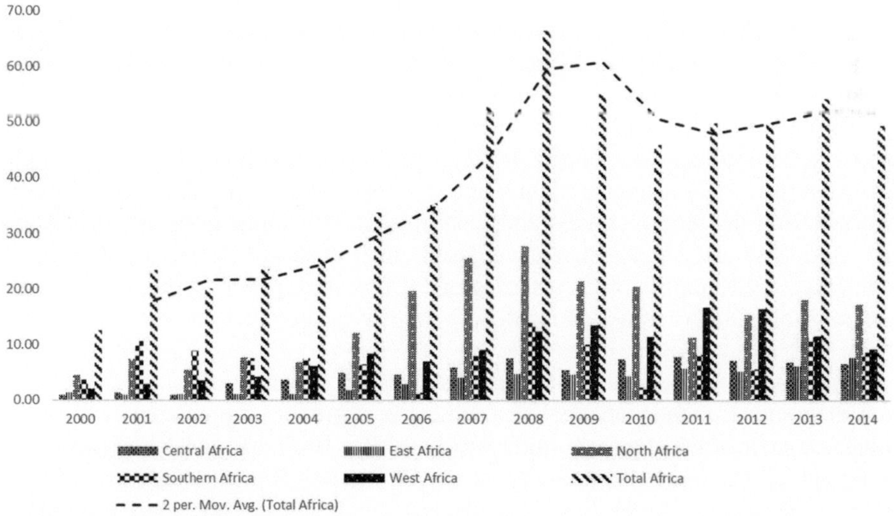

Fig. 20.1 Inward foreign direct investment by region, USD$ billion (2000–2014) Source: Author's computation with data from the IMF

Globalism is consequently influencing African nations' domestic economic policy directions. The lure of the prospects offered through the growth of global markets has enabled African nations to accept global integration. Already this is yielding incredible trends in economic growth and positively affecting the prosperity of millions of people in Africa. Meanwhile, since the 2000s, nations in Meanwhile, since the 2000s, nations in Africa are witnessing unprecedented robust real economic growth. For example, the economic growth of oil-exporting nations in Africa stands at an average rate of about 8.5% and a more modest 4% for others (AfDB, OECD, UNDP 2016, 2014). Evidence of the nature of African development initiatives is analyzed in depth in the next section.

The Nature of Africa's Development Initiatives

The uniqueness of African development experiences is evident in the nature of African development initiatives depending on the dominant philosophical viewpoints (Table 20.2). Colonialism is characterized by foreign dominated thoughts and policies. The various development initiatives reflect the priority of the home country and were simply imposed on the various colonial territories instead of being negotiated locally. Land-extensive and labor-intensive policies were geared to commodities for their industries back home rather than enhancing the productivity of Africans or capacity building (Palmer and Parsons 1977). Their development initiatives did not support the building of competences or critical skills acquisition in the locals except where it met their egocentric priorities. The imperialist had no intentions of conforming to any global convention or norms and did not encourage advocacy for African nations. They also failed to lay the foundation for robust economic development and regional or global integration. These issues are among the reasons why the legacy of European colonialism in Africa entrenched backwardness, mediocrity and under-development (Austin 2008).

The nature of Pan-Africanism, which has its roots in African thought, aspirations and ideals, immediately sought to lay the foundation for self-reliance, self-sufficiency and self-actualization through self-sustaining economic growth. As evidenced from the tenets, context and typologies of development initiatives, Africa and Africans seek a true renaissance based on their shared interests, passion and comparative advantage among other regions. This has propelled openness and cooperation within the African region and between Africa and other regions of the world (Fig. 20.2).

The nature of African development initiatives has clearly demonstrated a craving for integration into the global policies and markets and for intraregional integration. Besides, African development initiatives have also been affected by a number of geographic, economic and political factors. In the last 50 years, data from World Population Review (2016) shows that Africa's population size and growth has experienced an explosion, leapfrogging from about 229 million in 1950 to 1.2 billion in 2014 which represent 9.1 and 15.1% of the total world population respectively. The

Table 20.2 The nature of Africa's development initiatives

Philosophical viewpoint	Nature	Development initiatives
Colonialism	Entirely Foreign Land-extensive and labor-intensive Absence of competitive markets No desired competences Lacked negotiation No advocacy Did not conform to global development conventions and norms Did not promote regional and global integration Centralized administration	Direct rule Assimilation Building of empire states including settlers, peasants and plantations Resource extraction Export of raw materials
Pan-Africanism	Home-grown initiatives which includes: The OAU charter, the Monrovia declaration, the Lagos plan of action, the Abuja treaty, the AU constitutive act and, NEPAD, etc. (Adedeji 2002; NEPAD 2001) Creates the desired competences Shared common interests and aspirations Involves advocacy Leverages global development convention and norms Forms partnership with international organizations Follows global practices and standards Promotes regional and global integration Values human rights Influences, implements and monitors development agendas	AU/NEPAD planning and coordination agency (NPCA) capacity development strategic framework (CSDF) The Africa we want, (Africa Union Commission 2014). NEPAD-OECD Africa investment initiative at national and regional levels Peace and security council – AU Economic development – AAP, NEPAD, ADB, Infrastructure development – PIDA Single regional markets – WAEMU, CEMAC, COMESA, SACU, ACM/AMU, ACU, etc. Regional integration – ECOWAS, SADC, EAC, United States of Africa, single currency, etc. Free trade areas Democratic governance and so on.
Globalism	Global negotiation Supports and enhances human rights Pursues crisis recovery and reconstruction Strengthens regional cooperation Influences, implements and monitors development agendas Encourages funding and counterpart contribution	UN 10-year capacity building Programme for the African union Peace and security – UN security council, international criminal courts at The Hague Infrastructure consortium for Africa (ICA) Public health delivery – WHO, UNAIDS, Agriculture and food security – FAO Human migration and refugees – UNCHR Economic development – UNDP, UNCTAD, UNWTO, UNIDO, the World Bank, IMF, ECA, etc. Education and human development – UNESCO, UNICEF, ILO, etc. Gender – UN women Human settlement and environment – UNEP, UN–habitat, UNFCCC, IPCC, etc.

Source: Author's thoughts

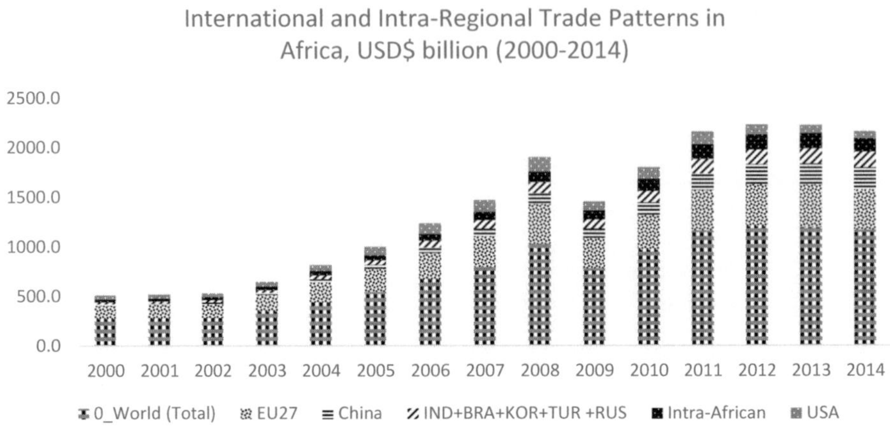

Fig. 20.2 International and intra-regional trade patterns in Africa, USD$ billion (2000–2014) (Source: Author's compilation with data from UN COMTRADE 2015)

report further indicates that Africa's population from recent projections will constitute 19.0% and 35.3% of the world population by 2034 and 2100 respectively. Furthermore, the demographic composition of Africa's population reveals a youthful population with a median age of about 20 years in 2014 compared to a world average of 30 years. These scenarios give Africa a comparative advantage in terms of expanding markets and labor force which cannot be ignored. Indeed, the increase in population especially the youth bulge is attracting investors and businesses to the African region and encouraging local private investors as well. This is gradually making Africa a significant economy, an epicenter of investment and a force to be reckoned with globally.

Similarly, there are numerous global initiatives including the Millennium Development Goals (MDGs) and the recent Sustainable Development Goals (SDGs), the Monetary Consensus, General Agreement on Tariffs and Trade, Global Alliance on Vaccines and Immunization, Global Environment Monitory Systems (GEMS) and Joint United Nations Programme on HIV/AIDs that are influencing, implementing and monitoring African development initiatives. Although these initiatives have been basically negotiated globally they are being implemented in Africa through several local programmes and institutions. Some of the main features of the global development initiatives include support for human rights, pursuit of crisis recovery and reconstruction, protection of environment and human settlements, encouragement of funding and financial contributions in core areas, as well as influencing, implementing and monitoring development agendas for economic growth and human development. There is tremendous influence from various United Nations (UN) development systems in Africa as indicated in Table 20.1. These development partnerships and strategies have resulted in peace keeping and security, humanitarian relief, human rights, poverty reduction, education and human development, health, infrastructure, global development conventions and norms, advocacy, crisis recovery and reconstruction and setting global technical standards as core development agendas.

Impacts of African Development Initiatives

Assessing the impacts of African development initiatives reveals both the constraints and opportunities facing Africa's development experience. Table 20.2 expounds the major domains and role of colonialism, pan-Africanism and globalism in defining the economic and human development trajectories of the region in all aspects of economic development, industrialization, democratic governance, education, health, human rights, regional cooperation, agriculture, social policy, science and technology, poverty reduction, security and peace, human settlements and environment. It enumerates the key policies and strategies of these viewpoints, stressing both their positive and negative impacts in relation to Africa's development paths.

Indeed, the development of the African region has been constrained or helped by what was done or undone in the various philosophical viewpoints. Colonialism failed to put the African people at the center of the various development initiatives. The achievements in the social and physical infrastructure only served the economic and political interests of the colonialists. Their failure has been very obvious even while colonialism lasted and became the foundation for many of the ills that have bedeviled development in the African region. Both in their spirit and letter the development initiatives as pursued through colonialism were anti-people, retrogressive and unsustainable. On the other hand, both pan-Africanism and globalism derived from people-focused considerations or aspirations of reducing injustice to enhance social inclusion. The development paradigm enumerated under these viewpoints supports and strengthens intraregional and global integration as fundamental to African development initiatives. Similarly, both pan-Africanism and globalism pursue African unity, peace and security. They encourage capacity building and empowerment based on the potential vested in the huge demographic dividends associated with the youths and women in Africa. These viewpoints also support and encourage the contributions of African nations to financing African development initiatives. Likewise, they promote inclusive and accountable governments and institutions to ensure inclusive economic growth and sustainable development (Table 20.3).

Strategies for Strengthening Africa's Development Initiatives

In order to strengthen African development initiatives to make Africa relevant in the modern global arena it will be necessary to identify some challenges which must be conquered. These challenges are highlighted as follows:

Table 20.3 Impacts of African development initiatives

Major indicators	Colonialism	Pan-Africanism	Globalism
Economic development	Land-extensive primary exports, self-supporting economy running on tax payments, extraversion, monoculture economy, introduction of money a platform for trade liberation and international trade	Encouraging intraregional and global integration such AAP, NEPAD, free trade areas, etc., pan-African banks	Economic recovery and adjustment packages of the IMF and the World Bank, ECA etc., commodity market regulation e.g. OPEC Aid from the WHO, UNICEF, UNDP and the World Bank for social and physical infrastructure Creating favorable trade tariffs Trade liberalization e.g. open market operations, etc. Providing favorable fiscal and monetary policies for Africa
Industrialization	Subsistence oriented, booming mineral industry, neglect of robust industrialization and local processing of raw materials	Supporting the growth of regional infrastructure Ambitious policies and strategies for Africa's industrialization through NEPAD, PIDA, AAP	Transformative industrial policy for Africa by the ECA Co-financing critical infrastructure for Africa's industrialization
Democratic governance	Centralized government, political fragmentation, lopsided political boundaries, judicial system, civil service, weakening of indigenous system of government Governance procedures, laws and structures alien to African tradition;	In collaboration with African nations and international development partners growing the culture of democratic structure for inclusive, transparent and accountable public institutions and governance	Supporting and funding the growth of structures for the democratization of African nations
Education	Provided the foundation for basic education and rise of African elites, introduction of lingua franca	Helping to increase the human development ratings of Africans through campaigns, funding and collaborations	Increased funding and scholarship opportunity towards capacity building, Knowledge production and dissemination

(continued)

Table 20.3 (continued)

Major indicators	Colonialism	Pan-Africanism	Globalism
Health	Basic health facility, malnutrition, massive reduction in maternal and infant mortality, eradication of endemic diseases, etc. created awareness for improved water and sanitation systems	Halting the loss of skilled health personnel through the creation of opportunities and world-class health facilities	Creating awareness, promoting collaboration, supporting campaigns and health care delivery systems, capacity building program etc.
Human rights	Loss of African sovereignty and independence and the right to deal directly with the outside world	Openly condemning human right abuses, criminalizing offenders and supporting, promoting and protecting genuine causes of the marginalized or vulnerable individuals or groups	Nurturing and sponsoring structures that strengthen and protect human rights
Regional integration	Fragmentation of the continent, foundation for alignment of sub-regional groups along political and cultural/linguistic inclinations	Establishing institutions and initiatives that enhance intraregional cohesion and integration	Policies that increase divergence in the region Launching and fostering regional peace and security
Agriculture	Support the growth of cash crops such as cocoa, rubber, coffee, groundnuts, sisal, etc. No deliberate efforts for value-added agricultural products	The activities of Africans and African institutions through research and development strategies are yielding tremendous results in improved agricultural productivity, food security and regional markets for farm products	Ensuring food security; high-yielding seedlings Improved agricultural technologies and practices etc.
Social policy	Provision of basic physical and social infrastructure including roads, railways, telephones, telegraphs and airports Transformation of the social culture	Instilling the consciousness of common history and interests among African nationals Nurturing social cohesion and interdependence and intraregional cooperation	Enshrining inclusive economic growth, enduring inclusive and accountable governance structures; Linking development initiatives to local needs and priorities Raising human dignity and promoting human rights; etc.

(continued)

Table 20.3 (continued)

Major indicators	Colonialism	Pan-Africanism	Globalism
Science and technology	Insulated and isolated the continent from scientific and technological world	Encouraging competition and platforms for innovative activities among Africans Learning and implementing best practices around the world Rejecting the temptation of turning Africa into dumpsites for science and technological waste etc.	Encouraging the brain drain Leading in technological transfer Capacity development; Protecting intellectual property right; etc.
Poverty reduction	Increase in purchasing power and demand for consumer goods, creation of wealth	Targeting and evolving programmes to reduce the proportion of Africans below the poverty line	Reducing capital flight Encouraging local industries
Security and peace	Encouraged the continuous harmonious co-habitation of a continent ravaged by intra-communal and inter-ethnic conflicts; helped in stabilizing the region	Organizing and coordinating regional peace-keeping activities Rejecting and/or opposing antidemocratic tendencies, practices and governments, etc.	Enforcement of peace and security initiatives and strategies
Sustainable human settlements and environments	Fostered the growth of urban centers through urban-biased policies, rising rural–urban migration	Attempting to halt rapid rural–urban migration through massive integrated rural–urban development policies and projects	Evolving and funding sustainable human settlements and environments Sharing of best practices; encouraging innovations and competitions, etc.

Source: Author's thoughts

Lack of Financial Resources This has been a major challenge facing African development initiatives. Mobilizing funds for African development initiatives has been hindered by the faulty structures of colonialism which failed to make self-reliance an economic culture in the continent. Self-reliance flourishes in an atmosphere of competition and capitalism. Although African nations got political independence, the absence of competition and capitalism has denied the region economic freedom from their colonial masters, which has also elevated state-controlled economy above the private sector.

Absence of Harmony and Internal Cohesion Another challenge facing African development initiatives is the lack of internal organizational cohesion. Several institutions have been created under pan-Africanism and globalism yet there have been a lot of inconsistencies, incompetence and ineffectiveness due to internal contentions and disagreements.

Threats of Competition from Other Regions Modern international competition in developing and developed regions has also influenced African development initiatives in negative ways. Globalism has not been particularly beneficial because Africa has a history of weak foundations for competition and capitalism. Other developing regions including Latin America and Asia are becoming rising economic forces. Their homegrown economic and political structures are indeed fundamental to their human and economic development. Global economic and human development indicators including GDP, foreign direct investment (FDI), the Human Development Index, trade flows, and so forth have put several nations in these areas far ahead of their African counterparts. Similarly, the advanced countries have demonstrated their superiority in the area of human security and peace, the eradication of poverty, hunger and disease, gender equality and climate change. African history is dotted with unpleasant experiences that have confined several nations within the continent to slavish and dependency tendencies.

Non-access to Desirable Competences The non-access to desirable competences has also slowed down African development initiatives. The nature of knowledge development in Africa has been unable to produce the relevant skills and competences required to drive economic growth and sustainable development. This has made Africa a largely dependent economy, importing almost everything from household commodities to office to industrial needs.

Effect of Colonial and Neocolonial Imperialists The influence of colonial and neocolonial imperialists is shown in the dominance of advanced economies over their past territories or colonies in the aspects of unequal economic exchanges. Trade balances have remained always in favor of the advanced countries. Even though this author is of the view that African nations with several years of political independence should have evolved home-grown self-reliance mechanisms, the political and economic legacies of colonialism in Africa have nevertheless not adequately established the right foundation for economic emancipation and prosperity.

Having said that, there are a number of strategies that are suggested here which can render African development initiatives able to deliver and fulfil the aspirations of the region. They include:

Sensitivity to Regional Needs African development initiatives should be rendered sensitive to regional needs (Elias et al. 2016). People-driven African development initiatives are needed to eliminate hunger and disease, insecurity, inequality and poverty. This is possible if African development initiatives are drawn from local knowledge, local conditions and local needs that truly guarantee distributive justice, social inclusion and common wealth.

Knowledge Driven Economy Another strategy is to encourage adequate knowledge of the economic and human conditions of the region. The knowledge economy is the panacea for the growing inequality and poverty in Africa. It is only through efficient knowledge that effective economic and human development policies and plans can be evolved to nurture sustainable development. This compels huge and continuous investment in the aspect of research and innovation to grow and sustain Africa's share of global markets.

Internal Cohesion and Harmony in the African Continent The need to nurture internal cohesion and harmony in the African continent is not debatable. Africa's strength lies in the rich human, ecological, social and cultural diversities of the region. Therefore, African nations must shun divisive ideologies and/or politics and commit to a united Africa with common background, interests and aspirations. Efforts must be geared towards minimizing differences and emphasizing shared interests and aspirations. African nations should embrace continuous dialogue to resolve differences and contribute the resources required to nurture African development initiatives. These will strengthen the various institutions and intraregional blocs as foundation for pursuing regional development.

Cooperation and Collaboration with International Partners African development initiatives should continue to recognize the influence of global ideologies, policies and programmes. Integrating African development initiatives into global initiatives will boost the design, implementation and monitoring of economic and human development strategies in the region. It will also increase access to international support and technical assistance in core sectors.

Independence of African Development Initiatives and Institutions African development initiatives and institutions should deliberately defend the independence of local interests and institutions while collaborating and cooperating with international development partners. Africa should not lose the noble ideologies and aspirations of pan-Africanism while adopting globalism.

Summary and Conclusion

This chapter has examined the nexus among the historical perspectives, nature and impacts of African development initiatives. The nature of African development initiatives cannot be divorced from the rich historical foundations which underpins the various deveploment experiences. The pattern of development in Africa is a product of several forces both locally derived and globally controlled. Therefore, the development indicators and performance should be understood in the context of the dominant controlling philosophical thoughts and associated African development initiatives. Different motivations and considerations influenced the various emphases of the proponents of the development initiatives under each, which have also contributed to the inconsistent nature of African development experiences. The suggested strategies for strengthening African development initiatives in this chapter depend on an adequate understanding of the various challenges which have constrained sustainable economic and human development.

It is clear that contextualizing African development initiatives in the three dominant phases, that is, the philosophical viewpoints of colonialism, pan-Africanism and globalism, enhances an evaluation of the foundational issues responsible for the state of Africa. The pattern of economic and human development in Africa remains a reflection of several forces both locally derived and globally controlled. Similarly, the various economic and human development indicators cannot be divorced from the dominant controlling philosophical thoughts which demonstrate the vision and mission of the proponents. The disparate foundations of colonialism, pan-Africanism and globalism are responsible for the uneven pattern of African development experiences. The foundation of colonialism and the dominance of globalism are still reflected in the aspirations of pan-Africanism. This is evident in the various efforts and strategies of intraregional and global integration. This compels further study to understand the controlling influence of the foundation of colonialism and the dominance of globalism on African development initiatives.

References

Adedeji, A. (2002, April 29). *From the Lagos Plan of Action to the New Partnership for African Development and from the Final Act of Lagos to the Constitutive Act: Wither Africa?* A keynote address at African Forum for Envisioning Africa, Nairobi, Kenya.

AfDB, OECD, UNDP. (2014). *Global value chains and Africa's industrialization: African economic outlook report*. doi:http://dx.doi.org/10.1787/aeo-2014-en

AfDB, OECD, UNDP. (2016). *African economic outlook: Sustainable cities and structural transformation*. pp. 51–113. doi:http://dx.doi.org/10.1787/aeo-2016-en

Africa Union Commission. (2014). *Agenda 2063: The Africa we want*. p. 92. http://www.un.org/en/africa/osaa/pdf/au/agenda2063-first10yearimplementation.pdf

AU/NEPAD. (2010). *Capacity Development Strategic Framework (CDSF)*. http://www.nepad.org/resource/au-nepad-capacity-development-strategic-framework-cdsf-1

Austin, G. (2008). Resources, techniques and strategies south of the Sahara: Revising the factor endowments perspective on African economic development, 1500–2000. *The Economic History Review, 61*, 587–624. doi:10.1111/j.1468-0289.2007.00409.x.

Baah, A. (2003, May 22–23). *History of African development initiatives*. A paper presented at the Africa Labour Research Network Workshop, Johannesburg.

Broadberry, S., & Gardner, G. (2013). *Africa's growth prospects in a European mirror: A historical perspective*. UK: The CAGE-Chatham House Series. No. 5.

Daron, A., Simon, J., & James, A. R. (2009). The colonial origin of comparative advantage. *The American Economic Review, 91*(5), 1369–1401.

Elias, P., & Babatola, O. (2016). Migration, globalization and tourism in Nigeria: Issues and policies. In J. Oyefara (Ed.), *Migration and urbanization in contemporary Nigeria: Policy issues and challenges* (pp. 435–645). Lagos: University of Lagos Press.

Elias, P., Babatola, O., & Omojola, A. (2016). Effective urban governance in Africa: Resolving the wealth-poverty paradox. In U. B. Benna & S. B. Garba (Eds.), *Population growth and rapid urbanization in the developing world* (pp. 125–148). Hershey: IGI Global.

Iweriebor, E. G. (2012). *The colonization of Africa: African Age*. Schomburg Center for Research in Black Culture. http://exhibitions.nypl.org/africanage-colonization-of-africa.html
Law, R. (Ed.). (1995). *From slave trade to "legitimate" commerce: The commercial transition in nineteenth-century West Africa*. Cambridge: Cambridge University Press.
Palmer, R., & Parsons, N. (Eds.). (1977). *Roots of rural poverty in central and Southern Africa*. London: Heinemann.

Peter Elias Holds a Ph.D. in Geography from the University of Ibadan. He is a Senior Lecturer in the Department of Geography, University of Lagos, where he teaches and conducts researches. His research interests include Regional Development and Planning, Sustainable Transformation in Urbanized Contexts, Inclusive and Sustainable Urban Development, Soils and Land Use Planning, Environmental Change and Climate Adaptation Planning. He has won several awards including as an ISSC/ICSU/CA Nominee in 2016 UN-Habitat III, a World Social Sciences Fellow and a Lead Author for the IPBES African Regional Assessment and Land Degradation (2015–2018). Email: pelias@unilag.edu.ng.

Chapter 21
Africa, Migration and Development: The Lagos Women of Bamenda Grassfields, Cameroon

Walter Gam Nkwi

Introduction

This chapter is about returned female migrants who lived in Lagos in the 1940s. Their return to the Bamenda Grassfields saw the introduction of new things and thus they distinguished themselves from their peers not only because they had introduced new things but also because these led to the development of the region. Migration has received attention in recent debates while internal migration has received even more significant attention in terms of the numbers of people involved and perhaps the quantum of remittances and poverty reduction potential of these. This has become an important livelihood strategy for many poor groups across the world (see McDowell and de Haan 2004; Nelson 1976; Murton 1997; Oberai and Singh 1980; Deshingkar and Start 2000). While it is no panacea for the poor it can likely bring many benefits and this is recognized in some policy and research circles. For example, a recent Club du Sahel report states unequivocally: "Population mobility is a necessary condition of sustainable development and poverty alleviation in West Africa. Any policy, program or action which tend to restrain mobility or to provide incentives for people to stay on their areas of origin would, in the long run, lead to unmanageable situations."(ILO 2015)

In a study in Asia, based on secondary data from Bangladesh, China, Vietnam and the Philippines, Anh (2003) has concluded that migration is a driver of growth and an important route out of poverty with significant positive ramifications for people's livelihoods and well-being. Anh further argues that attempts to control the geographical mobility of people will likely be counterproductive. In another incisive study, Afsar (2003) argues that migration has reduced poverty directly and indirectly in Bangladesh, as remittances have expanded the area under cultivation and rural labor markets by making land available for tenancy. Ping (2003, 23) draws our atten-

W.G. Nkwi (✉)
University of Buea, Buea, Cameroon
e-mail: nkwiwally@yahoo.com; nkwi.walters@ubuea.cm

O. Akanle, J.O. Adésìnà (eds.), *The Development of Africa*, Social Indicators Research Series 71, DOI 10.1007/978-3-319-66242-8_21

tion to the huge contribution of migrant labor to overall development in China and concludes that "without migrants there would be no Beijing, Shanghai, Guangzhou or Shenzhen". The potential of migration is also attracting attention in Latin America. For instance, Andersson (2002) has argued that rural–urban migration can bring many benefits to Bolivia where the low population density, poverty and mountainous terrain make it expensive and difficult to provide services in rural areas.

The root causes of migration therefore are numerous and complex. The push–pull framework gives insight into the different forces at work to explain migration. In Africa, poor socioeconomic conditions, such as low wages, high levels of unemployment, rural underdevelopment, poverty and lack of opportunity fuel out-migration (Bakewell and de Haas 2007). These factors are usually brought about by a mismatch between the rapid population growth and the available resources, a low level of requisite technology to exploit the available natural resources and lack of capacity to create employment and jobs in the countries of origin. In addition, various political and social factors induce migration. Among these are poor governance, nepotism and corruption, human rights violations, political instability, environmental factors, conflict and civil strife. The real or perceived opportunity for a better life, high income, greater security, better quality of education and health care at the destinations influence the decision to migrate. Lower costs of migration, improved communication, greater information availability and the need to join relatives, families and friends are among the factors that amplify push-pull factors (Nkwi 2015). Whereas well-managed migration may have a substantial positive impact on the development of countries of origin and yield significant benefits to destinations states, mismanaged or unmanaged migration can have serious negative consequences for states' and migrants' welfare, including potential destabilizing effects on national and regional security. In response to the challenge posed by migration, the Eighth Ordinary Session of the Executive Council of the African Union in Khartoum from 16 to 21 January 2006 adopted decision EX.CL/DEC.264 (VIII). In this context, Council decided to convene an experts meeting on migration and development in Algiers, Algeria at the invitation of the Algerian government in order to prepare a common African position.

Africa is experiencing important development which is rendered likely by its migratory flows. Some of these movements have occurred and are still occurring essentially within the continent. African migrants have recently been noted to be moving towards Europe, North America and some Middle East countries and this movement could be voluntary (as a result of pull factors in destination countries) or involuntarily/forced (due to push factors in countries of origin) (Mohielden & Ratha 2014). These movements have been legal and/or undocumented and encompass all social categories that could be imagined. They include refugees as well as internally displaced persons, nomads migrating in search of pasturelands, young men and women setting off from the countryside in search of job opportunities in the city, employment seekers and, increasingly, qualified persons, women and children under the age of 18. Migratory flows are occurring everywhere in the continent. Of the 150 million migrants in the world, more than 50 million are estimated to be Africans (Adepoju et. al. 2007).

Given that the number of migrants is rising and that this trend is likely to persist in the foreseeable future, the management of migration has necessarily become one of the critical challenges for states in the new millennium. In recent years, migration has been making its way steadily towards the top of the continental and international affairs agenda and now calls for the urgent attention of governments, whatever the nature of their involvement or interest in the management of migratory processes. There is a need for a comprehensive and balanced approach to migration, taking into account migration realities and trends as well as linkages between migration and other key economic, social, political and humanitarian issues. Another contemporary aspect of migration in Africa is the growing number of women who have also started to migrate in search for greater employment/economic opportunities (Orozco et al. 2015). However, there is an important relationship between migration and development which scholars have not failed to pay attention to in their various debates.

Migration and Development Debate Revisited

Migration and development are closely related. Migration and development discourses have recently appeared to be leaning much on remittances (Orozco et al. 2015; Klapper and Singer 2014; Jureidini 2014; Global Migration Group 2014). These discourses have displayed near neglect of historicizing the role of migrant women in the development of their regions.

At the same time development has become a buzzword with many-sided processes. This is both at the individual and collective levels. Each social group comes into contact with others and thence there is cross pollination of ideas and goods and also creativity. Development as employed in this chapter means the introduction of new things into society which helps to further the process of social change. The migrants whom we are dealing in this chapter are those who were at the forefront of introducing things like health, bakery, sewing, education and the brewing of local liquor. In concrete terms these are social remittances (Levitt & Lamba-Nieves 2011). Levitt (1998) was one of the first scholars to use the concept of social remittances. According to this author, social remittances collectively mean ideas, behaviors and social capital that flow from receiving to sending countries. This chapter further maintains that social remittances merit attention because they play an important yet understudied role in transnational migration. Secondly, social remittances bring the social impacts of migration to the fore and, finally, they are a potential community development aid because they travel through identifiable pathways to specific audiences. According to the Levitt, social remittances flow from the North to the South. In this chapter, although I will largely draw from Levitt, the view that social remittances flow from the North to the South is not taken seriously. South–South migration and its developmental implications seem not to have attracted serious attention.

There is no shortage of work on migration. Broadly speaking the red lines of the scholars could be categorized into three major parts. First, these scholars have shown us that migrations are not new to Africa and have been rural–rural; rural–urban, and urban–rural. Secondly, that Africa is a continent of considerable migration and people movements are dictated by political, social, economic and religious factors. Thirdly, since the imposition of colonial rule in Africa, most migration has been dictated by labor. But what has not been done relates to the returned labor migrants as viewed through visual representations (Amin 1974; Adepoju 1998, 2008, 2010; Harris 1994; Van Onselen 1980).[1] On the other side of the spectrum, return migration has also received considerable attention. The International Organization of Migration (IOM) in 2004 simply defined returned migration as a process of a person returning to his or her country of origin or habitual residence. However, scholars have handled this phenomenon from multifarious dimensions. This chapter hopes to contribute to this literature.

This chapter is about migration and its development implications for Africa. Migration is a major issue affecting Africa whether through mass emigration, immigration, remittances, policy backlashes or conflicts. A major issue, however, is the poor historicity of many existing works on migration and Africa. This chapter will therefore adopt a richly contemporary historical approach to understanding the nexus of migration and development in Africa. It will be comparative and pragmatic in exploring the migration and development spaces of Africa as a continent and body of countries. An empirical case study approach is also adopted through returned female migrants in Bamenda Grassfields, Cameroon, who lived in Lagos in the 1940s. This is to link the recent gendered migration paths of Africa to the current situations for very enriching chaptered discourse of the problematic. The return of the female migrants in Bamenda Grassfields, Cameroon to this sub-region saw the introduction of new things and thus they further distinguished themselves from their peers not only because they had introduced new things but because these led to the development of the region. The chapter has the following broad research questions: What are the mobility norms and discourses around migration in Africa? What are the migration norms, values and trajectories of women in the region? What was considered the norm in terms of women moving with or without a male (husband or chaperone)? What were/are the economic, social and cultural ramifications of such return migrations in Africa? Were the women then and now breaking new ground in terms of their move? Was/is what they were doing was the norm? What were/are the socioeconomic conditions they left behind and after their sojourn and what type of a society did they find on return. Did/does migrants' return intervention fit in with the broader social processes taking place at the time? What specific conditions trigger migration and return? Was/is it a life course? The methodology of this chapter includes secondary data on migration and development of African women and primary interviews with migrant women who were implicated in migration processes and those who only witnessed the returned migrants.

[1] The private sector from the three Regional Economic Communities met in Rwanda in February 2016 to express the view and recommendations on how the Tripartite Agreements can be of benefit to them.

Female migration needs further attention. The female dimension of migration is striking but has not received equal attention in academia to that of men. According to some scholars the migration of women is stated in the literature that it came much later than that of the male. For instance, the anthropologist, James Clifford, observes that: "Good travel (heroic, educational, scientific, adventurous, ennobling) is something men should do. Women are impeded from serious travel. *Some of them (women) go to distant places but largely as companions*" (1992). In other words, women always travelled in conjunction with men. This does not, however, mean that scholars have not studied the labor mobility of women as independent agents in Africa (Barnes 2002; Kihato 2009; Clifford 1992). What is indeed relevant here is that these authors have not seen these women in terms of independent migrants and their role in societal development, a lacuna which this chapter sets out to fill. This chapter therefore helps us to start by examining the migration of women who returned to the Cameroon Western Grassfields and further reinforces the historical perspective of migration.

Situating the Bamenda Grassfields

The Bamenda Grassfields is the present-day northwest region of Cameroon. Politically, it is organized around Fondoms. A Fondom is ruled by a Fon who exercises judiciary and executive powers over his people. There are centralized Fondoms of which the largest is Nso. The second largest is Kom while Bali and Bafut are third and fourth respectively. The Fons exercise quasi-religious functions and are the custodians of traditions (Chilver 1981; Nkwi and Warnier 1982; Rowlands 1978). Geographically, the Bamenda Grassfields is located at the point where the long West African coastline turns sharply south to run down to the Congo. The native population comprises a variety of ethnic and linguistic groups. The main ethnic groups are of Tikar origin: the Tikar, Widikums, Fulanis and Moghamo. They are found east of the Greenwich meridian, approximately between longitudes $5^{\circ}\ 3'$ and latitudes $9^{\circ}\ 5'$, $1'$ north of the equator (Terretta 2014; Dillon 1990). According to Chilver and Kaberry (1967), the region covers the former administrative divisions of Bamenda, Wum and Nkambe, which in 1953 had a total population of 429,000 including 10,000 nomadic Fulani (Chilver and Kaberry 1967). It covers a land surface area of 17,300 km^2 (6680 m^2). Following the 2005 census the population of this stood at 1,728,963. The dominant geographical feature of this area is the Bamenda High Plateau, which stretches from the north east and east of the Bamenda Grasslands over the center of the area at an average height of 4500 feet above sea level. It is studded with peaks, the highest and the most spectacular of them being the Akuafo Mountains between the Bamenda station and former French Cameroon frontier and the Oku Mountains which is 7357 feet above sea level (Nkwi 2010; Chilver 1981).

Economic, political and social globalization seem to have laid the foundation upon which the interconnectivity of people and places became possible and hence migration (Portes 1996; Appadurai 1990). The connection between Bamenda and

Lagos is worth appreciating, with a distance of more than 1723 km between them. After the First World War, the Germans were expelled from Cameroon and the British and French partitioned the territory. Britain took one-fifth while the French took four-fifths. The British administered their portion, of which the Bamenda Grassfields was part, as an integral part of the eastern provinces of Nigeria with their headquarters in Lagos. Therefore this region was administered from Lagos. There were preexisting communication networks there that had been established over centuries of human contact and these were transformed by the British administration through colonial networks such as pre-colonial trade between the eastern portion of Nigeria and Bamenda Grassfields. Bamenda and Lagos also shared socioeconomic connections. The English language was the official language and was introduced in the Bamenda region by the British to replace the German lingua franca. The two countries shared similar administrative systems, educational institutions and economic policies.

Methodology

Methodologically, the data used in this chapter was collected, firstly, during my PhD fieldwork which I conducted in Kom between 2006 and 2011 (Nkwi 2011). Secondly I spent more time in various areas of the Bamenda Grassfields between 2015 and 2016. During the fieldwork I used several methods ranging from archives, photographs and interviews. But mainly my research included just talking to people. Although the research was not on women per se, I happened on their itinerary and thought that I should make a deeper study of this class of women who had been to Lagos during the heydays of the colonial period in the 1940s for various reasons and were back now in the region. It was through talking to and interacting with them that I came to know the women. This method appears to have been very useful. In his piece ‘Fishing in troubled waters’, Nyamnjoh (2005, 295–324) observes that one of the fieldwork methods which he used was talking and interacting with people. He writes:

> The ethnography used in this paper has been harvested as I went along, propelled by a fascination with the theme in question and a background of similar interests pursued among students and youth elsewhere in Cameroon and Botswana. Over twenty-five years of research have taught me this: if you are passionate about a theme and have a way with people, rich ethnographic insights flow your way through interactions with others anywhere, anytime. One is always doing fieldwork, even when not formally in the field. While confining social research to formal field situations might yield ‘hard facts’, it detracts from those realities that may not immediately fit our practised instruments and scholarly *manière de faire* […].

Like Francis Nyamnjoh, I realized that the more one talked with people about the work, the more it was enriched and the more the researcher was also directed to other people. So obsessed was the researcher with the work that he practically talked with almost everybody who seemed at all relevant to the study. For instance, my research interest was shared with Andreas Ngongbi, a friend and classmate in primary school, who directed me to his mother who had lived in Lagos in the 1940s but was back in Kom. Her mother granted me an audience and narrated her experiences in Lagos and what she studied there and introduced to Kom. During the interview, she also spoke about the glamorous life in Lagos and how she had travelled there. She said she met with other women in Lagos from Kom, whom she directed me to. These women included Elizabeth Ngebo who lives at Mugoegoe and who was the first woman to introduce a bakery and tailoring in Kom. Elizabeth not only recounted her experiences in Nigeria but also showed some of the things she brought home, like the umbrella which she used in Surelele Stadium when the Queen of England visited Nigeria in 1956 and part of the luggage which she had brought home from Nigeria like the relics of the bakery. After the interview, she directed me to another friend, Grace Wuyum, whose husband worked with the military in Lagos.

Through this method I came to know these Lagos women and how they contributed in their own way to the social change of this region. In total I talked and interacted to more than thirty women and also tried to sketch their biographies. This was because generally in biographies, historians attempt to decipher the behavior of individuals and their influence on history. However, in this chapter, I work according to the views of the Georgian novelist, Henry Fielding (1973, 218), who once remarked that he depicted species and not individuals. While in the field I followed the people and their itineraries that together formed the Bamenda Grassfields region. The informants cited in this chapter are a representation of Bamenda/Lagos women's' geographical and social mobility and its ramifications for this region. This chapter depicts not only individuals but also processes and the dynamics of a society. The individual however matters. Individual and life history stories are significant but only when linked to the process and how they ignited development within their own society. The fundamental interest here is how the society has functioned over time and space with the focus on social change with women being the agents and conduits of the social change.

Historical Evidence

Health has been held as one of the key features for development and some of the migrants to Lagos introduced health facilities. For instance, the Kom women migrants who moved to Lagos also introduced health facilities in Kom after their sojourn. One of these migrants was Benedicta. Her profile will help us to understand her itinerary and how she came to introduce a medicine store in the region. Benedicta was born in 1937 at Njinikom. At a tender age she went to St. Anthony's Primary School, Njinikom and was one among a few girls. When she got to standard 4 the manager of the school, Rev. Fr. Groot, decreed that girls were to further their education at the Convent School at Shisong, Nso, Cameroon, some 140 km from Kom. She and other girls went to Shisong. At that time there were no drivable roads (*ndzi kfaang*). There were no vehicles (*afuem a kfaang)* as one would find today. There were no post offices and there were no telephones (*fincha fi kfaang).* Benedicta and the other girls trekked to Shisong. The journey to Shisong took Benedicta and her friends three days. A school of Nursing and Midwifery was opened in Shisong. Benedicta's parents preferred her to go to Shisong. She spent one year at Shisong and returned to Nigeria again for one more year. There she graduated from Abakiliki Nursing School. After graduating from Abakiliki, she got her first appointment in Cameroon with the Wum Rural Council in 1957 and her next job was in Tiko, Southwest Region of Cameroon situated some 450 km from Kom with the Cameroon Development Cooperation (CDC) hospital. She worked there for eight months, and then applied and was admitted to the University Teaching College, Ibadan, Nigeria. She studied in Ibadan for three years, obtained her diploma and then went to Lagos where she joined her elder brother. At Lagos she practiced there as well.

Back in Kom, Bendicta worked first at a government health center and then opened her own medicine store which she called the Royal Diamond Chemist. In this medicine store she sold palliative medicines such painkillers and also provided first aid for patients who visited the medicine store. She ran her medicine store to the admiration of those who felt the immediate impact of it. In her store she employed a night watchman and two girls whose jobs were to clean the store. She also employed a sales girl who generally helped to sell the medicines. Benedicta's movements and the opening of her health center was something out of the ordinary as she had grown up in an environment where the place of women was secondary. Women played second fiddle in the area as they were largely seen as child bearers and labor on the farms. Migration for a long time was thought as the affair of men, as Clifford (1992) maintained. Benedicta and other women had started breaking new ground by demystifying the notion.

Closely linked to Benedicta was Mamma Mumbang. She was born in 1930 in Fundong, another village in the Bamenda Grassfields. She attended preliminary school and then went to Lagos with her maternal uncle who was cook to a colonial officer. She was enrolled in a nursing school in Ibadan where she studied midwifery for four years. Upon her graduation she gained employment in a private maternity home in Lagos. When her uncle retired she stayed behind in Lagos and raised some money. Back in Fundong she opened her own maternity home. Although no documentation exists for the maternity home, from which I would have been able to gather how many women gave birth per annum, she testified that there were no less 150 women who gave birth in her maternity home. It meant that many women did not have to make a 13 km journey to the nearest maternity hospital. Mamma Mumbang also taught anti-natal lessons. In her maternity home she employed people whose job descriptions ranged from dry cleaning the maternity, watching the place both in the day and night and other auxiliary nurses who helped her out during the periods of women's delivery.

Another woman who migrated to Lagos was Elizabeth Ngehbo. Unlike the other women whom we have mentioned above who were unmarried, Elizabeth actually followed the husband first to Jos and later to Lagos. According to her,

> I was born in 1932 in Njinikom and grew up with catechist Ngongbi who was my uncle. I never went to school because in those days school meant nothing to a woman. Very few women went to school. During catechumen doctrine I fell in love with my husband who

> was a houseboy of Rev. Fr. Ivo Stockman. When Father Stockman was transferred to Mamfe he took him along. While in Mamfe negotiation started for our traditional wedding. Before the wedding came to an end my husband Ngehbo, was already in Jos and so I had to go and meet him in Jos. He had left Mamfe because the white priest had annoyed him. So I got married in St. Augustine's parish in Jos Nigeria. I was conducted to Jos by the eldest brother of my husband. I was taken alongside with one other small boy. We went on foot. We passed through Abuh, Achain, Bum, Misaje. From there we went through Takum, Wukari, Ibi and cross the Benue River into Jos. It took us more than three weeks and was constantly entering and staying in missions … After staying for a very long time in Jos, my husband left me there and went to Lagos. While in Lagos he was cooking for a one Whiteman. I was alone in Jos till he settled down in Lagos and called for me. I left Jos for Lagos by train. That was my first time I entered a train and it was very interesting. I was with my small son. I gave birth to all my children in Lagos and one of my children has remained in Lagos. I was always coming home on leave because the Mamfe-Bamenda-Kom road was opened to traffic. It was very difficult coming home because I had to carry children in a narrow lorry which was constantly galloping. From Lagos we stopped at Onitsha and from there we stopped at Ikom. From Ikom we took the lorry from there to Bamenda. While in Bamenda we were already tired and had to stay at Kubou's compound. That compound was really a Kom compound and all the Kom had to rest there before continuing. In Lagos I learnt how to bake bread and while in Kom here I opened a bakery and people were buying from it. In the bakery we employed several boys and some few girls who were working for us. I also learnt how to sew clothes and came home here with a sewing machine and taught many girls how to sew. My husband taught me how to bake cakes and make bread. I was a star when I came home here. The queen's visit was wonderful. When he was visiting the foyn of Kom was selected to be one of those who were to have an audience with the queen. The fon, Alo, came down to Lagos with many carriers and guards. There were more than 30 people following the fon (Elizabeth Ngebo, Personal Communication, 9 July 2012).

While in Kom Elizabeth and her husband opened a bakery and this was the first bakery in the region. They employed labor, mostly boys, who were working for them. These boys performed very robust jobs. They were charged with cutting wood since the local bakery survived through the use of excessive wood fuel to keep the temperature of the oven ready to bake the bread. In total they employed ten boys and three girls. The next thing Elizabeth did was to open a sewing shop in which she taught the girl child how to sew. This was very creative and more girls over the years learnt how to sew. The opening of these places with the subsequent employment of youths to work in such areas led to an increase in their standard of living. Living on a monthly wage and also gainfully employed ultimately led to the development of the area no matter how small.

Unlike Elizabeth and Benedicta, who introduced health facilities from Lagos, Grace Mandofi introduced a kindergarten school which was hitherto unknown in the region. Grace was born in 1946 at Abakwa in Markurdi, Northern Nigeria, of Nigerian and Cameroonian parents. She grew up and was schooled in Nigeria at Markurdi where she attended the St Louis Primary School between 1952 and 1954. In Lagos she attended the Oriel Girls School at Ebute Metta, Lagos, where she successfully obtained a standard 6 certificate in 1959. She then enrolled at a clerical school after which she gained employment as a sales girl with a petroleum company. While at the clerical school she got married to a husband who did not believe in the empowerment of women. But he had a family friend who was British but married to a Nigerian, Priscilla St Ledger Igiega. The wife of this British man introduced her to nursery school education and when they went to the United Kingdom, she made Grace the headmistress of the Hillside Nursery School.

In 1978, her husband retired to Cameroon and so Grace had to follow him and leave her job. When in Cameroon they settled in Bamenda which was the administrative capital of the Northwest region of Cameroon. While in Bamenda, Grace started the process of opening a nursery school. Both the administration and her peers found this very strange as it was a new idea coming above all from a woman. “I encountered a lot of bottlenecks when I started the procedure of opening a school. People did not understand why a woman should be opening a school and in some offices I was told that it was impossible,” Grace said (Grace Madoff, Personal Communication, 12 August 2016, Bamenda). However, the difficulty was soon overcome and in September 1982, the Minister of National Education, Rene Ze Nguele, authorized that the school should go operational. Consequently, at the start of the academic year, the school opened its doors as Ngi-Vichi Nursery School with five pupils. That was the first nursery school in the Bamenda metropolis. The number of the pupils increased with time; by 1985 the school already boasted 100 pupils and in 1993 the school had 400 pupils and a staff complement of 28 (16 women and 12 men) (Grace Madofi, Personal Communication, 2 July 2016, Bamenda).

Conclusion

Migration and development have been intertwined over time and space. In Africa migration has often been linked to remittances which are sent back to their areas of origin by migrants. This chapter has departed from this conventional position, stressing the role of women who migrated to Lagos as either married or single women. Their sojourn in Lagos led to the introduction of health services, bakeries and sewing shops that further led to the social transformation of the area. The concept of social remittance which has been borrowed from Levitt has largely been used in this chapter to buttress the fact that migrant women from the Bamenda Grassfields of Cameroon were also torchbearers of development in their various regions. Their employment of people in itself led to an increase in the standard of living of these people no matter how negligent their wages. This chapter made use of a myriad of methods and, building on my previous work, has offered fresh interpretations for the role of women in migration and development. The introduction of such services to their areas of origin put the role of men in migration in perspective and their over emphasis in the domain of remittances in further debate.

Health and education have been earmarked as prime drivers of development not only in Africa but the world over. The women discussed in this chapter contributed in their small way to the development of the region. Those who opened bakeries and tailoring shops helped in the employment of youths. Yet we should not lost sight of the fact that what these women were doing has also been done elsewhere. Petterson (1988), in his study of the Atlantic System, notes that return migrants to the West

Indies repatriated change while inducing ideologies which they had learnt from the Black Power movement in the United States., The Bamenda Grassfields women, like the returned migrants in the West Indies, repatriated what they acquired from Lagos. Accordingly, the position and the role of these women changed. Again, drawing from Petterson (1988), migrant women modified their ideas about women's role in response to their more active engagement.

This chapter concludes that these women of Bamenda Grassfields brought back new ideas to their areas of origin while the ramifications of what was introduced in the society was telling. Far from what the literature has provided thus far on migration and history and development, this chapter shows that women have played a role in development just like men have done over time and space. Furthermore, the chapter has contended that these women broke away with the traditional patriarchal norms of their societies which hitherto maintained that migration was not meant for them. More research therefore needs to be done on migrant African women and development than the literature has provided. On a final note, these women became 'new women' who further distinguished themselves from their peers and the durability of what they introduced to this society has caused it to continue to linger in the region to this day.

References

Adepoju, A. (1998). Linkages between internal and international migration: The African situation. *International Social Science Journal, 50*(157), 387–395.

Adepoju, A. (2008). *Migration in sub-Saharan Africa*. Uppsala: Nordic Inst.

Adepoju, A. (2010). *International migration within, to and from Africa in a globalized world*. Lagos: Sub-Saharan Pub and Traders.

Adepoju, A., Zoomers, A., & van Naerssen, T. (Eds.). (2007). *International migration and national development in sub Saharan Africa: Viewpoints and policy initiatives in the countries of origin*. Leiden: Brill Academic.

Afsar, R. (2003). Dynamics of poverty, development and population mobility: The Bangladesh case. Ad Hoc Expert Group Meeting on Migration and Development, Economic and Social Commission for Asia and the Pacific (ESCAP), Bangkok, August 27–29. Available from http://www.sdnpbd.org/sdi/internationaldays/wed/2005/bangladesh/migration/document/Bangladesh_rita.pdf.

Amin, S. (1974). *Modern migrations in Western Africa*. London: Oxford University Press.

Andersson, L. (2002). Rural-urban linkages in Bolivia: Advantages and disadvantages. Instituto de Investigaciones Socio-Económicas, Universidad Catolica Boliviana.

Appadurai, A. (1990). Disjuncture and difference in the global cultural economy. In M. Featherstone (Ed.), *Global culture: Nationalism, globalisation and modernity*. London and Newbury Park: Sage Publications.

Bakewell, O., & de Haas, H. (2007). African migrations: Continuities, discontinuities and recent transformations. In L. de Haan, U. Engel, & P. Chabal (Eds.), *African alternatives*. Leiden: Brill.

Barnes, T. (2002). Virgin territory? Travel and migration by African women in twentieth-century southern Africa. In J. Allman, S. Geiger, & N. Musisi (Eds.), *Women in African colonial histories* (pp. 164–185). Indiana: Indiana University Press.

Chilver, E. M. (1981). Chronological synthesis: The western region, comprising the western grassfields, Bamum, the Bamileke chiefdoms and the central Mbam. In C. Tardits (Ed.), *The con-*

tribution of ethnological research to the history of Cameroon cultures (pp. 453–475). Paris: Editions du Centre National de la Recherché Scientifique.
Chilver, E. M., & Kaberry, P. M. (1967). *Traditional Bamenda: The pre-colonial history and ethnography of the Bamenda grassfields*. Buea: Government Printers.
Clifford, J. (1992). Travelling cultures. In L. Grossberg, C. Nelson, & P. Treinch (Eds.), *Cultural studies* (pp. 97–98). New York: Routledge.
De Bruijn, M., & Van Dijk, H. (2003). Changing population mobility in West Africa: Fulbe pastoralists in Central and South Mali. *African Affairs, 102*(407), 285–307.
Deshingkar, P., & Start, D. (2000). Seasonal migration for livelihood in India: Coping accumulation and exclusion. In*Working Paper 220*. London: Overseas Development Institute.
Dillon, R. G. (1990). *Ranking and resistance: Pre-colonial Cameroonian polity in regional perspective* Stanford: University of California Press.
Fielding, H. (1973), *Joseph Andrews and Shamela* with an Introduction and notes by Arthur Friedman, University of Chicago.
Global Migration Group. (2014). Realizing the inclusion of migrants and migration in the post 2015 UN development agenda. October.
Harris, P. (1994). *Work, culture and identity: Migrant laborers in Mozambique and South Africa, c. 1860–1910: Social History of Africa*. London: James Currey.
International Labour Organisation. (2015). Geneva, Switzerland.
Jureidini, R. (2014). Arab Gulf States: Recruitment of Asian workers. GLMM; Explanatory note; 3/2014; Migration Policy Centre.
Kihato, C.W. (2009). Migration, gender and urbanisation in Johannesburg. PhD Thesis submitted to the Department of Sociology, University of South Africa
Klapper, L., & Singer, D. (2014). *The opportunities of digitizing payments*. World Bank Publication.
Levitt, P. (1998). Social remittances: Migration Driven local-level forms of cultural diffusion. *International Migration Review, 32*(4), 926–948.
Levitt, P., & Lamba-Nieves, D. (2011). Social remittances revisited. *Journal of Ethnic and Migration Studies, 37*(1), 1–22.
McDowell, Christopher, and Arjan de Haan. (2004). Migration and sustainable livelihoods: A critical review of literature. IDS Working Paper 65.
Mohieldin, M., & D. Ratha. (2014). Bonds of the Diaspora. Project Syndicate, July.
Murton, J. (1997). Sustainable livelihoods in marginal African environments? The social and economic impacts of agricultural intensification in Makueni District, Kenya. Paper presented at ESRC Conference on Sustainable Livelihoods in Marginal African Environments, University of Sheffield, 10–11 April.
Nelson, J. M. (1976). Sojourners versus new urbanites: Causes and consequences of temporary versus permanent cityward migration in developing countries. *Economic Development and Cultural Change, 24*, 721–757.
Nkwi, P. N., & Warnier, J. P. (1982). *Elements for a history of the western grassfields*. Yaounde: SOPECAM. Sponsored by the Department of Sociology, University of Yaounde.
Nkwi, W. G. (2010). *Voicing the voiceless: Contributions to closing gaps in Cameroon history, 1958–2009*. Mankon: Langaa Research and Publishing House.
Nkwi, W. G. (2011). *Kfaang and its technologies: Towards a social history of mobility in Kom, Cameroon, 1928–1998*. Leiden: ASC Publications.
Nkwi, W. G. (2015). *African mobilities and modernities: An historical ethnography of Kom, c. 1800–2008. Mankon*. Bamenda: Langaa RCIG.
Nyamnjoh, F. B. (2005). Fishing in troubled waters: Disquettes and thiofs in Dakar. *Africa, 75*, 295–324.
Oberai, A., & Singh, H. K. (1980). Migration, remittances and rural development: Findings of a case study in the Indian Punjab. *International Labour Review, 119*(2), 229–241.
Orozco, M., Porras, I., & Yansura, J. (2015). *Trends in remittances to Latin America and the Caribbean in 2014: Inter-American dialogue perspective*. Stanford and California: University of California Press.

Petterson, O. (1988). The emerging West Atlantic system: Migration, culture and underdevelopment in the United States and the circum-Carribean Region. In W. Alonso (Ed.), *Population in an interacting world*. Cambridge, MA: Harvard University Press.

Ping, H. (2003). China migration country study. Paper presented at the Regional Conference on Migration, Development and Pro-Poor Policy Choices in Asia organized by the Bangladesh Refugee and Migratory Movements Research Unit, Bangladesh/DFID.

Portes, A. (1996). Transnational communities: Their emergence and significance in the contemporary world system. In R. P. Korzeniewicz & W. C. Smith (Eds.), *Latin America in the world economy*. Connecticut: Greenwood Press.

Rowlands, M. (1978). Local and long-distance trade and incipient state formation in the Bamenda plateau in the late 19th century. *Paideuma, 25*, 1–19.

Terretta, M. (2014). *Nation of outlaws, state of violence: Nationalism, grassfields tradition and state building in Cameroon*. Ohio: Ohio University Press.

Van Onselen, C. (1980). *Chibaro: African mine labour in Southern Rhodesia, 1900–1933*. Johannesburg: Ravan Press.

Walter Gam Nkwi holds a PhD in Social History/ Social Anthropology from the University of Leiden, The Netherlands. He is teaching Social and Labour History at the Department of History, University of Buea, Cameroon. He has published in peer review journals, books and book chapters and encyclopedia entries. Dr. Nkwi's research interest is in the history of communication technology, social history, indigenous conflict management, pre-cultural history and global labour historical issues of Africa. e-mails : nkwi.walters@ubuea.cm,nkwiwally@yahoo.com

Chapter 22
Aid and Development in Africa

Simeon K. Koffi

Introduction

The mixed results of development aid in Africa and the conditionalities which are often associated with it, makes it a very controversial issue. Never has a good been so much desired and slandered. This ambivalence makes it a subject of immense interest in development issues. As an action by which developed countries transfer to others public resources in order to contribute to their development, assistance as apprehended today was born after the Second World War from the need to rebuild Europe and Asia, in a context influenced by the Cold War. The damage created by the Great War increased the need for international cooperation, which is how the International Bank for Reconstruction and Development, the International Monetary Fund and the United Nations were created. Development assistance appeared in Africa at the beginning of decolonization. The first forms of assistance to Africa appeared through the two major colonial empires, that is, the United Kingdom and France. Thus, in 1940, the UK passed the Colonial Development and Welfare Act which includes an entire section dedicated to the development of the health and education sectors as well as agricultural production in the British colonies. France took a little longer to join the movement, but in 1943 it created the Central Fund of France of overseas (Jacquet 2006).

However, the assistance granted to the colonies was not only for the welfare of the natives but for the development of resources for the colonial powers. Thus, self-interest and humanism were already mingled in donor motivations. In other words, assistance had, since the beginning, made use of development in favor of political and strategic interests. Other bilateral donors joined these two countries in the 1960s, a period during which development aid was broadened. The special feature

S.K. Koffi (✉)
Economic Community of West African States (ECOWAS), Abuja, Nigeria
e-mail: kkoffi@ecowas.int; ksimeon@yahoo.com

O. Akanle, J.O. Adésìnà (eds.), *The Development of Africa*, Social Indicators Research Series 71, DOI 10.1007/978-3-319-66242-8_22

of this development was not so much the aid itself but rather the extent of its spread since it covered all regions (Jacquet and Severino 2002). Africa is currently one of the largest development assistance recipients in the world, so chaptering the aid toward one of the poorest regions of the world appears appropriate and necessary to better understand the real impact of development assistance policy. The matter of development aid has always been a subject of intense discussion, sometimes contradictory. The most recent debates have largely focused on technocratic arguments, that is, on particular themes related to the effectiveness of aid.

However, this issue of the effectiveness or impact of aid remains controversial in development issues. Never has an issue so divided opinion and sparked passion. The arguments highlighted have long attested to its complexity, so much so that no single chapter alone can identify the total reality of aid effectiveness. This chapter, which aims to contribute to this debate, attempts to assess the impact of aid to Africa by asking whether it has achieved the desired changes in the beneficiary countries. However, the analysis may have some shortcomings because, in general, data on development assistance remain fragmented. They hardly fit the flow of aid from major emerging economies such as China and the analytical framework is therefore that of traditional donors. The argument in this chapter is structured into five parts. The first part is a brief review of existing studies on the contribution of aid. The second part deals with the dependence of development strategies vis-à-vis aid. The third part presents the evolution of aid flows since 1960, highlighting the differences between the major regions of the continent. The fourth part is an evaluation of the impact of aid in terms of development goals and economic indicators. Finally the fifth section provides elements that can be considered as additions and/or relevant alternatives to traditional aid policy in the African development process.

Review of Controversies Relating to Aid Policy

When one examines the literature on development aid policy in Africa, there is strong controversy in most analyses. There are generally two dominant approaches: the first considers that the aid to the continent has a negative impact while the second approach believes instead that the donor action is generally positive. Some studies attempt to overcome this cleavage, however they are a minority.

Theoretical Frameworks for Aid Policy Assessment

Studies evaluating the impact of aid policies are shaped by the motives their authors impute to donor countries. These motivations can be classified according to the theoretical framework in which they operate: neorealist, liberal, neoliberal, idealistic, etc. It is important to start by introducing the "theoretical frameworks of motivation" before treating the approaches mentioned above to better put them into perspective (Amprou and Chauvet 2005). The neorealist framework analyzes the motivations of aid policy in terms of power searching. According to this perspective, aid is an instrument of power that would allow the donor to "influence, reward or punish other countries." According to this view, assistance for example enables the donor to "ensure votes" in international institutions. It notes that the proponents of the negative impact approach model and issue some of its criticisms based on the neorealist theoretical framework (Charnoz and Severino 2007). The liberal theoretical approach envisages motivations of aid in terms of interest: the donor is implementing an aid policy because it serves its interests. The beneficiary country encourages this assistance because it allows it to "increase its material well-being." The logic of exchange is not one of power but of investment and "mutual benefit". This theoretical framework is favored by proponents of the positive impact approach and by several donor countries.

Liberal theory differs somewhat from the neoliberal framework in the sense that aid policies in the latter case meet private interests (Klein and Harford 2005). The aid is framed in terms of "rent to private agents' service", for instance exporters' lobbies. Similarly, in recipient countries, the assistance is diverted from its original purpose and serves private interests. Elements developed by liberal theory are taken up by the supporters of the negative impact approach. As for idealistic theory, it shows aid as a moral (unselfish) action. This approach is mostly used by some governments of the former colonial powers to justify their aid policy.

Positive Perception of Aid Policies

Conversely, supporters of the thesis of a positive impact see in the presence of external donors, economic opportunity, development catalysts, economic partners and foreign investors, which allow for the alleviation of the domestic resources shortage. For them, aid is an essential complement to the development of African states. Other aspects of aid in Africa (investment, trade, etc.) are also judged positively by the authors of the "positive impact" approach: "Africa has huge needs in capitals, technology and infrastructure and some foreign donors meet these needs. Some donors are perceived as development partners, sustainably involved on the continent," certainly driven by economic needs, but also committed to building a partnership with Africa. According to proponents of the approach of "positive impact", the structure of certain foreign investment confirms this development partner status, because these investments largely explain the growth of some African countries in recent years.

Finally, some authors believe that aid has a positive impact in terms of peace and political stability of the continent. Donor countries, in considering that a politically stable environment better suits their interests and the objectives of aid, seek to preserve this environment. This analysis, however, is controversial; other experts believe instead that the Western intervention in Africa is sometimes a factor of destabilization and tension. It is often argued that the support is provided by developed countries to dictators or undemocratic regimes to suit their interests.

Negative Perception of Aid Policies

This chapter opines that assistance in Africa is essentially negative. Aid policies are produced both by Western activists but also African, and by non-governmental organizations (Jacquet 2006). Analyses and works of this corpus generally present donors as 'predatory' powers, driven by a logic of plundering natural resources. According to this trend, the presence of some developed countries in the field of oil exploitation (Sudan, Nigeria, etc.), logging and extraction of mineral resources (Central Africa) demonstrates the looting logic of these countries. Similarly, the fact that some investors do not care about the environmental damage caused by their activities is an argument that reinforces the predatory appearance of the presence of some countries. Some advocates of the negative impact of aid accuse some donors of re-colonizing the continent, although this point remains extremely controversial.

Moreover, proponents of the negative impact approach define aid as of 'no real economic, financial and social impact', not contributing to sustainable development and meant to serve first the interests of donors, especially securing its energy and raw materials supplies. Regarding the impact of aid, it is the African critics who are more numerous. Some authors report on the one hand that aid is not applied in the productive sector (Beynon 2003). Many other analysts note that the projects carried out by donor countries "are in line for a extroversion" (Clemens and Moss 2005) and reinforce African countries in the role of producers of raw materials: "the revival of an annuity of raw materials seems punctual (because of proven reserves) and may lead to higher growth rates without driving the sustainable development". In addition, the conditionality grip is one of the most criticized aspects: it is not only a major obstacle to obtaining and absorbing aid but also an element of frustration for countries claiming their sovereignty. A final concern of the proponents of this approach is that of the phasing out of Africa by the developed countries in view of the shifting of their agenda.

Clear-Cut Positions to be Relativized

In reality, it is difficult to advocate exclusively for either of the approaches discussed above (Easterly et al. 2003). That is why some analysts are trying to overcome this simplistic cleavage. In general, their thoughts revolve around the fact that it is the African response which will give its positive or negative nature to development aid. The responsibility for deficiencies in the global aid policy cannot lie solely with donors. Reforms on the part of Africans themselves are necessary so that the impact of development aid becomes really positive: they should make a change in their rent seeking and assistance-based behavior, take measures to transform a windfall economy into a production economy and anchor their countries to a knowledge-based economy. African leaders ought to strengthen their negotiating skills when they face their donors and should be able to use the funds adequately to develop their countries.

Development Strategy Dependent on Aid

Following independence, most African countries have developed and implemented ambitious development programs. Although being relevant to their objectives, including the development of agriculture and the industrialization of the continent, these programs have somehow faltered over their financing strategies, including the mobilization of external resources, an indispensable addition to the weakness of domestic savings.

Development Goals

In the early 1960s, two major objectives were assigned to development policies implemented by newly independent African countries. This was to ensure, on the one hand, the modernization of the agricultural sector and, on the other hand, the diversification of economies particularly through the development of industry. Therefore, development strategies focused on the primary and secondary sectors. In most countries, different methods of rural modernization were explored. Some countries have tried the path of agrarian capitalism by developing small export crop plantations and others have moved towards the construction of large hydro-agricultural complexes for the production of food crops for local consumption or export (Gillis et al. 1997). Africa has also entered, although often timidly, the path of industrialization to take over export agriculture.

These policies, especially in relation to funding strategies, in particular the provision of aid, have been conducted in three major phases: the first from 1960 to 1970, with a predominance of public partners, then from 1970 until the late 1980s, with the emergence of private financing and, finally, from 1990 until now, with international organizations as the main actors.

Development Funding Phases

(i) From 1960 to 1970, aid policies adopted after independence were deeply inspired by the dominant model, in this case of the Marshall Plan implemented after the Second World War for the reconstruction of Europe and built on an intensive use of public funds to relay defective private flows caused by the crisis of the 1930s (Shaw 1973). Thus during this period, in the financing strategies of African countries' economic programs, public funding dominated mainly by development aid has been important. This consists of bilateral aid resulting from cooperation between the two countries and multilateral aid from international organizations like the World Bank and the United Nations. These funds are allocated in the form of grants or 'preferential' loans that is at lower rates than international markets. In many countries this aid has also taken the form of technical assistance (provided to resource persons) or capital.

(ii) From 1970 to 1990, thanks to the abundance of cash flows from the oil shocks, the private financing of development saw a remarkable boom. This included foreign direct investment and portfolio investment. However, North Africa benefited from the emergence of private funding, often non-concessional. In contrast, official development assistance (concessional) remained dominant for Sub-Saharan African countries; as the share of private funding in total flows they received was only 40% on average. Development assistance policy has been accompanied by the creation of development banks, mostly state banks, which use low interest rate policies or even negative real interest rates to ensure internal financing. However, these internal funding policies have not been particularly successful owing to low domestic savings and the strong presence of the state, combined with an unfavorable international economic situation. This has led to the bankruptcy of almost all these banks and the restructuring of the banking system in most countries.

(iii) From 1990, the imperfections found in development financing in the first decades after independence resulted in the failure of postcolonial strategies and led public authorities to vary the terms of intervention in development financing. Macroeconomic imbalances and the debt burden led to new strategies in early 1990. Adjustment and privatization policies stepped in, but it remains true that development aid has remained a central element of these policies. Thus, new strategies are focused on savings mobilization (financial markets) and testing of public–private partnerships within the framework of privatization policy. Development policies give an important place to the private sector and to the need to mobilize savings through appropriate rate policies, thus increasing internal and external resources to ensure the recovery of productive investment and lay the foundations for sustained growth. The idea is to resort to new financing methods mobilizing, to a greater extent, private flows on the one hand and the improvement of the performance of development aid through the flexibility and efficiency of this private financing on the other. So far the assessment of development strategies is rather mixed. The decade of the 1980s was marked by serious social and economic difficulties for Africa. Between 1980 and 1989, there was a steady and widespread decline in economic activity, social welfare and living standards in Africa. The serious crisis in Africa during the 1980s was manifested in three ways: the general deterioration of the main macroeconomic indicators, the disintegration of production structures and infrastructure, and the rapid deterioration of social welfare, including education, public health and housing, and accelerated ecological deterioration.

The Lagos Plan of Action (LPA) for the Economic Development of Africa 1980–2000, launched by the Organization of African Unity (OAU) at the XVIth Ordinary Session of the Conference of Heads of State and Government, held in Monrovia in July 1979, was intended as a solution to the socioeconomic decline of Africa. Through the Monrovia Declaration, the Heads of State and Government of the OAU "pledged, on behalf of their governments and peoples, to promote economic and social development and the integration of their economies with a view to increasing self-reliance and promote endogenous and self-sustaining development", to facilitate and strengthen their social and economic relations for the development of a dynamic and interdependent African economy at the national, sub-regional and regional levels, as well as for the establishment each year of specific programs to materialize this sub-regional, regional and continental economic cooperation.

The action plan covers areas as diverse as agriculture and food; the industrialization of the continent through the pursuit of long, medium and short-term objectives aimed at achieving at least 2% of world industrial production in 2000, in line with the objectives of the Lima Conference; the exercise of total sovereignty in African countries over their natural resources, relying on the training of people capable of mastering the appropriate technologies; the rational development and utilization of the human resources required for this action plan; the use of science and technology for the development of the continent at national, sub-regional and regional levels; the adoption and implementation of a general transport and com munications strategy; and the promotion and intensification of inter-African trade and financial exchanges. This non-exhaustive list shows the extent to which the LPA has been applied, as well as the high hopes it has generated during its adoption and promulgation. Despite this, the 90s showed poor results in achieving the objectives of the LPA.

Why did the LPA and the first generation of plans and the strong determination that inspired them not succeed in pushing Africa along the path of economic and social growth and development? Has the LPA been abandoned for the benefit of the Structural Adjustment Program (1981) or the United Nations Program of Action for Development of Africa (1986)? This list is not exhaustive because many other programs have been aborted, such as the various decades of 'industrial development', "transport and telecommunications" and an African Framework of Reference for Structural Adjustment Programs (AFRSAP) for the recovery and socioeconomic transformation of the continent. At the end of the day, the results were very much in the way of expectations, which justified severe assessments like "the decade spoiled", "the decade of hopes disappointed" or more frequently "the lost decade".

Africa as a whole has been unable to meet the socioeconomic performance targets set out in the LPA at sectoral and macroeconomic levels. Compared with the macroeconomic targets set for the 1980s in the LPA in 1988, the growth rate of GDP per capita reached only 0.88%, agriculture grew at 2.3%, industry at 4.9%, mining at 4.7%, while the share of investment in GDP dropped from 25.2% in 1978 to 15.8% in 1988, and export and import growth rates were only 3.8% and 0.3% respectively, which was well below the rates recorded in 1978. The question then arises as to why the actual performance of the economic indicators and the social situation could not be commensurate with the expectations aroused by the LPA. The gap between intentions and reality could be due to the following reasons: the chronic inability of African countries to translate the guidelines adopted at the continental level into national policies, programs and projects and the lack of determination to pursue continuously the agreed strategies and policies, with the consequent non-implementation of these policies and programs. Instead, national development plans and annual budgets tended to perpetuate or even strengthen the economic structures that Africa inherited from the colonial era; the difference in conception and perspective between Africa, on the one hand, and donors and multilateral institutions, on the other, as regards the way forward in Africa. There was a lack of enthusiasm on the part of Africa's development partners to help the continent achieve its goals and objectives; the illusion maintained in some countries that each country can do it alone, that each country, acting in its individual capacity, can overcome the enormous difficulties of socioeconomic transformation.

There is therefore a need for a new vision. And the means to solve the crisis of the African economies exist. Indeed, the global system has the technical and financial resources, while Africa possesses important assets of enormous potential for demographic and cultural growth. What is needed then is a new vision of sustainable development through integration as proposed by the Agenda 2063 of the African Union, the foundations of which would be first of all the improvement of the governance which stabilizes institutions and the fundamentals of the macroeconomic framework. Secondly, investments in the growth sectors which would then increase the competitiveness and diversification of economies and, thirdly, the sharp reduction in the dependency on binomial aid and indebtedness. This development model should overcome all obstacles and handicaps in order to create a democratic political system and an efficient economy capable of engaging in a process of steady, harmonious growth and at the highest possible rate, given the resources available. The Agenda 2063 proposed by the African Union is intended to be this approach, both strategic and original.

Evolution of Development Aid Flows

The evaluation of development assistance is often approximate as the statistics on aid flows are incomplete and inaccurate. There are so many elements, including the nature and volume, the actual beneficiaries, donors, the allocation and the impact of the aid, that it is difficult to determine this with accuracy. However, the aid granted by the twenty-two countries and the European Commission and members of the Development Assistance Committee (DAC), the OECD body that form nearly 90% of global aid, represents a good approximation of these flows (OECD 2014).

Attractiveness of the African Continent

Analysis of net financial flows between 1960 and 2014 shows a rather mixed evolution of development aid (Fig. 22.1 and Table 22.1 in the Annex). Aid to Africa has experienced a rather heterogeneous trajectory. Overall, five phases can be observed in the evolution of the official development assistance (ODA). The first phase, covering the first decade after the independence of most African countries, is characterized by sluggishness in aid flows towards the continent. These averaged 1.4 billion dollars and hardly exceeded US$1.6 billion over the decade. Compared to other developing regions of the world, a relative decline is observed in aid to Africa. Thus, the share of aid granted to Africa in the total assistance to developing countries

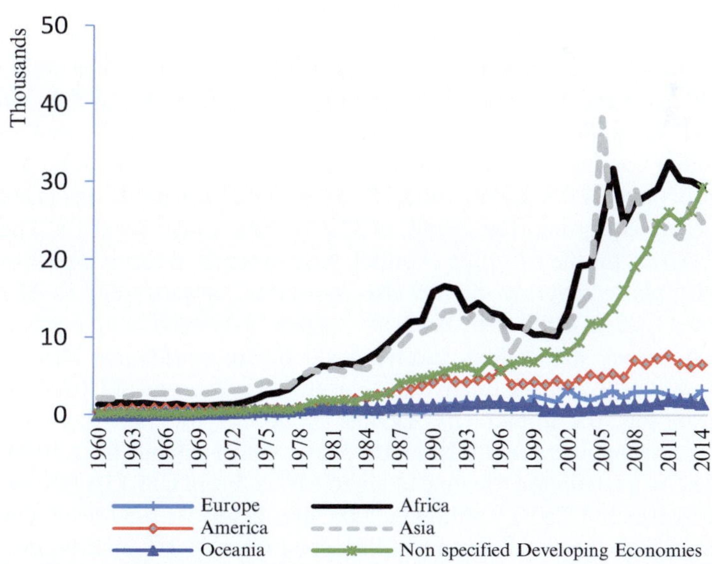

Fig. 22.1 Evolution of aid flows to the continents from 1960 to 2014 (Source: OECD data)

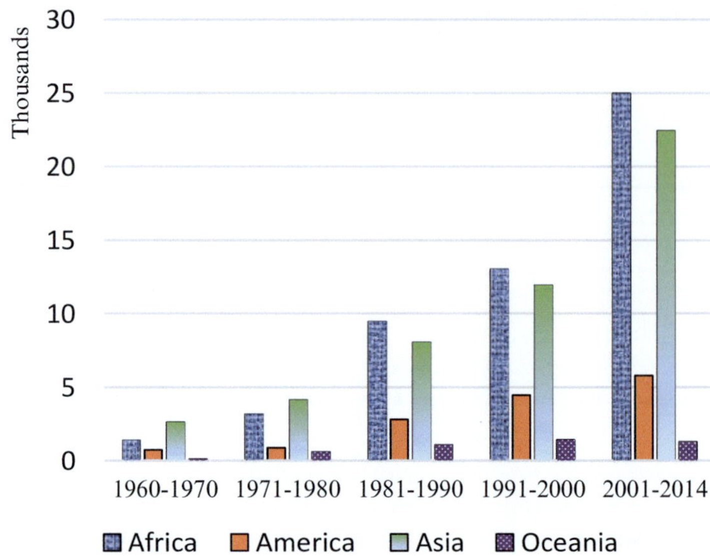

Fig. 22.2 Relative share of aid of the continents of the world (Source: OECD data)

(DCs) has shown a steady decline from 30.3% in 1960 to 21.9% in 1970. This progression contrasts for instance with that of Asia (another big beneficiary) where the relative aid has increased steadily around an average trend of 49% (Fig. 22.2 and Table 22.2 in Annex).

The second phase consisted of a more or less rapid increase in aid flows to Africa, breaking the sluggishness observed during the 60's. From US$1.3 billion in 1971, ODA towards the continent reached US$6.3 billion in 1980. The total level of African aid appeared this year for the first time higher than that of Asia which was US$5.6 billion. So the 70s were marked by a faster increase in aid to Africa compared to other continents. The relative share of African aid in the total aid to DCs rose steadily up to 22.1% in 1971 and 37.3% in 1980. Meanwhile, the share of Asia evolved negatively, going from 53.4% to 32.3% of the total aid to DCs. Thus, in the early 80s, Africa for the first time overtook Asia in terms of receiving assistance.

The third phase covering the 80s also showed an upward trend in African aid. This reached US$12.1 billion in 1989, having nearly doubled in nine years, making Africa first among the regions receiving aid in the world, just ahead of Asia. However, unlike the 70s, the relative share of Africa in the total aid to DCs remained stable during the 90's around 37%, against about 33% for Asia. In contrast, other DCs saw their share increased. The fourth phase, which extends from 1990 to 2001, was marked by a continuous decline of aid to Africa. From US$15.8 billion in 1990, the aid decreased to US$10.1 billion in 2001, thus below its 1987 level. During this period, the relative share of African aid dropped from 41.1% in 1990 to 28.7% in

2001, in favor of DCs other than Asia. Finally, the fifth phase, spreading from 2002 to 2014, occasioned a new upward trend in aid. However, from 2005, its evolution has been quite irregular alternating between periods of decline with a low of US$24.6 billion in 2007, and rising to a peak of US$32.5 billion in 2011. During this time, a weakness or even a decline in the share of African aid to the benefit of other DCs is observed.

Africa is one of the main beneficiaries of development assistance. However, this aid has not always had a smooth evolution since it has been characterized by successive phases of growth and contraction since 1960. In addition, the relative share of African aid in the total aid to DCs has been more or less stagnant.

However, the African reality is quite heterogeneous given the differences between the main African regions. Although there is a huge trend in terms of attractiveness of aid in Africa in general, disparities exist between the Central regions, East, North, West and South of the continent.

Regional Attractiveness

The evolution of aid flows towards Africa since 1960 confirms the existence of disparities between the major regions of the continent. In other words, the attractiveness of the aid has been quite variable over time and by region. Thus, in general, North Africa attracted more aid from 1960 until the mid-80s. However, while aid to countries in the North was declining, other parts of the continent experienced growth, albeit slow but sustained, for at least the next decade. In 1960, North Africa was the largest recipient of aid, with nearly 71% of all the aid to the continent. But this share recorded a downward trend and decreased to 30% in 1970 and 20% in the 90s; in 2014 it was only 7%.

The East African region was the second most attractive one in terms of aid during the first half of the 1960s. Its share of the total aid to the continent was 16% in 1963, far off the dominant share of North Africa. Interest in East Africa was further strengthened from 2000 when it appeared as the most attractive region in terms of purpose of the aid. Having obtained 27% of the total aid in 2000, the relative share of East Africa increased significantly to reach 40% in 2014 (Fig. 22.3). Aid to West Africa experienced more or less steady growth. Aid flows to West Africa were valued at US$53 million in 1960, 5% of total aid to Africa, but rose to US$243 million in 1964, representing a relative share of 18% of the total allocation of aid. Thus, from the second half of the 60s, West Africa became one of the most attractive regions on the continent.

Until the late 1970s, Central Africa was the fourth largest recipient area of the aid. Its share was 13% behind the three regions mentioned above. However, this

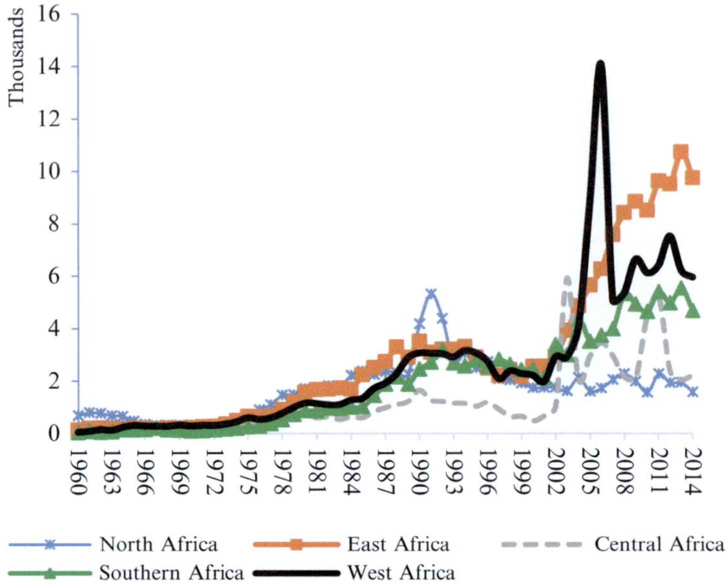

Fig. 22.3 Evolution of aid flows in the main African regions (Source: OECD data)

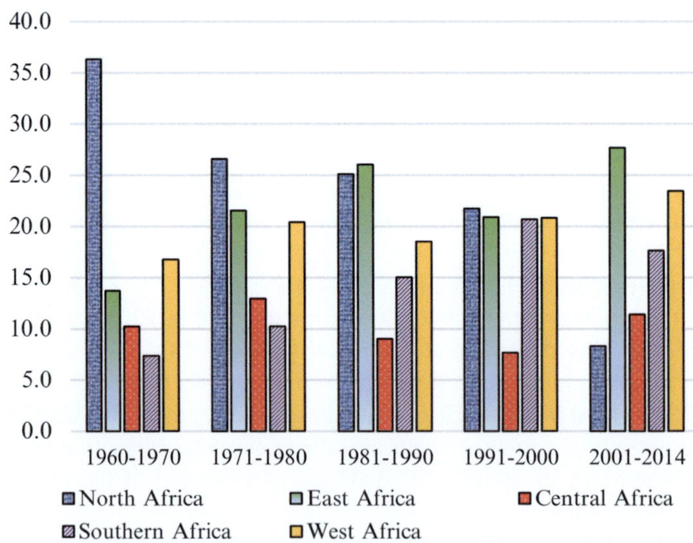

Fig. 22.4 Relative share of aid in the main African regions (Source: OECD data)

share has been in constant decline so that the region has become the least provided with support, although this position has been attributed to North Africa since the mid-2000s (Fig. 22.4 and Table 22.3 in Annex). With an average of 10% of the received aid, Southern Africa was until the late 70s the least endowed region. However, aid to this region rose sustainably, becoming most important in the late 90s. Since then, it is one of the three main beneficiary regions of aid in Africa.

Impact of Development Assistance

The impact of the various aid policies on Africa's development could be viewed from two perspectives: the first is related to the objectives defined, and the second is about the socioeconomic performance achieved.

Appraisal in the Light of the Development Goals

Compared to the aforementioned objectives assigned to economic policy in the early 1960s, especially agriculture upgrading and industrial sector development, the financing plans actually developed were not effective. They have not promoted the modernization of African agriculture as the agrarian structures remain archaic nor have they helped to create an industrial environment that allows for integrating into the world economy. Indeed, notwithstanding these objectives, most African countries did not set priorities for the use of resources received. Unlike Asian countries, where the governments selected strategic companies whose development required the improvement of their conditions, in Africa the spread of preferential interest rates nurtured corporate rent-seeking behavior. The modernization experiments of economic structures have not allowed for real change and economic diversification. Industrial development attempts have been limited to a few agricultural product processing activities, African economies still depend on the primary sector and the import of commodities from developed countries. The expected results were not achieved, with a lack of real processing industries.

Assessment Under the Socioeconomic Performance

A review of work that has been done on the impact of aid shows that the practical results are mixed at best. In the 1980s and 1990s, many studies endeavored to evaluate the effectiveness of aid. However, the pursuit of efficiency is naturally hindered by its definition. Most studies on the effectiveness of aid use as a starting assumption that it should promote growth in beneficiary countries. This approach is acceptable to the extent that economic growth is one of the interim goals for most purposes of aid (Boone 1995). Based on such an approach, this chapter attempts to show to what extent aid to Africa and to its major regions affects growth. The analysis of Africa's data from 1960 to 2014 reveals no material correlation between aid and economic growth. In other words, the aid received only slightly helped promote economic growth. The analysis hence corroborates the ambiguity in terms of aid effectiveness.

The low impact of aid in terms of improved growth is observable in all African regions. East Africa appears to be the region where the stimulatory effect of aid on growth is the most important, then come Central and Southern Africa. However, this relationship is only very weakly established in the North and West regions of the continent. Moreover, comparing aid data with that of expenses and investment, it appears that aid contributes to an increase in government expenditure rather than maximizing capital. Furthermore, the characteristics of funding for developing countries in the post-independence decades have placed an increasing financial risk on these nations. As a matter of fact, the unprecedented expansion of international credit, even concessional, coupled with economic conditions characterized by a deterioration in the terms of trade, with the decline in world raw material prices and climatic hazards, have resulted in excessive debt for developing countries. Showing large savings deficits, they are more indebted with more expensive conditions, creating enormous economic and financial imbalances with deficits in the balance of payments and with very important public finances.

The debt crisis that ensued in 1982 in Latin American and Asian countries, with the declaration of insolvency of Mexico whose debt was estimated at more than US$100 billion, also affected African countries. To illustrate this, as far as ECOWAS countries were concerned, the value of the debt stock rose, on average, from FCFA412.7 billion to FCFA3109.3 billion, from 1970–1977 to 1979–1984, being an increase of over 600% (Raffinot 1991). Therefore, there was an increase in the collapse of bank loans. The reduction of multilateral flows and the stagnation of official assistance, under the auspices of international financial institutions, led to the implementation of structural adjustment policies. These are recommended for restoring large external (balance of payments) and internal balances (public finances). The development of these policies was based on the monetary approach to the balance of payments, with the external imbalance being of a monetary nature. The treatment of external imbalances will therefore basically be done by reducing the money supply, that is, credit and especially credit to the government.

Internal financing, which was provided by the development banks, defected after their bankruptcy. Indeed, with their low rate policy, under the auspices of the government, coupled with recurring management problems, the financial situation of these banks worsened, calling their solvency into question. In the case of ECOWAS countries, the crisis has led monetary authorities to implement extensive restructuring and liquidation programs with regard to banks in order to restore their creditworthiness and organize a progressive disengagement of the government. In a nutshell, it is impossible to link aid to improved economic performance. In other words, aid has not played a significant role in accelerating the growth and diversification of production structures in African economies.

Rational Aid Ineffectiveness

Many reasons are given for what can be qualified as the ineffectiveness of development assistance (World Bank 1998). These reasons relate to the situation in the beneficiary countries, especially in their political, strategic, and economic dimensions, but also the quality of the official development assistance itself, particularly its instability and its absorption by the beneficiaries.

a) *Governance and political stability in the recipient countries*

The consideration of governance and stability has led to the concept of 'fragile state'. This was adopted as an important operational concept by the World Bank and the Development Assistance Committee (DAC) among many governmental and non-governmental donor agencies. It is a delicate way of saying that a country has weak or dysfunctional institutions or that it is characterized by poor governance. Development theory recognizes that economic growth requires above all good policies as well as good institutions to implement them. The term is also used to raise the possibility of political violence that aid agencies have long considered as not falling within their competence. Violent conflicts may be caused by poor policies and institutions, and may in turn generate poor policies, the breaking down of institutions and more severe poverty. Fragile states run the risk of being caught in a "conflict trap" (Collier et al. 2003). The various forms of instability have a negative impact on aid allocation, its efficiency and therefore on growth and development. The stability and the importance of the level of democratization are factors underlying an appeal for help. Indeed, countries with good results in democratization experience a relative increase in aid.

The results of aid efforts depend on its use by the recipients and its interaction with local conditions and institutions. Burnside and Dollar (1997, 2000), and others after them, sought to clarify the conditions under which the aid effort could be used effectively. But the idea of measuring governance in relation to standards of 'good governance' inspired from the experience of donor countries may be too simplistic. We still do not know what explains and determines a successful development process. The example of China's take-off shows that ideas on good governance perceived as Western ones do not exhaust the issue.

b) *Political and strategic interests of the donor countries*

Since aid consists of making international provision for domestic resources, ODA has a political dimension. This is obvious for its bilateral component, but it also exists for national contributions to multilateral institutions. As indicated by Alesina and Dollar (1998) in their work, the political and strategic interest of donor countries is one of the motivations for aid allocation. In this context, the development of recipient countries is not necessarily the objective sought by donors.

c) *Aid instability*

Aid volatility is often seen as one of the causes of its inefficiency. Aid is usually expected, and although it fails to eliminate often exogenous shocks, it does help to reduce them, thus affecting African economies. However, the conditions required to receive aid seem to favor countries in better economic health, a fact that negates the need for support in case of a negative shock. This obviously shows the unpredictable and often pro-cyclical nature of aid; that is, it is granted during periods of expansion in the beneficiary countries and is deferred or withheld during times of downturn. Moreover, the aid granted in the case of good economic performance is often quite low, which contributes to pro-cyclical dynamic aid for beneficiaries.

This self-reinforcing phenomenon of the cycle is a source of instability and reduces the potential for long-term growth of the countries under consideration (Ramey and Ramey 1995). The uncertainty of the aid may also influence its impact on growth (Lensink and Morrissey 1999). In this case, the contribution of aid to growth and long-term welfare seems to depend on economic policies for the recipients (Burnside and Dollar 1997). As a whole, there is a lack of predictability and continuity of aid.

d) *Low absorption by beneficiaries*

The absorption capacity of resources by beneficiaries determines the future aid flows. In many states, especially those in crisis, the rate of implementation of funded projects can be lower than 50% of the amounts programmed, which reduces the efficiency and effectiveness of aid. There is no specific explanation for the weakness of project implementation. In fact several factors are involved, specific to the country and to the terms and policies governing foreign aid. Unrealistic conditions, complex procedures sometimes unknown to countries, fragmentation of aid into many projects and donors, and lack of ownership of programs because of human and institutional deficiencies combine with and reinforce each other to lead to the underutilization of resources of the international aid (Cohen et al. 2006).

Both on bilateral and multilateral donors' side, disbursement procedures of loans and grants and the procurement of goods and services are often complex, cumbersome and bureaucratic. They are also generally subject to many conditionalities relating to policy reforms that a fragile administration cannot handle. The most problematic ones are the cross-conditionalities. Moreover, very often demands for reforms do not take into account existing institutional capacities in designing and implementing them.

Supplements to Traditional Aid

The various stakeholders involved in the international financing of developing economies, especially the various countries, multinational organizations and international banking institutions, should learn from the failures in the aid policies.

Traditional aid, often granted in the form of concessional loans and grants to governments, have become anachronistic with the extraordinary wealth of available funding instruments. The real question is not whether to lend cheaply or give, but how to use these resources to develop the most effective financing solutions for development, by combining them with any useful instrument available on the markets. Financial innovation is the missing link in development assistance.

Thus, to complement the efforts made by African countries, it is essential that the international community strengthen its support, by particularly focusing on instruments that could enable the continent to create the conditions for accelerated economic growth and sustainable development. To increase the effectiveness of their action, Africa and its external partners will need to develop new approaches that can support strategic priorities subject to a consensus on the continent and internationally. In this context, and in light of past experience and successes achieved in other parts of the world, it appears necessary to consolidate certain instruments and certain developments.

a) *Foreign direct investment*

As such, foreign direct investment (FDI) remains one of the most relevant instruments. It is therefore necessary to put in place policies to increase the attractiveness of African countries to attract more FDI. Its impact on the economic development of the beneficiary countries is clear as evidenced by the experiences of some emerging economies. Indeed, despite the various measures taken economically by many countries, including the development of an incentive code of investment for the establishment of economic zones to attract these investment flows, the African continent is still lagging behind other regions of the world. FDI increased in mid-1980 and its share in financing developing countries' economies has increased since the 1990s; however, the increase of the FDI in the world is mainly done for the benefit of the emerging countries of Latin America and Asia. In 2002, these countries attracted almost a quarter of global FDI flows, while Africa attracted only 7% of the FDI to developing countries. In 2015, Africa contributed negatively to the overall growth of global FDI. Although the continent barely held above US$50 billion of FDI for three years (US$54 billion inward FDI in 2014, 56 billion in 2013, and 53 billion in 2012), these flows fell by US$38 billion in 2015, thus decreasing by −31.4%. At the same time, FDI flows worldwide rebounded by +36% in 2015 to US$1700 billion (its highest level since the financial crisis of 2008–2009) after decreasing by −16% in 2014.

The decline recorded in the continent is largely due to a drop in FDI flows towards Sub-Saharan Africa, while they increased in North Africa. FDI flows in Egypt reversed a downward trend (US$6.7 billion in 2015 against US$4.3 billion in 2014). Central Africa and Southern Africa have experienced the most important slowdown: the end of the raw materials boom has impacted FDI flows towards this part of the continent. For example, inward flows to Mozambique declined by −21% (US$3.8 billion). They decreased by −27% in Nigeria, particularly affected by the fall in the oil price to reach US$3.4 billion. South Africa experienced a precipitous drop of −74% of US$1.5 billion.

b) *Loans preserving the creditworthiness of borrowers*

The debt crisis is not only, nor even firstly, due to the bad governance of the debtors, but to their vulnerability to economic shocks or natural disasters. Therefore, it is possible to set up loans preserving the solvency of borrowers: several formulas enable the debt burden to be reduced when facing a shock. These innovations are essential if we are to assist in the recovery of loans to developing countries nurturing a new debt crisis. What has been missing in lending strategy is to provide for the possible bankruptcy of debtors and mechanisms to deal with it. Indeed, due to its negative impact on the economic recovery efforts of African countries, the external debt issue requires sustained handling. African governments continue to further consolidate public finances, despite the economic and financial difficulties they are faced with. Despite the various measures taken by the international financial community for debt relief for poor countries, especially the enhanced Heavily Indebted Poor Countries (HIPC) Initiative, the annual service of Africa external debt still accounts for 17% of its export earnings (Ben 2000). So the continent's debt keeps on impairing the ability of the governments to finance the investments needed to accelerate growth. Sustainability should not be determined only by the HIPC initiative funding constraints.

c) *Rebalancing of international trade rules*

The tariff and non-tariff protection measures of developed countries are still preventing African countries from taking full advantage from international trade. Likewise, subsidies to producers in industrialized countries represent a source of immiseration in Africa, especially for farmers. In this regard, developed countries should comply with the commitments agreed upon in Doha in November 2001, which consisted of taking a series of tariff dismantling and fair trade rules and measures, as well as the implementation of a technical assistance program and capacity building. The failure of Cancun in 2003 must therefore be seen as an invitation to the international community to strongly commit to the use of trade policies for development.

d) *Support to private sector development*

Traditional aid is mainly oriented towards government projects and programs at the expense of the private sector. The private investment flows to Africa remain low despite the potential and the many economic and institutional reforms implemented. Yet the private sector is one of the main actors of the strategy accelerating the continent growth and development. It is therefore necessary to reverse this trend through specific actions to support the private sector. These actions include mainly:

- *Strengthening the guarantee strategies*. To attract private investment in Africa, partners could act to strengthen guarantee strategies against non-commercial risks and help mobilize private financial resources. For instance, the Multilateral Investment Guarantee Agency (MIGA) and the International Finance Corporation (IFC) could adapt their response mechanisms to the realities of Africa which include small and medium enterprises.

- *Financing economic infrastructures*. Private sector development also implies the availability of inputs at lower costs. One of the major areas of external support could therefore target the development of national and regional infrastructure in Africa. Also, funding for basic economic infrastructure could be listed in the priority interventions for external partners.
- Implementing other *conventional financing techniques,* widely used in developed countries, such as venture capital, project funding in the form of BOT (Build Operation Transfer) and BOOT (Build, Own, Operate, Transfer) and the stock exchange. In developing countries these techniques reveal emerging coverages to be explored while acknowledging specific constraints.

Conclusion

The review of data on aid concluded that aid flows have no significant impact on economic performance and on the African development process. From the political decolonization in the 1960s to the present date through the 1980–90s of structural adjustment, the contrasted political, economic and social outcomes evidence the ineffectiveness of development assistance to the African continent. Despite the reforms initiated in the early 1980s, the support of development partners failed to fundamentally transform the structure of African economies. The socioeconomic situation remains fragile as illustrated, on the one hand, by the instability of economic performance and, on the other, the reversibility of the results recorded socially. However, not all African regions are facing the same challenges. Even if the weak impact of aid in terms of growth improvement is observable throughout Africa, the continent's eastern region is where the stimulating effect of aid on growth is the most important, followed by Central and Southern Africa. However, this impact is only very weakly established in the Northern and Western regions of the continent. Similarly, it appears that aid contributes generally to increase government expenditure rather than capital accumulation, which is why aid has a very mixed effect on development goals.

It is also necessary to define a new approach enabling the implementation of a new aid policy to accelerate growth and sustainable development. This could correct the mistakes made in the past, removing obstacles to economic and social development, reflecting a new ambition and a new vision for the African continent, which, through the efficient exploitation of its potential, can subsequently have a better place in the global economy. For this to happen, there is the need to develop and approve appropriate financial instruments as they are indivisible from the debate on the objectives and effectiveness of development assistance. The ineffectiveness of aid is inherent in its definition, stating that it must be the demonstration of public structures and fund development objects, and take the form of grants or concessional loans (incorporating a grant so as to reduce the cost for the borrower in relation to the market loans terms) comprising at least 25% of gifts items. This restrictive and binary definition of aid has shown its limitations. Consequently, the new development agenda set out at global level (Sustainable Development Goals) should be an opportunity to go beyond the traditional agenda which has always involved aid. There is a need to use financial innovation for development funding.

The new kind of partnership around which African governments and the international community will be able to articulate a more ambitious program of strategic action should be an instrument that helps to increase the chances of achieving accelerated growth and effective poverty reduction in Africa.

Annex

Table 22.1 Aid inflows by recipients (US$ million)

Year	Total developing economies	Europe	Africa	America	Asia	Oceania	Non specified developing economies
1960	4238.4	385.56	1286.13	278.17	2144.77	23.18	120.59
1961	5202.74	570.23	1531.53	816.67	2089.53	25.87	168.91
1962	5311.31	463.93	1591.3	787.4	2185.54	40.68	242.46
1963	5581.18	452.45	1499.47	810.31	2530.61	43.28	245.06
1964	5331.33	320.56	1516.65	681.21	2628.65	42.34	141.92
1965	5687.14	336.63	1401.45	837.4	2770.73	148.72	192.21
1966	5524.48	335.89	1258.9	888.02	2780.27	149.3	112.1
1967	5841.65	222.83	1443.75	747.7	3155.75	161.85	109.77
1968	5370.1	202.29	1170.03	813.85	2845.13	194.01	144.79
1969	5248.16	221.47	1180.39	696.03	2715.65	220.74	213.88
1970	5420.7	146.86	1186.13	708.68	2815.22	257.72	306.09
1971	6033.67	182.17	1332.86	629.45	3219.21	275.38	394.6
1972	6246.81	268.63	1364.89	627.3	3162.65	372.79	450.55
1973	6683.73	223.58	1616.43	655.47	3277.01	432.65	478.59
1974	7793.05	93.82	2057.67	711.28	3761.76	502.32	666.2
1975	9219.06	82.81	2691.94	847.37	4314.88	597.01	685.05
1976	8818.81	151.46	2852.71	844.4	3734.62	551.44	684.18
1977	9306.07	203.9	3356.99	780.9	3717.17	593.31	653.8
1978	12271.71	304.61	4480.9	969.63	4845.08	733.79	937.7
1979	15340.79	582.14	5389.09	1198.3	5765.69	844.12	1561.45
1980	17022.97	892.95	6344.27	1331.75	5588.57	948.17	1917.26
1981	17201.74	659.37	6223.83	1629.54	5924.02	900.58	1864.4
1982	17635.02	634.54	6603.26	1883.33	5641.42	937.84	1934.63
1983	17778.19	391.09	6456.15	2074.06	6186.42	923.91	1746.56
1984	19047.91	301.1	7187.91	2194.99	5973.44	912.36	2478.11

(continued)

Table 22.1 (continued)

Year	Total developing economies	Europe	Africa	America	Asia	Oceania	Non specified developing economies
1985	21212.32	311.48	8079.88	2617.83	6880.54	851.04	2471.55
1986	25,229	430.93	9333.94	2866.11	8615.87	1098.69	2883.46
1987	28890.55	518.45	10687.12	3422.42	8901.09	1250.99	4110.48
1988	31966.48	478	11992.46	3342.72	10364.24	1291.53	4497.53
1989	32933.82	361.54	12139.77	3787.97	10647.18	1274.31	4723.05
1990	38469.19	775.19	15818.13	4188.48	11329.33	1215.03	5143.03
1991	43029.52	1487.41	16555.94	4860.28	13256.91	1214.08	5654.9
1992	42824.7	1456.96	16212.5	4296.7	13419.9	1316.47	6122.17
1993	39100.7	1767.26	13453.23	4267.58	12002.16	1445.67	6164.8
1994	41057.93	1140.42	14416.97	4553.54	13755.07	1667.04	5524.89
1995	40556.23	1349.64	13242.09	4810.98	12388.23	1712.31	7052.98
1996	39213.77	1186.52	12858.42	5768.73	12007.85	1699.82	5692.43
1997	32517.81	990.03	11407.7	3937.23	8197.56	1434.9	6550.39
1998	35350.69	1161.42	11251.32	4021.36	10451.78	1526.73	6938.08
1999	37995.46	2507.76	10359.72	4244.1	12675.29	1372.48	6836.11
2000	36,221	2092.99	10401.75	3862.34	11075.68	712.47	8075.77
2001	35338.28	1732.15	10158.72	4471.36	10817.48	702.22	7456.35
2002	41018.12	3398.53	13385.04	3913.55	11496.27	660.1	8164.63
2003	50107.44	2301.84	19174.75	4591.31	13923.74	747.73	9368.07
2004	54753.78	1941.4	19386.49	5147.2	15735.21	834.7	11708.78
2005	83075.66	2422.85	24661.76	4866.99	38228.99	974.42	11920.65
2006	77537.24	3174.49	31665.13	5289.97	22628.19	1073.24	13706.22
2007	73698.01	2230.1	24640.7	4868.19	24747.39	1176.85	16034.78
2008	87114.58	3063.94	27380.21	7015.5	29266.41	1313.05	19075.47
2009	83944.78	3052.08	28197.57	6579.5	23642.9	1351.68	21121.05
2010	90619.2	3088.2	29139.35	7282.88	24848.77	1616.18	24643.82
2011	94794.29	2662.88	32522.89	7682.93	23873.71	1979.24	26072.64
2012	88436.52	2064.87	30270.25	6603.32	22795.08	1875.7	24827.3
2013	93536.27	2013.17	30067.53	6320.55	27194.01	1760.01	26180.99
2014	94662.16	3221.68	29274.24	6503.62	24852.05	1566.78	29243.8

Source: OECD

Table 22.2 Proportion of aid per recipients

Year	Total developing economies	Europe	Africa	America	Asia	Oceania	Non specified developing economies
1960	100	9.1	30.3	6.6	50.6	0.5	2.8
1961	100	11.0	29.4	15.7	40.2	0.5	3.2
1962	100	8.7	30.0	14.8	41.1	0.8	4.6
1963	100	8.1	26.9	14.5	45.3	0.8	4.4
1964	100	6.0	28.4	12.8	49.3	0.8	2.7
1965	100	5.9	24.6	14.7	48.7	2.6	3.4
1966	100	6.1	22.8	16.1	50.3	2.7	2.0
1967	100	3.8	24.7	12.8	54.0	2.8	1.9
1968	100	3.8	21.8	15.2	53.0	3.6	2.7
1969	100	4.2	22.5	13.3	51.7	4.2	4.1
1970	100	2.7	21.9	13.1	51.9	4.8	5.6
1971	100	3.0	22.1	10.4	53.4	4.6	6.5
1972	100	4.3	21.8	10.0	50.6	6.0	7.2
1973	100	3.3	24.2	9.8	49.0	6.5	7.2
1974	100	1.2	26.4	9.1	48.3	6.4	8.5
1975	100	0.9	29.2	9.2	46.8	6.5	7.4
1976	100	1.7	32.3	9.6	42.3	6.3	7.8
1977	100	2.2	36.1	8.4	39.9	6.4	7.0
1978	100	2.5	36.5	7.9	39.5	6.0	7.6
1979	100	3.8	35.1	7.8	37.6	5.5	10.2
1980	100	5.2	37.3	7.8	32.8	5.6	11.3
1981	100	3.8	36.2	9.5	34.4	5.2	10.8
1982	100	3.6	37.4	10.7	32.0	5.3	11.0
1983	100	2.2	36.3	11.7	34.8	5.2	9.8
1984	100	1.6	37.7	11.5	31.4	4.8	13.0
1985	100	1.5	38.1	12.3	32.4	4.0	11.7
1986	100	1.7	37.0	11.4	34.2	4.4	11.4
1987	100	1.8	37.0	11.8	30.8	4.3	14.2
1988	100	1.5	37.5	10.5	32.4	4.0	14.1
1989	100	1.1	36.9	11.5	32.3	3.9	14.3
1990	100	2.0	41.1	10.9	29.5	3.2	13.4
1991	100	3.5	38.5	11.3	30.8	2.8	13.1
1992	100	3.4	37.9	10.0	31.3	3.1	14.3
1993	100	4.5	34.4	10.9	30.7	3.7	15.8
1994	100	2.8	35.1	11.1	33.5	4.1	13.5
1995	100	3.3	32.7	11.9	30.5	4.2	17.4
1996	100	3.0	32.8	14.7	30.6	4.3	14.5
1997	100	3.0	35.1	12.1	25.2	4.4	20.1
1998	100	3.3	31.8	11.4	29.6	4.3	19.6
1999	100	6.6	27.3	11.2	33.4	3.6	18.0

(continued)

Table 22.2 (continued)

Year	Total developing economies	Europe	Africa	America	Asia	Oceania	Non specified developing economies
2000	100	5.8	28.7	10.7	30.6	2.0	22.3
2001	100	4.9	28.7	12.7	30.6	2.0	21.1
2002	100	8.3	32.6	9.5	28.0	1.6	19.9
2003	100	4.6	38.3	9.2	27.8	1.5	18.7
2004	100	3.5	35.4	9.4	28.7	1.5	21.4
2005	100	2.9	29.7	5.9	46.0	1.2	14.3
2006	100	4.1	40.8	6.8	29.2	1.4	17.7
2007	100	3.0	33.4	6.6	33.6	1.6	21.8
2008	100	3.5	31.4	8.1	33.6	1.5	21.9
2009	100	3.6	33.6	7.8	28.2	1.6	25.2
2010	100	3.4	32.2	8.0	27.4	1.8	27.2
2011	100	2.8	34.3	8.1	25.2	2.1	27.5
2012	100	2.3	34.2	7.5	25.8	2.1	28.1
2013	100	2.2	32.1	6.8	29.1	1.9	28.0
2014	100	3.4	30.9	6.9	26.3	1.7	30.9

Source: Calculated from the data in Table 22.1

Table 22.3 Average aid per period

	1960–1970	1971–1980	1981–1990	1991–2000	2001–2014
Africa	1370	3149	9452	13,016	24,995
America	733	860	2801	4462	5795
Asia	2606	4139	8046	11,923	22,432
Oceania	119	585	1066	1410	1259
Non-specified developing economies	182	843	3185	6461	17,823

Source: Calculated from the data in Table 22.1

References

Alesina, A., & Dollar, D. (1998). *Who gives foreign aid, to whom and why? NBER working paper 6612*. Cambridge: Massachusetts.

Amprou J., & L. Chauvet. (2005). Efficacité et allocation de l'aide, revue des débats, Paris, Agence Française de Développement, Notes et documents, n° 6.

Ben, H. H. (2000). *Le post ajustement en stratégies en Afrique*. Dakar: CODESRIA.

Beynon, J. (2003). Poverty efficient aid allocations: Collier and dollar revisited. In *ESAU working paper 2*. London: Overseas Development Institutes.

Boone, P. (1995). *The impact of foreign aid on savings and growth*. London: London School of Economics.

Burnside, C., & D. Dollar. (1997). *Aid, policies, and grants*. Policy research working paper, no. 1777. Washington: Banque mondiale.

Burnside, C., & Dollar, D. (2000). Aid, policies, and growth. *American Economic Review, 90*, 847–868.

Charnoz, O., & J.M. Severino. (2007). *L'aide publique au développement*. Coll. Repères, Paris, La découverte, p. 37.

Clemens, M.A., & T.J. Moss. (2005). *Ghost of 0.7%: Origins and relevance of the International Aid Target*. Working paper no. 68. Washington, DC: Center for Global Development.

Cohen, D., S. Guillaumont-Jeanneney, & P. Jacquet (eds.). (2006). La France et l'aide publique au développement, Paris, La Documentation française, Rapport au Conseil d'analyse économique.

Easterly, W., R. Levine, & D. Roodman. (2003). *New data, new doubts : A comment on Burnside and Dollar's 'Aid, policies, and growth' (2000)*. NBER working paper, no. 9846. Cambridge, MA: National Bureau of Economic Research.

Gillis, M., D. Perkins, M. Roemer, & D. Snodgrass. (1997). Economie du développement. Nouveaux Horizons.

Jacquet, P. (2006). Les enjeux de l'aide publique au développement. *Politique étrangère* 4 (Hiver): 941–954.

Jacquet, P., & Severino, J.-M. (2002). L'aide au développement: Une politique publique au cœur du développement durable et de la gouvernance de la mondialisation. *Revue d'économie financière, no, 66.*

Klein, M., & Harford, T. (2005). *The market for aid*. Washington, DC: International Finance Corporation.

Lensink, R., & Morrissey, O. (1999). *Uncertainty of aid inflows and the aid growth relationship*. CREDIT: University of Nottingham.

OECD. (2014). Development aid statistics, Development Aid Committee.

Raffinot, R. (1991). Dette extérieure et ajustement structurel. EDICEF.

Ramey, G., & Ramey, V. A. (1995). Cross-country evidence on the link between volatility and growth. *American Economic Review, 85*(5), 1138–1151.

Shaw, E. (1973). *Financial deepening in economic development*. New York: Oxford University Press.

World Bank. (1998). *Assessing aid: What works, what doesn't and why*. New York: Oxford University Press.

Simeon K. Koffi holds a PhD in economics from the University of Aix-Marseille in France. He is currently Head of the Research and Development Division of the Economic Community of West African States (ECOWAS) Commission. He has previously been Lecturer and Researcher at the University of Abidjan and Senior officer in the Department of Research and Statistics at the Central Bank of West African States (BCEAO). His various functions allowed him to conduct research works on the economies of the Member States of ECOWAS. He contributed to the publication of some collective works. Email: kkoffi@ecowas.int/ksimeon@yahoo.com.

MIX
Papier aus verantwortungsvollen Quellen
Paper from responsible sources
FSC® C105338

If you have any concerns about our products,
you can contact us on
ProductSafety@springernature.com

In case Publisher is established outside the EU,
the EU authorized representative is:
Springer Nature Customer Service Center GmbH
Europaplatz 3, 69115 Heidelberg, Germany

Printed by Libri Plureos GmbH
in Hamburg, Germany